Human Relations

FOR CAREER AND PERSONAL SUCCESS

FOURTH
CANADIAN
EDITION

ANDREW J. DUBRIN
Rochester Institute of Technology

TERRI GEERINCK
Sir Sandford Fleming College

Pearson Canada
Toronto

To Rosie—and her sparkle
To Clare—and her spirit
To Camila—and her spontaneity
To Sofia—and her self-confidence
—*AJD*

For my family . . .
—*TG*

Library and Archives Canada Cataloguing in Publication

DuBrin, Andrew J.
Human relations for career and personal success / Andrew J. DuBrin, Terri Geerinck.—4th Canadian ed.

Includes bibliographical references and index.
ISBN 978-0-13-812787-9

1. Interpersonal relations. 2. Organizational behaviour. 3. Success in business. I. Geerinck, Terri, 1958- II. Title.

HF5386.D78 2012 650.1'3 C2010-907791-1

ISBN 978-0-13-812787-9

Vice-President, Editorial Director: Gary Bennett
Editor-in-Chief: Ky Pruesse
Editor, Humanities and Social Sciences: Joel Gladstone
Marketing Manager: Lisa Gillis
Developmental Editor: Rema Celio
Project Managers: Söğüt Y. Güleç, Renata Butera (Central Publishing)
Production Editor: Jogender Taneja (Aptara®, Inc.)
Copy Editor: Deepak Arora
Proofreader: Barnali Ojha
Composition: Aptara®, Inc.
Art Direction: Miguel Acevedo
Cover Designer: Sandra Friesen Design
Cover Image: Getty Images/David Lees

Photo Credits: Page 1: Ron Chapple, Getty Images, Inc.—Taxi, Page 24: Getty Images, Inc., Page 51: Ron Chapple, Getty Images, Inc.—Taxi, Page 79: Kelvin Murray, Getty Images Inc.—Stone Allstock, Page 108: Stephen Simpson, Getty Images, Inc.—Taxi, Page 133: Koester Axel, Corbis/Sygma, Page 168: Getty Images—Digital Vision, Page 196: Tom McCarthy, PhotoEdit Inc., Page 220: Getty Images—Stockbyte, Page 245: © iStockphoto.com/Teun van den Dries, Page 266: Alamy Images Royalty Free, Page 291: EyeWire Collection, Getty Images—Photodisc, Page 317: Getty Images—Stockbyte, Page 336: Steve Gottlieb, The Stock Connection, Page 366: © Thinkstock/Comstock Images, Page 390: SuperStock, Inc.

4 5 6 CP 15 14 13

Contents

HUMAN RELATIONS CASE STUDIES

Preface

Welcome to the fourth Canadian edition of *Human Relations for Career and Personal Success*. This new edition has been expanded to emphasize developing effective human relations skills for the workplace in the new economy, including material on life span challenges, teamwork, and the impact of technology. The purpose of this book is to show you how you can become more effective in your work and personal life through knowledge of and skill in human relations. A major theme of this book is that success in work and success in personal life are related. Success on the job often leads to success in personal life, and success in personal life can lead to job success. To progress in your career, you need to deal effectively with yourself and other people. Dealing effectively with people is an enormous asset in both work and personal life.

One major audience for this book is students who will meet human relations problems on the job and in personal life. The text is designed for human relations courses taught in colleges, career schools, vocational–technical schools, and other post-secondary schools. Another major audience for this book is managerial, professional, and technical workers who are forging ahead in their careers and for those who are thinking of or who are actively switching careers.

ORGANIZATION OF THE BOOK

The text is divided into three parts, reflecting the major issues in human relations. Part 1 covers aspects of understanding and managing yourself: Chapter 1 focuses on self-understanding and the interrelationship of career and personal success; Chapter 2 explains how to use goal setting and other methods of self-motivation to improve your chances for success; Chapter 3 explains the basics of solving problems and making decisions with an emphasis on creativity; Chapter 4 deals with achieving wellness by managing stress and burnout; Chapter 5 focuses on life span changes and dealing with personal problems such as counterproductive habits, and other forms of self-defeating behaviour; and Chapter 6 provides key ideas for finding happiness and enhancing your personal life.

Part 2 examines the heart of human relations—dealing effectively with other people. The topics in Chapters 7 through 12 are, respectively, communicating with people, improving intercultural competence, handling conflict with others and being assertive, getting along with your manager, getting along with your co-workers and customers, and developing self-confidence and leadership skills.

Part 3 provides information to help career-minded people capitalize on their education, experience, talent, and ambition. The topics of Chapters 13 through 16 are choosing a career, developing a portfolio career, conducting a job search, developing good work habits, and getting ahead in your career.

Human Relations for Career and Personal Success, Fourth Canadian Edition, is both a text and a workbook of experiential exercises, including role plays and self-assessment quizzes related to the text. (An experiential exercise allows for learning by doing, along with guided instruction.) Each chapter contains one or more exercises and has been improved to include two human relations case studies in most of the chapters. The experiential exercises, which can all be completed during a class session, emphasize human interaction and thinking while keeping class paperwork to a minimum.

CHANGES IN THE FOURTH CANADIAN EDITION

The fourth Canadian edition continues to emphasize Canadian content, with even more references to Canadian research and Canadian companies with updated statistics from the latest Canadian census. It also features more Canadian illustrations applicable to our culture and current economic environment. The text continues its emphasis on the internet, and each chapter contains an online skill-building exercise called an Internet Skill Builder. Also, websites are referred to throughout the text. There are also several new Canada Today boxes featuring Canadian research and Canadian companies.

Several new chapter openers feature leading North American business people. A new feature, "Human Relations in Practice" has been added to most chapters to showcase how chapter concepts and theories are being applied in workplaces today.

Chapter 1 contains more information on the importance of self-esteem. Chapter 2 has better coverage of risk taking and thrill seeking, and discusses generational differences in needs including the Millennials. Chapter 3 includes information about emotional intelligence and decision making, asking "but not" questions to sharpen problem solving. Chapter 4 describes how the body mass index relates to health, the tend-and-befriend explanation of stress, emotional labour as a stressor, sick buildings and job stress, and creating your own stress triggers. Chapter 5 has been redesigned in this edition and examines life span changes and challenges as well as managing personal problems that many of us face in life, both on and off the job. Chapter 6 expands emotional intelligence and adds information about attitudes and how companies can foster positive attitudes among employees.

Chapter 7 includes a new section about how good interpersonal communication aids in relationship building. In Chapter 8, the focus continues to be on developing intercultural competence, but with updated statistics and more strategies to overcome cultural barriers. Chapter 9 includes more information on aggressive personalities and bullies and newer sources of conflict. Chapter 10 includes strategies to get along with your boss including a disorganized boss. Chapter 11, on getting along with co-workers and customers, includes a new section on team member roles and more strategies to assist in becoming an effective team member. Chapter 12, on self-confidence and leadership includes new research on self-efficacy, courage and self-confidence.

Chapter 13 includes expanded coverage of using the internet for job search including social networking such as Twitter. Chapter 14 adds new information and research about using networking, especially online social networking for finding a new job. Chapter 15 includes more strategies for developing attitudes and values for the workplace and to improve concentration. Chapter 16, "Getting Ahead in Your Career," expands strategies and tips for getting ahead including mentoring.

Several more complex cases have been added, many self-assessment exercises have been revised, and many new ones added. Over 75 percent of the cases and examples are new. As well, there are several new Canada Today features and others have been updated with the most recent data available at the time of writing.

Many of the new additions were a direct result of Canadian research on the employability skills that will be required for workers now and in the future. Today's workplace looks very different from the workplace of 20 years ago. This book provides students with the skills required for this new workplace as well as the foundation for building a satisfying personal life.

SUPPLEMENTS

The following instructor supplements are available for downloading from a password-protected section of Pearson Canada's online catalogue (vig.pearsoned.ca). Navigate to your book's catalogue page to view a list of those supplements that are available. See your local sales representative for details and access.

Instructor's Manual and Test Item File

The Instructor's Manual for this text contains a large number of test questions, chapter outlines and lecture notes, answers to discussion questions and case problems, and comments about the exercises.

PowerPoint Presentations

PowerPoint Presentations are available for each chapter. They can be accessed by logging onto Pearson's password protected website at http://vig.pearsoned.ca.

Companion Website

Go to **www.pearsoncanada.ca/dubrin** to access links to online resources for each chapter. Here you will find additional exercises and quizzes for each chapter, including multiple-choice questions, true/false questions and essay questions.

CourseSmart for Instructors

CourseSmart goes beyond traditional expectations—providing instant, online access to the textbooks and course materials you need at a lower cost for students. And even as students save money, you can save time and hassle with a digital eTextbook that allows you to search for the most relevant content at the very moment you need it. Whether it's evaluating textbooks or creating lecture notes to help students with difficult concepts, CourseSmart can make life a little easier. See how, when you visit www.coursesmart.com/instructors.

CourseSmart for Students

CourseSmart goes beyond traditional expectations—providing instant, online access to the textbooks and course materials you need at an average savings of 50 percent. With instant access from any computer and the ability to search your text, you'll find the content you need quickly, no matter where you are. And with online tools like highlighting and note taking, you can save time and study efficiently. See all the benefits at www.coursesmart.com/students.

ACKNOWLEDGMENTS

This book was certainly not written in isolation and could not have been accomplished without the assistance of many people. Many thanks go to the team that helped put this book together.

On my work front at the college, Debora Windover also deserves mention as an exemplary team leader and supporter of my writing endeavours. I would also like to thank many of my co-workers who supported me through this and offered many wonderful ideas.

Thanks to the outside reviewers, Beverly A. Pederson, Red Deer College; Tanya Haye, Douglas College; Doug McLean, Vancouver Island University; and Rosalie McMullin, New Brunswick Community College, who provided many suggestions for improving this book.

Thanks also to my family members and friends, whose emotional and spiritual support also assisted me in this project. Without all of you this book would have not been possible.

ABOUT THE AUTHORS

An accomplished author, Andrew J. DuBrin, Ph.D., brings to his work years of research experience in human relations and business psychology. His research has been reported in *Entrepreneur, Psychology Today, The Wall Street Journal, Fortune Small Biz,* and more than 100 national magazines and local newspapers. He has published numerous articles, textbooks, and well-publicized professional books. Dr. DuBrin received his Ph.D. from Michigan State University and is professor emeritus at the College of Business, Rochester Institute of Technology, where he has taught organizational behaviour, leadership, and career management.

Terri Geerinck is a curriculum consultant and professor at Fleming College. She has spent over two decades teaching several courses including Human Relations, Interpersonal and Group Dynamics, and several courses in Psychology. Her portfolio as a consultant includes developing new college programs, program review and renewal, teaching workshops, and mentoring new faculty. As part of a team, she has also delivered human relations training to business and industry with a particular emphasis on problem solving, interpersonal communication skills, and conflict management. Her teaching interests are instructional design, methodology, prior learning assessment, and web-based instruction. Her formal education includes a Bachelor of Arts in psychology and a Master's Degree in Education.

Part 1 Understanding and Managing Yourself

Chapter 1

Human Relations and Yourself

Learning Outcomes

After studying the information and doing the exercises in this chapter, you should be able to

- explain the meaning of human relations;
- pinpoint how work and personal life influence each other;
- explain how the self-concept influences behaviour;
- summarize the nature and consequences of self-esteem;
- describe how to improve your self-concept and self-esteem;
- understand the major factors influencing job performance and behaviour.

When David Neeleman, founder, chair, and chief executive officer (CEO) of the highly successful airline JetBlue, was asked to describe his Golden Rule, he replied as follows:

> *My grandfather ran a general store, and if a customer needed something that wasn't in stock, he did whatever it took to get the item—even running across the street to a competitor—rather than asking the customer to take her business elsewhere. He never told me, "Take care of others, and they'll take care of you"—he didn't have to. I saw it happen.*
>
> *When I entered the aviation business, I never thought in terms of "passengers" or "tickets sold" but of "people" and "customers." It was distressing to hear airline colleagues complain about the customers—even going so far as to say how much easier it would be for them if there were fewer passengers.*
>
> *When JetBlue started flying in February 2000, my goal was to bring humanity back to air travel. We hire nice people and train them in the skills they require to help run the airline. . . . We are all servants in the best sense of the word, which brings amazing personal and professional rewards.*[1]

The comments by the highly successful and much admired business executive David Neeleman focus on the importance of effective human relations. You have to be nice to begin with (have good human relations skills and a positive attitude), and then you have to treat your customers well (more good human relations skills).

In other words, you can accomplish more in dealing with people in both personal and work life. You can do so by relying on guidelines developed by psychologists, counsellors, and other human relations specialists.

This book presents a wide variety of suggestions and guidelines for improving your personal relationships both on and off the job. Most of them are based on systematic knowledge about human behaviour. Our main concern, however, will be with the suggestions and guidelines themselves, not the methods by which these ideas were discovered.

WHAT IS THE NATURE AND IMPORTANCE OF HUMAN RELATIONS?

In the context used here, **human relations** is the art of using systematic knowledge about human behaviour to improve personal, job, and career effectiveness. Human relations is far more than "being nice to people" because it applies systematic knowledge to treating people in such a way that they feel better and are more productive, such as providing a more relaxed work atmosphere to enhance worker creativity.

Similar to the field known as organizational behaviour, human relations studies individuals and groups in organizations. Human relations, however, is essentially a less technical and more applied version of organizational behaviour. In this text we make some references to research and theory, but the emphasis is on a more personal and applied approach to the subject matter.

From the standpoint of management, human relations is quite important because it contributes to **organizational effectiveness**—the extent to which an organization is productive and satisfies the demands of interested parties, such as employees, customers, and investors. Steve Kent, an equity analyst (not a human relations specialist) at Goldman Sachs & Co., made extensive observations about the importance of treating employees well (using principles of human relations). He found that treating employees with respect and paying them fairly contributes to developing an efficient and creative organization. Business firms that go the extra mile to treat employees well often derive tangible benefits, such as a high quality of customer service.

Kent notes that Starbucks Corporation is at the forefront of treating workers with respect. CEO Howard Schultz has set the tone from the top and made it clear that workers will not be neglected. For example, employees who work at least 20 hours per week are eligible for health benefits and may get a chance to receive a stock option grant. (A stock option allows the employee to purchase stock at a specified price at a later date. So if the stock rises in price, the employee can buy it at a profit.) As a result of good human relations, Starbucks's employee turnover is low for the restaurant industry, and its customer service levels are high.[2]

Why does paying more attention to the human element improve business performance? The organizational behaviour professor Jeffery Pfeffer at Stanford University notes that people work harder when they have greater control over their work environment, and when they are encouraged by peer pressure from teammates. Even more advantage comes from people working smarter. People-oriented management practices enable workers to use their wisdom and receive the training they need to perform better. Another contribution to improved performance stems from eliminating positions that focus primarily on watching and controlling people.[3]

HOW WORK AND PERSONAL LIFE INFLUENCE EACH OTHER

Most people reading this book will be doing so to improve their careers. Therefore, the book focuses on relationships with people in a job setting. Keep in mind that human relationships in work and personal life have much in common. One such study conducted by Timothy A. Judge, psychology professor at the University of Florida, and Remus Ilies, psychology professor at Michigan State University, involved 74 university employees with administrative support positions, such as secretaries or office managers. The researchers collected reports of mood and job satisfaction at work, mood away from work, and job satisfaction. Data were collected using questionnaires posted on a website.

The major findings of the study were that mood influences job satisfaction, with a positive mood increasing satisfaction. The effect decreases rapidly because moods pass quickly. The researchers also found that employees' satisfaction with their jobs, measured at work, influences the mood at home. Workers who are more emotional by nature are more likely to experience these relationships, such as joy or anger, on the job spilling over to home life. A related finding was that a mood developed on the job spilled over to the home later in the day.[4] In short, this study confirmed the old cartoons about a worker who is chewed at by the boss coming home and swearing at his or her dog or kicking the furniture!

An earlier study by Judge and a colleague, based on a nationwide sample, supports the close relationship between job satisfaction and life satisfaction. The study also found that both job satisfaction and life satisfaction influence each other. Life satisfaction significantly influenced job satisfaction, and job satisfaction significantly influenced life satisfaction. The relationship between job and life satisfaction is particularly strong at a given time in a person's life. However, being satisfied with your job today has a smaller effect on future life satisfaction.[5]

Work and personal life influence each other in a number of specific ways. First, the satisfactions you achieve on the job contribute to your general life satisfactions. Conversely, if you suffer from chronic job dissatisfaction, your life satisfaction will begin to decline. Career disappointments have been shown to cause marital relationships to suffer. Frustrated on the job, many people start feuding with their partners and other family members.

Second, an unsatisfying job can also affect physical health, primarily by creating stress and burnout. Intense job dissatisfaction may even lead to heart disease, ulcers, intestinal disorders, and skin problems. People who have high job satisfaction even tend to live longer than those who suffer from prolonged job dissatisfaction. Finding the right type of job may thus add years to a person's life.

Third, the quality of your work relationships influences the quality of your personal relationships, and vice versa. If you experience intense conflict in your family, you might be so upset that you will be unable to form good relationships with co-workers. Conversely, if you have a healthy, rewarding personal life, it will be easier for you to form good relationships on the job. People you meet on the job will find it pleasant to relate to a seemingly positive and untroubled person.

Relationships on the job also influence personal relationships. Interacting harmoniously with co-workers can put one in a better mood for dealing with family and friends after hours. Crossing swords with employees and customers during working hours can make it difficult for you to feel comfortable and relaxed with people off the job.

Fourth, certain skills contribute to success in both work and personal life. For example, people who know how to deal effectively with others and get things accomplished on the job can use the same skills to enhance their personal lives. Similarly, people who are effective in dealing with friends and family members, and who can organize things, are likely to be effective supervisors.

Can you think of other ways in which success in work and success in personal life are related? The Human Relations in Practice and the Canada Today feature look more closely at balancing work and personal lives.

Many other companies offer similar programs and arrangements that allow better personal balancing of home and work demands. Many companies, such as IBM Canada, offer *flextime* arrangements. With flextime, all employees must be present for a certain number of core hours (such as 10 a.m. to 3 p.m.), but the employees design the rest of their days or hours according to their own schedule. According to Human Resources Development Canada, flextime is widespread in Canada. Almost one-fifth of the paid Canadian workforce reported being on a flextime arrangement in 1995, up significantly from previous years.

Compressed work weeks are another work option that some employers offer. According to Human Resources Development Canada, between 14 and 24 percent of Canadian

Human Relations in Practice

Eddie Bauer Knows the Impact of Home Life at Work

Eddie Bauer, the casual lifestyle retailer with locations in both the United States and Canada, is an example of a company that recognizes the close connection between work and personal life. Balance between home and work is a strong corporate value at Eddie Bauer. The company uses its work/life programs to help its associates (the company term for employees) lead more productive and balanced lives. Management at Eddie Bauer believes that physical and mental fitness contribute to a productive and satisfied workforce. The various programs help associates to be more focused at work because they know resources are available to help them manage the demands of their personal lives. Over the past several years, the company has introduced more than 20 programs to help associates run their lives more smoothly. For example, Balance Days are offered—a free day intended for associates to schedule a "call in well" absence, once a year. Also, the company offers a Customized Work Environment program that enables associates to choose job-sharing (where one job is divided between two people), a compressed work week (such as working 40 hours in four days), or working at home.

Source: Leslie Fraught, "At Eddie Bauer You Can Work and Have a Life," *Workforce*, April 1997, p. 8.

Canada Today

Work-Life Conflict

While Eddie Bauer may know about the importance of helping employees achieve work and personal life balance, not all companies have picked up on this notion. A comprehensive study by Health Canada, however, offers evidence that argues against the notion of supportive work arrangements by concerned and sensitive employers. For example, one finding of these studies is that one in four employees work more than 50 hours per week—up from one in ten in 1991. Also, employees donate a significant amount of time to unpaid overtime work and spend more time doing work at home after hours. Many working Canadians (38%) report moderate levels of work interferes with family. While just over one in four of the respondents (28%) report high interference from work to family (i.e. perceive that the demands they face at work make it very difficult to satisfy their non-work responsibilities), 35% are currently experiencing little work interference with family.

A comparison of the percentage of the 1991 sample with high work interferes with family to the percentage with high interference in 2001 shows that the proportion of Canadians with high work interferes with family has remained fairly constant over the decade. While in some senses this is a positive finding (this form of interference has not increased), it is also cause for concern as it indicates that little has been done to address this issue.

The study also found that there was more work life interference in workers (both men and women) when they had more life responsibilities (such as caring for children or parents). The work culture was also significant. Organizations that promote a culture of long work hours and/or a culture of work OR family created the most conflicts for workers.

If organizations are not going to help workers cope with after-work responsibilities, more than ever you will need to develop a variety of skills and facilities to balance the increasing demands of the workplace while seeking personal life satisfaction.

Source: Dr. Linda Duxbury and Dr. Chris Higgins, *The 2001 National Work-Life Conflict Study: Report Six*, Health Canada, January 2009. http://www.hc-sc.gc.ca/ewh-semt/pubs/occup-travail/balancing_six-equilibre_six/index-eng.php—accessed June 15, 2010.

workplaces offer this type of work, but only one-fifth to one one-third of employees take advantage of this offer.

Teleworking, another work arrangement, entails working at a location outside the workplace, usually at home. This type of work, also known as *telecommuting*, can be part-time or full-time and may involve the use of computers, the internet, and other electronic processing of information. See the Canada Today feature below to learn more about this work alternative.

HUMAN RELATIONS BEGINS WITH SELF-UNDERSTANDING

Before you can understand other people very well, you must understand yourself. All readers of this book already know something about themselves. An important starting point in learning more about yourself is self-examination. Suppose that instead of being about human relations, this book were about dancing. The reader would obviously need to know what other dancers do right and wrong. But the basic principles of dancing could not be fully grasped unless they were seen in relation to your own style of dancing. Watching a videotape of your dancing, for example, would be helpful. You might also ask other people for comments and suggestions about your dance movements.

Similarly, to achieve **self-understanding**, you must gather valid information about yourself. (Self-understanding refers to knowledge about oneself, particularly with respect to mental and emotional aspects.) Every time you read a self-help book, take a personality quiz, or receive an evaluation of your work from a manager or instructor, you are gaining some self-knowledge.

In achieving self-understanding, it is helpful to recognize that the **self** is a complex idea. It generally refers to a person's total being or individuality. However, a distinction is sometimes made between the self a person projects to the outside world and the inner self. The **public self** is what the person is communicating about himself or herself, and what others actually perceive about the person. The **private self** is the actual person that one is.[6] To avoid making continual distinctions between the various selves throughout this text, we will use the term *self* to refer to an accurate representation of the individual.

Although an entire chapter in this book is devoted to the self, that is not meant to imply that the other chapters do not deal with the self. Most of this text is geared toward using human relations knowledge for self-development and self-improvement. Throughout the text you will find questionnaires designed to improve insight. The self-knowledge emphasized here deals with psychological characteristics (such as personality traits and thinking style) rather than physical ones (such as height and blood pressure).

Here we discuss six types of information that contribute to self-understanding:

- General information about human behaviour
- Informal feedback from people including co-workers
- Feedback from employers, managers, and team leaders
- Feedback from self-assessment quizzes
- Insights gathered in psychotherapy and counselling

General Information about Human Behaviour

As you learn about people in general, you should also be gaining knowledge about yourself. Therefore, most of the information in this text is presented in a form that should be useful to you personally. Whenever general information is presented, it is your responsibility to relate such information to your particular situation. Chapter 7, for example, discusses some causes of conflicts in personal relationships. One such general cause is limited resources; that is, not everyone can have what he or she wants. Consider how this general principle applies to you. An example involving others is, "That's why I've been so angry with Melissa lately. She was the one given the promotion, while I'm stuck in the same old job."

In relating facts and observations about people in general to yourself, be careful not to misapply the information. Feedback from other people will help you avoid the pitfalls of introspection (looking into oneself).

Informal Feedback from People (Including Co-workers)

As just implied, feedback is information that tells you how well you have performed. You can sometimes obtain feedback from the spontaneous comments of others, or by asking them for feedback. A materials-handling specialist grew one notch in self-confidence when co-workers began to call him "Lightning." He was given this name because of the rapidity with which he processed orders. His experience illustrates that a valuable source of information for self-understanding is what the significant people in your life think of you. Although feedback of this type might make you feel uncomfortable, when it is consistent, it accurately reflects how you are perceived by others.

With some ingenuity you can create informal feedback. (In this sense, the term *informal* refers to not being part of a company-sponsored program.) A student enrolled in a human relations course obtained valuable information about himself from a questionnaire he emailed to 15 people. Here are his directions:

> I am hoping that you can help me with one of the most important assignments of my life. I want to obtain a candid picture of how I am seen by others—what they think are my strengths, weaknesses, good points, and bad points. Any other observations about me as an individual would also be welcome. Write down your thoughts and email them back to me.

A few skeptics will argue that friends never give you a true picture of yourself, but rather say flattering things about you because they value your friendship. Experience has shown, however, that if you emphasize the importance of their opinions, most people will give you a few constructive suggestions. You also have to appear to be sincere. Since not everyone's comments will be helpful, you may have to sample many people.

Similar to friends, co-workers can give you informal feedback as well. Open-ended questions work best such as, "How can I improve my communication with customers?", or "What kind of additional training would you recommend for me to improve my presentations?" Approach co-workers that you have good relations with and those who view your work regularly.

Feedback from Employers, Managers, and Team Leaders

Virtually all employers provide employees with formal and/or informal feedback on their performance. A formal method of feedback is called a *performance appraisal*. During a performance appraisal, your manager or team leader will convey to you what he or she thinks you are doing well and not so well. These observations become a permanent part of your personnel record. Informal feedback occurs when a manager or team leader discusses your job performance with you but does not record these observations.

The feedback obtained from managers in this way can help you learn about yourself. For instance, if two different managers say that you are a creative problem solver, you might conclude that you are creative. If several managers told you that you are too impatient with other people, you might conclude that you are impatient.

Given that work life consumes so much of a working adult's time, it becomes a valuable source of information about the self. Many people, in fact, base much of their identity on their occupations. Next time you are at a social gathering, ask a person "What do you do?" Most likely, the person will respond in terms of an occupation or a company affiliation. It is a rare person in our culture who responds, "I sleep, I eat, I watch television, and I talk to friends."

Feedback from Self-Examination Quizzes

Many self-help books, including this one, contain questionnaires and quizzes that you fill out by yourself, for yourself. The information that you pick up from these questionnaires often provides valuable clues to your preferences, values, and personal traits. Such self-examination questionnaires should not be confused with the scientifically researched tests you might take in a counselling centre or guidance department, or when applying for a job.

The amount of useful information gained from self-examination questionnaires depends on your candour. Since no outside judge is involved in these self-help quizzes, candour is usually not a problem. An exception is that we all have certain blind spots. Most people, for example, believe that they have considerably above-average skills in dealing with people.

As a starting point in conducting self-examination quizzes, fill out Human Relations Self-Assessment Quiz 1-1. The quiz will help get you into the self-examination mode.

Insights Gathered in Psychotherapy and Counselling

Many people seek self-understanding through discussions with a psychotherapist or other professional counsellor. **Psychotherapy** is a method of overcoming emotional problems through discussion with a mental health professional. However, many people enter into psychotherapy with the primary intention of gaining insight into themselves. A representative area of insight would be for the therapist to help the client detect patterns of self-defeating and self-destructive behaviour. For example, some people unconsciously do something to ruin a personal relationship or perform poorly on the job just when things are going well. The therapist might point out this self-defeating pattern of behaviour. Self-insight of this kind often—but not always—leads to useful changes in behaviour.

YOUR SELF-CONCEPT: WHAT YOU THINK OF YOU

Another aspect of self-understanding is your **self-concept**, or what you think of you and who you think you are. A successful person—one who is achieving his or her goals in work or personal life—usually has a positive self-concept. In contrast, an unsuccessful person often has a negative self-concept. Such differences in self-concept can have a profound influence on your career.[7] If you see yourself as a successful person, you will tend to engage in activities that will help you prove this view of yourself right. Similarly, if you have a limited view of yourself, you will tend to engage in activities that prove that limited view right. For example, you may often look for convenient ways to prevent yourself from succeeding.

Self-concepts are based largely on our perceptions of what others have said about us and others' reactions to us. This process of incorporating what others have said about us into our self-concept is known as **reflected appraisal.** Reflected appraisal tends to occur most often when the same thing is told to us by many different people. If enough people tell you that you are "terrific," after a while you will have the self-concept of a terrific person. When people tell you that you are not a worthwhile person, after a while your self-concept will become that of a not-worthwhile person.

Human Relations Self-Assessment

QUIZ 1-1 The Written Self-Portrait

A good starting point in acquiring serious self-knowledge is to prepare a written self-portrait in the major life spheres (or aspects). In each of the spheres listed below, describe yourself in about 25–75 words. For example, under the social and interpersonal sphere, a person might write: "I'm a little timid on the surface. But those people who get to know me well understand that I'm filled with enthusiasm and joy. My relationships with people last a long time. I'm on excellent terms with all members of my family. And my spouse and I have been together for five years. We are very close emotionally, and should be together for a lifetime."

A. ***Occupational and School:***

____

____

____

____

B. ***Social and Interpersonal:***

____

____

____

____

C. ***Beliefs, Values, and Attitudes:***

____

____

____

____

D. ***Physical Description (body type, appearance, grooming):***

____

____

____

____

People who say "I'm OK" are expressing a positive self-concept. People who say "I'm not OK" have a negative self-concept.

We also compare ourselves with others to examine how different we are from others. Through this process of **social comparison**, we describe ourselves in terms of the ways in which we stand out from others around us. These comparisons also become part of our self-concept. For example, you ask others in your class how they did on the last test. Your grade is far better than others in your class. If this is a pattern (your grades higher than others' grades), then you may describe yourself as smarter (at least academically) than the majority of the students in your business program.

Another important fact about the self-concept is that it usually has several components. Many people, for example, have an academic self-concept and a nonacademic self-concept.[8] One person might feel proud and confident in a classroom yet quite humble and shaky on the job. Another person might feel unsure and uneasy in the classroom yet proud and confident on the job. Following the same logic, a person's self-concept with respect to personal life may differ from his or her career self-concept.

The experiences that we have, our changing abilities and knowledge, and our interactions with others create a complex self-concept. The self-concept can change and we can improve how we feel about ourselves. Several strategies to improve your self-concept and self-esteem will be reviewed later in the chapter.

The Self-Concept and Self-Confidence

A strong self-concept leads to self-confidence, which has many important implications for job performance. People who are confident in themselves are more effective in leadership and sales positions. Self-confident workers are also more likely to set higher goals for themselves and to persist in trying to reach their goals.[9]

Why some people develop strong self-concepts and self-confidence while others have weak self-concepts and self-confidence is not entirely known. One contributing factor may be inherited talents and abilities. Assume that a person quickly learns how to perform key tasks in life such as walking, talking, swimming, running, reading, writing, computing, and driving a car. This person is likely to be more self-confident than a person who struggled to learn these skills.

Another contributing factor to a positive self-concept and self-confidence is lifelong feedback from others (as mentioned above). If, as a youngster, your parents, siblings, and playmates consistently told you that you were competent, you would probably develop a strong self-concept. However, some people might find you to be conceited.

Self-confidence also contributes heavily to leadership ability. How to build self-confidence will therefore be described in Chapter 12, which deals with becoming a leader.

Group Identification and the Self-Concept

Similar to the process of social comparison, another important source of the self-concept is the small groups people join. People not only compare themselves with others, but choose groups that are attractive to them. For example, if you feel that you are athletic you may join sports groups. As part of a baseball team or some other team, you begin to identify yourself as a baseball player as well as a member of this specific team.

Also, according to research by the social psychologist Marilynn Brewer, people join small groups to achieve some degree of individuality and identity.[10] People develop much of their self-concepts by comparing their own group with others. The group you identify with becomes part of your psychological self. Joining the group satisfies two conflicting needs. A person wants to retain some individuality, so being a member of a mega-group like students or General Motors employees does not quite do the job. Yet people also yearn to have some group affiliation. So joining a small group that is distinctive from others is a happy compromise.

The smaller group the person joins becomes part of the self-image and self-concept for many people. A sampling of the kinds of groups that could become part of a person's self-concept might include athletic teams, church groups, street gangs, musical bands, volunteer committees, and internet chat rooms. What group memberships have become part of your self-concept?

THE NATURE AND CONSEQUENCES OF SELF-ESTEEM

Although the various approaches to discussing the self may seem confusing and overlapping, all of them strongly influence your life. A particularly important role is played by **self-esteem**, the experience of feeling competent to cope with the basic challenges in life and of being worthy of happiness.[11] In more general terms, self-esteem refers to a positive overall evaluation of oneself. People with positive self-esteem have a deep-down, inside-the-self feeling of their own worth. Consequently, they develop a positive self-concept. Before reading further, you are invited to measure your current level of self-esteem by taking our Human Relations Self-Assessment Quiz 1-2. We look next at the nature of self-esteem and many of its consequences.

The Nature of Self-Esteem

The definition just presented tells a lot about self-esteem, yet there is much more to know about its nature. According to Nathaniel Branden, self-esteem has two interrelated components: self-efficacy and self-respect.[12] **Self-efficacy** is confidence in your ability to carry out a specific task in contrast to generalized self-confidence. When self-efficacy is high, you believe you have the ability to do what is necessary to complete a task successfully. Being confident that you can perform a particular task well contributes to self-esteem.

Self-respect, the second component of self-esteem, refers to how you think and feel about yourself. Self-respect fits the everyday meaning of self-esteem. Many street beggars are intelligent, able-bodied, and have a good physical appearance. You could argue that their low self-esteem leads them to beg. Also, people with low self-respect and self-esteem allow themselves to stay in relationships where they are frequently verbally and physically abused. These abused people have such low self-worth they think they deserve punishment. Another noteworthy aspect of self-respect is that when individuals are secure with themselves (high self-respect), they are less likely to be self-absorbed. As a consequence, they are more likely to focus on the needs of other people.[13]

The Development of Self-Esteem

Part of understanding the nature of self-esteem is knowing how it develops. As with the self-concept, self-esteem comes about from a variety of early-life experiences. People who were encouraged to feel good about themselves and their accomplishments by family members, friends, and teachers are more likely to enjoy high self-esteem. Early-life experiences play a key role in the development of both healthy self-esteem and low self-esteem, according to research synthesized at the Counselling and Mental Health Centre of the

University of Texas.[14] Childhood experiences that lead to healthy self-esteem include the following:

- being praised
- being listened to
- being spoken to respectfully
- getting attention and hugs
- experiencing success in sports or school

In contrast, childhood experiences that lead to low self-esteem include the following:

- being harshly criticized
- being yelled at or beaten
- being ignored, ridiculed, or teased
- being expected to be "perfect" all the time
- experiencing failures in sports or school
- often being given messages that failed experiences (losing a game, getting a poor grade, and so forth) were failures of their whole self.

A widespread explanation of self-esteem development is that compliments, praise, and hugs alone build self-esteem. Yet many developmental psychologists seriously question this perspective. Instead, they believe that self-esteem results from accomplishing worthwhile activities and then feeling proud of these accomplishments. Receiving encouragement, however, can help the person accomplish activities that build self-esteem.

The psychologist Martin Seligman argues that self-esteem is caused by a variety of successes and failures. To develop self-esteem people need to improve their skills for dealing with the world.[15] Self-esteem therefore comes about through genuine accomplishments, followed by praise and recognition. Heaping undeserved praise and recognition on people may lead to a temporary high, but it does not produce genuine self-esteem. The child develops self-esteem not from being told he or she can score a goal in soccer, but from scoring that goal.

Although early-life experiences have the major impact on the development of self-esteem, experiences in adult life also impact self-esteem. David De Cremer of the Tilburg University (Netherlands) and his associates conducted two studies with Dutch college students about how the behaviour of leaders and fair procedures influence self-esteem. The focus of the leaders' behaviour was whether they motivated the workers/students to reward themselves for a job well done, for example, giving self-compliments. Procedural fairness was measured in terms of whether the study participants were given a voice in making decisions. Self-esteem was measured by a questionnaire somewhat similar to Human Relations Self-Assessment Quiz 1-2 in this chapter. The study questionnaire reflected the self-perceived value that individuals have of themselves as organizational members.

The study found that self-esteem was related to procedural fairness and leadership that encourages self-rewards. When leadership that encouraged rewards was high, procedural fairness was more strongly related to self-esteem. The interpretation given of the findings is that a leader/supervisor can facilitate self-esteem when he or she encourages

Human Relations Self-Assessment

QUIZ 1-2 The Self-Esteem Checklist

Indicate whether each of the following statements is Mostly True or Mostly False, as it applies to you.

	Mostly True	Mostly False
1. I am excited about starting each day.	____	____
2. Most of any progress I have made in my work or school can be attributed to luck.	____	____
3. I often ask myself, "Why can't I be more successful?"	____	____
4. When I'm given a challenging assignment by my manager or team leader, I usually dive in with confidence.	____	____
5. I believe that I am working up to my potential.	____	____
6. I can set limits to what I will do for others without feeling anxious.	____	____
7. I regularly make excuses for my mistakes.	____	____
8. Someone else's bad mood will affect my good mood.	____	____
9. I care very much how much money other people make, especially when they are working in my field.	____	____
10. I feel like a failure when I do not achieve my goals.	____	____
11. Hard work gives me an emotional lift.	____	____
12. When others compliment me, I doubt their sincerity.	____	____
13. Complimenting others makes me feel uncomfortable.	____	____
14. I find it comfortable to say, "I'm sorry."	____	____
15. It is difficult for me to face up to my mistakes.	____	____
16. My co-workers think I should not be promoted.	____	____
17. People who want to become my friends usually do not have much to offer.	____	____
18. If my manager praised me, I would have a difficult time believing it was deserved.	____	____
19. I'm just an ordinary person.	____	____
20. Having to face change really disturbs me.	____	____

Scoring and Interpretation: The answers in the high-self-esteem direction are as follows:

1. Mostly True
2. Mostly False
3. Mostly False
4. Mostly True
5. Mostly True
6. Mostly True
7. Mostly False
8. Mostly False
9. Mostly False
10. Mostly False
11. Mostly True
12. Mostly False
13. Mostly False
14. Mostly True
15. Mostly False
16. Mostly False
17. Mostly False
18. Mostly False
19. Mostly False
20. Mostly False

17–20: You have very high self-esteem. Yet if your score is 20, it could be that you are denying any self-doubts.

11–16: Your self-esteem is in the average range. It would probably be worthwhile for you to implement strategies to boost your self-esteem (described in this chapter) so that you can develop a greater feeling of well-being.

0–10: Your self-esteem needs bolstering. Talk over your feelings about yourself with a trusted friend or with a mental health professional. At the same time, attempt to implement several of the tactics for boosting self-esteem described in this chapter.

self-rewards and uses fair procedures. Furthermore, fair procedures have a stronger impact on self-esteem when the leader encourages self-rewards.[16] A takeaway from this study would be that rewarding yourself for a job well done, even in adult life, can boost your self-esteem a little.

The Consequences of Self-Esteem

No single factor is as important to career success as self-esteem, as observed by the psychologist Eugene Raudsepp. People with positive self-esteem understand their own competence and worth, and have positive perceptions of their abilities to cope with problems and adversity.[17] Kendrick Melrose, former CEO of Toro, illustrates this fundamental point. Toro employees were bedraggled because of some rough time business years, and they were reluctant to make decisions. Melrose helped them learn how to make decisions as a team. He said, "The transformation in management philosophy built self-esteem. It built innovation, creativity, risk, ownership."[18]

One of the major consequences of high self-esteem is good mental health. People with high self-esteem feel good about themselves and have a positive outlook on life. One of the links between good mental health and self-esteem is that high self-esteem helps prevent many situations from being stressful. Few negative comments from others are likely to bother you when your self-esteem is high. A person with low self-esteem might crumble if somebody insulted his or her appearance. A person with high self-esteem might shrug off the insult as simply being the other person's point of view. If faced with an everyday setback such as losing keys, the high-self-esteem person might think, "I have so much going for me, why fall apart over this incident?"

Although people with high self-esteem can readily shrug off undeserved insults, they still profit well from negative feedback. Because they are secure, they can profit from the developmental opportunities suggested by negative feedback.

Workers with high self-esteem develop and maintain favourable work attitudes and perform at a high level. These positive consequences take place because such attitudes and behaviour are consistent with the personal belief that they are competent individuals. Mary Kay Ash, the legendary founder of a beauty-products company, put it this way, "It never occurred to me I couldn't do it. I always knew that if I worked hard enough, I could." Furthermore, research has shown that high-self-esteem individuals value reaching work goals more than do low-self-esteem individuals.[19]

The combined effect of workers having high self-esteem helps a company prosper. Long-term research by Branden, as well as more recent studies, suggests that self-esteem is a critical source of competitive advantage in an information-based society. Companies gain the edge when, in addition to having an educated workforce, employees have high self-esteem, as shown by behaviours such as the following:

- Being creative and innovative
- Taking personal responsibility for problems
- Feeling independent while still wanting to work cooperatively with others
- Trusting one's own capabilities
- Taking the initiative to solve problems[20]

Behaviours such as these help workers cope with the challenge of a rapidly changing workplace where products and ideas become obsolete quickly. Workers with high self-esteem are more likely to be able to cope with new challenges regularly because they are confident they can master their environment.

A major consequence of low self-esteem is poor mental health. People with low self-esteem are often depressed, and many people who appear to have "paranoid personalities" are suffering from low self-esteem. A store manager who continually accused store associates of talking behind his back finally said to a mental health counsellor, "Face it, I think I'm almost worthless, so I think people have negative things to say about me."

Low self-esteem can have negative consequences for romantic relationships because people with self-doubts consistently underestimate their partners' feelings for them. People with low self-respect distance themselves from the relationship—often devaluing their partner—to prepare themselves for what they think will be an inevitable breakup. John G. Holmes, a psychologist at the University of Waterloo in Ontario, Canada, says, "If people think negatively about themselves, they think their partner must think negatively about them—and they're wrong."[21]

The consequences of self-esteem are related to its source. People who evaluate their self-worth on how others perceive them and not on their value as human beings often suffer negative mental and physical consequences. In a series of studies, the developmental psychologist Jennifer Crocker found that college students who based their self-worth on external sources reported more stress, anger, academic problems, and interpersonal conflicts. In addition, these students had higher levels of drug and alcohol use and symptoms of eating disorders. (External sources of self-worth include appearance, approval from others, and grades in school.) Students who based their self-esteem (or self-worth) on internal sources generally received higher grades and were less likely to consume alcohol and drugs or develop eating disorders.[22] (An internal source would be thinking of yourself as a kind and charitable person.)

How to Enhance Self-Esteem

Improving self-esteem is a lifelong process because self-esteem is related to the success of your activities and interactions with people. The following are four approaches to enhancing self-esteem that are related to how self-esteem develops:

Legitimate Accomplishment and Self-Esteem To emphasize again, accomplishing worthwhile activities is a major contributor to self-esteem in both children and adults. Social science research suggests this sequence of events: Person establishes a goal → person pursues the goal → person achieves the goal → person develops esteem-like feelings.[23] The opposite point of view is this sequence: Person develops esteem-like feelings → person establishes a goal → person pursues the goal → person achieves the goal.

Similarly, giving people large trophies for mundane accomplishments is unlikely to raise self-esteem. More likely, the person will see through the transparent attempt to build his or her self-esteem and develop negative feelings about the self. What about you? Would your self-esteem receive a bigger boost by (1) receiving an A in a course in which 10 percent of the class received an A, or (2) receiving an A in a class in which everybody received the same grade?

Awareness of Strengths and Self-Esteem Another method of improving your self-esteem is to develop an appreciation of your strengths and accomplishments. Research with over 60 executives showed that their self-concepts became more positive after one month of practising this exercise for a few minutes every day.[24] A good starting point is to list your strengths and accomplishments on paper. This list is likely to be more impressive than you expected. The list of strengths and accomplishments requested in the Human Relations Self-Assessment Quiz 1-3 can be used for building self-esteem.

You can sometimes develop an appreciation of your strengths by participating in a group exercise designed for such purposes. A group of about seven people meet to form a support group. All group members first spend about ten minutes answering the question, "What are my three strongest points, attributes, or skills?" After each group member has recorded his or her three strengths, that person discusses them with the other group members.

Each group member then comments on the list. Other group members sometimes add to your list of strengths or reinforce what you have to say. Sometimes you may find disagreement. One member told the group: "I'm handsome, intelligent, reliable, athletic, self-confident, and very moral. I also have a good sense of humour." Another group member retorted, "And I might add that you're unbearably conceited."

Minimize Settings and Interactions That Detract from Your Feelings of Competence Most of us have situations in work and personal life that make us feel less than our best. If you can minimize exposure to those situations, you will have fewer feelings of incompetence. The problem with feeling incompetent is that it lowers your self-esteem. An office supervisor said she detested company picnics, most of all because she was forced into playing softball. At her own admission, she had less aptitude for athletics than any able-bodied person she knew. In addition, she felt uncomfortable with the small talk characteristic of picnics. To minimize discomfort, the woman attended only those picnics she thought were absolutely necessary. Instead of playing on the softball team, she volunteered to be the equipment manager.

A problem with avoiding all situations in which you feel lowly competent is that it might prevent you from acquiring needed skills. Also, it boosts your self-confidence and self-esteem to become comfortable in a previously uncomfortable situation.

Talk and Socialize Frequently with People Who Boost Your Self-Esteem The psychologist Barbara Ilardie says that the people who can raise your self-esteem are usually those with high self-esteem themselves. They are the people who give honest feedback because they respect others and themselves. Such high-self-esteem individuals should not be confused with yes-people who agree with others just to be liked. The point is that you typically receive more from strong people than weak ones. Weak people will flatter you but will not give you the honest feedback you need to build self-esteem.[25]

Model the Behaviour of People with High Self-Esteem

Observe the way people who are believed to have high self-esteem stand, walk, speak, and act. Even if you are not feeling so secure inside, you will project a high-self-esteem image

Human Relations Self-Assessment

QUIZ 1-3 The Self-Knowledge Questionnaire

Complete the following questionnaire for your personal use. You might wish to use a worksheet before putting your comments in final form.

I. Education

1. How far have I gone in school?
2. What is my major field of interest? art-Literature
3. Which are (or have been) my best subjects? Literature
4. Which are (or have been) my poorest subjects? Chemistry
5. What further educational plans do I have? Why? Ass diploma- higher salary higher education
6. What extracurricular activities have I participated in? I played theater and painted
7. Which ones did I enjoy? Why? both I Love art.

II. Work Experience

8. What jobs have I held since age 16? tranlator_teacher- writer
9. What aspect of these jobs did I enjoy? Why? Cominucat with people, improve my abilites
10. What aspect of these jobs did I dislike? Why? have a islamic Hijab at work
11. What were my three biggest accomplishments on the job? good writing - good speaking and Patiance
12. What kind of employee am (was) I? Hard worker-hounest
13. What compliments did I receive from my managers, co-workers, or customers? They enjoyed to work with me.
14. What criticisms or suggestions did I receive? Sometimes I was not very kind!
15. What would be an ideal job for me? writing is my dremwork.

III. Attitudes toward People

16. The kind of people I get along best with are ... most of them
17. The kind of people I clash with are ... liar
18. How many close friends do I have? What is it I like about each one? 2 / hounest and nice
19. Would I prefer working mostly with men or women? Why? men / easier!
20. How much contact with other people do I need? not much
21. My arguments with other people are mostly about ... politic

IV. Attitudes toward and Perceptions of Myself

22. What are my strengths? Strong fighter. hunest-Smart - hard worker
23. What are my weaknesses or opportunities for improvement? Sometimes I'm not ontime
24. What do I think of me? Improud of myself
25. What do I worry about most? my Kids
26. What is my biggest problem? I don't have a job
27. What things in life do I dislike? depretion
28. What have I accomplished in life so far? Writing-coming to Canada- Learning multpal Language
29. Has this been enough accomplishment? Not realy
30. So far, what has been the happiest period of my life? Why? when my Kids were born. I love mother hood
31. What gives me satisfaction in life? Writing
32. In what ways do I make life miserable for myself? Staying at home all the time
33. What motivates me? my children

(continued)

(continued)

V. How People outside of Work See Me

34. What is the best compliment my spouse (or a good friend) has paid me?
35. In what ways would my spouse (or a good friend) like me to change?
36. What do my friends like best about me?
37. What do my friends dislike about me?

VI. Hobbies, Interests, Sports

38. What activities, hobbies, interests, sports, and so forth do I actively participate in?
39. Which one of these do I really get excited about? Why?

VII. My Future

40. What are my plans for further education and training?
41. What positions would I like to hold within the next five years?
42. What are my career goals beyond five years?
43. Where would I like to be at the peak of my career?
44. What activities and interests would I like to pursue in the future?
45. What goals do I have relating to friends, family, and marriage?

Additional Thoughts

1. What other questions should have been asked of you in the Self-Knowledge Questionnaire?
2. To what use can you put all or part of this information?
3. What impact did completing this questionnaire have on your self-understanding?

if you act assured. Raudsepp recommends, "Stand tall, speak clearly and with confidence, shake hands firmly, look people in the eye and smile frequently. Your self-esteem will increase as you notice encouraging reactions from others."[26] (Notice here that self-esteem is considered to be about the same idea as self-confidence.)

Choose your models of high self-esteem from people you know personally as well as celebrities you might watch on television news and interview shows. Observing actors on the large or small screen is a little less useful because they are guaranteed to be playing a role. Identifying a teacher or professor as a self-esteem model is widely practised, as is observing successful family members and friends.

Building self-esteem is a major asset in life. Yet, as with self-efficacy, a danger exists in having highly inflated self-esteem. A controversial study conducted in England found that people with high self-esteem might have an unrealistic sense of themselves. "They expect to do well at things, discount failure, and feel beyond reproach." Furthermore, people with exaggerated self-esteem are sometimes intolerant of people who are different from them.[27]

HOW STUDYING HUMAN RELATIONS CAN BENEFIT YOU

A person who carefully studies the information in this book and incorporates its suggestions into his or her way of doing things should derive the five benefits discussed next. Knowledge itself, however, is not a guarantee of success. Since people differ greatly in learning ability, personality, and life circumstances, some will get more out of this book than will others.

You may, for example, be getting along so well with co-workers or customers that the chapter on this topic is unnecessary from your viewpoint. Or you may be so shy at this stage of your life that you are at present unable to capitalize on some of the tips for being assertive with people. You might have to work doubly hard to reap benefit from that particular chapter.

The major benefits from studying human relations are

- *Acquiring valid information about human behaviour.* To feel comfortable with other people and to make a favourable impression (both on and off the job), one needs to understand how people think and act. This book will provide you with some basic knowledge about interpersonal relationships such as the meaning of emotional security, openness, and nonverbal messages. You will even learn about such things as mimicking another person's body movements in order to improve rapport with that person.
- *Developing skills in dealing with people.* Anyone who aspires to high-level jobs or an enriched social life needs to be able to communicate with others, resolve conflict, and behave in a confident manner. Relating well to diverse cultural groups is also an asset. Studying information about such topics in this book, coupled with trying them out in practice, should help you develop such interpersonal skills.
- *Coping with job problems.* Almost everyone who holds a job inevitably runs into human relations problems. Reading about these problems and suggestions for coping with them could save you considerable inner turmoil. Among the job survival skills that you will learn about in the following chapters are how to cope with job stress and how to overcome what seems to be an overwhelming workload.
- *Coping with personal problems.* We all have problems. An important difference between the effective and ineffective person is that the effective person knows how to manage them. Among the problems this book will help you cope with are shyness, finding a job when you are unemployed, overcoming low self-confidence, and managing stress.
- *Capitalizing on opportunities.* Many readers of this book will someday spend part of their working time taking advantage of opportunities rather than solving daily problems. Every career-minded person needs a few breakthrough experiences in order to make his or her life more rewarding. Toward this end, the book discusses how to get ahead in your career and how to become a leader.

SUMMARY

Human relations is the art and practice of using systematic knowledge about human behaviour to improve personal, job, and career effectiveness.

Work and personal life often influence each other in several ways. A high level of job satisfaction tends to spill over to one's personal life. Conversely, an unsatisfactory personal life could lead to negative job attitudes. Another close tie between work and personal life is that one's job can affect physical and mental health. Severely negative job conditions may lead to a serious stress disorder, such as heart disease.

The quality of one's relationships with people in work and the quality of one's personal relationships influence each other. Also, certain skills (such as the ability to listen) contribute to success in work and personal life.

To be effective in human relationships, you must first understand yourself. Six methods for gaining self-understanding are: (1) acquire general information about human behaviour and apply it to yourself; (2) obtain informal feedback from people including co-workers; (3) obtain feedback from superiors; (4) obtain feedback from skill-building exercises and self-assessment quizzes; and (5) gather insights in psychotherapy and counselling.

An important aspect of self-understanding is your self-concept, or what you think of you and who you think you are. The self-concept is based largely on what others have said about us. A strong self-concept leads to self-confidence, which is a basic requirement for being successful as a leader or in sales.

Self-esteem refers to appreciating self-worth and importance, being accountable for your own behaviour, and acting responsibly toward others. People with high self-esteem develop a positive self-concept. Self-esteem has two interrelated components: self-efficacy (a task-related feeling of competence) and self-respect. Self-esteem develops from a variety of early-life experiences. People who were encouraged to feel good about themselves and their accomplishments by key people in their lives are more likely to enjoy high self-esteem. Most significantly, self-esteem also results from accomplishing worthwhile activities, and then feeling proud of these accomplishments. Praise and recognition for accomplishments also help develop self-esteem.

Good mental health is one of the major consequences of high self-esteem. One of the links between good mental health and self-esteem is that high self-esteem helps prevent many situations from being stressful. Workers with high self-esteem develop and maintain favourable work attitudes and perform at a high level.

A major consequence of low self-esteem is poor mental health. Schoolchildren with low self-esteem are more likely to be delinquents. Workers with low self-esteem often develop and maintain unfavourable work attitudes and perform below expectations.

Self-esteem can be enhanced in many ways. Accomplishing worthwhile activities is a major contributor to self-esteem in both children and adults. Developing an appreciation of your strengths and accomplishments is another self-esteem builder. It is also important to minimize settings and interactions that detract from your feelings of competence. In addition, talk and socialize frequently with people who boost your self-esteem. Finally, model the behaviour of people with high self-esteem to assist in boosting your own self-esteem.

QUESTIONS AND ACTIVITIES

1. Why is it difficult for a person with poor human relations skills to succeed in business?
2. How important are human relations skills in an era of high technology in the workplace?
3. Give an example of a business executive, politician, athletic coach, or professor whom you think has exceptional human relations skills. On what basis did you reach your conclusion?
4. How do some people attempt to combine work and personal life?
5. Give an example from your own experience of how work life influences personal life and vice versa.
6. Whom can a person turn to as the most reliable source of feedback about himself or herself?

7. Of the sources of information about the self described in this chapter, which one do you think is likely to be the most accurate? Why?
8. How can your self-concept affect your career?
9. Having workers with high self-esteem is supposed to give a company a competitive edge. If you were responsible for hiring a few new workers, how would you evaluate a given applicant's level of self-esteem?
10. Interview a person whom you perceive to have a successful career. Ask that person to describe his or her self-concept. Be prepared to discuss your findings in class.

INTERNET SKILL BUILDER

The Importance of Human Relations Skills in Business

One of the themes of this chapter and the entire book is that human relations skills are important for success in business. But what do employers really think? To find out, visit the websites of five of your favourite companies, such as www.apple.com or www.ge.com. Go to the employment section and search for a job that you might qualify for now or in the future. Investigate which human relations or interpersonal skills the employer mentions as a requirement, such as "Must have superior spoken communication skills." Make up a list of the human relations, or interpersonal skills, you find mentioned. What conclusion or conclusions do you reach from this exercise?

Log on to the **Companion Website** at **www.pearsoncanada.ca/dubrin** to access additional resources for this chapter.

CASE STUDY 1-1 HUMAN RELATIONS

Self-Esteem Building at Pyramid Remanufacturing

Pyramid Remanufacturing opened for business ten years ago in a cinder block building with four employees. Today Pyramid is housed in an old factory building in a low-rent district. The company has 100 full-time employees and about 50 part-timers. The nature of the company's business is to salvage parts from used or broken equipment sent to them by other companies. One of Pyramid's remanufacturing projects is to salvage the workable parts from single-use cameras and recycle the balance of the plastic parts. Another large company contract is to salvage parts from children's toys that purchasers have returned to retailers because they do not function properly. Both contracts also call for making new single-use cameras and toys, incorporating the salvaged parts.

The basic remanufacturing jobs can be learned in several hours. The work is not complex, but it is tedious. For example, a remanufacturing technician would be expected to tear down, salvage, and assemble about 100 single-use cameras per day. The jobs pay about twice the minimum wage, and full-time workers receive standard benefits.

Derrick Lockett, president and founder of Pyramid, believes that his company plays an important role in society. As he explains, "First of all, note that we are remanufacturers. We are helping save the planet. Think of the thousands and thousands of single-use cameras that do not wind up in landfills because of our recycling efforts. The same goes for plastic toys. Consider also that we hire a lot of people who would not be working if it were not for Pyramid. A lot of our employees would be on welfare if they were not working here. We hire a lot of people from the welfare rolls. We also hire a lot of troubled teenagers and seniors who can't find employment elsewhere.

"Some of our other employees have a variety of disabilities which make job-finding difficult for them. Two of our highest producers are blind. They have a wonderful sense of touch, and they can visualize the parts that have to be separated and assembled. Another source of good employees for us is recently released prisoners."

Lockett was asked if all Pyramid manufacturing employees were performing up to standard. He explained that about one-fourth of the workforce were either working so slowly or doing such sloppy work that they were a poor investment for the company. "Face it," said Lockett, "some of our employees are dragging us down. After a while we have to weed out the workers who just don't earn their salary."

Next, Lockett gave his analysis of why some remanufacturing technicians are unable to perform properly. "Lots of reasons," said Lockett. "Some can't read; some have a poor work ethic; some have attention deficit disorders. But the big problem is that many of the poor performers have such rotten self-esteem. They don't believe in themselves. They think nobody wants them and that they are incapable of being valuable employees."

Lucy Winters, the director of human resources and administration, explained what Pyramid was attempting to do about the self-esteem problem. "You have to realize," she said, "that it's not easy for a company to build the self-esteem of entry-level employees. Derrick and I would both like to save the world, but we can't do everything. But we are taking a few initiatives to build the self-esteem of our employees.

"One approach is that our supervisors give out brightly coloured badges imprinted with the words 'I'm a real remanufacturer.' The supervisors are supposed to give out the badges when a technician looks to be down in the dumps. We also have a newsletter that features stories about our remanufacturing technicians. Each month we choose somebody to be 'Remanufacturer of the Month.' Usually it's an employee whose self-esteem appears to be hurting."

"Another approach is more informal. We ask our supervisors to remember to be cheerleaders. They're supposed to lift the spirits of employees who don't think much of themselves by saying things like 'I know you can do it,' or 'I believe in you.'"

When asked how the self-esteem-building program was working, Winters and Lockett both said it was too early to tell with certainty. Winters did say, however, "I see a few bright smiles out there among our technicians. And the turnover rate is down about five percent. So the program might be working."

Questions

1. What is your evaluation of Lockett's analysis that low self-esteem could hurt the work performance of entry-level remanufacturing technicians?
2. What is your evaluation of the self-esteem-building program at Pyramid?
3. What other suggestions can you offer for building the self-esteem of the Pyramid employees who appear to be having a self-esteem problem?

CASE STUDY 1-2 HUMAN RELATIONS

Building Up Kristina

Kristina Wright entered the front door of the half of a house she was sharing with Wendy Lopez. Her housemate said, "I don't see a smile on your face. How did the job hunt go today?"

"Not too well," replied Wright. "I had two interviews, but I doubt I will be called back. After all there are dozens of applicants looking for administrative assistant positions with better qualifications than mine. In this economy you really have to know the right people to land a job."

"Will you please stop it, Kristina? You're as good as or better than the competition. You have your degree, and you have experience as an administrative intern. Besides that, you look great."

"That's easy for you to say, Wendy. You have a good job, and people like you. I'm simply average, average, average. Even Lucky [Kristina's cocker spaniel] has an average name. And thousands of girls are named Kristina."

"With an attitude like that," replied Lopez, "you won't get hired. Be proud of who you are. You are somebody special."

"Thanks for the ego boost, my ever-faithful friend. But I almost don't have the courage to go back out there tomorrow and face any more interviews."

Questions

1. What seems to be Wright's problem based on the brief information you have been given?
2. What recommendations can you make to Wright to boost her self-confidence enough to get through any upcoming job interviews she might have?
3. How helpful might be the words of encouragement and advice that Lopez has given Wright so far?

Chapter 2

Self-Motivation and Goal Setting

Learning Outcomes

After studying the information and doing the exercises in this chapter, you should be able to

- explain how needs and motives influence motivation;
- identify several needs and motives that could be propelling you into action;
- pinpoint how the hierarchy of needs could explain your behaviour;
- explain why and how goals contribute to self-motivation;
- describe how to set effective goals;
- specify the problems sometimes created by goals;
- describe several specific techniques of self-motivation;
- apply the self-discipline model to achieve your goals.

Gary Rogers is the president of Jasco Tools, a company that employs 300 people. He thinks that the employee work ethic is a big problem. According to Rogers, job applicants come to the firm asking what's in the job for them, not what they can do to make the company a success. "It used to be that you would find job applicants dressed up for an interview. They would wear a suit and tie or dress and try to make a good impression. Now they come in jeans and hats turned around backwards." Rogers said that Jasco tries to teach virtues such as punctuality and teamwork. But basic attitudes won't change until schools and parents start to instill a work ethic.[1]

Whether or not you agree with Gary Rogers that the work ethic (belief in the dignity of work) is declining, his comments emphasize an important truth. You have to be motivated to achieve success in work. Strong motivation is also important for personal life. Unless you direct your energies toward specific goals, such as improving your productivity or meeting a new friend, you will accomplish very little. Knowledge of motivation and goal setting, when applied, can therefore pay substantial dividends in improving the quality of your life. Understanding motivation and goal setting is also important when attempting to influence others to get things accomplished. Motivating others, for example, is a major requirement of a manager's job.

Being well motivated is also important just to meet the demands of employers. Even when unemployment is low, most organizations insist on high productivity and quality from workers at all levels. Assuming you have the necessary skills, training, and equipment, being well motivated will enable you to achieve high productivity and quality. Furthermore, workers in professional-level positions are often expected to work about 55 hours per week, which includes doing work at home.

The general purpose of this chapter is to present information that can help you sustain a high level of motivation by focusing on the importance of needs and goals.

HOW NEEDS AND MOTIVES INFLUENCE MOTIVATION

According to a widely accepted explanation of human behaviour, people have needs and motives that propel them toward achieving certain goals. Needs and motives are closely related. A **need** is an internal striving or urge to do something, such as a need to drink when thirsty. It can be regarded as a biological or psychological requirement. Because the person is deprived in some way (such as not having enough fluid in the body), the person takes action toward a goal. In this case, the goal might be simply getting something to drink.

A **motive** is an inner drive that moves a person to do something. The motive is usually based on a need or desire, and results in the intention to attain an appropriate goal. Because needs and motives are so closely related, the two terms are often used interchangeably. For example, "recognition need" and "recognition motive" refer to the same thing.

The Need Theory of Motivation

The central idea behind need theory is that unsatisfied needs, whether physiological or psychological, motivate us until they become satisfied. When people are dissatisfied or anxious about their present status or performance, they will try to reduce this anxiety.[2] This need cycle is shown in Figure 2-1. Assume that you have a strong need or motive to achieve recognition. As a result, you experience tension that drives you to find some way of being recognized on the job. The action you take is to apply for a position as the team leader of your group. You reason that being appointed as team leader would provide ample recognition, particularly if the team performs well.

You are appointed to the position, and for now your need for recognition is at least partially satisfied as you receive compliments from your co-workers and friends. Once you receive this partial satisfaction, two things typically happen. Either you will soon require a stronger dose of recognition, or you will begin to concentrate on another need or motive, such as achievement.

In either case, the drive cycle will repeat itself. You might seek another form of recognition, or satisfaction of your need for power. For example, you might apply for a position as

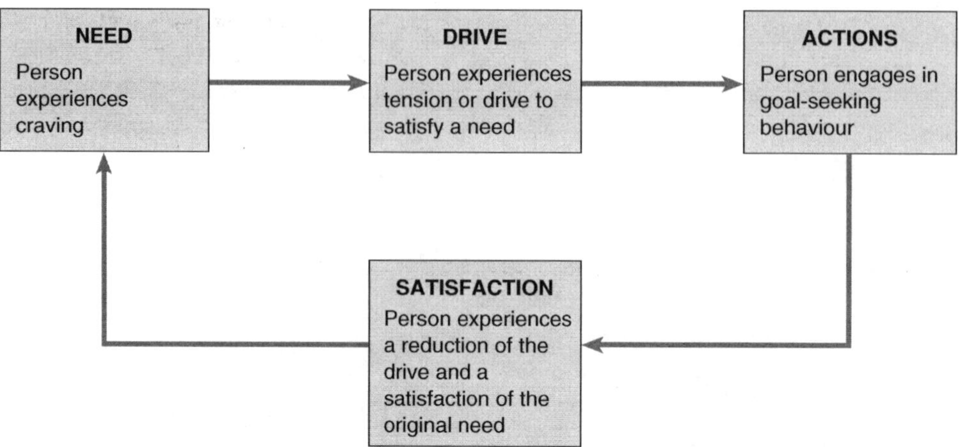

Figure 2-1 The Need Cycle

department manager. Ideally, in this situation your boss would give you more responsibility. This could lead to more satisfaction of your recognition need and to some satisfaction of your need for achievement. (The needs mentioned so far, and others, are defined next.)

The need theory suggests that self-interest plays a key role in motivation.[3] People ask, "What's in it for me?" or "WIIFM" (pronounced *wiff'em*) before engaging in any form of behaviour. In one way or another people act in a way that serves their self-interest. Even when people act in a way that helps others, they are doing so because helping others helps them. For example, a person may give money to poor people because this act of kindness makes him or her feel wanted and powerful.

Important Needs and Motives People Attempt to Satisfy

Work and personal life offer the opportunity to satisfy dozens of needs and motives. In this and the following section, we describe important needs that propel people into action. As you read these needs and motives, relate them to yourself. For example, ask yourself, "Am I a power-seeking person?"

Achievement The need for achievement is the desire to accomplish something difficult for its own sake. People with a strong need for achievement frequently think of how to do a job better. Responsibility seeking is another characteristic of people with a high need for achievement. They are also concerned with how to progress in their careers. Workers with a high need for achievement are interested in monetary rewards primarily as feedback about how well they are achieving. They also set realistic yet moderately difficult goals, take calculated risks, and desire feedback on performance. (A moderately difficult goal challenges a person but is not so difficult as to most likely lead to failure and frustration.) In general, those who enjoy building business, activities, and programs from scratch have a strong need for achievement. Figure 2-2 outlines the preferences of workers with strong achievement needs.

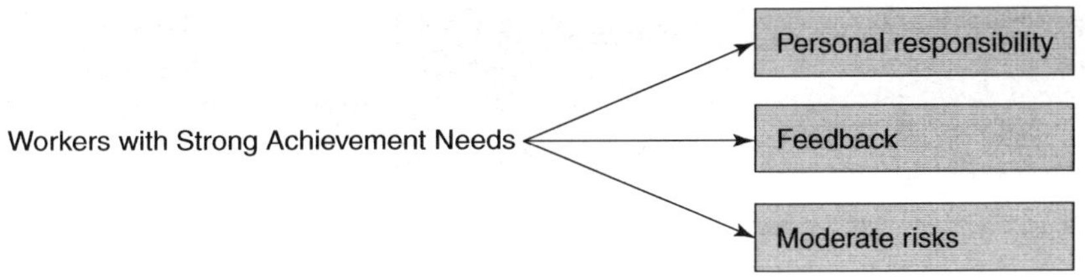

Figure 2-2 Preferences of Workers with Strong Achievement Needs

Power People with a high power need feel compelled to control resources, such as other people and money. Successful executives typically have a high power motive and exhibit three dominant characteristics: (1) they act with vigour and determination to exert their power; (2) they invest much time in thinking about ways to alter the behaviour and thinking of others; and (3) they care about their personal standing with those around them.[4] The power need can be satisfied through occupying a high-level position or by becoming a highly influential person. Or you can try to acquire a National Hockey League Team like Jim Balsillie, the co-CEO of Research in Motion.

Affiliation People with a strong affiliation need seek out close relationships with others and tend to be loyal as friends or employees. The affiliation motive is met directly through belonging to the "office gang," a term of endearment implying that your co-workers are an important part of your life. Many people prefer working in groups to individual effort because of the opportunity the former provides for socializing with others.

Recognition People with a strong need for recognition want to be acknowledged for their contribution and efforts. The need for recognition is so pervasive that many companies have formal recognition programs in which outstanding or long-time employees receive gifts, plaques, and jewellery inscribed with the company logo. The recognition motive can be satisfied through means such as winning contests, receiving awards, and seeing one's name in print.

Order People with a strong need for order have the urge to put things in order. They also want to achieve arrangement, balance, neatness, and precision. The order motive can be quickly satisfied by cleaning and organizing one's work or living space. Occupations offering the opportunity to satisfy the order motive almost every day include accountant, computer programmer, and paralegal.

Risk Taking and Thrill Seeking Some people crave constant excitement on the job and are willing to risk their lives to achieve thrills. The need to take risks and pursue thrills has grown in importance in the high-technology era. Many people work for employers, start businesses, and purchase stocks with uncertain futures. The search for giant payoffs and the desire for daily thrills motivate these individuals.[5] A strong craving for thrills may have some positive consequences for the organization, including willingness to perform such dangerous feats as setting explosives, capping an oil well, controlling a radiation leak, and introducing a new product in a highly competitive environment. However, extreme risk takers and thrill seekers can also create problems such as being involved in a disproportionate number of vehicular accidents and making imprudent investments. Take Human Relations Self-Assessment Quiz 2-1 to measure your tendency toward risk taking.

Human Relations Self-Assessment

QUIZ 2-1 The Risk-Taking Scale: We Dare You to Take This Quiz

How can you size up your capacity for risk and thrills? Here's an informal quiz. Although some of the questions seem obvious, your final score reflects the range of risk that you are comfortable with, not just whether you like taking risks or not. Answer True or False:

	True	False
1. I eat sushi or other raw fish.	❑	❑
2. I would rather be a stock broker than an accountant.	❑	❑
3. I think that amusement park roller coasters should be abolished	❑	❑
4. I enjoy doing creative work.	❑	❑
5. I enjoy (or did enjoy) the excitement of looking for new dates.	❑	❑
6. I don't like trying foods from other cultures.	❑	❑
7. I would choose bonds over growth stocks.	❑	❑
8. Friends would say that I do not like to take risks.	❑	❑
9. I like to challenge people in positions of power.	❑	❑
10. I don't always wear seat belts while driving.	❑	❑
11. I sometimes talk on my cell phone while driving at highway speeds.	❑	❑
12. I would love to be an entrepreneur (or I love being one).	❑	❑
13. I purposely avoid traveling overseas.	❑	❑
14. Most days are boring for me.	❑	❑
15. I would like helping out in a crisis such as a product recall.	❑	❑
16. On the highway, I usually drive at least 10 miles per hour beyond the speed limit.	❑	❑
17. I would like to go cave exploring (or already have done so).	❑	❑
18. I like to have a daily dose of simulation.	❑	❑
19. I would be willing to have at least one-third of my compensation based on a bonus for good performance.	❑	❑
20. I would be willing to visit a maximum security prison on a job assignment.	❑	❑

Scoring and Interpretation

1. T	**5.** T	**9.** T	**13.** F	**17.** T
2. T	**6.** F	**10.** T	**14.** F	**18.** T
3. F	**7.** T	**11.** T	**15.** T	**19.** T
4. T	**8.** F	**12.** T	**16.** T	**20.** T

Give yourself one point each time your answer agrees with the key. If you score 16–20, you are probably a high risk taker. 10–15: You're a moderate risk taker. 5–9: You are cautious. 0–4: You're a very low risk taker.

Questions

1. How does your self-evaluation of your risk-taking tendencies compare with your score on this quiz?
2. Do you see any needs for improvement in terms of becoming more (or less) of a risk taker?

Source: The idea of a test about risk-taking comfort, as well as several of the statements on the quiz come from psychologist Frank Farley.

Generational Differences in Needs

Popular opinion strongly suggests that the various generations have different needs, which are based on their values. A **value** is the importance a person attaches to something that serves as a guide to action. If you value cleanliness, you will strive to keep your work area neat. Values are also tied in with needs. If you value love, your need for love and affection will be strong. Generational differences in needs and values are reflected in the stereotypes about differences between older people (Baby Boomers) and younger people (Generation X and Generation Y, or the Net generation). Older people will more frequently have strong needs for security. In contrast, younger people might have a stronger need for thrill seeking.[6] This is one of several reasons that middle-aged people are more likely to be hired as pilots of large commercial airplanes.

Exhibit 2-1 summarizes stereotypes about generational differences in values. The values in turn can be translated into needs. For example, "appreciating hierarchy" may be based on a need for order and security. Keep in mind, of course, that not everybody fits these stereotypes. Some 70-year-olds enjoy skydiving, and some 23-year-olds are looking for secure, low-risk jobs.

Exhibit 2-1
Value Stereotypes for Several Generations of Workers

Baby Boomers (1946–1964)	Generation X (1965–1977)	Generation Y (1978–1984)	Net Generation (approx 1982–2003)
Uses technology as necessary tool	Techno-savvy	Techno-savvy	Very techno-savvy
Appreciates hierarchy	Teamwork very important	Teamwork very important	Multi-taskers
Tolerates teams but values independent work	Dislikes hierarchy	Culturally diverse	Want job to fit lifestyle
Strong career orientation	Strives for work/life balance but will work long hours for now	Dislikes hierarchy	Feel pressure to succeed/ understand economic votility
More loyalty to organization	Loyalty to own career and profession	Strives for work/family balance but will work long hours for now	Communicate visually
		Believes in informality	Express feelings easily
		Wants to strike it rich quickly	Relationships a priority
		Highly regards start-up companies	Very aware of competitive job market
Favours diplomacy	Candid in conversation	Candid in conversation	
Favours old economy	Appreciates old and new economy	Prefers the new economy	
Expects a bonus based on performance	Would appreciate a signing bonus	Expects a signing bonus	

Source: Several of the ideas in this table are from Robert McGarvey, "The Coming of Gen X Bosses," *Entrepreneur,* November 1999, pp. 60–64; Joanne M. Glenn, "Teaching the Net Generation," *Business Education Forum*, February 2000, pp. 6–14; Charlene Marmer Solomon, "Ready or Not: Here Come the Kids," *Workforce*, February 2000, pp. 62–68; Ronald A. Burke, "Teaching Strategies for the Net Generation," Transformative Dialogues: Teaching and Learning Journal, November 2009, Volume 3, Issue 2.

MASLOW'S NEED HIERARCHY

The best known categorization of needs is **Maslow's need hierarchy**. At the same time, it is the most widely used explanation of human motivation. According to the psychologist Abraham H. Maslow, people strive to satisfy the following groups of needs in step-by-step order:

1. *Physiological needs* refer to bodily needs, such as the requirements for food, water, shelter, and sleep.
2. *Safety needs* refer to actual physical safety and to a feeling of being safe from both physical and emotional injury.
3. *Social needs* are essentially love or belonging needs. Unlike the two previous levels of needs, they centre on a person's interactions with other people.
4. *Esteem needs* represent an individual's demands to be seen by others as a person of worth.
5. *Self-actualizing needs* are the highest levels of needs, including the needs for self-fulfillment and personal development.[7]

A diagram of the need hierarchy is presented in Figure 2-3. Notice the distinction between higher-level and lower-level needs. With few exceptions, higher-level needs are more difficult to satisfy. A person's needs for affiliation might be satisfied by being a member of a friendly work group. Yet to satisfy self-actualization needs, such as self-fulfillment, a person might have to develop an outstanding reputation in his or her company.

The need hierarchy implies that most people think of finding a job as a way of obtaining the necessities of life. Once these are obtained, a person may think of achieving friendship, self-esteem, and self-fulfillment on the job. When a person is generally satisfied at one

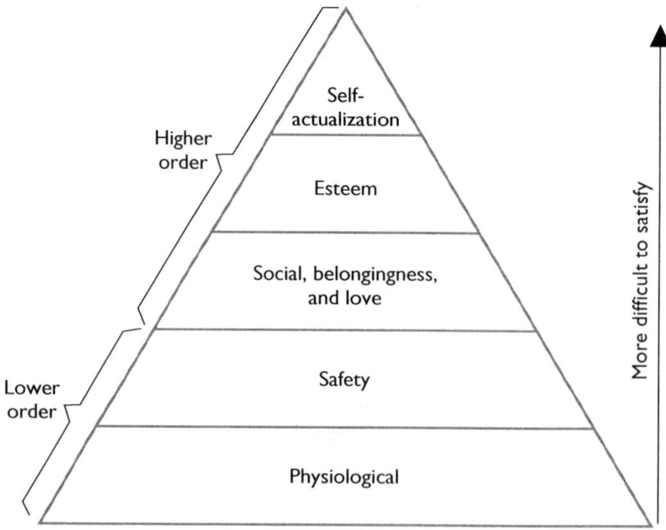

Figure 2-3 Maslow's Need Hierarchy

level, he or she looks for satisfaction at a higher level. As Maslow describes it, a person is a "perpetually wanting animal." Very few people are totally satisfied with their lot in life, even the rich and famous.

How do Maslow's needs and the other needs described in this chapter relate to self-motivation? First you have to ask yourself, "Which need do I really want to satisfy?" After answering the question honestly, concentrate your efforts on an activity that will most likely satisfy that need. For instance, if you are hungry for power, strive to become a high-level manager or a business owner. If you crave self-esteem, focus your efforts on work and social activities that are well regarded by others. The point is that you will put forth substantial effort if you think the goal you attain will satisfy an important need. Many businesspeople still use Maslow's need hierarchy to guide their thinking about motivation in the workplace, and many university and college courses teach it as a method of understanding how needs influence motivation.

GOALS AND MOTIVATION

One writer says this about success: "All truly successful men or women I have met or read about have one thing in common. At some point in their lives, they sat down and wrote out their goals. The first great key to success begins with you, a piece of paper, and a pencil."[8] This statement indicates why goal setting is so important. A **goal** is an event, circumstance, object, or condition a person strives to attain. A goal thus reflects your desire or intention to regulate your actions. Here we look at two related topics: (1) the advantages of goals, and (2) the underlying reasons why they are motivational.

Advantages of Goals

Goal setting is well accepted as a motivational tool. Substantial research indicates that setting specific, reasonably difficult goals improves performance.[9] Goals are useful for several reasons. First, when we guide our lives with goals, we tend to focus our efforts in a consistent direction. Without goals, our efforts may become scattered in many directions. We may keep trying, but we will go nowhere unless we happen to receive more than our share of luck.

Second, goal setting increases our chances for success, particularly because success can be defined as the achievement of a goal. The goals we set for accomplishing a task can serve as a standard to indicate when we have done a satisfactory job. A sales representative might set a goal of selling $300,000 worth of merchandise for the year. By November she might close a deal that places her total sales at $310,000. With a sigh of relief she can then say, "I've done well this year."

Third, goals serve as self-motivators and energizers. People who set goals tend to be motivated because they are confident that their energy is being invested in something worthwhile. Aside from helping you become more motivated and productive, setting goals can help you achieve personal satisfaction. Most people derive a sense of satisfaction from attaining a goal that is meaningful to them. The sales representative mentioned above probably achieved this sense of satisfaction when she surpassed her quota.

The Learning and Performance Orientations toward Goals

Another useful perspective on understanding how goals influence motivation is that goals can be aimed at either learning or performing.[10] A learning-goal orientation means that an individual is focused on acquiring new skills and mastering new situations. For example, you might establish the goal of learning how to develop skill in making a computerized-presentation package. You say to yourself, "My goal is to learn how to use PowerPoint (or similar software)."

A performance-goal orientation is different. It is aimed at wanting to demonstrate and validate the adequacy of your competence by seeking favourable judgments about your competence. At the same time, you seek to avoid negative judgments. For example, your goal might be to make PowerPoint presentations that would highly impress whoever watched them. Your focus would be on looking good and avoiding negative evaluations of your presentations.

A person's goal orientation usually affects his or her desire for feedback. People with a learning-goal orientation are more likely to seek feedback on how well they are performing. In contrast, people with a performance-goal orientation are less likely to seek feedback. If you focus too much on setting performance goals, you might have a tendency to overlook the value of feedback. Yet the feedback could help you improve your performance in the long run. It is also important to recognize that if you, the goal setter, seek feedback, you will create a good impression.

Goal orientation is also important because it can affect work performance. Attempting to master skills often leads to better results than does attempting to impress others. A study of the effects of the two different goal orientations was conducted with 167 salespeople working for a medical supplies distributor. The salespeople were paid mostly on the commission of the gross profits they generated. The researchers found that a learning-goal orientation was associated with higher sales performance. In contrast, a performance-goal orientation was unrelated to sales performance. An important implication of the study for managers and workers is that a focus on skill development, even for an experienced workforce, is likely to lead to higher performance.[11]

Another positive consequence of a mastery (or learning-goal) orientation is that it often prompts workers to develop better relationships with their supervisors. A study in a Dutch energy supply company found that workers with a mastery orientation had stronger job performance and job satisfaction than those workers with a performance orientation. The positive outcomes of stronger job performance and satisfaction appeared to take place because the workers developed better relationships with their supervisors.[12]

A recent synthesis of evidence points to a key reason why a learning (or mastery) goal orientation is so important in today's business world. The purpose of a learning goal is to stimulate a person's imagination, to engage in discovery, and to think imaginatively. A performance goal focuses more on exerting effort to attain an objective using the knowledge one already possesses. When an effective strategy requires innovation that has yet to emerge—as is often the case—specific, high-learning goals should be set.[13] An example of a learning goal of high importance would be figuring out how to dispose of debris after a hurricane.

Before studying more about goals, do Human Relations Self-Assessment Quiz 2-2. It gives you an opportunity to think through your readiness to accept goals as part of your life.

Human Relations Self-Assessment

QUIZ 2-2 Are You Ready for Goal Setting?

Answer each of the following questions spontaneously and candidly. As with all self-help quizzes, if you try to answer the question in a way that will put you in a favourable light, you will miss some potentially valuable diagnostic information. For each question answer 1 for strongly disagree, 2 for disagree, 3 for a neutral attitude, 4 for agree, and 5 for strongly agree.

1. I almost always know what day of the month it is. ____
2. I regularly prepare to-do lists. ____
3. I make good use of my to-do lists. ____
4. I can tell you almost precisely how many times I engaged in my favourite sport or hobby this year. ____
5. I keep close tabs on the win and lose record of my favourite athletic team. ____
6. I have a reasonably accurate idea of the different income tax brackets. ____
7. I use a budget to control my personal expenses. ____
8. I know how much money I want to be making in five years. ____
9. I know what position I want to hold in five years. ____
10. Careful planning is required to accomplish anything of value. ____

Total ____

Scoring and Interpretation: Add up your point score. If your score is 40 points or higher, you are probably already convinced of the value of goal setting. If your score is between 20 and 39 points, you are in the middle range of readiness to incorporate goal setting into your life. You probably need to study more about goal setting to capitalize on its value. If your score is between 10 and 19 points, you are far from ready to accept goal setting. Carefully review the information about the advantages of goal setting mentioned previously. Until you change your attitudes about the contribution of goals to your life, you will not become an active goal setter and planner.

GOAL SETTING ON THE JOB

If you are already well into your career, you have probably been asked to set goals or objectives on the job. Virtually all modern organizations have come to accept the value of goal setting in producing the results they want to achieve.

You participate in the goal-setting process by designing goals to fit into the overall mission of the firm. If you were a teller in the bank mentioned above, you might set a personal goal of this nature: "During rush periods, and when I feel fatigued, I will double-count all the money that I handle." In some goal-setting programs, employees are requested to set goals that will lead to their personal improvement. A federal auditor set this goal for herself: "Within the next 12 months, I will enroll in and complete a supervisory training course in a local college." This woman aspired to become a supervisor.

Figure 2-4 Memo Form Used in Automobile Dealership for Statement of Goals

Job Title and Brief Job Description

Manager, Service Department:

Responsible for supervision of service department of automobile dealership. Responsible for staffing service department with appropriate personnel and for quality of service to customers. Work closely with owner of dealership to discuss unusual customer problems. Handle customer complaints about mechanical problems of cars purchased at dealership.

Objectives for Scott Gilley

1. By December 31 of this year, decrease by 10 percent customer demands for rework.
2. Hire two general mechanics within 45 days.
3. Hire two body specialists within 45 days.
4. Decrease by 30 percent the number of repairs returned by customers for rework.
5. Reduce by 10 percent the discrepancy between estimates and actual bills to customers.

An important part of goal setting, both on and off the job, is priority setting. You pursue with more diligence those goals that can have the greatest impact on performance or are most important to top management. Suppose that one of a purchasing associate's goals for the month is to learn how to use his new cell phone features to be able to do emails to stay in touch with the company to save time while on the road to visit more suppliers. His priority is to achieve higher sales to earn more bonuses.

A sample set of work goals is shown in Figure 2-4. The service and repair shop supervisor who set these objectives took into account the requirements of his boss and the automobile dealership. Even if you set goals by yourself, they must still take into account the needs of your employer. As you read through the goals listed in Figure 2-4, see if they conform to the suggestions made in the section "Guidelines for Goal Setting" that follows.

PERSONAL GOAL SETTING

Personal goals are important in their own right. If you want to lead a rewarding personal life, your chances of doing so increase if you plan it. Personal goals heavily influence the formulation of career goals as well. For this reason it is worthwhile to set personal goals in conjunction with career goals. Ideally, they should be integrated. Two examples follow:

- A young man may have a strong interest in hiking, camping, skiing, and appreciating nature. One personal goal he might formulate is to have enough money for this lifestyle and to live in an area where it would be available. His occupational goals should then include developing skills that are needed in smaller and more remote communities. Another personal goal may be to learn wilderness and survival skills. His career planning might then focus on obtaining employment in a geographic location such as northern British Columbia, where skiing and hiking are readily accessible.

- A woman might develop a preference early in life for the outdoors, particularly for hunting, fishing, and camping. She might also be interested in raising a large family. Part of her career planning should include developing skills that are in demand in rural areas where her preferences are easier to satisfy than in a city. When she learns that many manufacturing facilities have been developed in rural and semi-rural areas, her career planning might then include the goal of developing job skills that are in demand in a factory or mill. Computer skills, of course, are in demand everywhere. Another alternative for this woman might be to develop technical computer skills so that she could work for a city company through teleworking.

Types of Personal Goals

Personal goals can be subdivided into those relating to social and family life, hobbies and interests, physical and mental health, and finances. Examples of each type follow:

Social and family: "By age 30 I would like to have a spouse and two children." "Have my own apartment by age 23."

Hobbies and interests: "Become a black belt in karate by age 28." "Qualify as a downhill ski instructor by age 21."

Physical and mental health: "Be able to run four miles without stopping or panting for breath by April 15 of next year." "Get my dermatitis under control within six months from now." "Maintain normal blood pressure for the indefinite future."

Financial: "Within the next four years be earning $40,000 per year, adjusted for inflation." "Build my mutual fund accounts into a total value of at least $20,000 within five years."

The Human Relations Skill-Building Exercise 2-1 accompanying this discussion will give you an opportunity to set both work and personal goals. Ideally, reading this chapter and doing the exercises in it will start you on a lifelong process of using goals to help you plan your life. But before you can capitalize on the benefits of goal setting, you need a method for translating goals into action.

Action Plans to Support Goals

An **action plan** describes how you are going to reach your goal. The major reason you need an action plan for most goals is that without a method for achieving what you want, the goal is likely to slip by. Few people ever prepare a road map or plan that will lead them to their goal. If your goal were to build your own log cabin, part of your action plan would be to learn how to operate a buzz saw, to read a handbook on log cabin building, to learn how to operate a tractor, and so forth.

Some goals are so difficult to reach that your action plan might encompass hundreds of separate activities. You would then have to develop separate action plans for each step of the way. If your goal is to lead a rewarding and satisfying career, the techniques presented in this book can help you formulate many of your action plans. Among these skill-building techniques are assertiveness, resolving conflict, developing good work habits, and managing stress.

Human Relations Skill Building

Exercise 2-1 Goal-Setting and Action Plan Worksheet

The purpose of this activity is to help you gain some experience in setting both work and personal goals and action plans to accompany them. Before writing down your actual goals, consult the "Guidelines for Goal Setting" section that follows. For each of the following levels of goals, set a work goal, a personal goal, and a brief action plan for each. If you are not currently employed, set up hypothetical goals and action plans for a future job.

Long-Range Goals (beyond five years)

Work: ____________________

Action plan: ____________________

Personal: ____________________

Action plan: ____________________

Medium-Range Goals (two to five years)

Work: ____________________

Action plan: ____________________

Personal: ____________________

Action plan: ____________________

Short-Range Goals (within two years)

Work: ____________________

Action plan: ____________________

Personal: ____________________

Action plan: ____________________

Some immediate goals do not really require an action plan. A mere statement of the goal may point to an obvious action plan. If your goal is to start painting your room, it will not be necessary to draw up a formal action plan such as: "Go to hardware store to purchase paint, brush, and rollers; borrow ladder and drop cloth from Ken; put furniture in centre of room"; and so on.

GUIDELINES FOR GOAL SETTING

Goal setting is an art in the sense that some people do a better job of goal setting than others. The following paragraphs provide suggestions on setting effective goals—those that lead to achieving what you hoped to achieve.

Formulate Specific Goals A goal such as "To attain success" is too vague to serve as a guide to daily action. A more useful goal would be to state specifically what you mean by success and when you expect to achieve it. For example, "I want to be the manager of customer service at a telephone company by January 1, 2006."

Formulate Concise Goals A useful goal can usually be expressed in a short, punchy statement. An example: "Decrease input errors in bank statements so that customer complaints are decreased by 25 percent by September 30 of this year." People new to goal setting typically commit the error of formulating lengthy, rambling goal statements. These lengthy goals involve so many different activities that they fail to serve as specific guides to action.

Set Realistic Goals as well as Stretch Goals A **realistic goal** is one that represents the right amount of challenge for the person pursuing the goal. On the one hand, easy

Human Relations Skill Building

Exercise 2-2 Goal Sharing and Feedback

Each person in the class selects one work-related and one personal goal from Human Relations Skill-Building Exercise 2-1, exactly as stated on the worksheet, that he or she would be willing to share with other members of the class. Other class members have the opportunity of providing feedback to the person sharing his or her goals. Here are a few types of errors commonly made in goal setting that you should avoid:

1. Is the goal too lengthy and complicated? Is it really a number of goals rather than one specific goal?
2. Is the goal so vague that the person will be hard-pressed to know if he or she has reached the goal (e.g., "I intend to become a good worker.")?
3. Is the action plan specific enough to serve as a useful path for reaching that goal?
4. Does the goal sound sincere? (Admittedly, this is a highly subjective judgment on your part.)

goals are not very motivational—they may not spring you into action. On the other hand, goals that are too far beyond your capabilities may lead to frustration and despair because there is a good chance you will fail to reach them.[14] The extent to which a goal is realistic depends upon a person's capabilities. An easy goal for an experienced person might be a realistic goal for a beginner. Self-efficacy is also a factor in deciding whether a goal is realistic. The higher your self-efficacy, the more likely you are to think that a particular goal is realistic. A person with high self-efficacy for learning Chinese might say, "I think learning two new Chinese words a day is realistic."

Several goals that stretch your capability might be included in your list of goals. The goal of becoming CEO of a national chain of department stores when you are in your third year of a college management program would be considered a "stretch goal." Another type of stretch goal is striving for a noble cause. A logging supervisor may not get excited about having the crew load a certain number of felled trees on a flatbed truck. However, she might get excited about the trees being used to build homes, schools, and hospitals.

Human Relations Skill-Building Exercise 2-2 gives you an opportunity to improve your goal-setting skills.

Set Goals for Different Time Periods Goals are best set for different time periods, such as daily, short-range, medium-range, and long-range. Daily goals are essentially a "to do" list. Short-range goals cover the period from approximately one week to one year into the future. Finding a new job, for example, is typically a short-range goal. Medium-range goals relate to events that will take place within approximately two to five years. They concern such things as the type of education or training you plan to undertake and the next step in your career.

Long-range goals refer to events taking place five years into the future and beyond. As such they relate to the overall lifestyle you wish to achieve, including the type of work and family situation you hope to have. Although every person should have a general idea of a desirable lifestyle, long-range goals should be flexible. You might, for example, plan to stay single until age 40. But while on vacation next summer you might just happen to meet the right partner for you.

Short-range goals make an important contribution to attaining goals of longer duration. If a one-year work goal is to reduce mailing and shipping costs by 12 percent for the year, a good way to motivate workers is to look for a 1 percent saving per month. Progress toward a larger goal is self-rewarding.

Include Some Fantasy in Your Personal Goal Setting Breakthrough goals greatly enlarge your horizons. Fantasy goals take you one step further. Such fantasies can bridge the gap between personal and career goal setting. A fantasy goal would be difficult to attain at any stage in your life. Fantasy goals also reflect your vision of the ideal type of life you would like to lead. They help you dream the impossible dream. However, difficult they may be to attain, some people *do* eventually live out their wildest dreams.

Here is a sampling of fantasy goals found in the career reports of students in a career development course:

- "I'd like to become a big tycoon by owning about ten office buildings in Toronto along with the Maple Leafs and the Argonauts."
- "I hope to become a freelance photographer for major news magazines. My specialty would be shooting civil unrest and border wars."
- "I hope to become a millionaire philanthropist and have a high school named after me in a poor neighbourhood."

Aside from being exciting to pursue, fantasy goals are important for another reason. Research suggests that your fantasy life can help with personal adjustment and overcoming stress. A well-developed fantasy can result in a pleasurable state of physical and mental relaxation. Furthermore, fantasy goals can help you cope with an unpleasant current situation by giving you hope for the future.[15]

Canada Today

Linking Goals and Motivation: Do You Have the Characteristics of a Good Employee

In an interesting article about hiring the "right" employees, Brian Scudamore founder and CEO of 1-800-GOT-JUNK? listed seven traits that management should look for in a potential employee. Interestingly, two of the seven traits are on motivation and goal setting. He analyzed his hires from the past twenty years—good and bad—and came up with seven specific things that every business owner should look for in a potential employee. As you read, see if you have these characteristics:

Cultural fit

Hire people who seem to share the core values of the company. Many times, I've made the mistake of hiring someone who excelled in a particular skill but didn't fit the company or team's culture, and it has come back to haunt him. Lesson: Fit first, skills second.

A shared vision

Is there a clear and compelling company vision? A potential employee should share that vision. If their eyes light up and sparkle when they read it, then they share your vision—which means we will all be rowing powerfully in the same direction. Look for people who have a clear vision for themselves: what are their goals, and can your company help them reach them; what do they aspire to do, and is your company the place for them? People join a company for reasons beyond simply making money. Scudamore believes most of us genuinely want to do meaningful work.

A fire within you hear a lot about how to "motivate" employees, but he does not believe you can motivate people. You can encourage behaviours in the short term with celebrations, bonuses and the like, but your people "gotta wanna." In other words, they have to want to do the work they've been asked to do for their own reasons. There has to be something in your business that people find intrinsically stimulating. Do they believe they can positively impact the world through their work with your business? Do they firmly believe in your BHAG (big hairy audacious goal) and the challenge of doing something that seems almost impossible? Motivation comes from within; and for it to be long-lasting, there has to be a fire burning inside that drives someone beyond what any amount of money can.

A love of goals

You are more likely to build a winning company by hiring winners, and in his opinion, winners are people who routinely set clear goals and achieve them. He has found goal-setters are more focused, disciplined and successful.

That said, you have to ensure that your people are set up to win. All 1-800-GOT-JUNK? employees post their three biggest priorities for the week and month above their desks. Those priorities define and display what winning is in their position, and trickle up to support winning for the team. He is a big believer in "what gets measured gets done." If you define winning, you are much more likely to come out ahead.

A sunny outlook

A company culture manifests itself through the leadership within the organization. He looks for people who are optimistic, positive and see the potential in the company and its people. If you have too many negative forces at work in your office, your culture will eventually turn sour and unproductive. Inevitably, things will go wrong in business; for instance, you will miss a goal or lose a great employee. People who lean toward the bright side will help you overcome those obstacles.

Tenacity

All businesses go through change, and it is the right people who will help you get through it. As the old cliché goes: "When the going gets tough, the tough get going." Look for people who will step up and push through hard times. His company's rapid growth has created plenty of challenging times for us, and I see the same core people rise to the challenge each and every time.

The ability to have fun

His company integrates fun into everything they can at 1-800-GOT-JUNK? and they try not to take themselves too seriously. Why? Because when people are having fun, they collaborate more, they communicate more and they achieve better results. So, look for people who can be loose and relaxed. They will be more creative and come up with better solutions to complex problems.

Finding the right people is an ongoing challenge every entrepreneur faces. Apply discipline and rigour to recruiting, and you will have far better success. Understand who the right people are for your business—what has worked for you in the past; what have you learned about people? Do more of what works and never, ever compromise. It's never worth it.

Source: Brian Scudamore, The 7 Traits of Super Staff: It Starts with Hiring: *PROFIT, December 2009; accessed February 15, 2010 at http://www.canadianbusiness. com/columnists/brian_scudamore/article. jsp?content=20091201_ 30017_ 30017&page=1.* Used with permission of the author.

Review Your Goals from Time to Time A sophisticated goal setter realizes that all goals are temporary to some extent. In time, one particular goal may lose its relevance for you and therefore may no longer motivate you. At one time in your life you may be committed to earning an income in the top 10 percent of the population. Along the way toward achieving that goal, some other more relevant goal may develop. You might decide that the satisfactions of being self-employed are more important than earning a particular amount of money. You might therefore open an antique store with the simple financial goal of "meeting my expenses."

PROBLEMS SOMETIMES CREATED BY GOALS

Despite the many advantages of goals, they can create problems. A major problem is that *goals can create inflexibility*. If you become so focused on achieving a 90 percent in one course, you may neglect your other courses. Goals can also make a person inflexible with respect to missing out on opportunities. Some people may actually miss out on career opportunities as an offered job is not in their chosen field. Rather than seeing this position as a possible stepping stone, they flat out refuse the opportunity.

Goals can contribute to *a narrow focus, thus neglecting other worthwhile activities*. While studying hard is a worthy goal, some students miss out on physical fitness or other activities to help maintain health and well-being. In other words, when a goal becomes the primary focus of all efforts, other important areas of life can become neglected.

Another problem is that *performance goals can sometimes detract from an interest in the task*. People with a performance-goal orientation (focusing on being judged as competent) will sometimes lose interest in the task. The loss of interest is most likely to occur when the task is difficult.[16] This potential problem could be stated in another way. If you focus too much on success (as being defined by reaching your goal), you will become frustrated when the means to reaching the goal is difficult. For example, assume that your primary goal for working as a salesperson is to perform well enough so that you will be in line for promotion. If you encounter some hurdles selling your product, you may easily become frustrated with selling. However, if your orientation is primarily to learn how to sell effectively, you will not be readily frustrated when you encounter problems. You might even look on it as a learning opportunity!

A tight focus on goals can also encourage unethical behaviour and a disregard for *how* the goals are attained. A sales representative might give kickbacks simply to gain a sale, and a CEO might lay off needed workers and neglect investing in new-product research simply to make certain profit figures.

Despite the problems that can arise in goal setting, goals are valuable tools for managing your work and personal life. Used with common sense, and according to the ideas presented in this chapter, they could have a major positive impact on your life.

TECHNIQUES FOR SELF-MOTIVATION

Many people never achieve satisfying careers and never realize their potential because of low motivation. They believe they could perform better but admit, "I'm just not a go-getter" or "my motivation is low." Earlier we described how identifying your most important needs could enhance motivation. Here we describe eight additional techniques for self-motivation.

1. Set goals for yourself.
2. Find intrinsically motivating work.
3. Get feedback on your performance.
4. Apply behaviour modification to yourself.
5. Improve your skills relevant to your goals.

6. Raise your level of self-expectation.
7. Develop a strong work ethic.
8. Develop psychological hardiness.

To think through your own tendencies toward being self-disciplined, you are invited to take Human Relations Self-Assessment Quiz 2-3.

1. *Set Goals for Yourself* As shown throughout this chapter, goal setting is one of the most important techniques for self-motivation. If you set long-range goals and back them up with a series of smaller goals set for shorter time spans, your motivation will increase.
2. *Find Intrinsically Motivating Work* A major factor in self-motivation is to find work that is fun or is its own reward. **Intrinsic motivation** refers to the natural tendency to

Human Relations Self-Assessment

Quiz 2-3 The Self-Discipline Quiz

On the following scale, indicate the extent to which each of the following statements describes your behaviour or attitude by circling one number for each: disagree strongly (DS), disagree (D), neutral (N), agree (A), agree strongly (AS). Consider asking someone who knows your behaviour and attitudes well to help you respond accurately.

	DS	D	N	A	AS
1. I have a strong sense of purpose.	1	2	3	4	5
2. Life is a pain when you are always chasing goals.	5	4	3	2	1
3. My long-range plans in life are well established.	1	2	3	4	5
4. I feel energized when I have a new goal to pursue.	1	2	3	4	5
5. It is difficult for me to picture an event in my mind before it occurs.	5	4	3	2	1
6. When success is near, I can almost taste, feel, and see it.	1	2	3	4	5
7. I consult my daily planner or a to-do list almost every day.	1	2	3	4	5
8. My days rarely turn out the way I had planned.	5	4	3	2	1
9. What I do for a living is not (or would not be) nearly as important as the money it pays.	5	4	3	2	1
10. Some parts of my job are as exciting to me as any hobby or pastime.	1	2	3	4	5
11. Working 60 hours per week for even a short period of time would be out of the question for me.	5	4	3	2	1
12. I have personally known several people who would be good role models for me.	1	2	3	4	5
13. So far I have never read about or known anybody whose lifestyle I would like to emulate.	5	4	3	2	1
14. My work is so demanding that it's difficult for me to concentrate fully on my personal life when I'm not working.	5	4	3	2	1
15. When I'm involved in an important work project, I can enjoy myself fully at a sport or cultural event after hours.	1	2	3	4	5

(continued)

(*continued*)

16. If it weren't for a few bad breaks, I would be much more successful today.	5	4	3	2	1
17. My best helping hand is at the end of my arm.	1	2	3	4	5
18. I get bored easily.	5	4	3	2	1
19. Planning is difficult because life is so unpredictable.	5	4	3	2	1
20. I feel that I'm moving forward a little bit each day toward achieving my goals.	1	2	3	4	5

Scoring and Interpretation:

Calculate your score by adding the numbers circled.

90–100 points:	You are a highly self-disciplined person who should be able to capitalize on your skills and talents. Studying about self-discipline might help you capitalize even further on your strong self-discipline.
60–89 points:	You have an average degree of self-discipline, so studying the self-discipline model could point to areas for personal improvement.
40–59 points:	You may be experiencing problems with self-discipline. Start putting into practice the ideas contained in the self-discipline model.
20–39 points:	If your answers are accurate, you have enough problems with self-discipline to limit achieving many of the things in life important to you. In addition to studying the self-discipline model, study about work habits and time management.

Questions

1. How does this score agree with your evaluation of your self-discipline?
2. Who might you use as a role model of a person with high self-discipline?

seek out novelty and challenges, to extend and use one's capacities, to explore, and to learn.[17] The intrinsically motivated person is involved in the task at hand, such as a netizen surfing the Web for hours at a time. With some serious introspection (and assisted by the Self-Knowledge Questionnaire in Chapter 1), you should be able to find work you perceive to be intrinsically motivating. Next, find a job that offers your motivators in ample supply. For example, you might have good evidence from your past experience that the opportunity for close contact with people is a personal motivator. Find a job that involves working in a small, friendly department or team.

Owing to circumstances, you may have to take whatever job you can find, or you may not be in a position to change jobs. In such a situation, try to arrange your work so you have more opportunity to experience the reward(s) that you are seeking. Assume that solving difficult problems excites you, but that your job is 85 percent routine. Develop better work habits so that you can take care of the routine aspects of your job more quickly. This will give you more time to enjoy the creative aspects of your job.

3. *Get Feedback on Your Performance* Few people can sustain a high level of motivation without receiving information about how well they are doing. Even if you find your work to be challenging and exciting, you will need feedback. One reason feedback is valuable is that it acts as a reward. If you learn that your efforts achieved a worthwhile purpose, you will feel encouraged. For example, if a graphics display you designed was well received by company officials, you would probably want to prepare another graphics display.

4. *Apply Behaviour Modification to Yourself* **Behaviour modification** is a system for motivating people that emphasizes rewarding them for doing the right things and punishing them for doing the wrong things. In recent years, behaviour modification has been used by many people to change their own behaviour. Specific purposes include overcoming eating disorders, tobacco addiction, nail biting, and procrastination.

   To boost your own motivation through behaviour modification you would have to first decide what specific motivated actions you want to increase (such as working 30 minutes longer each day). Second, you would have to decide on a suitable set of rewards and punishments. You may choose to use rewards only, since rewards are generally better motivators than punishments.

5. *Improve Your Skills Relevant to Your Goals* The **expectancy theory of motivation** states that people will be motivated if they believe that their efforts will lead to desired outcomes. According to this theory, people hold back effort when they are not confident that their efforts will lead to accomplishments. For example, some people are hesitant to attempt to operate a new piece of software because they suspect they will flounder. One way to increase their effort (motivation) toward learning the software would be to give them step-by-step training, thus increasing their skills.

   Expectancy theory has an important implication for self-motivation. Seek adequate training to ensure that you have the requisite abilities and skills to perform your work. The training might be provided by the employer or through a course or self-study. Appropriate training gives you more confidence that you can perform the work. The training also increases your feelings of self-efficacy (as described in Chapter 1).[18] By recognizing your ability to mobilize your own resources to succeed, your self-confidence for the task will be elevated.

6. *Raise Your Level of Self-Expectation* A final strategy for increasing your level of motivation is to simply expect more of yourself. If you raise your level of self-expectation, you are likely to achieve more. Because you expect to succeed, you do succeed. The net effect is the same as if you had increased your level of motivation.

   The technical term for improving your performance through raising your own expectations is the **Galatea effect**. In one experiment, for example, the self-expectations of subjects were raised in brief interviews with an organizational psychologist. The psychologist told the subjects they had high potential to succeed in the undertaking they were about to begin (a problem-solving task). The subjects who received the positive information about their potential did better than those subjects who did not receive such encouragement.[19]

   High self-expectations and a positive mental attitude take a long time to develop. However, they are critically important for becoming a well-motivated person in a variety of situations.

7. *Develop a Strong Work Ethic* A highly effective strategy for self-motivation is to develop a strong work ethic. If you are committed to the idea that most work is valuable and that it is joyful to work hard, you will automatically become strongly motivated. A person with a weak work ethic cannot readily develop a strong one, because the change requires a profound value shift. Yet if a person gives a lot of serious thought to the importance of work and follows the right role models, a work ethic can be strengthened. The shift to a strong work ethic is much like a person who has a casual

attitude toward college or a job who then becomes conscious of the quality of his or her schoolwork or job activities.

8. *Develop Psychological Hardiness.* A comprehensive approach to becoming better self-motivated would be to develop a higher degree of psychological hardiness—a mental state in which the individual experiences a high degree of commitment, control, and challenge. *Commitment* is a tendency to involve oneself in whatever one is doing or encounters, such as being committed to developing a successful video game. *Control* is a tendency to feel and act as if one is influential, rather than helpless, in facing the twists and turns in life. *Challenge* is a belief that change rather than stability is normal in life and that changes lead to growth and are not threats to security. (Moving in these three directions would involve substantial personal development.) A study with more than 600 college students demonstrated that those who scored higher on psychological hardiness tended to have stronger motivation to study and learn.[20] Psychological hardiness would also be helpful in work motivation.

DEVELOPING THE SELF-DISCIPLINE TO ACHIEVE GOALS AND STAY MOTIVATED

Another perspective on achieving goals and staying motivated is that it requires **self-discipline**, the ability to work systematically and progressively toward a goal until it is achieved. The self-disciplined person works toward achieving his or her goals without being derailed by the many distractions faced each day. Self-discipline incorporates self-motivation, because it enables you to motivate yourself to achieve your goals without being nagged or prodded with deadlines. Recent articles suggest that self-discipline is a requirement for many new jobs.[21] For example, working from home requires self-motivation, the ability to set goals, and the ability to discipline yourself in order to achieve those goals.[22] Our discussion of how to develop self-discipline follows the model shown in Figure 2-5. You will observe that the model incorporates several of the ideas about goals already discussed in this chapter. Without realizing it, you have already invested mental energy into learning the self-discipline model.

Component 1. *Formulate a mission statement.* Who are you? What are you trying to accomplish in life? If you understand what you are trying to accomplish in life, you have the fuel to be self-disciplined. With a mission, activities that may appear mundane to others become vital stepping stones for you. An example would be learning Spanish grammar to help you become an international businessperson. To help formulate your mission statement, answer two questions: What are my five biggest wishes? What do I want to accomplish in my career during the next five years?

Component 2. *Develop role models.* An excellent method of learning how to be self-disciplined is to model your behaviour after successful achievers who are obviously well disciplined. To model yourself on another person does not mean you will slavishly imitate every detail of that person's life. Instead, you will follow the general pattern of how the person operates in spheres related to your mission and goals. An ideal role model is the type of person whom you would like to become, not someone you feel you could never become.

Component 3. *Develop goals for each task.* Your mission must be supported by a series of specific goals that collectively will enable you to achieve your mission. Successfully

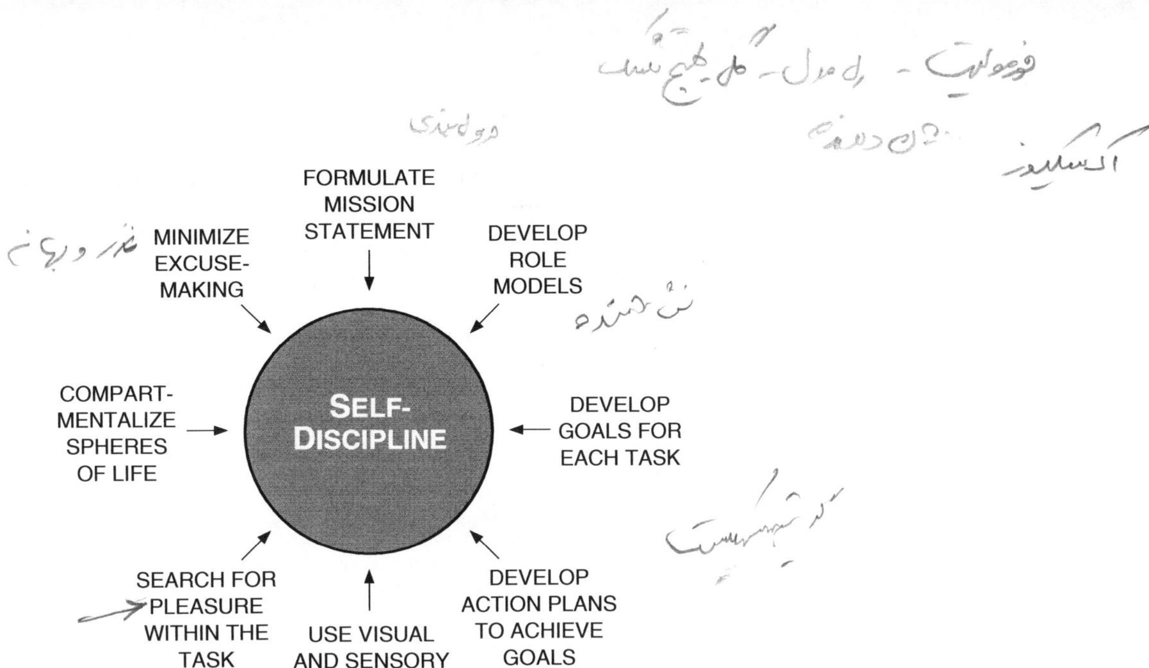

Figure 2-5 The Self-Discipline Model

Source: Andrew J. DuBrin, *Getting It Done: The Transforming Power of Self-Discipline* (Princeton, NJ: Peterson's, 1995), p. 18.

completing goals eventually leads to fulfilling a mission. Each small goal achieved is a building block toward larger achievements.

Component 4. *Develop action plans to achieve goals*. Self-disciplined people carefully follow their action plans because they make goal attainment possible. It is helpful to chart your progress against the dates established for the sub-activities.

Component 5. *Use visual and sensory stimulation*. A self-disciplined person relentlessly focuses on a goal and persistently pursues that goal. To accomplish this consistent focus, self-disciplined people form images of reaching their goals—they actually develop a mental image of the act of accomplishing what they want. As mysterious as it sounds, visualization helps the brain convert images into reality. The more senses you can incorporate into your visual image, the stronger its power. Imagine yourself seeing, tasting, hearing, smelling, and touching your goal. Can you imagine yourself sitting in your condo overlooking the ocean, eating a great meal to celebrate the fact that the business you founded now has 10,000 employees?

Component 6. *Search for pleasure within the task*. A self-disciplined person finds joy, excitement, and intense involvement in the task at hand and therefore finds intrinsic motivation. Instead of focusing on the extrinsic (or external) reward, the love of the task helps the person in pursuit of the goal. An axiom of becoming wealthy is not to focus on getting rich. Instead, focus on work. If the task at hand does not thrill you, at least focus on the pleasure from the most enjoyable element within the task. An expressway toll collector might not find the total task intrinsically motivating, but perhaps he or she enjoys meeting so many people on the job!

Component 7. *Compartmentalize spheres of life*. Self-disciplined people have a remarkable capacity to divide up (or compartmentalize) the various spheres of their lives to stay focused on what they are doing at the moment. While working, develop the knack of concentrating on work and putting aside thoughts about personal life. In the midst of social and family activities, concentrate on them rather than half-thinking about work. This approach will contribute to both self-discipline and a better integration of work and family life.

Component 8. *Minimize excuse making*. Self-disciplined people concentrate their energies on goal accomplishment, rather than making excuses for why work is not accomplished. Instead of trying to justify why they have been diverted from a goal, high-achieving, self-disciplined people circumvent potential barriers. Undisciplined people, in contrast, seem to look for excuses. If you are an excuse maker, conduct a self-audit, writing down all the reasons blocking you from achieving any current goal. Be brutally honest in challenging each one of your excuses. Ask yourself, "Is this a valid excuse, or is it simply a rationalization for my getting sidetracked?"

The belief that self-discipline contributes to goal attainment and success is about as strong as the belief that a healthy diet and exercise contribute to physical health. Nonetheless, a study conducted with 325 working adults provides reassurance about the benefits of self-discipline. The study participants completed the self-discipline questionnaire previously presented, and they also answered questions about their age, education, salary, and how they felt about their career success and goal accomplishment. As shown in Figure 2-6, positive relationships were found between being self-disciplined and education, salary, career success, and goal attainment. Self-ratings of career success and goal accomplishment were the most strongly related.[23] In conclusion, self-discipline pays. Why do you think it was found that self-discipline was positively associated with years of formal education?

Key Factor	Average Score on Factor for 325 Adults	Relationship to Self-Discipline Score
1. Age	34.7 years	Almost zero
2. Years of formal education	15.9	Slightly positive
3. Salary in U.S. dollars	$45,899	Slightly positive
4. Self-rating of career on scale of 1 to 7	4.9	Quite positive
5. Self-rating of goal accomplishment on scale of 1 to 7	5.6	Quite positive
6. Self-discipline score on scale of 20 to 100	76.9	------

Figure 2-6 Relationship between Self-Discipline Score and Key Factors

Score: Table derived from data presented in Andrew J. DuBrin, "Career-Related Correlates of Self-Discipline," *Psychological Reports*, 2001, Vol. 89, p. 109.

Chapter 3

Problem Solving and Creativity

Learning Outcomes

After studying the information and doing the exercises in this chapter, you should be able to

- understand how personal characteristics influence the ability to solve problems and make decisions;
- explain the four major decision-making styles as defined by the Myers-Briggs Type Indicator;
- apply the problem-solving and decision-making steps to complex problems;
- summarize the characteristics of creative people;
- describe various ways of improving your creativity.

Peter Labaziewicz, an Eastman Kodak Co. scientist, was riding on the train to work one day in Japan when he reached back across the decades for an idea that could push the digital era to new frontiers. He started thinking about the old "turret" film cameras—beastly looking models containing multiple lenses on a "plate" that rotates in front of a shutter. His concept: building similar flexibility in choice of lenses into a digital camera. "Wouldn't it be interesting?" Labaziewicz says he wondered.

> *It's not only interesting but also possible, and very, very successful, as Labaziewicz and his colleagues have found out. His musings helped trigger the creation of the Kodak imaging into an important new phase. The V750 is the first camera with two lenses and image sensors—one for wide-angle picture taking, the other for regular zoom. It's considered the first attempt by an industry mainstay to design digital products with attributes that are unique in their own right, free of the constraints of the film era.*
>
> *Since its introduction in early January 2006, the V750 has become a miniphenomenon, capturing the imagination of snap shooters and*

celebrities alike. It has drawn thousands of emails and numerous requests for product placements and donations. Kodak gave out diamond-encrusted models of the V750 to nominees for best actress at the 2006 Academy Awards. The attention is largely because of its sleek, unusual, space-age look and the allure of the camera offering something different.[1]

The new turret digital camera may not rival the light bulb or the computer as creative brilliance. Yet it does illustrate a few basic facts about problem solving, decision making, and creativity. The inventor of the new camera found a **problem**, a gap between what exists and what you want to exist. His employer was looking to push the digital era to new frontiers. Part of being a creative problem solver is to rely on a storehouse of information, such as knowledge about old turret film cameras. **Decision making** refers to choosing one alternative from the various alternative solutions that can be pursued. The developers of the new camera undoubtedly were sifting through hundreds of new product ideas to find a breakthrough camera.

The general purpose of this chapter is to help you become a more effective problem solver when working individually or in groups. Recent research by the Conference Board of Canada listed the ability to think critically and solve problems as a requirement for successful employees.[2] Companies require workers who can solve problems and make effective and smart decisions. Whether you are solving problems by yourself or as part of a group at work or home, most of the principles apply equally well. Most of the information in this chapter is designed to help you make unique and/or major decisions such as developing a new product, purchasing major equipment, or weighing a job offer.

PERSONAL CHARACTERISTICS THAT INFLUENCE YOUR PROBLEM-SOLVING ABILITY

Many personal characteristics and traits influence the type of problem solver and decision maker you are now or are capable of becoming. Fortunately, some personal characteristics that influence your decision-making ability can be improved through conscious effort. For instance, if you make bad decisions because you do not concentrate on the details of the problem, you can gradually learn to concentrate better. Most of the personal characteristics described next and outlined in Figure 3-1 can be strengthened through the appropriate education, training, and self-discipline.

Cognitive Intelligence, Education, and Experience

In general, if you are intelligent, well-educated, and experienced you will make better decisions than people without these attributes. Cognitive intelligence helps because, by definition, intelligence denotes the ability to solve problems. (The term *cognitive*

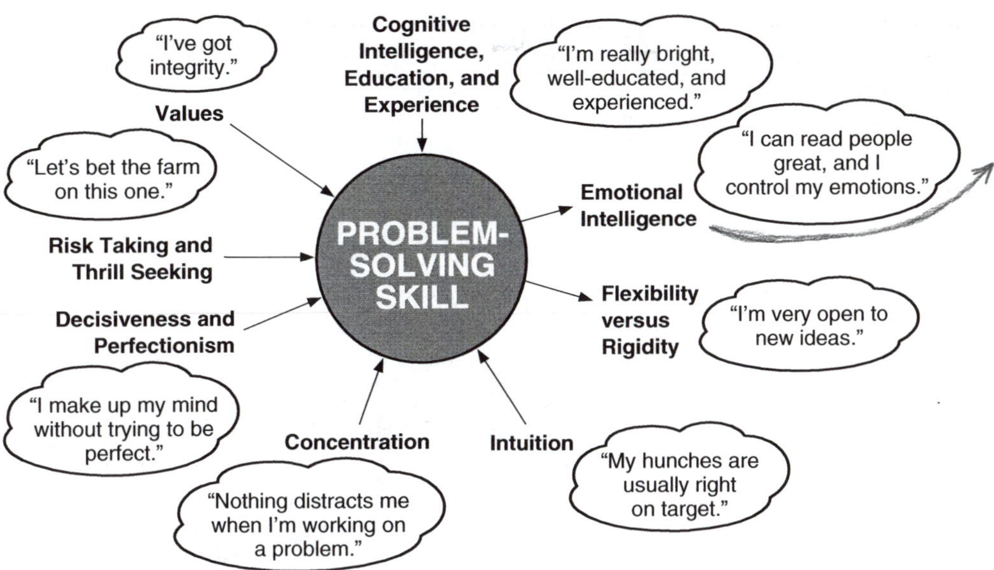

Figure 3-1 Influences on Problem-Solving Skill

intelligence refers to the intellectual, or traditional, type of intelligence that is necessary for such tasks as solving math problems and conjugating verbs.) Education improves the problem-solving and decision-making process because it gives you a background of principles and facts to rely on.

Experience facilitates decision making because good decisions tend to be made by people who have already faced similar situations in the past. This is one of the many reasons that experienced people command higher salaries. All things being equal, would you prefer to take your computer problem to an experienced or inexperienced specialist?

Emotional Intelligence

Being able to deal effectively with your feelings and emotions and those of others can help you make better decisions. **Emotional intelligence** refers to qualities such as understanding one's own feelings, empathy for others, and the regulation of emotion to enhance living. This type of intelligence has to do with the ability to connect with people and understand their emotions. A worker with high emotional intelligence would be able to engage in such behaviours as sizing up people, pleasing others, and influencing them.[3]

Emotional intelligence is important for decision making because effectiveness in managing your feelings and reading other people can affect the quality of your decisions. For example, if you cannot control your anger you are likely to make decisions that are motivated by retaliation, hostility, and revenge. An example would be shouting and swearing at your team leader because of a work assignment you received. Your emotional intelligence could also influence your career decision making. If you understand your own feelings, you are more likely to enter an occupation or accept a position that matches your true attitude.

Flexibility versus Rigidity

Some people are successful problem solvers and decision makers because they approach every problem with a fresh outlook. They are able to avoid developing rigid viewpoints. Flexible thinking enables the problem solver to think of original—and therefore creative—alternative solutions to solving a problem. Another perspective on the same issue is that being open-minded helps a person solve problems well. For example, a person might face the problem of wanting to purchase a high-quality PC but lacks sufficient funds. So the person keeps searching for a high-quality PC at a bargain price. If the person were more open-minded, he or she might investigate a "Netbook." These less expensive computers have fewer applications available, but are still useful for basic web applications and general computing needs. The link between flexibility and creativity will be described in more detail in the discussion of the characteristics of creative people.

Intuition

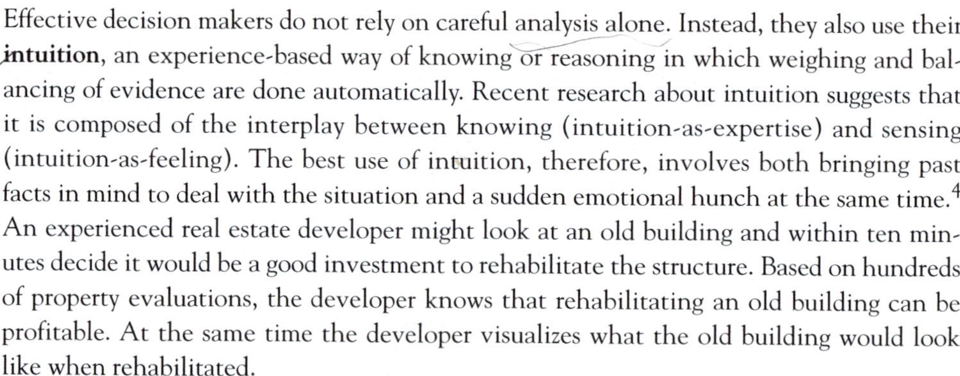

Effective decision makers do not rely on careful analysis alone. Instead, they also use their **intuition**, an experience-based way of knowing or reasoning in which weighing and balancing of evidence are done automatically. Recent research about intuition suggests that it is composed of the interplay between knowing (intuition-as-expertise) and sensing (intuition-as-feeling). The best use of intuition, therefore, involves both bringing past facts in mind to deal with the situation and a sudden emotional hunch at the same time.[4] An experienced real estate developer might look at an old building and within ten minutes decide it would be a good investment to rehabilitate the structure. Based on hundreds of property evaluations, the developer knows that rehabilitating an old building can be profitable. At the same time the developer visualizes what the old building would look like when rehabilitated.

Relying on intuition is like relying on your instincts when faced with a decision. Intuition takes place when the brain gathers information stored in memory and packages it as a new insight or solution. Intuitions, therefore, can be regarded as stored information that is reorganized or repackaged. Developing good intuition may take a long time because so much information has to be stored. The cognitive psychologist Gary Klein explains it this way:

> We sometimes think that experts are weighted down by information, by facts, by memories—that they make decisions slowly because they must search through so much data. But in fact, we've got it backward. The accumulation of experience does not weight people down—it lightens them up. It makes them fast.[5]

Intuition has become perhaps the hottest topic in decision making, including being the subject of a bestseller (*Blink* by Malcolm Gladwell).[6] Nevertheless, intuition has its drawbacks. Our hunches based on the combination of experience and emotion can sometimes lead us astray when a more analytical approach would have led to a better decision. For example, a charming and articulate job candidate might be chosen mostly on the basis of intuition. A background check based on rational analysis might have revealed that the candidate is a procrastinator and a criminal. One way to improve intuition is to get feedback on the decisions we make, so we can sharpen future decisions.[7] For example, a credit analyst in a bank profits from feedback about the future payment records of the loans he or she approved.

Concentration 

Mental concentration is an important contributor to making good decisions. Many people who solve problems poorly do so because they are too distracted to immerse themselves in the problem at hand. In contrast, effective problem solvers often achieve the **flow experience**—total absorption in their work. When flow occurs, things seem to go just right. The person feels alive and fully attentive to what he or she is doing. As a by-product of the flow experience, a good solution to a problem may surface. If you fail to concentrate hard enough you may overlook an important detail that could affect the outcome of the decision. For example, a person about to purchase an automobile might be excited about the high gas mileage but forget to research the vehicle's ability to withstand a crash.

Decisiveness and Perfectionism 

Some people are ill-suited to solving problems and making decisions because they are fearful of committing themselves to any given course of action. "Gee, I'm not sure, what do you think?" is their typical response to a decision forced upon them. If you are indecisive, this characteristic will have to be modified if you are to become a success in your field. A manager has to decide which person to hire. And a photographer has to decide which setting is best for the subject. As the old saying goes, at some point you have to "fish or cut bait."

People can be indecisive because they are perfectionists. With regard to decision making, **perfectionism** is a pattern of behaviour in which the individual strives to accomplish almost unattainable standards of flawless work. The combination of being indecisive and a perfectionist can lead to procrastination. Also, being a procrastinator can make one indecisive. Perfectionism contributes to delayed decision making because the person keeps working on a project before deciding to submit it to somebody else. Have you noticed any students or work colleagues with this type of procrastination? Chapter 15, about work habits, examines procrastination in depth.

Risk Taking and Thrill Seeking 

The need for taking risks and seeking thrills is yet another personality characteristic that influences problem-solving skill. For some types of problems, the risk taker and thrill seeker is at an advantage. Firefighters have to take risks to save people from burning buildings and to remove people trapped in collapsed buildings. An information technology specialist might have to engage in a risky manoeuvre to salvage data from a crashed hard drive. Risk taking and thrill seeking can also lead to poor problem solving and decision making, such as a merchandiser buying a huge inventory of highly original fashions. The experienced decision maker needs to know when to take high risks and seek thrills and when to be more conservative.

Values of the Decision Maker 

Values influence decision making at every step. The right values for the situation will improve problem solving and decision making, whereas the wrong values will lead to poor decisions. Ultimately, all decisions are based on values. A manager who places a high value on the well-being of employees tries to avoid alternatives that create hardships for workers. Another value that significantly influences problem solving and decision making is the pursuit of excellence. A worker who embraces the pursuit of excellence (and is therefore conscientious) will search for the high-quality alternative solution.

Attempting to preserve the status quo is a value that can negatively influence problem solving. Clinging to the status quo is perceived as a hidden trap in decision making that can prevent making the best decisions. People tend to cling to the status

Canada Today

So You've Decided to Be a CEO (Chief Executive Officer)—How Do You Get There?

A recent article in *Canadian Business* went looking for and found five of the brightest young executives in Canada. All five were young, powerful, driven, and very ambitious, often with their sights on attaining a CEO position within the next few years. The five included Andrew Nevin, Managing Director of TD Green Line Investor Services for the Asia-Pacific Region; Michael McCain, President and COO (Chief Operating Officer), Maple Leaf Foods Inc.; Dawn Farrell, VP, independent power projects, TransAlta Corp.; Paula Zivot, Marketing Manager of private brands, Zellers Inc.; and Kathy McLaughlin, VP, Western Canada Microcell Telecommunications Inc. These five people have all worked hard in school and since leaving school. Another common characteristic that stands out in this article is their ability to not only manage change, but to embrace and be excited by changes in their various industries. They all meet challenges head on and demonstrate flexibility and creativity. For example, Paula Zivot was pivotal in the successful launch of the Martha Stewart and Cherokee lines at Zellers.

This article also included "A Brilliant Career Path," a graph of where a number of experts think you should be at specific points in your life to launch your CEO career. If you want to attain these milestones, you will have to make many decisions and solve many problems. You should complete your MBA (if you plan to get one) by your early 30s. It can be too difficult to take time off and get it later on. If you want to take time off and travel or do other things, do them in your early 20s. In your 20s and 30s you should be changing jobs and titles regularly. Before the age of 40, you need to get noticed and start earning the big money; as a general rule, you should be making about two-and-a-half times your age. By your early 40s you should be at least vice-president and have headhunters trying to get you to switch firms. If this has not happened by your early 40s, you may want to set your sights on something else.

However, take note: this is just one article on CEOs. The key is to make effective decisions once you have some ideas about where you want to be in your career. Many of us may not want to be CEOs, but if you do, you may want to jot a few of these ideas down or, better yet, read the complete article.

Source: David Berman, "Looking Great for 2008," *Canadian Business*, July 31/August 14, 1998, pp. 40–71. Used with permission.

quo because, by *not* taking action, they can prevent a bad decision.[8] If you value the status quo too highly, you may fail to make a decision that could bring about major improvements.

PROBLEM-SOLVING STYLES

A well-documented observation is that people go about solving problems in various ways. You may have observed, for example, that some people are more analytical and systematic while others are more intuitive. The most widely used method of classifying problem-solving styles is the Myers-Briggs Type Indicator (MBTI).[9] A key aspect of the MBTI is to understand how people gather and evaluate information to solve problems. The MBTI is also used as a methodology to classify learning styles.

To solve problems it is necessary to gather information. Styles of information gathering range from sensation to intuition. **Sensation-type individuals** prefer routine and order. They search for precise details when gathering information to solve a problem. These people would prefer to work with established facts rather than search for new possibilities. **Intuitive-type individuals** prefer an overall perspective—the big picture. Such people enjoy solving new problems. In addition, they dislike routine and would prefer to look for possibilities rather than work with facts.

When shopping for an automobile, a sensation-type individual would want to gather a large number of facts about such matters as kilometres per litre, provisions of the warranty, finance charges, and resale value. In contrast, the intuitive-type individual would be more concerned about the overall style of the car and how proud he or she would be as the owner.

The evaluation aspect of problem solving involves judging how to deal with information after it has been collected. Styles of information evaluation range from an emphasis on feeling to an emphasis on thinking. **Feeling-type individuals** have a need to conform, and they attempt to adapt to the wishes of others. Because of these tendencies, they try to avoid problems that might result in disagreements. **Thinking-type individuals** rely on reason and intellect to deal with problems. They downplay emotion in problem solving and decision making.

Assume that a manager asks a group of employees their opinions on an idea for a new product. Feeling-type people in the group are likely to look for the good in the proposal and express approval for the new project. Thinking-type group members are likely to be more independent in their evaluation of the new product idea. As a result, they will express their opinion even if it is not what the manager wants to hear.

The two dimensions of information gathering and evaluation are combined to produce a four-way classification of problem-solving styles, as shown in Exhibit 3-1. The four styles are (1) sensation-thinking, (2) sensation-feeling, (3) intuitive-thinking, and (4) intuitive-feeling. Listed below each type are examples of occupations well suited for people of that particular type.

If you take the Myers-Briggs Type Indicator assessment, often available in career centres, you will discover your type. You can also study these four types and make a tentative judgment as to your problem-solving style. Recognizing your problem-solving style can help you identify work that you are likely to perform well. For example, a person with an intuitive-feeling style is likely to be skillful in resolving customer complaints. The same person might not be well suited by temperament to bookkeeping.

Exhibit 3-1
Four Problem-Solving Styles and Work Matchup[10]

Sensation-Thinking: decisive, dependable, and alert to details
Accounting and bookkeeping
Computer programming
Manufacturing technology

Intuitive-Thinking: creative, progressive, and perceptive
Design of systems
Law, paralegal work
Middle manager

Sensation-Feeling: pragmatic, analytical, methodical, and conscientious
Supervision
Selling
Negotiating

Intuitive-Feeling: colourful, people person, and helpful
Customer service
Business communications
Human resources

PROBLEM-SOLVING AND DECISION-MAKING STEPS

Whatever complex problem you face, it is best to use the standard problem-solving and decision-making steps as a guide. The steps in this model are similar to the systematic approach used in the scientific method. Although based on the scientific method, the decision-making and problem-solving steps presented here do not exclude the role of intuition. Rather, finding creative alternatives to your problem is actually at the heart of this method. Paying attention to this model is important because deviating too far from the model will often result in decision failure. Paul C. Nutt studied 356 decisions in medium to large organizations in the United States and Canada. He found that one-half of these decisions failed, mostly because the decision makers did not take a systematic approach, such as searching for many alternative solutions. The managers involved also committed the human relations error of not involving enough other people in helping with the decisions.[11]

Figure 3-2 summarizes the steps involved in problem solving and decision making. It is based on the assumption that decision making and problem solving should take place in an orderly flow of steps.

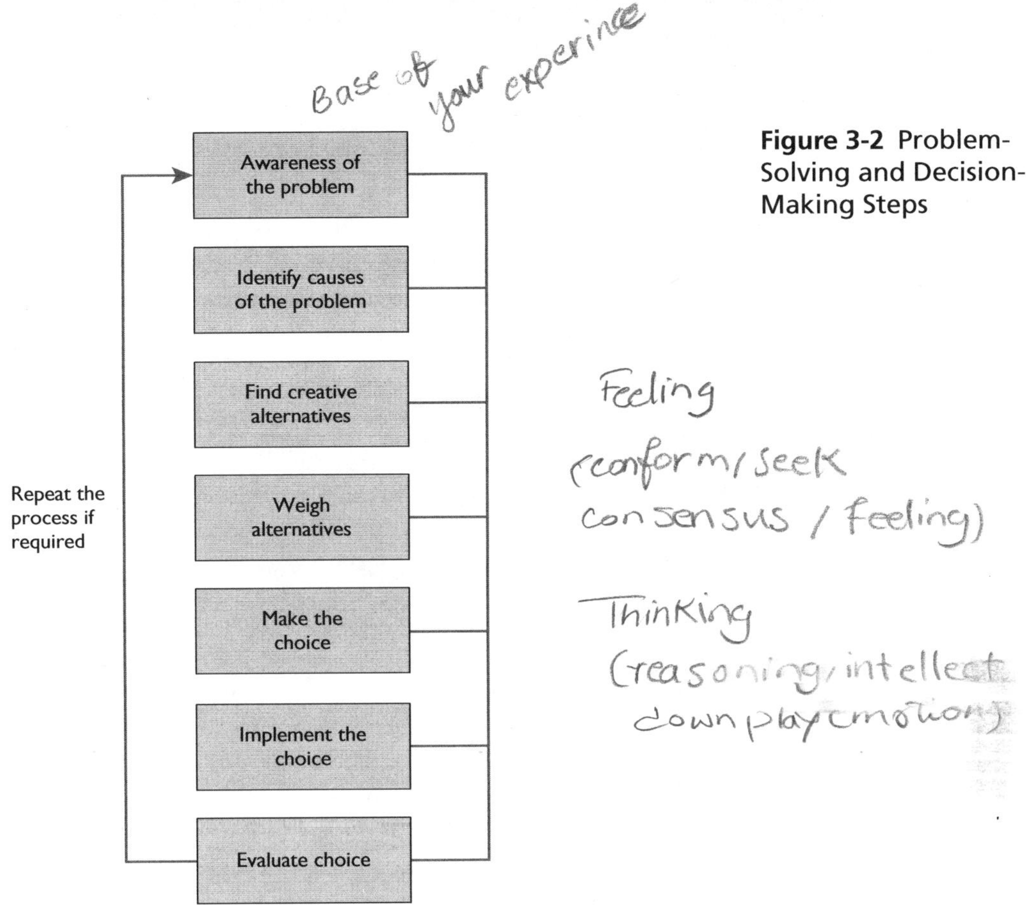

Figure 3-2 Problem-Solving and Decision-Making Steps

Awareness of the Problem

Problem solving and decision making begin when somebody is aware that a problem exists. In most decision-making situations, problems are given to another person. At other times, people create their own problems to solve, or they find problems. When one man decided that there were too many potholes in the streets of his town, he campaigned for the town supervisor to take decisive action on the problem.

After you have identified the problem, recognize that it may represent an important opportunity. For example, if you are bothered enough by a problem facing your company, you might volunteer to be the person in charge of overcoming the problem.

Identify Causes of the Problem

The causes of problems should be diagnosed and clarified before any action is taken because they are not always what they seem to be on the surface. Some problems may be more complicated than suspected. You may even be facing the wrong problem—not the one you need to solve in a particular situation. The person who found the potholes was thinking about treating the symptoms and not the real problem. Although it certainly would be advisable for the town to patch its potholes, the best solution would be to attend to the cause of potholes. The town would never be able to change the weather conditions, of course, but it could strengthen all new pavement.

Identifying the root cause of a problem can sometimes be facilitated by asking a series of questions. Five key elements to ask questions about (along with some sample questions) are as follows:

- *People.* What do the people involved contribute to the problem? Are they competent? Do they have an attitude problem?
- *Materials.* Do we have the right materials available? Is the quality of the materials adequate?
- *Machines and facilities.* Do we have the right machines and facilities to do the job? Have the machines and facilities changed?
- *Physical environment.* Is anything wrong with the environment (such as toxic fumes making people sick)? Has the environment changed?
- *Methods.* Are the processes and procedures adequate? Have new methods been introduced that workers do not understand?

The approach to analyzing causes is often placed in a cause-and-effect diagram, as shown in Figure 3-3. The approach is sometimes referred to as a fishbone diagram because of the angles of the lines leading to the various causes. Notice that all the causes contribute to the problem at the right. Even when you have identified the general source of a problem, you may still need to dig further to discover what, when, and where a problem *did not* occur. Suppose a friend talks about a fear of public speaking. By asking a few "but not" questions, you might be able to identify a major cause of the problem. Let's try out the method:

YOUR FRIEND: I'm horribly afraid of public speaking. I hate going up in front of the class.

YOU: But have you ever not been afraid of speaking to a group of people?

YOUR FRIEND: Yes, I can remember once feeling OK speaking at a victory dinner for my high school soccer team. We came in first in the region.

YOU: What did you talk about?

YOUR FRIEND: I told a cute story about how my mother and father put a soccer ball in my crib. I hugged it every day like it was a teddy bear.

YOU: So why weren't you afraid of giving that talk?

YOUR FRIEND: I knew what I was talking about. I didn't have to rehearse.

YOU: What else was different about the talk?

YOUR FRIEND: It wasn't like talking to strangers. I was just there with my buddies and our coaches.

YOU: What you are really telling me is that public speaking is OK when you are well prepared and you are in comfortable surroundings.

YOUR FRIEND: Thanks for helping me understand my problem.

Find Creative Alternatives

Here creativity and imagination enter into problem solving and decision making. Successful decision makers have the ability to think of different alternatives. The person

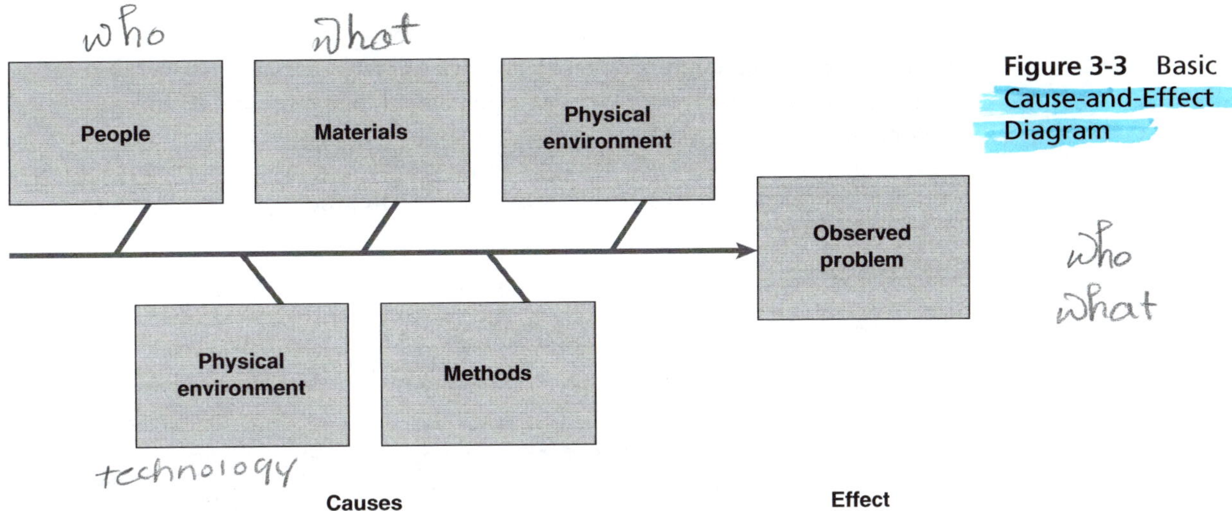

Figure 3-3 Basic Cause-and-Effect Diagram

who pushes to find one more alternative to a problem is often the person who finds a breakthrough solution. The more alternatives you generate, the more likely you will find a useful solution to your problem. Creativity plays such an important role in decision making that it will be discussed again in the next two major sections of this chapter.

Weigh Alternatives

This stage refers simply to examining the pros and cons of the various alternatives in the previous stages. In a major decision, each alternative would have to be given serious consideration. In practice, weighing alternatives often means jotting down the key good and bad points of each possible choice.

Make the Choice

The essence of decision making is selecting the right course of action to follow. You have to choose an alternative, even if it is not to go ahead with a new plan of action. For instance, after conducting a job campaign you could decide not to change jobs. Experienced business executives have often criticized well-educated young people for their lack of decisiveness. Instead of coming to a decision, the young people are accused of over-analyzing a problem. Do you suffer from "analysis paralysis," or do you make up your mind after a reasonable amount of thought?

In choosing an alternative, it is helpful to remember that most problems really have multiple solutions. You therefore do not have to be overly concerned with finding the only correct answer to your problem. For instance, there might be several effective ways of reducing the costs of running a department.

Implement the Choice

After you decide which course of action to take, you have to put the choice into effect. Some decisions are more difficult to implement than others. Decisions made by top management, for example, are sometimes so difficult to implement that they have to be reversed. An executive announced a new policy that all employees would be restricted to 45-minute lunch breaks. Few employees took the edict seriously, and most continued to spend about 60 minutes at lunch. The executive gave up and reconsidered the decision in terms of its effect on morale. The general point is that to implement many decisions, the human element must be taken into consideration.

Evaluate the Choice

The decision-making sequence is not complete until the decision has been evaluated. Evaluation may take a considerable period of time because the results of your decision are not always immediately apparent. Suppose you receive two job offers. It might take several months to a year to judge whether you are satisfied with the job you accepted. It would be necessary to look at the factors you think are most important in a job. Among them might be "Is there opportunity for advancement?" "Are the people here friendly?" "Is the work interesting?" Evaluating your choice would be further complicated by the difficulty of determining how you might have fared in the job you didn't accept. Now and then you might obtain some information to suggest what that alternative held in store for you, as did a woman who turned down a job offer with a new and promising company. She questioned that decision until she read one morning a year later that the company had gone into bankruptcy.

What happens when your evaluation of a decision is negative? You go back to the drawing board, as the line and arrow on the left-hand side of Figure 3-2 indicates. Since your first decision was not a good one, you are faced with another problem situation.

A helpful decision-making aid is to visualize what you would do if the alternative you chose proved to be dreadful—the **worst-case scenario**. Suppose, for example, you choose a job that proves to be unsuited to your talents. Would you resign as soon as your mistake became apparent, or would you sweat it out for a year in order to show some employment stability? Or would you retain the job while starting to look around for a more suitable job? Developing a worst-case scenario helps prevent you from becoming overwhelmed by the fear of making a bad decision. Closely related to the worst-case scenario is establishing an **exit strategy** that determines in advance how you will get out of a bad decision, such as having joined a failing family business.

To gain practice in developing your skills in making major decisions, do Human Relations Skill-Building Exercise 3-1. You will be given some additional practice in using the problem-solving method in the end-of-chapter case study.

CREATIVITY IN DECISION MAKING

Creativity is helpful at any stage of decision making, but it is essential for recognizing problems, analyzing them, and searching for creative alternatives. Simply put, creativity is the ability to develop good ideas that can be put into action. Finding a creative idea usually involves a flash of insight about how to solve a problem. If you have above-average creativity you will be more adept at solving problems in both work and personal life.

Human Relations Skill Building

Exercise 3-1 Using the Problem-Solving Process

Imagine that you have received $1,000,000 in cash. The only stipulation is that you will have to use the money to establish some sort of enterprise, either a business or a charitable foundation. Solve this problem, using the worksheet provided below. Describe what thoughts you have or what actions you will take for each step of problem solving and decision making.

1. *Awareness of the problem:* Have you found your own problem or was it given to you?
2. *Identify causes of the problem:* What is your underlying problem? What is the true decision that you are facing?
3. *Find creative alternatives:* Think of the many alternatives facing you. Let your imagination flow and be creative.
4. *Weigh alternatives:* Weigh the pros and cons of each of your sensible alternatives.

	Alternatives	Advantages	Disadvantages
a.			
b.			
c.			
d.			
e.			

5. *Make the choice:* Based on your analysis in step 4, choose the best alternative.
6. *Implement the choice:* Outline your action plan for converting your chosen alternative into action.
7. *Evaluate the choice:* Do the best you can here by speculating how you will know if the decision you reached was a good one.

When people see or hear the word *creativity*, many think of a rarefied talent. A more helpful perspective is to recognize that not all creativity requires wild imagination. The emphasis here is on creativity applied to business and personal life rather than on creativity in science, technology, and the arts. Creativity is important for companies of all sizes, not only for large firms. As explained in the Encyclopedia of Creativity, creativity can be taught and learned, enhanced, and mastered. Enough is known about creativity that it can be integrated into every level in the educational system.[12]

Measuring Your Creative Potential

One way to gain an understanding of creativity is to try out exercises used to measure creative potential, such as those presented in Human Relations Self-Assessment Quizzes 3-1 and 3-2. Do not be overly encouraged or dejected by any results you achieve on these exercises, as both of them only measure creativity based on verbal ability.

Characteristics of Creative Workers

Creative workers tend to have different intellectual and personality characteristics from their less creative counterparts. In general, creative people are more mentally flexible than others, which allows them to overcome the traditional ways of looking at problems. This flexibility often shows up in practical jokes and other forms of playfulness such as making up a rap song about the company's product line.

The characteristics of creative workers can be grouped into three broad areas: knowledge, intellectual abilities, and personality.[13]

Human Relations Self-Assessment

QUIZ 3-1 Creative Personality Test

The following test will help you determine if certain aspects of your personality are similar to those of a creative individual. Since our test is for illustrative and research purposes, proceed with caution in mind. This is not a standardized psychological instrument. Such tests are not reprinted in general books. Answer each of the following statements as "mostly true" or "mostly false." We are looking for general trends; therefore, do not be concerned if you answer true if they are not entirely true and false if they are not entirely false.

	Mostly True	***Mostly False***
1. I think novels are a waste of time, so I am more likely to read nonfiction books.	_____	_____
2. You have to admit, some crooks are very clever.	_____	_____
3. People consider me to be a fastidious dresser. I despise looking shaggy.	_____	_____
4. I am a person of very strong convictions. What's right is right; what's wrong is wrong.	_____	_____
5. I enjoy it when my boss hands me vague instructions.	_____	_____
6. Business before pleasure is a hard and fast rule in my life.	_____	_____
7. Taking a different route to work is fun, even if it takes longer.	_____	_____
8. Rules and regulations should not be taken too seriously. Most rules can be broken under unusual circumstances.	_____	_____
9. Playing with a new idea is fun even if it doesn't benefit me in the end.	_____	_____
10. People say that I have an excellent sense of humour.	_____	_____
11. Writers should try to avoid using unusual words and word combinations.	_____	_____
12. Detective work would have some appeal to me.	_____	_____
13. Crazy people have no good ideas.	_____	_____
14. Why write letters to friends when there are so many clever greeting cards available in the stores today?	_____	_____
15. Pleasing myself means more to me than pleasing others.	_____	_____
16. If you dig long enough, you will find the true answer to most questions.	_____	_____

Scoring the Test: The answer in the creative direction for each question is as follows:

1. Mostly False	**5.** Mostly True	**9.** Mostly True	**13.** Mostly False
2. Mostly True	**6.** Mostly False	**10.** Mostly True	**14.** Mostly False
3. Mostly False	**7.** Mostly True	**11.** Mostly False	**15.** Mostly True
4. Mostly False	**8.** Mostly True	**12.** Mostly True	**16.** Mostly False

Give yourself a point for each answer you gave that agreed with the keyed answers.

Interpreting Your Score: A score of 12 or more suggests that your personality and attitudes are similar to those of a creative person. A score of 5 or less suggests that your personality is dissimilar to that of a creative person. You are probably more of a conformist (and somewhat categorical) in your thinking, at least at this point in your life. Don't be discouraged. Most people can become more creative.

Human Relations Self-Assessment

QUIZ 3-2 Rhyme and Reason[14]

A noted creativity expert says that exercises in rhyming release creative energy; they stir imagination into action. While doing the following exercises remember that rhyme is frequently a matter of sound and does not have to involve similar or identical spelling. This exercise deals with light and frivolous emotions. After each "definition," write two rhyming words to which it refers.

Examples:

1. Large hog	Big	pig
2. Television	Boob	tube
3. A computer control for the home	House	mouse

Now try these:

1. Happy father	___	___
2. False pain	___	___
3. Formed like a simian	___	___
4. Highest-ranking police worker	___	___
5. Voyage by a large boat	___	___
6. Corpulent feline	___	___
7. Melancholy fellow	___	___
8. Clever beginning	___	___
9. Heavy and unbroken slumber	___	___
10. Crazy custom	___	___
11. Lengthy melody	___	___
12. Weak man	___	___
13. Instruction at the seashore	___	___
14. Criticism lacking in effectiveness	___	___
15. A person who murders for pleasurable excitement	___	___
16. Musical stringed instrument with full, rich sounds	___	___
17. Courageous person who is owned as property by another	___	___
18. Mature complaint	___	___
19. Strange hair growing on the lower part of a man's face	___	___
20. Drooping marine crustacean	___	___
21. A computer whiz with a bizarre sense of humour	___	___

(continued)

(continued)

Answers and Interpretation: The more of these rhymes you were able to come up with, the higher your creative potential. You would also need an advanced vocabulary to score very high (for instance, what is a "simian" or a "crustacean"?). Ten or more correct rhymes would tend to show outstanding creative potential, at least in the verbal area. Here are the answers:

1. Glad dad
2. Fake ache
3. Ape shape
4. Top cop
5. Ship trip
6. Fat cat
7. Sad lad
8. Smart start
9. Deep sleep
10. Mad fad
11. Long song
12. Frail male
13. Beach teach
14. Weak critique
15. Thriller killer
16. Mellow cello
17. Brave slave
18. Ripe gripe
19. Weird beard
20. Limp shrimp
21. Absurd nerd

If you can think of a sensible substitute for any of these answers, give yourself a bonus point.

Knowledge Creative thinking requires a broad background of information, including facts and observations. Knowledge supplies the building blocks for generating and combining ideas. This is particularly true because some experts say that creativity always comes down to combining things in a new and different way. The introductory case about the scientist who linked knowledge of old turret cameras with knowledge about digital cameras illustrates how combining facts can be helpful.

Intellectual Abilities In general, creative workers tend to be bright rather than brilliant. Extraordinarily high intelligence is not required to be creative. Yet creative people are good at generating alternative solutions to problems in a short period of time. According to Yale University professor of psychology and education, Robert Sternberg, the key to creative intelligence is **insight**, an ability to know what information is relevant, to find connections between the old and the new, to combine facts that are unrelated, and to see the "big picture."[15] Creative people also maintain a youthful curiosity throughout their lives. And the curiosity is not centred on just their own field of expertise. Instead, their range of interests encompasses many areas of knowledge, and they generate enthusiasm toward almost any puzzling problem.

Creative people are able to think divergently. They can expand the number of alternatives to a problem, thus moving away from a single solution. Yet the creative thinker also knows when it is time to think convergently, narrowing the number of useful solutions. For example, the divergent thinker might think of 27 different names for a website that sells high-fashion buttons. Yet at some point he or she will have to converge and choose the best URL, such as **www.chicbutton.com**.

Creativity can stem from both *fluid intelligence* and *crystallized intelligence*. Fluid intelligence depends on raw processing ability, or how quickly you learn information and solve problems. Like raw athletic ability, fluid intelligence begins to decline by age 30, particularly because nerve conduction slows. Crystallized intelligence is accumulated knowledge that increases with age and experience.[16]

Personality The emotional and other nonintellectual aspects of a person heavily influence creative problem solving. Creative people tend to have a positive self-image without being blindly self-confident. Because they are self-confident, creative people are able to cope with criticism of their ideas. Creative people have the ability to tolerate the isolation necessary for developing ideas. Talking to others is a good source of ideas. Yet at some point the creative problem solver has to work alone and concentrate.

Creative people are frequently nonconformists, and do not need strong approval from the group. Many creative problem solvers are thrill seekers who find developing imaginative solutions to problems to be a source of thrills. Creative people are also persistent, which is especially important for seeing that a new idea is implemented. Selling a creative idea to the right people requires considerable follow-up. Creative people enjoy dealing with uncertainty and chaos. A creative person, for example, would enjoy the challenge of taking over a customer service department that was way behind schedule and ineffective. Less creative people become frustrated quickly when their job is unclear and disorder exists.

Self-reflection and a concentration on feelings are characteristic of many creative people. The quiet thinking is helpful in finding useful ideas, as in thinking of how to solve a difficult problem while walking alone or taking a shower. Creative people are also open and responsive to feelings and emotions in the world around them.

The Conditions Necessary for Creativity

Creativity is not just a random occurrence. Well-known creativity researcher Teresa M. Amabile has summarized 22 years of her research about creativity in the workplace. Her findings are supported by others.[17] Creativity takes place when three components come together: expertise, creative thinking skills, and the right type of motivation.

Expertise refers to the necessary knowledge to put facts together. The more ideas floating around in your head, the more likely you are to combine them in some useful way. *Creative thinking* refers to how flexibly and imaginatively individuals approach problems. If you know how to keep digging for alternatives and how to avoid getting stuck in the status quo, your chances of being creative multiply. Along these same lines, you are much more likely to be creative if you are intentionally seeking ideas, such as always being on the lookout for money-saving ideas. Persevering, or sticking with a problem to a conclusion, is essential for finding creative solutions. A few rest breaks to gain a fresh perspective may be helpful, but the creative person keeps coming back until a solution emerges.

The right type of *motivation* is the third essential ingredient for creative thought. A fascination with or passion for the task is much more important than searching for external rewards. People will be most creative when they are motivated primarily by the satisfaction and challenge of the work itself. A Dutch psychologist attempted to analyze what separated chess masters from chess grand masters. He subjected groups of each to a variety of mental ability tests, but found no difference between the two groups. The only difference found was in motivation: Grand masters simply loved chess more and had more passion and commitment for the game.[18]

Passion for the task and high intrinsic motivation contribute to a total absorption in the work and intense concentration, resulting in the flow experience. (Refer to the section in Chapter 2 about self-motivation.) Flow also means *being in the zone*. A creative businessperson, such as an entrepreneur developing a plan for worldwide distribution of a product, will often achieve the experience of flow.

In addition to the internal conditions that foster creativity, five factors external to a person are key:

1. An environmental need must stimulate the setting of a goal. This is another way of saying that necessity is the mother of invention. Here's an example for animal lovers:

   > A dairy farmer in Ontario, Canada, was concerned that his cows suffered so many diseases from the bacteria that accumulate in their surroundings. Bacteria is also hazardous because it can contaminate milk. Another adverse environmental condition the farmer noticed was that cows took too many falls, often suffering serious injuries. The farmer's solution to the problem was a cow mattress. (Just think of the size of the untapped market.) Farmers in Canada, the east coast of the United States, and Europe have been the biggest customers for the mattresses because they are especially effective in cold, rainy climates. The mattresses, made of thick tarp and stuffed with ground-up auto tires, are installed on slanted concrete foundations. The slant keeps rainwater and manure from collecting and becoming a breeding ground for bacteria. The rubber-filled columns on the mattresses serve as shock absorbers that prevent the cows from slipping and injuring themselves.
   >
   > A California dairy farmer observed that after installing the mattresses, milk production increased, diseases decreased, and the cows were more blissful. Pointing to a cow lying on a mattress and lazily chewing her feed, the farmer said, "See how peaceful and stress-free she looks? That's a happy cow."[19]

2. Another condition that fosters creativity is enough conflict and tension to put people on edge. Robert Sutton advises managers to prod happy people into fighting among themselves to stimulate creativity. The fights should be about ideas, not personality conflicts and name calling. For example, a group member should be given time to defend his or her work, and then the ideas should be sharply criticized by the other group members.[20] Cirque du Soleil, the world-famous circus, capitalizes on the importance of conflict for creativity. Cirque officials generally ensure there is a mix of nationalities and viewpoints when they assemble a creative team. Daniel Lamarre, the troupe's president, says that easy consensus is the enemy of groundbreaking ideas. The ideas, in this context, usually refer to fascinating acts.[21]
3. Another external factor for creativity is encouragement, including a permissive atmosphere that welcomes new ideas. A manager or team leader who encourages imagination and original thinking and does not punish people for making honest mistakes is likely to receive creative ideas from people. For example, 3M is highly regarded as a company with many innovations including Scotch Tape and Post-it® Notes. The company encourages creativity in many ways, such as granting people time off from regular responsibilities just to think about new ideas.
4. Humour is a key environmental condition for enhancing creativity. Humour has always been linked to creativity. Humour gets the creative juices flowing, and effective humour requires creativity. Thomas Edison started every workday with a joke-telling session. Mike Vance, chairman of the Creative Thinking Association of America, says that "Humour is unmasking the hypocritical. What makes us

laugh often is seeing how things are screwed up—then sometimes seeing how we can fix them. Whenever I go into a company and don't hear much laughter, I know it's not a creative place."[22]

5. A final key environmental condition to be considered here is how much time pressure the problem solver should face to trigger creativity. Conventional wisdom says that people produce the best when pressure is highest, for example, thinking of ways to keep a business running after a disaster, such as a fire, flood, or terrorist attack. Yet studies show that the more workers feel pressed for time, the less likely they are to produce creative output, such as solving a tricky problem or envisioning a new product, or to have other such "aha" experiences that result in innovation. Time pressures may diminish creativity because they limit a worker's freedom to think through different options and directions. A subtle finding, however, is that time pressures may help creativity if the worker is focused on a single task he or she considers important.[23] So if you are under heavy time pressure to arrive at a creative solution, focus on one task.

Despite the theme of permissiveness in several of the conditions for enhancing creativity, constraints also have their place. Individuals or teams with budget constraints and time constraints sometimes find that these constraints help them rise to the occasion. Marissa Ann Mayer, the vice-president for search products and user experience at Google contends that constraints can actually speed product development. Google often gets a sense of just how good a new concept is if they simply prototype it (try it out) for a single day or week. Another constraint would be limiting team size to two or three people.[24]

IMPROVING YOUR CREATIVITY

Because of the importance of creative problem solving, many techniques have been developed to improve creativity. Let us look at both specific techniques and general strategies for becoming more creative. The goal of these experiences is to think like a creative problem solver. Such a person lets his or her imagination wander. He or she ventures beyond the constraints that limit most people.

Concentrate Intensely on the Task at Hand

The ability to concentrate was mentioned earlier as a characteristic that contributes to effective problem solving in general. The ability to eliminate distractions also contributes mightily to generating new ideas. At times we think we are thinking intently about our problem (such as how to make cows more comfortable), yet in reality we may be thinking about something that interferes with creativity.[25] Among the office distractions that interfere with concentration are phone calls, a computer beep informing you of an incoming message, a fax machine in the receiving mode, and a friendly hello from a work associate walking past your cubicle. All of the following methods for enhancing creativity require concentration.

Overcome Traditional Mental Sets

An important consequence of becoming more intellectually flexible is that you can overcome a **traditional mental set**, a fixed way of thinking about objects and activities.

Overcoming traditional mental sets is important because the major block to creativity is perceiving things in a traditional way. All creative examples presented so far in this chapter illustrate the power of overcoming a traditional mental set. In the anecdote about the storage space in the SUV, the designer solved an apparently impossible problem by thinking in a mental set different from that suggested by the original request. Instead of adding another six inches of room, the designer reframed the question: "How can we find more storage space?"

An effective way of overcoming a traditional mental set is to challenge the status quo. If you want to develop an idea that will impress your boss or turn around an industry, you must use your imagination. Question the old standby that things have always been done in a particular way. To make the information superhighway possible, many old standby assumptions had to be questioned. Among them were that (1) the only way to obtain videos for home use is to bring a videocassette into the home, and (2) only telephone cables can be used to transmit digital information.

Discipline Yourself to Think Laterally

A major challenge in developing creative thinking skills is to learn how to think laterally in addition to vertically. **Vertical thinking** is an analytical, logical process that results in few answers. The vertical thinker is looking for the one best solution to a problem, much as if he or she were solving an equation in algebra. In contrast, **lateral thinking** spreads out to find many different alternative solutions to a problem. In short, critical thinking is vertical and creative thinking is lateral.

A vertical thinker might say, "I must find a part-time job to supplement my income. My income is not matching my expenses." The lateral thinker might say, "I need more money. Let me think of the various ways of earning more money. I can find a second job, get promoted where I am working, cut my expenses, run a small business out of my home. . . ."

To learn to think laterally, you have to develop the mental set that every problem has multiple alternative solutions. Do not leave the problem until you have sketched out multiple alternatives. Use a pencil or pen and paper or a computer screen, but do not walk away from your problem until you have thought of multiple alternatives. The accompanying Human Relations in Practice box insert provides an industrial example of lateral thinking.

Conduct Brainstorming Sessions

The best-known method of improving creativity is **brainstorming**, a technique by which group members think of multiple solutions to a problem. Using brainstorming, a group of six people might sit around a table generating new ideas for a product. During the idea-generating part of brainstorming, potential solutions are not criticized or evaluated in any way. In this way spontaneity is encouraged. The original device for programming VCRs by simply punching one number was a product of brainstorming. The product retails for about $75. It is designed for people who are unable or unwilling to learn how to program a VCR. Rules for brainstorming are presented in Exhibit 3-2. Brainstorming has many variations, including an electronic approach, creative twosomes, brainwriting, and forced associations.

Human Relations in Practice

Robot Maker Thinks Laterally to Find New Use for Product

The KR 500, designed to lift car parts, is sold by Kuka Robotics, Europe's largest manufacturer of automated industrial machines. In 2000, several Kuka engineers wondered aloud whether the KR 500 could also lift people. "We could attach a chair to the end of it," one said. "It could make a fun ride." At any other industrial manufacturer, such an idea might have been laughed at and forgotten. But at Kuka, which has long built robots not only to perform but also to delight, it breathed new life into the company.

Only five years ago, Kuka was a century-old supplier of manufacturing equipment whose profits were disappearing because of its overreliance on automakers. By taking on its engineers' challenge to break down the barrier between man and machine, Kuka has found lucrative customers in a range of new industries and made its robots the stars of internationally renowned movies (for example, Die Another Day) and theme parks. Says Donald Vincent, executive vice-president of Robotic Industries Association, "Kuka has stretched the envelope in growing new markets."

Questions

1. Why is the new use for an industrial robot an example of lateral thinking?
2. Why are Kuka's ideas for new uses for their products more about business creativity than scientific creativity?

Source: Siri Schubert, "Taking Robots for a Ride," Business 2.0, August 2005, p. 46.

Electronic Brainstorming In electronic brainstorming, group members simultaneously enter their suggestions into a computer. The ideas are distributed to the screens of other group members. Although the group members do not talk to each other, they are still able to build on each other's ideas and combine ideas.

Electronic brainstorming helps overcome certain problems encountered in traditional brainstorming. Shyness, domination by one or two members, and participants who loaf tend to be less troublesome than in face-to-face situations.

Exhibit 3-2
Rules and Guidelines for Brainstorming

1. Use groups of about five to seven people.
2. Encourage the spontaneous expression of ideas. All suggestions are welcome, even if they are outlandish or outrageous. The least workable ideas can be edited out when the idea-generation phase is completed.
3. Quantity and variety are very important. The greater the number of ideas, the greater the likelihood of a breakthrough idea.
4. Encourage combination and improvement of ideas. This process is referred to as "piggybacking" or "hitchhiking."
5. One person serves as the secretary and records the ideas, perhaps posting them on a chalkboard.
6. Do not overstructure by following any of the above rules too rigidly. Brainstorming is a spontaneous process.

Ted Talked David Kelky Founder of IDEO and Stanford Professor) How to Bild your Creative confidence (12 min)

Tim Brown: Tales of creativity and Play

Brainwriting In many situations brainstorming by yourself produces as many or more useful ideas as does brainstorming in groups. **Brainwriting**, or solo brainstorming, is arriving at creative ideas by jotting them down yourself. The creativity-improvement techniques discussed so far will help you to develop the mental flexibility necessary for brainstorming. After you have loosened up your mental processes, you will be ready to tackle your most vexing problems. Self-discipline is very important for brainwriting because some people have a tendency to postpone something as challenging as thinking alone.

An important requirement of brainwriting is that you set aside a regular time (and perhaps place) for generating ideas. The ideas discovered in the process of routine activities can be counted as bonus time. Even five minutes a day is much more time than most people are accustomed to spending thinking creatively about job problems. Give yourself a quota with a time deadline.

Forced Associations A widely used method of releasing creativity is the **forced-association technique**. Using this technique, individuals or groups solve a problem by making associations between the properties of two objects. A link is found between the properties of the random object and the properties of the problem object. The forced association is supposed to help solve the problem. An individual (working alone or in a group) selects a word at random from a dictionary or textbook. If you happen to choose a preposition, try again until you find a noun to give you something more to work with. Next, the person (or group) lists many of the properties and attributes of this word. Assume you randomly chose the word *ladder*. Among its attributes are "durable," "foldable," "aluminum or wood," "moderately priced," and "easy to use." If you were trying to improve a bow tie to increase sales, for example, you might make the tie more durable and easier to use.

In the various types of brainstorming just discussed, collecting wild ideas is just the start of the process. After ideas are collected, the group or each member carefully evaluates and analyzes the various alternatives. It is usually important to also specify the implementation details. For example, how do you actually convert an industrial robot into an amusement park ride?

Borrow Creative Ideas

Copying the successful ideas of others is a legitimate form of creativity. Be careful, however, to give appropriate credit. Knowing when and which ideas to borrow from other people can help you behave as if you were an imaginative person. Creative ideas can be borrowed through such methods as:

Speaking to friends, relatives, classmates, and co-workers

Reading newspapers, newsmagazines, trade magazines, textbooks, nonfiction books and novels, and surfing the internet

Watching television and listening to radio programs

Subscribing to computerized information services (expensive but worth it to many ambitious people)

Business firms borrow ideas from each other regularly as part of quality improvement. The process is referred to as *benchmarking* because another firm's product, service, or process is used as a standard of excellence. Benchmarking involves representatives from one company visiting another to observe firsthand the practices of another company. The company visited is usually not a direct competitor. It is considered unethical to visit a competitor company for the purpose of appropriating ideas.

Challenge Your Ruts

A major hurdle to thinking creatively is getting locked into so many habits and routines that our thinking becomes too mechanical. According to Kathleen R. Allen, "We do the same things, the same way, every day. This is a primary barrier to creativity. Often we need to feel a little uncomfortable—we need to experience new things—to get creative sparks."[26] Challenging your ruts, or habitual way of doing things, can assist you in developing mental flexibility. Anything you do that forces you out of your normal environment will help you see things in new and different ways. Here is a sampling of everyday ruts worth challenging:

- Eating lunch with the same friends at work or school
- Watching the same television shows or reading only the same sections of the newspaper
- Restricting your internet browsing to only your favourite sites
- Befriending only those people in your same demographic group, such as age range, race, and ethnic background
- Engaging in the same pastimes exclusively
- Using the same form of physical exercise each time you exercise

Play the Roles of Explorer, Artist, Judge, and Lawyer

A method for improving creativity has been proposed that incorporates many of the suggestions already made. The method calls for you to adopt four roles in your thinking.[27]

First, be an explorer. Speak to people in different fields and get ideas that you can use. For example, if you are a telecommunications specialist, speak to salespeople and manufacturing specialists.

Second, be an artist by stretching your imagination. Strive to spend about 5 percent of your day asking "what if" questions. For example, a sales manager at a fresh-fish distributor might ask, "What if some new research suggests that eating fish causes intestinal cancer in humans?" Also, remember to challenge the commonly perceived rules in your field. For example, a bank manager challenged why customers needed their cancelled cheques returned each month. This questioning led to some banks not returning cancelled cheques unless the customer paid an additional fee for the service. (As a compromise, some banks send customers photocopies of about ten cheques on one page.)

Third, know when to be a judge. After developing some wild ideas, at some point you have to evaluate them. Do not be so critical that you discourage your own imaginative thinking. However, be critical enough to prevent attempting to implement weak ideas.

Fourth, achieve results with your creative thinking by playing the role of a lawyer. Negotiate and find ways to implement your ideas within your field or place of work. The explorer, artist, and judge stages of creative thought might take only a short time to develop a creative idea. Yet you may spend months or even years getting your brainstorm implemented. For example, it took a long time for the developer of the electronic pager to finally get the product manufactured and distributed on a large scale.

SUMMARY

Problem solving occurs when you try to remove an obstacle that is blocking a path you want to take, or when you try to close the gap between what exists and what you want to exist. Decision making takes place after you encounter a problem. It refers to selecting one alternative from the various courses of action that can be pursued.

Many traits and characteristics influence the type of problem solver you are now or are capable of becoming. Among them are (1) flexibility versus rigidity; (2) cognitive intelligence, education, and experience; (3) emotional intelligence; (4) intuition; (5) concentration; (6) decisiveness and perfectionism; (7) risk taking and thrill seeking; and (8) values.

The Myers-Briggs Type Indicator is a widely used method of determining problem-solving styles. Information gathering is divided into two main types. Sensation-type individuals prefer routine and order. Intuitive-type individuals prefer an overall perspective. Information evaluation is also divided into two types. Feeling-type individuals have a need to conform. Thinking-type individuals rely on reason and intellect to deal with problems. The two dimensions of information gathering and evaluation are combined to produce a four-way classification of problem-solving styles. Recognizing your problem-solving style can help you identify work you are likely to perform well. (See Exhibit 3-1.)

The decision-making process outlined in this chapter uses both the scientific method and intuition for making decisions in response to problems. Decision making and problem solving follow an orderly flow of events:

1. You are aware of a problem or create one of your own.
2. You identify causes of the problem.
3. You find creative alternatives.
4. You weigh the alternatives.
5. You make the choice.
6. You implement the choice.
7. You evaluate whether you have made a sound choice. If your choice was unsound, you are faced with a new problem and the cycle repeats itself.

Creativity is the ability to develop good ideas that can be put into action. Being creative helps you in both work and personal life. Creative workers tend to have different intellectual and personality characteristics from their less creative counterparts. In general, creative people are more mentally flexible than others, which allows them to overcome the traditional way of looking at problems.

Creative thinking requires a broad background of information, including facts and observations. Creative workers tend to be bright rather than brilliant. The emotional and other nonintellectual aspects of a person heavily influence creative problem solving. For example, creative people are frequently nonconformists and thrill seekers. Creativity takes place when three components come together: expertise, creative thinking skills, and personality. Creative thinking refers to being flexible and imaginative. The right type of motivation refers to passion for the task and intrinsic motivation. Four factors external to a person play a key role in fostering creativity: an environmental need, enough conflict and tension to put people on edge, encouragement from management, and the presence of humour.

Methods of improving your creativity include (1) concentrating intensely on the task at hand, (2) overcoming traditional mental sets, (3) disciplining yourself to think laterally (instead of only vertically), (4) conducting brainstorming sessions, (5) borrowing creative ideas, and (6) playing the roles of explorer, artist, judge, and lawyer.

QUESTIONS AND ACTIVITIES

1. What would be some of the symptoms or signs of "rigid thinking"?
2. How might being a perfectionist create performance problems for a team leader? For a paralegal? For a computer programmer?
3. Why does concentration improve problem solving?
4. Furnish an example from your own life in which you became aware of a problem. What led to this awareness?
5. Which of the four problem-solving styles shown in Exhibit 3-1 would you prefer to be characteristic of your boss? Explain your reasoning.
6. How might you use the internet to improve major decisions you face on the job and in your personal life?
7. Give two examples of decisions you have faced, or will face, that justify running through the problem-solving and decision-making steps.
8. Think of the most creative person you know. Describe his or her personal characteristics and compare them with the characteristics of creative people presented in this chapter.
9. Ask an experienced manager or professional how important creative thinking has been in her or his career. Report back to the class with your findings.
10. Give an example of one work problem and one personal problem for which brainstorming might be useful.

INTERNET SKILL BUILDER

Learning about Creativity Training

Many websites offer creativity training. One such site is www.before-after.com, which mentions many reasons for improving creativity, including "Bring greater creativity to our sales process," "Infuse our meeting with creative energy," and "I'm just looking for creative inspiration." We especially recommend going to the two-minute Creative IQ test. How do the results of this test compare to the creativity test you took in this chapter? If before-after.com is no longer in operation, insert "creativity training" in your search engine to find a comparable site.

Log on to the **Companion Website** at **www.pearsoncanada.ca/dubrin** to access additional resources for this chapter.

CASE STUDY 3-1 HUMAN RELATIONS

L.L. Bean Changes Its Mind

A few years ago, outdoor-clothing retailer L.L. Bean Inc. began building a call center near Waterville, Maine. Then, in November, mobile-phone carrier T-Mobile USA Inc. said it would build its own call center next door. Within a week, Bean chief executive Christopher McCormick halted construction—literally stopping bulldozers in their tracks. A few weeks later, Bean said it would abandon the Waterville site; it ultimately chose to open the new call center in Bangor, about 55 miles away.

McCormick wasn't concerned about appearing wishy-washy. He simply wanted to make the best decision for the closely held Freeport, Maine, retailer. A 23-year veteran who was named CEO in 2001, 50-year-old McCormick is the first chief executive from outside the founding family.

Bean, which does much of its business through catalog telephone sales, opened a call center in an old Waterville shopping center in 1997. But the storefront was cramped and offered limited parking, so Bean executives in early 2004 began scouting for another site. By summer, they had settled on the FirstPark business center in nearby Oakland. Bean purchased the land, drew up the plans for a 50,000-square-foot office that could accommodate up to 800 workers and began grading the site.

Then T-Mobile disclosed plans for a 77,000 square-foot center in FirstPark, housing 700 or more employees. McCormick says he worried immediately whether Waterville, a city of 16,000 had enough workers to supply both companies. He was especially concerned because much of Bean's workforce is seasonal, peaking near the Christmas holidays. He feared that experienced call-center workers would prefer relatively stable year-round employment with T-Mobile, leaving Bean out in the cold.

Within days, he called a meeting of his top lieutenants and told them he wanted to stop work at FirstPark. "You want to do what?" he recalls one asking. "There were certainly some shocked looks." It didn't help that the reappraisal came at Bean's busiest time of the year, when executives were already stretched thin to accommodate holiday sales. Moreover, McCormick wanted the new call center ready by the fall of 2005, then only about nine months away.

McCormick says he has never before reversed such a significant decision. Beyond the land cost, Bean had already sunk more than $500,000 into plans and preliminary construction. But he also wanted to send a signal to other executives. "I want my people to consider all the options. I want objective decision making," he says. "I don't want them to be a champion of one point of view."

Bean began searching for a new call-center site, employing the same real estate broker that had steered T-Mobile to FirstPark. By spring, Bean executives settled on a vacant office building in Bangor, where the city offered the company a break on the rent. When it came time to formally abandon the Waterville deal and commit to Bangor, McCormick says the Bean executive team agreed unanimously.

In disagreement with state officials, McCormick says he couldn't take the chance on moving forward with the Waterville call center. "It was too risky to build this huge building" without more confidence about the potential labor supply. McCormick briefly considered locating the call center outside Maine. He says Bean could have saved money, but he rejected the move because Bean's connection to the state is crucial to the company's branding.

Questions

1. To what extent did McCormick use the problem-solving and decision-making steps described in the chapter?
2. How will CEO McCormick know if he made a good decision?
3. What is your opinion of the ethics of McCormick backing off on the deal to construct a call center in Waterville?

Source: Adapted from Scott Thurm, "Seldom-Used Executive Power: Reconsidering," The Wall Street Journal, February 6, 2006, p. B3.

CASE STUDY 3-2 HUMAN RELATIONS

Hanging on to a Vulnerable Account

Henry Sanderson is an outsourcing manager at Mercury Products, an office equipment manufacturer. He manages 17 customer sites and 35 employees who work at the sites. Sanderson described a recent problem his group faced. Business was good in that the customers were pleased with the management of their office equipment but had concerns over their monthly costs, which ranged from $37,000 to $43,000. It seemed like a great deal of money to them.

About two years before the five-year account was going to be up for renewal, Alice Reuben, an on-site technician telephoned Sanderson and said there had been a couple of sales reps from one of their competitors in to visit with a customer. Furthermore, the customer had agreed to allow them to make a formal presentation the following week.

Sanderson realized that this account could be taken by a worthy outsourcing competitor, so he listed this major account as vulnerable in his customer database. The consequences of losing an account were tremendous because of lost revenues and layoffs of the on-site employees.

Sanderson decided to conduct a brainstorming session to deal with possible loss of the account. After this the brainstorming began, Betty Yang acted as the scribe to capture every thought on a flip chart. The big question the team sought answers to was, "What can we do better with the customer?" The ideas thrown out included the following: (A few of the ideas were accompanied by action plans.)

- We need to do better training of end users. A lot of the service calls were needed because the end users did not know how to perform certain functions on our copiers. Although all end users had been trained three years earlier when the equipment was installed, this growing business had added a lot of new employees who didn't know how to use the equipment. Fewer calls to service meant techs would spend less time at this site. This would have a positive effect on their overall performance and budget.
- Improve overall customer service.

- Seek an early renewal to the contract.
- Find a way to lock out the competition. One of the sales strategies for the new contract was to remove the labor component. This would bring the cost down by $3,800 per month.
- Take the misery out of billing.
- Create a roles and responsibilities document. The document will help organize our individual efforts so we can present a unified organization to the customer.
- Give more value to the customer. The sales team, led by Shawn Elliot will determine the appropriate new equipment for the account and determine the pricing with the standard net profit margin. The monthly charge to the customer will probably be higher because of the buyout and the fact that installing networked equipment costs more. However, it will be the task of sales and technical to present a value-added solution that also saves the customer money in terms of time-in-motion, while increasing their productivity.
- Respond more quickly to service problems. Stephanie Johnson reported that the group's average response time to service calls has been 2.4 hours. This is at the very high end of acceptability as the industry average is more than 7 hours.
- Find some quick ways to delight the customer. Mercury's invoice would be put on "auto-pay," meaning it did not need any corporate-level approval and the company could be paid immediately.
- Go for seven-year contracts instead of the traditional five-year contract.

Sanderson scheduled another day for solution presentations in one week. The sales group was asked to present their results. Based on a seven-year contract, we would accomplish all of our goals:

- The on-site labor component would remain at 100 percent.
- The cost to the customer would be reduced by $1,719 per month.
- The biggest possible savings for the customer would be $8,000 per month.

The customer would save approximately four cents for each print. The sales group concluded that the customer was printing about 200,000 prints to desktop printers per month, at a cost of about five cents per print; $10,000 for printing documents. The cost of printing with our products would only be one cent, or $2,000 per month, representing a new savings of $8,000 per month. Additional savings would come through the removal of the desktop printers and the supplies and service that accompanied them. A new contract was signed four days after this presentation.

Questions

1. In what way did the Mercury group make effective use of brainstorming?
2. In what way did the Mercury group deviate from traditional brainstorming?
3. What advice can you offer Sanderson when he conducts his next brainstorming session?

Source: Case researched by Henry Soric, Liverpool, New York, March 2006.

Chapter 4
Achieving Wellness and Managing Stress

Learning Outcomes

After studying the information and doing the exercises in this chapter, you should be able to

- define and understand the meanings of wellness and stress;
- explain the major strategies for achieving wellness;
- identify several positive and negative consequences of stress;
- pinpoint potential stressors in personal and work life;
- describe key methods for managing the potential adverse effects of stress.

To be successful in a competitive business world it is not enough simply to cope with job pressures and overcome health problems. You also have to feel and be at your best. Similarly, treating and curing physical and mental health problems is still important, but considerable emphasis is now being placed on preventing illness and staying well. Well people are not simply those who are not sick. Instead, they are vibrant, relatively happy, and able to cope with life's problems. Many companies have come to the realization that prevention rather than intervention is important to company productivity and company success. Therefore, there has been an increase in companies that offer company programs aimed at maintaining employees' wellness. **Wellness** is thus a formalized approach to preventive health care. By promoting health, company wellness programs help prevent employees from developing physical and mental problems often associated with excessive job pressures.

An excellent example of a wellness program is the state-of-the-art wellness centre at Husky Injection Molding Systems Ltd. in Bolton, Ontario. The facility houses a daycare centre for employees' children, a fully equipped weight and training room, and a library of health care books and videos. It is staffed and equipped with offices and treatment rooms for a physician, chiropractor, fitness-management specialist, massage therapist, naturopath (who is also an acupuncturist and dietician), and nurses. According to Dr. Angelo Pinto, the centre's physician, Husky has one of the lowest rates of absenteeism and industrial injuries. The team at the centre works closely together and thus provides a fuller range of care than traditional medical practice only.[1]

Companies that embrace family-friendly policies have a more holistic focus, believing that stress-free workers are more productive and productive employees are good for the company. For example, Pfizer Canada Pharmaceutical Group in Kirkland, Quebec, has on-site daycare and provides flexibility for employees trying to balance family and work life. B.C. Biomédical Laboratories in Surrey, British Columbia—rated as one of the best Canadian workplaces—encourages innovation and flexibility with such options as job-sharing.[2]

Technology has also helped with wellness initiatives at many organizations. Webinars and videoconferencing allow employees to stay at home rather then travelling to work or other cities for meetings and training. Group discussions can be held using such web meeting platforms as *Elluminate* or *Webex* saving time for employees and money for companies who can reduce travel expenses considerably.

One of the primary challenges in achieving wellness is to understand and manage stress. As the term is currently used, **stress** is an internal reaction to any force that threatens to disturb a person's equilibrium. The internal reaction usually takes the form of emotional discomfort. Notice that in general use the term *stress* typically refers to the stimulus or force that creates the problem.[3]

A **stressor** is the external or internal force that brings about the stress. The fact that something is dangerous, challenging, or disturbing in any way makes it a stressor. Your perception of an event or thought influences whether or not a given event is stressful. Your confidence in your ability to handle difficult situations also influences the amount of stress you experience. Most people find speaking in front of an audience to be a stressor, yet some experienced speakers can breeze through such an event with "no sweat." These people have learned how to handle the challenges involved in giving a talk.

Despite the importance of a person's size-up of an event, there are certain universal stressors. Almost everybody on a passenger plane experiences heavy stress when told to prepare for a crash landing. Can you think of a few other universal stressors?

In this chapter we describe the achievement of wellness and managing work stress. In the next chapter we continue with a stress-related topic: coping with personal problems.

STRATEGIES FOR ACHIEVING WELLNESS

The increasing costs of health care and recent cutbacks to medical care in many provinces are causing people to listen more carefully to ideas that many health care professionals and psychologists have advocated for years. An increasing number of people believe that we can live longer, healthier lives if we choose to do so.

An important principle of behavioural medicine is now widely accepted: that the body and mind must work together for a healthy lifestyle.[4] Consider also that lifestyle decisions contribute to seven of the ten principal causes of mortality. And about half of the deaths resulting from these causes could be prevented by changes in behaviour.[5] A person who smokes two packs of cigarettes per day, eats mostly fatty food and sweets, drinks a litre of wine per day, and leads a sedentary life has a below-average life expectancy. Note that all of these life-threatening activities are under the person's control.

In this section we describe achieving wellness through exercise, diet, competence, resilience, developing a health-prone personality, and minimizing health and safety risks. Another key component of achieving wellness—stress management—is described later.

Exercising Properly

The right amount and type of physical exercise contributes substantially to wellness. A recent poll from Statistics Canada about recent measures that individuals are taking to improve their health indicated that more than half of the men and women polled exercise more than three times weekly.[6] To achieve wellness it is important to select an exercise program that is physically challenging but that does not lead to overexertion and muscle injury. Competitive sports, if taken too seriously, can actually increase a person's stress level. In 1998–1999, 22 percent of Canadians in the household population over 11 years old engaged in some sort of vigorous activity that included such activities as walking for an hour, biking for 45 minutes, or jogging for 20 minutes.[7] The most beneficial exercises are those classified as aerobic, because they make you breathe faster and raise your heart rate.

The physical benefits of exercise include increased respiratory capacity; increased muscle tone; reduced risk of heart disease; improved circulation; reduced cholesterol level; increased energy; increased rate of metabolism; reduced body weight and improved fat metabolism; and slowed-down aging process. Of enormous importance, physical activity strengthens the heart and reduces harmful cholesterol (LDL) while increasing the level of beneficial cholesterol (HDL).

The mental benefits of exercise are also plentiful. A major benefit is the euphoria that often occurs when morphine-like brain chemicals called *endorphins* are released into the body. This experience is often referred to as "runner's high." Other mental benefits of exercise include increased self-confidence; improved body image and self-esteem; improved mental functioning, alertness, and efficiency; release of accumulated tensions; and relief from mild depression.[8]

Research suggests that people who find intrinsic motivation in exercise are the most likely to maintain a successful program. The idea is to shift the focus from long-term, external outcomes like losing weight to positive, internal experiences you can enjoy now. Exercise, like work, is the most fun when it leads to the flow experience. When exercise is fun for its own sake, you are more likely to persist and therefore derive the many benefits already mentioned.[9]

Sleeping Adequately

Getting enough sleep plays a major role in wellness, yet about 80 million people in North America suffer from sleep deprivation. Work-related problems such as increased stress, inattention, and lowered productivity are caused by workers getting too little sleep or poor-quality sleep. Also, sleep deprivation is a major contributor to vehicular accidents. The average person requires seven and a half hours of sleep per 24 hours, yet the average amount of sleep is six and a half hours. (Some people require more sleep, others less.)

Sleep deprivation appears to be cumulative, resulting in *sleep debt*. If you need eight hours of sleep per night and only get seven, by the end of the week your sleep debt is five hours. (Also, you may have noticed that some people sleep until noon on Saturday or Sunday!)

A survey conducted by the National Sleep Foundation found that 44 percent of the 1,014 adults surveyed said they slept more on the weekends—about 40 extra minutes. Yet it is better for wellness to have a fixed sleep pattern, going to bed at the same time each night and waking up at the same time each morning, weekends included. Here are some suggestions for staying alert and getting a wellness advantage from sleep:

- At home, set a regular bedtime and observe it carefully.
- Near bedtime, avoid exercise, caffeine, and heavy food.
- Don't consume any alcohol within two hours of bedtime.
- Generally eat healthy snacks and avoid eating too much or too little.
- At work, exercise during breaks. Exercise improves mood and promotes alertness.[10]

As implied by the preceding bit of wisdom, exercise, diet, appropriate sleep, and wellness are linked to each other.

Maintaining a Healthy Diet

Eating nutritious foods is valuable for mental as well as physical health. To illustrate, many nutritionists and physicians believe that eating fatty foods such as red meat contributes to colon cancer. Improper diet, such as consuming less than 1,300 calories per day, can weaken you physically. In turn, you become more susceptible to stress.

The subject of proper diet has been debated continuously. Advice abounds on what to eat and what not to eat. Some of this information is confusing and contradictory, partly because not enough is known about nutrition to identify an ideal diet for each individual. For example, many people can point to an 85-year-old relative who has been eating the wrong food (and perhaps consuming considerable alcohol) most of his or her life. The implication is that if this person has violated sensible habits of nutrition and has lived so long, how important can good diet be? But whether we can point to this 85-year-old relative or not, it is clear that people are eating better and paying more attention to their diet.

The food requirements for wellness differ depending on age, sex, body size, physical activity, and other conditions such as pregnancy and illness. Canada's Food Guide to Healthy Eating (which can be accessed at Health Canada's website http://www.hc-sc.gc.ca) is an excellent resource for improving and maintaining the healthy eating habits that help promote physical well-being.

The guide consists of five categories. The first category is grain products and includes breads, cereal, rice, and pasta. Five to twelve servings from this category are recommended daily. The second category is fruit and vegetables, which should comprise five to ten servings per day. Grain products and vegetables and fruit should make up a large part of an individual's diet. Milk products comprise the third category and two to four servings should come from this category daily. Meat and alternatives comprise the fourth category and two to three servings are recommended daily. The fifth category consists of foods that do not fall into any of the four categories. Examples of these foods include butter, margarine, oils, salad dressings, sugar, sweets, many snack foods, beverages like soft drinks, herbs, spices, and condiments. Foods from this category should be consumed in moderation.[11]

Alcohol should also be used only in moderation. Alcoholic beverages are high in calories and low in nutrients. Heavy drinkers, especially those who also smoke, frequently develop nutritional deficiencies. They also develop more serious diseases such as cirrhosis of the liver and certain types of cancer. However, one standard-size drink per day appears to cause no harm in normal healthy, non-pregnant adults. Some medical specialists believe that moderate doses of alcohol actually help prevent heart disease by preventing arteries from becoming clogged with fatty deposits. Of special interest here is some recent information concerning Canadian wines, which contain greater amounts of resveratrol, a substance that decreases the risk of heart attacks, than most wines produced elsewhere in the world. Wine is also a powerful antioxidant, "eliminating free radicals which cause aging and other degenerative problems." Consuming moderate amounts of wine also increases the "good cholesterol," HDL, which removes other damaging types of cholesterol from the blood.[12]

These dietary guidelines are intended only for populations with eating habits similar to those of people in Canada. Also, the guidelines are for people who are already healthy and do not require special diets because of diseases or conditions that interfere with normal nutritional requirements. No guidelines can guarantee health and well-being. Health depends on many things in addition to diet, including heredity, lifestyle, personality traits, mental health, attitudes, and the environment. However, good eating habits based on moderation and variety keep you healthy and can even improve your health.

An approach to estimating whether you are achieving the right balance of food intake and exercise is the *body mass index (BMI)*, an estimation of body fat based on a person's height and weight. The National Heart, Lung and Blood Institute developed this approach to estimating body fat. People who measure high on the scale are supposedly more at risk for such ailments as heart disease, high blood pressure, and some cancers. Results from the Canadian Health Measures Survey 2007–2009 indicate that Canadian adults have become much heavier over the past 25 to 30 years, a growing concern for health care professionals.[13]

Exhibit 4-1 provides a chart for determining your BMI, along with the actual method of calculation. According to the BMI categories endorsed by the World Health Organization, a normal BMI is 18.6 to 24.9; overweight is 25 to 29.9; and obesity is 30 or higher. Having a large frame or being muscular is likely to elevate your BMI. One reason is that muscle weighs more than fat. When interpreting your BMI, recognize also that many factors other than body fat influence your susceptibility to disease. Among them are blood pressure, cholesterol level, and family history.

Developing Competence

Emory L. Cowen, a major contributor to the wellness movement, says that **competence** is an important part of wellness. Competence refers to both job skills and social skills, including the ability to solve problems and control anger. The presence of these skills has been shown to be related to wellness, and their absence to poor adaptation to one's environment. Although acquiring such capabilities is a lifelong undertaking, Cowen recommends that childhood is the best time to lay the groundwork for competency.[14] If

Exhibit 4-1
Calculating Your Body Mass Index (BMI)

Body Mass Index: Does your weight put you at risk of health problems?

Height \ Weight	110	115	120	125	130	135	140	145	150	155	160	165	170	175	180	185	190	195	200	205	210	215	220	225	230	235	240	245	250
5′0″	21	22	23	24	25	26	27	28	29	30	31	32	33	34	35	36	37	38	39	40	41	42	43	44	45	46	47	48	49
5′1″	21	22	23	24	25	26	26	27	28	29	30	31	32	33	34	35	36	37	38	39	40	41	42	43	43	44	45	46	47
5′2″	20	21	22	23	24	25	26	27	27	28	29	30	31	32	33	34	35	36	37	37	38	39	40	41	42	43	44	45	46
5′3″	19	20	21	22	23	24	25	26	27	27	28	29	30	31	32	33	34	35	35	36	37	38	39	40	41	42	43	43	44
5′4″	19	20	21	21	22	23	24	25	26	27	27	28	29	30	31	32	33	33	34	35	36	37	38	39	39	40	41	42	43
5′5″	18	19	20	21	22	22	23	24	25	26	27	27	28	29	30	31	32	32	33	34	35	36	37	37	38	39	40	41	42
5′6″	18	19	19	20	21	22	23	23	24	25	26	27	27	28	29	30	31	31	32	33	34	35	36	36	37	38	39	40	40
5′7″	17	18	19	20	20	21	22	23	23	24	25	26	27	27	28	29	30	31	31	32	33	34	34	35	36	37	38	38	39
5′8″	17	17	18	19	20	21	21	22	23	24	24	25	26	27	27	28	29	30	30	31	32	33	33	34	35	36	36	37	38
5′9″	16	17	18	18	19	20	21	21	22	23	24	24	25	26	27	27	28	29	30	30	31	32	32	33	34	35	35	36	37
5′10″	16	17	17	18	19	19	20	21	22	22	23	24	24	25	26	27	27	28	29	29	30	31	32	32	33	34	34	35	36
5′11″	15	16	17	17	18	19	20	20	21	22	22	23	24	24	25	26	26	27	28	29	29	30	31	31	32	33	33	34	35
6′0″	15	16	16	17	18	18	19	20	20	21	22	22	23	24	24	25	26	26	27	28	28	29	30	31	31	32	33	33	34
6′1″	15	15	16	16	17	18	18	19	20	20	21	22	22	23	24	24	25	26	26	27	28	28	29	30	30	31	32	32	33
6′2″	14	15	15	16	17	17	18	19	19	20	21	21	22	22	23	24	24	25	26	26	27	28	28	29	30	30	31	31	32
6′3″	14	14	15	16	16	17	17	18	19	19	20	21	21	22	22	23	24	24	25	26	26	27	27	28	29	29	30	31	31
6′4″	13	14	15	15	16	16	17	18	18	19	19	20	21	21	22	23	23	24	24	25	26	26	27	27	28	29	29	30	30

The Actual Calculation: To calculate your BMI, follow these steps:

1. Divide your weight in pounds by your height in inches squared.
2. Multiply the result by 704.5.

For example, the BMI of a 5-foot 11-inch, 185-pound person would be calculated as follows:

$$5 \text{ ft } 11 \text{ in} = 71 \text{ in}$$
$$71^2 = 5{,}041$$
$$185 \text{ lb} \div 5{,}041 = 0.0367$$
$$0.0367 \times 704.5 = 25.85 \text{ (rounded to 26 for the chart)} = \text{low to moderate risk}$$

Note: People under 5 feet or over 6 feet 4 inches will have to extrapolate the data.

Source: National Institutes of Health, 1998.

you are a well-rounded person who has performed satisfactorily in school and on the job, and you have a variety of friends, you have probably achieved competency.

The importance of competence in developing wellness illustrates how different wellness strategies produce similar results. Developing competence improves self-confidence and self-esteem. Physical exercise also contributes to enhanced self-confidence and self-esteem.

Developing Resilience

The ability to overcome setbacks is an important characteristic of successful people. It therefore follows that resilience, the ability to withstand pressure and emerge stronger for it, is a strategy for achieving wellness.[15] Most people at times in their lives experience threats to their wellness. Among these threats are the death of a loved one, having a fire in one's home, a family breakup, or a job loss. Recovering from such major problems helps a person retain wellness and become even more well in the long term. Learning how to manage stress, as described later in this chapter, is an important part of developing resilience.

Resilience also deals with being challenged and not breaking down. The ability to bounce back from a setback, resilience is another aspect of emotional intelligence. In the context of emotional intelligence, resilience refers to being persistent and optimistic when faced with setbacks.[16] Learning how to manage stress, as described later, is an important part of developing resilience. Being resilient is also closely associated with self-confidence, as described in Chapter 12.

Human Relations Self-Assessment Quiz 4-1 gives you an opportunity to examine your level of resilience.

Human Relations Self-Assessment

QUIZ 4-1 Find Out How Resilient You Are

On a scale of 1 to 5, rate how much each of the following applies to you (1 = very little, 5 = very much):

1	2	3	4	5	You are curious. You ask questions, want to know how things work, experiment.
1	2	3	4	5	You constantly learn from your experience and the experience of others.
1	2	3	4	5	You need and expect to have things work well for yourself and others. You take good care of yourself.
1	2	3	4	5	You play with new developments, find the humour, laugh at yourself, chuckle.
1	2	3	4	5	You adapt quickly to change and are highly flexible.
1	2	3	4	5	You feel comfortable with paradoxical qualities.
1	2	3	4	5	You anticipate problems and avoid difficulties.
1	2	3	4	5	You develop better self-esteem and self-confidence every year. You develop a conscious self-concept of professionalism.
1	2	3	4	5	You listen well and read others, including difficult people, with empathy.
1	2	3	4	5	You think up creative solutions to challenges, invent ways to solve problems, and trust your intuition and hunches.
1	2	3	4	5	You manage the emotional side of recovery. You grieve, honour, and let go of the past.
1	2	3	4	5	You expect tough situations to work out well, and you keep on going. You help others and bring stability to times of uncertainty and turmoil.
1	2	3	4	5	You find the gift in accidents and bad experiences.
1	2	3	4	5	You convert misfortune into good fortune.

Add numbers to get your total: If you scored 60 to 70, you're highly resilient; 50 to 60, you're better than most; 40 to 50, adequate; 30 to 40, struggling; under 30, seek help! *Note:* To improve your resilience, practise more of the preceding traits.

Source: Adapted from Al Siebert, *The Survivor Personality* (Encitas, CA: Perigree/Berkeley Books 1999).

Minimize Obvious Risks to Health and Safety

Part of staying well is staying alive. Perhaps the most effective strategy for achieving wellness is to minimize exposure to activities that can readily contribute to disease, injury, and death. The list of these environmental threats is endless, including riding in helicopters, skydiving, bungee jumping, inhaling cleaning fluid or rubber cement, playing "highway chicken," walking in a high-crime area at night, or having unprotected sex with prostitutes and intravenous drug users. Add to the list drunken driving, not wearing seat belts, and motorcycle riding or bicycle riding without a helmet. All of the activities just mentioned have a common element: They are conscious behavioural acts that can in almost all cases be avoided.

To relate the concept of wellness and stress to yourself, take Human Relations Self-Assessment Quiz 4-2. Taking the inventory will give you many useful ideas for improving your well-being.

THE PHYSIOLOGY AND CONSEQUENCES OF STRESS

An important aspect of learning about stress is to understand its underlying physiology and its consequences to the person. The physiological changes taking place within the body are almost identical for both positive and negative stressors. Riding a roller coaster, falling in love, or being fired, for example, make you feel about the same inside. The experience of stress helps activate hormones that prepare the body to either fight or run when faced with a challenge. This battle against the stressor is referred to as the **fight-or-flight response**. (The "response" is really a conflict because one is forced to choose between struggling with the stressor or fleeing from the scene.) This response helps you deal with emergencies.

Recent studies suggest the possibility that women, along with females of other species, react differently to major stressors. Instead of the fight-or-flight response typical of males, they *tend and befriend*. When stress levels mount, women are more likely to protect and nurture their children (tend) and turn to social networks of supportive females (befriend). The researchers speculate that the tend-and-befriend behaviour became prevalent over the centuries because women who tended and befriended were more likely to have their offspring survive and pass on their mother's traits. The tend-and-befriend response can be traced to a hormone, oxytocin, produced in the brain. Although this research may not be politically correct, it has stimulated the interest of many scientists.[17]

Another useful explanation of how stress affects people is that, when faced with stress, the brain acts much like a thermostat. When outside conditions deviate from an ideal point, the thermostat sends a signal to the furnace to increase heat or air-conditioning. The brain senses stress as damage to well-being and therefore sends out a signal to the body to cope. The purpose of coping is to modify the discrepancy between ideal (low-stress) and actual (high-stress) conditions.[18] The brain is thus a self-regulating system that helps us cope with stressors.

The activation of hormones when the body has to cope with a stressor produces a short-term physiological reaction. Among the most familiar reactions are increases in heart rate, blood pressure, blood glucose, and blood clotting. To help you recognize these symptoms, try to recall the internal bodily sensations you felt the last time you were

Human Relations Self-Assessment

QUIZ 4-2 The Wellness Inventory

Answer Yes or No to each question.

1.	I rarely have trouble sleeping.	Yes	No
2.	My energy level is high when I get up in the morning and it stays high until bedtime.	Yes	No
3.	In the past year, I've been incapacitated by illness less than five days.	Yes	No
4.	I am generally optimistic about my chances of staying well.	Yes	No
5.	I do not smoke or drink alcoholic beverages habitually.	Yes	No
6.	I am pain-free except for minor ailments, which heal quickly.	Yes	No
7.	I am generally considered to be slim, not fat.	Yes	No
8.	I am careful about my diet. I restrict my intake of alcohol, sugar, salt, caffeine, and fats.	Yes	No
9.	I am moderate in food and drink, and I choose fresh, whole foods over processed ones.	Yes	No
10.	I strenuously exercise at least three times a week for at least 20 minutes.	Yes	No
11.	I do not need any medicine (prescribed or self-prescribed) every day or most days to function.	Yes	No
12.	My blood pressure is 120/80 or lower.	Yes	No
13.	I am concerned about the future, but no one fear runs through my mind constantly.	Yes	No
14.	My relationships with those around me are usually easy and pleasant.	Yes	No
15.	I have a clear idea of my personal goals and choices.	Yes	No
16.	Disappointments and failures might slow me down a bit, but I try to turn them to my advantage.	Yes	No
17.	Taking care of myself is a high priority for me.	Yes	No
18.	I spend at least 20 minutes a day by myself, for myself.	Yes	No
19.	I know how much sleep I require, and I get it.	Yes	No
20.	I accept the fact that daily life can be stressful, and I am confident I can handle most problems as they arise.	Yes	No
21.	I have at least one hobby or form of creative expression (e.g., music, art, or gardening) that is a passion for me.	Yes	No
22.	I can share my feelings with others and allow them to share their feelings with me.	Yes	No
23.	I enjoy and respect my connection to nature and the environment.	Yes	No
24.	I am aware of what my body feels like when I am relaxed and when I am experiencing stress.	Yes	No
25.	I find meaning in life and generally anticipate death with minor fear.	Yes	No

Score: ______________

Scoring: Give yourself four points for each Yes answer.

88–100: Excellent health/wellness awareness. You are probably well adapted to handle stress.

76–88: Good awareness, but there are areas where improvement is needed. Look at your no answers again.

Less than 76: You need to evaluate your health and lifestyle habits to improve the quality of your life and your ability to handle stressful situations.

Source: Anita Schambach, Wellness Coordinator of the Holistic Health & Wellness Center at Mercy Hospital Anderson, Cincinnati, Ohio. Reprinted with permission.

almost in an automobile accident or heard some wonderful news. Less familiar changes are a redirection of the blood flow toward the brain and large muscle groups and a release of stored fluids from places throughout the body into the bloodstream.

If stress is continuous and accompanied by these short-term physiological changes, annoying and life-threatening conditions can occur. A stressful life event usually leads to a high cholesterol level (of the unhealthy type) and high blood pressure. Men who respond most intensely to mental stress run a higher risk of blocked blood vessels. The result is a higher risk of heart attack and stroke. One explanation of this problem is that mental stress may over time injure blood vessels and foster the buildup of arterial plaque.[19] Other conditions associated with stress are cardiac disease, migraine headaches, ulcers, allergies, skin disorders, and cancer. To make matters worse, stress can hamper the immune system, thus increasing the severity of many diseases and disorders. For example, people whose stress level is high recover more slowly from colds and injuries, and are more susceptible to sexually transmitted diseases. Stress symptoms vary considerably from one person to another. A sampling of common stress symptoms is listed in Exhibit 4-2.

Figure 4-2 depicts the relationship between stress and performance. Current research adds credence to this well-established finding. In a learning situation, when the stress takes the form of challenging material, learning performance improves. In contrast, when the stress is associated with hindrances (such as not knowing what is expected of you), it lowers performance.[20] An exception to this relationship is that certain negative forms of stress are likely to lower performance even if the stress is moderate.[21] For example, the stress created by an intimidating boss or a fear about radiation poisoning—even in moderate amounts—will not improve performance.

Multitasking contributes to the relationship between stress and performance, based on a study conducted by information technology professors Gloria Mark and Victor Gonzalez at the University of California at Irvine. The participants were 36 information technology workers at an investment firm. For most workers, as the number of tasks juggled increased, stress rose and performance decreased. However, a little multitasking raised the challenge bar and often led to enhanced performance.[22]

Stress has enormous consequences to employers as well as individuals. By some estimates, work-related stress costs the national economy a staggering amount in sick pay, lost productivity, health care, and litigation costs.[23] We emphasize again that positive stress is not associated with negative consequences to the employer.

Where does burnout fit into the stress picture? One of the major problems of prolonged stress is that it may lead to **burnout**, a condition of emotional, mental, and physical exhaustion in response to long-term job stressors. The burned-out person often becomes cynical. Burnout is most likely to occur among those whose jobs call for frequent and intense interactions with others, such as a social worker, teacher, or customer service representative. Yet people in other occupations also suffer from burnout, especially when not much support from others is present and the rewards are few.[24] Also, a hostile work environment, such as being harassed by co-workers and managers, is a major contributor to burnout.[25] Students can also experience burnout because studying is hard work. Conscientiousness and perfectionism also contribute to burnout because people with these characteristics feel stressed when they do not accomplish everything they would like.

Exhibit 4-2
A Variety of Stress Symptoms

Mostly Physical

Shaking or trembling	Upper- and lower-back pain
Dizziness	Frequent headaches
Heart palpitations	Low energy and stamina
Difficulty breathing	Stomach problems
Chronic fatigue	Constant cravings for sweets
Unexplained chest pains	Increased alcohol or cigarette consumption
Frequent teeth grinding	Frequent need to eliminate
Frequent nausea and dizziness	

Mostly Emotional and Behavioural

Difficulty concentrating	Anxiety or depression
Nervousness	Forgetfulness
Crying	Restlessness
Anorexia	Frequent arguments with others
Declining interest in sex	Feeling high-strung much of the time

Despite all the problems previously mentioned, stress also plays a positive role in our lives. The right amount of stress prepares us for meeting difficult challenges and spurs us on to peak intellectual and physical performance. An optimum amount of stress exists for most people and most tasks. In general, performance tends to be best under moderate amounts of stress. If stress is too great, people become temporarily ineffective because they may freeze or choke. Under too little stress, people may become lethargic and inattentive. Stress can lower job performance because the stressed person makes errors in concentration and judgment.

Burnout can be treated in many ways, just as with the negative effects of stress. Showing gratitude for hard work by employees is particularly helpful in preventing and treating burnout, because many cases of burnout are caused by intense feelings of being unappreciated.

SOURCES OF STRESS IN PERSONAL LIFE

Almost any form of frustration, disappointment, setback, inconvenience, or crisis in your personal life can cause stress. The list is dynamic because new sources of stress emerge continuously. For example, legislation in Quebec forbids new drivers from having even one alcoholic beverage before driving. Drinkers there who recently obtained an operator's licence have something new to worry about. Our life stage also helps determine which events are stressors. Being snubbed by a friend at age 16 may be more stressful than being snubbed at age 40. Also,

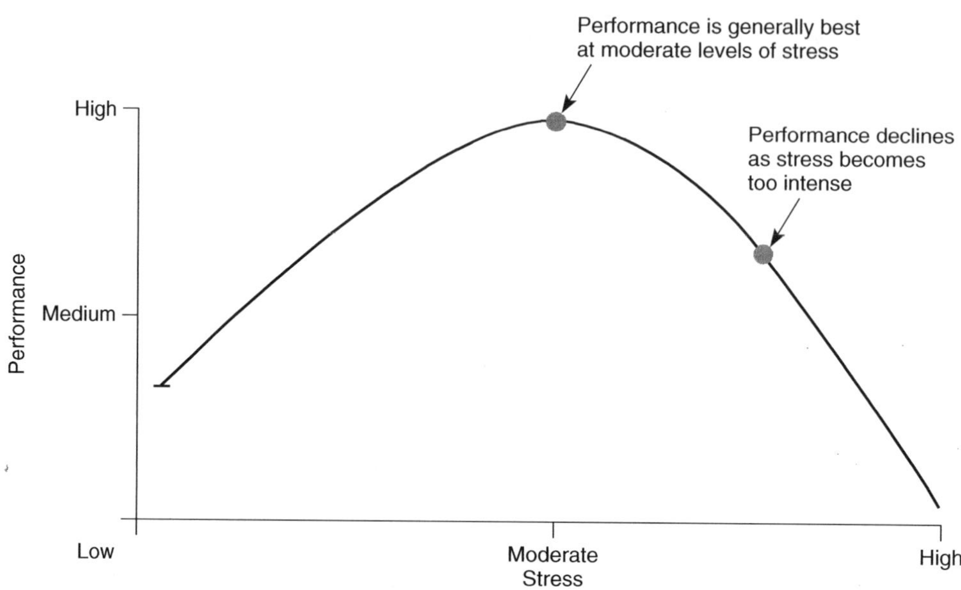

Figure 4-1 The Relationship between Stress and Job Performance

although we have separated work and personal life stressors into discrete categories, in reality they overlap. Seven different sources of stress encountered in personal life are described here.

Significant Life Change

A general stressor that encompasses both work and personal life is having to cope with significant change. According to many years of research conducted by Thomas Holmes and Richard Rahe, the necessity of a significant change in an individual's life pattern creates stress. The more significant the change you have to cope with in a short period of time, the greater the probability of experiencing a stress disorder.[26] As shown in Exhibit 4-3, the maximum negative change is the death of a spouse. Twenty-four other stressors created by change are listed in the table, in decreasing order of impact. Individual differences are important in understanding the stressful impact of life changes. The rank order shown in Exhibit 4-3 represents averages that do not hold true for everybody. For example, a person who could fall back into working for a family business might not find being fired from the job (number 8) to be so stressful.

Low Self-Esteem

A subtle cause of stress is having low self-esteem. People who do not feel good about themselves often find it difficult to feel good about anything. Low self-esteem has several links to stress. One is that being in a bad mood continually functions like a stressor. People with low self-esteem drag themselves down into a funk, which creates stress. Another link between low self-esteem and stress-proneness is that people with low self-esteem get hurt more by insults. Instead of questioning the source of the criticism, the

Canada Today

Canadians: Stress at Home and Work

No matter what you want to call it, many Canadians are feeling stressed, and they are feeling stressed in both life and at work. Data from the National Population Health Survey, conducted by Statistics Canada in 1994 and 1995, indicates some interesting trends. Personal stress was defined as "trying to take on too much at once; feeling pressure to be like other people; feeling that others expect too much; feeling that your work around home was not appreciated; and feeling that others are too critical of you."

The survey reported that 26 percent of Canadians rated themselves as experiencing high chronic stress. Women were more likely than men to report a high stress level in their lives, with the most stress being felt by women between the ages of 20 and 24. As people age, stress both in life and at work appears to decline. Also, people with higher levels of educational attainment were not as stressed as those with lower levels of education. People in Manitoba and Ontario reported higher levels of life stress than those from other provinces. Newfoundland reported the least amount of life stress. Single parents also reported more stress than individuals who are unattached or couples with children.[i]

A more recent survey conducted by Statistics Canada, in which respondents were asked to indicate their level of stress at work, revealed that 38.8% of Canadians between the ages of 15 and 75 are slightly stressed at work, 25% are relatively stressed at work, while 5.4% are extremely stressed at work (Statistics Canada, 2002, updated in September 2004). Stress is becoming increasingly recognized as a phenomenon that has a negative effect on a growing number of people in the workplace.[ii]

What are the sources of this work stress? According to the National Population Health Survey, work stress stems from a number of sources including physically demanding labour, low support from co-workers and managers, job strain, and job insecurity. About 40 percent of workers aged 15 to 64 reported that their jobs were physically demanding, 30 percent reported low support, and 20 percent experienced job strain. Job strain was caused by such factors as conflicting job demands and having little freedom in controlling the pace of work. Also, substantial numbers of those surveyed felt that their jobs were insecure (18 percent).[iii]

A more recent international survey of over 9,000 employees echoed many of the earlier findings, finding that Canadian workers feel the most stressed, with 41 percent of the respondents stating that they "often" or "almost always" experience stress at work. According to the researchers the main cause of work-related stress is long working hours. The more hours that you work, the more stress you are likely to experience. The second largest stressor found in this study was demanding job content or dangerous work conditions. Other job conditions that led to stress included poor communication between co-workers and management, lack of support, conflicting work roles, career concerns such as job insecurity, and unpleasant environmental conditions. People experiencing high levels of job stress were also more likely to be absent and more likely to quit or have intentions of leaving.[iv]

With so much reported stress in our home and work lives, stress management becomes critical to maintaining wellness. Visualizing pleasant experiences, exercise, eating right, getting proper rest, massages, and deep breathing all have beneficial effects. It seems that in such a fast-paced society, the answer may be in learning how to "gear down" for at least a few minutes each day!

Notes:

i. Statistics Canada, *Health Reports*, Volume 12 (3), April 2001, Catalogue No. 82-003-Xpe, Xie; The Federal, Provincial, and Territorial Advisory Committee on Population Health, *Statistical Report on the Health of Canadians*. Prepared for the Meeting of Ministers of Health, September 1999. Statistics Canada Catalogue No. 82-570-X1e.

ii. Statistics Canada. (2002, updated in September 2004). Canadian Community Health Survey—Mental health and well-being (Catalogue No. 82-617, Table 26). Statistics Canada.

iii. Statistics Canada, *Health Reports*.

iv. "Canadian Workers among Most Stressed," *Worklife* (14)2, pp. 8–10, 2002.

Exhibit 4-3
The Top 25 Stressors as Measured by Life-Change Units

1. Death of a spouse
2. Divorce
3. Marital separation
4. Jail term/imprisonment
5. Death of a family member
6. Personal injury or illness
7. Marriage +
8. Fired from the job
9. Marital reconciliation
10. Retirement
11. Change in health of family member
12. Pregnancy +
13. Sexual difficulties
14. Change in financial status
15. Number of arguments with spouse
16. Major mortgage
17. Foreclosure of a loan
18. Change in responsibilities at work
19. Son or daughter leaves home
20. Trouble with in-laws
21. Outstanding personal achievement
22. Spouse begins or stops work
23. Begin or end school +
24. Change in living conditions
25. Revision of personal habits

Sources: These stressors have changed over time. This version is from Thomas H. Holmes and Richard H. Rahe, "The Social Adjustment Rating Scale," *Journal of Psychosomatic Research*, 15, 1971, pp. 210–23, with an interview updating from Sue Macdonald, "Battling Stress," *The Cincinnati Enquirer*, October 23, 1995, p. C4.

person with self-doubt will accept the opinion as valid.[27] An insult accepted as valid acts as a stressor because it is a threat to our well-being.

Low self-esteem is linked to stress in yet another way. People with low self-esteem doubt their ability to work their way out of problems. As a result, minor challenges appear to be major problems. For example, a person with low self-esteem will often doubt he or she will be successful in conducting a job search. As a result, having to conduct a job search will represent a major stressor. A person with high self-esteem might feel better prepared mentally to accept the challenge. (As you will recall, your perception of an event influences whether it is stressful.)

Everyday Annoyances

Managing everyday annoyances can have a greater impact on your health than can major life catastrophes. "Sweating the small stuff" can hurt you more than dealing with the significant changes mentioned above, according to several studies.[28] Everyday annoyances that create stress for many people include concerns about weight, the health of a family member, crashing a computer file, overcrowded schedules, yardwork and home maintenance, taxes, crime, and physical appearance. Several of these hassles are discussed here as separate categories.

An important finding of these studies is that people who are able to cope well with daily hassles tend to have good health. They are resilient enough to tailor-make a coping strategy for each hassle they face, such as overcoming a billing error made by a credit-card company. Another method of coping with this general category of stress is to recognize that these annoyances happen to everybody. You are not being singled out for harassment; you are not a loser; it's just part of modern living.

Social and Family Problems

Friends and family are the main source of love and affection in your life. But they can also be the main source of stress. Most physical acts of violence are committed among friends and family members. One of the many reasons we encounter so much conflict with friends and family is that we are emotionally involved with them.

Physical and Mental Health Problems

Prolonged stress produces physical and mental health problems, and the reverse is also true. Physical and mental illness can act as stressors—the fact of being ill is stressful. Furthermore, thinking that you might soon contract a life-threatening disease is stressful. Many people who find they are HIV positive (yet do not have AIDS) experience overwhelming stress. If you receive a serious injury, that too can create stress. The stress from being hospitalized can be almost as severe to some patients as the stress from the illness or injury that brought them to the hospital.

Stress operates in a cycle: stress can bring about illness and injury; the illness and injury, in turn, serve as stressors themselves, thus exacerbating the discomfort. You must learn to break the cycle by using the appropriate method of stress management.

Financial Problems

A major life stressor is financial problems. Although you may not be obsessed with money, not having enough money to take care of what you consider the necessities of life can lead to anxiety and tension. If you do not have enough money to replace or repair a broken or faulty personal computer or automobile, the result can be stressful. In the current economic climate, many people have lost long-term jobs and may be overwhelmed with how to pay off debts. Even worse, imagine the stress of being hounded by bill collectors. Lack of funds can also lead to embarrassment and humiliation (both stressors).

School-Related Problems

The life of a student can be stressful. Recent research has indicated that many college students find campus life stressful and often perceive their experiences as being quite traumatic.[29] Among the stressors to cope with are exams in subjects you do not understand well, having to write papers on subjects unfamiliar to you, working your way through the complexities of registration, or having to deal with instructors who do not see things your way. Another source of severe stress for some students is having too many competing demands on their time. On most campuses you will find someone who works full-time, goes to school full-time, and has a family. This type of three-way pull often leads to marital problems. You do not have to be a middle-aged executive to develop ulcers!

PERSONALITY FACTORS AND STRESS-PRONENESS

Some people are more stress-prone than others because of personality factors. Three key personality factors predisposing people to stress are Type A behaviour, belief that one's life is controlled by external forces, and a negative disposition.

Type A Behaviour

People with **Type A behaviour** characteristics have basic personalities that lead them into stressful situations. Type A behaviour has two main components. One is a tendency to try to accomplish too many things in too little time. This leads the Type A individual to be impatient and demanding. The other component is free-floating hostility. Because of this combined sense of urgency and hostility, these people are irritated by trivial things. On the job, people with Type A behaviour are aggressive and hard-working. Off the job, they keep themselves preoccupied with all kinds of errands to run and things to do.

Certain features of the Type A behaviour pattern are related to coronary heart disease. Hostility, anger, cynicism, and suspiciousness lead to heart problems, whereas impatience, ambition, and being work-driven are not associated with coronary disease.[30] Many work-driven people who like what they are doing—including many business executives—are remarkably healthy and outlive less competitive people.

Belief in External Locus of Control

If you believe that your fate is controlled more by external than internal forces, you are probably more susceptible to stress. People with an **external locus of control** believe that external forces control their fate. Conversely, people with an **internal locus of control** believe that fate is pretty much under their control.

The link between locus of control and stress works in this manner: If people believe they can control adverse forces, they are less prone to the stressor of worrying about them. For example, if you believe that you can always find a job, you will worry less about unemployment. At the same time, the person who believes in an internal locus of control experiences a higher level of job satisfaction. Work is less stressful and more satisfying when you perceive it to be under your control.

The everyday problem of lost computer files illustrates the importance of an internal locus of control. When a hard drive crashes or a valuable file is lost in some other way, the externally oriented person blames the computer or the software for the stressful event. An internally oriented person, in contrast, would most likely have created backup files along the way. When a crash occurs, that person is less stressed because he or she has lost relatively little data.

What about your locus of control? Do you believe it to be internal? Or is it external?

Negative Affectivity

A major contributor to being stress-prone is **negative affectivity**, a tendency to experience aversive (intensely disliked) emotional states. In more detail, negative affectivity is a predisposition to experience emotional stress that includes feelings of nervousness, tension, and worry. Furthermore, a person with negative affectivity is likely to experience emotional states such as anger, scorn, revulsion, guilt, and self-dissatisfaction.[31] Such negative personalities seem to search for discrepancies between what they would like and what exists. Instead of attempting to solve problems, they look for them. Although negative affectivity is a relatively stable personality characteristic, new research suggests that the circumstances a person faces can trigger such behaviour.[32] For example, a four-hour wait in an airplane parked on the tarmac might trigger a person's mild tendencies toward negative affectivity.

People with negative affectivity are often distressed even when working under conditions that co-workers perceive as interesting and challenging. In one company, a contest was announced that encouraged customer-contact workers to compete against each other in terms of improving customer service. An employee with a history of negative affectivity said: "Here we go again. We're already hustling like crazy to please customers. Now we're being asked to dream up even more schemes to make sure the customer is right. It's about time the company thought of ways to please employees as well as customers."

SOURCES OF STRESS IN WORK LIFE

No job is without potential stressors for some people, and dozens of sources of stress on the job have been identified. Here we discuss six major job stressors you might encounter or might already have encountered, as listed in Figure 4-2.

High Job Demands—Low Job Control

Many workers experience stress when they are faced with a heavy workload combined with limited ability to control key features of the job.[33] Among these features would be how many phone calls to handle, when to perform certain tasks, and how fast to perform the work. Imagine being required to write more reports than you thought you

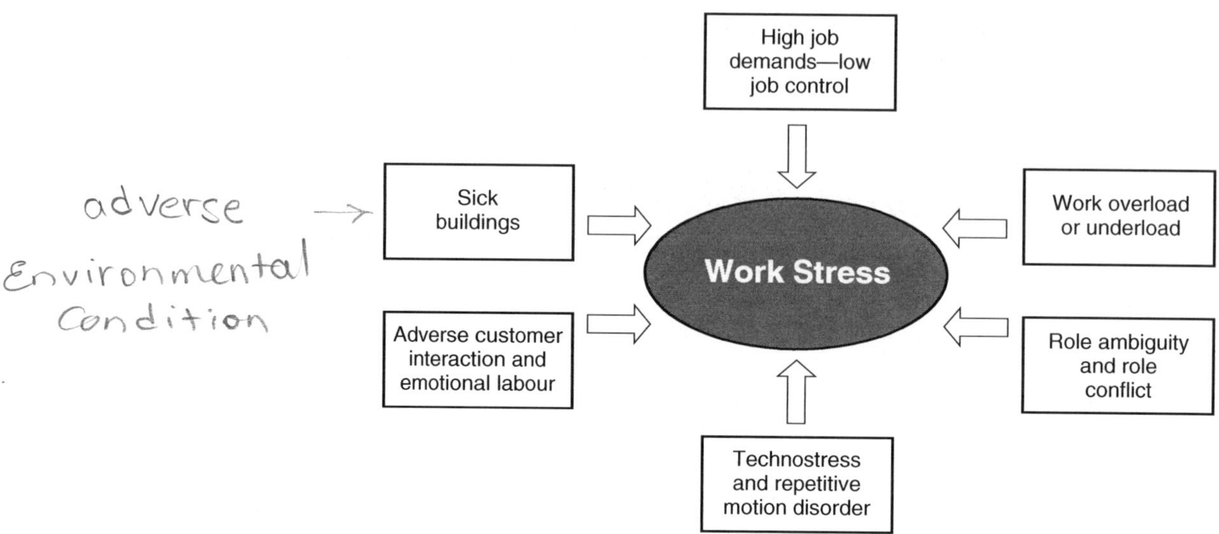

Figure 4-2 Six Major Job Stressors

could handle, yet being unable to concentrate on them for more than a few minutes at a time. The impediments to your concentration might include demands from customers, co-workers, and your boss.

Why a combination of high demand and low control creates stress can be explained as follows: High job demands produce a state of arousal that is typically reflected in such responses as increased heart rate and flow of adrenalin. When the worker has low control the arousal cannot be properly channelled into a coping response. As a result, the physiological stress reaction is even larger and persists for a longer time.[34]

Self-efficacy can influence the impact of high job demands with low control. A study of health professionals showed that having high self-efficacy (being confident of one's abilities) softens the stress consequences (as measured by blood pressure) of demanding jobs. However, people with high self-efficacy were disturbed by having low control because it conflicts with their feelings of wanting to be in control. Also, people with low self-efficacy were stressed by demanding jobs even when they had control. The responsibility of having control was stressful for those workers with low self-efficacy.[35]

The high job demands–low job control model is illustrated by a service station mechanic suffering from migraine headaches. Asked by a health professional if he was experiencing job stress, the mechanic replied: "My job is killing me. Half the time we're shorthanded. That means while I'm doing repair work I also have to work the cash register. Sometimes I have to pump gas for the people who don't use self-serve. Every time the bell rings I have to stop what I'm doing. I can't do decent repair work when I'm being jerked around like this."

Work Overload or Underload

As just described, having limited control over a heavy workload creates job stress. A heavy workload itself, however, can also be a stressor. **Role overload**, a burdensome workload, can create stress for a person in two ways. First, the person may become fatigued and thus be less able to tolerate annoyances and irritations. Think of how much easier it is to become provoked over a minor incident when you lack proper rest. Second, a person subject to unreasonable work demands may feel perpetually behind schedule, a situation that in itself creates an uncomfortable, stressful feeling.

Another form of work overload is demanding higher and higher speed from workers. Speed is important to companies because delivering goods and services very quickly brings a competitive edge. Making matters worse is that a sagging economy (or one that goes up and down) has forced employers to make increasing demands on employees.[36] One of the main causes of such demands is the effects of **downsizing**. A company first downsizes (reduces its workforce to operate more efficiently and save money). Next, the remaining workers are expected to carry a heavier workload, at a faster pace than previously. The combination of additional responsibility and high speed can be a major stressor. Among the problems are that the hurried employees have very little time to ask for help, or to carefully study what they are doing.

A disruptive amount of stress can also occur when people experience **role underload**, or too little to do. Some people find role underload frustrating, because it is a normal human desire to want to work toward self-fulfillment. Also, making a contribution on the job is one way of gaining self-respect. As with any facet of human behaviour, there are exceptions. Some people find it relaxing not to have much to do on the job. One direct benefit is that it preserves their energy for family and leisure activities.

Role Ambiguity and Role Conflict

Not being certain of what they should be doing is a stressor for many people. **Role ambiguity** is a condition in which the job holder receives confusing or poorly defined expectations. A typical complaint is "I'm not really sure I know what I'm supposed to be doing around here." You will recall, however, that creative people enjoy ambiguity because they can define problems for themselves when clear directions are lacking. Role ambiguity is related to job control. If you lack a clear picture of what you should be doing, it is difficult to get your job under control.

Role conflict refers to having to choose between two competing demands or expectations. Many workers receive conflicting demands from two or more managers. Imagine being told by your manager to give top priority to one project. You then receive a call from your manager's manager, who tells you to drop everything and work on another project. It's often up to you to resolve such a conflict. If you don't, you will experience stress.

Adverse Environmental Conditions

A variety of adverse organizational conditions are stressors, as identified by the National Institute of Occupational Safety and Health. Among these adverse organizational conditions are unpleasant or dangerous physical conditions, such as crowding, noise, air pollution, or ergonomic problems. Enough polluted air within an office building can create a sick building in which a diverse range of airborne particles, vapours, moulds, and gases pollute the indoor environment. The result can be headaches, nausea, and respiratory infections as well as the stress created by being physically ill.

Working at a computer monitor for prolonged periods of time can lead to adverse physical and psychological reactions. (These computer-related stressors could be considered part of techno stress.)[37] The symptoms include headaches and fatigue, along with eye problems. Common visual problems are dry eyes and blurred or double vision. An estimated one out of five visits to vision care professionals is for computer-related problems. Another vision-related problem is that people lean forward to scan the monitor, leading to physical problems such as back strain.

A repetitive motion disorder most frequently associated with keyboarding and the use of optical scanners is **carpal tunnel syndrome**. The syndrome occurs when repetitive flexing and extension of the wrist causes the tendons to swell, thus trapping and pinching the median nerve. Carpal tunnel syndrome creates stress because of the pain and misery. The thoughts of having to permanently leave a job requiring keyboarding is another potential stressor. Repetitive motion disorders can be prevented somewhat by computer workers taking frequent rest breaks and using a well-designed combination of the worktable, chair, and monitor. Wearing elasticized wrist bands provides enough support to the wrist tendons to prevent many cases of repetitive motion disorders. Being comfortable while working prevents much physical strain. Figure 4-3 presents the basics of a workstation designed on ergonomic principles. (Ergonomics has to do with making machines and equipment fit human capabilities and demands.)

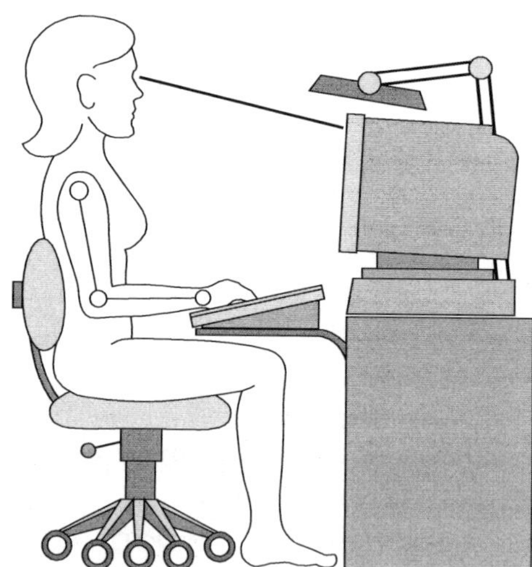

An Ergonomic Workstation

- Keep the screen below your eye level.
- Keep your elbows on the same level with home-key row, with your wrists and lower arms parallel to floor.
- Support your back and thighs with a well-constructed chair.
- Position your feet flat on the floor.
- Use lamp to supplement inadequate room lighting.

Figure 4-3 How to Minimize Cumulative Trauma Disorder

Adverse Customer Interaction and Emotional Labour

In one study, interviews conducted with 93 employees revealed that interactions with customers can be a major stressor. Stressful events frequently cited were customers losing control, using profanity, badgering employees, harassing employees, and lying. The employees interviewed said that these adverse interactions with customers negatively affected the quality of their work environment.[38] Part of the problem is that the sales associate often feels helpless when placed in conflict with a customer. The sales associate is told that "the customer is always right." Furthermore, the store manager usually sides with the customer in a dispute with the sales associate.

Related to adverse customer interaction is the stressor of having to control the expression of natural emotion in order to please, or avoid displeasing, a customer. Imagine having to smile at a customer who belittles you or makes unwanted sexual advances. Alicia A. Grandey defines **emotional labour** as the process of regulating both feelings and expressions to meet organizational goals.[39] The process involves both surface acting and deep acting. Surface acting means faking expressions such as smiling, whereas deep acting involves controlling feelings, for instance suppressing anger toward a customer whom you perceive to be annoying. Sales workers and customer service representatives carry the biggest emotional labour among all workers because so often they have to fake facial expressions and feelings to please customers.

Engaging in emotional labour for prolonged periods of time can lead to job dissatisfaction, stress, and burnout. A contributing cause is that faking expressions and emotion takes a physiological toll, such as the intestines churning. Workers who engage in emotional labour may also develop cardiovascular problems and weakened immune systems.

MANAGING STRESS

Because potentially harmful stressors surround us in work and personal life, virtually everybody needs a program of stress management in order to stay well. Stress management techniques are placed here into two categories: attacking the source of stress, including getting close to people, and relaxation techniques.

Dealing with Stress by Attacking Its Source

Stress can be dealt with in the short range by indirect techniques such as exercise and relaxation. However, to manage stress in the long range and stay well you must also learn to deal directly with stressors. Several of these techniques are described in the next few paragraphs.

Eliminate or Modify the Stressor The most potent method of managing stress is to eliminate the stressor that is giving you trouble. For example, if your job is your primary stressor, your stress level would be reduced if you found a more comfortable job. At other times, modifying the stressful situation can be equally helpful. Using the problem-solving method, you search for an alternative that will change the stressor. Here is a useful model to follow:

> A retailing executive repeatedly told her boss that she wanted to open a new branch of the business. He agreed with her, but took no action. Feeling rejected, frustrated, and stressed, she took another approach to the problem. She drew up the plans for opening

a new branch, presented them to her boss, and informed him she was ready to move ahead. To the executive's surprise, he said, "Great! I was only hesitating to ask you to do this because I thought you were overworked."

Everything worked out just as she wanted after she pursued the alternative of restating her plans in writing.[40]

Place the Stressful Situation in Perspective Stress comes about because of our perception of the situation. If you can alter your perception of a threatening situation, you are attacking the source. A potentially stressful situation can be put into perspective by asking, "What is the worst thing that could happen to me if I fail in this activity?"[41]

The answer to the above question is found by asking a series of questions, starting with the grimmest possibility. For instance, you are late with a report that is due this afternoon. Consider the following questions and answers:

- Will my reputation be damaged permanently? *(No.)*
- Will I get fired? *(No.)*
- Will I get reprimanded? *(Perhaps, but not for sure.)*
- Will my boss think less of me? *(Perhaps, but not for sure.)*

Only if the answer is yes to either of the first two questions is negative stress truly justified. The thought process just described allows stressful situations to be properly evaluated and kept in perspective. You therefore avoid the stress that comes from overreacting to a situation.

Gain Control of the Situation As implied in the discussion of low job control, feeling that a bothersome situation is out of control is almost a universal stressor. A key method of stress management is therefore to attack the stressor by gaining control of the situation. A multipurpose way of gaining control is to improve your work habits and time management, as described in Chapter 14. By being "on top of things," you can make heavy work and school demands less stressful. A trend related to reducing stress by gaining control is to simplify your life by getting rid of unessential activities. Andrew Weil, the natural health guru, recommends that you downsize your life. He believes that significant stress stems from the complexity of our lives, a major contributor being our material possessions. Many people have too many physical objects that require attention and maintenance. Weil recommends that you get rid of what you can spare.[42] You will gain control of your life situation by having less clutter.

A note of caution is that an oversimplified life can also be an impoverished life, creating stress of its own. Throw out or give to charity those physical possessions that contribute virtually nothing to your life. Yet save the sources of an enriched life. For example, why give up your digital camera, cell telephone, and I-Pod if all three are major sources of pleasure and satisfaction?

Reduce Stress through Social Support An ideal way of managing stress is one that provides side benefits. Getting close to people falls into this category. You will reduce some of your tension and form healthy relationships with other human beings in the process. Closeness suggests getting in touch with your feelings or tuning into others. By getting close to others you build a **support system**, a group of people you can rely on for encouragement and comfort. The trusting relationship you have with these people is critically important. People you can go to with your problems include family members, friends, co-workers, and other students. In addition, some people in turmoil reach out to strangers to discuss personal problems. An effective way of developing a social support network is to become a good listener so others will reciprocate when you need to talk through your problems. Recent research findings indicate that having good work relations with colleagues and/or management significantly reduces workplace stress.[43] Working with people you enjoy being with and can talk to regularly can lend you support right where the stress occurs!

The usual method of reducing stress is to talk over your problems while the other person listens. Switching roles can also help reduce stress. Listening to other people will make you feel better because you have helped them. Another advantage of listening to the feelings and problems of others is that it helps you get close to them.

Relaxation Techniques for Handling Stress

"You ought to relax" is the advice family physicians, relatives, and friends have always offered the stressed individual. Stress experts today give us similar advice but also offer specific techniques. Here we describe four do-it-yourself techniques that can help you to relax and consequently reduce stress and its accompanying tension. In addition, Exhibit 4-4 from the Canadian Mental Health Association lists a variety of tips to reduce stress and tension, many of which are relaxation-oriented. Recognize that several of these techniques are aimed at achieving wellness. Pick and choose from these brief suggestions and those presented in more detail for dealing with stressors.

Relaxation Response A standard technique for reducing stress is to achieve the relaxation response. The **relaxation response** is a bodily reaction in which you experience a slower respiration and heart rate, lowered blood pressure, and lowered metabolism. The response can be brought about in several ways, including meditation, exercise, or prayer. By practising the relaxation response you can counteract the fight-or-flight response associated with stress.

According to the cardiologist Herbert Benson, four things are necessary to practise the relaxation response: a quiet environment, an object to focus on, a passive attitude, and a comfortable position. You are supposed to practise the relaxation response for 10 to 20 minutes, twice a day. To evoke the relaxation response, Dr. Benson advises you to close your eyes. Relax. Concentrate on one word or prayer. If other thoughts come to mind, be passive, and return to the repetition.[44] Human Relations Skill-Building Exercise 4-1 gives you an opportunity to practise the relaxation response.

Similar to any other relaxation technique, the relaxation response is harmless and works for most people. However, some very impatient people find it annoying to disrupt their busy day to meditate. Unfortunately, these may be the people who most urgently need to learn to relax.

Deep Breathing The natural process of inhaling and exhaling slowly, filling your lungs with air and slowly letting it escape is a powerful stress reducer for many people. Deep breathing has immediate and long-term benefits. It lowers the heart rate and blood pressure and

Exhibit 4-4
18 Tips for Dealing with Stress and Tension

1. Recognize your symptoms of stress.
2. Look at your lifestyle and see what can be changed—in your work situation, your family situation, or your schedule.
3. Use relaxation techniques—yoga, meditation, deep breathing, or massage.
4. Exercise—Physical activity is one of the most effective stress remedies around!
5. Time management—Do essential tasks and prioritize the others. Consider those who may be affected by your decisions, such as family and friends. Use a check list so you will receive satisfaction as you check off each job as it is done.
6. Watch your diet—Alcohol, caffeine, sugar, fats, and tobacco all put a strain on your body's ability to cope with stress. A diet with a balance of fruits, vegetables, whole grains, and foods high in protein but low in fat will help create optimum health. Contact your local branch of the Heart and Stroke Foundation for further information about healthy eating.
7. Get enough rest and sleep.
8. Talk with others—Talk with friends, professional counsellors, support groups, or relatives about what is bothering you.
9. Help others—Volunteer work can be an effective and satisfying stress reducer.
10. Get away for a while—Read a book, watch a movie, play a game, listen to music, or go on vacation. Leave yourself some time that's just for you.
11. Work off your anger—Get physically active, dig in the garden, start a project, get your spring cleaning done.
12. Give in occasionally—Avoid quarrels whenever possible.
13. Tackle one thing at a time—Don't try to do too much at once.
14. Don't try to be perfect.
15. Ease up on criticism of others.
16. Don't be too competitive.
17. Make the first move to be friendly.
18. Have some fun! Laugh and be with people you enjoy!

Used with the permission of the Canadian Mental Health Association, Toronto Branch. Visit their website at www.toronto.cmha.ca (accessed April 30, 2003). Visit the National site at www.cmha.ca.

increases your skin temperature. Deep breathing also relaxes you emotionally and helps you gain perspective. The following steps explain how to use deep breathing for stress reduction.

1. Sit or lie down in a quiet spot. Place one hand on your waist, the other in the centre of your chest. Breathe several times. The hand on your belly should move more because it indicates you are breathing from your diaphragm.

Human Relations Skill Building

Exercise 4-1 The Relaxation Response

Think of one of the most stressful moments you have experienced in recent weeks. Visualize yourself as experiencing stress. If you are currently experiencing significant stress, visualization will not be necessary. Now carry out the relaxation response. Close your eyes. Relax. Concentrate on one simple word. Repeat the word several times.

Describe to yourself, in writing, how effective this technique has been in reducing your stress. Share experiences with the rest of the class. Discuss what you see as the strengths and limitations of this technique.

2. Now inhale slowly, filling up the lungs. As you exhale slowly, push air out from the bottom of your lungs.
3. Take long, slow breaths. If you become dizzy or lightheaded, you are breathing too fast.
4. As you inhale, elevate your shoulders and collarbone slightly to fill the lungs fully with air.
5. After you have mastered the breathing technique, with each outward breath blow out your worrisome thoughts and pains. Breathe in relaxation and calmness.[45]

Create Your Own Relaxation Triggers Marriage and family therapist Jeff Herring has developed a relaxation technique that allows you to relax anywhere, any time. It derives from a widely used visualization technique. Three simple steps are involved:

Step 1. Visualize yourself in a very relaxing place. Create as much detail as you can in the image, making it bright and colourful. Make sure you are seeing the scene through your own eyes, as if you were there. See it, hear it, and feel it.

Step 2. While you are picturing yourself in this place, create an immediate trigger that will instantly remind you of the relaxed feeling. It could be a snap of the fingers, a word or phrase, or a mental picture. It can be anything that quickly and strongly reminds you of your relaxing place.

Step 3. When you find yourself in a stressful situation, simply go for your relaxation trigger, fire it off, and feel the almost instant relaxation.[46]

Human Relations Skill-Building Exercise 4-2 will give you and your classmates an opportunity to learn more about what stress-management techniques others use.

Human Relations Skill Building

Exercise 4-2 The Stress-Buster Survey

Each class member thinks through carefully which techniques he or she uses to reduce work or personal stress. Class members then come to the front of the room individually to make a brief presentation of their most effective stress-reduction technique. After the presentations are completed, class members analyze and interpret what they heard. Among the issues to explore are:

1. Which are the most popular stress-reduction techniques?
2. How do the stress-reduction techniques used by the class compare with those recommended by experts?

SUMMARY

Wellness is a formalized approach to preventive health care. By promoting health, company wellness programs help prevent employees from developing physical and mental problems often associated with excessive job pressures.

Six strategies for achieving wellness were described in this chapter. First, the right amount and type of physical exercise contributes substantially to wellness. Second, getting adequate sleep also contributes substantially to wellness. Third, maintaining a healthy diet is valuable for mental and physical health. Canada's Food Guide to Healthy Eating contains many useful suggestions. Fourth, developing competence, including both job and social skills, helps us stay well. Fifth, being resilient is another wellness strategy. And sixth, minimizing obvious risks to health and safety improves the chance of achieving wellness.

The body's battle against a stressor is the fight-or-flight response. Stress always involves physiological changes such as an increase in heart rate, blood cholesterol, and blood pressure. The right amount of stress can be beneficial. Performance tends to be best under moderate amounts of stress, yet certain negative forms of stress almost always decrease performance. Prolonged stress may lead to burnout, a condition of emotional, mental, and physical exhaustion in response to long-term job stressors.

Almost any form of frustration, disappointment, setback, inconvenience, or crisis in your personal life can cause stress. The categories of situations that can produce stress include significant life changes; low self-esteem; everyday annoyances; social and family problems; physical and mental health problems; financial problems; and school-related problems.

Personality factors contribute to stress-proneness. People with Type A behaviour are impatient and demanding, and have free-floating hostility, all of which lead to stress. Another personality factor related to stress is locus of control. If you believe that your fate is controlled more by external than internal forces, you are more susceptible to stress. Another major contributor to stress-proneness is negative affectivity (a predisposition to negative mental states).

Sources of job stress are quite varied. Among them are high job demands and low job control; work overload or underload; role ambiguity and role conflict; adverse environmental conditions; and adverse customer interaction and emotional labour.

To successfully manage stress in the long range you have to deal with stressors directly. Four direct approaches are to eliminate the stressor; put the situation into proper perspective; gain control of the situation; and find humour in the situation.

Getting close to people in order to develop a support system is another useful strategy for managing stress. Discussing your problems with others can reduce your tension.

Three relaxation techniques for reducing stress are the relaxation response; deep breathing; and creating your own relaxation triggers.

QUESTIONS AND ACTIVITIES

1. How can a company wellness program improve profits and productivity?
2. If exercise contributes so much to wellness, why are so many athletes stressed out?
3. How does a person judge the strength or impact of a stressor he or she is facing?
4. Does a "well person" ever eat such foods as pizza, hamburgers, and hot dogs, and drink milkshakes and beer? Explain.

5. What responsibility should an employer have in helping employees minimize obvious risks to health and safety?
6. Identify several stressors created by cellular phones. What can be done to lessen these stressors?
7. How does carefully choosing a career help a person reduce stress?
8. Do students tend to suffer from the stress of high job demands and low job control with respect to their schooling? Explain your reasoning.
9. How can a person who becomes stressed from having to interact with co-workers several hours a day compete in the modern world?
10. Get in touch with a person you consider to be much more relaxed than most people. Ask your contact which (if any) of the relaxation or stress-busting techniques listed in this chapter he or she uses. Report your findings back to the class.

INTERNET SKILL BUILDER

Learn Something New about Your Health

Connect with Health Canada (www.hc-sc.gc.ca). From this link, investigate an area of interest that pertains to material in this chapter, such as exercise or proper diet. Find one interesting piece of research, health tip, or fitness idea that you did not know prior to this investigation and share it with a class member.

Log on to the **Companion Website** at **www.pearsoncanada.ca/dubrin** to access additional resources for this chapter.

CASE STUDY 4-1 HUMAN RELATIONS

The New Marketing Assistant

One year ago Wanda Diaz returned enthusiastically to the workforce after 12 years of being a full-time homemaker and a part-time direct sales representative for beauty products. Diaz's major motive for finding a full-time professional job was to work toward her career goal of being a marketing manager in a medium-size or large company. To help prepare for this career, Diaz completed a business administration degree over a five-year period.

Another compelling reason for returning to full-time employment was financial need. Diaz's husband owned and operated an appliance and electronics store that was becoming less profitable each year. Several large appliance stores had moved into the area, which resulted in fewer customers for Northside Appliances (the name of the family business). Diaz and her husband, Miguel, concluded that the family could not cover its bills unless Wanda earned the equivalent of a full-time income.

After three months of searching for full-time employment, Wanda responded to a newspaper ad for a marketing assistant position. The ad described the position as part of a management training program with an excellent future. Ten days after submitting her cover letter and résumé, Wanda was invited for an interview. The company proved to be a national provider of long-distance telephone service. The human resources interviewer and hiring manager both explained that Wanda's initial assignment would be as a telemarketer. Both people advised Wanda that large numbers of people were applying for these telemarketing positions.

Wanda would be required to telephone individual consumers and small-business owners and make a sales pitch for them to transfer their long-distance telephone service to her company. The company supplied an almost inexhaustible computerized list of names and telephone numbers across the country. In this way, Wanda could take advantage of time-zone differences to telephone people during their dinnertime, as well as other times. Wanda would receive a small commission for customers who made the switch to her company. Her major responsibilities in addition to telephone soliciting would be to enter the results of her conversations into a computer and to prepare summaries.

One week after the interviews, Wanda was offered a job. She accepted, despite some concern that the position was a little too far removed from the professional marketing position she sought. Wanda was assigned to a small cubicle in a large room with about 25 other telemarketers. She found the training program exciting, particularly with respect to techniques for overcoming customer resistance. Wanda reasoned that this experience combined with her direct selling of beauty products would give her excellent insights into how consumers think and behave. For the first two weeks, Wanda found the calls to be uplifting. She experienced a surge of excitement when a customer agreed to switch to her company. As was the custom in the office, she shouted "Yes" after concluding each customer conversion to her company.

As the weeks moved slowly on, Wanda became increasingly restless and concerned about the job. Her success ratio was falling below the company standard of a three percent success rate on the cold calls. A thought kept running through Wanda's mind: "Even if I'm doing well at this job, 97 percent of people I call practically hang up on me. And I can't stand keyboarding all these worthless reports explaining what happened as a result of my calls. It's a horrible waste of time."

Wanda soon found it difficult to sleep peacefully, often pacing the apartment after Miguel had fallen asleep. She also noticed that she was arguing much more with Miguel and their two children. Wanda's stomach churned so much that she found eating uncomfortable. She often poked at her food, but she drank coffee and diet soft drinks much more than previously. After six months of working at the long-distance carrier, her weight plunged from 135 pounds to 123 pounds. Wanda's left thumb and wrists were constantly sore. One night when Miguel asked her why she was rubbing the region below her thumb, Wanda said, "I keep pushing around the mouse so much during the day that my thumb feels like it's falling off."

During the next several months, Wanda spoke with her supervisor twice about her future in the company. Both times the supervisor explained that the best telemarketers become eligible for supervisory positions, providing they have proved themselves for at least three years. The supervisor also cautioned Wanda that her performance was adequate but not exceptional. Wanda thought to herself, "I'm banging my head against the wall, and I'm considered just average."

As Wanda approached a full year in her position, she and Miguel reviewed the family finances. He said, "Sales at the store are getting worse and worse. I predict that this year your salary will be higher than profits from the store. It's great that we can count on at least one stable salary in the family. The kids and I really appreciate it."

Wanda thought to herself: "Now is the worst time to tell Miguel how I really feel about my job. I'm falling apart inside, and the family needs my salary. What a mess."

Questions

1. What aspects of work stress are revealed in this case?
2. What suggestions can you make to the company for decreasing the stressors in the position of telemarketer?
3. What advice can you offer Wanda to help her achieve wellness?

CASE STUDY 4-2 HUMAN RELATIONS

Not Enough to Do

Kristina Henry began her career as a government contractor in the early 1990s. Her company provided services to the U.S. government, and much of the company's work was classified. Henry was ambitious and looked to her job as a source of learning new skills and professional growth. She had heard stories about the demanding nature of government contracting, with its emphasis on precise bids and every detail of the contract spelled out carefully. Her understanding was that even the specifications for a computer mouse used for a government project had to be presented in fine detail.

Soon Henry's job left her so stressed that she started grinding her teeth and was constantly looking for new work. "My stress came from having nothing to do," she explains. "It was like Dilbert," she said. "I learned a lot about FAA regulations and flight rules. And I learned a lot of acronyms. A lot of times it was just tedious, and I was thinking, I can't believe I'm here and being paid for this."

Her coworkers were facing the same problem. Occasionally, they too sneaked out to movies and museums. And Henry brought a copy of War and Peace to work. She finished it in two weeks.

Questions

1. What is the technical term for the stressor Kristina Henry was facing?
2. What should Henry have done about her problem?
3. What should company management have done about Henry's problem?
4. Explain whether you think Henry really had a dream job.

Source: The basic facts in this case are from Amy Joyce, "Even at Highest Levels, Boredom on the Job Takes Toll on Workers," *Washington Post* syndicated story, August 15, 2005.

Chapter 5
Dealing with Life Changes and Personal Problems

Learning Outcomes

After studying the information and doing the exercises in this chapter, you should be able to

- identify the stages of the life cycle;
- understand the challenges of responding to changes in adolescence, adulthood, and late adulthood;
- describe the impact of the life span on life and job satisfaction;
- be better prepared to cope with change;
- recognize how self-defeating behaviour contributes to personal problems;
- recognize the career impact of absenteeism and tardiness;
- understand the impact of depression and neurobiological disorders at work;
- develop a strategy for managing anger.

Gerry Salvo, age 43, worked happily for many years as the bumper assembly supervisor for an automotive parts manufacturer in Oshawa, Ontario. He supervised a department of 24 skilled and unskilled workers. Over 90 percent of the company's products were sold to the three major North American automotive manufacturers. Sales volume at the company started a decline a decade ago. The decline accelerated as the Big Three automotive customers bought more auto and truck components from lower-priced overseas suppliers and sales declined for all three automakers. Salvo watched as his company went through a series of layoffs, hoping that he would never be "tapped." In January 2009, the unpleasant reality finally hit. Salvo's department was folded because his company could no longer compete in the sale of auto and truck bumpers. Salvo was given four months severance pay. He and his wife Michelle, a part-time home health aide, figured that the family, including two primary-age schoolchildren could last about eight months before going bankrupt. So Gerry Salvo realized he had to find new employment quickly that would pay at least 75 percent of what he was making as a supervisor.

A four-month job search turned up no job inside or outside of manufacturing that paid much more than $8 per hour. Salvo thought that if he obtained a degree, or even a certificate, in manufacturing such as tool design or computer-aided manufacturing, he could rebuild his own career related to what he was doing. But for now, he had to act quickly.

Looking through self-employment opportunities in magazines and on the internet, Salvo hit on the idea of operating a window-blind franchise. His wife agreed that she could help with installations and customer contact. The Salvo's pulled together $11,000 through savings and credit-card loans to invest in a franchise. After ten days of company headquarters training, Salvo became a certified window blinds installer for homes and small businesses. Michelle's parents were their first customer, followed by an aunt of Jerry's. Salvo thought to himself, "I never thought that in my early 40s I would be selling and installing blinds for a living. But it's no time for self-pity. Michelle and I need to focus on four installations per week to break even."

Perhaps no reader of this book is in the same boat as Gerry Salvo, but his story illustrates an important point about the world of work and the reality of life changes. It is possible that at any stage of our life cycle we may be required to make major adaptations and changes. In this chapter we deal with a series of issues and topics that enable a person to develop career thrust and stay on track: life span changes and challenges and the major challenges people face at different stages of their life and how to cope with change. We will also examine some behaviours that impede coping with these changes including self-defeating behaviour, coping with the loss of a relationship, absenteeism and tardiness, depression and neurobiological disorders and finally managing anger, a major personal issue that impacts upon workplaces.

HOW DO WE RESPOND TO LIFE SPAN CHANGES AND CHALLENGES?

At different stages in life we face different challenges, beginning with the embryo struggling for enough oxygen, and ending with the 99-year-old fretting about physical well-being and passing on his or her estate. Here we overview the stages of the life cycle and challenges associated with adolescence and beyond.

Stages of the Life Cycle

Several approaches have been developed over the years to explain the various stages of human development, or the tasks people face at different periods in life. Among the best known is the eight stages of human development formulated by psychiatrist Erick H. Erikson

8 stages

STAGES AND AGES	THE PRIMARY CRISIS AND RELATED COMMENT
1. Infancy (0–1 year)	*Learning basic trust versus basic mistrust (hope)* A well-nurtured child develops trust and security.
2. Toddler (1–2 years)	*Learning autonomy versus shame (will)* The well-parented child emerges from this stage proud rather than feeling shamed.
3. Preschool (3–5 years)	*Learning initiative versus guilt (purpose)* Healthy children broaden their skills at this stage through active play.
4. Elementary school (6–12 years)	*Learning industry versus inferiority (competence)* Here the child learns the more formal life skills such as mastering reading and arithmetic, and some self-discipline.
5. Adolescence (13–19 years)	*Learning identity versus identity diffusion (fidelity)* The adolescent can now answer satisfactorily and happily the question, "Who am I?"
6. Young adulthood (20–40 years)	*Learning intimacy versus isolation (love)* The successful young adult experiences the type of intimacy that makes possible a good marriage or a genuine or enduring friendship.
7. Middle adulthood (40–65 years)	*Learning generativity (building a generation) versus self-absorption* In adulthood, the successful adult engages in a partnership and raises children.
8. Late adulthood (65 and over)	*Learning Integrity versus despair (wisdom)* The mature adult has integrity, is independent, and enjoys people and work. If the earlier psychosocial crises have not been resolved, he or she may have a self-view of disgust and despair.

Figure 5-1 Erikson's Eight Stages of Development and Associated Crisis

Source: Erick H. Erikson, Childhood and Society (New York: Norton, 1963); Child Development Institute, "Stages of Social-Emotional Development in Children and Teenagers," available at www.childdevelpmentinfo.com, retrieved May 10, 2006.

in the 1950s.[1] Figure 5-1 presents an outline of these stages and the associated primary crisis for each one. According to Erikson, the socialization process consists of the "eight stages of man," with each stage representing a psychosocial crisis. The crisis must be resolved at each stage before the next stage can be satisfactorily negotiated.

Satisfactory learning and resolution of each stage is necessary if the child is to manage the next and later stages successfully. The building of a skyscraper is an appropriate metaphor. Each floor, including the foundation and ground level, must be built correctly or the next floor will collapse. An example of this stage-by-stage development is that if the young adult cannot experience intimacy at stage 6, he or she will not be successful at the marriage or parenting that takes place at stage 7.

Erikson's stages of human development have prompted later investigation into how humans develop through different phases of their life. Despite these analyses of life stages, there are huge cultural and individual differences in the successful development of an adult. For example, what about Russians whose life expectancy is only about 50 years old? Do Russians never deal with Stage 8, integrity versus despair? And is it not possible to be a successful, well-adjusted adult even if you are not in a committed relationship and have no children?

Next, we summarize briefly challenges people face in adolescence, adult life, and late life.[2] The first stage, infancy and childhood is an important building block for later stages but lies outside the purview of our treatment of human relations.

Responding to Challenges in Adolescence

In its technical meaning **adolescence** is the period in life from approximately ages 13 to 20. From a biological standpoint, adolescence begins with puberty, the beginning of sexual maturation marked by rising levels of sex hormones and rapid growth. During adolescence many people start building work-related human skills, such as teamwork, and also engage in career choice and career preparation. Adolescents (or teenagers) vary considerably in their accomplishments with some teenagers being successful entrepreneurs, information technology consultants, professional athletes, and movie stars. Industries such as retailing and food service depend on the adolescent workforce, suggesting that even average teenagers occupy an important work role in society.

Cognitive Challenges Adolescents headed for a successful career must rise to the challenge of developing logic, abstract thought, and hypothetical reasoning. Many adolescents are studying five different subjects at once and feel compelled to think well enough to perform well in school and on college entrance exams. Adolescents must also deal with the development of moral reasoning in which they attempt to learn acceptable versus unacceptable codes of conduct. According to Lawrence Kohlberg, former moral education professor at Harvard University, adolescents begin to develop three levels of moral thought:[3]

- At the *preconventional level* moral dilemmas are resolved in a self-centred way. An act is moral if it enables someone to avoid punishment or obtain reward. Obeying safety rules or returning a lost wallet might fit this category of moral development.
- At the *conventional level* moral dilemmas are resolved in ways that reflect laws or norms set by parents and other influential adults. Making a complete stop at a stop sign on a country road when no one else is watching would fit the conventional level of moral development.
- At the *postconventional level* moral dilemmas are resolved by relating to abstract principles such as equality, justice, and the value of life. An adolescent at this level of moral development might start a food-and-clothing campaign for homeless people in the community.

One reason offered for the unethical behaviour of many adults in executive positions in business is that they did not advance to the postconventional level of moral development.

Personality and Social Challenges As an adolescent struggles to establish a reliable self-concept, or personal identity, he or she faces an **identity crisis**. In a multicultural world, the adolescent may need to establish an ethnic identity. Adolescents often struggle with whether to retain close ties with the family or invest more energy in developing peer relations. Adolescents struggle with sexuality, with some happily engaging in sex whereas others face unintended negative consequences such as parenthood, paternity suits, dropping out of school, and sexually transmitted diseases. Another conflict many adolescents face is one of body image, with discontent possibly leading to anorexia and excessive body piercing.

Responding to Adult Life Challenges

Adulthood is not marked by the same more predictable milestones as childhood and adolescence. Assuming that a person lives until about age 80, he or she spends more than half the life in the adult stage, so adults face an enormous number of challenges, including managing social life, work, and finances; raising children; keeping a blended family working together; staying current with technology; and investing for retirement.

Cognitive Challenges Adults face the unique challenge of applying the many cognitive skills they have acquired during study. For example, some people who performed well in math exams have no clue as to how to calculate kilometres per litre on a vehicle or balance a chequebook. To prosper in a career, the adult must often learn creative-thinking skills and apply wisdom. For example, in the chapter opener, facing a job loss and trying to find employment may require some creativity. An entrepreneur has to "sell" investors on his or her idea for the launch of a new product or service. An adult faces the challenge of learning to think more flexibly rather than finding the "correct" answer to a problem—the essence of creative thinking.

Personality and Social Challenges Adults must learn to become less self-centred and refine their interpersonal skills, including developing business etiquette. For some young people a major adjustment is to learn to take off their sports cap when eating at a restaurant or being interviewed for a job. Many adults in their 40s face a **midlife crisis**, when they feel unfulfilled and search for a major shift in career or lifestyle. Adults facing a midlife crisis often wonder whether their choice of career or life partner was the right decision. During the more common **midlife transition**, adults may take stock of their life and formulate new goals, such as an engineer working for IBM deciding to teach high school math. (IBM encourages such transitions to foster math and science knowledge and skills.) Among the dozens of other personality and social challenges facing adults are the loss of a youthful appearance and a decreased reproductive or sexual capacity. Such challenges have spurred the development of plastic surgery, youth-enhancing cosmetics, and lifestyle drugs such as those designed to enhance sexual performance.

Responding to Late Life Challenges

The challenges of late life have increased because more people live longer beyond the traditional retirement age, and many remain active and in good health. A major challenge for the older adult is to lose a job before retirement eligibility. Many people in late life are infirmed, impoverished, and dependent on family and government to maintain their well-being.

Cognitive Challenges Many people in late adulthood face cognitive decline, whereas many others do not. The ability to learn rapidly and reason abstractly and logically may decline through adulthood, starting at age 30. However, wisdom and judgment based on the accumulation of knowledge may increase up into the 80s. The issue of the cognitive skills of late life adults has been the subject of much opinion and research in recent years because the life span of people has increased, and so many old people hold responsible positions, drive cars, and even fly airplanes solo.

Common wisdom suggests that staying in shape mentally by such activities as doing crossword puzzles, surfing the internet, or studying a foreign language can slow the decline of an aging brain. A long-term study called Active trained 2,832 adults 65 to 94 years old in memory, reasoning, or visual attention and perception. Although the trainees performed better on the skill they practised, that training did not translate to improvement in the other skills. Many mentally active, late life adults show smaller cognitive decline than their less mentally active counterparts. Yet, the mentally active people most likely had a stronger cognitive reserve (mental capacity) that led them to stay mentally active.[4] Though this study did not support the use-it-or-lose-it hypothesis, it demonstrates that older adults can still master specific cognitive tasks with practice. So your grandmother who studies Mandarin Chinese may not then be able to decipher a manual for a digital camera easily, but at least she now knows Mandarin.

An optimistic note about cognitive decline is that the intake of about one alcoholic beverage a day appears to slow the decline, perhaps because moderate use of alcohol helps preserve the blood vessels in the brain. The research—not sponsored by a wine or beer distributor—was conducted by researchers from Harvard University, and Brigham and Women's Hospital in Boston. The study compared the cognitive functions in more than 11,000 nurses, ages 70 to 81, divided into alcoholic intakes of one, two, or no drinks per day.[5]

Personality and Social Challenges A change noted in late adulthood is that people begin to value the present more because they correctly perceive that they have a shorter future than do younger adults. As a result, late life adults are less concerned about activities that may have a payoff in the long run, such as networking. Instead, they look to spend times with good friends and family already available. Practical problems for those in the most advanced years are that many friends die and family members move away. Thus, the late life adult may have to seek out new friends. Retirement communities, including assisted living, provide an opportunity for affluent older people to make new social contacts, to help compensate for the loss of friends and family members.

A challenge for some late life adults is to engage in fulfilling physical activities to replace favoured activities of previous years. For example, a 75-year-old with a hip and knee replacement may not be able to play tennis or golf any longer and may have to find satisfaction in a replacement activity such as light hiking.

Life and Job Satisfaction throughout the Life Span

People at various stages of their life span often wonder what type of satisfaction and happiness awaits them at later stages. Typical self-questions are these: "Will I enjoy my work more in late career?" "Will I be more (or less) happy in my later years?" Although the research evidence about life and job satisfaction throughout the life span is not entirely consistent, some trends are notable.

Life Satisfaction and Age Life satisfaction tends to increase throughout adulthood, partially because many of the major challenges in life are met as one reaches one's 50s and 60s. For example, by middle age most people have completed their formal education, chosen a career, and reared children. According to a study by Daniel Mroczek, a psychology professor at Fordham University, life satisfaction for men tends to peak at age 65. His study synthesized more than 20 years of data from almost 2,000 men in the Veterans Affairs Normative Aging Study. The life satisfaction and personal traits of the subjects were measured over almost a 30-year span.

After life satisfaction peaking around 65, the men around age 95 were about as happy as they were in their mid-40s. Nevertheless, there was considerable variation among individuals with some people peaking in satisfaction early, and then experiencing a permanent decline in happiness. In contrast, some of the men in the study continued to gain in happiness. Personality factors influenced the happiness and satisfaction curve. Highly extroverted people were more likely to have high levels of life satisfaction and more stability in life satisfaction. (One interpretation of these findings is that extroversion helps a person develop friends, and positive human contact contributes to life satisfaction.) Another finding was that life satisfaction dropped considerably during the last year of life—often because a person has poor physical health during his or her final year.[6]

Women also tend to gain in life satisfaction as they become older. Psychology students Brian Scott Ehrlich and Derek Isaacowitz guided by their professors at the University of Pennsylvania, conducted a study of subjective well-being, including life satisfaction, among young, middle-aged, and older people. The sample consisted of 190 women and 90 men, ranging in age from 18 to 93 years old. Young adults and middle-aged adults showed relatively the same degree of life satisfaction, and older adults tended to be the most satisfied with life. The findings about older people having higher life satisfaction were of modest magnitude, but they did support similar evidence from other studies.[7]

Not all researchers have found that life satisfaction increases with age. Yet, the bulk of evidence is at least that the ratings of life satisfaction do not decline with age. Apparently, as long as people have a reasonable amount of love and satisfying work, they tend to stay happy.[8]

Job Satisfaction and Age Job satisfaction also tends to increase with age, as would be predicted because work satisfaction is such a major component of life satisfaction. A study conducted by the Conference Board in 2005 found that Americans were growing increasingly unhappy with their job in comparison to previous years. However, the smallest decline in job satisfaction took place among workers 65 and older. Overall job satisfaction slipped from 60.8 to 58.0 percent, making people in this age group the most satisfied with their jobs.[9] (It is possible that still being part of the workforce during an era of so many downsizings would add to an older person's appreciation and job satisfaction.)

A general explanation for the many studies indicating the increase in job satisfaction during a person's career is that with more work experience older workers understand better which needs work can and cannot satisfy. In addition, they have a more realistic view

Who moved my cheese? Spencer Johnson

of life and work.[10] Experience also contributes to income, and a higher income in turn contributes to job satisfaction for many workers.

Changes in life, as we age, can be a challenge but become more difficult to deal with if other behaviours are present that negatively affect us. Self-defeating behaviours, lateness and tardiness, and anger are three behaviours we examine next. Behaviours such as alcohol or drug abuse can be considered a classification of self-defeating behaviour.

WHAT ARE SOME TACTICS FOR COPING WITH CHANGE?

We have all heard that adapting to changes including life span and career changes is necessary for career success, and even survival. Here we present a few tactics for coping with change. To begin, look for the personal value that could be embedded in a forced change.[11] If you are downsized, take the opportunity to assume responsibility for your own career rather than being dependent on the organization. Many downsizing victims find a new career for themselves that better fits their interests or try self-employment in search of more job security.

When faced with a significant change, ask "What if?" questions such as "What if my company is sold tomorrow?" "What if I went back to school for more education?" and "What if I did accept that one-year assignment in China?" When confronting major change, force yourself to enjoy at least some small aspect of the change. Suppose the edict comes through the organization that purchases can now only be made over the internet. This means you will no longer be able to interact with a few of the sales reps you considered to be buddies. With the time you save, however, you will have spare hours each week for leisure activities.

You are less likely to resist change if you recognize that change is inevitable. Dealing with change is an integral part of life, so why fight it? Keep in mind also to change before you have to, which can lead to a better deal. If your manager announces a new plan, get on board as a volunteer before you are forced to accept a lesser role. If your company has made the decision to start a Six Sigma (companywide quality improvement) program, study the subject early and ask for a role as a facilitator or team leader. Stop trying to be in control all the time because you cannot control everything. Many changes will occur that you cannot control, so relax and enjoy the ride. Finally, recognize that change has an emotional impact, which will most likely cause some inner turmoil and discomfort. Even if the change is for the better, you might remain emotionally attached to your old system—or neighbourhood, car, or PC.

Continuing to acquire useful knowledge is also helpful in dealing with change because you have the new knowledge at hand to get past the change.[12] When digital photography became dominant, the operators of many portrait studios felt threatened and were too slow to offer digital services to their customers. Many of these photographers who waited too long to offer digital services were forced out of business. In contrast, many other portrait photographers were early learners of digital technology and survived the transition well.

The bestseller, *The World Is Flat: A Brief History of the Twenty-First Century* (2005) by Thomas L. Friedman, has made thousands of educators and individuals aware of the potential changes imposed on us by globalization and outsourcing. One key point of the book is that the global economic playing field has been levelled by information technology that enables people to collaborate regardless of their location. Another key point is that the success of individual workers will depend on the development of specialized skills. Furthermore, to cope with these changes workers must constantly upgrade their skills. At the same time they should search for jobs that cannot be outsourced or that are anchored because they must be done at a specific location, such as calling on an industrial customer.[13]

Many personal service jobs cannot be outsourced or sent offshore, including hairdressers, massage therapists, custodial technicians, and auto mechanics. Yet even here, some personal service workers in North America complain that residents from lower-wage countries are willing to perform these services at lower wages than the North American workers are. Some corporate professional jobs are more difficult to outsource than others. The positions less likely to be outsourced are those requiring the combination of technical (or discipline) skills plus connections with people.[14] A real estate agent with hundreds of personal contacts cannot be replaced by a website. An information systems specialist who performs hands-on work with internal clients cannot be replaced by an information technology specialist working 8,000 miles away in another country. The change-management lesson here is building relationships with work associates helps ward off some of the threats of the "flat world."

SELF-DEFEATING BEHAVIOUR

Many problems on the job and in personal life arise because of factors beyond our control. A boss may be intimidating and insensitive, an employer might lay you off, or a significant other might abruptly terminate your relationship. Nevertheless, many personal problems arise because of **self-defeating behaviour**. A person with self-defeating tendencies intentionally or unintentionally engages in activities or harbours attitudes that work against his or her best interests. A person who habitually is late for important meetings is engaging in self-defeating behaviour. Using drugs or drinking excessively to forget troubles or dropping out of school for no reason other than being bored with studying are other examples. In short, self-defeating behaviour means the same as being your own worst enemy.

Let's examine several leading causes of self-defeating behaviour, and how to reverse the pattern.

Why People Engage in Self-Defeating Behaviour

Many different forces lead people to work against their own best interests, often sabotaging their careers. The major cause of self-defeating behaviour is a *loser life script*.[15] Early in life, our parents and other influential forces program our brains to act out certain life plans. These plans are known as *scripts*. People fortunate enough to have winner scripts consistently emerge victorious. When a tough assignment needs doing, they get the job done. For example, they figure out how to fix a jammed computer program that baffles everybody else in the office.

In contrast, others have scripts that program them toward damaging their careers and falling short of their potential. Much of this damage paradoxically occurs just when things seem to be going well. For example, a person might steal equipment from a company shortly after receiving an outstanding performance appraisal.

The simplest explanation for self-defeating behaviour is that some people suffer from a personality that fosters defeat. People with a *self-defeating personality pattern* have three notable characteristics. First, they repeatedly fail at tasks they have the ability to perform. Second, they place themselves in very difficult situations and respond helplessly. Third, they typically refuse to take advantage of escape routes, such as accepting advice and counsel from a manager.[16]

Self-defeating beliefs put many people on the road to career self-sabotage. In this context, a self-defeating belief is an erroneous belief that creates the conditions for failure. For example, some people sabotage their job campaigns before even starting. They think to themselves: "I lack the right experience," "I'm not sharp enough," "I'm too old," "I'm too young," and so forth.

To examine your present tendencies toward self-defeating behaviour, take the self-sabotage quiz presented in Human Relations Self-Assessment Quiz 5-1. Taking the quiz will help alert you to many self-imposed behaviours and attitudes that could potentially harm your career and personal life.

Human Relations Self-Assessment

QUIZ 5-1 The Self-Sabotage Questionnaire

Indicate how accurately each of the statements below describes or characterizes you, using a five-point scale: (0) very inaccurately, (1) inaccurately, (2) midway between inaccurately and accurately, (3) accurately, and (4) very accurately. Consider discussing some of the questions with a family member, close friend, or work associate. Another person's feedback may prove helpful in providing accurate answers to some of the questions.

		Answer
1.	Other people have said that I am my own worst enemy.	Yes
2.	If I don't do a perfect job, I feel worthless.	NO
3.	I am my own harshest critic.	____
4.	When engaged in a sport or other competitive activity, I find a way to blow a substantial lead right near the end.	____
5.	When I make a mistake, I can usually identify another person to blame.	No
6.	I have a sincere tendency to procrastinate.	____
7.	I have trouble focusing on what is really important to me.	Yes
8.	I have trouble taking criticism, even from friends.	____
9.	My fear of seeming stupid often prevents me from asking questions or offering my opinion.	____
10.	I tend to expect the worst in most situations.	____

(continued)

11.	Many times I have rejected people who treat me well.	____
12.	When I have an important project to complete, I usually get sidetracked and then miss the deadline.	____
13.	I choose work assignments that lead to disappointments even when better options are clearly available.	____
14.	I frequently misplace things, such as my keys, then get very angry at myself.	____
15.	I am concerned that if I take on more responsibility people will expect too much from me.	____
16.	I avoid situations, such as competitive sports, where people can find out how good or bad I really am.	____
17.	People describe me as the "office clown."	____
18.	I have an insatiable demand for money and power.	____
19.	When negotiating with others, I hate to grant any concessions.	____
20.	I seek revenge for even the smallest hurts.	____
21.	I have an overwhelming ego.	____
22.	When I receive a compliment or other form of recognition, I usually feel I don't deserve it.	____
23.	To be honest, I choose to suffer.	____
24.	I regularly enter into conflict with people who try to help me.	____
25.	I'm a loser.	____
	Total score	____

Scoring and Interpretation: Add your answers to all the questions to obtain your total score. Your total score provides an approximate index of your tendencies toward being self-sabotaging or self-defeating. The higher your score, the more probable it is that you create conditions to bring about your own setbacks, disappointments, and failures. The lower your score, the less likely it is that you are a self-saboteur.

0–25: You appear to have very few tendencies toward self-sabotage. If this interpretation is supported by your own positive feelings toward your life and yourself, you are in good shape with respect to self-defeating behaviour tendencies. However, stay alert to potential self-sabotaging tendencies that could develop at later stages in your life.

26–50: You may have some mild tendencies toward self-sabotage. It could be that you do things occasionally that defeat your own purposes. Review actions you have taken during the past six months to decide if any of them have been self-sabotaging.

51–75: You show signs of engaging in self-sabotage. You probably have thoughts, and carry out actions, that could be blocking you from achieving important work and personal goals. People with scores in this category characteristically engage in negative self-talk that lowers their self-confidence and makes them appear weak and indecisive to others. People in this range frequently experience another problem. They sometimes sabotage their chances of succeeding on a project just to prove that their negative self-assessment is correct. If you scored in this range, carefully study the suggestions offered in this chapter.

76–100: You most likely have a strong tendency toward self-sabotage. (Sometimes it is possible to obtain a high score on a test like this because you are going through an unusually stressful period in your life.) Study this chapter carefully and look for useful hints for removing self-imposed barriers to your success. Equally important, you might discuss your tendencies toward undermining your own achievements with a mental health professional.

Strategies and Techniques for Overcoming and Preventing Self-Defeating Behaviour

Overcoming self-defeating behaviour requires hard work and patience. Here we present six widely applicable strategies for overcoming and preventing self-defeating behaviour. Pick and choose among them to fit your particular circumstance and personal style.

Examine Your Script and Make the Necessary Changes Much importance has been attached to the influence of early-life programming in determining whether a person is predisposed to self-defeat. Note carefully the word *predisposed*. A person may be predisposed to snatch defeat from the jaws of victory, but that does not mean the predisposition makes defeat inevitable. It does mean that the person will have to work harder to overcome a tendency toward self-sabotage. A good starting point is to look for patterns in your setbacks:

- Do you blow up at people who have the authority to make the administrative decisions about your future?
- Do you get so tense during your command performances (stumbling over your words in an important presentation, for instance) that you are unable to function effectively?
- Do you give up in the late stages of projects, saying, "I just can't get this done"?

Stop Blaming Others for Your Problems Blaming others for your problems contributes to self-defeating behaviour and career self-sabotage.[17] Projecting blame onto others is self-defeating because doing so relieves you of most of the responsibility for your setback and failure. Consider this example: If someone blames favouritism for not receiving a promotion, he or she will not have to worry about becoming a stronger candidate for future promotions. Not to improve one's suitability for promotion is self-sabotaging. If you accept most of the blame for not being promoted, you are more likely to make the changes necessary to qualify in the future.

An underlying theme to the suggestions for preventing and overcoming self-defeating behaviour is that we all need to engage in thoughts and actions that increase our personal control. This is precisely the reason that blaming others for our problems is self-sabotaging. By turning over control of your fate to forces outside yourself, you are holding them responsible for your problems.

Solicit Feedback on Your Actions Feedback is essential for monitoring whether you are sabotaging your career or personal life. A starting point is to listen carefully to any direct or indirect comments from your superiors, subordinates, co-workers, customers, and friends about how you are coming across to them. Consider the case of Bill, a technical writer:

> Bill heard three people in one week make comments about his appearance. It started innocently with "Here, let me fix your collar." Next, an office assistant said, "Bill, are you coming down with something?" The third comment was, "You look pretty tired today. Have you been working extra hard?" Bill processed this feedback carefully. He used it as a signal that his steady late-night drinking episodes were adversely affecting his image. He then cut back his drinking enough to revert to his normal healthy appearance.

An assertive and thick-skinned person might try the technique described for soliciting feedback described in Chapter 1. Approach a sampling of people both on and off the job with this line of questioning: "I'm trying to develop myself personally. Can you think of anything I do or say that creates a bad impression in any way? Do not be afraid of offending me. Only people who know me can provide me with this kind of information."

Take notes to show how serious you are about the feedback. When someone provides any feedback at all, say, "Please continue, this is useful." Try not to react defensively when you hear something negative. You asked for it, and the person is truly doing you a favour.

Learn to Profit from Criticism As the above example implies, learning to profit from criticism is necessary to benefit from feedback. Furthermore, to ignore valid criticism can be self-defeating. People who benefit from criticism are able to stand outside themselves while being criticized. It is as if they are watching the criticism from a distance and looking for its possible merits. People who take criticism personally experience anguish when receiving negative feedback. The following are several specific suggestions for benefiting from valid criticism.[18]

1. *See yourself at a distance.* Place an imaginary glass shield between you and the person making the criticism. Attempt to be a detached observer looking for useful information.
2. *Ask for clarification and specifics.* Ask politely for more details about the negative behaviour in question, so you can change if change is warranted. If your boss is criticizing you for being rude with customers, you might respond: "I certainly don't want to be rude. Can you give me a couple of examples of how I was rude? I need your help in working on this problem." After asking questions you can better determine if the criticism is valid.
3. *Decide on a response.* An important part of learning from criticism is to respond appropriately to the critic. Let the criticizer know what you agree with. Apologize for the undesirable behaviour, saying something like, "I apologize for being rude to customers. I know what I can do differently now. I'll be more patient, so as not to appear rude." If the feedback was particularly useful in helping you overcome self-defeating behaviour, thank the person for the constructive feedback.

Stop Denying the Existence of Problems Many people sabotage their careers and personal lives because they deny the existence of a problem and therefore do not take appropriate action. Denial takes place as a defensive manoeuvre against a painful reality. An example of a self-sabotaging form of denial is to ignore the importance of upgrading one's credentials, despite overwhelming evidence that it is necessary. Some people never quite complete a degree program that has become an informal qualification for promotion. Consequently, they sabotage their chances of receiving a promotion for which they are otherwise qualified. Many people in recent years have damaged their chances for career progress by not upgrading their computer skills.

Visualize Self-Enhancing Behaviour Visualization is a primary method for achieving many different types of self-improvement. It is therefore an essential component of overcoming self-defeating behaviour. To apply visualization, program yourself to overcome self-defeating actions and thoughts. Imagine yourself engaging in self-enhancing, winning actions and thoughts. Picture yourself achieving peak performance when good results count the most.

A starting point in learning how to use visualization for overcoming career self-sabotage is to identify the next job situation you will be facing that is similar to ones you have flubbed in the past. You then imagine yourself mentally and physically projected into that situation. Imagine what the room looks like, who will be there, and the confident expression you will have on your face. Visualization is akin to watching a video of yourself doing something right.

COPING WITH THE LOSS OF A RELATIONSHIP

A major personal problem many people encounter is the loss of a valued personal relationship. The loss may take the form of separation, divorce, or the breakup of a non-married couple. A more subtle loss is when a couple stays together, yet the intimacy in the relationship vanishes. Loneliness and conflict result from the lost intimacy. The next chapter presents ideas on maintaining and revitalizing relationships. Our attention here is directed toward specific suggestions for dealing with the loss of an important personal relationship. When you are emotionally and romantically involved with another person, the loss of that relationship usually has a big impact. Even if you believe strongly that splitting up is in your best interest, the fact that you cared at one time about that person leads to some hurt. The major reason we need tactics for dealing with lost relationships is that many upsetting feelings surface in conjunction with the loss.

A newly unattached person might feel lonely, guilty, angry, or frightened. Your role in the breakup will usually dictate which emotion surfaces. For instance, if you dumped your partner, you will probably experience guilt. If you were the person dumped, you will probably experience anger. If you survive a spouse, you might feel guilty about not having been nice enough to your partner during your years together.

A number of suggestions to help a person recover from a lost relationship are presented below.[19] Choose the tactics that seem to fit your personality and circumstances. As with the other personal problems described in this chapter, professional counselling may be helpful in making a recovery.

1. *Be thankful for the good in the relationship*. An excellent starting point in recovering from a broken relationship is to take stock of what went right when the two of you were together. Looking for the good in the relationship helps place the situation in proper perspective. It also helps prevent you from developing the counterproductive attitude that your time together was a total waste.
2. *Find new outlets for spare time*. Some of the energy you were investing in your partnership can now be invested in spare-time activities. This activity provides a healthy form of the defence mechanism called *compensation* or *substitution*.
3. *Get ample rest and relaxation*. A broken relationship is a stressor. As a result, most people need rest and relaxation to help them overcome the emotional pain associated with the departure of a partner.

4. *Pamper yourself.* Pampering involves finding little ways of doing nice things for yourself. These could take the form of buying yourself a new outfit, taking a weekend vacation, eating pizza at midnight, or getting a body massage.
5. *Seek emotional support.* Friends and relatives can also be an important source of emotional support to help you cope with post-separation blues. Be careful, however, not to let your loss of a relationship dominate conversations with friends to the point of boring them. Another source of emotional support is groups specifically designed to help people cope with recent separation or divorce. Parents Without Partners is an example of such a group. A caution here is that some people stay too long with such groups rather than taking the initiative to find a new partner.
6. *Get out and go places.* The oldest suggestion about recovering from a lost relationship is perhaps the most valid—keep active. While you are doing new things you tend to forget about your problems. Also, as you go places and do things, you increase your chances of making new friends. And friends are the only true antidote to the loneliness of being unattached.
7. *Give yourself time to heal.* The greater the hurt, the more time it will take to recover from the broken relationship. Recognizing this fact will help to curb your impatience over disentangling yourself emotionally from the former spouse or partner.
8. *Anticipate a positive outcome.* While you are on the path toward rebuilding your social life, believe that things will get better. Also believe that all the emotional energy you have invested into splitting and healing will pay dividends. Self-fulfilling prophecies work to some extent in social relationships. If you believe you will make a satisfactory recovery from a broken relationship, your chances of doing so will increase. The underlying mechanism seems to be that if you believe in yourself, you exude a level of self-confidence that others find appealing.

ABSENTEEISM AND TARDINESS

Absenteeism and tardiness are the leading causes of employee discipline. Developing a poor record of attendance and punctuality is also a form of career self-sabotage. Employees who are habitually absent or late develop a poor reputation and receive negative employment references. It becomes difficult to find a good job with another employer after having established a poor record of attendance and punctuality. Maintaining good attendance and punctuality is more important today than ever, because worldwide competition has forced many private organizations to trim costs. Government organizations are also under constant pressure to control costs. The person who is habitually absent or late therefore risks termination.

Here we will first look at data about absenteeism and tardiness standards. We will then discuss how a person might overcome the problem of high absenteeism and tardiness.

During a person's career, many unexpected situations arise in which it is necessary to be absent or late. Accidents, illnesses, severe family problems, and family deaths all may require time away from the job. A serious-minded worker should therefore strive to attain near-perfect attendance and punctuality when not faced with an emergency. Some suggestions follow to help a person develop the right mental set for achieving an excellent record of attendance and punctuality.

1. *Recognize that not to have excellent attendance and punctuality is self-defeating.* For reasons already described, poor attendance and punctuality can lead to a poor reputation and job loss. Why self-handicap your chances for career success?
2. *Look upon your job as self-employment.* Few people operating their own business will take a day off, or begin late, for no valid reason. The smaller the business, the better the attendance and punctuality, because so little help is available. You can therefore improve your attendance and punctuality by imagining that your area of responsibility is your own business.
3. *Regard your job responsibilities as equally important to those of the person in charge of opening the bank's doors in the morning.* People in charge of opening banks, department stores, movie theatres, and other retail businesses have excellent records of attendance and punctuality. A poor performance in these areas would create panic, especially in the case of the bank. To improve your attendance and punctuality, think of your responsibilities as being as important as opening the doors in the morning.
4. *Reward yourself for good attendance and punctuality and punish yourself for the opposite.* Following the suggestions for self-motivation described in Chapter 2, modify your behaviour in relation to attendance and punctuality. Treat yourself after six months of excellent attendance and punctuality. Punish yourself for a poor record. For example, if you miss one day of work for a flimsy reason, punish yourself by working all day on a national holiday.
5. *Think through carefully the consequences if all company employees were absent and late frequently.* Some people argue that they are entitled to take the maximum number of sick days allowable under company policy. If everybody took the maximum number of sick days and was late as often as possible without incurring discipline, companies would suffer. Customer service would deteriorate, productivity would decrease, and more people would have to be hired just to cover for employee "no-shows." Less money might be available for salary increases and employee benefits. Even worse, the company might have to lay off employees because of low profits.
6. *Think of the consequences to co-workers if you are absent and late frequently.* Being absent or late may hurt the company. The same behaviour can adversely affect your relationships with co-workers. Co-workers become annoyed and irritated quickly when they have to cover for a negligent peer. The worker who is frequently absent or late runs the risk of losing the cooperation of co-workers when he or she needs assistance.

DEPRESSION AND NEUROBIOLOGICAL DISORDERS

Many employees perform poorly on the job because of reasons beyond their control. They would like to perform well, but disturbed emotions or physical or neurological impairments interfere with handling some aspects of their job responsibilities well. To illustrate this kind of obstacle, we describe two problems faced by many workers: depression and neurobiological disorders.

Depression

Depression is a widespread emotional disorder. A depressed person has difficulties such as sadness, changes in appetite, sleeping difficulties, and a decrease in activities, interests, and energy. Depression is the most commonly diagnosed mental illness. According to Public Health Agency of Canada, approximately 8 percent of adults will experience major depression at some time in their lives.[20] In 1998–1999, an estimated 4 percent of Canadians of age 12 or older reported symptoms that would suggest that they had suffered at least one episode of major depression during the previous year. Also, women were twice as likely to report depression, and their depressive episodes last longer.[21]

Most cases of depression are believed to be caused primarily by a chemical imbalance in the brain whereby the functioning of the neurotransmitters is disturbed. A person's psychological makeup also contributes to susceptibility to depression. People with low self-esteem, who are pessimistic, and who manage stress poorly are prone to depression. To treat depression successfully, antidepressant medication usually needs to be accompanied by psychotherapy and counselling.

In recent years, much attention has been paid to **seasonal affective disorder (SAD)**, a form of depression that develops during the fall and winter months and disappears as the days lengthen in the spring. Because darkness stimulates the production of melatonin, some researchers believe that people who experience SAD may produce an excess of melatonin or may be particularly sensitive to the hormone. SAD sufferers become lethargic in the winter and fall, and show other symptoms of depression. In one survey study done in Toronto, almost 3 percent of respondents indicated that they suffered from SAD.[22] "Winter blues" is the everyday term for this problem.

The farther north of the equator you live, the more likely you are to experience SAD. However, people who enjoy outdoor winter activities like skiing, ice skating, curling, and shovelling snow are less prone to SAD (based on one author's observations).

Being depressed on the job creates many problems. Depression drains energy and reduces productivity and quality. The reduced effectiveness triggers a cycle of failure. As effectiveness decreases, the person's thinking, acting, and feeling become more damaged. As relationships with co-workers and job performance deteriorate, the person becomes more depressed.[23] Here is an example of how depression affects job behaviour:

> A sales manager known for his exuberance and enthusiasm slowly began to withdraw from face-to-face contact with team members. During one team meeting the manager abruptly terminated the meeting, telling the group, "I'm just too emotionally drained to continue today." Soon, he rarely communicated with others in the firm except through email. At times he was observed just staring out the window. Reports of his unusual behaviour soon reached his manager, who in turn urged the sales manager to visit a mental health professional. A combination of antidepressant drugs and psychotherapy helped the sales manager to overcome his problems enough to function satisfactorily on the job.

Human Relations Self-Assessment Quiz 5-2 and the Canada Today feature will help you better appreciate the symptoms of depression as they apply to the job. These symptoms are easier to recognize in another person than in oneself. Having more than a few of these symptoms is an indicator that treatment by a mental health professional is important. Many people who commit suicide are extremely depressed.

Canada Today

Depression and Job Impairment

As a common mental illness, depression affects many Canadians both on and off the job. Below is some information from two Canadian studies:

Around half a million Canadian workers experience depression and most of them say the symptoms interfere with their ability to work, according to a new study.

Data from the 2002 Canadian Community Health Survey, which focused on mental health and well-being, show that almost 4 percent of workers aged 25 to 64 had experienced depression in the 12 months before the survey.

The *Health Reports* study "Depression and work impairment," revealed that the workers most prone to depression were those who regularly worked evening or night shifts, along with those employed in sales or service.

Nearly 8 out of 10 (79%) workers who had experienced depression in the year before they were interviewed reported that the symptoms had interfered with their ability to work, at least to some extent. Almost one in five (19%) reported a very severe degree of interference.

Depressed workers reported an average of 32 days in the previous year when their symptoms left them either unable to carry out normal activities or totally unable to work.

This study reinforces other research, which found that several crucial elements of job performance, such as time management, concentration, teamwork and overall output, are particularly vulnerable to depressive symptoms.

A number of job-related factors, such as shift work, hours of work, work stress and occupation, were associated with depression.

Men and women who worked evening or night shifts were more likely to be depressed than those who had a regular day-time schedule.

The prevalence of depression was relatively high among workers who spent fewer than 30 hours a week on the job, and lower among those who worked more than 40 hours.

Source: Excerpt: "In Canada: Depression and Job Impairment," adapted from Statistics Canada publication *The Daily,* Catalogue 11-001, Friday January 12, 2007. http://www.statcan.gc.ca/daily-quotidien/070112/dq070112a-eng.htm.

Neurobiological Disorders

Personal problems on the job are sometimes the result of a **neurobiological disorder**, a quirk in the chemistry or anatomy of the brain that creates a disability. The quirk is usually inherited, but could also be caused by a brain injury or poisoning, such as exposure to harmful vapours. The disabilities take the form of reduced ability to control one's behaviour, movements, emotions, or thoughts.[24] If you experience sudden changes in your job behaviour, a thorough neurological examination is strongly recommended. The most common neurobiological disorders on the job are described next. Depression, described in the previous section, is sometimes classified as a neurobiological disorder when it stems from chemical or anatomical factors.

Attention Deficit Disorder People with this disorder have difficulty concentrating that may be accompanied by hyperactivity. The person might therefore engage in a flurry of activity on the job, yet much of the activity might be wasted effort. Many children's difficulties in paying attention in school are attributed to attention deficit disorder.

Obsessive-Compulsive Disorder People with this disorder have uncontrollable and recurring thoughts or behaviour relating to an unreasonable fear. A job example of obsessive-compulsive disorder would be a person who becomes obsessed with cleaning

Human Relations Self-Assessment

QUIZ 5-2 Symptoms of Depression on the Job

Workers suffering from depression often experience a combination of one or more of the following symptoms. Not every depressed person will experience them all. (Most of these symptoms are also present off the job.)

- Slow movement, drooped posture
- Decreased energy, fatigue, and frequent complaints of being tired
- Decreased ability to concentrate, remember, or make decisions
- Taking an unusually long time to complete tasks
- Speaking only when spoken to
- Crying on the job
- Attributing any personal successes to luck
- Loss of interest in activities that were once enjoyable, such as having lunch with co-workers
- Mentions of suicide, even in a joking manner
- Deterioration in grooming such as rumpled clothing, unkempt hair, neglected facial shaving
- Increased absenteeism
- Alcohol and drug abuse
- Increasing intensity and frequency of any of the above symptoms

Sources: Canadian Mental Health Association, 1995; *Health Guide*, America's Pharmaceutical Research Companies, 1996 (www.phrma.org); John Lawrie, "Coping with Depression on the Job," *Supervisory Management*, June 1992, pp. 6–7.

his or her work area. The person could be motivated by fear of being contaminated by impurities in the ventilation system.

Narcolepsy People with this disorder have uncontrollable sleepiness, even after receiving adequate sleep. A person with narcolepsy may fall asleep at the desk, or while driving a company vehicle or operating dangerous machinery.

Tourette's Syndrome People suffering from this disorder experience uncontrollable movement or utterances, and often shout profanities at inappropriate times. A person with Tourette's syndrome is often misinterpreted as consciously attempting to create a disturbance.

Although damaging to work performance, neurobiological disorders can be treated successfully. In addition to the proper medication, the person usually needs a supportive environment both at home and on the job. Most people with neurobiological disorders can function close to normally after appropriate medication is prescribed and they are taught how to cope with their symptoms.

Training others to understand their condition is an important part of the treatment. The person with Tourette's syndrome, for example, should explain to co-workers that at times he or she may appear insulting and abusive. Furthermore, co-workers can be advised not to take such behaviour seriously, and that the behaviour is under medical control and may soon disappear entirely. Discussing a personal problem with co-workers may help to reduce their fears about your problem and lead to better understanding.

DEALING WITH ANGER

Limited ability to manage anger damages the career and personal life of many people. **Anger** is a feeling of extreme hostility, displeasure, or exasperation. The emotion of anger creates stress, including the physiological changes described in Chapter 4. One noticeable indicator of anger is enlargement of the pupils, causing the wide-eyed look of people in a rage. Blood may rush to the face, as indicated by reddening in light-skinned people. Anger often leads to aggression, which is the verbal or physical attacking of another person, animal, or object. Workplace violence, such as an ex-employee shooting a former boss who fired him, is an extreme example of expressing anger. What angry behaviour have you observed on the job?

The ability to manage anger is an important interpersonal skill, now considered to be part of **emotional intelligence**. This concept refers to qualities such as understanding your feelings, empathy for others, and the regulation of emotion to enhance living.[25] A person who cannot manage anger well cannot take good advantage of his or her regular intelligence. As an extreme example, a genius who swears at the boss regularly will probably lose his or her job despite being so talented. Our concern here is with several suggestions that will help you manage (not necessarily eliminate) anger so it does not jeopardize your career or personal success.

A starting point is to recognize that at its best, *anger can be an energizing force*. Instead of being destructive, channel your anger into exceptional performance. If you are angry because you did not get the raise you thought you deserved, get even by performing so well that there will be no question you deserve a raise next time. Develop the habit of *expressing your anger before it reaches a high intensity*. Tell your companion that you do not appreciate his or her using a cell phone while you are having dinner together the first time the act of rudeness occurs. If you wait too long, you may wind up grabbing the cell phone and slamming it to the floor.

As you are about to express anger, *slow down*. (The old technique of counting to ten is still effective.) Slowing down gives you the opportunity to express your anger in a way that does not damage your relationship with the other person. Following your first impulse, you might say to another person, "You're a stupid fool." If you slow down, this might translate into, "You need training on this task." Closely related to slowing down is saying to yourself as soon as you feel angry, "Oops, I'm in the anger mode now. I had better calm down before I say something or do something I will regret later." To gauge how effectively you are expressing your anger, ask for feedback. Ask a friend, co-worker, or manager, "Am I coming on too strong when I express my negative opinion?"[26]

Anger has also become widespread throughout society and we have even labelled it depending upon where it occurs—we have "road rage," "air rage," and uncivil workplaces. Anger can erupt into violence. Many companies have been asking ill-tempered employees

Human Relations Skill Building

Exercise 5-1 Learning to Manage Anger

The next few times you are really angry with somebody or something, use one or more of the good mental health statements described below. Each statement is designed to remind you that you are in charge, not your anger. For starters, visualize something that has made you angry recently. Practise making the statements below in relation to that angry episode.

- I'm in charge here, not my emotional outbursts.
- I'll breathe deeply a few times and then deal with this.
- I feel _____ when you _____.
- I can handle this.
- I'm going to take time out to cool down before I deal with this.
- Yes, I'm angry and I'll just watch what I say or do.

Now describe the effect making the above statements had on your anger.

Source: Based on Lynne Namka, "A Primer on Anger: Getting a Handle on Your Mads," http://members.aol.com/angriesout/grown2.htm (July 7, 1997), p. 4. (Accessed April 14, 2003)

to attend anger management classes. Anger management is often included in drug treatment and couples counselling. A major part of these classes is to help clients learn self-control by such means as thinking through the consequences of unchecked anger. Another approach is to help people learn to look at the big picture and not let little things bother them. These classes are a start, but overcoming anger issues may take most people at least one year.[27] Human Relations Skill-Building Exercise 5-1 will give you an opportunity to develop your anger-management skills. However, the exercise will require some work outside class.

SUMMARY

Life span challenges and changes impact us in both our personal and work lives. According to Erickson, the socialization process consists of the "eight stages of man," with each state representing a psychosocial crisis. The crisis must be resolved at each stage before the next stage can be successfully negotiated. The challenges of adolescence include the cognitive challenge of developing logic and abstract thought as well as developing moral reasoning. A key personality and social challenge is the identity crisis. The challenges of adulthood include applying cognitive skills to real-life problems. Adults must also learn to become less self-centred and refine their interpersonal skills. Adults may also face a midlife crisis and a midlife transition. The challenges of late adulthood include cognitive decline, even though older people can be trained to learn new, complex tasks. A change facing late life adults is more of a focus on the present. Life satisfaction tends to increase throughout adulthood but may peak for men at about age 65. Job satisfaction also tends to increase with age, partially because older adults understand better which needs work can and cannot satisfy.

Suggestions for managing change well include searching for the personal value that could be embedded in forced change, asking "What if," forcing yourself to enjoy at least some small aspect of the change, recognizing that change is inevitable, and understanding that change has an emotional impact. To help cope with possible changes caused by outsourcing and offshoring of one's job is to incorporate building relationships into one's job.

Unless personal problems are kept under control, a person's chances of achieving career and personal success diminish. Many personal problems arise out of self-defeating behaviour. The major cause of this behaviour is a loser life script, a life plan of coming out a loser in important situations. Other causes of self-defeating behaviour include a self-defeating personality pattern, self-defeating beliefs, and fear of success. Approaches to overcoming and preventing self-defeating behaviour include these strategies:

1. Examine your "script" and make the necessary changes.
2. Stop blaming others for your problems.
3. Solicit feedback on your actions.
4. Learn to profit from criticism.
5. Stop denying the existence of problems.
6. Visualize self-enhancing behaviour.

A major personal problem many people encounter is the loss of a valued personal relationship. Suggestions for dealing with this problem include the following: (1) be thankful for the good in the relationship, (2) find new outlets for spare time, (3) get ample rest and relaxation, (4) pamper yourself, (5) seek emotional support, (6) get out and go places, (7) give yourself time to heal, and (8) anticipate a positive outcome.

Absenteeism and tardiness are the leading causes of employee discipline, and thus can be a major personal problem. Workers must develop the right mental set to achieve excellent attendance and punctuality. For example, a person might look upon the job as self-employment.

Many employees perform poorly on the job because they are depressed. Depression drains energy and reduces productivity and quality. As job performance deteriorates, the person becomes more depressed. Many job problems are also caused by neurobiological disorders, a quirk in the chemistry or anatomy of the brain that creates a disability. The disabilities take the form of reduced ability to control one's behaviour, movements, emotions, or thoughts. Major neurobiological disorders are attention deficit disorder, obsessive-compulsive disorder, narcolepsy, and Tourette's syndrome. These disorders can be treated with medication, but a supportive environment is also needed.

Limited ability to deal with anger damages the career and personal lives of many people. Eating disorders can also have an impact on a person's life and can cause severe health problems.

The ability to manage anger is an important interpersonal skill, considered to be a component of emotional intelligence. To manage anger well, recognize that it can be an energizing force. Express anger before it reaches a high intensity. As you are about to express anger, slow down, and then express it in a constructive way. Ask others for feedback on how well you are expressing anger. Anger management classes are also an option for coping with anger.

QUESTIONS AND ACTIVITIES

1. How do you interpret the old saying, "Youth is wasted on the young?"
2. Based on information in this chapter, what advice can you offer a person in her or his late 40s who is fearful of becoming old?
3. What is your strategy for dealing with the biggest change you will have to face during the next 12 months?
4. What is the difference between making a bad mistake once and self-defeating behaviour?
5. Describe a person you know who appears to have a "winner" life script, and justify your reasoning.
6. Some companies offer awards for good attendance. Why is this necessary from a motivational standpoint?
7. Do you think people who have poor attendance records in school will probably have poor attendance records on the job? Explain your reasoning.
8. What is the difference between having a depression disorder and "having the blues"?
9. What are some effects that an eating disorder could create for a person on the job? Should employers have programs in place to help employees eat well, just as many employers have substance abuse programs? Explain your answer.
10. Why is it that hockey players become so angry that they regularly physically attack their opponents, whereas tennis and golf players almost never act this way?

INTERNET SKILL BUILDER

The Millenial

Although opinions vary as to the precise meaning of a millennial, the term generally refers to the last generation born in the twentieth century. Search the internet to identify about ten life span challenges facing the millenials—in other words challenges facing members of this generation attributed to their stage in life. You can probably supplement the list with reading you have done or personal observations. Did you find the World Wide Web useful for this type of search, or did you have better luck with a library database?

Log on to the **Companion Website** at **www.pearsoncanada.ca/dubrin** to access additional resources for this chapter.

CASE STUDY HUMAN RELATIONS

A Concern about Violence

Vernon Bigsby is the CEO and owner of a large soft-drink bottling company in Vancouver. The company invests money periodically in training to help the management and supervisory staff stay abreast of important new trends in technology and managing human resources. Bigsby recently became concerned about workplace violence. Although the company had not yet experienced an outbreak of violence, Bigsby was intent on preventing violence in the future. To accomplish his goal, Bigsby hired a human resources consultant, Sara Toomey, to conduct a seminar on preventing workplace violence.

The seminar was given twice, with one-half the managers and supervisors attending each session. Chad Ditmar, a night-shift supervisor, made the first wisecrack during the seminar. He said, "What are we here for? To prevent workers from squirting 'pop' at each other?" Toomey responded, "My job would be easy if I were here only to prevent horseplay. Unfortunately the reality is that there are thousands of lethal weapons going past your workers every day. Just think how much damage one angry worker could do to an innocent victim with one slash of a broken bottle." The laughter in the room quickly subsided.

About one hour into the seminar, Sara Toomey projected a PowerPoint slide outlining characteristics of a worker with potential for violence. She said, "Recognize that not every person who has many of these characteristics will become violent. However, they do constitute early-warning signals. I would watch out for any worker with a large number of these traits and behaviours."

Ditmar supervises 45 workers directly involved in the bottling of three company brands of soft drinks. The workers in his department range in age from 18 to 57. The nature of the job can usually be learned within three days, so the workers are classified as semiskilled. After his initial wisecrack, Ditmar took the seminar quite seriously. He made extensive notes on what the consultant said and took back to his office a printed copy of the computer slide, which looked something like this:

Profile of the Violent Employee

- Socially isolated (a loner) white male between the ages of 30 and 40
- Fascination with the military and weapons
- Temper control problem with a history of threats
- Alcohol and/or drug abuser
- Makes unwanted sexual advances toward other employees
- Accepts criticism poorly and holds grudge against the criticizer
- Shows paranoid thinking and believes that management is out to get him (or her)
- Blames others for his problems
- Makes violent statements, such as spoken threats about beating up other employees

The morning following the seminar, Chad sent an email to Gary Bia, the vice-president of operations. Chad said, "I must see you today. I'm worried about a potentially explosive personnel problem." Bia made arrangements to see Ditmar at 5:45 p.m., before Ditmar's shift began.

"What's up, Chad?" said Bia.

"Here's what's up," said Ditmar. "After attending the seminar on violence, I think I've found our suspect. As you know, you do get some strange types working the night shift. Some of them don't have a normal life. I've got this one guy, Freddie Watkins. He's a loner. He wears his hair weird with pink-coloured spikes. He's got a tattoo and a huge gun collection that he brags about. I doubt the guy has any friends. He talks a lot about how he plays violent video games. Freddie told about how he once choked to death a dog that bit him.

"What really worries me is that," Freddie once said he would punch out the next person who made a smart comment about his hair.

"Do you agree or not that we might have a candidate for workplace violence right here in my department? I'm talking to you first, Gary, but maybe I should be speaking to the antiviolence consultant or to our security officer. What should we do next?"

Bia said, "I'm happy that you are bringing this potential problem to my attention, but I need some more facts. First of all, have you had any discipline problems yet with Freddie?"

Chad responded, "Not yet, Gary, but we're talking about a potential killer right here on my shift. I think we have to do something."

Bia said, "Chad, I'm taking your concerns seriously, but I don't want to jump too fast. Let me think over your problem for at least a day."

Questions

1. What actions, if any, should Gary Bia take?
2. What evidence does Chad Ditmar have that Freddie Watkins has significant personal problems?
3. What career advice can you offer Freddie Watkins?

Chapter 6

Finding Happiness and Enhancing Your Personal Life

Learning Outcomes

After studying the information and doing the exercises in this chapter, you should be able to

- define emotional intelligence and its key components;
- understand the components of attitudes, and explain how they are acquired and changed;
- explain how attitudes can be changed;
- display effective organizational citizenship behaviour;
- explain how happiness is contingent upon keeping the spheres of life in balance;
- specify factors that contribute to personal happiness.

Andrea Jung, the chair and CEO of Avon Products, told *Harvard Business Review*, "Emotional intelligence is in our DNA here at Avon because relationships are critical at every stage of our business. It starts with the relationships our 4.5 million independent sales reps have with their customers and goes right up through senior management to my office.

"So the emphasis on emotional intelligence is much greater here than it was at other companies in which I've worked. We incorporate emotional intelligence education into our development training for senior managers, and we factor in emotional intelligence competence when we evaluate employee's performance.

"Of all a leader's competencies, emotional and otherwise, self-awareness is the most important. Without it, you can't identify the impact you have on others. Self-awareness is very important for me as CEO. At my level, few people are willing to tell me the things that are hardest to hear. We have a CEO advisory counsel—10 people chosen each year from Avon offices throughout the world—and they tell me the good, the bad, and the ugly about our company. Anything can be said. It helps keep me connected to what people really think and how my actions affect them. . . ."[1]

The comments offered by Andrea Jung of Avon illustrate how one of the key themes of this chapter, emotional intelligence including self-awareness, figures into success in business. Other major sections of the chapter deal with related aspects of using emotion constructively: attitudes and happiness.

WHAT IS EMOTIONAL INTELLIGENCE?

Research into the functioning of the human brain has combined personality factors with wisdom and common sense, indicating that how effectively people use their emotions has a major impact on their success. The topmost layers of the brain govern intelligence functions, such as analytical problem solving. The innermost areas of the brain govern emotional functions, such as dealing with anger when being criticized by a customer.

The term **emotional intelligence** has gathered different meanings; all relating to how effectively a person makes constructive use of his or her emotions. John D. Mayer, a professor of psychology at the University of New Hampshire, along with Yale psychology professor Peter Saloey, originated the concept of emotional intelligence. Mayer explains that from a scientific (rather than a popular) viewpoint, emotional intelligence is the "ability to accurately perceive your own and others' emotions; to understand the signals that emotions send about relationships; and to manage our own and others' emotions."[2] A person with high emotional intelligence would be able to engage in such behaviours as sizing up people, pleasing others, and influencing them.

Key Components of Emotional Intelligence

Four key factors included in a current analysis of emotional intelligence are as follows:[3]

1. *Self-awareness.* The ability to understand your moods, emotions, and needs as well as their impact on others. Self-awareness also includes using intuition to make decisions you can live with happily. (A person with good self-awareness knows whether he or she is pushing other people too far.) In the chapter opener, Andrea Jung emphasized the importance of self-awareness for a leader.
2. *Self-management.* The ability to control one's emotions and act with honesty and integrity in a consistent and acceptable manner. The right degree of self-management helps prevent a person from throwing temper tantrums when activities do not go as planned. Effective workers do not let their occasional bad moods ruin their day. If they cannot overcome the bad mood, they let co-workers know of their problem and how long it might last. (A person with low self-management would suddenly decide to drop a project because the work was frustrating.)
3. *Social awareness.* Includes having empathy for others and having intuition about work problems. A team leader with social awareness, or empathy, would be able to assess whether a team member has enough enthusiasm for a project to assign him to that project. Another facet of social skill is the ability to interpret nonverbal communication, such as frowns and types of smiles.[4] (A supervisor with social awareness, or empathy, would take into account the most likely reaction of group members before making a decision affecting them.)

4. *Relationship management*. Includes the interpersonal skills of being able to communicate clearly and convincingly, disarm conflicts, and build strong personal bonds. Effective workers use relationship management skills to spread their enthusiasm and solve disagreements, often with kindness and humour. (A worker with relationship management skill would use a method of persuasion that is likely to work well with a particular group or individual.)

Emotional intelligence thus incorporates many of the skills and attitudes necessary to achieve effective interpersonal relations in organizations. Many topics in human relations, such as resolving conflict, helping others develop and positive political skills would be included in emotional intelligence.

A review of many studies concluded that low emotional intelligence employees are more likely than their high emotional intelligence counterparts to experience negative emotional reactions to job insecurity, such as high tension. Furthermore, workers with low emotional intelligence are more likely to engage in negative coping behaviours, such as expressing anger and verbally abusing an immediate supervisor for the organization failing to provide job security.[5]

Tests of emotional intelligence typically ask you to respond to questions on a 1-to-5 scale (never, rarely, sometimes, often, consistently). For example, indicate how frequently you demonstrate the following behaviours:

I can laugh at myself.	1	2	3	4	5
I help others grow and develop.	1	2	3	4	5
I watch carefully the nonverbal communication of others.	1	2	3	4	5

Human Relations Self-Assessment Quiz 6-1 gives you an opportunity to measure your emotional intelligence.

Human Relations Self-Assessment

QUIZ 6-1 What Is Your Emotional Intelligence?

Psychologists have developed various measures of emotional intelligence. The EQ (Emotional Quotient) test found by visiting www.myskillsprofile.com deals with 16 emotional competencies. The feedback report provides a chart of your emotional competencies together with a detailed description of your profile. An advantage of this quiz is that it is based on the work of two of the original researchers in emotional intelligence, not the later popularizers of the concept.

Demonstrating good emotional intelligence is impressive because it contributes to performing well in the difficult arena of dealing with feelings. A worker with good emotional intelligence would engage in such behaviours as (1) recognizing when a co-worker needs help but is too embarrassed to ask for help, (2) dealing with the anger of a dissatisfied customer, (3) recognizing that the boss is facing considerable pressure also, and (4) being able to tell whether a customer's "maybe" means "yes" or "no." The accompanying Human Relations in Practice provides another illustration of how a businessperson might make good use of emotional intelligence.

Human Relations in Practice

Colleen Barrett, President and COO of Southwest Airlines Tunes into Feelings

Reflecting on her ability to read people, Barrett said, "The other day I was talking to one of our officers, and he said, 'How did you do that?' and I said 'How do I do what?' He was referring to a meeting we'd both been at earlier. I'd asked one of the presenters at the meeting, a fellow who reported to this officer, if he was feeling OK. The officer thought the employee was fine, but, it turns out, the poor guy had a pretty traumatic experience in his personal life the night before. His presentation went well, but he seemed off to me, distracted. I suppose in order to have seen that, I must have been fairly attuned to what his fellow's presentations were usually like.

"I often communicate on a passionate, emotional level—which can be a detriment, particularly for a woman in a predominantly male leadership group, as ours was for many years."

Questions

1. Which aspect of emotional intelligence was Barrett demonstrating?
2. How might it have helped the presenter to be asked if he were doing OK?

Source: "Leading by Feel: Watch the Language," *Harvard Business Review*, January 2004, p. 29.

Acquiring and Developing Emotional Intelligence

Many people believe that emotional intelligence can be acquired and developed, much like a person can learn to become more extraverted or learn to control his or her intelligence. Many consultants offer training programs for helping employees develop emotional intelligence, and school systems throughout North America provide students some training in emotional intelligence. Elkhonon Goldberg, a clinical professor of neurology at New York University School of Medicine explains that emotional intelligence can be learned to a degree, much like musical talent or numerical ability can be developed. Having the right natural talent, however, is an important starting point. The combination of biological endowment (such as being aware of your emotions) and training will enable most people to enhance their emotional intelligence.[6]

Given that emotional intelligence is composed of different components, to acquire and develop such ability would usually require working on one component at a time. For example, if a person had difficulty in self-management, he or she would study and be coached in an aspect of self-management such as anger control. Training in anger management is widespread today because so many people have difficulty in managing their anger. Skill-Building Exercise 6-1 presented later in the chapter provides a step-by-step approach to the development of emotional intelligence.

A criticism of the ideal of emotional intelligence is that it might simply be part of analytical (or traditional) intelligence. For example, if you can read the feelings of other people, aren't you just being smart? Another concern is that the popularized concept of emotional intelligence has become so broad it encompasses almost the entire study of personality.

WHAT ARE THE COMPONENTS OF ATTITUDES, AND HOW ARE THEY ACQUIRED AND CHANGED?

"You've got an attitude," said the supervisor to the store associate, thus emphasizing the importance of attitude to job performance. For mysterious reasons, the term attitude in colloquial language often connotes a negative attitude. More accurately, an **attitude** is a predisposition to respond that exerts an influence on a person's response to a person, a thing, an idea, or a situation. Attitudes are an important part of human relations because they are linked with perception and motivation. For example, your attitude toward a co-worker influences your perception of how favourably you evaluate his or her work, and you will be better motivated if you have a positive attitude toward your work. Having and displaying positive attitudes will also help you build better relationships with co-workers, managers, and customers.

Our study of attitudes includes the components of attitudes, how attitudes are acquired, how they are changed, the importance of positive attitudes, how companies attempt to enhance positive attitudes and job satisfaction, and organizational citizenship behaviour.

Components of Attitudes

Attitudes are complex, having three components as shown in Figure 6-1. The **cognitive component** refers to the knowledge or intellectual beliefs an individual might have about an object (an idea, a person, a thing, or a situation). A market researcher might have accumulated considerable factual information about statistics (such as sampling procedures)

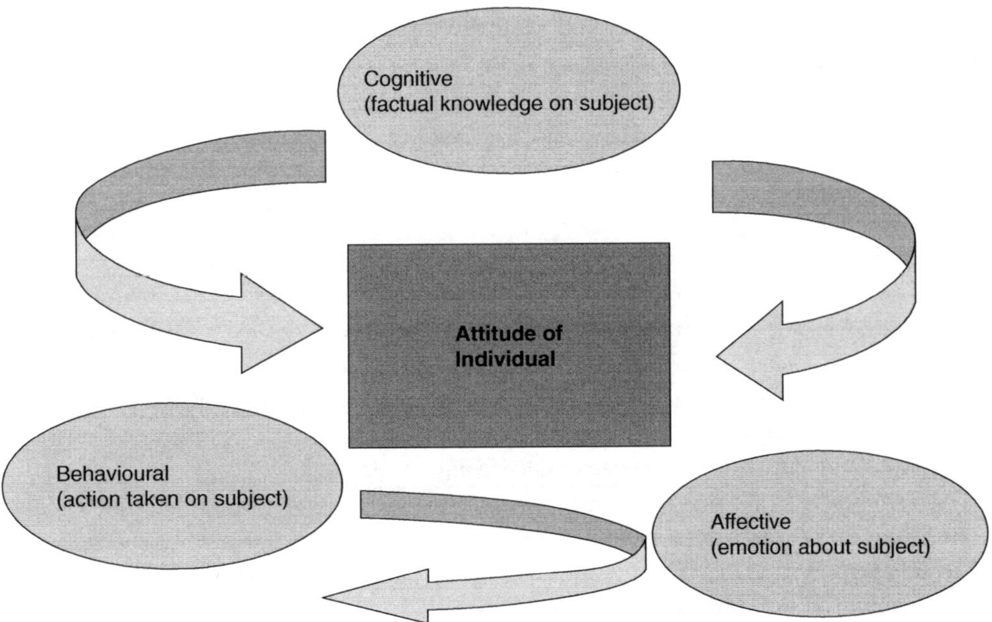

Figure 6-1 The Three Components of Attitudes

Observe that the three components of attitudes influence each other and that the attitude toward a subject, person, object, or thing is the combined effect of the cognitive, affective, and behavioural components.

and software for running data. The researcher might, therefore, have a positive attitude toward statistics.

The feeling or **affective component** refers to the emotion connected with an object or a task. The market researcher mentioned might basically like statistical analysis because of some pleasant experiences in college associated with statistics. The **behavioural component** refers to how a person acts. The market researcher might make positive statements about statistical methods or emphasize them in his or her reports.

The cognitive, affective, and behavioural aspects of attitudes are interrelated. A change in one of the components will set in motion a change in one or more of the others. If you have more facts about an object or process (cognitive), you form the basis for a more positive emotional response to the object (affective). In turn, your behaviour toward that object would probably become more favourable. For example, if you have considerable information about the contribution of feedback to personal development, you might have a positive feeling toward feedback. When receiving feedback, therefore, you would act favourably.

At times, people do not experience the type of consistency previously described and feel compelled to search for consistency. **Cognitive dissonance** is the situation in which the pieces of knowledge, information, attitudes, or beliefs held by an individual are contradictory. When a person experiences cognitive dissonance, the relationship between attitudes and behaviours is altered. People search for ways to reduce internal conflicts when they experience a clash between the information they receive and their actions or attitudes. The same process is used when a person has to resolve two inconsistent sets of information.

A typical example of cognitive dissonance on the job might occur when a worker believes that the report she submits to team members is of high quality; her teammates, however, tell her the report is flawed and requires substantial revisions. To reduce the dissonance, the worker might conveniently ignore the criticism. Or the worker might reason that she is the resident expert on the topic of the report, and her teammates, therefore, are not qualified to judge the merits of her report.

How Attitudes Are Formed

Attitudes usually are based on experience. Assume that you visited a convenience store, and you left your wallet on the counter without realizing it. Your wallet contained your credit cards, debit cards, driver's licence, $150 in cash, and personal memories. On returning home, you receive a telephone call from the clerk, informing you that he is holding your wallet for you. You most likely develop an immediate positive attitude toward the convenience store, the clerk, and perhaps toward other people of his ethnic group. Next we look more closely at the processes underlying attitude formation.[7]

A starting point in developing attitudes is to receive direct instruction from another individual. A friend whose opinion you respect tells you that e-filing of income tax is fast, efficient, and modern. You might quickly have a positive attitude toward e-filing. Similarly, you might develop a positive attitude through modelling the behaviour of another person. You have seen that your trusted friend e-files her income tax, so you develop a positive attitude toward e-filing.

Conditioning, or making associations, also contributes to attitude formation, as in the example of the convenience store. The attitudes that we develop based on conditioning or associations usually develop after at least several exposures. You might develop a favourable attitude toward the human resources (HR) department if you asked for help several times, and each time you received useful advice. In contrast, you might have developed negative attitudes toward HR if a department representative was unhelpful at each visit.

The way we think about things, or our cognitions, can influence attitude formation. You might be quite content with your salary and benefits provided by your employer. You then visit www.salary.com and discover that you make much less than other workers in your city performing the same work. As a result, your attitude toward your salary and benefits plunges.

The deepest contributor to attitude formation could be a person's standing on the personality trait of optimism. People with a high degree of optimism are predisposed toward viewing events, persons, places, and things as positive, which in turn leads to a positive attitude. In contrast, people who have a high standing on pessimism will harbor many negative attitudes. Many workers who have chronically low job satisfaction are pessimistic at the core.[8]

The Importance of Positive Attitudes

Positive attitudes have always been the foundation of effective human relations, as reflected in the writings of Dale Carnegie, the pioneer of the popular (rather than scientific) approach to human relations. A sampling of Carnegie's wisdom is presented in Figure 6-2. In recent years, positive attitudes have also become of interest to human relations specialists, as reflected in the fields called positive psychology and positive organizational studies. A major thrust of these fields is to enhance our experiences of enjoyment of work, as well as love, and play. The assumption is that when employees are in a positive mood, they are typically more creative, better motivated to perform well, and more helpful toward co-workers.[9]

The name "Dale Carnegie" is synonymous with a popularized approach to human relations. Carnegie (1888–1955) authored several best-sellers, including *How to Win Friends and Influence People* first published in 1937. More than 50 million copies of Carnegie's books have been printed and published in 38 languages. Nine of Carnegie's suggestions for becoming a positive, friendlier person follow:

1. Don't criticize, condemn, or complain.
2. Give honest, sincere appreciation.
3. Arouse in the other person an eager want.
4. Become genuinely interested in other people.
5. Smile.
6. Remember that a person's name is to that person the sweetest and most important sound in any language.
7. Be a good listener. Encourage others to talk about themselves.
8. Talk in terms of the other person's interests.
9. Make the other person feel important—and do it sincerely.

Source: *Dale Carnegie's Golden Book*, Dale Carnegie® Training, www.dalecarnegie.com, undated.

Figure 6-2 The Wisdom of Dale Carnegie

A worker who consistently maintains a genuine positive attitude will accrue many benefits. Being genuine is important because people with good emotional intelligence can readily detect a phony smile used as a cover up for anger. Assuming the worker with a positive attitude backs it up with good performance, he or she is more likely to (a) be liked by customers, (b) close more sales, (c) receive good performance reviews, (d) receive favourable work assignments, and (e) be promoted.

A mild note of caution is that there is a negative side to workers being too positive. As analyzed by Judge and Ilies, putting on a happy face can lead to stress, burnout, and job dissatisfaction. Workers who have an unrealistically positive self-concept might become self-centred and manipulative and think they deserve more attention and rewards than other workers.[10] Also a little negativity and cynicism is helpful in jobs such as auditor, budget analyst, tax accountant, and store detective. Sometimes being suspicious and negative contributes to a job role.

How Attitudes Are Changed

In general, attitudes can be changed by reversing the processes by which they were formed. Yet, we can look at the process of attitude change more specifically. First, we might receive information from a source we trust. A manager might have negative attitudes toward the value of employee training, then reads in a reliable business magazine that IBM spends more than $100 million annually on employee training. As a consequence, the manager develops a more favourable attitude toward training. A person might also be reconditioned to bring about attitude change. A small-business owner might have a negative attitude toward e-filing income taxes because of the need to learn new skills combined with a fear of security. After trying e-filing for two consecutive years because of being almost forced to by the law, the business owner receives refunds promptly and find the process not really so complicated. So her attitude toward e-filing becomes reconditioned in a positive direction.

Another way to change attitudes is to learn to look at the positive or negative aspect of situations, if you are a pessimist or optimist, respectively. A pessimistic person should concentrate on searching for the positive elements of a situation, such as a supervisor saying to himself or herself, "Okay this employee is a pill, but maybe there is something good about him."

In contrast, a naturally optimistic person might learn to say, "I tend to fall in love with the credentials of most job candidates. So maybe I should scrutinize this candidate more carefully."

How Companies Encourage Positive Attitudes and Job Satisfaction

From the standpoint of management it is beneficial for employees to have positive attitudes and job satisfaction. These two emotional states contribute to better customer service, less absenteeism and tardiness, less turnover, and often higher productivity. Much of the effort of human resource professionals is aimed at making employees more content. Among the hundreds of possible company initiatives to foster positive attitudes and high job satisfaction among employees are flexible working hours, recognition awards, company picnics, financial bonuses, time off for birthdays, on-site haircuts, and on-premises childcare centres. The following are three specific examples of small and medium-sized companies voted among the 50 Best Companies to Work For (as featured by *Profit Magazine*) to enhance employee attitudes and satisfaction:[11]

> Intuit Canada, Edmonton (financial and tax preparation software developer). Balanced workflow is a priority: production cycles are planned a year in advance to more evenly distribute workload throughout the year. And when the work is done, Intuit schedules time for play, too. During the last week of tax season, employees are treated to free ice cream sundaes in the lobby, juggling lessons and other games. This commitment to a "happy-employees-equals-motivated-employees" philosophy earned Intuit the No. 18 ranking among the 30 best workplaces in the country as named in 2006 by the Great Place to Work Institute Canada. There is also a wellness program with monthly sessions on different topics.
>
> R.L. Solutions, Toronto (software for the health care industry). This company motivates employees through a variety of incentives. In 2009, every staff member was given an HD television for meeting their team goals. Other programs include profit-sharing, an employee stock plan and matching every dollar that employees donate to a qualified charity.
>
> CBCI Telecom Canada Inc. Lachine, Quebec (video conferencing and audiovisual solutions integrator). CBCI Telecom has a flex-time policy to help its people balance their work and family life, above-average benefits, and monthly and yearly recognition programs. CBCI also offers employees financial support to encourage them to fundraise for charity.

Organizational Citizenship Behaviour

An employee attitude highly valued by employers is **organizational citizenship behaviour** (OCB), the willingness to go beyond one's job description to help the company, even if such act does not lead to an immediate reward. Being a good organizational citizen is also tied in with values because the person who goes beyond the job description to help others most likely has a strong work ethic and values helping others. Several examples of good organizational citizenship follow:

- Adelaide helps an employee in another department with a currency exchange problem because she has skill in this area, but Melissa's job does not involve working with currency exchange.
- Jeff is walking into the company from the company parking lot. He notices that a few beer bottles have been scattered on the lot. Worried about possible flat tires to employee vehicles, Jeff collects the bottles and disposes of them properly. He does not tell anybody about his good deed.
- Penelope, an information technology-gifted person, is walking down the aisle toward her cubicle. She notices a worker from another department with a panicked look on his face as he stares into his computer monitor. Penelope asks if there is anything she can do to help and proceeds to transfer valuable data from a corrupted file to a new file for the employee in panic.

Organizational citizenship behaviour is so important to organizations that this set of attitudes has been the subject of many studies. A general finding has been that as a result of many workers being good organizational citizens, the organization functions more effectively in such ways as improved product quantity and quality.[12]

Three management professors from Indiana University at Bloomington, Philip M. Podsakoff, Michael Ahearne, and Scott B. MacKenzie, conducted one of the first studies about the impact of organizational citizenship behaviour on work unit performance. They studied the effects of citizenship behaviour on the quantity and quality of the performance of 218 people working in 40 machine crews in a paper mill in the northeastern United States that produced bond and catalogue paper. Three different aspects of OCB were measured—helping behaviour, sportsmanship, and civic virtue—by having the crew members fill out questionnaires about each other. An example of a questionnaire statement measuring helping behaviour was "Help each other out if someone falls behind in his or her work." An example of a civic virtue statement was "Provide constructive suggestions about how the crew can improve its performance." And for sportsmanship, "Consume a lot of time complaining about trivial matters" (reverse scoring). All three aspects of organizational citizenship behaviour were rated on a scale of 1 to 7.

Quantity was measured by the amount of paper produced as a percentage of total machine capacity for the year. Quality was measured as the percentage of paper produced that was rejected by the mill's quality department or the customer.

The results of the study showed that helping behaviour and sportsmanship had a significant effect on performance quantity and that helping behaviour had a significant impact on performance quality. Somehow, civic virtue had no effect on quality or quantity of the work produced by the crews.[13] In conclusion, organizational citizenship behaviour was associated with higher quality and quantity of paper production by mill crews.

ACHIEVING HAPPINESS

When asked what is the most important thing in life, most people respond, "happiness." Research and opinion on the topic indicate that people can take concrete steps to achieve happiness. Planning for happiness is possible because it appears to be somewhat under people's control. Unhappiness, in contrast, seems to be more predetermined by genes. Sadness tends to run in families.[14] Our approach to the unlimited topic of understanding how to achieve happiness involves a model of happiness, a listing of keys to happiness, and the five principles of psychological functioning.

The Spheres of Life and Happiness

A practical way of understanding happiness is that it is a by-product of having the various components of life working in harmony and synchrony. To understand this approach, visualize about six gears with teeth, spinning in unison. As long as all gears are moving properly (and no teeth are broken), a state of equilibrium and fluid motion is achieved. Similarly, imagine that life has six major components. The exact components will differ among people. For most people, the components would be approximately as follows:

1. Work and career
2. Interpersonal life including loved ones and romantic life
3. Physical and mental health

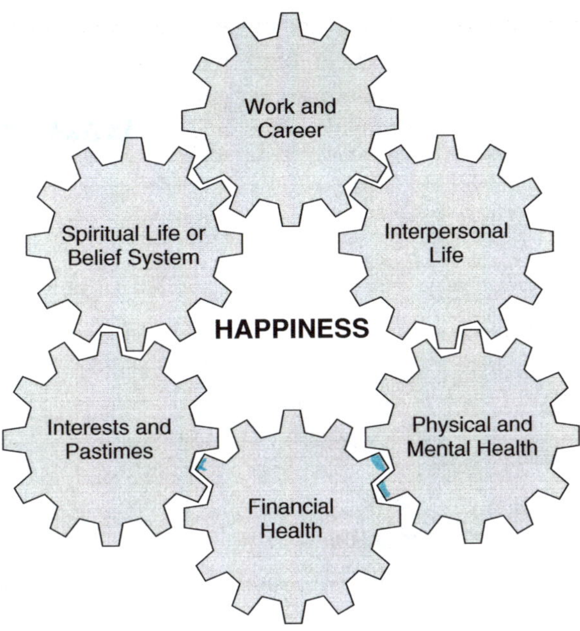

Figure 6-3 The Spheres-of-Life Model of Happiness

4. Financial health
5. Interests and pastimes, including reading, surfing the internet, and sports
6. A spiritual life or belief system including religion, science, or astrology

When a person has ample satisfactions in all six spheres, he or she achieves happiness. However, when a deficiency occurs in any of these six factors, the person's spheres are no longer in harmony, and dissatisfaction, or unhappiness, occurs. Yet sometimes if a person is having problems in one sphere, satisfaction in the other spheres can compensate temporarily for a deficiency in one. For the long range, a state of happiness is dependent on all six spheres working in harmony. In short, the theme of this book surfaces again: Work and personal life are mutually supportive. Figure 6-3 presents the spheres-of-life model of happiness.

People vary as to how much importance they attach to each sphere of life. A person with intense career ambitions, for example, might place less weight on the interests sphere than would a more leisure-oriented person. However, if any of these spheres are grossly deficient, total happiness will not be forthcoming. Another source of variation is that the importance people attach to each sphere may vary according to the stage of life. A full-time student, for example, might need just enough money to avoid worrying about finances. However, after about ten years of full-time career experience, a person's expenses might peak. The person would then attach more importance to the financial sphere.

The Keys to Happiness

Many people, including psychologists and other human relations specialists, have conducted research and made observations about the ingredients of happiness. If you are aware of these contributors to happiness, you might be able to enhance your happiness. The spheres-of-life model of happiness also furnishes direction for the person seeking happiness: Strive for acceptable levels of achievement in all six spheres. Here we summarize and synthesize a wide range of research and opinion on the keys to happiness.[15]

1. *Give high priority to the pursuit of happiness.* Discover what makes you happy and make the time to pursue those activities. Spending time doing what you enjoy contributes directly to happiness.
2. *Experience friendship and love, and find a life partner.* A happy person is one who is successful in personal relationships, who exchanges care and concern with loved ones. Happy people are able to love and be loved. Hugging people you like, or being hugged by them, is an important part of having enjoyable personal relationships. Married adults, in general, are happier than unmarried ones, and the results are similar for men and women.[16] Despite the consistency of this finding, it must be interpreted cautiously. It takes a satisfying marriage to bring happiness, and unmarried partners who have a long-term, caring relationship are also likely to be happy.
3. *Develop a sense of self-esteem.* Self-love must precede love for others. High self-esteem enables one to love and be loved. Developing a good self-image leads to the self-esteem required for loving relationships. A feeling of self-worth is important because it helps prevent one from being overwhelmed by criticism. An important part of developing self-esteem is not wanting financial success more than other things. Insecure people often seek society's approval in the form of purchasing consumer goods and accumulating investments.[17]
4. *Work hard at what you enjoy.* Love may be the most important contributor to happiness, with staying involved in work you like coming in second. To achieve happiness, it is necessary to find a career inside or outside the home that fits your most intense interests. Hard work contributes to happiness. A fundamental secret of happiness is accomplishing things and savouring what you have accomplished. A contributor to unhappiness is comparing one's successes, or lack of them, with those of other people. To be happy you must be happy with what *you* achieve.
5. *Appreciate the joys of day-to-day living.* Another key to happiness is the ability to live in the present without undue worrying about the future or dwelling on past mistakes. Be on guard against becoming so preoccupied with planning your life that you neglect to enjoy the happiness of the moment. The essence of being a happy person is to savour what you have right now.
6. *Be fair, kind, and helpful to others.* The Golden Rule is a true contributor to happiness: "Do unto others as you would have them do unto you." It is also important to practise charity and forgiveness. Helping others brings personal happiness. Knowing that you are able to make a contribution to the welfare of others gives you a continuing sense of satisfaction and happiness. Related to fairness and kindness is trusting others. Happy people have open, warm, and friendly attitudes.
7. *Have recreational fun in your life.* A happy life is characterized by fun, zest, joy, and delight. When you create a time for fun, you add an important element to your personal happiness. However, if you devote too much time to play, you will lose out on the fun of work accomplishments. In choosing fun activities, don't overplan. Because

novelty contributes to happiness, be ready to pursue an unexpected opportunity or to try something different.

8. *Learn to cope with grief, disappointment, setbacks, and stress.* To be happy one must learn how to face problems that occur in life without being overwhelmed or running away. It is also important to persevere in attempting to overcome problems, rather than to whine or engage in self-pity. Once you have had to cope with problems, you will be more able to appreciate the day-to-day joys of life.
9. *Live with what you cannot change.* Psychologist Martin Seligman says that attempting to change conditions unlikely to change sets us up for feeling depressed about failing. Weight loss is a prime example. Nineteen out of twenty people regain the weight they lose. It is therefore better to worry less about weight loss and concentrate on staying in good physical condition by engaging in moderate exercise. Good conditioning contributes much more to health than does achieving a weight standard set primarily to achieve an aesthetic standard.[18] You can then concentrate on being happy about your good physical condition instead of being unhappy about your weight.
10. *Energize yourself through physical fitness.* Engage in regular physical activity, such as dancing or sports, that makes you aerobically fit. Whether it is the endorphins released by exercise, or just the relaxed muscles, physical fitness fosters happiness.
11. *Satisfy your most important values.* Based on a survey of over 6,000 individuals, Steven Reiss concluded that people cannot find lasting happiness by aiming to have more fun or seeking pleasure. Instead, you have to satisfy your basic values or desires and take happiness in passing. To increase your value-based happiness, you have to first identify your most important desires and then gear your life toward satisfying these values. Among these key values are curiosity, physical activity, honour, power, family, status, and romance.[19] For example, if power and romance are two of your basic values, you can achieve happiness only if your life is amply provided with power and romance.

The Five Principles of Psychological Functioning

According to Richard Carlson, the best way to achieve inner serenity (or happiness) is to follow the five principles of psychological functioning.[20] These principles act as guides toward achieving a feeling of inner happiness. The first is *thinking*, which creates the psychological experience of life. Feelings come about only after you think about something or somebody. If you think of another person as attractive, it will lead to a warm feeling toward that person. People who learn to direct their thinking in positive directions will contribute to their own happiness. Remember that you produce your own thoughts.

The second principle is *moods*, meaning that the positive or negative content of your thinking fluctuates from moment to moment and day to day. Practise ignoring your low (bad) moods rather than analyzing them, and you will see how quickly they vanish. Developing this skill will contribute substantially to healthy psychological functioning. The third principle is *separate psychological realities*. Because each person thinks in a unique way, everyone lives in a separate psychological reality. Accept the idea that others think differently from you, and you will have much more compassion and fewer quarrels. As a result you will be happier. Also, if you accept the principle of separate realities, you will waste less time attempting to change people. At the same time, others will like you more, thus contributing to your happiness.

The fourth principle of psychological functioning is *feelings*. Combined with emotions, feelings are a built-in feedback mechanism that tells us how we are doing psychologically. If your feelings turn negative suddenly, you know that your thinking is dysfunctional. It is then time to make a mental readjustment. If you feel discontented, for example, it is necessary to clear the head and start thinking positively. As a consequence, you will experience contentment and happiness. A key point is that the person will maintain a sense of well-being as long as he or she does not focus on personal concerns.

The fifth principle is *the present moment*. Learning to pay attention to the present moment and to your feelings enables people to live at peak efficiency, without the distraction of negative thinking. Much like the flow experience, the present moment is where people find happiness and inner peace. Carlson advises, "The only way to experience genuine and lasting contentment, satisfaction, and happiness is to learn to live your life in the present moment."[21] (This supports happiness key number 5.)

Now that you have studied attitudes and activities that contribute to happiness, you are invited to do Human Relations Skill-Building Exercise 6-1. It is designed to bring about a state of happiness.

A PLANNED APPROACH TO FINDING A RELATIONSHIP

How many people have you heard complain about a poor social life because of circumstances beyond their control? Such complaints take various forms: "The women in this school are all unappreciative," "The men at my school don't really respect women," "There's absolutely nobody to meet at work," or "This is the worst town for meeting people."

Some of the people expressing these attitudes are systematic when it comes to handling business or technology problems. Under those circumstances they use the problem-solving method. But when it comes to their social lives, they rely heavily on fate or chance.

The approach recommended here is to use your problem-solving skills to improve your personal life. Whatever the problem, try to attack it in a logical, step-by-step manner. We are not ruling out the influence of emotion and feeling in personal life. We are simply stating that personal life is too important to be left to fate alone. With good fortune you might form a relationship with a stranger you meet at a rapid-oil-change-and-lubrication centre. Unfortunately, such good fortune is infrequent.

Too many people leave finding a new relationship to chance or to a few relatively ineffective alternatives. Too many unattached adults lament, "Either you go to a bar or you sit at home." In reality, both men and women can find dates in dozens of constructive ways. It is a matter of identifying some of these alternatives and trying out a few that fit your personality and preferences. See Exhibit 6-1 for more details.

An important consideration in searching for a relationship is to recognize when you are experiencing **quest fatigue**. This is the feeling of demoralization and disappointment that takes place when all our efforts at finding a date or mate fail.[22] When quest fatigue sets in, give yourself some time off from the search. Enjoy your activities without a partner, and revitalize yourself before resuming the quest.

Human Relations Skill Building

Exercise 6-1 Achieving Happiness

The following exercises will help you develop attitudes that contribute mightily to happiness.

1. **Start the day off right.** Begin each day with five minutes of positive thought and visualization. Commit to this for one week. When and how do you plan to fit this into your schedule?

   ____
   ____
   ____

2. **Make a list of five virtues you believe in.** Examples would include patience, compassion, and helping the less fortunate.

   ____
   ____
   ____

3. **Each week, for the next five weeks, incorporate a different virtue into your life.** On a simple index card, write this week's virtue in bold letters, such as "helping the less fortunate." Post the card in a prominent place. After you have completed one incident of helping the less fortunate, describe in about 10 to 25 words what you did. Also record the date and time.

   ____
   ____
   ____

4. **Look for good things about new acquaintances.** List three students, customers, or co-workers you have just met. List three *positive* qualities about each.

   ____
   ____
   ____

5. **List the *positive* qualities of fellow students or co-workers you dislike or have trouble working with.** Remember, keep looking for the good.

   ____
   ____
   ____

6. **Think of school assignments or job tasks you *dislike*, and write down the *merits* of these tasks.** Identify the benefits they bring you.

   ____
   ____
   ____

7. **Look at problems as opportunities.** What challenges are you now facing? In what way might you view them that would inspire and motivate you?

   ____
   ____
   ____

Source: Adapted from Stu Kamen, "Turn Negative into Positive," *Pryor Report Success Workshop*, May 1995, pp. 1–2.

The steps to take after making contact with someone are not clear-cut. Some people recommend that you have at least two phone conversations before arranging a meeting. This advice is particularly applicable when you have not seen the person, as when meeting through an ad or introduction service, or through the internet such as through a chat room. It is generally recommended that the first date be informal and in a public place, such as meeting for coffee and dessert, or a glass of wine.

Susan Page, who runs singles workshops, recommends several actions to take after the initial meeting.[23] First, cast a wide net. "Most of your catches will be tossed back in the sea." Nevertheless, the more people you meet, the better the chances of one sharing your interests and values. Second, limit the first date to about one or two hours. Mention that you have a prior commitment. The limited time frame guards against the unpleasantness

Exhibit 6-1
In Search of a Date?

Every relationship begins with one person meeting another. In order to find one good relationship, you may need to date more than a dozen people. Next is a sampling of potentially effective methods for making a social contact.

HIGHLY RECOMMENDED

1. Participate in an activity that you do well and enjoy. For example, if you are a good Frisbee player, use Frisbee playing as a vehicle for meeting people.
2. Get involved in your work or another activity not logically related to dating. People naturally gravitate toward a busy, serious-minded person.* Besides, the workplace has now become the number one natural meeting place for singles.
3. Take courses in which the male–female ratio is in your favour, such as automotive technology for women and cooking for men.
4. Ask your friends for introductions and describe the type of person you are trying to meet—but don't be too restrictive.
5. Get involved in a community or political activity in which many single people participate. A good example is to become a political-party worker.
6. For men, join almost any formal singles group. The membership of these clubs is overwhelmingly female.
7. For women, join an armed forces reserve unit. The membership of these units is overwhelmingly male.
8. Take advantage of every social invitation to a party, picnic, breakfast, or brunch. Social occasions are natural meeting places.
9. Place a personal ad in a local newspaper or magazine, stating the qualifications you are seeking in a companion and how you can be reached. Personal ads have achieved such popularity that several national magazines now accept them. Personal ads are frequently integrated with voice mail. (You leave a voice message for the person who placed the ad.) Under many systems, your personal ad consists of a voice message to which people respond.
10. Participate in internet chat rooms (*cyberdating*). Many people rely on the internet as their exclusive method of finding romance. Chat rooms can be selected according to interests, including movie fans, gays and lesbians, and astrology believers. After exchanging emails or instant messages, the two people arrange for an in-person meeting. Many of the people you meet might live in a faraway location. Another problem is that many chat room participants badly misrepresent themselves, and a few have proved to be deranged sex criminals. Dating services on the internet are modestly priced and offer the advantage of sorting people out by geographic area.

11. Join special-promotion singles groups such as indoor tennis for singles or a singles ski weekend. Similarly, join singles groups associated with churches, temples, or mosques. Singles groups outside of religious institutions are also worth exploring.

AT LEAST WORTH A TRY

1. While networking for career purposes, also prospect for social companions.
2. Join an introduction (dating) service, particularly one that has an established reputation.
3. Shop at supermarkets from 11 p.m. to 2 a.m. You will frequently find other single people shopping at that time.
4. Spend a lot of time in laundromats and rapid-oil-change service centres.
5. Strike up a conversation while waiting in line for tickets at the movies or concerts.
6. Congregate, or float around, in large gatherings such as rallies for causes, registration for courses, or orientation programs.
7. Organize a singles party, and require each person invited to bring along an unattached person of the opposite sex—no regular couples allowed.
8. Find valid reasons for visiting other departments at your place of work. Chance meetings at photocopying machines, for example, have allegedly spawned thousands of romances.

*Although these suggestions are primarily geared to meeting people of the opposite sex, these same principles will also apply to meeting people and making friends of the same sex.

of an uncomfortable first date. If the date is pleasant, you will look forward with strong anticipation to the next date. Third, screen for compatibility with what you are looking for in a relationship. Initial physical attraction is important, but also look for clues to the type of relationship the person is seeking. Talk about your own general opinions and desires in a relationship and see how your new prospective friend responds.

WHY PEOPLE ARE ATTRACTED TO ONE ANOTHER

As part of enriching social life, it is helpful to understand why people are attracted to each other. Understanding these forces may help in choosing a compatible person for a long-term relationship. Three different psychological explanations of why two people develop a strong attraction to each other are balance theory, exchange theory, and the need for intimacy. Attraction can also be attributed to chemical or hormonal reasons. All four of these explanations can apply in a given situation.

Balance Theory of Attraction

According to **balance theory**, people prefer relationships that are consistent, or balanced. If we are very similar to another person, it makes sense (it is consistent or balanced) to like that person. We are also attracted to similar people because they reinforce our opinions and values. It is usually reassuring and rewarding to discover that another person agrees with you or has similar values.[24]

Balance theory explains why we are eager to stay in a relationship with some people, but it does not explain why opposites often attract each other. People sometimes get along best with those who possess complementary characteristics. A talkative and domineering person may prefer a partner who enjoys listening. The explanation is that a dominant person needs someone to dominate and therefore might be favourably disposed toward submissive people.

Social Exchange Theory of Attraction

A long-standing explanation of why two people become a couple is **social exchange theory**, the idea that human relationships are based mainly on self-interest. This research shows that people measure their social, physical, and other assets against a potential partner's. The closer the match, the more likely they are to develop a long-term relationship.

Exchange theory has been able to predict the permanence of a relationship based on the way each partner feels he or she stacks up against the other. One study of 537 dating men and women found that partners who thought they were getting far more in exchange for what they were giving felt guilty and insecure. In comparison, those who believed they gave more than they got were angry.

The giving was mostly psychological. It included such things as being more physically attractive than the partner, kinder, or more flexible. The greater the imbalance, the more likely the couple was to split up; the more equitable the partners believed the exchange to be, the more likely they were to remain partners. A researcher on the topic of love offered this explanation of the findings just presented:

> It's terribly corroding if one person feels taken advantage of. And it is just as disturbing to feel you can take advantage of your partner.[25]

Need for Intimacy

For some, the balance and exchange theories of mutual attraction are too mechanical and logical. The psychologist David McClelland proposes instead that love is an experience seated in the nonrational part of the brain (the right side). People who believe that they are in love have a strong **need for intimacy**. This craving for intimacy is revealed in the thoughts of people in love who are asked to make up stories about fictitious situations. Their stories reveal a preoccupation with harmony, responsibility, and commitment, and a preference for a relationship that includes warmth and intimacy.

McClelland and his associates say that these themes show up repeatedly in many guises in the stories told by people who say they are in love. The same stories are told by people in situations where love feelings run high, such as just having seen a romantic movie.[26]

A Biochemical Explanation of Attractiveness

Another explanation of why certain people are attracted to one another is based on chemicals and specifically hormones. According to this theory, our hormones direct us to sense or screen potential mates. After the initial biochemical attraction, our conscious, psychological preferences—like, Does he enjoy action movies and golfing?—come into play. The interests and lifestyle preferences of the potential mate carry more weight after the initial attraction. While the biochemical factors are at work, the brain is processing the external clues people use to measure sex appeal. Among these personality factors are appearance, clothing, makeup, scent, body language, and voice.[27]

A more specific explanation of attraction between people is based on the presence of pheromones. These are chemical substances released by a person (or animal) to influence the behaviour of another member of the same species. A person who emits high doses of pheromones will therefore attract more partners. Conversely, we are physically attracted to people with high doses of pheromones.

The pheromone theory is particularly geared toward explaining why one person is strongly attracted to another person at first sight. After the initial physical attraction, however, other more rational factors (e.g., Is this person employed?) enter into the picture. Several companies sell cologne that allegedly contains pheromones, thus making it easier for you to attract Prince or Princess Charming. Because these "attractant" substances are considered cosmetics, and not drugs, they are free from government regulation. Buyer beware.

The Importance of Choosing a Partner Carefully

Having a plan for meeting a partner and understanding why people are attracted to each other should be regarded as helpful information for making the right choice. A principal problem in many poor relationships is that the couple used faulty judgment in choosing each other. Of course, it is difficult to be objective when choosing a partner. Your needs at the time may cloud your judgment. Many people have made drastic mistakes in choosing a spouse because they were lonely and depressed when they met the person they married. Being on the rebound from a relationship that went bad makes you particularly vulnerable.

The problem of mate selection is indeed complicated. Do you marry for love, companionship, infatuation, or all three? It has been pointed out that the success rate of the arranged marriages still practised in a few countries is about as good as that of nonarranged marriages. Since most people have only a limited amount of time to invest in finding the ideal mate, they are content to marry a good fit.

An in-depth study of 300 happy marriages provides a practical clue about mate selection. The most frequently mentioned reason for an enduring and happy marriage was having a generally positive attitude toward each other.[28] If you view your partner as your best friend and like him or her "as a person," you will probably be happy together. As obvious as it sounds, choose only a life partner whom you genuinely like. Some people deviate from this guideline by placing too much emphasis on infatuation.

Research about selecting the right partner emphasizes finding a mate with a similar *love story*. According to Robert J. Sternberg, love between people follows a story. To understand love, it is necessary to understand the stories that dictate our beliefs and expectations of love. These stories form in childhood and become the basis for romance in later life. The story indicates how people describe love. For example, a person who strongly agrees with the statement, "I believe that in a good relationship, partners change and grow together" tells a travel story (in the sense that the partners are taking a journey together). A person who agrees strongly with the statement, "I enjoy making sacrifices for the sake of my partner" believes in a sacrifice story.

Sternberg contends that the key to compatibility with a romantic partner is whether their stories match, such as two people believing the business story of love (i.e., marriage as a partnership with divided responsibilities). To determine if your story matches that of a prospective partner's, you would first have to study the many stories contained in the research about love stories.[29] Should you meet someone with an incompatible love story who would otherwise make an excellent mate, another option exists. You can learn to modify your stories until they fit. However, the change would have to be sincere and involve a different way of looking at love.

Human Relations Self-Assessment Quiz 6-2 gives you an opportunity to sample a love story analysis. The love story evaluated has proven to be a workable one for many

Human Relations Self-Assessment

QUIZ 6-2 What's Your Love Story?

Rate each statement on a scale from 1 to 9, with 1 meaning that it doesn't characterize your romantic relationships at all and 9 meaning that it describes them extremely well. Then average your scores for the story below. In general, averaged scores of 7 to 9 are high, indicating a strong attraction to a story, and 1 to 3 are low, indicating little or no interest in the story. Moderate scores of 4 to 6 indicate some interest, but probably not enough to generate or keep a romantic interest.

1. I believe that close relationships are partnerships.
2. I believe that in a romantic relationship, just as in a job, both partners should perform their duties and responsibilities according to their "job description."
3. Whenever I consider having a relationship with someone, I always consider the financial implications of the relationship as well.

Score: _______

A business story has several potential advantages, not the least of which is that the bills are more likely to get paid than in other types of relationships. That's because someone is always minding the store. Another potential advantage is that the roles tend to be more clearly defined than in other relationships. The partners are also in a good position to get ahead in terms of whatever they want.

One potential disadvantage occurs if only one of the two partners sees their relationship as a business story. The other partner may quickly become bored and look for interest and excitement outside the marriage. The story can also turn sour if the distribution of authority does not satisfy one or both partners. If the partners cannot work out mutually compatible roles, they may find themselves spending a lot of time fighting for position. It is important to maintain the option of flexibility.

Source: Robert J. Sternberg, "What's Your Love Story?" *Psychology Today*, July/August 2000, pp. 55, 57.

people. Also, see the Canada Today that follows about relationship trends in Canada. The message here is to recognize that when you are contemplating choosing a life partner, you are facing one of life's major decisions. Put all of your creative resources into making a sound decision.

WORKING OUT ISSUES WITHIN RELATIONSHIPS

People emotionally involved with each other often find themselves in conflict over a variety of issues, especially when they are emotionally dependent upon each other. Without conflict, relationships would be artificial.

Human relations specialists have formulated some ground rules for resolving the many types of conflicts that frequently occur in relationships. These rules supplement the techniques for conflict resolution presented in Chapter 9.

1. *Listen carefully and give feedback.* Many conflicts intensify because the people involved never stop to listen carefully to what the other side is trying to say. After listening to your partner's point of view, express your feelings about the issue. Expressing your feelings leads to more understanding than expressing your judgments. It is therefore preferable to say "I feel left out when you visit your mother" than to say "You're insensitive to my needs; look at the way you visit your mother all the time."

   To help improve understanding, provide mutual feedback. Although you may disagree with your partner, communicate your understanding: "From your point of view it's frivolous of me to spend so much money on bowling. You would prefer that I invest that money in baby furniture."
2. *Use more positive than negative behaviours during arguments.* A ten-year study of arguments between partners in relationships, involving hundreds of couples, supported several basic ideas about good human relations. Some negative emotions used in arguments are more toxic than others. At the top of the corrosive list are criticism, contempt, defensiveness, and stonewalling (withdrawing from a discussion). On the positive side, the team of researchers found that happy couples use five times more positive behaviours in their arguments than negative behaviours. One way to be positive is to use humour to ease the tension in an argument. The humour is considered an effort to mend the conflict.[30] To illustrate, Jennifer might be upset that her husband Larry spent most of his time at an office party they attended together talking to other women. On their way home, Jennifer said, "I don't know whether to be angry at you for flirting all evening or to compliment you for networking with every woman at the party sharp enough to have a future in business."
3. *Define the real problem.* What your partner or you grumble about at first may not be the real issue in the conflict. It will require mutual understanding combined with careful listening and sympathy to uncover the real problem. A man might be verbally attacking a woman's dress when he really means that she has gained weight. A woman might verbally attack a man's beer drinking when her real complaint is that he should be out in the yard raking leaves instead of sitting inside playing video games.

Canada Today

Changing Patterns in Conjugal Relationships

There is little doubt that times are changing and so are our love relationships. Data from the General Social Survey conducted in 1995 show some interesting trends. A comprehensive survey of 11,000 respondents aged 15 years and over remains one of the best sources for data on relationships. The survey collected statistics on all marital and common-law unions, separation (not the legal one), divorce, and the death of a partner, along with a wide range of background information.

Whether born in the 1920s or the 1960s, over 94 percent of all women, ranging in age from 30 to 69, have been in a marriage or common-law relationship. While the tendency to form unions has remained fairly constant, the real change is the choice of the relationship. Although marriage still accounts for the majority of relationships, common-law has become more popular and has become the most favoured type of first conjugal relationship for younger people. Of women aged 20–29, 52 percent started their conjugal lives with common-law partners, compared with only one percent of the women aged 60–69.

How does this newer and more popular type of first-time union fare over time? Well, according to the statistics, not as well as marriage. For example, in the 30–39 age group, 63 percent of those whose first relationship was common-law had separated by 1995, compared with 33 percent of those who had married first. In general, recent research shows that common-law relationships tend to be temporary and transitory, that they rarely transform into marriage, and that men are more likely to end this type of relationship. Women who have a better economic status are the least likely to marry a common-law partner. While choosing to live together over marriage may seem to be a better option, it appears that it is also the most temporary option.

This study, although one of the best and most comprehensive is 15 years old. Do these statistics apply today? Why or why not?

Source: Celine Le Bourdais, Ghyslaine Neill, and Pierre Turcotte with collaboration of Nathalie Bachon and Julie Archambault, "The Changing Face of Conjugal Relationships," *Canadian Social Trends*, Spring 2000, Statistics Canada, Catalogue No. 11-008.

4. *Don't hit below the belt.* The expression "below the belt" refers to something that is unfair. Some issues are just plain unfair to bring up in a marital dispute. When you are intimate with another person, you are bound to know one or two vulnerable areas. Here are two below-the-belt comments:

   > "You're lucky I married you. What other woman would have married a man who was so much of a loser that he had to declare bankruptcy?"
   >
   > "Don't complain so much about being mistreated. Remember, when I married you, you were down on your luck and had no place to live."

   Is anyone really as cruel as the above quotes would suggest? Yes, in the heat of a tiff between partners, many cruel, harsh things are said. If two people want to live harmoniously after the conflict, they should avoid below-the-belt comments.

5. *Be prepared to compromise.* For many issues compromise is possible. The compromise you reach should represent a willingness to meet the other person halfway, not just a temporary concession. On some issues the only compromise can be letting the other person have his or her way now, and waiting to have your turn later. Among such issues that cannot be split down the middle are whether to have children, whether to live in an apartment or a house, whether to go to Miami or London for a vacation, or

whether to run a kosher or nonkosher household. Several of these issues should be settled before marriage or living together, since no real compromise on the basic issue is possible in these instances.

6. *Minimize an accusatory tone*. You lessen the accusatory tone when you make "I" statements instead of "you" statements. The door to dialogue is opened when you make a statement such as, "I felt really disappointed when you did not call me to ask about how my promotion interview went." You shut off dialogue when you say, "You don't care about my happiness. You didn't even call to ask about how my promotion interview went."
7. *Use email as a substitute for face-to-face confrontations*. At times, a couple may be so emotionally charged that resolving conflicts face-to-face is not possible. To back off temporarily from the difficulty of in-person conflict resolution, it may be worthwhile to correspond through email, messaging, or hard-copy letters. While sending notes to each other, it is valuable to put down in writing what you think the other side is angry about. For instance, "You are ticked off at me because I think your family is intolerant of people who are not like themselves." After dealing with the conflict in writing, the couple may be calm enough to move on to a face-to-face discussion.
8. *Be alert to gender differences in communication style*. As will be described in more detail in Chapter 8, men and women tend to have differences in communication style. One example is that men are more likely to focus on objects and things, and thus will gloss over feelings. In contrast, women are more likely to focus on interpersonal relationships and are eager to communicate feelings. If a couple does face these forms of stereotyped behaviour, it is helpful not to devalue the other side for simply acting in a gender-appropriate way. In dealing with the differences just described, the man should not be angry with the woman for focusing too much on feelings and wanting open communication. The woman should not be angry with the man for being somewhat tightlipped about feelings. Instead, the partners should accept these gender differences and not expect major changes in communication style. As well, when not in a conflict situation, partners can help each other to overcome gender barriers in communication. The man can help the woman understand his discomfort with feelings, and the man can learn more about sharing feelings from the woman.

MEETING THE CHALLENGES OF BEING A DUAL-INCOME COUPLE

The number of couples in which both partners have full-time jobs continues to increase. In 1997, dual-earner families comprised over 61 percent of families. Two critical factors influencing this steady growth are women's career aspirations and the high cost of living. Housing, in particular, costs more today than in the past. Many families need two incomes to own their own home.

If the couple has children, women, more than men, may have the most difficulty trying to manage a home life and a work life. In families, women report more time stress than men, as they still are the primary caregivers in the home.[31] Mothers, in particular, who try to balance the demands of earning a paycheque while still maintaining a traditional homemaker role may feel especially stressed.[32] The division of labour in two-income families has virtually remained unchanged.[33] Women are still doing the bulk of home management and child management. Therefore, women in particular may have to learn new strategies and behaviours to manage this additional stress in their lives. Managing a home, children, and a career can be extremely stressful for the dual-income couple, and both partners need to take responsibility for the family. Even without children, two-income partners may experience stress as they try to balance work, home lives, and responsibilities.

It is challenging to run a two-income household in a way that will enhance the couple's personal life. In Chapter 9 we present information about using organizational support systems to help reduce work–family conflicts. Following are some suggestions that couples themselves can implement to increase the chances of a dual-income couple or family running more smoothly.

1. *Establish priorities and manage time carefully.* A major contributor to the success of a dual-income relationship is careful time management.[34] Each partner must establish priorities, such as ranking quality time together ahead of adding a community activity to the schedule. Or both partners might inform their employer of a certain date they would be taking as a vacation day to celebrate their wedding anniversary.
2. *Deal with feelings of competitiveness.* Feelings of competitiveness between husband and wife about each other's career often exist even when both have a modern outlook. Competitive feelings are all the more likely to surface when both parties are engaged in approximately the same kind of work. One man became infuriated with his wife when she was offered a promotion before he was. They had both entered the same big company at the same time in almost identical jobs. In contrast, the working couple with traditional views is less likely to have a problem if the husband outdistances his wife in career advancement.

   The familiar remedy of discussing problems before they get out of hand is offered again here. One partner might confess to the other, "Everybody is making such a fuss over you since you won that suggestion award. It makes me feel somewhat left out and unimportant." A sympathetic spouse might reply, "I can understand your feelings. But don't take all this fuss too seriously. It doesn't take away from my feelings for you. Besides, two months from now maybe people will be making a fuss over you for something."
3. *Share big decisions equally.* A distinguishing characteristic of today's two-income families is that both partners share equally in making important decisions about the domestic side of life. Under such an arrangement, neither has exclusive decision-making prerogatives in any particular area. One may make a decision without consulting the other over some minor matter (such as the selection of a plant for the living room). The other may make the decision the next time a plant is to be selected for inside the house. But on major decisions—such as relocating to another town, starting a family, or investing in the stock market or real estate—both partners collaborate.

4. *Divide household tasks equitably.* Many women who work outside the home rightfully complain that they are responsible for too much of the housework. As stated previously, they often have the equivalent of two full-time jobs. Under this arrangement, conflict at home is highly probable. The recommended solution is for the working couple to divide household tasks in some equitable manner. Equity could mean that tasks are divided according to preference or the amount of effort required. In one family, the husband might enjoy food shopping while the wife enjoys cleaning. Assignments could be made accordingly. Each couple should negotiate for themselves what constitutes an equitable division of household tasks.

5. *Take turns being inconvenienced.* In a very traditional family, the woman assumes the responsibility for managing inconvenient household tasks even if she, too, has a job outside the home. The underlying assumption may be that her work is less important than his work. For more modern couples, a more equitable solution is to take turns being inconvenienced. If Sue has to go to work late one day to be around for the plumber, Ted can go to work late when the dog has to be taken to the veterinarian. A working couple with children will frequently have to miss work because of a child's illness or accident, parent–teacher conferences, or school plays.

6. *Develop adequate systems for child care.* Any working couple with a young child or children will attest to the challenge of adequately balancing work and child demands. Imagine this scenario: Your spouse has already left for work, and you discover that your four-year-old child has a fever of 39°C. The childcare centre will not accept a sick child, nor will your neighbour who helps out occasionally. She fears contaminating her own children. The logical solution is to stay home from work, but you have a crucial work meeting scheduled for 11 a.m.

   One solution to dilemmas of this nature, and less serious problems, is to have a diverse support system. Make arrangements with at least three people, including relatives, who could help you out in an emergency. Retired people, for example, often welcome the challenge of helping out in an emergency.

7. *Share parenting roles.* A dual-income family functions best when both parents take an active interest in child-rearing. Mother and father have to regard spending extensive amounts of time with their child or children as an appropriate activity.

8. *Decide who pays for what.* Unfortunately, the problem of negotiating who pays for what arises for many two-income families. Many couples find that the additional expenses of being a working couple prevent them from getting ahead financially. Childcare expenses are often involved; restaurant meals become more frequent; and a second car is usually a necessity.

A division of income that minimizes conflict for many two-income families is to allocate some money for common expenses (such as rent or mortgage payments) and some money for personal expenses. The specific allocation of the latter does not have to be discussed with the partner. For instance, one partner is free to buy a new CD player with his or her personal money. But an item like new draperies would be a joint expense and a joint decision. Another helpful practice is to have one joint chequing account and two personal chequing accounts.

KEEPING YOUR RELATIONSHIP VIBRANT

One of the major challenges in personal life is to keep a relationship with a partner alive, healthy, and vibrant. For many people, relationships that begin with enthusiasm, rapport, and compatibility end in a dull routine or in splitting up. Human Relations Self-Assessment Quiz 6-3 pinpoints some of the symptoms of a relationship gone bad. Here we will describe major factors in achieving a mutually rewarding long-term relationship.

Keep Romantic Love in Proper Perspective

A speaker told an audience that you can tell you are infatuated with your partner if your heart begins pounding at a chance meeting with him or her. An 80-year-old in the audience responded, "I know just what you mean. The Mrs. and I have been married for 55 years, and that's exactly how I feel whenever I run into her downtown." This happy husband is an exception; although infatuation or romantic love is vital in getting a relationship started, it usually cools down within several years. When infatuation declines, instead of being disappointed, the couple should realize that the relationship has grown more mature and lasting.

A relationship counsellor observes that as full of rapture and delight as the first phase of a relationship is, it is essentially a trick of nature designed to bring us together. Nature knows that without the illusion of perfection, we might not choose each other. After the emotional bond is secure, nature lifts the veil.[35] To avoid discouragement and disillusionment, it is important to keep romantic love in proper perspective. It helps launch a relationship, but does not have to be kept at its initial high intensity for a relationship to endure. However, the spark should not be extinguished.

Another significant key to keeping romantic love in perspective is to review your expectations in the relationship. Over the years, the expectations for relationships have increased. People want more from marriage than in times past. Fifty years ago, for example, more people thought of a marriage as an institution primarily to raise a family and gain economic security. According to marriage therapist Rita DeMaria, many more people today want marriages to be gratifying and satisfying and intimate. When these expectations are not met, one or both partners may become discouraged.[36] In reviewing your expectations, you might decide that you have set the bar too high and are therefore creating the opportunity for disappointment.

Have Communication Sessions

Good communication is vital for creating and maintaining a loving relationship. Therefore, one way to keep a relationship alive is to hold formal communication sessions in which you tell each other almost anything on your mind. The topics can be both positive and negative. A man may want to tell his partner of something she did that he appreciated very much. Or a woman may want to talk about the way her partner offended her in public. Or a couple may want to discuss concerns about finances, a child, in-law relations, or anything else.

Human Relations Self-Assessment

QUIZ 6-3 Early Warning Signs of a Relationship in Trouble

You know your relationship is in trouble, and in need of revitalization, when several or more of the indicators below are present. The term "partner" refers to a spouse, boyfriend, girlfriend, or significant other.

- You observe that your partner has terrible table manners.
- You perceive that your partner is not as attractive or cute as you thought previously.
- The sound your partner makes with his or her teeth annoys you.
- Your conversation is confined to routine matters such as "Did you put gas in the car?" or "Why are you 15 minutes late?"
- A significant change in routine takes place, such as the partner calling every other day instead of at least once a day.
- You rarely plan ahead for social occasions, such as parties, dinner, or movies, but decide to go out at the last moment—such as making plans for Saturday night at 4 p.m. that day.
- You spend progressively less time together.
- You nitpick each other frequently, and all your partner's quirks begin to bother you.
- You touch each other less and less, including holding hands while walking or driving the car.
- Your fights are more frequent and last longer.
- Small tokens of affection, such as sending love notes, almost disappear.
- You rarely mention your partner favourably to a third party.
- You notice frequent criticisms including backhanded compliments such as, "You look nice today for a person with so little taste in clothing."
- You jump into binding commitments with little planning, such as having a baby, moving, or buying a house. (Quite often partners think that such major joint activities will save a sinking relationship.)
- You look for an opportunity to spend time with your friends, watching television, or surfing the internet rather than with your partner.
- You rarely look forward to spending time alone with your partner.
- Neither partner ever says "I love you" any longer.

Source: Several of the signs were collected from relationship experts by Elaine Gross, "Love on the Edge," Gannett News Service story, March 12, 1996, and from "The Relationship Quiz" used by Worldwide Marriage Encounter (undated).

A vital aspect of these sessions is that both facts and feelings are expressed. The statement "I am really afraid we are drifting apart" communicates much more than "You and I haven't been talking too much lately." The role play at the end of this chapter explores the type of communication that can keep a relationship thriving.

Communication sessions are also important because they can sometimes revive a failing relationship. This is true because communication breakdowns often lead to failed relationships. Typically, in the early stages of a relationship, the couple is keenly attuned to each other's thoughts and feelings. The partners look for small verbal and nonverbal signals of contentment and discontent in each other.

After the relationship seems secure, couples often replace the intense monitoring of the early stages with a nonrevealing style of communication. For example, the man and woman may mechanically say to each other, "How was your day?" or "Love ya." This shorthand style of communication obstructs the sending and receiving of messages that could indicate the relationship is in trouble.[37] Introducing communication sessions can make it possible for the couple to deal with subtle problems in the relationship.

Strive for Novelty in Your Relationship

An unfortunate aspect of many relationships is that they drift toward a routine. A married couple might go to the same place for vacation, meeting the same family and friends for years on end. A man dating a woman might call her every night at the same time. Or a couple's sex life may turn into a routine. Many people have suggested that you try pleasant surprises to keep your relationship vibrant and fun. Make up a list of your own, but here are a few ideas to jog your thinking:

- Ask your mate out for dinner on a *Monday* evening.
- Write your partner a poem instead of sending a commercial greeting card.
- Take up a new activity together in which you are both beginners (such as country dancing or scuba diving) and learn with each other.

Maintain a Nonpossessive Relationship

A **nonpossessive relationship** is one in which both partners maintain separate identities and strive for personal fulfillment, yet are still committed to each other. Such a relationship is based on interdependent love—love involving commitment with self-expression and personal growth.[38] A nonpossessive relationship does not mean that the partners have sexual relationships with other people.

A nonpossessive relationship is helpful because some people find the traditional form of marriage stifling. For example, many married people feel compelled to give up a hobby or interest because the partner does not share the interest. In a nonpossessive relationship, the couple can take many separate paths and pursue different interests and have friends of their own. Unfortunately, if couples pursue nonpossessive relationships too far, they can wind up drifting away from each other. The reason is that happy partners spend considerable time with each other enjoying shared activities. Each couple must find the right balance between maintaining separate identities yet spending sufficient time together to remain close.

collectively as **paralanguage**. These make up the remaining 38 percent of communication.[5] As a case in point, *how* you say "Thank you" makes a big difference in the extent to which your sense of appreciation registers. In **nonverbal communication** we use our body, voice, or environment in numerous ways to help put a message across. Sometimes we are not aware how much our true feelings colour our spoken message.

One problem of paying attention to nonverbal signals is that they can be taken too seriously. Just because some nonverbal signals (such as yawning or looking away from a person) might reflect a person's real feelings, that doesn't mean that every signal can be reliably connected with a particular attitude. Jason may put his hand over his mouth because he is shocked; Parmo may put her hand over her mouth because she is trying to control her laughter about the message; and Ken may put his hand over his mouth as a signal that he is pondering the consequences of the message. Here we will look at six categories of nonverbal communication. While we are dividing these types into discrete categories, be aware that usually these cues occur simultaneously. Much of the content below is based on North American studies that did not include cultural differences. Not all of these rules and examples will apply to all cultures.

The Environment around Us: Personal Appearance, Artifacts, and Time

Your external image plays an important role in communicating messages to others. Clothing and personal appearance constitute one of the most personal ways in which we state things about ourselves to others. Job seekers show recognition of this aspect of nonverbal communication when they carefully groom for a job interview. People pay more respect and grant more privileges to people they perceive as being well dressed and attractive. Furthermore, some research indicates that a favourable personal appearance leads to higher starting salaries and, later, salary increases.[6] In other words, we are judged by how we look, and projecting a positive image by paying attention to how we look is important.

Artifacts are the personal objects that we select and display to announce who we are and to personalize our environments. Artifacts also help to personalize and claim our space. Often personal areas are jammed with objects that are important to us and reflect our values, ideas, and beliefs. If an individual values home and family, pictures of family members and pets may be displayed. Religious individuals often decorate their homes and offices with religious symbols. A doctor may have her office decorated with pictures of all the babies she has delivered over several years. In residence, students decorate their rooms with objects that remind them of home, pictures of current musical groups, and other items that are important to them to personalize an often-drab room. The next time you are in an office of a teacher or other professional, see what artifacts are present and try to determine what this says about the person.

Also surrounding us, much as our physical space does, is time. **Chronemics** refers to how we perceive and use time. We use time to define identities, interaction, and even status.[7] In the fast-paced Western society, time is highly valued and therefore so is speed. We often talk about the fast pace of life and look for ways to manage this pace. We want faster computers, faster highways, faster food, and so on. Being used to this fast pace and the high value placed on time and speed can be frustrating for Westerners who visit other cultures that don't share this value.

Maintain a Differentiation of Self

Closely related to having a nonpossessive relationship is for each partner to achieve a reasonable degree of autonomy by maintaining a **differentiation of self**. The term refers to an individual who is secure and not desperate for signals of approval and affection from others. If you have a differentiation of self, you are not so subject to social pressures from your partner and other family members. Another key characteristic of a person with high differentiation of the self is that he or she is not highly judgmental and not obsessed with his or her place in the family hierarchy.[39] As a consequence, the person is not so demanding and can appreciate the reality that he or she does not dominate the partner's life. The person with self-differentiation can comfortably say, "I'm happy that you are going out to dinner with your co-workers. I'll use that time this evening for learning more about digital photography."

This sense of autonomy and laid-back nature makes the person easier to live with, thus avoiding some of the conflict over affection and control that takes place in many relationships. In turn, the relationship has a chance to remain more vibrant. A mildly detached person is easier to live with; however, the same caution about nonpossessive relationships is in order. If your differentiation of self and detachment are too pronounced, you will not participate in the closeness required of a vibrant relationship.

To further develop your sensitivity to keeping a relationship vibrant, do Human Relations Skill-Building Exercise 6-2.

Human Relations Skill Building
Exercise 6-2 Keeping Your Relationship Vibrant

The role-playing exercise described here will help you experience the type of communication and interaction required for keeping a relationship vibrant. As with any other role play, visualize yourself in the role briefly described. Try to develop the feel and the flavour of the person depicted.

The man in this relationship is becoming concerned that his wife does not enthusiastically participate in activities involving his family. He prefers that he and his wife spend their Sunday afternoons with his parents and other relatives. He thinks they are all loads of fun and cannot imagine why his wife is beginning to drag her heels about spending time with them. Twice in the last month she has come up with excuses for not going along with him to visit his folks on Sunday.

The woman in this relationship still loves her husband but thinks his preference for Sunday afternoons with his folks is unreasonable. She prefers to pursue her own interests on Sunday afternoons. She plans to confront her husband about the situation this evening.

Two people act out this role play for about five to ten minutes. Other members of the class can act as observers. Among the observation points will be: (1) How well did the couple get to the key issues? (2) How much feeling was expressed? (3) Do they appear headed toward a resolution of this problem?

According to Richard Carlson, the best way to achieve inner serenity (or happiness) is to follow the five principles of psychological functioning. First is thinking, which brings about feelings. Second is moods, including the idea that you can ignore bad moods. Third is separate psychological realities, meaning that each person thinks in a unique way. Fourth is feelings, which can be turned from negative to positive. Fifth is the present moment, which is where people find happiness and inner peace.

A good social life begins with finding the people you want to date. Such an important activity in life should not be left to chance or fate alone. Instead, use a planned approach that includes exploring many sensible alternatives.

Understanding why people are attracted to one another helps in choosing a compatible partner. The balance theory of attraction contends that people prefer relationships that

(continued)

are consistent or balanced, and therefore they are comfortable with people similar to themselves. According to social exchange theory, people seek relationships in which there is an even match of personal assets. A third explanation is that people are attracted to each other because their need for intimacy prompts them to fall in love. A fourth explanation is based on biochemistry, suggesting that our hormones direct us to sense or screen potential mates. After the initial biochemical attraction, our conscious, psychological preferences come into play.

Whatever the basis for attraction, choose a partner carefully. One factor in mate selection is choosing a person with a similar *love story,* or description of love.

To keep intimate relationships healthy, you should resolve issues as they arise. Suggestions for accomplishing this include: listen carefully and give feedback; define the real problem; avoid old wounds; don't hit below the belt; be willing to go the extra mile; and be alert to gender differences in communication.

Dual-income couples are subject to unique pressures. To sustain a good relationship, a two-income couple should consider these approaches: (1) establish priorities and manage time carefully; (2) deal directly with feelings of competitiveness; (3) share big decisions equally; (4) divide household tasks equitably; (5) take turns being inconvenienced; (6) develop adequate systems for child care; (7) share parenting roles; and (8) decide who pays for what.

Keeping a relationship vibrant is a major challenge. Among the strategies proposed to meet this goal are (1) keep romantic love in perspective; (2) have communication sessions; (3) strive for novelty in your relationship; (4) maintain a nonpossessive relationship; and (5) maintain a differentiation of self.

SUMMARY

Emotional intelligence generally refers to how effectively a person makes constructive use of his or her emotion. The four key components of emotional intelligence are

- self-awareness (understanding the self)
- self-management (emotional control)
- social awareness (includes empathy and intuition)
- relationship management (includes interpersonal skills)

The combination of biological endowment and training will enable most people to enhance their emotional intelligence.

Attitudes are complex, having three components

- cognitive (knowledge or beliefs)
- affective (emotional)
- behavioural (how a person acts)

Cognitive dissonance occurs when the three components are not consistent with each other. Attitudes are formed based on experience, including receiving instruction from another person, conditioning, and cognitions (the way we think about something). The trait of optimism versus pessimism influences attitudes strongly. A worker who maintains a genuine positive attitude will accrue many benefits, yet being too positive can have disadvantages.

Attitudes can be changed by reversing the process by which they were formed. Looking at the positive or negative aspect of a situation can also lead to attitude change. From the standpoint of management it is beneficial for employees to have positive attitudes

and job satisfaction. Organizational citizenship behaviour is highly valued by employers because such attitudes can lead to improved product quality and quantity.

A satisfying and rewarding personal life can help a person absorb a career setback and also contributes to a satisfying and rewarding career. Planning for happiness is somewhat under a person's control. A practical way of understanding happiness is that it is a by-product of having the spheres of life working in harmony and synchrony. For most people these spheres would be: (1) work and career; (2) interpersonal life, including romance; (3) physical and mental health; (4) financial health; (5) interests and pastimes; and (6) a spiritual life or belief system.

Contributors or keys to happiness are somewhat under a person's control. They include (1) giving priority to happiness; (2) experiencing love and friendship; (3) developing self-esteem; (4) working hard at things enjoyed; (5) appreciating the joys of day-to-day living; (6) being fair, kind, and helpful to others; (7) having fun; (8) coping with grief, disappointment, setbacks, and stress; (9) living with what you cannot change; (10) energizing yourself through physical fitness; and (11) satisfying your most important values.

QUESTIONS AND ACTIVITIES

1. After reading this chapter, do you believe a person can learn how to be happy?
2. What are some of the skills involved in being happy?
3. How do your "spheres of life" compare with those in Figure 6-1?
4. In this chapter you were told that the office has become the best place to meet a mate. In Chapter 11, you will be cautioned about the hazards of an office romance. How will you integrate these two opinions?
5. What is your reaction to the practice of having a third party conduct a background investigation of a prospective mate? Also, should the prospective mate be informed of the investigation after it is completed?
6. What do you perceive to be the advantages and disadvantages of finding a romantic relationship over the internet?
7. In Chapter 7, devoted to communication, you will be told that a problem with email is that it may not be well-suited to conveying feelings. In this chapter, email is recommended as a way of dealing with some of the emotional issues in a relationship. How do you reconcile this apparent contradiction?
8. When one person in a two-income couple loses a job, should that person be responsible for all the household chores? Explain your reasons.
9. Find a couple that has been together for 20 years or more. Ask them what they perceive to be the secret of their successful relationship. Share your findings with class members.

INTERNET SKILL BUILDER

Finding Romance on the Net

Search for five different methods of finding romance online. Evaluate which one of these methods offers the greatest promise of finding romance while minimizing the chance of being deceived by another person.

Log on to the **Companion Website** at **www.pearsoncanada.ca/dubrin** to access additional resources for this chapter.

CASE STUDY 6-1 HUMAN RELATIONS

The Love Lab

Psychologist John Gottman began his research on the quality of marital relationships 30 years ago. Since then, his University of Washington laboratory, called the "Love Lab," has focused on determining exactly what makes marriages thrive or fail. The conversation that follows is taken from the records of the Love Lab. Valerie, 24, and Mark, 25, have a young baby. They have recently moved, and both have new jobs.

VALERIE: (Laughter) We don't go that long without talking.

MARK: I know, I just start going stir-crazy.

VALERIE: The problem . . .

M: Huh?

V: . . . is, you told me that when you took the job as manager at Commonwealth that you'd come home in the afternoons and spend some time with us.

M: That's right, but I did not say that it would start in the first week when I'm trying to do two different jobs. I gotta get myself replaced. Right now, I'm not just a manager.

V: It's been three weeks.

M: Well, I just don't go out on the street and say, "Hey you. Want to sell insurance?" It's not that easy. There's two people in the program. One of them is probably gonna be hired within the next couple of weeks. But in the meantime it's tough. It's just the way it's gotta be.

V: I realize that.

M: Okay.

V: But.

M: At midnight when you get off work and you're all keyed up, I'm all worn out.

V: I realize that. That doesn't bother me that much, you going to sleep at night.

M: I'll just be starting to go to sleep and you'll go "Are you listening to me?" I'll be trying to stay awake . . .

V: I'm laughing about it usually. I'm not upset about it.

M: I don't know by then. I'm half out.

V: But now with me having a car, you'll be able to go to sleep early and get up with Stephanie a little bit. That's one of my big problems. I'm not getting any sleep. I don't get to sleep until two.

M: I've been getting up with her.

V: You've been real good about that.

M: Okay.

V: I guess I just wish that you didn't have to go in early.

M: Yeah, we don't get a whole lot of time together.

V: When I have the car, I can get out and get stuff then. I feel like I'm stuck at home and here you are . . .

M: I'll be able to meet you for lunch and stuff. I guess that wasn't any big problem.

V: It is a problem. It seems like we talk about it every day.

M: Yeah, we do.

V: That's about the only thing we really complain about.

M: Yeah. The last couple of nights I tried to take you out to the lake and look at the stars and stuff, so . . .

V: I know.

M: We just need to get used to our schedules.

V: That first week I was so, I was real upset 'cause it seemed like all I did was stay home with Stephanie all morning till three and just work all evening. I wasn't doing anything. It didn't seem like we had family gatherings every weekend. We never had time to go out, just the two of us.

M: I got a little surprise for the next weekend.

V: Yeah, it's always next weekend. It's never this weekend.

M: Eight weekends in a row.

V: I just went from not working at all and being home. We've both been through major job changes and all.

M: And I can't breathe.

V: But we're getting used to it and I feel so much better about going to work at three (o'clock), three-thirty now than I did that first week.

M: Um.

V: I just wish I had more time to do what I wanted to do. I, it's just being . . .

M: I'll be able to stay . . .

V: . . . a wife and mother.

M: . . . to stay at home during the days a little bit more. I'll have to go in early but then I can take a couple of hours off in the afternoons.

V: Do you have to go in early every day?

M: 'Cause there are things I need to do every morning.

V: I think you just like going in to your office.

M: You don't know a thing about it then. Randy was in there early every day, tell me why?

V: Yeah, but he was home at a decent hour too.

M: He stays out late.

V: Eight to eight or eight to nine every day.

M: Every day.

V: Now, then, I don't want you taking that job. You forget it.

M: No.

Questions

1. What evidence do you find in this transcript that Valerie and Mark have conflict and low levels of marital satisfaction?
2. What evidence do you find that Valerie and Mark have reasonably good marital satisfaction?
3. What recommendations can you offer Valerie and Mark to improve their relationship?

Source: John Gottman and Sybil Carrere, "Welcome to the Love Lab," *Psychology Today*, September/October 2000, pp. 44–45. Reprinted with permission.

CASE STUDY 6-2 HUMAN RELATIONS

The Very Positive Kelly Malibu

Kelly Malibu, twenty-seven, is the manager of Deco, a woman's store that features clothing with an art deco design. Deco is one of several specialty retail stores owned by Max and Mary Lowenstein. When the store opened three years ago, Malibu was hired as the manager. Max Lowenstein said, "Kelly was a wonderful fit. She had retailing in her blood, having worked at women's stores since age seventeen. She also had supervisory experience, and is so upbeat. Our one concern was that she might be too nice to be a tough boss when needed."

Malibu is responsible for merchandising. Twice a year she makes trips to New York to buy designs imported from Asia in bulk, and also purchases some clothing online. Malibu contends that the most difficult part of her responsibilities is dealing with employees and customers. "When I deal with vendors, things usually go pretty smoothly," she says. "The vendors are usually trying to please me. We sometimes haggle a little bit about price, but we can usually work out a deal. We have the occasional dispute about returning merchandise that we cannot sell. I know that some big retailers insist on a generous return policy."

"My attitude is that our vendors are themselves small outfits operating on slim margins. So I hate to cut too deeply into their profits. If I can't sell a few dresses at Deco unless we practically give them away, it's as much my fault as that of the manufacturer or distributor. I guessed wrong on what our clientele wants. Max and Mary don't agree with my philosophy 100 percent, but they do respect my right to manage the store as I see fit."

Malibu notes that keeping her store associates productive and happy can be a challenge. Deco Style has two full-time associates and three part-time associates. One challenge is that her part-time associates make frequent requests for a change of schedule to fit their personal life or school demands. A recent Victoria Day was a good example of this problem.

She says, "Victoria Day is usually one of our best days outside of the holiday season. So I wanted to make sure we had two part-time sales associates on board to supplement the two full-time associates." Three days before Victoria Day, Tracy, one of the part-timers, told her she had to complete a mammoth project for her computer science class so

she wouldn't be able to work that day. "My instinct was to tell Tracy that if she couldn't be here on Victoria Day, she could set sail for another job. Then I thought of my own experiences in college. A computer science project can suck up all your mental energy and make it difficult to concentrate on anything else. So I let Tracy off the hook.

"Kim, another one of our associates, said she would be out of town for her brother's wedding. She had given me two month's notice about the wedding, so I couldn't insist that she be here. Bruce, another one of our associates, said he couldn't work on Victoria Day because he would be running a marathon. My first thoughts were to tell Bruce that running a marathon was no excuse for missing work. However, as I thought it through I realized that completing a marathon would add considerably to Bruce's self-esteem. As a result, I simply wished Bruce the best of luck in the marathon. I know that Bruce appreciated my understanding.

"That left me with one sales associate, Nicki, who could work on Victoria Day. I made up for one of the missing sales associates with my mom, who isn't a bad last-minute substitute.

"My biggest hassle with customers is when they want to see the manager because of a dispute with the associate about a return. You know that quite often they bought the dress, blouse, or suit with the intention of using it for a special occasion, and then returning it for a full refund. I usually go along with the return as a way of building customer goodwill. But I have my limits. No returns when clothing has food or perspiration stains."

A good social life begins with finding the people you want to date. Use a planned approach that includes exploring many sensible alternatives. Understanding why people are attracted to one another helps in choosing a compatible partner. The balance theory of attraction contends that people prefer relationships that are consistent or balanced, and therefore they are comfortable with people similar to t themselves. According to social exchange theory, people seek relationships in which there is an even match of personal assets. A third explanation is that people are attracted to each other because their need for intimacy prompts them to fall in love. A fourth explanation is based on biochemistry, suggesting that our hormones direct us to sense or screen potential mates. To keep intimate relationships healthy, you should resolve issues as they arise. Suggestions for accomplishing this include: listen carefully and give feedback; define the real problem; avoid old wounds; don't hit below the belt; be willing to go the extra mile; and be alert to gender differences in communication.

Dual-income couples are subject to many pressures. In order to sustain good relationships, these couples should consider some of these approaches: establish priorities and manage time; deal directly with feeling of competitiveness; share big decisions; take turns being inconvenienced; develop adequate systems for child care; share parenting roles; and decide who pays for what.

Keeping a relationship vibrant is a major challenge. Among the strategies proposed to meet this goal are keep romantic love in perspective, communicate, strive for some novelty in the relationship, maintain a non-possessive relationship, and maintain a differentiation of self.

Questions

1. In what way does Malibu demonstrate empathy?
2. In what way does Malibu demonstrate a positive attitude?
3. To what extent do you think Malibu would be a more effective manager if she were less empathic and positive?

Part 2 Dealing Effectively with People

Chapter 7

Communicating with People

Learning Outcomes

After studying the information and doing the exercises in this chapter, you should be able to

- explain the basic communication process;
- explain the relationship-building aspect of interpersonal communication;
- describe the nature and importance of nonverbal communication in the workplace;
- identify roadblocks to communication;
- know how to build bridges to communication;
- enhance your listening skills.

The president of a chain of sporting and athletic goods stores was touring several of the chain's stores located in one province. The chain itself was doing very well, but some stores were showing more profits than others. The president visited one store where profits had been consistently lower than elsewhere. While not contemplating closure of this location, the president was interested in an overall picture of it, including how it was being run, what the sales targets were, and what the possible problems were. The store's manager, who had requested a promotion to a larger store with more responsibilities, greeted the president. The president asked the manager, Dominique, about the possible reasons for the lack of profit at this location. Dominique replied, "Like, I'm not really sure. It's a really busy mall and it gets pretty crazy, if you know what I mean. Like, there's lots of reasons, eh? See where I'm coming from?" The president did not know where Dominique was coming from, but he knew one thing: Dominique was not going to get her promotion.

You may feel sorry for Dominique. After all, it was only one interaction. Maybe she was nervous. Yet one thing is very clear. Communication barriers can easily be created between yourself and key people in your organization. There are side effects for choosing the wrong communication style. Not communicating properly on and off the job can have serious consequences.

Communication is so vital that it has been described as the glue that holds organizations and families together. Most job foul-ups and marital tiffs are considered to be communication problems. ***Communication***, as the term is used here, is the sending and receiving of messages. Furthermore, to be successful in work or personal life, you usually have to be an effective communicator. You can't make friends or stand up against your enemies unless you can communicate with them. And you can't accomplish work through others unless you can send and receive messages effectively.

In this chapter we explain several important aspects of communication such as the communication process and overcoming various communication barriers. Many factors contribute to enhanced communication, leading in turn to more effective human relations. Explanation should also lead to skill improvement. For example, if you understand the steps involved in getting a message across to another person, you may be able to prevent many communication problems.

HOW COMMUNICATION TAKES PLACE

A convenient starting point in understanding how people communicate is to look at the steps involved in communicating a message. A diagram of how the process takes place is shown in Figure 7-1. The theme of the model is that two-way communication involves three major steps and that each step is subject to interference, or noise.[1]

Assume that Tony, a customer, wishes to inform Crystal, a used-car sales representative, that he is willing to make an offer of $5,500 on a used car. The price tag on the car is $8,000.

Step 1. *Encoding the Message* **Encoding** is the process of organizing ideas into a series of symbols, such as words and gestures, designed to communicate with the receiver. Word choice has a strong influence on communication effectiveness. The better a person's grasp of language, the easier it is for him or her to encode. Tony says, "Crystal, this car obviously is not in excellent condition, but I am willing to give you $5,500 for it."

Step 2. *Transmission over Communication Media* The message is sent via a communication medium, such as voice, telephone, paper, or email. It is important to select a medium that fits the message. It would be appropriate to use the spoken word to inform a co-worker that he swore under his breath at a customer. It would be inappropriate to send the same message through email. Many messages on and off the job are sent nonverbally, through the use of gestures and facial expressions. For example, a smile from a superior during a meeting is an effective way

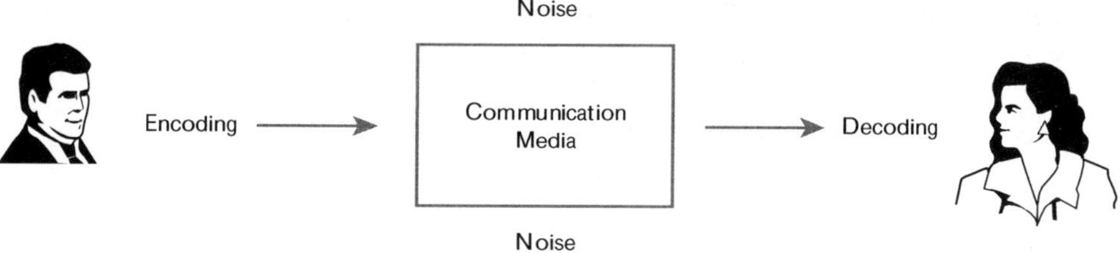

Figure 7-1 The Communication Process

of communicating the message, "I agree with you." Tony has chosen the oral medium to send his message.

Step 3. *Decoding* In **decoding**, the receiver interprets the message and translates it into meaningful information. Decoding is the process of understanding a message. Barriers to communication are most likely to surface at the decoding step. People often interpret messages according to their psychological needs and motives. Crystal wants to interpret Tony's message as saying that he is very eager to purchase this car. She may therefore listen attentively for more information demonstrating that he is interested in purchasing the car.

Decoding the message leads naturally to action—the receiver does something about the message. If the receiver acts in the manner the sender wants, the communication has been successful. If Crystal says, "It's a deal," Tony had a successful communication event.

Unfortunately, not all communication experiences are so successful. Many missteps can occur between encoding and decoding a message. **Interference**, or **noise**, often distorts or blocks a message and leads to misinterpretation by the receiver. If Tony has an indecisive tone and raises his voice at the end of his statement, it could indicate he is not really serious about offering a maximum of $5,500 for the car.

Noise is usually divided into three main types.[2] *Physical noise* is interference with the physical transmission of a message. An example would be trying to listen to someone in a loud and noisy restaurant. *Psychological noise* is interference inside a person that produces barriers in the decoding and processing of information, such as if you are distracted while trying to listen to someone. *Semantic noise* is interference created when the receiver does not decode the message as it was intended by the sender. If you do not know the meaning of a word, it makes it more difficult to decode the message.

A final note about this process. The diagram shows an arrow going one way from sender to receiver. Most communication between people is ongoing, with messages being sent back and forth. At any point, problems can occur in the process. These problems may be caused by interference as mentioned above. Psychological noise as well as other internal characteristics or problems can create many types of interference. Our thoughts, personalities, current physiological state, health, and other internal characteristics affect our encoding and decoding of messages. For example, have you ever found it hard to listen to someone when you have a really bad cold or have just received other disturbing information? Other sources of interference may be cultural differences, values, and beliefs. In some cultures people do not maintain eye contact during conversation.

HOW DOES INTERPERSONAL COMMUNICATION RELATE TO RELATIONSHIP BUILDING?

Another way of understanding the process of interpersonal communication is to examine how communication is a vehicle for building relationships. According to business communication professors Rich Sorenson, Grace De Bord, and Ida Ramirez, we establish relationships along two primary dimensions: dominate–subordinate and cold–warm. In the process of communicating we attempt to dominate or subordinate. When we dominate, we attempt to control communication. When we subordinate, we attempt to yield control, or think first of the wishes and needs of the other person. Dominators expect the receiver of messages to submit to them; subordinate people send a signal that they expect the other person to dominate.[3]

We indicate whether we want to dominate or subordinate by the way we speak or write, or by the nonverbal signals we send. The dominator might speak loudly or enthusiastically; write forceful messages filled with exclamation points; or gesture with exaggerated, rapid hand movements. He or she might write a harsh email message such as, "It's about time you started taking your job seriously and put in some real effort."

In the subordinate mode, we might speak quietly and hesitantly, in a meek tone, being apologetic. A subordinate person might ask, "I know you have better things on your mind than to worry about me, but I was wondering when I can expect my reimbursement for travel expenses?" In a work setting we ordinarily expect people with more formal authority to have the dominant role in conversations. However, in more democratic, informal companies, workers with more authority are less likely to feel the need to dominate conversations.

The cold–warm dimension also shapes communication because we invite the same behaviour that we send. Cold, impersonal, negative messages evoke similar messages from others. In contrast, warm verbal and nonverbal messages evoke similar behaviour from others. Getting back to the inquiry about the travel-expense check, here is a colder versus warmer response by the manager:

COLDER: Travel vouchers really aren't my responsibility. You'll just have to wait like everybody else.

WARMER: I understand your problem. Not getting reimbursed on time is a bummer. I'll follow up on the status of your expense check sometime today or tomorrow.

The combination of dominant and cold communication sends the signal that the sender of the message wants to control and to limit, or even withdraw from, a personal relationship. A team leader might say that she cannot attend a Saturday morning meeting because she has to go out of town for her brother's wedding. A dominant and cold manager might say, "I don't want to hear about your personal life. Everyone in this department has to attend our Saturday meeting."

Subordinate actions combined with warm communication signal a desire to maintain or build the relationship while yielding to the other person. A manager communicating in a warm and subordinate manner in relation to the wedding request might say, "We'll miss you on Saturday morning because you are a key player in our department. However, I recognize that major events in personal life sometimes take priority over a business meeting."

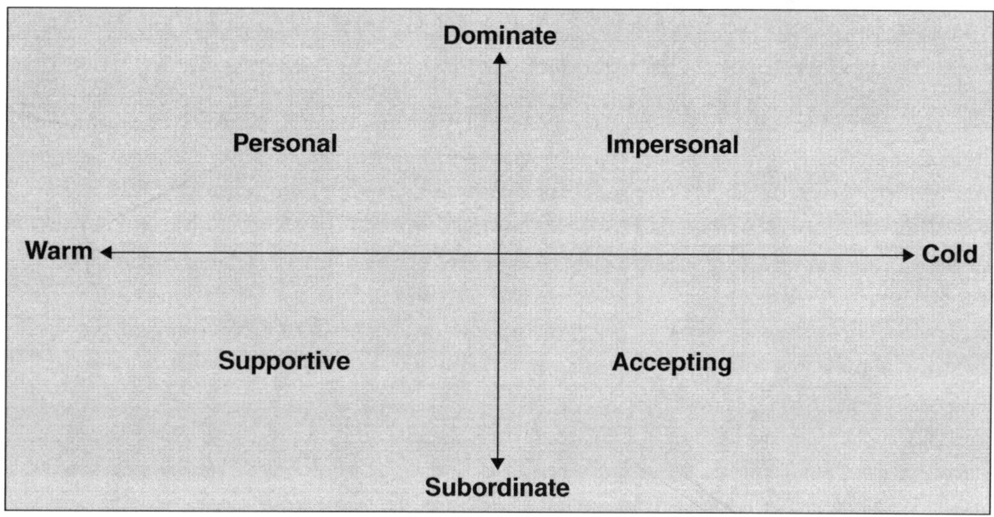

Figure 7-2 Communication Dimensions of Establishing a Relationship

Source: Adapted with permission from Rich Sorenson, Grace De Bord, and Ida Ramirez, *Business and Management Communication: A Guide Book*, 4th ed. (Upper Saddle River, NJ: Prentice Hall, 2001), p. 7.

Figure 7-2 summarizes how the dual dimensions of dominant–subordinate and cold–warm influence the relationship building aspects of communication. Rather than regarding these four quadrants of relationships as good or bad, think of your purposes. In some situations you might want to dominate and be cold, yet in most situations you might want to submit a little and be warm in order to build a relationship. For example, being dominant and cold might be necessary for a security officer who is trying to control an unruly crowd at a sporting event.

Observe that the person in the quadrant dominate–cold has an impersonal relationship with the receiver and the person in the warm–subordinate quadrant has a supportive relationship with the receiver. Being dominant and warm leads to a personal relationship, whereas being subordinate and cold leads to an accepting relationship. The combinations of dominate–cold and warm–subordinate are more likely to produce the results indicated.

NONVERBAL COMMUNICATION (SENDING AND RECEIVING SILENT MESSAGES)

So far we have been talking mostly about spoken communication. However, much of the communication among people consists of messages that are neither spoken nor written. These nonverbal signals are a critical part of everyday communication. According to Albert Mehrabian,[4] in the verbal communication of a message, only 7 percent of the meaning of a message is verbal content. This means that 93 percent of what we communicate to others is through nonverbal channels. Nonverbal behaviours (physical cues), for instance, account for 55 percent of our meaning. These include facial expressions, movement and gestures, territory and space, touch, and personal appearance, to name a few. Vocal cues, which include voice volume, tone, pitch, and intensity, are referred to

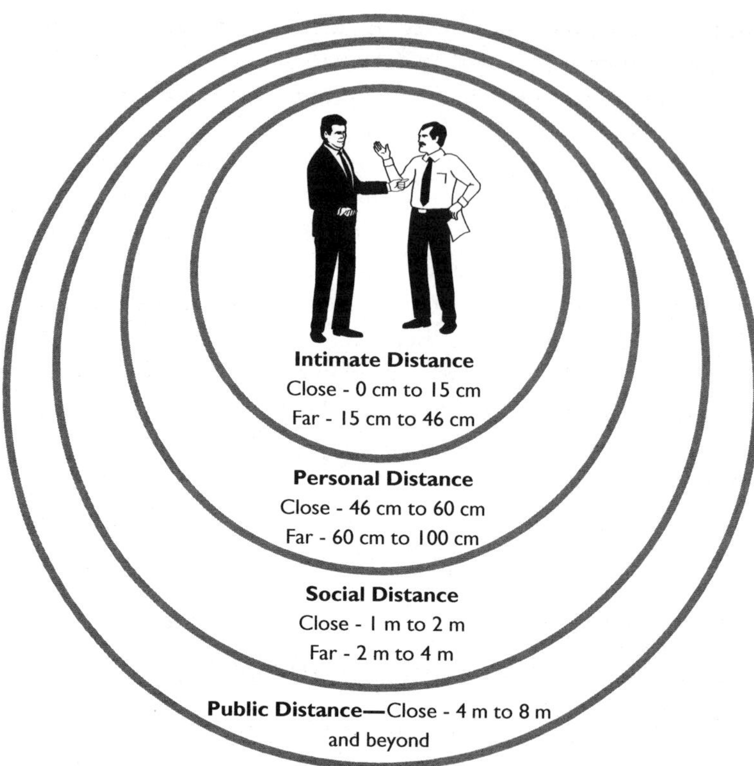

Figure 7-3 Four Interpersonal Distances

The Space around Us

All of us carry around an invisible bubble that is called our personal space. **Proxemics**, the study of spatial communication, was pioneered by Edward T. Hall.[8] Often, we are not aware of our invisible bubble until someone gets too close or does not get close enough. In fact, many of our sayings use space to demonstrate feelings. "Get out of my face," "too close for comfort," and "get off my back" are just a few of the statements that we use when people are overstepping their boundaries in a relationship. When people we do not know get too close, we feel uncomfortable and we will attempt to increase the distance to regain our comfort. According to Hall, there are four interpersonal distances or circles that correspond to types of relationships: intimate, personal, social, and public (see Figure 7-3).

Intimate Distance *Intimate distance* ranges from actual touching to 46 centimetres. This distance is for close and intimate relationships where touching is important. When strangers cross over into intimate distance, we feel threatened or very uncomfortable. For instance, in a crowded elevator, we do not look at each other and focus our eyes ahead on the floor numbers.

Personal Distance Within *personal distance*, your comfort zone is from 46 centimetres to a far range of one metre. Many of our friendly relations and friendly business relations stay in this zone. At 46 centimetres you can still touch a person, such as by shaking hands or patting backs, but the zone is less intimate.

Social Distance Ranging from one to four metres, *social distance* is the distance at which we conduct impersonal business and have less personal interaction. Conducting business across a desk is usually in this zone, and many office areas are designed to maintain this distance.

Public Distance *Public distance* ranges from four to eight metres and beyond—the outer limit being defined as the distance at which the speaker can no longer be heard. If someone is behaving in a bizarre manner, you will choose this as your safe distance because at this distance you can readily flee from a situation. Stage productions, lectures, and speeches are given using this distance.

These distances are general distances and are not always followed in interaction. For example, some cultures are more comfortable with closer contact. To illustrate, a French male is likely to stand closer to you than a British male, even if they have equally positive attitudes toward you.

Body Language: Posture, Gestures, and Movement

Think back to a time when you were really happy. Maybe it was the phone call that landed you a job you really wanted. What did you do after you hung up the phone? Some people literally jump up and down with joy! Your **body language** reflected your mood and feelings at that moment in time. Your posture can also indicate how you feel about yourself. People who walk and stand erectly, hold their heads up, and do not slouch appear calm and self-assured. On the other hand, people who shuffle along, slouch over, and keep their heads down appear to be unsure of themselves. Students who do not want to participate in a discussion often slouch over, look down, and avoid looking at the teacher. We also use posture to let others know whether or not we wish to interact. We may sit slightly forward and smile to invite interaction. Flirting signals our sexual or romantic interest to a prospective partner and involves postures and other nonverbal behaviours such as women swaying their hips and men swaying their pelvises.[9]

Related to posture are the nonverbal signals sent by standing versus sitting. Sitting down during a conversation is generally considered to be more intimate and informal than standing. If you do sit down while conversing, be sure to stand up when you wish the conversation to end. Standing up sends a message to the other person that it is time to leave. It also gives you the chance to be more attentive and polite in saying goodbye.[10]

Gestures are used to emphasize or replace verbal communication and are culturally determined. In North America, "thumbs-up" means "great" or "way to go," making an "o" with your thumb and forefinger means "OK," nodding your head up and down means "yes," and displaying your middle finger up is a gesture of aggressive contempt. To illustrate the cultural determination of gestures, the North American gesture for OK means a big zero in Germany and a part of female or male anatomy in Russia.[11]

Facial Expressions and Eye Contact

When used in combination, the head, face, and eyes provide the clearest indications of attitudes toward other people. Your face can assume a vast number of expressions, and much research has been devoted to the expression of emotion. Lowering your head and peering over your glasses, for instance, is the nonverbal equivalent of the expression, "You're putting me on." As is well known, maintaining eye contact with another person usually improves communication with that person. In order to maintain eye contact, it is usually necessary to correspondingly move your head and face. Moving your head, face, and eyes away from another person is often interpreted as a defensive gesture or one suggesting a lack of self-confidence. Would you lend money to someone who didn't look at you directly?

The face is often used as a primary source of information about how we feel. We look for facial clues when we want to determine another person's attitude. You can often judge someone's current state of happiness by looking at his or her face. The expression "sourpuss" attests to this observation. Happiness, apprehension, anger, resentment, sadness, contempt, enthusiasm, and embarrassment are but a few of the emotions that can be expressed through the face.

Voice Quality

More significance is often attached to the *way* something is said than *what* is said. A forceful voice with a consistent tone and no vocalized pauses connotes power and control. Closely related to voice tone are volume, pitch, and rate of speaking. Anger is noted when the person speaks loudly, with a high pitch and at a fast rate. Boredom is indicated by a monotone. A tip-off to joy is when the person speaks loudly with a high pitch and fast rate. Joy is also indicated by loud volume.

Avoiding an annoying voice quality can make a positive impact on others. The research of voice coach Jeffrey Jacobi provides some useful suggestions. He surveyed a sample of 1,000 American men and women, asking, "Which irritating or unpleasant voice annoys you the most?" The most irritating quality was a whining, complaining, or nagging tone.

Jacobi notes that we are judged by the way we sound. He also notes that careers can be damaged by voice problems such as those indicated in the survey. Jacobi continues: "We think about how we look and dress. And that gets most of the attention. But people judge our intelligence much more by how we sound than how we dress."[12] Human Relations Self-Assessment Quiz 7-1 provides more detail about his findings.

ROADBLOCKS TO COMMUNICATION

Communication rarely proceeds as swiftly or as effectively as we would like. Many different factors filter our message on its way to the intended receiver. In this section we will look at some of the human, rather than physical or mechanical, roadblocks to communication. If you are aware of their presence, you will be better able to overcome them.

Routine or neutral messages are the easiest to communicate. Communication roadblocks are most likely to occur when a message is complex or emotionally arousing, or clashes with the receiver's mental set. An emotionally arousing message would deal with such topics as a relationship between two people, or money. A message that clashes with a receiver's mental set requires that person to change his or her familiar pattern of receiving messages. The next time you order a meal in a restaurant, order dessert first and an entrée

Human Relations Self-Assessment

QUIZ 7-1 Voice Quality Checkup

Jacobi's study of voice quality (cited in the text) ranked voice quality, in decreasing order of annoyance, as follows:

- Whining, complaining, or nagging tone—44.0%
- High-pitched, squeaky voice—15.9%
- Mumblers—11.1%
- Very fast talkers—4.9%
- Weak and wimpy voice—3.6%
- Flat, monotonous tone—3.5%
- Thick accent—2.4%

Ask yourself, and two other people familiar with your voice, if you have one or more of the above voice-quality problems. If your self-analysis and feedback from others does indicate a serious problem, get started on self-improvement. Tape your voice and attempt to modify the biggest problems. Another avenue of improvement is to consult with a speech coach or therapist.

second. The server will probably not "hear" your dessert order because it deviates from the normal ordering sequence. The roadblocks or barriers described here are as follows:

1. Limited understanding of people
2. One-way communication
3. Different interpretation of words
4. Credibility of the sender and mixed signals
5. Distortion of information
6. Different perspectives and experiences
7. Emotions and attitudes
8. Communication overload
9. Improper timing
10. Poor communication skills
11. Cultural and language barriers

Limited Understanding of People

If you do not understand people very well, your communication effectiveness will be limited. To take a basic example, if you frame your message in terms of what can be done for you, you may be in trouble. It's much more effective to frame your message in terms of what you can do for the other person. Suppose a person in need of money wants to sell

Exhibit 7-1
A Short Course in Human Relations

- The six most important words are "I admit I made a mistake."
- The five most important words are "You did a good job."
- The four most important words are "What is your opinion?"
- The three most important words are "If you please."
- The two most important words are "Thank you."
- The one most important word is "We."
- The one least important word is "I."

Some people react negatively to this "short course" when they first read it. Among their reservations are that "It is corny," "It's so obvious; anybody with common sense knows that," or "Good for people in kindergarten." Yet if you put these seven rules into practice, you will find they do help overcome the communication roadblock called limited understanding of people. As one example, if you use "I" too frequently in your conversation, you will create communication roadblocks.

magazine subscriptions to a friend. Mentioning financial need is a very self-centred message. It could be made less self-centred:

- *Very self-centred:* "You've got to buy a few subscriptions from me. I can't meet my credit card payments."
- *Less self-centred:* "Would you be interested in subscribing to a few magazines that would bring you enjoyment and help you get ahead in your career? If your answer is yes, I can help you."

Limited understanding of people can also result in false assumptions about the receiver. The false assumption serves as a communication roadblock. A supervisor might say to a telemarketer (a person who sells over the phone), "If you increase sales by 15 percent, we will give you an outside sales position." When the telemarketer does not work any harder, the supervisor thinks the message did not get across. The false assumption the supervisor made was that the telemarketer wanted an outside sales position. What false assumptions have you made lately when trying to communicate with another person? Guidelines for helping a person overcome a limited understanding of people are presented in Exhibit 7-1.

One-Way Communication

Effective communication proceeds back and forth. An exchange of information or a transaction takes place between two or more people. Person A may send messages to person B to initiate communication, but B must react to A to complete the communication loop. One reason written messages (including email) fail to achieve their purpose is that the person who writes the message cannot be sure how it will be interpreted. One written message that is subject to many interpretations is "Your idea is of some interest to me." (How much is *some*?) Face-to-face communication helps to clarify meanings.

Instant messaging helps overcome the one-way barrier because the receiver reacts immediately to your message. An example: "You said ship the first batch only to good customers. What do you consider to be a *good* customer?" Ten seconds later comes the reply, "A good customer bought at least $4,000 worth of goods last year and is up to date on payments." Three seconds later, the first person writes, "Got it." Chat features of sites such as Facebook illustrate how much we often prefer two-way rather than one-way communication.

Different Interpretation of Words (Semantics)

Semantics is the study of the meaning and changes in the meaning of words. These different meanings can create roadblocks to communication. Often the problem is trivial and humorous; at other times, semantic problems can create substantial communication barriers. Consider first an example of trivial consequence:

> Two American first-time visitors to Montreal entered a restaurant for dinner. After looking over the menus, the husband suggested they order the shrimp cocktail entrées. He said to his wife, "A whole shrimp dinner for $9.95 Canadian is quite a deal. I guess it's because Montreal is a seaport." When the entrées arrived, the visitors were sadly disappointed because the entrées were the size of an appetizer.
>
> The husband asked the server why the entrées were so small in Montreal. With a smile, the server replied: "You folks must be Americans. In French-speaking countries the entrée is the beginning of the meal, like the word *enter*. In the United States it's just the reverse: the entrée is the main meal. Are you now ready to order your main meal?"

Of greater consequence is the experience of a trainer of airplane pilots who inadvertently contributed to a crash. As a rookie pilot navigated down the runway, the trainer shouted, "Takeoff power." The pilot shut off the engine and skidded off the runway. What the trainer really meant was to *use* takeoff power—a surge of energy to lift the airplane off the ground. He was using "takeoff" as an adjective, not a verb.

Credibility of the Sender and Mixed Signals

The more trustworthy the source or sender of the message, the greater the probability that the message will get through clearly. In contrast, when the sender of the message has low credibility, many times it will be ignored. Has someone ever lied to you? If so, the next time this person asked you to believe him or her, you probably had more trouble trusting what you were being told. He or she had lost some credibility and may have had to work to achieve it once again.

Communications can also break down as the result of a subtle variation of low credibility. The disconnect occurs from **mixed signals**—sending different messages about the same topic to different audiences. For example, a company might brag about the high quality of its products in its public statements. Yet on the shop floor and in the office the company tells its employees to cut corners whenever possible to lower costs. Another type of mixed signal occurs when you send a message to a person about desired behaviour yet behave in another way yourself. As a team leader, you might tell others that a tidy worker is a productive worker. However, your own cubicle contains a four-month supply of empty soft drink cans, and old papers consume virtually every square inch of your desk.

Distortion of Information

A great problem in sending messages is that people receiving them often hear what they want to hear. Without malicious intent, people modify your message to bolster their self-esteem or improve their situation. An incident that occurred between Danielle and her supervisor is fairly typical of this type of communication roadblock. Danielle asked her supervisor when she would be receiving a salary increase. Regarding the request as far-fetched and beyond the budget at the time, Danielle's supervisor replied, "Why should the company give you a raise when you are often late for work?"

Danielle heard her supervisor say, "If you come to work on time regularly, you will receive a salary increase." One month later Danielle said to her supervisor that she had not been late for work in a month and should now be eligible for a raise. Her supervisor replied, "I never said that. Where did you get that idea?"

Different Perspectives and Experiences

People perceive words and concepts differently because their experiences and vantage points differ. On the basis of their perception of what they have heard, many Latino children believe that the opening line of the "Star-Spangled Banner" is "José, can you see . . ." (note that few children have *seen* the U.S. national anthem in writing).

Cultural differences create different perspectives and experiences, such as workers from Eastern cultures having more respect for authority. A worker from India might more readily accept a message from the boss than would his or counterpart from British Columbia or Sweden. Generational differences also create different perspectives. An older person may express disapproval of a younger person texting at a family function whereas the person texting sees this as necessary communication with friends.

Emotions and Attitudes

Have you ever tried to communicate a message to another person while that person is emotionally aroused? Your message was probably distorted considerably. Another problem is that people tend to say things when emotionally aroused that they would not say when calm. Similarly, a person who has strong attitudes about a particular topic may become emotional when that topic is introduced. The underlying message here is try to avoid letting strong emotions and attitudes interfere with the sending or receiving of messages. If you are angry at someone, for example, you might miss the merit in what that person has to say. Calm down before proceeding with your discussion or attempting to resolve the conflict.

Improper Timing

Many messages do not get through to people because they are poorly timed. You have to know how to deliver a message, but you must also know when to deliver it. Sending a message when the receiver is distracted with other concerns or is rushing to get somewhere is a waste of time.[13] Furthermore, the sender may become discouraged and therefore will not repeat the message later.

The art of timing messages suggests not to ask for a raise when your boss is in a bad mood, or to ask a new acquaintance for a date when he or she is preoccupied. On the other hand, do ask your boss for a raise when business has been good. And do ask someone for a date when you have just done something nice for that person and have been thanked.

Communication Overload

A major communication barrier facing literate people is being bombarded with information. **Communication (or information) overload** occurs when people are so overloaded with information that they cannot respond effectively to messages. As a result, they experience work stress. Workers at many levels are exposed to so much printed, electronic, and spoken information that their capacity to absorb it is taxed. In meetings, some employees may be attending to text messages and emails on their cell phones, attempting to listen to a presentation, and trying to ignore the chatter of others. The problem is worsened when low-quality information is competing for your attention.[14] One example is a pop-up ad flashing in front of you informing that you have won a free i-phone, and all you have to do is follow a link to claim your prize. An influx of irrelevant emails, usually advertisements, can load up your email in-box and require time and effort to sort through and delete. The human mind is capable of processing only a limited quantity of information at a time.

Poor Communication Skills

A message may fail to register because the sender lacks effective communication skills. The sender might garble a written or spoken message so that the receiver finds it impossible to understand. Also, the sender may deliver the message so poorly that the receiver does not take it seriously. A common deficiency in sending messages is to communicate with low conviction by using wimpy words, backpedalling, and qualifying. Part of the same idea is to use affirmative language, such as saying "when" instead of "if." Also, do not use phrases that call your integrity into question, such as "to be perfectly honest" (implying that you usually do not tell the truth).[15] To illustrate, here are three statements that send a message of low conviction to the receiver: "I think I might be able to finish this project by the end of the week." "It's possible that I could handle the assignment you have in mind." "I'll do what I can."

Another communication skill deficiency that can serve as a communication barrier is to have a regional accent so strong that it detracts from your message. Your regional accent is part of who you are, so you may not want to modify how you speak. Nevertheless, many public personalities and salespeople seek out speech training or speech therapy to avoid having an accent that detracts from their message.[16]

Communication barriers can result from deficiencies within the receiver. A common barrier is a receiver who is a poor listener. Improving listening skills is such a major strategy for improving communication skills that it receives separate mention later in this chapter.

Cultural and Language Barriers

Communication barriers in work and personal life can be created when the sender and receiver come from different cultures and are not fluent in each other's language. Quite often cultural differences and language differences exist at the same time. An example of a cultural difference creating a barrier to communication often takes this form: A supervisor from a culture that emphasizes empowering (giving power to) employees is giving instructions to an employee from a culture that believes the boss should make all the decisions. In response to a question from the subordinate, the supervisor says, "Do what you think is best." The subordinate has a difficult time understanding the message because he or she is waiting for a firm directive from the boss.

A language communication barrier is sometimes amusing, such as a Canadian worker complimenting another by saying "You have been working like a dog" on this project. The second person might interpret the comment as suggesting he or she must be punished to work hard. The Canada Today below illustrates an amusing misunderstanding of the word "Canuck." At other times, language barriers cause accidents. Many foreign-language speaking construction workers in Canada encounter accidents because they do not clearly understand the instructions about danger.

To help overcome cultural and language barriers, many companies invest considerable time and money into cross-cultural training. In addition to learning more about another culture, many employees are able to enhance a second language in which they already have some proficiency.

Canada Today

Canuck or Not Canuck?

Although an older story, students still enjoy this one! A newspaper article in 1999 discussed the use of the word "Canuck" to describe Canadians. According to the article, a writer for a campus newspaper had used the word when referring to the large number of Canadians moving into American entertainment. The newspaper, *The Statesman*, is the paper at Indiana State University. Because of this incident and other prior incidents that were not reported, the writer was fired. However, the writer was rehired later after the editor received many letters from Canadians saying that they were not offended by the use of the term. Interestingly, Merv Hendricks, the university's director of student publications, had complained that the term was a derogatory label for French Canadians.

There appears to have been some confusion at the university as to what the term "Canuck" means and whether or not it is offensive or politically incorrect. As mentioned in the article, the Vancouver Canucks is one of our hockey teams. "Canuck" has been around for at least a century. Johnny Canuck was a cartoon character that appeared in papers in the 1860s. During World War II, he became a cartoon hero in comic books, protecting Canadians from the Nazi threat. If you are looking for Canadian content on the internet, many sites have "Canuck" in their address or title. There is even a Canuck site of the day! So is the label of Canuck offensive? It would appear that Canadians themselves use this term to describe much about their own country and the people who inhabit this nation. What do you think? Is this an offensive term or is it OK to call ourselves Canucks?

Sources: "'Canuck' No Slur, Editor Rehired," *Peterborough Examiner*, Sunday, February 28, 1999, reprinted with permission from the Associated Press; and Andrew Phillips, "Fear and Hope at Home: Social Changes Caused by WWII," *Maclean's*, June 6, 1994.

BUILDING BRIDGES TO COMMUNICATION

With determination and awareness that communication roadblocks and barriers do exist, you can become a more effective communicator. It would be impossible to remove all barriers, but they can be minimized. The following techniques are helpful in building better bridges to communication:

1. Appeal to human needs and time your messages.
2. Have an empowered attitude.
3. Repeat your message, using more than one channel.
4. Discuss differences in frames of reference.
5. Check for comprehension and feelings through feedback.
6. Minimize defensive communication.
7. Counter information overload.
8. Use mirroring to establish rapport.
9. Engage in small talk and constructive gossip.

Appeal to Human Needs and Time Your Messages

People are most receptive to messages that promise to do something for them. In other words, if a message promises to satisfy a need that is less than fully satisfied, you are likely to listen. The hungry person who ordinarily does not hear low tones readily hears the whispered message, "How would you like a pizza with everything on it?" Somehow, we have always been able to communicate this message to our class: "Unfortunately the class will not meet a week from today." We wonder to which need we have been appealing.

Timing a message properly is related to appealing to human needs. If you deliver a message at the right time, you are taking into account the person's mental condition at the moment. A general principle is to deliver your message when the person might be in the right frame of mind to listen. The right frame of mind includes such factors as not being preoccupied with other thoughts, not being frustrated, being in a good mood, and not being stressed out. (Of course, all this severely limits your opportunity to send a message!)

Have an Empowered Attitude

According to Sharon Lund O'Neill, professor of business education, a person's communication effectiveness is directly proportional to his or her attitude. The point is that a positive attitude helps a person communicate better in speaking, in writing, or nonverbally. *Empowerment* is involved here because the person takes charge of his or her own attitude.[17] Developing a positive attitude is not always easy. A starting point is to see things from a positive perspective, including looking for the good in people and their work. If your work is intrinsically motivating, you are likely to have a positive attitude. You would then be able to communicate about your work with the enthusiasm necessary. Figure 7-4 summarizes key ideas about persuasive communication, a topic most readers have most likely studied in the past.[18] If you can learn to implement most of the nine suggestions, you are on your way toward becoming a persuasive communicator. In addition,

Figure 7-4 Key Principles of Persuasive Communication

1. *Know exactly what you want.* Clarify ideas first in your own mind.
2. *Never suggest an action without telling its end benefit.* Explain how your message will benefit the receiver.
3. *Get a yes response early on.* It is helpful to give the persuading session a positive tone by establishing a "yes pattern" at the outset.
4. *Use powerful words.* Sprinkle your speech with words such as *bonding with customers*, and *vapourizing the competition.*
5. *Minimize raising your pitch at the end of sentences.* Part of being persuasive is to not sound unsure and apologetic.
6. *Back up conclusions with data.* You will be more persuasive if you support your spoken and written presentations with solid data, but do not become an annoyance by overdoing it.
7. *Minimize "wimp" phrases.* (As discussed earlier in this chapter.)
8. *Avoid or minimize common language errors.* Do not say "could care less" when you mean "couldn't care less," or "orientated" when you mean "oriented."
9. *Avoid overuse of jargon and clichés.* To feel "in" and hip many workers rely heavily on jargon and clichés, such as referring to their "fave" (for *favourite*) product, or that "At the end of the day," something counts.

you will need solid facts behind you, and you will need to make skillful use of nonverbal communication.

Repeat Your Message, Using More Than One Channel

In general, you can overcome roadblocks to communication by repeating your message several times. It is usually advisable to say the same thing in different ways so as to avoid annoying the listener with straight repetition. In any case, your message may not have been understood in its first form. If there is too much repetition, however, people no longer listen to the message. They think they already understand the message.

Repetition, like any other means of overcoming communication roadblocks, does not work for all people. Many people who repeatedly hear the message "Drinking and driving do not mix" are not moved by it. It is helpful to use several methods of overcoming roadblocks or barriers to communication.

A generally effective way of repeating a message is to use more than one communication channel. For example, follow up a face-to-face discussion with an email or telephone call or both. Your body can be another channel or medium to help impart your message. If you agree with someone about a spoken message, state your agreement and also shake hands over the agreement. Can you think of another channel by which to transmit a message?

Discuss Differences in Frames of Reference

Another way of understanding differences in perspectives and experiences is to recognize that people often have different paradigms that influence how they interpret events. A **frame of reference** is a model, framework, viewpoint, or perspective. When two people look at a situation with different paradigms, a communication problem may occur. For instance, one person may say, "Let's go to Montreal for the computer show." The other person may respond, "A ridiculous idea. It costs too much money and takes too much time. Besides, the company would never approve." These objections are based on certain unstated beliefs:

- Air travel is the most suitable mode of transportation.
- Travelling over 800 kilometres a day by auto is fatiguing and dangerous.
- Travelling over a weekend for business and using vacation days cannot be considered seriously.
- Paying for such a trip with personal money is out of the question.

The other person has a different set of unstated beliefs:

- It is possible, travelling on expressways and using two drivers, to cover 800 kilometres in one day.
- Travelling over a weekend and taking vacation days is sensible.
- Paying for the trip with personal money is a sound educational investment.

The solution to this communication clash is to discuss the differences in frames of reference. Both people live by different rules or guidelines. If the two people can recognize that they are operating with different frames of reference, the chances for agreement are improved. Keep in mind that people can change their frames of reference when the reasons are convincing.[19] For example, the first person in the preceding situation may never have thought about using personal funds for a trip as being an educational investment.

Check for Comprehension and Feelings through Feedback

Don't be a hit-and-run communicator. Such a person drops a message and leaves the scene before he or she is sure the message has been received as intended. It is preferable to ask receivers their understanding or interpretation of what you said. For example, you might say after delivering a message, "What is your understanding of our agreement?" Also use nonverbal indicators to gauge how well you delivered your message. A blank expression on the receiver's face might indicate no comprehension. A disturbed, agitated expression might mean that the receiver's emotions are blocking the message.

A comprehension check increases in importance when possible cultural and language barriers exist. A simple direct inquiry about comprehension is often effective, such as "Is what I said OK with you" or "Tell me what I said." A friendly facial expression should accompany such feedback checks, otherwise your inquiry will come across like a challenge.

In addition to looking for verbal comprehension and emotions when you have delivered a message, check for feelings after you have received a message. When a person speaks, we too often listen to the facts and ignore the feelings. If feelings are ignored, the true meaning and intent of the message are likely to be missed, thus creating a communication barrier. Your boss might say to you, "You never seem to take work home." To clarify what your boss means by this statement, you might ask, "Is that good or bad?" Your boss's response will give you feedback on his or her feelings about getting all your work done during regular working hours.

When you send a message, it is also helpful to express your feelings in addition to conveying the facts. For example, "Our defects are up by 12 percent [fact], and I'm quite disappointed about those results [feelings]." Because feelings contribute strongly to comprehension, you will help overcome a potential communication barrier.

Minimize Defensive Communication

Distortion of information was described previously as a communication barrier. Such distortion can also be regarded as **defensive communication**, the tendency to receive messages in such a way that our self-esteem is protected. Defensive communication is also responsible for people sending messages to make themselves look good. For example, when criticized for achieving below-average sales, a store manager might shift the blame to the sales associates in her store.

Overcoming the barrier of defensive communication requires two steps. First, people have to acknowledge the existence of defensive communication. Second, they have to try not to be defensive when questioned or criticized. Such behaviour is not easy because of **denial**, the suppression of information we find uncomfortable. For example, the store manager just cited would find it uncomfortable to think of herself as being responsible for below-average performance.

Defensive communication sometimes takes the form of answering the wrong question. Being touchy about a particular issue, you might regard a request for information as a criticism. David's manager might say to him, "Have you collected the data yet that we need for the trade show?" Angrily defensive because he feels criticized, David might say, "You know that I'm covering for two employees who are out ill." If he had simply said no, the boss might have said, "Oh, I just wanted to offer my help."

Combat Information Overload

You will recall that a flood of information reaching a person acts as a communication barrier because people have a tendency to block out new information when their capacity to absorb information becomes taxed. You can decrease the chances of suffering from communication overload by such measures as carefully organizing and sorting information before plunging ahead with reading. Speed-reading may help, provided you stop to read carefully the most relevant information. Or you can scan through hard-copy reports, magazines, and websites looking for key titles and words that are important to you. Recognize, however, that many subjects have to be studied carefully if you are to derive benefit. It is often better to read a few topics thoroughly than to skim through lots of information.

Being selective about your email and internet reading goes a long way toward preventing information overload. Suppose you see an email message titled "Car Lights Left On in Parking Lot." Do not retrieve the message if you distinctly remember having turned off your lights or you did not drive to work. Email programs and internet search software are available to help users sort messages according to their needs. You can help prevent others from suffering from communication overload by being merciful in the frequency and length of your messages in email and texts. Also, do not join the ranks of pranksters who send loads of jokes on email, or be misled by those who prepare bogus websites that look authentic but are unofficial (and unreliable) sources of information.

Use Mirroring to Establish Rapport

Another approach to overcoming communication barriers is to improve rapport with another person. A form of nonverbal communication called **mirroring** can be used to establish such rapport. To mirror someone is to subtly imitate another's breathing pattern. If you adjust your own breathing rate to someone else's, you will soon establish rapport with that person. Mirroring sometimes takes the form of imitating the boss in order to communicate better and win favour. Many job seekers now use mirroring to get in sync with the interviewer. Is this a technique you would be willing to try?

Mirroring will take practice before it can contribute to overcoming communication barriers. It is a subtle technique that requires a moderate skill level. If you mirror (or match) another person in a rigid, mechanical way you will appear to be mocking that person. And mocking, of course, erects rather than tears down a communication barrier.

Engage in Small Talk and Constructive Gossip

The terms small talk and gossip have negative connotations for the career-minded person with a professional attitude. Nevertheless, the effective use of small talk and gossip can help a person melt communication barriers. Small talk is important because it contributes to conversational skills, and having good conversational skills enhances interpersonal communication. Trainer Randi Fredeig says, "Small talk helps build rapport and eventually trust. It helps people find common ground on which to build conversation."[20] A helpful technique is to collect tidbits of information to use as small talk to facilitate work-related or heavy-topic conversation in personal life. Keeping informed about current events, including sports, television, and films, provides useful content for small talk.

Being a source of positive gossip brings a person power and credibility. Workmates are eager to communicate with a person who is a source of not-yet-verified developments. Having such inside knowledge enhances your status and makes you a more interesting communicator. Positive gossip would include such tidbits as mentioning that the company will be looking for workers who would want a one-year assignment in Europe or that more employees will soon be eligible for stock options. In contrast, spreading negative gossip will often erode your attractiveness to other people.[21]

ENHANCING YOUR LISTENING SKILLS

Improving your receiving of messages is another part of developing better communication skills. Unless you receive messages as they are intended, you cannot perform your job properly or be a good companion. Listening is a particularly important skill for anybody whose job involves solving problems for others because you need to gather information in order to solve problems.

Another reason that improving employee listening skills is important is that insufficient listening is extraordinarily costly. Listening mistakes lead to reprocessing letters, rescheduling appointments, reshipping orders, and recalling defective products. Effective listening also improves interpersonal relationships because the people listened to feel understood and respected. Human Relations Self-Assessment Quiz 7-2 gives you the opportunity to think through possible listening traps you may have developed. The accompanying Human Relations in Practice illustrates how being a good listener can enrich the lives of others.

A major component of effective listening is being an active listener. The **active listener** listens intensely, with the goal of empathizing with the speaker. **Empathy** is simply understanding another person's point of view. If you know "where the other person is coming from," you will be a better receiver and sender of messages. Empathy does not necessarily mean that you sympathize with the other person. For example, you may understand why some people are forced to beg in the streets, but you may have very little sympathy for their plight.

A useful way of showing empathy is to accept the sender's figure of speech. This makes the sender feel understood and accepted. Also, if you reject the person's figure of speech by rewording it, the sender may become defensive. Many people use the figure of speech "I'm stuck" when they cannot accomplish a task. You can facilitate smooth communication by a response such as "What can I do to help you get unstuck?" If you respond with something like "What can I do to help you think more clearly?" the person is forced to change mental channels and may become defensive.[22]

As a result of listening actively, the listener can feed back to the speaker what he or she thinks the speaker meant. Feedback of this type relies on both verbal and nonverbal communication. Active listening also involves **summarization**. When you summarize, you pull together, condense, and thereby clarify the main points the other person communicates. Here are two examples of summarization statements:

> "What I heard you say during our meeting is that . . ."
>
> "As I understand it, your position is that . . ."

To be an active listener, it is also important to **paraphrase**, or repeat in your own words, what the sender says, feels, and means. You might feel awkward the first several times you paraphrase. Therefore, try it with a person with whom you feel comfortable. With some practice, it will become a natural part of your communication skill kit. Here is an example of how you might use paraphrasing:

OTHER PERSON: I'm getting ticked off at working so hard around here. I wish somebody else would pitch in and do a fair day's work.

YOU: You're saying that you do more than your fair share of the tough work in our department.

OTHER PERSON: You bet. Here's what I think we should be doing about it . . .

Human Relations Self-Assessment

QUIZ 7-2 Listening Traps

Communication specialists have identified certain behavior patterns that interfere with effective hearing and listening. After thinking carefully about each trap, check how well the trap applies to you: Not a Problem or Need Improvement. To respond to the statements accurately, visualize how you acted when you recently were in a situation calling for listening.

	Not a Problem	Need Improvement
1. Mind reader. You will receive limited information if you constantly think "What is this person really thinking or feeling?"	❑	❑
2. Rehearser. Your mental rehearsals for "Here's what I'll say next" tune out the sender.	❑	❑
3. Filterer. You engage in selective listening by hearing only what you want to hear. (Could be difficult to judge because the process is often unconscious.)	❑	❑
4. Dreamer. You drift off during a face-to-face conversation, which often leads you to an embarrassing "What did you say?" or "Could you repeat that?"	❑	❑
5. Identifier. If you refer everything you hear to your experience, you probably did not really listen to what was said.	❑	❑
6. Comparer. When you get sidetracked sizing up the sender, you are sure to miss the message.	❑	❑
7. Derailer. You change the subject too quickly, giving the impression that you are not interested in anything the sender has to say.	❑	❑
8. Sparrer. You hear what is said but quickly belittle or discount it, putting you in the same class as the derailer.	❑	❑
9. Placater. You agree with everything you hear just to be nice or to avoid conflict. By behaving this way, you miss out on the opportunity for authentic dialogue.	❑	❑

Interpretation

If you checked "Need Improvement" for five or more of the above statements, you are correct—your listening needs improvement! If you checked only two or fewer of the above traps, you are probably an effective listener and a supportive person.

Source: Reprinted with permission from *Messages: The Communication Skills Book* (Oakland, CA: New Harbinger Publications, 1983).

Human Relations Skill-Building Exercise 7-2 gives you an opportunity to practise your listening skills.

To help become an active listener, consider several additional suggestions. If feasible, keep papers and your computer screen out of sight when listening to somebody else. Having distractions in sight creates the temptation to glance away from the message sender. Avoid answering your cell phone unless you are anticipating an emergency call. At the start of your conversation, notice the other person's eye colour to help you establish

Human Relations Skill Building

Exercise 7-2 Active Listening

Before conducting the following role plays, review the suggestions for active listening in this chapter. The suggestions about paraphrasing the message are particularly relevant because the role plays involve emotional topics.

The Elated Co-worker. One student plays the role of a co-worker who has just been offered a promotion to supervisor of another department. She will be receiving ten percent higher pay and be able to travel overseas twice a year for the company. She is eager to describe full details of her good fortune to a co-worker. Another student plays the role of the co-worker to whom the first co-worker wants to describe her good fortune. The second worker decides to listen intently to the first worker. Other class members will rate the second student on his or her listening ability.

The Discouraged Co-worker. One student plays the role of a co-worker who has just been placed on probation for poor performance. His boss thinks that his performance is below standard and that his attendance and punctuality are poor. He is afraid that if he tells his girlfriend, she will leave him. He is eager to tell his tale of woe to a co-worker. Another student plays the role of a co-worker he corners to discuss his problems. The second worker decides to listen intently to his problems but is pressed for time. Other class members will rate the second student on his or her listening ability.

eye contact. (But don't keep staring at his or her eyes!) A major technique of active listening is to ask questions rather than making conclusive statements. Asking questions provides more useful information. Suppose a teammate is late with data you need to complete your analysis. Instead of saying, "I must have your input by Thursday afternoon," try, "When will I get your input?"

Be sure to let others speak until they have finished. Do not interrupt by talking about yourself, jumping in with advice, or offering solutions unless requested.[23] A final suggestion is not to smile continuously during your conversation. Although you may appear friendly, the smiling could also be interpreted as you not taking the other person seriously.[24]

Research with employees from a Swedish insurance company provides some evidence that listening skills can be improved. A small group of employees received 24 hours of training in reflective listening that involves empathizing with the listener and then paraphrasing what he or she said (as in active listening). A 27-year-old female undergraduate psychology student was paid to act as a customer in evaluations of the listening skills before and after training. She acted in the roles of (1) a customer who was waiting for the results of whiplash injury investigation and (2) a person who had been accused by her insurance agent of having staged a burglary. The student dealt with both the trained group and an untrained, or comparison, group. She rated the listening skills of the employees, using a scale provided by the experimenters.

Later, the employees were also rated on their listening skills based on audiotapes with actual customers. The judges this time were a group of 54 psychology students. The results of the study showed that training increased reflective listening and that these skills were transferred to work with live customers. However, training did not result in higher evaluations of their conversation skills.[25] The training in reflective listening provided some assistance to the insurance agents, even if their conversational skill did not appear to be better.

SUMMARY

Communication is the sending and receiving of messages. Therefore, almost anything that takes place in work and personal life involves communication. The steps involved in communication are encoding, transmission over a communication medium, and decoding.

Nonverbal communications, or silent messages, are important parts of everyday communication. Aspects of nonverbal communication include the environment; distance or space from the other person; body language; facial expressions and eye contact; and voice quality.

Many potential roadblocks or barriers to communication exist. These roadblocks are most likely to occur when messages are complex, emotional, or clash with the receiver's mental set. Communication roadblocks can result from limited understanding of people; one-way communication; semantics; low credibility of the sender and mixed messages; distortion of information; different perspectives and experiences; emotions and attitudes; improper timing; communication overload; poor communication skills, and cultural and language barriers.

Strategies to overcome communication roadblocks include appealing to human needs, timing your messages, and having an empowered attitude; repeating your message using more than one channel; discussing differences in frames of reference; checking for comprehension and feelings; minimizing defensive communication; combating information overload; using mirroring to establish rapport; and engaging in small talk and constructive gossip. Unless you receive messages as intended, you cannot perform your job properly or be a good companion. A major component of effective listening is to be an active listener. The active listener uses empathy and can feed back to the speaker what he or she thinks the speaker meant. Active listening also involves summarizing the speaker's key ideas and paraphrasing what the speaker says, feels, and means. Another major technique of active listening is to ask questions rather than making conclusive statements.

QUESTIONS AND ACTIVITIES

1. How can knowing the three major steps in communication help a person communicate more effectively?
2. Why is nonverbal communication so important for the effectiveness of a manager or sales representative?
3. Would you classify a handshake as a form of nonverbal communication? Explain your reasoning.
4. In what ways might an email message contain nonverbal communication?
5. How might instant messaging distract you while you are doing homework or other work on the internet? What are some suggestions that you might offer to reduce these distractions?
6. What barriers to communication typically exist in a classroom? What can be done to reduce these barriers?
7. Based on your own observations, identify a term or phrase that creates semantic problems.
8. During your next three work- or school-related phone calls, analyze what the people you speak to are doing right and wrong from the standpoint of telephone communication. Be prepared to report your findings to the class.
9. Why is a high level of face-to-face speaking skill very important for a successful business career?

INTERNET SKILL BUILDER

Infoplease offers some practical suggestions for improving your listening skills that both support and supplement the ideas offered in this chapter. Infoplease divides listening into three basic steps: hearing, understanding, and judging. Visit the site at www.infoplease.com/homework/listeningskills1.html.

Log on to the **Companion Website** at **www.pearsoncanada.ca/dubrin** to access additional resources for this chapter.

CASE STUDY 7-1 HUMAN RELATIONS

The Scrutinized Team Member Candidate

HRmanager.com is a human resources management firm that provides human resource services such as payroll, benefits administration, affirmative action programs, and technical training to other firms. By signing up with HRmanager, other firms can outsource part or all of their human resources functions. During its seven years of operation, HRmanager has grown from 3 to 50 employees and last year had total revenues of $21 million.

Teams perform most of the work, led by a rotating team leader. Each team member takes an 18-month turn at being a team leader. CEO and founder Jerry Clune regards the four-person new ventures team as vital for the future of the company. In addition to developing ideas for new services, the team members are responsible for obtaining clients for any new service they propose that Clune approves. The new ventures team thus develops and sells new services. After the service is launched and working well, the sales group is responsible for developing more clients.

As with other teams at HRmanager, the team members have a voice as to who is hired to join their team. In conjunction with Clune, the new ventures team decided it should expand to five members. The team posted the job opening for a new member on an Internet recruiting service, ran classified ads in the local newspaper, and also asked present employees for referrals. One of the finalists for the position was Gina Cleveland, a 27-year-old business graduate. In addition to interviewing with Clune and the two company vice presidents, Cleveland spent one-half day with the new ventures team, breakfast and lunch included. About two-and-one-half hours of the time was spent in a team interview in which Gina sat in a conference room with the four team members.

The team members agreed that Cleveland appeared to be a strong candidate on paper. Her education and experience were satisfactory, her résumé was impressive, and she presented herself well during a telephone-screening interview. After Cleveland completed her time with the new ventures team, Lauren Nielsen, the team leader, suggested that the group hold a debriefing session. The purpose of the session would be to share ideas about Cleveland's suitability for joining the team.

Nielsen commented, "It seems like we think that Gina is a strong candidate based on her credentials and what she said. But I'm a big believer in nonverbal communication. Studying Gina's body language can give us a lot of valuable information. Let's each share our observations about what Gina's body language tells us she is really like. I'll go first."

LAUREN: I liked the way Gina looked so cool and polished when she joined us for breakfast. She's got all the superficial movements right to project self-confidence. But did anybody else notice how she looked concerned when she had to make a choice from the menu? She finally did choose a ham-and-cheese omelet, but she raised her voice at the end of the sentence when she ordered it. I got the hint that Gina is not very confident.

I also noticed Gina biting her lips a little when we asked her how creative she thought she was. I know that Gina said she was creative and gave us an example of a creative project she completed. Yet nibbling at her lips like that suggests she's not filled with firepower.

MICHAEL: I didn't make any direct observations about Gina's being self-confident or not, but I did notice something that could be related. I think Gina is on a power trip, and this could indicate high or low self-confidence. Did anybody notice how Gina put her hands on her hips when she was standing up? That's a pure and clear signal of somebody who wants to be in control. Her haircut is almost the same length and style as most women who've made it to the top in Fortune 500 companies.

Another hint I get of Gina's power trip is the way she eyed the check in the restaurant at lunch. I could see it in her eyes that she really wanted to pay for the entire team. That could mean a desire to control and show us that she is very important. Do we want someone on the team with such a strong desire to control?

BRENDA: I observed a different picture of Gina based on her nonverbal communication. She dressed just right for the occasion—not too conservatively, not too far business casual. This tells me she can fit into our environment. Did you notice how well groomed her shoes were? This tells you she is well organized and good at details. Her attaché case was a soft, inviting leather. If she were really into power and control, she would carry a hard vinyl or aluminum attaché case. I see Gina as a confident and assertive person who could blend right into our team.

LARRY: I hope that because I'm last, I'm not too influenced by the observations that you three have shared so far. My take is that Gina looks great on paper but that she may have a problem in being a good team player. She's too laid back and distant. Did you notice her handshake? She gave me the impression of wanting to have the least possible physical contact with me. Her handshake was so insincere. I could feel her hand and arm withdrawing from me as she shook my hand.

I also couldn't help noticing that Gina did not lean much toward us during the roundtable discussion. Do you remember how she would pull her chair back ever so slightly when we got into a heavy discussion? I interpreted that as a sign that Gina does not want to be part of a close-knit group.

LAUREN: As you have probably noticed, I've been typing as fast as I can with my laptop, taking notes on what you have said. We have some mixed observations here, and I want to summarize and integrate them before we make a decision. I'll send you an email with an attached file of my summary observations by tomorrow morning. Make any changes you see fit and get back to me. After we have finished evaluating Gina carefully, we will be able to make our recommendations to Jerry [Clune].

Questions

1. To what extent are new ventures team members making an appropriate use of nonverbal communication to size up Gina Cleveland?
2. Which team member do you think made the most realistic interpretation of nonverbal behaviour? Why?
3. Should Lauren, the team leader, have told Gina in advance that the team would be scrutinizing her nonverbal behaviour? Justify your answer.

CASE STUDY 7-2 HUMAN RELATIONS

The Dental Floss Communication Challenge

Claudia Telfair has worked as a dental hygienist for five years in the same large dental practice in suburban Winnipeg, Manitoba. She treats patients about 25 hours per week. In her words, "If I work too much more than 25 hours per week I'm liable to get tendonitis and carpal tunnel syndrome. All that precision scraping takes a toll on my right hand, and to some extent on my left hand. Hovering over patients can also give me back pains, if I do it for too long each week.

"I feel that my work is so important that I am willing to put up with a little physical pain to help my patients have healthy teeth and gums."

"You would then say that the biggest frustration in your work is its physical demands?" asked the case researcher.

"I never said that. You said that," replied Telfair. "The part of my job with the biggest impact on the health of patients is getting across my message about healthy habits to prevent tooth decay and gum disease. I lecture my patients. I demonstrate how they should be brushing and flossing, and how they should use softwood plaque removers [such as Stim-u-Dents]. I give out samples.

"I do everything I can think of to convince my patients to take good care of their teeth and gums between cleaning appointments."

"What is so frustrating about what you have just described?"

"The frustration is that my patients don't seem to listen. They smile, they nod in agreement, and they pack the samples. Yet four months later when the patients return, it appears that most of them are engaging in the same old sloppy dental habits. They continue with superficial brushing with an old toothbrush instead of using an electric one. It looks like they forgot my message about using wooden plaque removers. Yet flossing is the least used preventive treatment of them all."

"When you ask patients why they neglect flossing between their cleaning appointments, what do they say?" asked the case researcher.

"I hear more excuses than you get from violators in traffic court," said Telfair. "Some of the typical excuses are that the patients forget, that they are too busy, and that flossing is too painful. A patient told me the other day that he dislikes flossing because the ritual is so ugly and weird."

"What do you tell the patients when you observe that they are not following your advice?"

"I usually just tell them that are doing a poor job of taking care of their teeth and gums. Also, I will usually give them more samples of floss and plaque remover so they will be reminded to do better. Sometimes I give them another brochure about an electric tooth brush.

"I guess you could say that I'm doing a much better job treating tooth and gum problems than preventing them."

Questions

1. What communication problems is Claudia Telfair facing in her role as a dental hygienist?
2. What communication errors might Telfair be making?
3. Offer Telfair a couple of suggestions to help her accomplish her goal of being more effective at preventing dental and gum problems, based on your knowledge of interpersonal communication.

Chapter 8
Developing Intercultural Competence

Learning Outcomes

After studying the information and doing the exercises in this chapter, you should be able to

- define culture;
- define beliefs and values;
- identify six major ways in which cultures differ from one another;
- identify barriers to effective intercultural communication;
- appreciate and understand gender differences in communication;
- identify and be able to practise various strategies to reduce cross-cultural barriers.

Leanne was very excited when she was chosen to fly to China to discuss the details of a tender that her company had succeeded in obtaining. The company that she worked for builds intricate measuring equipment used in mining and other geographic and geologic operations. As part of the marketing division, Leanne was to fly to China and meet with company officials for the final signing of all documentation and to become familiar with the company in China.

Leanne had learned in similar dealings elsewhere in Canada and the United States that the giving of a small gift when being treated to a meal is proper business etiquette. And she had brought an elegant gift wrapped in beautiful white and black paper just in case such an occasion arose. The contracts had all been signed, and she had done the necessary tours and become familiar with the operation, when, on her last evening she was invited out to dinner with Yen Lo, the owner, and his wife. Pleased with her gift of a carving done by a Canadian artist, she was surprised with the stony reception of her gift. The rest of the evening was not very pleasant. When Leanne returned home, she decided to approach an Asian friend of hers. When she told her about the gift, her friend suddenly interjected, "Oh my, you gave them a gift for mourning. We wrap gifts in black and white paper for those who have had a loved one die!"

Leanne made a common mistake when interacting with those from other cultures. She assumed that there were few differences between people with a North American upbringing and those with an Asian upbringing. People often assume that with technology, a global marketplace, and instant communication, differences between people are diminishing. And while this may be true in some cultures, this assumption may hurt future business. Cultures still have differences and work to maintain their own unique set of beliefs, ideas, and ways of doing things, including how to do business. Being part of a global economy and the global marketplace means that employees will need to be more aware of cultural differences and other issues in diversity. A competent employee would have researched China before landing at the airport. With some prior knowledge of cultures, Leanne would not have made such an embarrassing, and perhaps costly, mistake.

While many employees may have the opportunity to visit other countries, an extensive knowledge of cultural differences and diversity is also required in our own country. There is little doubt that Canada is a diverse nation. Canada is made up of people from diverse cultures with diverse lifestyles, and a wide range of needs and challenges. Human Relations Self-Assessment Quiz 8-1 will provide you with the opportunity to assess how ready you are to work in a culturally diverse environment.

Understanding and managing diversity and developing intercultural competence will help you become a better worker and better citizen, as many of your co-workers and clients will be very different from you. When you complete this chapter, you will have an increased depth of understanding and will be better prepared to manage the diverse relationships that you will undertake both on and off the job. The facts and statistics in Exhibit 8-1 illustrate the powerful changes that are occurring in our population with regard to cultural diversity.

Keep in mind that cultures include a number of different groups, peoples, and lifestyles, including individuals with a different sexual orientation, people of the opposite gender, people with different religious affiliations and beliefs, people with disabilities, people older or much younger, and other groups that are different from your own group. For the first part of this chapter, we will explore cultural differences. Then, the barriers to effective intercultural communication will be explored. The chapter will conclude with several strategies to assist in communicating with people from diverse backgrounds, including a special section on gender differences.

Human Relations Self-Assessment

QUIZ 8-1 Cross-Cultural Skills and Attitudes

Here are some skills and attitudes that various employers and cross-cultural experts think are important for relating effectively to co-workers in a culturally diverse environment.

	Applies to Me Now	Not There Yet
1. I have spent some time in another country.	✓	
2. At least one of my friends is deaf, blind, or uses a wheelchair.		✓
3. Currency from other countries is as real as the currency from my own country.	✓	
4. I can read a language other than my own.	✓	
5. I can speak a language other than my own.	✓	
6. I can write a language other than my own.	✓	
7. I can understand people who speak a language other than my own.	✓	
8. I use my second language regularly.	✓	
9. My friends include people of races different from my own.	✓	
10. My friends include people of different ages.	✓	
11. I feel (or would feel) comfortable having friends with a sexual orientation different from mine.	✓	
12. My attitude is that cultures different from my own are equally as good.	✓	
13. I would be willing to (or already do) hang art from different countries in my home.	✓	
14. I would accept (or have already accepted) a work assignment of more than several months in another country.	✓	
15. I have a passport.		✓

Interpretation: If you answered Applies to Me Now to 10 or more of the preceding questions, you most likely function well in a multicultural work environment. If you answered Not There Yet to 10 or more questions, you need to develop more cross-cultural awareness and the skills to work effectively in a multicultural work environment. Notice that being bilingual gives you at least five points on this quiz.

Source: Several ideas for statements in this quiz are derived from Ruthann Dirks and Janet Buzzard, "What CEOs Expect of Employees Hired for International Work," *Business Education Forum,* April 1997, pp. 3–7; and Gunnar Beeth, "Multicultural Managers Wanted," *Management Review,* May 1997, pp. 17–21.

UNDERSTANDING CULTURE

Culture comes in many shapes and sizes. **Culture** can be defined as a learned and shared system of knowledge, behaviour, **beliefs,** attitudes, **values,** and norms. Culture in many ways refers to the lifestyle or way of living of a group. This system or way of life is shared by a group of people. Beliefs are the ways in which you structure your view or understanding of reality: what is true and what is false. For instance, you may have a religious belief

Exhibit 8-1
Canada Today

- The 2006 Census enumerated 6,186,950 foreign-born people in Canada. They accounted for virtually one in five (19.8%) of the total population, the highest proportion in 75 years.
- Recent immigrants born in Asia (including the Middle East) made up the largest proportion (58.3%) of newcomers to Canada. This was virtually unchanged from 59.4% in 2001. In contrast, in 1971, only 12.1% of recent immigrants for this period were born in Asia.
- Newcomers born in Europe made up the second largest group (16.1%) of recent immigrants. Europe used to be the main source region of immigrants. In 1971, they accounted for 61.6% of newcomers to Canada.
- In addition, an estimated 10.8% of recent immigrants were born in Central and South America and the Caribbean, up slightly from 8.9% in 2001. Another 10.6% of newcomers to Canada in 2006 were born in Africa, also up slightly from 8.3% in 2001.
- The Toronto, Montreal and Vancouver census metropolitan areas (CMAs) were home to 68.9% of the recent immigrants in 2006. In contrast, slightly more than one-quarter (27.1%) of Canada's total population lived in these three CMAs.
- Between 2001 and 2006, higher proportions of recent immigrants chose to settle in smaller CMAs. Fully 16.6% of newcomers in 2006 settled in the CMAs of Calgary, Ottawa–Gatineau, Edmonton, Winnipeg, Hamilton and London. In 2001, by comparison, 14.3% of newcomers lived in these CMAs.
- A majority (70.2%) of the foreign-born population in 2006 reported a mother tongue other than English or French. (Mother tongue is defined as the first language learned at home in childhood and still understood by the individual at the time of the census.)
- For the first time, allophones, that is, people whose mother tongue is neither English nor French, represented fully one-fifth of the population of Canada, according to the census. These include Aboriginal languages.
- Between 2001 and 2006, language groups from Asia and the Middle East recorded the largest gains. These language groups include the Chinese languages, Punjabi, Arabic, Urdu, Tagalog and Tamil.
- The 2006 Census reaffirmed the position of the Chinese languages as Canada's third most common mother tongue group, behind English and French.

Source: Statistics Canada, The Daily: *2006 Census: Immigration, citizenship, language mobility and migration,* 11-001-XWE Tuesday, December 4, 2007 http://www.statcan.gc.ca/daily-quotidien/071204/dq071204a-eng.htm

that Jesus was the son of God. Values are more enduring than beliefs and are central to who you are. They can be defined as a set of central and enduring goals in life and ways of living that you feel are important, right, and true. The belief in Jesus may be part of a much larger value that you have in Christianity as an important part in your life. Others may have different religious beliefs and a different religious value system. Religions are part of a cultural heritage for many people. Your cultural background and all the things that make up your culture affect how you communicate with others.

Your culture came from others around you as you grew up. Through a process of **enculturation**, culture is passed on or transmitted from one generation to another. We learn our culture through the teachings of our parents, teachers, peers, various institutions, and government agencies.[1] But as we come into contact with other cultures and other cultures come into contact with us, acculturation occurs. **Acculturation** is the process through which a person's culture is modified by contact with another culture. Through contact with people from other cultures—intercultural communication—our own beliefs, values, attitudes, and ideas may change. If we look at North American culture today, there are many examples of acculturation. Many of us undergo acupuncture, take part in karate and judo, enjoy East Indian foods, eat hot dogs and watch baseball, or other things that were not initially part of our "home culture." Intercultural communication can occur between many different types of cultures and co-cultures (cultures within a culture, such as women who are also Hindu). Communication can occur between different religions, different cultures, different races, different nations, different co-cultures, and different groups within a culture. However, we need to be aware that as we communicate with others from different cultures, we are always communicating from our own cultural perspective. For example, many Western women criticize the wearing of hijab by Muslim women due to their Western views. On the other hand, Muslim women who wear hijab believe that Western women are slaves to their appearance and see their own choice of dress as being more liberated. Both sides are expressing their beliefs based on their cultural perspective.

Dimensions of Cultural Differences

Although cultures can be very different, research has identified six dimensions (or facets) of cultural values that help us understand how cultures differ from one another.[2] In other words, various cultures value different types of behaviour.

Materialism versus Concern for Others Some cultures emphasize more materialistic values with an emphasis on assertiveness and the acquisition of money and material objects. It also means a de-emphasis on caring for others. At the other end of the continuum is concern for others, an emphasis on personal relations, and a concern for the welfare of others.[3] Materialistic cultures include Japan and Italy. Canada and the United States are considered to be moderately materialistic, as evidenced by the high participation rates in charities. Scandinavian countries all emphasize caring as a national value.

Formality versus Informality A country that values formality attaches considerable importance to tradition, ceremony, social rules, and rank. At the other extreme, informality refers to a casual attitude toward these same aspects of culture. Workers in Latin countries highly value formality, such as lavish public receptions and processions. Americans, Canadians, and Scandinavians are much more informal. Casual observation suggests that most of the industrialized world is becoming more informal through such practices as using only first names during business introductions.

Acceptance of Power and Authority People from some cultures accept the idea that members of an organization have different levels of power and authority. In a culture that believes in concentration of power and authority, the boss makes many decisions simply because he or she is the boss. Group members readily comply because they have a positive orientation toward authority, including high respect for elders. In a culture with less acceptance of power and authority, employees do not recognize a power hierarchy. They accept directions only when they think the boss is right or when they feel threatened. Cultures that readily accept power and authority include France, China, and India. Countries that have much less acceptance of power and authority are Canada and the United States and, particularly, the Scandinavian countries (e.g., Sweden).

Individualism versus Collectivism At one end of the continuum is individualism, a mental set in which people see themselves first as individuals and believe that their own interests take priority. Individualistic cultures emphasize the individual person and give priority to personal goals over the goals of the group. Members of society who value individualism are more concerned with their careers than with the goals of their employers. Western cultures such as those of the United States, Canada, and Great Britain emphasize the importance of individual goals and being responsible to oneself and one's immediate family.[4] Collectivistic cultures emphasize the importance of larger social groups, and individual identity is based on one's identity within a unit or group. Priority is given to group goals over personal or individual goals.[5] Members of a collectivist society are typically more concerned with the organization or the work group than with themselves. Japan and Mexico are among the countries that strongly value collectivism. Interestingly, some research indicates that African Americans tend to be more oriented to collective interests such as family than European North Americans.[6]

Urgent Time Orientation versus Casual Time Orientation Individuals and nations value time differently. People with an urgent time orientation perceive time as a scarce resource and tend to be impatient. People with a casual time orientation view time as an unlimited resource and tend to be patient. Americans are noted for their urgent time orientation. They frequently impose deadlines and are eager to get started doing business. Asians and Middle Easterners, in contrast, are patient negotiators. Many corporate workers and entrepreneurs engaged in international business recognize the importance of building relationships slowly overseas.

High-Context Cultures versus Low-Context Cultures Cultures differ in how much importance they attach to the surrounding circumstances, or context, of an event. People from a high-context culture place more emphasis on how something is said rather than what is said. (They emphasize nonverbal communication.) For example, a person from a high-context culture is not likely to take you seriously if you smile when you say that you do not like his or her service.

High-context cultures make more extensive use of body language as part of their emphasis on nonverbal communication. Some cultures, such as the Hispanic and African American cultures, are high context. In contrast, northern European cultures are low context and make less use of body language. The Anglo-American culture is considered to be medium-low context. People in low-context cultures seldom take time in business dealings to build relationships and establish trust.

Work Orientation versus Leisure Orientation A major cultural difference is the number of hours per week and weeks per year people expect to invest in work versus leisure or other nonwork activities. American and Canadian corporate professionals typically work about 55 hours per week, take 45-minute lunch breaks, and take two weeks of vacation. Japanese workers share similar values with respect to time invested in work. In contrast, many European countries have steadily reduced the workweek in recent years while lengthening vacations.

Multicultural Identities and the Cultural Mosaic

Another complexity about understanding cultural differences is that many people have multicultural identities because they identify with both their primary culture and another culture or cultures. As a consequence, these people may incorporate the values of two cultures. Young people develop a global identity that gives them a feeling of belonging to a worldwide culture. The feeling of belongingness enables them to communicate with people from diverse places when they travel, when others travel to where they live, and when they communicate globally using email and the telephone. Television, movies, and the internet also help us develop a global identity.

Further, according to this theory, people retain a local identity along with their global identity. Young people in India provide an apt example. The country has a rapidly growing high-tech sector led mostly by young people. Yet most of these well-educated young people still cling to local traditions, such as a marriage arranged by the parents and the expectation that they will care for their parents in old age.[7]

Another complexity of culture is that a person's country is but one cultural influence. For example, people from the upper-socioeconomic group within one country or ethnic group might value education and the use of grammatically correct speech more than people from a lower-socioeconomic group.

The fact of multicultural identities and different values among people from the same country and ethnic groups has recently been labelled the **cultural mosaic** by management professors Georgia T. Chao from Michigan State University and Henry Moon of Emory University. The cultural mosaic refers to an individual's unique mixture of multiple cultural identities that yields a complex picture of the cultural influences on that person. Rather than choosing a particular "tile" such as race, gender, or country of origin, people develop an identity based on a mix of smaller tiles.[8] Every reader of this book is probably an example of a cultural mosaic. One of thousands of possible examples is that one person could derive a cultural identity from being a (1) Canadian citizen, (2) Italian, (3) Buddhist, (4) male, (5) musician, (6) football player, (7) accountant, and (8) East Coaster.

The religious value part of the cultural mosaic often affects when people are willing to work or not work. One potential cultural clash is that the rights of an individual to freely practice and observe religious beliefs sometimes collide with company goals. Differences in religious practices must be recognized because the number of religions in the workplace has increased substantially.

Religious diversity can create problems as more companies move to 24/7 (around-the-clock, seven-days-per-week) schedules. Employers, therefore, need more flexibility from employees, yet religious beliefs often limit times at which employees are willing to work. The message for improved understanding is that employers must recognize workers' religious beliefs. At the same time, workers must understand the importance of a company meeting the demands of the marketplace, such as having 24-hour customer service support. Workers, for example, can trade off working on each others' religious holidays.

Applying Knowledge of Cultural Differences in Values

How might you use this information about cultural differences to improve interpersonal relationships on the job? A starting point would be to recognize that a person's national values might influence his or her behaviour. Assume that you wanted to establish a good working relationship with a person from a high-context culture. Make sure your facial expression fits the content of your words. For example, do not smile when, as a supervisor, you say, "No, you cannot take off tomorrow afternoon to have your French Poodle groomed." You would also want to emphasize body language when communicating with that individual. A related point is that people from high-context cultures are more likely to touch and kiss strangers. As Fernando, who was raised in the Dominican Republic and is studying in the United States, said, "In my country I hug people I meet for the first time. When I do it here, they think I'm very rude."

BARRIERS TO EFFECTIVE INTERCULTURAL COMMUNICATION

In a multicultural society, problems in communication are bound to happen as we attempt to communicate with those different from ourselves. It is not the struggle that occurs as we attempt to understand others' messages that creates true problems; it is the barriers that we consciously or even unconsciously erect. Here we look at several of the underlying factors that create problems in developing smooth cross-cultural relations. Not being aware of the type of barriers presented next blocks effective cross-cultural relations because such lack of awareness often leads to misunderstandings. The techniques presented in the following section of the chapter are designed to overcome some of these barriers.

Perceptual Expectations

Achieving good cross-cultural relations is hampered somewhat by people's predisposition to discriminate. They do so as a perceptual shortcut, much like stereotyping. The psychologist Diane Halpern explains how the process works: "Even if you have absolutely no prejudice, you are influenced by your expectations. A young-looking woman doesn't look like a corporate executive. If you look at the heads of corporations, they are tall, slender, white males. They are not fat. They are not in a wheelchair. They are not too old. Anything that doesn't conform to expectations is a misfit."[9]

Halpern made this comment several years ago, and it is still generally true. However, many women today occupy top-level positions in business, there are many overweight male executives, and many executives are old. Yet the message about perceptual expectations is important. We have to overcome this form of discrimination to enhance cross-cultural relations.

Positive expectations or stereotypes can also create some barriers to cross-cultural relations. Two company representatives were entertaining Sophie, a work associate from Jamaica. They assumed that because Sophie was black and Jamaican, she enjoyed dancing, so they invited her to a dance club. Sophie was a little taken aback and said, "What makes you think I like to dance? Not every Jamaican lady has natural rhythm." Similarly, on the job, we sometimes think that everybody from a certain national group has the characteristics of that group. For example, not all Chinese workers are methodical and precise, and have good eye–hand coordination and exceptional math skills.

Stereotypes, Prejudice, and Discrimination

Stereotypes are formed as part of the categorization process of perception. When we **stereotype**, we place people into categories or groups based on broad generalizations and assumptions that we perceive about a particular group. The problem with stereotypes is that we "lump" large numbers of people into the same category, often with a minimum of knowledge and experience about that particular category. For example, if you were to find out that Terri wears glasses, had extremely high marks during high school, and writes textbooks, you might categorize her as a "brain" or "nerd." Such an assumption would not be based on knowledge of all the other things that make up her personality.

Once we have a stereotype of a person, we tend to treat him or her according to this stereotype, and so our responses to that person become biased and limited. For example, if a sales associate has identified a prospective customer as "poor," the associate may not give the individual the same service he or she would have if the customer had been identified as "rich." When the sales associate notices the person browsing through a rack of reduced-price merchandise, this is used to support the stereotype of "poor." If we start to treat someone differently due to this stereotyping, we have developed a prejudicial attitude and may discriminate against members of this group. **Prejudice** is an unjustifiable negative attitude toward a group and its members; **discrimination** is the resulting unjustifiable negative behaviour based on this attitude.[10] Such behaviour may include verbal expressions of dislike, avoidance of group members, actual discriminatory practices such as excluding group members from certain activities or rights, and physical attacks.

Ethnocentrism

A key barrier to good cross-cultural relations is **ethnocentrism**, the assumption that the ways of one's culture are the best ways of doing things. Another part of ethnocentrism is to believe that our own way of living is essentially the only way. Most cultures consider themselves to be the centre of the world. One consequence of ethnocentrism is that people from one culture prefer people from other cultures similar to themselves. English people, therefore, would have more positive attitudes toward Australians than they would toward Mexicans. Despite this generalization, some countries that appear to have similar cultures are intense rivals. Many Japanese and Korean people dislike each other, as do the French and Belgians. In what way do you feel your country's way of doing something is the best?

Different Norms and Codes of Conduct

Norms are guidelines (usually unwritten) that govern the behaviour of members in a specific group. It should come as no surprise to you that different groups have norms that may differ from those of other groups. Also, what is permissible conduct in one group may be frowned upon and even punished in another group.

At times, we may also make the mistake of assuming that others are similar to us and then become confused when they act differently from our expectations. We may unknowingly insult others from a different culture or they may unknowingly insult us. If you are from a culture that highly values time such as the Austrians, the Swiss, or the English, you may feel anger when your new Italian acquaintance arrives 30 minutes late for a party. Since most Italians do not adhere to rigid time schedules for social events, you have just experienced a clash of different cultural norms.

Microinequities Many barriers to effective cross-cultural relations surface because a person is unaware that he or she is slighting another individual, according to Mary Row, a researcher on gender and racial differences. These slights are referred to as microinequities, as you may have studied in relation to interpersonal conflict. Understanding microinequities can lead to changes in one-on-one relationships that may profoundly irritate others.[11] For example, a manager was introducing a new office assistant to the group, mentioning the name of each member one by one. However, the manager omitted mentioning the name of the one Philippine American group member.

As part of a training program in understanding microinequities, the people who are slighted are taught to confront the issue rather than let resentment build. The Philippine Canadian worker might say tactfully to the manager, "Diane, the new assistant, was introduced to everybody but me. And I am the only Philippine in the department. Was this a coincidence?"

GENDER DIFFERENCES IN COMMUNICATION STYLE

Before we move on to discussing strategies for improving intercultural competence, we need to examine gender differences. If there are differences in how the genders communicate, an understanding of these differences will help us to communicate with the opposite sex. Despite the movement toward equality of sexes in the workplace, substantial interest has arisen in identifying differences in communication style between men and women. Interest in this topic was fuelled by the extraordinarily successful book *Men Are from Mars, Women Are from Venus*.[12] People who are aware of these differences face fewer communication problems between themselves and members of the opposite sex. As we describe these differences, recognize that they are group stereotypes. Individual communication styles are usually more important than group ones (men versus women). Furthermore, many research studies fail to show significant gender differences in communication style.[13] Here we will describe the major findings of gender differences in communication patterns.[14]

1. *Women prefer to use conversation for rapport building.* For most women, the intent of conversation is to build rapport and connections with people. It has been said that men are driven by transactions while women are driven by relations. Women are therefore more likely to emphasize similarities, to listen intently, and to be supportive.

2. *Men prefer to use talk primarily as a means to preserve independence and status by displaying knowledge and skill.* When most men talk, they want to receive positive evaluation from others and maintain their hierarchical status within the group. Men are therefore more oriented to giving a report while women are more interested in establishing rapport.
3. *Women want empathy, not solutions.* When women share feelings of being stressed out, they seek empathy and understanding. If they feel they have been listened to carefully, they begin to relax. When listening to a woman sharing these feelings, a man may feel blamed for her problems or that he has failed the woman in some way. To feel useful, the man might offer solutions to the woman's problem.
4. *Men prefer to work out their problems by themselves, whereas women prefer to talk out solutions with another person.* Women look on having and sharing problems as an opportunity to build and deepen relationships. Men are more likely to look on problems as challenges they must meet on their own. One communication consequence of these differences is that men may become uncommunicative when they have a problem.
5. *Men tend to be more directive and less apologetic in their conversation, while women are more polite and apologetic.* Women are therefore more likely to frequently use the phrases "I'm sorry" and "Thank you," even when there is no need to express apology or gratitude. Men less frequently say they are sorry, for the same reason they rarely ask directions when they are lost while driving: They perceive communications as competition, and they do not want to appear vulnerable.
6. *Women tend to be more conciliatory when facing differences, while men become more intimidating.* Again, women are more interested in building relationships, while men are more concerned about coming out ahead.
7. *Men are more interested than women in calling attention to their accomplishments or hogging recognition.* One consequence of this difference is that men are more likely to dominate discussion during meetings. Another consequence is that women are more likely to help a co-worker perform well. In one instance, a sales representative who had already made her sales quota for the month turned over an excellent prospect to a co-worker. She reasoned, "It's somebody else's turn. I've received more than my fair share of bonuses for the month."
8. *Men and women interrupt others for different reasons.* Men are more likely to interrupt to introduce a new topic or complete a sentence for someone else. Women are more likely to interrupt to clarify the other person's thought or offer support.
9. *Women are more likely to use a gentle expletive, while men tend to be harsher.* For example, if a woman locks herself out of the car she is likely to say, "Oh dear." In the same situation a man is likely to use a more "colourful" four-letter word. (Do you think this difference really exists?)

How can the information just presented help overcome communication problems on the job? As a starting point, remember that gender differences often exist. Understanding these differences will help you interpret the communications behaviour of people. For example, if a male co-worker is not as polite as you would like, remember that he is simply engaging in gender-typical behaviour. Do not take it personally.

A woman can remind herself to speak up more in meetings because her natural tendency might be toward holding back. She might say to herself, "I must watch out to avoid gender-typical behaviour in this situation." A man might remind himself to be more polite and supportive to co-workers. The problem is that, although such behaviour is important, his natural tendency might be to skip saying "thank you."

A woman should not take it personally when a male co-worker or subordinate is tight-lipped when faced with a problem. She should recognize that he may need more encouragement to talk about his problems than a woman would. If a man persists in not wanting to talk about the problem, the woman might say: "It looks like you want to work out this problem on your own. Go ahead. I'm available if you want to talk about it."

Men and women should recognize that when women talk over problems, they might not be seeking hard-hitting advice. Instead, they may simply be searching for a sympathetic ear so they can deal with the emotional aspects of the problem.

IMPROVING INTERCULTURAL COMMUNICATION AND FOSTERING UNDERSTANDING

Depending on where you choose to work, your contact with various cultures and groups will vary. If you work in a large urban centre, the cultural and ethnic diversity will be more pronounced than in a more rural setting. However, all settings will have a large diversity of groups. It is in your best personal and professional interest to learn skills that will help you communicate in this diverse nation. The methods and techniques for such improvement are outlined in Figure 8-1. Human Relations Skill-Building Exercise 8-1 may be a good way to start learning about another culture.

Methods and techniques

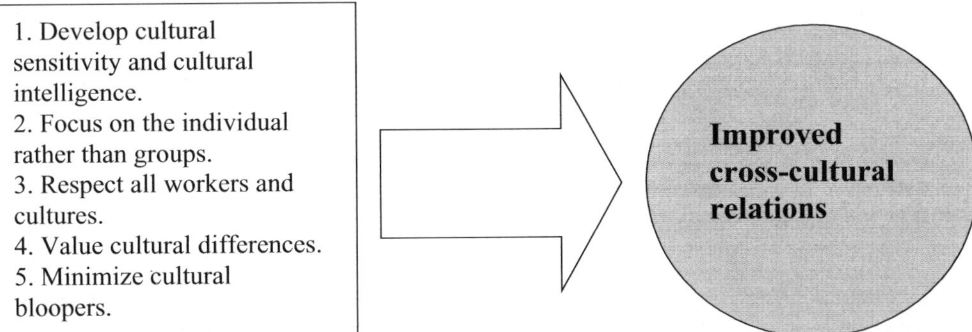

Figure 8-1 Improving Cross-Cultural Relations

Human Relations Skill Building

Exercise 8-1 A Plan for Learning

Identify a culture, race, or group that you have had very little experience with and limited knowledge about. Develop a plan that will help you learn the following things about this culture:

- How do they greet friends and strangers?
- What are some special holidays and celebrations?
- What is the structure of the family?
- What are the foods they typically eat and how do they organize their meals?
- Are there significant religious practices or rites of passage in this culture?

While these are only a few questions, you may want to add a few of your own. Where can you get this information? Consult the library or travel agencies, conduct personal interviews of members of this culture, telephone community associations, or try the internet. You may be surprised by what you learn, and you'll have developed at least one skill (knowledge) to help you adapt to diversity!

Develop Cultural Sensitivity and Cultural Intelligence

In order to relate well to someone from a foreign country, a person must be alert to possible cultural differences. When working in another country, one must be willing to acquire knowledge about local customs and learn how to speak the native language, at least passably. When working with people from different cultures, even from one's own country, the person must be patient, adaptable, flexible, and willing to listen and learn.

These characteristics mentioned are part of **cultural sensitivity**, an awareness of and a willingness to investigate the reasons why people of another culture act as they do.

A person with cultural sensitivity will recognize certain nuances in customs that will help build better relationships with people from cultural backgrounds other than his or her own. A culturally sensitive person will also recognize that humour does not easily translate from one culture to another, and that some types of humour might be offensive in another culture. Assume, for example, you are having lunch with a group of Japanese workers on a trip to Japan. You begin your joke with, "This old guy walks into a bar. . . . " The Japanese workers might take offense because older people are highly respected in Japan.

One approach to enhancing cultural sensitivity is to keep in mind the types of cultural differences mentioned throughout this chapter, even down to such details as holding a fork in your left hand when dining in England and India. Another approach is to raise your antenna and observe carefully what others are doing. Suppose you are on a business trip to a different region of your country and are invited to have dinner at the plant general manager's house. You notice that she takes off her street shoes on entering the house. You do likewise to establish better rapport, even if your host says, "Oh, please don't bother." It is obvious from your host's behaviour that she observes a "shoe code" in her house.

An advanced aspect of cultural sensitivity is to be able to fit in comfortably with people of another culture by observing the subtle cues they give about how a person should act in their presence. **Cultural intelligence (CQ)** is an outsider's ability to interpret someone's unfamiliar and ambiguous behaviour the same way that person's compatriots would.[15] (CQ refers to a cultural quotient.) With high cultural intelligence a person would be able to figure out what behaviour would be true of all people and all groups, such as rapid shaking of a clenched fist to communicate anger. Also, the person with high cultural intelligence could figure out what is peculiar to this group, and those aspects of behaviour that are neither universal nor peculiar to the group. These ideas are so abstract, that an example will help clarify.

> *A Canadian manager served on a design team that included two German engineers. As other team members floated their ideas, the engineers condemned them as incomplete or underdeveloped. The manager concluded that the Germans in general are rude and aggressive.*
>
> *With average cultural intelligence the Canadian would have realized he was mistakenly equating the merit of an idea with the merit of the person presenting it. The Germans, however, were able to make a sharp distinction between the two. A manager with more advanced cultural intelligence might have tried to figure out how much of the two German's behaviour was typically German and how much was explained by the fact that they were engineers.*

Similar to emotional intelligence, cultural intelligence encompasses several different aspects of behaviour. The three sources of cultural intelligence relate to the cognitive, emotional/motivational, and the physical, explained as follows:[16]

1. *Cognitive (the head).* The cognitive part of CQ refers to what a person knows and how he or she can acquire new knowledge. Here you acquire facts about people from another culture such as their passion for football (soccer in North America), their business practices, and their promptness in paying bills. Another aspect of this source of cultural intelligence is figuring out how you can learn more about the other culture.
2. *Emotional/motivational (the heart).* The emotional/motivational aspect of CQ refers to energizing one's actions and building personal confidence. You need both confidence and motivation to adapt to another culture. A man on a business trip to the Ivory Coast in Africa might say to himself, "When I greet a work associate in a restaurant, can I really pull off kissing him on both cheeks. What if he thinks I'm weird?" With strong motivation, the same person might say, "I'll give it a try. I kind of greet my grandfather the same way back in Canada."
3. *The body (physical).* The body aspect of CQ is the action component. The body is the element for translating intentions into actions and desires. Kissing the same-sex African work associates on both cheeks is the physical aspect previously mentioned. We often have an idea of what we should do, but implementation is not so easy. You might know, for example, that when entering an Asian person's home you should take off your shoes, yet you might not actually remove them—thereby offending your Asian work (or personal life) associate.

To practice high cultural intelligence, the mind, heart, and body would have to work together. You would have to figure out how you have to act with people from another culture; you would need motivation and confidence to change; and you would have to translate your knowledge and motivation into action. So when you are on a business trip to Tokyo, go ahead and bow when you are introduced to the plant manager.

Focus on Individuals Rather Than Groups

Understanding broad cultural differences is a good starting point in building relationships with people from other cultures. Nevertheless, it is even more important to get to know the individual rather than relying exclusively on an understanding of his or her cultural group. Instead of generalizing about the other person's characteristics and values (such as assuming that your Mexican American co-worker chooses to be late for meetings), get to know his or her personal style. You might find that this particular Mexican American values promptness and becomes anxious when others are late for a meeting. A consultant in the area of cross-cultural relations suggests that the best way to know individuals is to build personal relationships with people and not to generalize. [17]

Respect All Workers and Cultures

An effective strategy for achieving cross-cultural understanding is to simply respect all others in the workplace, including their cultures. An important component of respect is to believe that although another person's culture is different from yours, it is equally good. Respect comes from valuing differences, such as one person speaking standard English and the other favouring American Sign Language. Respecting other people's customs can translate into specific attitudes, such as respecting one co-worker for wearing a yarmulke on Friday or another for wearing an African costume to celebrate Kwanzaa. Another way of being respectful would be to listen carefully to the opinion of a senior worker who says the company should never have converted to voice mail in place of assistants answering the phone (even though you disagree). An aspect of respecting all workers is the importance of respecting the rights of majorities, including white males.

Another way of showing respect for all workers and cultures is to develop supportive peer relations in the workplace with people from different cultural groups. A supportive relationship includes a feeling of closeness and trust, the sharing of thoughts and feelings, and the feeling that one is able to seek assistance from another. Such respect in the form of support doubles in importance because the creativity advantage of a diverse group is more likely to surface when there is a supportive relationship among co-workers who differ demographically.

A major consequence of lack of respect is that it can lead to job discrimination intentionally or unintentionally. In 2006, the trendy retailer Abercrombie & Fitch settled sex discrimination and racial lawsuits. The company agreed to modify its well-known collegiate, all-American, mostly white, image by adding more African Americans, Hispanics, and Asians to its marketing materials. Abercrombie paid $40 million in fines, and agreed to hire 25 diversity recruiters and a vice president for diversity so that its hiring and promotion of minorities and women was in proportion to its applicant pool. The settlement also called for the company to increase diversity not only in hiring and promotions but also in advertisements and in catalogues.

When Abercrombie & Fitch was sued in June 2003, several Hispanic, African American, and Asian plaintiffs said that when they applied for jobs, they were steered toward backroom operations rather than sales positions.[18] If these charges were true, it would reflect lack of respect for the affected groups.

Value Cultural Differences

Recognizing cultural differences is an excellent starting point in becoming a **multicultural worker**, one who can work effectively with people of different cultures. More importantly, however, is to value cultural differences. The distinction goes well beyond semantics. If you place a high value on cultural differences, you will perceive people from other cultures to be different but equally good. Gunnar Beeth, an executive placement specialist in Europe, notes that you cannot motivate anyone, especially someone of another culture, until that person first accepts you. A multilingual sales representative has the ability to explain the advantages of a product in other languages. In contrast, a multicultural sales rep can motivate foreigners to make the purchase. The difference is substantial.[19]

A challenge in showing respect for other cultures is not to act revolted or shocked when a member of another culture eats something that lies outside your area of what is acceptable as food. Some westerners are shocked and repelled to find that some easterners eat insects, cats, horses, sheep's eyeballs, chicken soup containing the feet, and rattlesnakes. Some easterners are shocked and repelled to find that westerners eat a sacred animal such as cow and are surprised about popcorn.[20]

Other cross-cultural differences in customs also represent a challenge when trying to respect another culture. A Canadian might find it difficult to respect the Pakistani practice of having young children work in factories. In contrast, the Pakistani might find it difficult to respect the North American practice of putting old relatives in nursing homes and hospices. Sometimes it takes careful reflection on one's own culture to be able to respect another culture.

A current trend in valuing cultural differences, as well as showing respect, is to be mindful of the rights of gay, lesbian, bisexual, and transgender (GLBT) employees. A leading example is Eastman Kodak Company that has earned an award from the Human Rights Campaign, a gay rights organization. Kodak executives believe that providing equitable treatment toward gay employees makes its products more appealing to the 15 million domestic gay consumers who tend to be brand-loyal.[21]

Minimize Cultural Bloopers

An effective way of being culturally sensitive is to minimize actions that are likely to offend people from another culture because of differing values. Cultural bloopers are most likely to take place when you are visiting another country. The same bloopers, however, can also be committed with people from a different culture within your own country. To avoid these bloopers, you must carefully observe persons from another culture. Studying another culture through reading is also helpful.

Ecommerce and other forms of internet communication have created new opportunities for creating cultural bloopers. Website developers and content providers must have good cross-cultural literacy, including an awareness of how information might be misinterpreted. Here is a sampling of potential problems:

- Numerical date formats are often used for convenience. However, to an American, 4/9/01 means April 9, 2001 (or 1901!), whereas many Europeans would interpret the same numerical expression as September 4, 2001.

- Colours on websites must be chosen carefully. For example, in some cultures purple is the colour of royalty, whereas in Brazil, purple is associated with death.
- Be careful of metaphors that may not make sense to a person for whom your language is a second language. Examples include "We've encountered an ethical meltdown" and "Our biggest competitor is over the hill."

International business specialist Rick Borelli recommends communicating your message directly in your customer's native tongue for a competitive advantage.[22] The translator, of course, must have good knowledge of the subtleties of the language to avoid a blooper. An English-to-French translator used the verb *baiser* instead of *baisser* to describe a program of lowering prices. *Baisser* is the French verb "to lower," whereas *baiser* is the verb "to kiss." Worse, in everyday language, *baiser* is a verb that refers to having intimate physical relationships!

Keep two key facts in mind when attempting to avoid cultural mistakes. One is that members of any cultural group show individual differences. What one member of the group might regard as an insensitive act, another might welcome. Recognize also that one or two cultural mistakes will not peg you permanently as a boor. Human Relations Skill-Building Exercise 8-2 will help you minimize certain cultural bloopers.

Human Relations Skill Building

Exercise 8-2 Cultural Mistakes to Avoid with Selected Cultural Groups

Western Europe

Great Britain

- Asking personal questions. The British protect their privacy.
- Thinking that a businessperson from England is unenthusiastic when he or she says, "Not bad at all." English people understate positive emotion.
- Gossiping about royalty.

France

- Expecting to complete work during the French two-hour lunch.
- Attempting to conduct significant business during August—*les vacances* (vacation time).
- Greeting a French person for the first time and not using a title such as "sir" or "madam" (or monsieur, madame, or mademoiselle).

Italy

- Eating too much pasta, as it is not the main course.
- Handing out business cards freely. Italians use them infrequently.

Spain

- Expecting punctuality. Your appointments will usually arrive 20 to 30 minutes late.
- Making the American sign for OK with your thumb and forefinger. In Spain (and many other countries) this is vulgar.

(*continued*)

Scandinavia (Denmark, Sweden, Norway)

- Being overly rank-conscious. Don't expect Scandinavians to pay close attention to a person's place in the hierarchy.
- Introducing conflict among Swedish work associates. Swedes go out of their way to avoid conflict.

Asia

All Asian

- Pressuring an Asian job applicant or employee to brag about his or her accomplishments. Asians feel self-conscious when boasting about individual accomplishments. They prefer to let the record speak for itself. In addition, they prefer to talk about group, rather than individual, accomplishments.

Japan

- Shaking hands or hugging Japanese (as well as other Asians) in public. Japanese consider the practices to be offensive.
- Not interpreting "We'll consider it" as a no when spoken by a Japanese businessperson. Japanese negotiators mean no when they say, "We'll consider it."
- Not giving small gifts to Japanese when conducting business. Japanese are offended by not receiving these gifts.
- Giving your business card to a Japanese businessperson more than once. Japanese prefer to give and receive business cards only once.

China

- Using black borders on stationery and business cards because black is associated with death.
- Giving small gifts to Chinese when conducting business. Chinese are offended by these gifts.
- Making cold calls on Chinese business executives. An appropriate introduction is required for a first-time meeting with a Chinese official.

Korea

- Saying no. Koreans feel it is important to have visitors leave with good feelings.

India

- Telling Indians you prefer not to eat with your hands. If the Indians are not using cutlery when eating, they expect you to do likewise.

Mexico and Latin America

Mexico

- Flying into a Mexican city in the morning and expecting to close a deal by lunch. Mexicans build business relationships slowly.

Brazil

- Attempting to impress Brazilians by speaking a few words of Spanish. Portuguese is the official language of Brazil.

Most Latin American countries

- Wearing elegant and expensive jewellery during a business meeting. Most Latin Americans think people should appear more conservative during a business meeting.

Note: A cultural mistake for Canadians and Americans to avoid when conducting business in most countries outside North America is to insist on getting down to business quickly. Other stereotyped North American traits to avoid are aggressiveness, impatience, and frequent interruptions to get your point across. North Americans in small towns also like to build a relationship before getting down to business.

HOW DO YOU OVERCOME CROSS-CULTURAL COMMUNICATION BARRIERS?

A key part of developing good cross-cultural relations is to overcome or prevent communication barriers stemming from cultural differences. Personal life, too, is often more culturally diverse today than previously, leading to culturally based communication problems. The information about avoiding cultural bloopers presented in this chapter might also be interpreted as a way to prevent communication barriers. Here we describe eight additional strategies and tactics to help overcome cross-cultural communication barriers.

1. *Be alert to cultural differences in customs and behaviour.* To minimize cross-cultural communication barriers, recognize that many subtle job-related differences in customs and behaviour may exist. For example, Asians typically feel uncomfortable when asked to brag about themselves in the presence of others. From their perspective, calling attention to yourself at the expense of another person is rude and unprofessional.
2. *Use straightforward language and speak slowly and clearly.* When working with people who do not speak your language fluently, speak in an easy-to-understand manner. Be patient for many reasons including the fact that your accent in your native tongue may not be the same as the person from whom your target learned your language. (For example, English as learned in India is quite different from English as learned in Ontario.) Minimize the use of idioms and analogies specific to your language. For example, in North America the term "over the hill" means outdated or past one's prime. A person from another culture may not understand this phrase yet be hesitant to ask for clarification. Speaking slowly is also important because even people who read and write a second language at an expert level may have difficulty catching the nuances of conversation. Facing the person from another culture directly also improves communication because your facial expressions and lips contribute to comprehension.
3. *When the situation is appropriate, speak in the language of the people from another culture.* Canadians who can speak another language are at a competitive advantage when dealing with businesspeople who speak that language. The language skill, however, must be more advanced than speaking a few words and phrases. A new twist in speaking another language has surged recently: As more deaf people have been integrated into the workforce, knowing American Sign Language can be a real advantage to a worker when some of his or her co-workers or customers are deaf.
4. *Observe cultural differences in etiquette.* Violating rules of etiquette without explanation can erect immediate communication barriers. A major rule of etiquette is that in some countries older people in high-status positions expect to be treated with respect. Formality is important, unless invited to do otherwise. When visiting a company in Asia, for example, it is best to be deferent (appeal to the authority of) to company dignitaries. Visualize yourself as a company representative of a high-tech American firm that manufactures equipment for legally downloading music over the internet. You visit Sony Corporation in Japan to speak about a joint venture. On meeting the marketing vice president, bow slightly and say something to the effect; "Mr. ____________, it is my honour to discuss doing business with Sony." Do not commit the etiquette mistake of saying something to the effect, "Hi Charlie, how's the wife and kids?" (An American actually said this at a Japanese company shortly before being escorted out the door.)
5. *Be sensitive to differences in nonverbal communication.* Stay alert to the possibility that a person from another culture may misinterpret your nonverbal signal. To use positive reinforcement, some managers will give a sideways hug to an employee or will touch an employee's arm. People from some cultures resent touching from workmates and will be offended. Koreans in particular dislike being touched or touching others in a work setting. (Refer back to the discussion of cultural bloopers.)

6. *Do not be diverted by style, accent, grammar, or personal appearance.* Although all these superficial factors are related to business success, they are difficult to interpret when judging a person from another culture. It is, therefore, better to judge the merits of the statement or behaviour.[23] A brilliant individual from another culture may still be learning your language and thus make basic mistakes in speaking your language. He or she might also not have developed a sensitivity to dress style in your culture.
7. *Listen for understanding, not agreement.* When working with diverse teammates, the differences in viewpoints can lead to conflict. To help overcome such conflict, follow the LUNA rule: Listen for Understanding, Not Agreement. In this way you gear yourself to consider the viewpoints of others as a first resort. For example, some older workers may express some intense loyalty to the organization, whereas their younger teammates may speak in more critical terms. By everyone listening to understand, they can begin to appreciate each other's paradigms and accept differences of opinion.[24] Listening is a powerful tool for overcoming cross-cultural communication barriers.
8. *Be attentive to individual differences in appearance.* A major cross-cultural insult is to confuse the identity of people because they are members of the same race or ethnic group. Psychological research suggests that people have difficulty seeing individual differences among people of another race because they code race first, such as thinking, "He has the nose of an African American." However, people can learn to search for more distinguishing features, such as a dimple or eye colour.[25]

Human Relations in Practice

The Toronto Police Service: Recruiting for Diversity

The Toronto Police Service was selected as one of Canada's Best Diversity Employers (2008) for:

1. developing a recruitment strategy to hire from under-represented groups, with impressive results—nearly half of their new recruits in 2006 were members of equity groups, including women, Aboriginal people, visible minorities, LGBT and persons with a disability
2. attending job fairs, community events and other functions to recruit new officers from the city of Toronto's various cultural and ethnic groups establishing a Diversity Management Unit in 2006 to oversee their diversity policy and procedures, diversity management and training programs and other related matters
3. reviewing their promotional process to ensure it is equitable and accessible for women, visible minorities, Aboriginal people, LGBT employees and persons with disabilities

In 2006, The Toronto Police Service established a Diversity Management Unit, to oversee diversity management training, human rights issues, and a diversity policy and procedure review of policies at the Service. The Unit's mandate is to develop a more inclusive workplace environment for members of equity groups throughout the Toronto Police Service. Diversity training is also mandatory for all civilian officers, and includes components in areas such as human rights, religious and cultural awareness, and issues related to Aboriginal, LGBT and disabled employees.

In an effort to ensure that officers more accurately reflect the communities they serve, Toronto Police Service also has developed a recruiting strategy to increase the number of new recruits from the various equity groups. As part of this, the Service also sets up recruitment booths at numerous ethnic community affairs and celebrations throughout the year to attract potential visible minority candidates. The collective results of these efforts are demonstrated through the Service's appointment of its first visible minority Deputy Chief of Police, and the recent fact that fully one-third of the Service's new recruits were from visible minority groups last year.

SUMMARY

In this chapter, we have explored diversity in Canada. We have defined and looked at what a culture is and how culture is transmitted to others through acculturation and enculturation. Six dimensions of cultural values help us understand how cultures differ from one another: (1) materialism versus concern for others, (2) formality versus informality, (3) acceptance of power and authority, (4) individualism versus collectivism, (5) urgent time orientation versus casual time orientation, and (6) high context versus low context cultures. Another complexity about understanding cultural differences is the cultural mosaic whereby people identify with both their primary culture and another culture or cultures.

Significant barriers to effective intercultural communication include our perceptual expectations and stereotyping, prejudice, and discrimination. Often stereotypes and prejudicial attitudes lead to discrimination, which can take a number of forms ranging in severity from negative feelings about a group to actual elimination of the group members. Other barriers include ethnocentrism, and different norms and codes of conduct. Gender differences can also lead to misunderstanding between men and women at work as well as in other settings.

Five specific methods and techniques for improving cross-cultural relations are as follows:

- Develop cultural sensitivity (being aware of differences) and cultural intelligence (cognitive, emotional, and body components).
- Focus on individuals rather than groups.
- Respect all workers and cultures.
- Value cultural differences (this also involves showing respect).
- Minimize cultural bloopers (embarrassing mistakes).

QUESTIONS AND ACTIVITIES

1. What do you feel are the main reasons for intolerance and prejudice? Support your views.
2. Several well-known companies conduct an *awareness week* to celebrate diverse groups such as Aboriginal groups or homosexuals. What is your opinion of the effectiveness of such activities for bringing about workplace harmony?
3. Have you been a victim of prejudice or discrimination? How did it feel? What was your reaction?
4. In what way might having a high acceptance for power and authority make it difficult for a person to work well on a team that has very little supervision?
5. Differences in communication patterns between men and women have been identified. What impact will this information have on your communications with men and women?
6. Develop a list of what you perceive to be essential skills for working with others from different cultures or groups. Identify which skills you currently possess. How could you learn the other skills?
7. When you meet someone from another culture, what can you do to demonstrate that you respect that person's culture?
8. Many people speak loudly to deaf people, blind people, and those who speak a different language. Based on the information presented in this chapter, what mistakes are these people making?

9. Interview a person who has moved to Canada recently. What difficulties did he or she have after first arriving in Canada? What helped the person adjust to a new life in Canada?

INTERNET SKILL BUILDER

Cultural Exploration

A useful way to learn about another culture is to discover new information, and the internet is a great source. Choose a culture you would like to learn more about. This culture could be anything you want, from same-sex orientation to a different ethnic group to a physical or mental challenge. To get started, use a search engine such as Yahoo, Excite, or Google and type in your choice. After examining several sites, bookmark your favourite site so that you can visit it frequently to learn more. You might even choose a language you don't speak and study it for a few minutes every day!

Log on to the **Companion Website** at **www.pearsoncanada.ca/dubrin** to access additional resources for this chapter.

CASE STUDY 8-1 HUMAN RELATIONS

The Ethnocentric Marketing Assistant

Tamara graduated from a small college in her hometown and moved to a large city. With a diploma in marketing, she was particularly interested in the clothing industry. Although not exactly sure what she wanted to do, she was hired by a small clothing manufacturer in their shipping and receiving department. Here she assisted with packaging clothing for exporting to other countries. She also helped in receiving when different supplies arrived such as cloth and other sewing requirements. Tamara had a bubbly personality, always seemed to have fun at work, and was popular with her co-workers who were for the most part young, white, and also recent graduates. With her excellent work record and personality, she was promoted "upstairs" in two years as a marketing assistant to the head of marketing. As employees of a small company, everyone participated in all areas of the business. Ideas were freely exchanged between marketing, design, and manufacturing. Tamara was enthusiastic about her new job and let everyone know how exciting this was for her. She quickly engaged in conversation with everybody.

As part of her "cute" style, she developed nicknames for everyone, just as she had in shipping and receiving. She called her new boss "Chow Mein" instead of Chow Ling Su. As she whirred past people she gave affectionate pats to everyone. She often imitated the accent of the head of manufacturing, an older German-born man, and called him "Herbie" instead of Mr. Hermann as others did. She performed all of her duties enthusiastically and loved to tell jokes, sing, and chew gum while she worked. Although people often frowned at her antics, she seemed oblivious to any signals that her behaviour was any kind of problem. A couple of people had jokingly asked her to calm down a little and not to be continually so personal with them. Tamara just laughed it off. At Christmas, she gave out cards with Christian themes and kissed people while she dangled mistletoe over their heads. To Chow Ling Su, she asked, "Hey, what animal is it for you people this New Year?"

At her three-month performance appraisal she was told by Chow Ling Su, "You have some good knowledge of marketing, especially for the younger crowd, and we are pleased by many of your ideas. However, your behaviour leaves much to be desired. Your manner is insulting to many of us, and you have not changed even though many of us have asked you to do so. If you do not change, I fear that we may have to terminate your employment here."

Devastated, Tamara replied, "I don't understand, Chow Mein! I come to work on time, I help out, and my ideas have been adopted and appear to be working. What do you mean my manner is insulting? I treat everyone like old friends." Tamara burst into tears. "I don't understand what you mean. For over two years, I've been a good employee."

Questions

1. What cultural mistakes is Tamara making?
2. In what ways is Tamara displaying an ethnocentric attitude?
3. Offer Tamara several suggestions to improve her intercultural competence.
4. What basic communication skills do you feel that Tamara should use to improve her relations with her co-workers?

CASE STUDY 8-2 HUMAN RELATIONS

The Multicultural Dealership

Manuel Ortiz is the owner and operator of Futura Motors, a large automobile and small-truck dealership in Toronto, Ontario. The dealership represents several Japanese and Korean vehicle manufacturers. For more than a decade, Ortiz and his management team have invested time, effort, and money into building culturally diverse sales and service staffs to better serve the many ethnic, cultural, and racial groups that make up the dealership's customer base. Ortiz brags that in total his sales staff speaks 13 different languages. "In this way we can communicate in the native tongue of almost any customer or sales prospect who shows up on the floor," says Ortiz. (A sales prospect is anyone who visits Futura without the full intention of purchasing a vehicle from the dealership, including the people who are "just looking.")

The culturally diverse sales and service staffs apparently have contributed to the growth and profitability of Futura, although such an assertion would be difficult to prove. For example, Ortiz has not been able to compare the dollar volume of Futura to a comparable size foreign dealership in Brooklyn that has a more homogeneous workforce.

Penny Shakelford, the office manager at Futura, has recently brought a potential problem to Ortiz's attention that has caused him some concern about how well he and his staff are managing diversity. According to Shakelford, the multicultural sales staff appears to be well accepted by most customers and prospects, yet some problems are surfacing. Based on direct concerns expressed by both customers and prospects, Shakelford believes that they are being patronized on the basis of their demographic group. She explains:

"My impression is that some customers think we are bending over backwards to make them feel at home. If a person who walks on the floor appears to be an African American, immediately an African American sales rep walks up to him or her. The same goes for several other visible ethnic or racial groups. Two different Asiatic Indians wrote down on customer service survey cards that they thought it was too obvious that an Indian rushed out on the floor as soon as they appeared.

"A Spanish Canadian woman said she thought it was a little bit much that three minutes after she and her husband walked into the dealership, a young sales rep introduced himself in Spanish. The customer said she was in Toronto, not Madrid, and wanted to be treated like a Canadian."

Ortiz said that it appears that the vast majority of customers and prospects find no problem with our attempt to make a direct appeal to their racial or ethnic group but that maybe some adjustment needs to be made.

"We need to give this problem some thought. We don't want to insult anybody, but neither do we want to lose our competitive edge of having a multicultural workforce."

Questions

1. What is your opinion of the merits of a vehicle dealership attempting to match the demographic group of a customer with a sales rep of the same demographic group?
2. What do you recommend Ortiz and his management team do about the several complaints the Futura dealership has received.
3. To help you analyze this case, get the input from a few people in your network about how they would feel about having a person from their demographic group approach them when they visited a dealership. (Perhaps a few classmates representing different ethnic groups can provide useful input.)

Human Relations Skill Building

Exercise 8-3 Developing Sensitivity to Other Cultures

With one person playing the role of Tamara and another playing the role of Chow Ling Su, continue the scene of the performance appraisal described above. Chow Ling Su will use appropriate communication skills to assist Tamara in developing cultural awareness. Tamara must also use good communication skills as she responds to the feedback of Chow Ling Su.

Chapter 9
Handling Conflict and Being Assertive

Learning Outcomes

After studying the information and doing the exercises in this chapter, you should be able to

- understand why conflict between people takes place so often;
- pinpoint several helpful and harmful consequences of conflict;
- resolve conflict more effectively;
- improve your negotiating skills;
- practise various techniques to improve your assertiveness with others.

Both on and off the job, we face a wide array of problems. Some of these problems include conflict with others. For example, Sunai is a mid-level manager. Another manager persists in verbally harassing her by telling her that she is incompetent. As they are both managers in different departments, they report to different supervisors. Sunai does her best to avoid this man, but it is not always possible. Over time, this continued hostility is getting to her. What is Sunai to do? As this behaviour is persisting, her only option is to confront the person directly. If the harassment continues, she may be able to go to Human Resources and find out her rights to work in a harassment-free workplace.

This situation illustrates the underlying nature of **conflict**, a condition that exists when two sets of demands, goals, or motives are incompatible. You cannot work both on an eleven-to-seven and a nine-to-five schedule; and you cannot be engaged and not engaged at the same time. Such differences in demands often lead to a hostile or antagonistic relationship between two or more parties. A conflict can also be considered a dispute, a feud, a controversy, or even a private war!

A major purpose of this chapter is to describe ways of resolving conflict so that a win–win solution is reached. Both sides should leave the conflict feeling that their needs have been satisfied without resort to extreme behaviour. Both parties get what they deserve yet preserve the dignity and self-respect of the other side. Another purpose of this chapter is to explain assertiveness, because being assertive helps to prevent and resolve conflict.

WHY SO MUCH CONFLICT EXISTS

Many reasons exist for the widespread presence of conflict in all aspects of life. All of these reasons are related to the basic nature of conflict—the fact that not every person can have what he or she wants at the same time. As with other topics in this book, understanding conflict will help you develop a better understanding of why people act as they do. Here we describe seven key sources of conflict.

Competition for Limited Resources

A fundamental reason you might experience conflict with another person is that not everybody can get all the money, material, supplies, or human help they want. Conflict also ensues when employees are asked to compete for prizes such as bonuses based on individual effort, or for company-paid vacation trips. Because the number of awards is so limited, the competition becomes intense enough to be regarded as conflict. Conflict stemming from limited resources has become prevalent as so many companies attempt to reduce expenses. Many units of the organization have to compete for the limited money available to hire new people or purchase new technology.

Personality Clashes

Various value and personality differences among people contribute to workplace conflict. Many disagreements on the job stem from the fact that some people simply dislike each other. A **personality clash** is an antagonistic relationship between two people based on differences in personal attributes, preferences, interests, values, and styles. People involved in a personality clash often have difficulty specifying why they dislike each other. The end result, however, is that they cannot maintain an amiable work relationship. A strange fact about personality clashes is that people who get along well may begin to clash after working together for a number of years. Many business partnerships fold because the two partners eventually clash.

Aggressive Personalities Including Bullies

Coworkers naturally disagree about topics, issues, and ideas. Yet some people convert disagreement into an attack that puts down other people and damages their self-esteem. As a result, conflict surfaces. **Aggressive personalities** are people who verbally and sometimes physically attack others frequently. Verbal aggression takes the form of insults, teasing, ridicule, and profanity. The aggression may also be expressed as attacks on the victim's character, competence, background, and physical appearance. When people are verbally abused, they are put on the defensive making them feel uncomfortable.[1]

Aggressive personalities are also referred to as bullies. Among their typical behaviours are interrupting others, ranting in a loud voice, and making threats. A typical attitude of a bullying boss is "My way or the highway," sending the message that the employee's suggestions are unwelcome. One bullying manager would frequently ask people, "Are you going to be stupid the rest of your life?" Bullied workers complain of a range of psychological and physical ailments such as anxiety, sleeplessness, headache, irritable bowel syndrome, skin problems, panic attacks, and low self-esteem. Human relations specialist Gary Namie of The Work Doctor—a firm that works with companies to help reduce hostility—says that bullying can have negative effects on employees and the organization. Bullying reduces morale and productivity by increasing absenteeism and sick leave. "If you have been pummeled and denigrated long enough, you will not be a peak performer," he said.[2]

Aggressiveness can also take the extreme form of the shooting or knifing of a former boss or colleague by a mentally unstable worker recently dismissed from the company. According to the Canadian 2004 General Social Survey on victimization, 17 percent of self-reported incidents of violent victimization occurred in the workplace. These incidents included sexual assault, robbery, and physical assault, adding up to 356,000 violent workplace incidents in the ten provinces in 2004. In Newfoundland and Labrador, the victim's workplace was the location of 40 percent of all violent incidents—a proportion two times higher than in any other province.[3]

Culturally Diverse Teams and Factional Groups

Conflict often surfaces as people work in teams whose members vary in many ways. Ethnicity, religion, and gender are three of the major factors that lead to clashes in viewpoints. Differing educational backgrounds and work specialties can also lead to conflict. Workers often shut out information that doesn't fit comfortably with their own beliefs, particularly if they do not like the person providing the information. When these conflicts are properly resolved, diversity lends strength to the organization because the various viewpoints make an important contribution to solving a problem. Groups that are reminded of the importance of effective communication and taught methods of conflict resolution usually can overcome the conflict stemming from mixed groups.[4]

Another form of diversity occurs when groups contain different factions, such as those representing two different companies that merged. Often the factional group consists of two subgroups, each with several representatives, such as a cost-cutting task force consisting of three representatives each from marketing, operations, and finance. The potential for conflict within factional groups increases when the subgroups differ substantially in demographic characteristics such as age, gender, and educational levels. Professors Jiatao Li of Hong Kong University of Science and Technology and Donald C. Hambrick of the Pennsylvania State University studied factional groups at 71 Sino-foreign ventures in China. Five hundred and thirty-five managers completed surveys in either English or Chinese. Among the findings were that when there were large demographic differences between members of the joint venture teams, stereotyping, distrust, and discord mounted. These negative emotions led to conflict and a decrease in performance.[5]

Microinequities as a Source of Conflict

Growing attention is being paid to snubbing, or ignoring others, as a source of conflict. A **microinequity** is a small, semiconscious message we send with a powerful impact on the receiver. A microinequity might also be considered a subtle slight. Conflict occurs because a person's feelings are hurt, and he or she feels trivialized. Two examples of workplace microinequities follow:

- You check your messages on a cell phone, Blackberry, or computer screen while a co-worker is talking to you. [You are devaluing the other person's time, and trivializing his or her importance.]
- A manager dismisses the first idea offered in a meeting by responding, "Okay, so who would like to get the ball rolling?" [The person who offered the idea feels like his or her suggestion is not even worth consideration and, therefore, has hurt feelings.]

Many companies, including IBM, offer training seminars to help managers avoid microinequities, including those already mentioned as well as mispronouncing the name of subordinates and looking at a watch while someone else is talking.[6]

Harassment

A substantial number of employees experience conflict because they are harassed by a manager, co-worker, or customer. In Canada, the Canada Labour Code, the Canadian Human Rights Act, and provincial and territorial human rights codes prohibit all types of harassment, including sexual harassment (which is dealt with in its own section below). The Canadian Human Rights Act, which applies to the federal government and federally regulated business, took effect in March 1978 and prohibits all harassment including harassment due to race, ethnicity, religion, sexual orientation, disability, or gender. The Canada Labour Code also establishes that all employees have the right to be free from any type of harassment and that employers must take steps to ensure a harassment-free workplace. The *Canadian Employment Equity Act*, 1995, was designed to ensure that no Canadians are denied jobs for reasons unrelated to their abilities and to help correct the employment disadvantages of four groups: women, members of visible minorities, Aboriginal peoples, and persons with disabilities. These acts and codes attempt to ensure that no one will be harassed for any reason in the workplace and mandate that employers put into place policies and practices for fair and equitable treatment of all employees. If you are being harassed, whether sexually or otherwise, there are steps that you can take. The Canada Today feature below outlines some agreed upon steps that you can take to prevent or manage harassment.

Sexual Harassment

Division XV.1 of Part III of the Canada Labour Code establishes that all employees have the right to be free of sexual harassment in the workplace and requires employers to take

Canada Today

Dealing with Harassment

What do you do if you feel you are being harassed by a co-worker (or worse yet, your manager)? You do not have to take it and you do not have to quit your job. Most organizations, large and small, typically have formal or informal policies and procedures. Do not be afraid to deal with the harassment.

Larger organizations typically have formal policies and procedures for dealing with all types of harassment. Most include a formal and informal complaint and resolution process based on the Ontario Human Rights Code or other provincial codes based on the Human Rights Act and formal Labour Codes.

In general, many harassment policies start with an informal complaint process. This process may include discussion with the person giving rise to the complaint, meeting with an organizational harassment adviser, or reporting the complaint to his or her immediate supervisor (or another supervisor if the immediate supervisor is the harasser). In many cases, resolution is accomplished at this informal level. Although it can be difficult to confront the person you feel is harassing you, this type of confrontation often successfully ends the behaviour. Being assertive, stating your case firmly, and if necessary stating that a formal complaint process will be initiated is often all that is required to end the harassment. The harassment adviser or other member of Human Resources may also be very helpful in planning a strategy to deal with the person.

A more formal process is usually initiated if the informal process is not successful. The formal process is most often activated with a written complaint. This written request should document all incidents. As such, it is important that if you feel you are being harassed, sexually or otherwise, it is imperative that you document all incidents of harassment. Although it can be difficult, you have to discuss the harassment with others who will investigate the complaint. However, your confidentiality will be respected and you must give permission if others become involved in the resolution process.

When a formal complaint has been made and investigated, the investigative team decides whether or not the complaint is substantiated. This team makes recommendations about further action, if any, to resolve the dispute.

In general, then, here are the steps that you can take:

- Record the incident(s) in detail. Make sure to record the names of any witnesses to the event.
- Often, confronting the person for smaller transgressions immediately works. Sometimes, the person may be unaware that you find a behaviour offensive. For example, a co-worker who continually calls you sweetie or tells racially discriminating jokes may not realize that this is offensive to you. Be assertive and say something like, "I would prefer that you do not tell such jokes in my presence. I find them offensive."
- If the person continues, you can then add, "If you persist in this (name the behaviour), I will have no choice but to report this matter to (name your supervisor). And follow through—idle threats will not change the behaviour.
- If the behaviour is very harassing (such as patting your behind, making lewd comments or overt sexual advances, destroying your personal property, and so on), go immediately to your supervisor. Again, make sure that you record the behaviour in writing including dates of the incidents. This may launch an informal investigation, but if the behaviour is severe, ask for an immediate formal investigation.
- If the workplace is not helpful, call the Labour Board or crisis centre in your area for immediate assistance. Remember that no one deserves to be harassed and you do not have to put up with it in any employment setting.
- You may also want to call a lawyer. Many organizations have an Employee Assistance Program and the consultation may be free of charge.

positive action to prevent sexual harassment in the workplace. The Code defines **sexual harassment** as

> any conduct, comment, gesture, or contact of a sexual nature that is likely to cause offence or humiliation to any employee or that might, on reasonable grounds, be perceived by that employee as placing a condition of a sexual nature on employment or on any opportunity for training or promotion.[7]

Harassment can include something as violent as rape or as subtle as making a sexually oriented comment about another person's body or appearance. Decorating the work area with pictures of nude people is another example of behaviour that can be categorized as sexual harassment. The most frequent form of harassment involves men against women, but harassment also takes the form of women sexually harassing men and people of the same sex harassing each other.

A Canadian Human Rights Tribunal identified three characteristics of sexual harassment. The first characteristic is that the encounters must be unsolicited and unwelcome to the complainant. An example of this type of behaviour is unwanted sexual remarks. The second characteristic is that the conduct continues despite the complainant's protests, or if it does stop, there are negative employment consequences, such as being denied a promised promotion. Third, any perceived cooperation by the complainant must be due to employment-related threats or promises.[8]

As a result of the *Canadian Human Rights Act*, each province has put in place legislation to protect employees from all types of harassment, including sexual harassment. For example, Ontario has its own Human Rights Code, which prohibits harassment, and employers are responsible to prevent and discourage harassment. If an employer fails to do so, the employee may file a complaint with the Ontario Human Rights Commission.[9]

Sexual harassment creates conflict because the harassed person has to make a choice between two incompatible motives. One motive is to get ahead or at least keep the job. But to satisfy this motive, the person is forced to sacrifice the motive of holding on to his or her moral values or preferences. This chapter's Canada Today feature presents suggestions for dealing with harassment.

Competing Work and Family Demands

Balancing the demands of career and family life has become a major challenge facing today's workforce. The increasing proportion of full-time, dual-earner Canadian families continues to make work-life balance an important issue. Around one in four men in full-time, dual-earner families with young children at home, and more than one in three women, reported feeling severely time stressed.[10] Attempting to meet work and family demands is also a frequent source of conflict because the demands are often incompatible. Imagine having planned to attend your child's solo recital, and then being ordered at the last minute to work late because of an emergency.

The conflict over work versus family demands intensifies when the person is serious about both work and family responsibilities. The average professional working for an organization works approximately 55 hours per week, including five hours on weekends. Adhering to such a schedule almost inevitably results in some incompatible demands from work versus those from family members and friends. Conflict arises because the person wants to work sufficient hours to succeed on the job yet still have enough time for personal life.

Employers have taken major steps in recent years to help employees balance the competing demands of work and family. These programs help reduce conflict that arises from competing work and family demands. A sampling of these programs follows:

1. *Flexible work arrangements*. Many employers allow employees to use flexible work arrangements such as flextime, compressed workweeks, job sharing, and working from home. Technology today makes it easier to work from just about any location including home. Web conferencing, teleconferencing, computer chat and so on have increased work flexibility for many employees including women. For example, flextime arrangements reduce stress and the "time crunch" many women feel as they try to balance home and work demands.[11] A related program is the compressed workweek whereby the person works 40 hours in four days or less. Some employees prefer the compressed workweek because it gives them longer weekends with their families. (For many others, however, ten-hour workdays create family problems.)

   The Royal Bank Financial Group, in a recent survey, found that allowing employees to utilize a variety of alternative work arrangements improved efficiency, morale, commitment, and customer service while reducing absenteeism. Forty-eight percent of the 1,700 Royal Bank Financial Group employees surveyed said that flexible work arrangements helped them deal with family responsibilities including child- and eldercare. The Royal Bank, one of Canada's largest employers, has over 1,100 job-share arrangements, more than any other company in Canada. Approximately 30 percent (more than 13,000) of the Royal Bank Financial Group's employees utilize some form of alternative work arrangement.[12]

2. *Family leave programs*. Family leave programs allow employees to take extended time off work, without pay, to meet family responsibilities. The employee's benefits continue while on leave, and the employee is guaranteed a job upon return. The leave applies to any combination of family and/or medical leaves. Recent legislation has extended parental leave up to one year.

3. *Dependent care programs*. Assistance in dealing with two categories of dependents—children and elderly parents—lies at the core of many programs and policies to help employees balance the demands of work and family. Many companies offer financial assistance for childcare, including pre-tax expense accounts that allow employees to deduct childcare and eldercare expenses.

4. *Recognition that work and personal life can be complementary*. A case history study of managers in a variety of companies revealed that some managers see work and personal life as complementing each other. The manager gets to know the goals and personal responsibilities of each member of the group and then helps each person achieve success on and off the job. A worker who needs to care for a dying parent, for example, might be able to work four days a week for a stretch and then make up the time later in the year. One positive result is that an individual with a satisfying personal life can produce more work in a shorter period of time than one who experiences work–family conflict.[13] As you have probably concluded, recognition that work and personal life can be complementary leads to taking individual cases into consideration. Read the Human Relations in Practice box below to see how one company helps families resolve work-family conflicts.

Human Relations in Practice

Best Buy Helps Employees Resolve Work–Family Conflicts

Cali Ressler, manager of the work–life balance program for Best Buy, helped a troubled division of the retail group in Minneapolis deal with sinking employee morale. Ressler encouraged the manager to try flexible scheduling, trusting his team to work as it suited them. "He said, 'Well, trust doesn't cost me anything,'" she recalls. The innovation was that the whole team did it together. Although the sample size was fewer than 300 employees, the early results were promising. Turnover in the first three months of employment fell from 14 to 0 percent, job satisfaction rose 10 percent, and their team-performance scores rose 13 percent.

When Jody Thompson, Best Buy's "organizational change" guru, heard about Ressler's work, she pushed the company's management to make total flexibility available to everyone. No one is forced into it; teams sign up when they're ready. Best Buy expects that ROWE (results-oriented work environment) one day will apply to the whole company. Under ROWE, headquarters employees can work when and where they like, as long as they get the job done. At the moment, it is working on a version for the 100,000 retail employees in its stores, a much more difficult task because most of those employees are hourly, and their work is regulated by federal law.

Source: Jyoti Thottam, "Reworking Work," *Time*, July 25, 2005, pp. 51, 52.

THE GOOD AND BAD SIDES OF CONFLICT

Conflict over significant issues is a source of stress. We usually do not suffer stress over minor conflicts such as having to choose between wearing one sweater or another. Since conflict is a source of stress, it can have both positive and negative consequences to the individual. Like stress in general, we need an optimum amount of conflict to keep us mentally and physically energetic.

You can probably recall an incident in your life when conflict proved to be beneficial in the long run. Perhaps you and your partner or spouse hammered out an agreement over how much freedom each one has in the relationship. Handled properly, moderate doses of conflict can be advantageous. Some of the benefits that might arise from conflict are summarized in these key points. Figure 9-1 outlines the positive as well as the negative consequences of conflict.

1. *Talents and abilities may emerge in response to conflict.* When faced with a conflict, people often become more creative than they are in a tranquil situation. Assume that your company would no longer pay for your advanced education unless you used the courses to improve your job performance. You would probably find ways to accomplish such an end.
2. *Conflict can help you feel better because it satisfies a number of psychological needs.* By nature, many people like a good fight. As a socially acceptable substitute for attacking others, you might be content to argue over a dispute on the job or at home.
3. *As an aftermath of conflict, the parties in conflict may become united.* Two adolescents engaged in a fistfight may emerge bloodied but good friends after the battle. And two warring supervisors may become more cooperative toward each other in the aftermath of confrontation.

Interpersonal Conflict

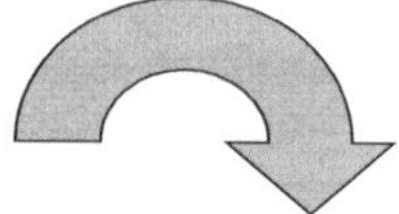

Positive Consequences

--Talents and abilities emerge

--Need satisfaction leads to good feelings

--Unity after conflict

--Prevents premature agreement and poor decisions

Negative Consequences

--Poor well-being

--Wasted time and energy

--Financial and emotional costs

--Fatigue

--Self-interest dominates

--Workplace violence

Figure 9-1 The Good and Bad Side of Conflict

Conflict between people and groupscan have both positive and negative consequences.

4. *Conflict helps prevent people in the organization from agreeing too readily with each other, thus making some very poor decisions*. **Groupthink** is the situation that occurs when group members strive so hard to get along that they fail to critically evaluate each other's ideas.

Despite the positive picture of conflict just painted, it can also have some detrimental consequences to the individual, the organization, and society. These harmful consequences of conflict make it important for people to learn how to resolve conflict:

1. *Prolonged conflict can be detrimental to some people's emotional and physical well-being*. As a type of stress, prolonged conflict can lead to such problems as heart disease and chronic intestinal disorders.
2. *People in conflict with each other often waste time and energy that could be put to useful purposes*. Instead of fighting all evening with your roommate, the two of you might fix up your shared space. Instead of writing angry email messages back and forth, two department heads might better invest that time in thinking up ideas to save the company money.

3. *The aftermath of extreme conflict may have high financial and emotional costs.* Sabotage—such as ruining machinery—might be the financial consequence. At the same time, management may develop a permanent distrust of many people in the workforce, although only a few of them are saboteurs.
4. *Too much conflict is fatiguing, even if it does not cause symptoms of emotional illness.* People who work in high-conflict jobs often feel spent when they return home from work. When the battle-worn individual has limited energy left over for family responsibilities, the result is more conflict. (For instance, "What do you mean you are too tired to go to the movies?" or "If your job is killing your appetite, find another job.")
5. *People in conflict will often be much more concerned with their own interests than with the good of the family, organization, or society.* A married couple in conflict might disregard the welfare of their children. An employee in the shipping department who is in conflict with his supervisor might neglect to ship an order. And a gang in conflict with another might leave a park or beach strewn with broken glass.[14]
6. *Workplace violence can erupt, including the killing of managers, previous managers, co-workers, and customers, as well as spouses and partners.* The number of violent incidents at work causing death or serious injury has risen dramatically in recent years.[15] According to the 2004 Canadian General Social Survey, 17 percent of all self-reported incidents of violent victimization, including sexual assault, robbery, and physical assault, occurred at the respondent's place of work. This represents over 356,000 violent workplace incidents in Canada's ten provinces.[16] Disgruntled employees, such as those recently fired, may attempt revenge by assassinating work associates. People involved in unresolved domestic disputes sometimes storm into a partner's workplace to physically attack him or her.

TECHNIQUES FOR RESOLVING CONFLICTS WITH OTHERS

Because of the inevitability of conflict, a successful and happy person must learn effective ways of resolving conflict. Here we concentrate on methods of conflict resolution that you can use on your own. Most of them emphasize a collaborative or win–win philosophy.

Confrontation and Problem Solving Leading to Win–Win

The most highly recommended way of resolving conflict is **confrontation and problem solving**. It is a method of identifying the true source of conflict and resolving it systematically. The confrontation in this approach is gentle and tactful rather than combative and abusive. Reasonableness is important because the person who takes the initiative in resolving the conflict wants to maintain a harmonious working relationship with the other party.

Imagine that Jason, the person working at the desk next to you, whistles loudly while he works. You find the whistling to be distracting and annoying; you think Jason is a noise polluter. If you don't bring the problem to Jason's attention, it will probably grow in proportion with time. Yet you are hesitant to enter into an argument about something a person might regard as a civil liberty (the right to whistle in a public place).

An effective alternative is for you to approach Jason directly in this manner:

YOU: Jason, there is something bothering me that I would like to discuss with you.

JASON: Go ahead, I don't mind listening to other people's problems.

YOU: My problem concerns something you are doing that makes it difficult for me to concentrate on my work. When you whistle it distracts me and grates on my nerves. It may be my hang-up, but the whistling does bother me.

JASON: I guess I could stop whistling when you're working next to me. It's probably just a nervous habit.

An important advantage of confrontation and problem solving is that you deal directly with a sensitive problem without jeopardizing the chances of forming a constructive working relationship in the future. One reason that the method works so effectively is that the focus is on the problem at hand, and not on the individual's personality.

The intent of confrontation and problem solving is to arrive at a collaborative solution to the conflict. The collaborative style reflects a desire to fully satisfy the desires of both parties. It is based on an underlying philosophy of **win–win**, the belief that after conflict has been resolved, both sides should gain something of value. The user of a win–win approach is genuinely concerned about arriving at a settlement that meets the needs of both parties, or at least does not badly damage the welfare of the other side. When a collaborative approach to resolving conflict is used, the relationships among the parties are built on and improved.

Here is an example of a win–win approach to resolving conflict. A manager granted an employee a few hours off on an occasional Friday afternoon because she was willing to be on call for emergency work on an occasional weekend. Both parties were satisfied with the outcome and both accomplished their goals.

Human Relations Skill-Building Exercise 9-1 gives you an opportunity to practise the win–win approach to conflict resolution. Confrontation and problem solving typically paves the way for getting to win–win.

The opposite approach to win–win conflict resolution is win–lose, in which one side attempts to maximize gain at the expense of the other side. Win–lose is also referred to as a zero-sum game in which one side wins nothing, and the other side wins everything. Common sense tells us that win–lose is the best approach to resolving conflict—and that is one reason so much conflict goes unresolved in the form of physical attacks on people and bankruptcies. A person with a competitive orientation is likely to engage in power struggles in which one side wins and the other loses. "My way or the highway" is a win–lose strategy. An extreme example of a win–lose strategy would be to bad-mouth a rival so he or she gets fired.

If faced with an adversary who has a win–lose orientation, a plausible defense is to keep on pointing out the benefits of finding a solution that fits both sides. A sales representative for a company that makes steel buildings (often used for warehousing) was about to be laid off because of poor business. He proposed to his boss, "Please give me one more chance. Give me just enough salary to pay my rent and feed our newborn child. All the rest of my income will come from commissions on the sales I make." The owner conceded, and the sales rep did earn his way, so a win–lose situation emerged into a win–win.

Human Relations Skill Building

Exercise 9-1 Win–Win Conflict Management

The class is organized into groups of six, with each group being divided into conflict-resolution teams of three each. The members of the team try to find a win–win solution to an issue separating the two sides. The team members are free to invent their own pressing issue or choose among the following:

Management wants to control costs by not giving cost-of-living adjustments in the upcoming year. The employee group believes that a cost-of-living adjustment is absolutely necessary.

The marketing team claims it could sell 250,000 units of a toaster large enough to toast bagels if the toasters could be produced at $15 per unit. The manufacturing group says it would not be feasible to get the manufacturing costs below $20 per unit.

Starbucks would like to build in a new location, adjacent to a historic district in one of the oldest cities in North America. The members of the town planning board would like the tax revenue and the jobs that the Starbucks store would bring, but they do not want a Starbucks next to the historic district.

After the teams have developed win–win solutions to the conflicts, the creative solutions can be shared with other teams.

Disarm the Opposition

The armament your criticizer has is valid negative criticism of you. The criticizer is figuratively clobbering you with knowledge of what you did wrong. If you deny that you have made a mistake, the criticism intensifies. A simple technique has been developed to help you deal with this type of manipulative criticism. **Disarm the opposition** is a method of conflict resolution in which you disarm the criticizer by agreeing with his or her criticism of you. The technique assumes that you have done something wrong. Disarm the opposition generally works more effectively than counterattacking a person with whom you are in conflict. Another reason this technique is effective is that it implies you are apologizing for a mistake or error you have made. An apology often gets the other person on your side, or at least softens the animosity

Agreeing with criticism made of you by a superior is effective because by doing so you are then in a position to ask for that superior's help in improving your performance. Most managers realize that it is their responsibility to help employees overcome problems, not merely to criticize them. Imagine that you have been chronically late in submitting reports during the last six months. It is time for a performance review and you know you will be reprimanded for your tardiness. You also hope that your boss will not downgrade all other aspects of your performance because of your tardy reports. Here is how disarming the situation would work in this situation:

YOUR BOSS: Have a seat. It's time for your performance review and we have a lot to talk about. I'm concerned about some things.

YOU: So am I. It appears that I'm having a difficult time getting my reports in on time. I wonder if I'm being a perfectionist. Do you have any suggestions?

YOUR BOSS: I like your attitude. I think you can improve on getting your reports in on time. Maybe you are trying to make your reports perfect before you turn them in. Try not to figure out everything to four decimal places. We need thoroughness around here, but we don't want to overdo it.

Cognitive Restructuring

An indirect way of resolving conflict between people is to lessen the conflicting elements in a situation by viewing them more positively. According to the technique of **cognitive restructuring**, you mentally convert negative aspects into positive ones by looking for the positive elements in a situation.[17] How you frame or choose your thoughts can determine the outcome of a conflict situation. Your thoughts can influence your actions. If you search for the beneficial elements in a situation, there will be less area for dispute. Although this technique might sound like a mind game to you, it can work effectively.

Imagine that a co-worker of yours, Jennifer, has been asking you repeated questions about how to carry out a work procedure. You are about ready to tell Jennifer, "Go bother somebody else. I'm not paid to be a trainer." Instead, you look for the positive elements in the situation. You say to yourself, "Jennifer has been asking me a lot of questions. This does take time, but answering these questions is valuable experience. If I want to become a manager, I will have to help group members with problems."

After having completed this cognitive restructuring, you can then deal with the conflict more positively. You might say to Jennifer, "I welcome the opportunity to help you, but we need to find a mutually convenient time. That way, I can better concentrate on my own work."

Appeal to a Third Party

Now and then you may be placed in a conflict situation in which the other party either holds most of the power or simply won't budge. Perhaps you have tried techniques such as confrontation and problem solving or disarming the opposition, yet you cannot resolve your conflict. In these situations, you may have to enlist the help of a third party with power—more power than you or your adversary has. Among such third parties are your common boss, union officials, or personnel managers. Taking your opponent to court is another application of the third-party technique.

In some situations, just implying that you will bring in a third party to help resolve the conflict situation is sufficient for you to gain advantage. One woman felt she was repeatedly passed over for promotion because of her sex. She hinted that if she were not given fairer consideration she would speak to the province's Human Rights Commission. She was given a small promotion shortly thereafter. Mediation, a formal type of third-party intervention, is discussed separately below.

Negotiation and Bargaining Tactics

Conflicts can be considered situations calling for **negotiating and bargaining**, conferring with another person to resolve a problem. When you are trying to negotiate a fair price for an automobile, you are also trying to resolve a conflict. At first the demands of both parties seem incompatible. After haggling for a while, you will probably reach a price that is satisfactory to both sides.

Negotiation has many applications in the workplace, including buying, selling, arriving at a starting salary or raise, and deciding on a relocation allowance. Negotiation may also take place with co-workers when you need their assistance. For example, you might need to strike a bargain with a co-worker to handle some of your responsibilities if you are faced with a temporary overload.

A sampling of five negotiating tactics to help you resolve conflict successfully is presented next. As with the other techniques of resolving conflict already presented, choose the ones that best fit your style and the situation.

Create a Positive Negotiating Climate Negotiation proceeds much more swiftly if a positive tone surrounds the session. So it is helpful to initiate a positive outlook about the negotiation meeting. A good opening line in a negotiating session is, "Thanks for fitting this meeting into your hectic schedule." Nonverbal communication such as smiling and making friendly gestures helps create a positive climate.

In negotiating with co-workers for assistance, a positive climate can often be achieved by phrasing demands as a request for help. Most people will be more accommodating if you say to them, "I have a problem that I wonder if you could help me with." The problem might be that you need the person's time and mental energy. By giving that person a choice of offering you help, you have established a much more positive climate than by demanding assistance.[18]

Allow Room for Compromise but Be Reasonable The basic strategy of negotiation is to begin with a demand that allows room for compromise and concession. Anyone who has ever negotiated the price of an automobile, house, or used furniture recognizes this vital strategy. If you are a buyer, begin with a low bid. (You say, "I'll give you $35 for that painting" when you are prepared to pay $70.) If you are the seller, begin with a high demand. (You say, "You can have this painting for $100" when you are ready to sell it for as low as $70.) As negotiations proceed, the two of you will probably arrive at a mutually satisfactory price. This negotiating strategy can also be used for such purposes as obtaining a higher starting salary or dividing property after a divorce or legal separation.

Common sense propels many negotiators to allow *too much* room for compromise. They begin negotiations by asking way beyond what they expect to receive, or offering far less than they expect to give. As a result of these implausible demands, the other side may become hostile, antagonistic, or walk away from the negotiations. Imagine that you've spotted a DVD player that you really want in a retail store. The asking price is $298.95. In an attempt to negotiate the price, you offer the store manager $98.95. Most likely the store owner will move on to the next customer. However, if you begin with a plausible offer such as $240, the store manager will likely take you seriously. Beginning with a plausible demand or offer is also important because it contributes to a positive negotiating climate.

Focus on Interests, Not Positions Rather than clinging to specific negotiating points, keep your overall interests in mind and try to satisfy them. A negotiating point might be a certain amount of money or a concession that you must have. Remember that the true object of negotiation is to satisfy the underlying interests of both sides. The interests you and the other side are trying to protect might include money, lifestyle, power, or the status quo. For example, instead of negotiating for a particular starting salary, your true interests might be to afford a certain lifestyle. If the company pays all your medical and

Common sense propels many negotiators to allow **too much** room for compromise.

dental coverage, you can get by with a lower salary. Or your cost of living might be much lower in one city than in another. You can therefore accept a lower starting salary in the city with a lower cost of living.

Make a Last and Final Offer In many circumstances, presenting a final offer will break a deadlock. You might frame your message something like this, "All I can possibly pay for your guitar is $280. You have my number. Call me when it is available at that price." Sometimes the strategy will be countered by a last and final offer from the other side: "Thanks for your interest. My absolute minimum price for this guitar is $300. Call us if that should seem OK to you." One of you will probably give in and accept the other person's last and final offer.

Allow for Face-Saving We have reserved one of the most important negotiating and conflict-resolution strategies for last. Negotiating does not mean that you should try to squash the other side. You should try to create circumstances that will enable you to continue working with that person if it is necessary. People prefer to avoid looking weak, foolish, or incompetent during negotiation or when the process is completed. If you do not give your opponent an opportunity to save face, you will probably create a long-term enemy.

Face-saving could work in this way. A small-business owner winds up purchasing a computer, monitor, and printer for about twice what he originally budgeted. After the sale is completed, the sales rep says, "I know you bought a more professional rig than you originally intended. Yet I know you made the right decision. You will be able to do desktop publishing and save enough in printing costs to pay back the cost of the computer system in two years."

Use a Mediator

Some conflicts cannot be resolved between two parties, and a third party or **mediator** is required for successful resolution. For example, when two people refuse to listen to each other or refuse to see the "other side," chances are the conflict will not be resolved. **Mediation** is a formal method of conflict resolution that includes an objective third party. A mediator who has no vested interest in the resolution is more objective and will work to find a win–win outcome that will satisfy both parties.

Mediation is similar to, but not the same as, negotiation. In a mediation situation, an independent third party assists the involved parties in resolving the dispute on their own. Negotiation, on the other hand, often occurs between the parties and does not always involve a third person. A mediator helps the conflicting parties to clarify their solution choices, identifies possible resources, and assists in reaching decisions by recognizing each side's perspectives.[19] The mediator does not make the final decision but assists in finding possible alternatives that satisfy both sides in the dispute. Growing in popularity, **alternative dispute resolution** involves a professional mediator hired to help people arrive at a mutually acceptable solution. The goal in alternative dispute resolution is to arrive at a solution that both parties can agree to and feel that their goals have been achieved. These professional mediators are often used in divorce situations as well as in business negotiations and other legal matters.

DEVELOPING ASSERTIVENESS

Several of the techniques for resolving conflict require assertiveness. Without forthrightness, confrontation and problem solving could not be achieved. Learning to express your feelings and make your demands known is also an important aspect of becoming an effective individual in general. Expressing your feelings helps you establish good relationships with people. If you aren't sharing your feelings and attitudes with other people, you will never get close to them.

Let's examine the nature of assertiveness in some detail, and then examine several techniques for building assertiveness. However, first take Human Relations Self-Assessment Quiz 9-1 to relate assertiveness to yourself.

Assertive, Nonassertive, and Aggressive Behaviour

As implied above, **assertive** people state clearly what they want or how they feel in a given situation without being abusive, abrasive, or obnoxious. People who are assertive are open, honest, and "up-front" because they believe that all people have an equal right to express themselves honestly. Assertive behaviour can be more fully understood by comparing it with that shown by two other types of people. **Nonassertive** people let things happen to them without letting their feelings be known. **Aggressive** people are obnoxious and overbearing. They push for what they want with almost no regard for the feelings of others.

Another way of explaining these differences is to say that the nonassertive person is stepped on and the aggressive person steps on others, while the assertive person deals with a problem in a mature and direct manner. Suppose a stranger invites you to accompany

Human Relations Self-Assessment

QUIZ 9-1 Are You Nonassertive, Assertive, or Aggressive?

The following questionnaire is designed to give you tentative insight into your current tendencies toward submissiveness, assertiveness, or aggressiveness. As with other questionnaires presented in this book, the Assertiveness Scale is primarily a self-examination and discussion device. Answer each question Mostly True or Mostly False, as it applies to you.

	Mostly True	*Mostly False*
1. It is extremely difficult for me to turn down a sales representative when that individual is a nice person.	______	______
2. I express criticism freely.	______	______
3. If another person were being very unfair, I would bring it to that person's attention.	______	______
4. Work is no place to let your feelings show.	______	______
5. No use asking for favours; people get what they deserve on the job.	______	______
6. Business is not the place for tact; say what you think.	______	______
7. If a person looked as if he or she were in a hurry, I would let that person go in front of me in a supermarket line	______	______
8. A weakness of mine is that I'm too nice a person.	______	______
9. If my restaurant bill is even 25¢ more than it should be, I demand that the mistake be corrected.	______	______
10. I have laughed out loud in public more than once.	______	______
11. I've been described as too outspoken by several people.	______	______
12. I am quite willing to have the store take back a piece of furniture that is scratched.	______	______
13. I dread having to express anger toward a co-worker.	______	______
14. People often say that I'm too reserved and emotionally controlled.	______	______
15. Nice guys and gals finish last in business.	______	______
16. I fight for my rights down to the last detail.	______	______
17. I have no misgivings about returning an overcoat to the store if it doesn't fit me properly.	______	______
18. If I have had an argument with a person, I try to avoid him or her.	______	______
19. I insist on my spouse (or roommate or partner) doing his or her fair share of undesirable chores.	______	______
20. It is difficult for me to look directly at another person when the two of us are in disagreement.	______	______
21. I have cried among friends more than once.	______	______
22. If someone near me at a movie kept up a conversation with another person, I would ask him or her to stop.	______	______
23. I am able to turn down social engagements with people I do not particularly care for.	______	______
24. It is in poor taste to express what you really feel about another individual.	______	______
25. I sometimes show my anger by swearing at or belittling another person.	______	______
26. I am reluctant to speak 236up in a meeting.	______	______
27. I find it relatively easy to ask friends for small favours such as giving me a lift to work when my car is being repaired.	______	______

28. If another person were talking very loudly in a restaurant and it bothered me, I would inform that person. ______ ______
29. I often finish other people's sentences for them. ______ ______
30. It is relatively easy for me to express love and affection toward another person. ______ ______

Scoring and Interpretation: Give yourself a point for each of your answers that agrees with the scoring key. If your score is 15 or less, it is probable that you are currently a nonassertive individual. A score of 16 through 24 suggests that you are an assertive individual. A score of 25 or higher suggests that you are an aggressive individual. Retake this quiz about 30 days from now to give yourself some indication of the stability of your answers. You might also discuss your answers with a close friend to determine if that person has a similar perception of your assertiveness. Here is the scoring key.

1. Mostly False
2. Mostly True
3. Mostly True
4. Mostly False
5. Mostly False
6. Mostly True
7. Mostly False
8. Mostly False
9. Mostly True
10. Mostly True
11. Mostly True
12. Mostly True
13. Mostly False
14. Mostly False
15. Mostly True
16. Mostly True
17. Mostly True
18. Mostly False
19. Mostly True
20. Mostly False
21. Mostly True
22. Mostly True
23. Mostly True
24. Mostly False
25. Mostly True
26. Mostly False
27. Mostly True
28. Mostly True
29. Mostly True
30. Mostly True

him or her to a party and you do not wish to go with that person. Here are the three ways of responding according to the three-way classification under discussion:

ASSERTIVE: Thank you for the invitation but I prefer not to go.

NONASSERTIVE: I'm not sure, I might be busy. Could you call me again? Maybe I'll know for sure by then.

AGGRESSIVE: I'd like to go to a party, but not with you. Don't bother me again.

Gestures as well as words can communicate whether the person is being assertive, nonassertive, or aggressive. Exhibit 9-1 illustrates these differences.

Becoming More Assertive and Less Shy

There are a number of everyday actions a person can take to overcome shyness and lack of assertiveness. Shyness is a serious communication barrier for many individuals and can become part of feeling negative about oneself. **Shyness** can be defined as discomfort or an inhibition in interpersonal situations that interferes with the pursuit of personal or professional goals.[20] It has been estimated that as many as 40 percent of North Americans suffer from shyness, ranging from extreme to mild levels, at some point in their lives.[21] The following techniques are most helpful for less severe cases of shyness.

Exhibit 9-1
Assertive, Nonassertive, and Aggressive Gestures

Assertive	*Nonassertive*	*Aggressive*
• Well-balanced • Straight posture • Hand gestures, emphasizing key words	• Covering mouth with hand • Excessive head nodding • Tinkering with clothing or jewellery • Constant shifting of weight • Scratching or rubbing head or other parts of body • Wooden body posture	• Pounding fists • Stiff and rigid posture • Finger waving or pointing • Shaking head as if other person isn't to be believed • Hands on hips

Source: Donna E. Ledgerwood, "Workplace Relationships in the Federal Sector: Implications of Employees' Perceptions of Behavior," Presentation for Employees of Dallas Region United States Office of Personnel Management, 1989.

Even if the ones described here do not elevate your social skills, they will not backfire and cause you pain. After reading these techniques, you might be able to think of others that will work for you.[22]

Set a Goal Clearly establish in your mind in what ways you want to behave differently. Do you want to date more often? Speak out more in meetings? Be able to express dissatisfaction to co-workers? You can only overcome shyness by behaving differently; feeling differently is not enough.

Appear Warm and Friendly Shy people often communicate to others through their body language that they are not interested in reaching out to them. To overcome this impression, smile, lean forward, uncross your arms and legs, and unfold your hands.

Conduct Anonymous Conversations Try starting a conversation with a stranger in a safe setting such as a political rally, the waiting room of a medical office, a waiting line at the post office, or in a laundromat. Begin the conversation by addressing the common experience you are sharing at the time. Your conversation starters might resemble these:

- "I wonder if there will be any tickets left by the time we get to the box office?"
- "How long does it usually take before you get to see the doctor?"
- "Where did you get that laundry basket? I've never seen one so sturdy before."

Greet Strangers For the next week or so, greet every person you pass. Smile and make a neutral comment such as "How ya doing?" "Great day, isn't it?" Since most people are unaccustomed to being greeted by a stranger, you may get a few quizzical looks. Many other people may smile and return your greeting. A few of these greetings may turn

Human Relations Skill Building

Exercise 9-2 Becoming More Assertive by Being Decisive

An important part of being assertive is to be decisive. To enhance your decisiveness, follow these steps:

1. Make a list of the requests people make of you that are a burden. Review the list and select one or two requests that you will refuse in the next week. Think about how you will politely, but firmly, inform someone of your need to say "no," then carry out your plan. What happened? Did you feel less guilty than you thought you would?
2. Review the requests you want to make of others to help you meet your own needs. Select one or two. Get clear in your mind what you specifically want. Formulate each request so that it is as reasonable as possible for the person you will ask, then make your request(s). Did you get a positive response? Are you happy with the support you obtained?

Source: Adapted from Mel Silberman, with Freda Hansburg, *PeopleSmart: Developing Your Interpersonal Intelligence* (San Francisco: Berrett-Koehler Publishers, 2000), pp. 90–91.

into conversations. A few conversations may even turn into friendships. Even if the return on your investment in greetings is only a few pleasant responses, it will boost your confidence.

Practise Being Decisive An assertive person is usually decisive, so it is important to practise being decisive. Some nonassertive people are even indecisive when asked to make a choice from a restaurant menu. They communicate their indecisiveness by asking their friend, "What are you going to have?" or asking the server, "Could you please suggest something for me?" or "What's good?" Practise quickly sizing up the alternatives in any situation and reaching a decision. This will help you be assertive and also project an image of assertiveness. Human Relations Skill-Building Exercise 9-2 is designed to improve decisiveness.

SUMMARY

Conflict occurs when two sets of demands, goals, or motives are incompatible. Such differences often lead to a hostile or antagonistic relationship between people. A conflict can also be considered a dispute, feud, or controversy.

Among the reasons for widespread conflict are (1) competition for limited resources; (2) personality clashes; (3) culturally diverse teams; (4) microinequities; (5) harassment including sexual harassment; and (6) competing work and family demands. The *Canadian Human Rights Code* prohibits all forms of harassment, including sexual harassment.

The benefits of conflict include the emergence of talents and abilities, constructive innovation and change, and increased unity after the conflict is settled. Among the detrimental consequences of conflict are physical and mental health problems, wasted resources, the promotion of self-interest, and workplace violence.

Techniques for resolving conflicts with others include

1. Confrontation and problem solving leading to win–win—get to the root of the problem and resolve it systematically. The intention of confrontation and problem solving is to arrive at a collaborative solution to conflict.
2. Disarm the opposition—agree with the criticizer and enlist his or her help.
3. Cognitive restructuring—mentally convert negative aspects to positive ones by looking for the positive elements in the situation.
4. Appeal to a third party.
5. Use negotiation and bargaining tactics.
6. Use a mediator. Some conflicts may seem impossible to resolve and an objective third party with no vested interests may help find a mutually satisfying solution.

Negotiation and bargaining tactics include (1) create a positive negotiating climate; (2) allow room for compromise but be reasonable; (3) focus on interests, not positions; (4) make a last and final offer; and (5) allow for face-saving.

Several of the techniques for resolving conflict require assertiveness, or stating clearly what one wants and how one feels in a given situation. Being assertive also helps you develop good relationships with people and get more of what you want in life.

People can become more assertive and less shy by using techniques such as these:

1. Set a goal in relation to assertiveness.
2. Appear warm and friendly.
3. Conduct anonymous conversations.
4. Greet strangers.
5. Practise being decisive.

QUESTIONS AND ACTIVITIES

1. Why are conflict resolution skills considered so important in a culturally diverse workplace?
2. What differences in goals might management and workers have that would lead to conflict?
3. Give an example from your own life of how competition for limited resources can breed conflict.
4. A manager invites a subordinate to dinner. The subordinate declines the offer, yet the manager repeats the invitation every week for five weeks. Is this persistent asking a form of harassment? Explain.
5. Suppose a police officer catches you making a right turn on a red light without stopping. Which conflict-resolution method do you think would be best suited to handling the conflict with the officer? Explain.
6. Identify several occupations in which conflict-resolution skills are especially important.
7. You are dining in an expensive restaurant with a special person in your life. A person seated at the next table starts making a series of calls, in a loud voice, on his cell phone. You and your partner are upset about the calls interrupting your romantic dinner. Make up an assertive statement to tell the phone caller.

8. Some people with very successful careers are apparently aggressive, even to the point of being obnoxious. Why, then, is there an emphasis on being assertive on the job rather than aggressive?
9. How might extreme shyness interfere with personal and career goals?
10. Ask a successful person how much conflict he or she experiences in balancing the demands of work and personal life. Be prepared to report your findings in class.

INTERNET SKILL BUILDER

Conflict Management Advice on the Web

Resolving conflict is such an important life activity that most people need all the help they can get. Search the Web for advice about conflict resolution and see if you can acquire information to supplement the contents of this chapter. For this activity, you might first try a search engine that enables you to ask questions (e.g., "How do I resolve conflict?"), such as **google.**

Log on to the **Companion Website** at **www.pearsoncanada.ca/dubrin** to access additional resources for this chapter.

CASE STUDY 9-1 HUMAN RELATIONS

Generation X Meets Baby Boomer

While studying hotel and restaurant management at college, Cindy worked two part-time jobs: as a desk clerk at the Windmere Hotel and as a hostess at a restaurant. As graduation approached, Cindy sent résumés to many hotels around the country. She received a few encouraging responses, mostly advising her to contact the hotel after she had relocated to the area. In assessing her employment opportunities, Cindy decided that it would make sense to discuss a full-time position with the head manager at the Windmere. Much to Cindy's delight and amazement, the manager offered her a full-time position as assistant general manager. Cindy expressed a little hesitation about her ability to handle so much responsibility at this stage in her career. The manager assured Cindy that he had observed her handle difficult situations as a desk clerk and that she could easily become a competent assistant general manager. He also told Cindy that he and other staff members would be available to give her whatever assistance she needed.

Several weeks into her new position, Cindy felt confident that she was successfully handling her responsibilities, with one exception. The exception took the form of Stephanie, a night auditor with 20 years of experience at the Windmere. While attending high school, Stephanie worked part-time in housekeeping. Shortly after graduation, she married and became a parent. Cramped for money after her second child was born, Stephanie returned to the Windmere as the bell desk coordinator. She soon recognized that working during the day was not profitable because of the high child-care expenses she incurred. Stephanie transferred to the night auditor position, which she held for 14 years.

Stephanie was disturbed to learn that her new boss was Cindy, whom she described as "a Generation Xer half my age." Each night while auditing her boss's mistakes, Stephanie became increasingly frustrated. Finally, she decided to send Cindy an email message about her unacceptable performance, which initiated a series of emails sent back and forth between the two women:

TO: Cindy
FROM: Stephanie
I am starting to wonder if you are really qualified for your new position. I found loads of mistakes made by you and your staff in last night's audit. I knew this was going to happen! I have circled numerous errors from yesterday's transactions. Please fix them immediately.

TO: Stephanie
FROM: Cindy
Thank you for your ever so kind note! It is unfortunate you're having difficulty dealing with me in my new position. I *am* your boss, you know. I can imagine that this is a difficult thing for you to accept, but it's the truth. Be patient with me and my staff. We are not perfect!!!!

TO: Cindy
FROM: Stephanie
Your life as a student and part-time worker is over now. It's time you get cracking and take your new job a little bit more seriously. We've got a business to run here. Again, I remind you to inform your staff of their errors.

TO: Stephanie
FROM: Cindy
We've got to stop meeting like this! Ha ha! Please forgive me. The desk clerks and I have been so wild and crazy that we haven't had a free minute to work. By the way, whatever transactions you have been referring to are no longer errors. If you would read the updated procedures manual you would know this. Please keep current on the many changes being made by management.

TO: Cindy
FROM: Stephanie
Please find my letter of resignation in the envelope I placed on your desk this afternoon. Perhaps if the Windmere had hired an adult to replace Mr. Benton this would not have happened. Good luck finding a new night auditor who will stay with the hotel for 19.8 years. And one who was an entirely devoted employee.

Cindy thought to herself, "Did I do something terribly wrong, or am I dealing with a nut case? I wonder what I might have done differently. The general manager will not be too happy about Stephanie resigning."

Questions

1. What is the most likely source (or sources) of the conflict between Cindy and Stephanie?

2. What could Cindy have done to better resolve conflict with Stephanie?
3. What could Stephanie have done to better resolve conflict with Cindy?

Source: Case researched by Nicol0065 Harwood, Rochester Institute of Technology, May 1997.

CASE STUDY 9-2 HUMAN RELATIONS

Wal-Mart Plays Tough in Quebec

In electronics, only "Le Gros Albert" (Fat Albert) and a few other leftover DVDs remain. Over in household goods, liquidation tags dangle beside thin skillets as the Wal-Mart in Jonquiere, Quebec (Canada), prepares to close. The company shut the doors here May 6, 2005, after workers voted to make this the first unionized Wal-Mart in North America.

The closure left 190 bitter employees out of work and the town uneasy over the future of unions. Supporters of organized labor also say it serves as a warning for workers at other Wal-Mart stores who might contemplate defying founder Sam Walton's sharp distaste for unions. The world's largest retail chain has fiercely and successfully resisted unionization attempts at its 3,600 stores in the United States.

In Canada, the battle has been pitched, pitting the country's still-healthy union movement against what is now its largest retailer. Wal-Mart Stores Inc. now takes 52 percent of the retail market share in Canada and is opening about 30 stores a year. Jonquiere was the first store to be unionized.

Andrew Pelletier, head of corporate affairs for Wal-Mart Canada Corp., said that, although the union may have succeeded in organizing a store in Jonquiere, Wal-Mart workers have on five other occasions voted against unionization. "I think that says we are a good employer," Pelletier said.

Jonquiere, 120 miles north of Quebec City, is a French-speaking mill town of 60,000. Its bland neighborhoods of square clapboard homes attest to its origins a century ago as a center for the pulp-and-paper industry. The Wal-Mart here is one of three in the area, and it was welcomed when it opened more than three years ago. The town's manufacturing legs are getting old: The two paper mills closed lines in their plants in 2004, costing 1,200 jobs. "Economically, it's not a good time for us," said the mayor of the Saguenay area, Jean Tremblay. The new Wal-Mart was swamped with applications, and those who were hired thought themselves lucky.

"I never had a job as good as this before," said Lynn Morissette, 44, who tracks inventory in the store. "I worked in the daytime. I thought I had a good wage, and I was a shareholder, too, so I could save up some money. I was going to retire here." But others were not so thrilled about Wal-Mart's pay—starting at about $6.20 (U.S.) an hour, its floating shifts for part-timers, or the rules that limited some full-time employees to 28 hours of work a week. In an area built on union jobs, with higher wage scales, it wasn't long before some employees tried to organize.

Those involved in the organizing effort claim they were harassed by the company. "We were targeted fairly quickly by Wal-Mart," said Pierre Martineau, a 60-year-old maintenance man who helped organize the union. He said he was humiliated and ridiculed by managers at a storewide meeting and followed around by supervisors who made implied threats.

Those who did not want a union, say organizers, harassed them to join. "People signed the cards just to get some peace" from the union organizers, said Noella Langlois, 53, who works in the clothing department. "They thought they would vote against it in a secret vote." In fact, there was a vote last April that rejected the union. But under Quebec labor laws, the organizers could try again. When they collected signed union cards from 51 percent of the employees, the law declared the Jonquiere Wal-Mart a union shop.

Pelletier, the Wal-Mart spokesperson, says the Quebec laws are unfair, and only a secret ballot would show the true feelings of the workers. "Signing a union card, when there's someone on your doorstep at night saying, 'Sign this card,' should not be the last word," he said. "A democratic, secret vote is the only way to avoid intimidation by either the union or an employer."

But it became moot in February, when Wal-Mart announced it would close the store. Company officials said it was losing money, and the demands of the union would have made it even less tenable. "You can't take a store that is a struggling store anyway and add a bunch of people and a bunch of work rules," said Wal-Mart chief executive H. Lee Scott, Jr.

Some here in Jonquiere don't believe the company's claim that the store was losing money. They say the chain sacrificed the store to make a point to its employees across Canada and the United States, where union organizers are involved in dozens of organizing drives and court battles. "They closed it to be a threat to other unions," said Tremblay, the mayor. "We know that for Wal-Mart, Jonquiere is nothing. They wanted to close it to make a lesson to other Wal-Marts."

The announcement deepened animosities among the employees. Those who liked their jobs and said they were happy at Wal-Mart are bitter at the union for its tactics, which they blame for the store closure.

Sylvie Lavoie, 40, said she is unsure how, as a single mother, she will support herself and her 10-year-old daughter after the store closes. But the backup cashier, who earns $7.55 an hour, said she does not regret joining the union drive. "We can't regret trying to make our lives better," she said at the union hall. "I don't know what I'll do, but I know my daughter will be proud of me."

Questions

1. Which technique of conflict resolution might have made it possible for Wal-Mart to stay open in Jonquiere?
2. How might the Wal-Mart workers who opposed the union and those that favoured the union have approached their differences?
3. What has this case got to do with human relations skills?

Source: Excerpted from Doug Struck, "Wal-Mart Leaves Bitter Chill: Quebec Store Closes after Vote to Unionize," *Washington Post Foreign Service*, April 14, 2005, p. E01.

Chapter 10

Getting Along with Your Manager or Team Leader

Learning Outcomes

After reading the information and doing the exercises in this chapter, you should be able to

- recognize the impact your manager has on your future;
- select several tactics for creating a favourable impression on your present or future manager;
- select several tactics for dealing with your manager in a constructive manner;
- prepare to deal effectively with a manager whom you perceive as being intolerable.

Kevin, an accountant in receivables for a recycling company, had an idea that would save the company time and money when contracting out work to truck owners for the local recycling pickups. Some truck drivers took longer hours to run a route than other trucks from other companies. Current practice was that the truck owners billed the company for the number of hours the truck was en route. This practice resulted in a great deal of work for those in accounting, who had to tally hours monthly, often using scraps of paper that the drivers handed in. This system had led to serious errors in both overpaying and underpaying some drivers. Also, it was believed that some drivers were billing for hours that were not used or that drivers were taking too much time. On the other hand, some drivers with faster, state-of-the-art trucks were earning less than those with the older and slower rigs.

Kevin's idea was that each route should be averaged based on the last year of payment for each route and that each independent driver would be paid the same based on the yearly average. In this way, the route itself was the basis of the payment rather than the number of hours it took for each driver to complete the circuit. As well, by using averaging, areas where the pickups were bigger would be factored into the time that it took to complete the route. By simplifying the process, records could be quickly computerized and payments made on time and more accurately.

Kevin, supported by his team leader, took the idea to the owner of the company. Upon hearing his idea, the owner stated, "Why, I like the idea in principle.

I need to hear more and get more data. I'll have to let your team leader know how impressed I am with your work and creativity. Good work!" Upon hearing from the owner, Kevin's team leader commented on how well Kevin had done and that this would be included in his file for his next performance appraisal.

In this chapter, we present a variety of strategies and tactics that lead to constructive relationships with an immediate superior, manager, or team leader. Getting along with your manager as well as co-workers is regarded by many as having good **political skills**, an interpersonal style that combines awareness of others with the ability to communicate well. People with political skill are charming and engaging, which inspires confidence, trust, and sincerity.[1] The strategies and tactics are grouped for convenience into three categories: creating a favourable impression on your manager, dealing with your manager directly, and coping with an intolerable manager.

CREATING A FAVOURABLE IMPRESSION ON YOUR MANAGER OR TEAM LEADER

The strategies and tactics in this section all help you create a favourable impression on the boss. The term *impression* refers to a true impression, not a false one. Following these straightforward suggestions helps you deserve a positive reputation.

Achieve Good Job Performance

Good performance remains the most vital strategy for impressing your manager. When any rational manager evaluates a group or team member's performance, the first question asked is "Is this employee getting the job done?" And you cannot get the job done if you are not competent.

Many factors contribute to whether you can become a competent performer. Among them are your education, training, personality characteristics, job experience, and special skills, such as being able to solve problems, resolve conflict, and organize your work. Much of this book discusses skills, techniques, and strategies that are designed to contribute to job competence.

An advanced way of displaying good job performance is to assist your manager or team leader with a difficult problem he or she faces. Your manager or team leader, for example, might need to know how to operate equipment outside his or her area of expertise. If you show your manager or team leader how to operate the equipment, he or she will think more highly of your job performance. Being part of a team means being helpful and cooperative to all team members including the team leader. In teams where each member may have a specialized skill including the leader, this type of assistance is essential to team success. If you demonstrate these characteristics, you are displaying good job performance as well as demonstrating good teamwork.

Display a Strong Work Ethic

A major factor contributing to good job performance is a strong **work ethic**, a firm belief in the dignity and value of work. People with a strong work ethic have strong internal motivation. An employee with a strong work ethic will sometimes be excused if his or her performance is not yet exceptional. This is true because the manager assumes that a strong work ethic will elevate performance eventually. A strong work ethic is more in demand today than ever because many organizations are thinly staffed. With fewer people performing the same amount of work, everybody has to work harder. The best overall way to display a strong work ethic is to work hard and enjoy the task. Six specific suggestions for demonstrating a strong work ethic follow:

1. *Work hard and enjoy the task.* By definition, a person with a strong work ethic works diligently and has strong internal motivation. The person may appreciate external rewards yet recognize the importance of any work that adds value to society.
2. *Demonstrate competence even on minor tasks.* Attack each assignment with the recognition that each task performed well, however minor, is one more career credit. A minor task performed well paves the way for your being given more consequential tasks.
3. *Assume personal responsibility for problems.* An employee with a problem will often approach the manager and say, "We have a tough problem to deal with." The connotation is that the manager should be helping the employee with the problem. A better impression is created when the employee says, "I have a tough problem to deal with, and I would like your advice." This statement implies that you are willing to assume responsibility for the problem and for any mistake you may have made that led to it.
4. *Assume responsibility for free-floating problems.* A natural way to display a strong work ethic is to assume responsibility for free-floating (nonassigned) problems. Taking on even a minor task, such as ordering lunch for a meeting that is running late, can enhance the impression one makes on a manager.
5. *Get your projects completed promptly.* A by-product of a strong work ethic is an eagerness to get projects completed promptly. People with a strong work ethic respect deadlines imposed by others. Furthermore, they typically set deadlines of their own that are even more tight than those imposed by their boss.
6. *Accept undesirable assignments willingly.* Another way of expressing a strong work ethic is to accept undesirable assignments willingly. Look for ways to express the attitude, "Whether or not this assignment is glamorous and fun is a secondary issue. What counts is that it is something that needs to be done for the good of the company."

Demonstrate Good Emotional Intelligence

A worker who deals effectively with the emotional responses of co-workers and customers is impressive, because feelings and emotions are a big challenge on the job. Such behaviour reflects emotional intelligence, defined in Chapter 5 in relation to dealing with anger. Emotional intelligence can also be regarded as the use of nonverbal cues, emotions, feelings, and mood. The person with good emotional intelligence recognizes and understands his or her own feelings and those of others.[2]

Demonstrating good emotional intelligence is impressive because it contributes to performing well in the difficult arena of dealing with feelings. A worker with good emotional intelligence would engage in such behaviours as (1) recognizing when a co-worker needs help but is too embarrassed to ask, (2) dealing with the anger of a dissatisfied customer, (3) recognizing that the boss is facing considerable pressure also, and (4) being able to tell whether a customer's "maybe" means "yes" or "no."

Be Dependable, Honest, and Ethical

Dependability is a critical employee virtue. If an employee can be counted on to deliver as promised, and to be at work regularly, that employee has gone a long way toward impressing the boss. A boss is uncomfortable not knowing whether an important assignment will be accomplished on time. If you are not dependable, you will probably not get your share of important assignments. Honesty is tied to dependability because a dependable employee is honest about when he or she will have an assignment completed.

Dependability and honesty are important at all job levels. One of the highest compliments a manager can pay an employee is to describe the employee as dependable. Conversely, it is considered derogatory to call any employee undependable. As one company president put it when describing a subordinate: "When he's great, he's terrific, but I can't depend on him. I'd rather he be more consistent even if he delivered fewer peak successes—at least I could rely on him."[3]

People who are *ethical* have high morals and treat others with respect and dignity. They do not engage in backstabbing or bad-mouthing their managers, team leaders, or co-workers. Ethical employees make sound judgments when completing their assignments and report their decisions to the manager. For example, if one of your responsibilities is to find out the costs of some new equipment, you get several quotes in a straightforward and honest manner. You do not engage in such activities as promising the company more favours later on if the price can be reduced, getting prices only from friends, or engaging in other questionable methods of "doing business." Such unethical conduct will reflect not only upon you, but upon your manager and company as well.

Ethical workers also do not mislead customers by stating a product is better than it really is or that an item can do more than stated in the product brochure. Lying about a product or pretending that something is a real "deal" or "steal" is also unethical. Dissatisfied customers who return with complaints about the item reflect poorly upon you, your manager, and your company. Lastly, "bad-mouthing" about competitors to customers is also considered unethical and many managers will not appreciate this behaviour. Remember that managers attend seminars, trade fairs, and the like where they do interact with competitors, and your manager may hear about your behaviour from the manager whose company you have been disparaging. Competition does not mean unfriendly relations.

Appreciate Your Manager's Strengths

You may not admire every boss you work for, particularly early in your career. Your young boss might be inexperienced and therefore less than ideal. Older managers you work for early in your career might be people who have been passed over for promotion many times. In other words, the company recognizes they are not the strongest supervisors. But they are usually competent enough to perform their jobs satisfactorily.

If you focus only on the weaknesses of your boss, you will probably communicate many negative nonverbal messages to that individual. For instance, when your boss is making general suggestions, you might display a bored expression on your face. Instead of thinking primarily about your boss's weakness, look for strengths. Look for answers to such questions as, "What knowledge does he or she have that can help me advance my career?" "What good points about my boss led to his or her promotion?" or "What do some of my co-workers see as my boss's strengths?" A case in point is Bruce, a young sales representative:

> Having recently graduated from business school, Bruce was fired up with modern techniques of selling, such as identifying the customer's most pressing problems. He was somewhat perplexed about why his boss, Arlie, was considered such an outstanding sales manager. He displayed few of the management techniques that Bruce had studied in school. Bruce then spoke to an aunt who worked in another department of the same company. "How come old Arlie is so highly regarded? He doesn't seem to know much about sales techniques or management." Bruce's aunt replied, "You could be right, Bruce. But Arlie knows how to read people and how to form good relationships. He's what is known as a good personal salesman."
>
> From that point on, Bruce began to look at techniques that Arlie used for forming good relationships with people. As he showed a sincere interest in learning more from Arlie, their relationship improved.

Show an Interest in Your Firm's Products or Services

Showing a genuine interest in your company and its products or services impresses superiors in both commercial and not-for-profit firms. This tactic works because so many workers do not identify with their employers. Many employees are not even familiar with what their organization is trying to accomplish. A natural opportunity for showing interest in your firm's products and services is to promote them. Find a way to promote your company's products or services and you will endear yourself to top management. The next step is to casually mention that you are actively using the product. As an administrative assistant working for a printer manufacturer told a vice president:

> My husband and I bought one of our desktop colour printers two years ago. We've become the neighbourhood print shop whenever somebody wants to prepare a fancy graphic. So far, the printer has never been back for service. Our neighbours are so impressed with the printer that two of them plan to buy one of their own.

Another way of showing an interest in your firm's product and services is to become familiar with the company website by visiting it regularly. In this way you can make informed comments about the website after speaking to key people about other matters. A question such as the following reflects legitimate interest: "How is the direct sale program over the internet going?"

Be a Good Organizational Citizen

An especially meritorious approach to impressing key people is to demonstrate organizational citizenship behaviour, the willingness to work for the good of the organization even without the promise of a specific reward. A good organizational citizen would do such things as assisting a person with a computer problem outside his or her team or department, or picking up a broken bottle on the company lawn. Organizational citizenship behaviour is increasing in importance as organizations face the challenge of global competition and the need for continuous innovation. The good organizational citizen goes above and beyond the call of duty.[4]

An effective way of being a good organizational citizen is to step outside your job description. Job descriptions are characteristic of a well-organized firm. If everybody knows what he or she is supposed to be doing, there will be much less confusion, and goals will be achieved. This logic sounds impressive, but job descriptions have a major downside. If people engage only in work included in their job description, the prevailing mentality becomes, "It's not my job." An effective way to impress your manager is therefore to demonstrate that you are not constrained by a job description. If something needs doing, you will get it done whether or not it is your formal responsibility.

An impressive way of stepping outside your job description is to anticipate problems, even when the manager had not planned to work on them. Anticipating problems is characteristic of a resourceful person who exercises initiative. Instead of working exclusively on problems that have been assigned, the worker is perceptive enough to look for future problems. Anticipating problems impresses most managers because it reflects an entrepreneurial, take-charge attitude.

Create a Strong Presence

A comprehensive approach to impressing your manager or team leader and other key people in the workplace is to create a strong presence, or keep yourself in the forefront. Such actions impress key people and simultaneously help advance your career. Stephanie Sherman, a career consultant, offers this advice for creating a strong presence:

- Get involved in high-visibility projects such as launching a new product or redesigning work methods. Even an entry-level position on such a project can be impressive.
- Get involved in teams because they give you an opportunity to broaden your skills and knowledge.
- Get involved in social and community activities of interest to top management, such as those sponsored by the company. Behave professionally and use your best manners.
- Create opportunities for yourself by making constructive suggestions about earning or saving money. Even if an idea is rejected, you will still be remembered for your initiative.
- Show a willingness to take on some of the tasks that your manager doesn't like to do but would be forced to do if you did not step in.[5]

DEALING DIRECTLY WITH YOUR MANAGER

To develop a good relationship with your manager, you need to create a favourable impression, as already described. You also need to focus directly on your relationship with your manager in terms of your work transactions with him or her. In this section, we emphasize techniques geared toward transactions with the boss, rather than focusing on the impression you create. (Do not be concerned about overlap in the categories.)

Understand Your Manager

A crucial aspect of developing a good working relationship with the boss is to understand the boss, including the environment in which the boss works. An important starting point in understanding your manager is to recognize his or her style. A **style** is a person's way of doing things. Walter St. John identifies some questions that need to be answered to understand one's manager.[6]

1. What is your manager's position in the company hierarchy? What are his or her relationships with his or her manager?
2. What are your manager's blind spots, prejudices, pet peeves, and sore spots? What constitute positive and negative words to your manager?
3. Does your manager understand better as a reader (should you send a memo) or as a listener (should you tell him or her in person)?
4. Is your manager a morning or evening person? When is the best time of the day to approach your manager?
5. What is your manager's preference for getting things done?
6. What is most important to your manager?
7. What nonverbal signals does your manager communicate to you?

Finding answers to these questions, including understanding your manager's style, may involve discussions with co-workers as well as with the boss directly. Concentrate on "how" questions, such as "This is my first report for Julie. How does she like it done? Does she want a one-page summary at the beginning of the report or at the end?" Speaking to co-workers can also reveal what kinds of attitudes your boss expects you to have. For example, does the boss really believe that the customer is always right? Your question may also reveal that your manager is jumping to please a demanding superior. If this is true, you may be expected to do the same.[7]

Find Out What Your Manager Expects of You

You have little chance of doing a good job and impressing your manager unless you know what you are trying to accomplish. Work goals and performance standards represent the most direct ways of learning your manager's expectations. Review your work goals and ask clarifying questions. An example would be, "You told me to visit our major customers who are 60 days or more delinquent on their accounts. Should I also visit the three of these customers who have declared bankruptcy?" In addition to having a clear statement of your goals, it is helpful to know the priorities attached to them. In this way you will know which task to execute first.

A **performance standard** is a statement of what constitutes acceptable performance. These standards can sometimes be inferred from a job description. For example, part of the job description of a payroll specialist is to "calculate and maintain provincial and federal tax returns." The payroll specialist would therefore be meeting a standard by accurately computing these taxes. Performance standards are sometimes stated in quantitative terms, such as, "process an average of 50 medical insurance claims per day."

A subtle aspect of understanding the expectations of your boss is adapting to his or her preferred style of work. Managers vary in terms of wanting written versus oral briefings. Some managers prefer to receive email messages from you regularly, others once a week. Some managers want to be treated informally, much like being a co-worker. A minority of managers wanted to be treated as if they were royalty. Matching your work style to the work style of your boss can help build a strong relationship between the two of you.

Bring Forth Solutions as Well as Problems

An advanced tactic for developing a good working relationship with your immediate superior is to bring solutions to your boss's attention, not just problems. Too often, group members ask to see their bosses only when they have problems requiring help. A boss under pressure may thus anticipate additional pressure when a group member asks for an appointment. The subordinate who comes forth with a solved problem is thus regarded as a welcome relief. In short, you can ease your manager's suffering by walking into his or her office and saying, "Here's what I did about that mess that was plaguing us yesterday. Everything is under control now."

Minimize Complaints

In the previous chapter we extolled the virtues of being open and honest in expressing your feelings and opinions. Nevertheless, this type of behaviour when carried to excess could earn you a reputation as a whiner. Few managers want to have a group member around who constantly complains about working conditions, co-workers, working hours, pay, and so forth. An employee who complains too loudly and frequently quickly becomes labelled as a pill or a pest.

Another important reason a boss usually dislikes having a subordinate who complains too much is that listening to these complaints takes up considerable time. Most managers spend a disproportionate amount of time listening to the problems of a small number of ineffective or complaining employees. Consciously or unconsciously, a manager who has to listen to many of your complaints may find a way to seek revenge.

How then does an employee make valid complaints to the manager? The answer is to complain only when justified. And when you do offer a complaint, back it up with a recommended solution. Anyone can take potshots at something. The valuable employee is the person who backs up these complaints with a constructive action plan. The following are two examples of complaints, backed up by action plans for remedying the complaint:

- "I've noticed that several of us get very tired feet by the end of the working day. Maybe we could perform this work just as well if we sat on high stools."
- "We have a difficult time handling emergency requests when you are away from the department. I would suggest that when you will be away for more than one or two hours, one of us can serve as the acting supervisor. It could be done on a rotating basis to give each of us some supervisory experience."

One possibility for minimizing the need for complaints is to attempt to look at decisions from the boss's point of view. The company might decide to block access to instant messaging and facebook from company computers. Instead of complaining that the prohibition on instant messages is unjust, the worker might attempt to understand why the company management thinks instant messages lower productivity.

Avoid Bypassing Your Manager

A good way to embarrass and sometimes infuriate your manager is to repeatedly go to his or her superior with your problems, conflicts, and complaints. Such bypasses have at least three strongly negative connotations. One is that you don't believe your boss has the power to take care of your problem. Another is that you distrust his or her judgment in the matter at hand. A third is that you are secretly launching a complaint against your manager.

The boss bypass is looked on so negatively that most experienced managers will not listen to your problem unless you have already discussed it with your immediate superior. There are times, however, when running around your manager is necessary, for example, when you have been unable to resolve a conflict directly with him or her (see the following section). But even under these circumstances, you should politely inform your manager that you are going to take up your problem with the next level of management.

In short, if you want to keep on the good side of your manager, bring all problems directly to him or her. If your boss is unable or unwilling to take care of the problem, you might consider contacting your boss's superior. Nonetheless, considerable tact and diplomacy are needed. Do not imply that your manager is incompetent, but merely that you would like another opinion about the issues at stake.

Suggest Improvements during the Performance Evaluation

An effective method of enhancing your relationship with your manager is to use the performance evaluation session as an opportunity to suggest a variety of work improvements. Making suggestions for improvement during the performance evaluation is logical because one purpose of an evaluation is to bring about improvements. After your manager has completed his or her agenda, volunteer ideas for such topics as these:

- Helping the department run more smoothly
- Making better use of your skills
- Saving time or money for the company
- Increasing productivity and quality[8]

Suggesting ideas of this nature communicates the fact that you perceive performance evaluation as an opportunity for both individual and company improvements. An attitude of this type will usually strengthen the relationship with your manager. If your company uses a peer evaluation system (as described in Chapter 1), look for an opportunity to make improvement suggestions to peers as well. However, also be aware that performance evaluations are not always the most positive of experiences as indicated by the Canada Today feature below.

Canada Today

Performance Appraisals—What Do They Really Accomplish?

Performance appraisals or performance evaluations are nearly universal in professionally managed organizations. A performance appraisal or evaluation usually involves a session where the employee sits down with an immediate supervisor (sometimes more than one) and reviews performance over a specified time. In some companies, such evaluations are used to decide upon such issues as promotions and pay or merit raises, and to plan for future performance changes. For the most part, these appraisals are a "top-down" process based on the ideas of what the manager thinks about the employee's past performance.

A 1997 survey of 2,004 Canadian workers, conducted by Watson Wyatt Worldwide, a consulting firm, discovered that performance appraisals are not an employee growth process but can actually be a disturbing and negative experience for many workers. According to this survey, only 57 percent of employees thought that they were evaluated fairly. Only 39 percent stated that the appraisal was useful for improving their performance (supposedly a major goal of evaluations and appraisals). Also of interest, only 42 percent reported that they had regular performance reviews. For many employees, performance appraisal time may be the only extensive communication with their upper-level managers. Fewer than two out of every five respondents in the survey stated that they talk with their leader or manager regularly about performance-related issues.

What can we conclude from this survey? First, many appraisals are a top-down meeting where the employer talks and the employee listens. Second, many of these appraisals are not done effectively, as they do not encourage better performance or allow employees any input or involvement in increasing their productivity. So while performance evaluations may be one avenue to impress your manager or team leader, such evaluations should not be the only time that you take an opportunity to do so. Instead, use a variety of the techniques that are discussed in this chapter.

Resolve Competing Demands of Two Managers

A substantial change in the modern workplace is that many workers report to more than one manager. A typical arrangement is for a person to report to a manager in his or her regular or *home* department. At the same time the person also reports to the head of a project, or task force, or team. Many people like this arrangement because it adds variety and excitement to the workday. An unfortunate consequence of having two bosses, however, is that you might be caught in conflict. One boss might make a demand that is incompatible with a demand made by the other boss. You might be asked to attend two meetings at the same time, or told by both bosses that some task has to be done immediately.

A recommendation for resolving the competing demands of two managers is to assemble a list of possible solutions that you can sell to both parties. After you have prepared your solutions, explain to both managers the pros and cons of each solution. Recommend which one you think would work best, and describe how it would be implemented. Get a reaction from each manager. After you have taken the steps just indicated, you and the two bosses might have a three-way discussion to resolve the issue.[9] The three of you might decide, for example, that the only way you can get both their projects done immediately is to hire an office temporary for the duration of the project.

Use Discretion in Socializing with Your Manager

A constant dilemma facing employees is how much and what type of socializing with the manager is appropriate. Advocates of socializing contend that off-the-job friendships lead to more natural work relationships. Opponents of socializing with the boss say that it leads to **role confusion** (being uncertain about what role you are carrying out). For example, how can your manager make an objective decision about your salary increase on Monday morning when he or she had dinner with you on Sunday? To avoid cries of favouritism, your boss might recommend you for a below-average increase.

One guideline to consider is to have cordial social relationships with the manager, of the same kind shared by most employees. "Cordial" socializing includes activities such as company-sponsored parties, group invitations to the boss's home, and business lunches. Individual social activities, such as camping with the boss, double-dating, and so forth, are more likely to lead to role confusion.

Socializing should not include a casual romantic involvement. Romantic involvements between a superior and a subordinate are disruptive to work and morale. Co-workers usually suspect that the manager's special friend is getting special treatment and resent the favouritism.

What should you do if you and your boss seem suited for a long-term commitment? Why walk away from Mr. or Ms. Right? Our suggestion is that if you do become romantically involved, one of you should request a transfer to another department. Many office romances do lead to happy marriages and other long-term relationships. At the start of the relationship, however, use considerable discretion. Engaging in personal conversation during work time and holding hands in the company cafeteria are unprofessional and taboo.

Engage in Favourable Interactions with Your Manager

The many techniques described previously support the goal of engaging in favourable interactions with your manager. A study of interactions between bank employees and their supervisors showed that purposely trying to create a positive impression on the supervisor led to better performance ratings.[10] Although the finding is not surprising, it is reassuring to know that it is backed by quantitative evidence. Human Relations Self-Assessment Quiz 10-1 contains a listing of behaviours used by employees in the study to create positive interactions with their supervisors. Use these behaviours as a guide for skill building.

Although favourable interactions with a manager are valuable for relationship building, there are times when a group member has to deliver bad news. For example, you might have to inform the manager about a burst water pipe in the mainframe computer room or a bunch of customer complaints about a new product. You want to avoid being the messenger who is punished because he or she delivered bad news. Attempt to be calm and businesslike. Do not needlessly blame yourself for the problem. Mention that *we* (or *the company*) are facing a serious challenge. If possible, suggest a possible solution such as, "I have already investigated a backup computer service we can use until the damage is repaired."

Human Relations Self-Assessment

QUIZ 10-1 Supervisor Interaction Checklist

Use the following behaviours as a checklist for achieving favourable interactions with your present manager or a future one. The more of these actions you are engaged in, the higher the probability that you are building a favourable relationship with your manager.

1. Agree with your supervisor's major opinions outwardly even when you disagree inwardly. ______
2. Take an immediate interest in your supervisor's personal life. ______
3. Praise your supervisor on his or her accomplishments. ______
4. Do personal favours for your supervisor. ______
5. Do something as a personal favour for your supervisor even though you are not required to do it. ______
6. Volunteer to help your supervisor with a task. ______
7. Compliment your supervisor on his or her dress or appearance. ______
8. Present yourself to your supervisor as being a friendly person. ______
9. Agree with your supervisor's major ideas. ______
10. Present yourself to your supervisor as being a polite person. ______

Source: Adapted from Sandy J. Wayne and Gerald R. Ferris, "Influence Tactics, Affect, and Exchange Quality in Supervisor–Subordinate Interactions: A Laboratory Experiment and Field Study," *Journal of Applied Psychology*, October 1990, p. 494.

COPING WITH A PROBLEM MANAGER

Up to this point, we have prescribed tactics for dealing with a reasonably rational boss. At some point in their careers many people face the situation of dealing with a problem manager—one who makes it difficult for the subordinate to get the job done. The problem is sometimes attributed to the boss's personality or incompetence. At other times, differences in values or goals could be creating the problem. However, also realize that some behaviours of managers go beyond problematic to more serious concerns about harassment or bullying. These suggestions are not designed to deal with this type of behaviour, and suggestions for these more serious behaviours were presented in Chapter 9. However, Exhibit 10-1 later in this section offers some suggestions if you perceive your manager as a bully. Our concern here is with constructive approaches to dealing with the delicate situation of working for a problem manager, not one who harasses or bullies you.

Re-evaluate Your Manager

Some problem managers are not really a problem. Instead, they have been misperceived by one or more group members. Some employees think they have problem managers when they simply have major role, goal, or value differences with their boss. (A role in this context consists of the expectations of the job.) The problem might also lie in conflicting personalities, such as being outgoing or shy. Another problem is conflicting perspectives, such as being detail-oriented as opposed to taking an overall perspective. The differences just noted can be good or bad, depending on how they are viewed and used. For example, a detail-oriented group member working with an "overall perspective" boss can be a winning combination.[11]

Another approach to being more cautious in evaluating your manager is to judge slowly and fairly. Many decisions your manager makes may prove to be worthwhile if you give the decisions on time.[12] Top management at your company might issue an order that employees cannot surf the Web for personal reasons on the job. You might think this rule is unfair and treats workers like adolescents. If you wait for the result of the decisions, you might find that productivity improves. Another benefit might be that many workers no longer have to work late because they save time by not surfing.

Confront Your Manager about the Problem

A general-purpose way of dealing with a problem manager is to use confrontation and problem solving as described in Chapter 9. Because your manager has more formal authority than you, the confrontation must be executed with the highest level of tact and sensitivity. A beginning point in confronting a manager is to gently ask for an explanation of the problem. Suppose, for example, you believe strongly that your team leader snubs you because he or she dislikes you. You might inquire gently, "What might I be doing wrong that is creating a problem between us?"

Another situation calling for confrontation would be outrageous behaviour by the manager, such as swearing at and belittling group members. Since several members, or all group members, are involved, a group discussion of the problem might be warranted. Exhibit 10-1 gives some suggestions as to how to deal with a manager who is a bully. You and your co-workers might meet as a group to discuss the impact of the manager's style on group morale and productivity. This tactic runs the risk of backfiring if the manager becomes defensive and angry. Yet career adviser Jim Miller believes it is worth the risk, because the problem of abuse will not go away without discussion.[13]

Confrontation can also be helpful in dealing with the problem of **micromanagement**, the close monitoring of most aspects of group member activities by the manager. "Looking over your shoulder" constantly is an everyday way of describing micromanagement. If you feel that you are being supervised so closely that it is difficult to perform well, confront the situation. Say something of this nature: "I notice that you check almost everything I do lately. Am I making so many errors that you are losing confidence in my work?"[14] As a consequence, the manager might explain why he or she is micromanaging or begin to check on your work less frequently.

Learn from Your Manager's Mistakes

Just as you can learn from watching your manager do things right, you can also learn from watching him or her do things wrong. In the first instance, we are talking about using your manager as a positive model. "Modelling" of this type is an important source of learning on the job. Using a superior as a negative model can also be of some benefit. As an elementary example, if your manager criticized you in public, and you felt humiliated, you would have learned a good lesson in effective supervision: Never criticize a

Exhibit 10-1
Is Your Boss a Bully?

Many managers might think of themselves as being very effective as they work hard to keep employees in line. These managers push employees, adjusting goals and micro-managing the tasks they assign to be completed. These are tough managers who may yell, insult, and patronize their subordinates. But when does "pushing hard" become bullying, and do you have to put up with it?

Bullying is any behaviour that intimidates, humiliates, or demeans you. If your boss yells at you and you just roll your eyes and it does not bother you, this might not be bullying. But if it does bother you, humiliate you, or stress you out, and you are the particular target, then you are being bullied. Bullying can range from personal insults and unjustified criticism to physically abusive or aggressive behaviour. Historically, bullying has gone on basically unchecked, often dismissed as a personality conflict or the strong management style of the supervisor. However, due to more public cases in Canada (such as the case of Pierre Lebrun, who went on a shooting spree at his workplace in Ottawa after being continually bullied by colleagues because of his speech impediment and facial tic), many companies are including behaviours like bullying under the same category as harassment in their policies, with the same consequences.

Here are a few suggestions if you feel you are being bullied by your manager (or even another co-worker), based on procedures for reporting and dealing with harassment:

- Confront the person with his or her behaviour and the effect it is having upon you. Your manager may not have thought the behaviour was problematic, particularly if he or she has always treated employees in this fashion.
- Consult fellow workers. If the manager treats them as he or she treats you and they don't have a problem with it, you may need to re-evaluate your feelings. For example, if co-workers say, "Oh, she yells at everyone. After a while, you just ignore it, especially when you see the Christmas bonus cheques."
- Keep a log of all incidents. If you report the bullying, you will need the dates of the incidents as well as a clear and concise record of what happened. One recent case in Canada that did go to court awarded an RCMP officer over $90,000 in lost earnings and nervous shock after she was bullied by fellow officers and her immediate supervisor.
- Report the behaviour to the human resources department using company policies and procedures. It is up to Human Resources then to investigate your complaint and resolve the issue either formally or informally.
- Above all, remember that you do have rights. You do not have to tolerate a poisonous work environment. If you have questions, call your local Labour Board office or Human Rights Office.

Source: Lauren M. Bernardi, "Management by Bullying: The Legal Consequences," *Canadian Manager,* 26(3), Fall 2001, pp. 13–16.

subordinate publicly. By serving as a negative example your manager has taught you a valuable lesson.

Learning from a problem manager's mistakes can also occur when a manager or team leader is fired. Should your manager be fired, analyze the situation to avoid the mistakes he or she made. Enlist the help of others in understanding what went wrong. Did the manager get along poorly with the higher-level managers? Was the manager lacking in technical expertise? Did the manager not work hard enough? Did the manager commit ethical or legal violations such as sexual harassment or stealing company property? Whatever the reason, you will learn quickly what behaviour the company will not tolerate. If your manager was fired simply as a way to downsize or cut costs, there is still a lesson to be learned. Attempt to prove to the company that your compensation is a good investment for the company because your work is outstanding. In lean and mean times, your continued excellent performance may be your only ticket to promotion and continued employment!

What to Do When Your Manager Ignores Your Suggestions

One subtype of a problem manager is the one who ignores suggestions because he or she prefers to maintain the status quo. These managers see their jobs as simply running a smooth operation, and they perceive employees who continue to bring forth suggestions as troublemakers. The problem with not bringing forth innovative ideas is that you will never earn the reputation of being imaginative and ambitious.

A management research report offers several suggestions for coping with this form of problem manager. One approach is to implement your idea without his or her approval. If your idea works out well, your manager may embrace your suggestion. Another tactic is to cultivate your boss's superior. Tactfully tell your boss's boss about your innovative idea. He or she might support your idea and give you the green light to implement it.[15]

A real problem with cultivating your boss's boss is that a boss bypass is generally frowned upon. However, so long as you do not say or imply anything negative about your manager, it could be worth a try. You might say to his or her superior, "I have brought this to Ms. McHendry's attention, but she's too busy with other projects now to dig into my proposal."

What to Do When Your Manager Takes Credit for Your Accomplishments

Imagine that you have been assigned the job of making the arrangements for a company meeting. Everything runs so smoothly that at the banquet your manager is praised for his or her fine job of arranging the meeting. You smoulder while he or she accepts all the praise without mentioning that you did all the work. How should you handle a problem manager of this type—one who takes credit for your accomplishments?

Remember, first, that in one sense your manager does deserve much of the credit. Managers are responsible for the accomplishments and failures of their subordinates.

Your boss had the good sense to delegate the task to the right person. Nevertheless, a self-confident manager would share the credit with you. To get the credit you deserve for your ideas and accomplishments, try these suggestions:

1. *Try a discreet confrontation.* The manager who is taking credit for your accomplishments may not realize that you are being slighted. A quiet conversation about the issue could prevent recurrences. You might gently ask, for example, "At what point do I get recognition for doing an assigned task well? I noticed that my name was not mentioned when our department received credit for setting up a new billing system." (It was you who did 95 percent of the work on the system.)
2. *Take preventive measures.* A sensible way to receive credit for your accomplishments is to let others know of your efforts while you are doing the work. This is more effective than looking for recognition after your manager has already taken credit for your accomplishments. Casually let others know what you are doing, including your boss's boss and other key people. In this way you will not sound immodest or aggressive—you are only talking about your work.
3. *Present a valid reason for seeking recognition.* By explaining why you want recognition, you will not seem unduly ambitious or pushy to your manager. You might say, "I am trying to succeed in this company. It would help me to document my performance. Would it therefore be possible for my name to also appear on the report of the new billing system?"[16]

How to Work with a Disorganized Manager

Many well-organized people report to disorganized managers, creating the opportunity for tension and personality clashes. Under these circumstances, the well-organized subordinate faces the challenge of creating a good working relationship. In contrast, a well-organized boss is unlikely to put up with a disorganized subordinate for long. Given that the well-organized group member cannot readily fire the boss, he or she faces the task of forever compensating for the boss's disorganization. For example, many assistants have to spend time searching for the misplaced files of their boss—both hard-copy and disk files.

According to management consultant Deborah Zeigler, you can take several steps to facilitate a good working relationship with a disorganized manager.[17] Begin by identifying goals and priorities. Find out what the organization and department are attempting to accomplish, and what your boss expects of you. This basic information can be used as a wedge to encourage your boss to be better organized.

The second step is to communicate your concerns to your manager about how his or her work habits could be interfering with goal attainment. Tact and diplomacy are essential. You might say, for example, "I want to prepare a chart explaining our need for more salespeople, but I can't do it without the figures you promised me last week."

Third, rely on co-workers and others throughout the company to supplement your boss as an information source. When your manager is unavailable (disorganized people are often difficult to find) or does not have the information you need, network members might be able to help. In the example above, maybe somebody else can provide the figures you need.

A fourth step is to become familiar with your boss's primary problems in organization. If you know your manager has difficulty getting projects completed on time, step in well before the deadline to offer encouragement and assistance. You might present a chart to your boss estimating how close the project should be to completion. If you offer help, rather than criticism, your contribution will be valued.

A unifying theme exists to the aforementioned approaches for dealing with a problem manager. Continue to perform well despite your short-term problems. If your manager is indeed a poor performer or has a personality problem, top management is probably aware of the situation. You will be admired for your ability to cope with the situation. Performing poorly because you perceive your manager as a problem is self-defeating.

SUMMARY

Developing a favourable relationship with your manager or team leader is the most basic strategy of getting ahead in your career. Your manager or team leader influences your future because he or she is often asked by other prospective superiors to present an opinion about your capabilities.

A general strategy for developing a good relationship with your manager or team leader is to create a favourable impression. Specific tactics of this type include these:

1. Achieve good job performance.
2. Display a strong work ethic.
3. Demonstrate good emotional intelligence.
4. Be dependable, honest, and ethical.
5. Appreciate your manager's strengths.
6. Show an interest in your firm's products or services.
7. Be a good organizational citizen.
8. Create a strong presence.

Many tactics for developing a good relationship with your manager or team leader require that you deal directly with him or her:

1. Try to understand your manager.
2. Find out what your manager expects of you.
3. Bring forth solutions as well as problems.
4. Minimize complaints.
5. Avoid bypassing your manager.
6. Suggest improvements during the performance evaluation.
7. Resolve competing demands of two managers.
8. Use discretion in socializing with your manager.
9. Engage in favourable interactions with your manager.

Coping with a manager you perceive to be a problem is part of getting along with him or her. Re-evaluate your manager to make sure you have not misperceived him or her. It is important to confront your manager about your problem. Often this problem is a case of being micromanaged. Learning from your problem manager's mistakes is recommended, including if he or she is fired.

When your manager takes credit for your accomplishments, consider these tactics: discreetly confront your manager, take preventive measures by keeping others informed of work in progress, and present a valid reason for seeking recognition.

Working with a disorganized manager can lead to tension and a personality clash. Under these circumstances, tactfully explain how your manager's work habits create problems in attaining work goals. Rely on others to help you attain the information you need to accomplish work for your manager. Also, recognize your manager's biggest problems in organization and offer direct assistance.

When your relationship with your manager does not improve, it may be necessary to seek a transfer. The best method is to market yourself to other key managers in the company. This may involve establishing a network of contacts. Also, speak to your manager about a transfer without indicating your dissatisfaction, and present your case to the human resources department.

QUESTIONS AND ACTIVITIES

1. Suppose your manager reads this chapter. How might this influence the effectiveness of your using the strategies and tactics described here?
2. Identify three of the tactics described in this chapter that you are least likely to use. Explain.
3. How can a worker implement the tactic "engage in favourable interactions with your manager" without appearing to be "kissing up" to the boss?
4. Aside from suggestions in the text, how else can an employee show an interest in the firm's products or services?
5. Assuming team leaders don't have as much power as a regular manager, why is it still important to build a good relationship with your team leader?
6. Why is "creating a strong presence" considered a key strategy for getting ahead in the workplace?
7. Suppose you and a co-worker are best friends. Your friend gets promoted and becomes your manager. What should be your policy about socializing with this person?
8. What would your manager have to do before you would be willing to organize a group confrontation about his or her behaviour?
9. Interview an experienced manager. Ask his or her opinion about what an employee can do to create a favourable impression.

INTERNET SKILL BUILDER

Management Skills for the Workplace

Visit www.workforce.com, the website of the American magazine *Workforce*. Scroll through the site with the goal of identifying three interpersonal skills that you think would be advantageous for you to develop to get along with your manager or team leader. Develop an action plan that will assist you in developing at least one of these skills. You may have to make some inferences as the articles may not be directly related to interpersonal skills for getting along with your boss.

Log on to the **Companion Website** at **www.pearsoncanada.ca/dubrin** to access additional resources for this chapter.

CASE STUDY 10-1 HUMAN RELATIONS

The Problem Manager[18]

Read the case below and answer the questions that follow. Once you've done that, attempt Human Relations Skill-Building Exercise 10-1.

Kaled was a hard-working supervisor whose demonstrated ability gave him a strong shot at a middle-management position. One morning Kaled was reviewing next year's budget. He was distressed when he discovered that his budget was being cut and that he was losing one person in his department. "Sorry, things are tight and there's nothing we can do," said his manager, Ruth. Later, Kaled found out that Phil, another supervisor (whose division was doing poorly), was getting a budget increase. Kaled became furious and said to himself, "Of course Phil gets what he wants. He's always so buddy-buddy with Ruth."

Phil did regularly take time to chat with Ruth. He would ask about her grandchild and suggest having lunch together. Kaled had a cordial relationship with Ruth, but he mostly kept to himself and tended to his job.

Kaled thought over who in the company might be able to help him work out his dispute with Ruth. He remembered that he and the president had struck up an acquaintance when they met at a music concert several months ago. "Maybe if I talk to him," Kaled thought, "I can get my budget restored."

Kaled sent an email message to the president's office justifying why he wanted his budget and group member restored. The president thought Kaled's points were sound, and he requested that Ruth reverse her decision. Although miffed, Ruth complied with the president's request.

Kaled was relieved at first, but Ruth started making life miserable for him. Working over the problem in his head, Kaled thought there might be one way Ruth would change her attitude toward him. "Maybe a well-placed memo asking why Ruth was never available until 11:00 in the morning might work, or saying that I can't ever talk with her because she's always showing Phil photos of her grandchild."

Kaled sent another email to his "friend" the president, sending a copy to Ruth. He didn't hear from the president, but he did hear from Ruth. "I'm putting you on notice," she said, "for gross insubordination."

Kaled said calmly, "We'll see about that." He then returned to his office and put a call through to the president, who was in a day-long meeting. Finally, at 3:00 the president called and asked him to come to his office. "Ah, sweet revenge," thought Kaled.

"I understand you're not happy here, Kaled," said the president.

"But . . ." Kaled tried to protest.

"You know we would hate to lose someone as competent as you, but I do have some connections in other companies. I strongly suggest you let me help you find a suitable position elsewhere."

Questions

1. What errors in boss relationships did Kaled commit?
2. How might Kaled have attempted to improve his relationship with Ruth?
3. How should Kaled respond to the president's suggestion about looking for another job elsewhere?

Human Relations Skill Building

Exercise 10-2 Discussing a Sensitive Issue with Your Manager

Assume Kaled decided to work directly with Ruth rather than go to the president with the budget controversy. Assume also that Kaled did learn about Phil receiving a budget increase. One student plays the role of Kaled, who is trying to get back in good graces with Ruth. Another student plays the role of Ruth, who has granted Kaled an appointment to further discuss the budget issue. The person who plays the role of Kaled should work diligently at creating a favourable impression on Ruth.

CASE STUDY 10-2 HUMAN RELATIONS

The Downhill Insurance Company

A large insurance company established a small sales office in the Detroit, Michigan, area. In addition to sales, the office would also provide the field staff with training in new product knowledge and sales skills. The four key people in the office were transferred from both inside and outside the geographic area of the office. The group worked well together, and within several months the sales and training goals established for the office were met. As the goals were reached, the office was expanded to a total of 30 staff members, most of whom were sales agents. Soon the office was producing $300,000 monthly in insurance premiums. In addition to commissions for the initial sale, the agents would receive residuals, or additional commissions, as the policies were renewed.

Tim Draper, the vice president who established the new office, suddenly decided to return to his hometown so he could spend more time with his family. The company then appointed Gordon Bracker, an experienced sales manager with the company, to replace Draper. Bracker created a strong initial impression within the office. He appeared ambitious, powerful, and socially smooth. He remarked in a sales meeting that about one-half of the agents were producing 85 percent of the sales volume, but he never brought up the matter again or took action on the problem. The previous vice president would make sure that low-producing sales agents had more training.

Soon Bracker began to behave quite differently from how he had at first. During the late morning and early afternoon, Bracker was often seen with an open bottle of Jack Daniels on his desk. He made no attempt to hide the bottle when visitors entered his office. The office staff also noticed that porn sites were regularly displayed on his desktop computer. Bracker began inviting others into the office to visit porn sites with him. The agents and trainers became increasingly uncomfortable with the behavior and actions of the new vice president.

The first person to quit was Bracker's secretary who told others she could no longer support her boss and that she would not work for a boss for whom she had lost respect. Two other sales agents soon quit. The volume of commissions in the office was declining steeply, and new policies being issued were often lost. Insufficient information was being furnished to the home office for the agents to receive their proper commissions. When a trainer invited field sales reps into the office, she was often greeted with wisecracks about "Hard-drinking, Gordon, the porno guy."

The three remaining staff members got into a huddle one afternoon to decide what they should do about the office and their livelihoods falling apart.

Questions

1. In what way is Gordon Backer a problem manager?
2. What should the remaining staff members do to restore a professional workplace?
3. Is bypassing the boss in this situation a possibility?

Source: Case researched by Tammy Riggs, Rochester Hills, Michigan, March 2006.

Chapter 11
Getting Along with Co-workers and Customers

Learning Outcomes

After studying the information and doing the exercises in this chapter, you should be able to

- describe several strategies for developing good relationships with co-workers;
- explain several strategies to deal with difficult people;
- explain the process of team development using one model of team development;
- explain several barriers that interfere with effective team behaviours;
- list possible barriers to effective team development;
- describe several methods to become an effective team member;
- specify approaches to building good relationships with customers.

When Sue Nokes joined T-Mobile as a senior vice president of customer service a few years back, the cell phone company had a little problem: Lousy customer service was driving T-Mobile users crazy. Calling with a question or complaint, they got put on hold for what seemed like eons. Users then spoke with customer service reps who weren't much help. J. D. Power's customer satisfaction surveys ranked T-Mobile dead last in the industry.

Nokes launched a total overhaul. The first step: getting T-Mobile's human resources people and its marketing department to sit down and talk. The idea was to revamp the company's hiring practices, thus increasing the odds of selecting customer service staffers willing and able to follow through on the marketing maven's promises.

A new set of hiring criteria at T-Mobile emphasized traits such as empathy and quick thinking. Nokes then set up a rigorous evaluation process. "In our business, customers want their problems resolved fast, in one phone call—and courtesy matters," she says. "So we created a system that gives a lot of weight to those two elements. And we made sure that everyone knows exactly how he'll be evaluated. Nokes started an employee-rewards program called Do More, Get More, which bestows restaurant dinners and exotic trips on workers who meet stringent standards for courtesy and speed.

With all the improvements, J. D. Power has ranked T-Mobile number one in customer service for two consecutive years.[1]

The story about upgrading the cell phone company customer service representatives illustrates once again that unless front-line workers have good human relations skills a company's reputation can go downhill rapidly. Developing effective relationships with work associates, including customers, has been seen as having good political skills, an interpersonal style that combines awareness of others with the ability to communicate well. People with political skill are charming and engaging, which inspires confidence, trust, and sincerity.[2] Based on these attributes, the person with political skill effectively influences others. This chapter presents information about developing productive relationships with two major groups of work associates: co-workers and customers. As teams are such an integral part of the workplace, it is dealt with separately but it is part of many of the strategies for developing good relations with others at work.

BUILDING GOOD CO-WORKER RELATIONSHIPS

The approaches in this section are both *proactive* and *reactive*. In other words, there are really two ways to get along with others. You can lead in the spirit of cooperation—in other words, be proactive. Your second choice is to react to the behaviours of others in positive ways, even when the other person is being difficult. These are reactive strategies. In reality, each of us chooses and uses a variety of behaviours listed below to maintain harmonious workplace relations. Your job, then, is to pick and choose from these strategies and apply them to your advantage.

Develop Allies through Being Civil

People who are courteous, kind, cooperative, and cheerful develop allies and friends in the workplace. Practising basic good manners such as being pleasant and friendly is also part of being civil. While being civil may seem obvious to most of us, lack of such civility appears to be a growing concern in the workplace. Such incivility exists not just in violence or conflict, but also in the "thousand small slings and arrows that day after day, eat away. . . ."[3] Examples of incivility include the following:

- A salesperson makes sarcastic comments about another employee in front of a customer.
- A co-worker initiates cell phone calls while listening to a presentation at a meeting.
- One worker continues responding to email messages while another is talking to him in person.
- One worker texts during a team meeting.[4]

Being civil will help you stand out in the face of such disrespectful or impolite behaviour. Being civil also involves not snooping, spreading malicious gossip, or weaseling out of group presents such as shower or retirement gifts. In addition, it is important to be available to co-workers who want your advice as well as your help in times of crisis.

Closely related to being civil is maintaining a positive outlook. Everyone knows that you gain more allies by being optimistic and positive than by being pessimistic and negative. Nevertheless, many people ignore this simple strategy for getting along well with others. Co-workers are more likely to solicit your opinion or offer you help when you are perceived to be a cheerful person.

Make Other People Feel Important

A fundamental principle of fostering good relationships with co-workers and others is to make them feel important. Leadership and change consultant, Sheila Murray Bethela, advises us to make use of the Please-Make-Me-Feel-Important concept. Visualize that everyone in the workplace is wearing a small sign around the neck that says, "Please make me feel important."[5] Although the leader has primary responsibility for satisfying this recognition need, co-workers also play a key role. One approach to making a co-worker feel important would be to bring a notable accomplishment of his or hers to the attention of the rest of the group. Human Relations Self-Assessment Quiz 11-1 gives you an opportunity to think through your tendencies to make others feel important.

Maintain Honest and Open Relationships

In human relations we attach considerable importance to maintaining honest and open relationships with other people. Giving co-workers frank but tactful answers to their

Human Relations Self-Assessment

QUIZ 11-1 How Important Do I Make People Feel?

Indicate on a one-to-five scale how frequently you act (or would act if the situation presented itself) in the ways indicated below: very infrequently (VI); infrequently (I); sometimes (S); frequently (F); very frequently (VF). Circle the number underneath the column that best fits your answer.

	VI	*I*	*S*	*F*	*VF*
1. I do my best to correctly pronounce a co-worker's name.	1	2	3	4	5
2. I avoid letting other people's egos get too big.	5	4	3	2	1
3. I brag to others about the accomplishments of my co-workers.	1	2	3	4	5
4. I recognize the birthdays of friends in a tangible way.	1	2	3	4	5
5. It makes me anxious to listen to others brag about their accomplishments.	5	4	3	2	1
6. After hearing that a friend has done something outstanding, I shake his or her hand.	1	2	3	4	5
7. If a friend or co-worker recently received a degree or certificate, I would offer my congratulations.	1	2	3	4	5
8. If a friend or co-worker finished second in a contest, I would inquire why he or she did not finish first.	5	4	3	2	1
9. If a co-worker showed me how to do something, I would compliment that person's skill.	1	2	3	4	5
10. When a co-worker starts bragging about a family member's accomplishments, I do not respond.	5	4	3	2	1

Scoring and Interpretation: Total the numbers corresponding to your answers. Scoring 40 to 50 points suggests that you typically make people feel important; 16 to 39 points suggests that you have a moderate tendency toward making others feel important; 0 to 15 points suggests that you need to develop skill in making others feel important. Study this chapter carefully.

requests for your opinion is one useful way of developing open relationships. Suppose that a co-worker asks your opinion about a memo that he intends to send to his boss. As you read it, you find it somewhat incoherent and filled with spelling and grammatical errors. An honest response to this letter might be: "I think your idea is a good one. But I think your memo needs more work before that idea comes across clearly."

As described in Chapter 7, accurately expressing your feelings also leads to constructive relationships. If you arrive at work upset over a personal problem and appearing obviously fatigued, you can expect some reaction. A peer might say, "What seems to be the problem? Is everything all right?" A dishonest reply would be, "Everything is fine. What makes you think something is wrong?" In addition to making an obviously untrue statement, you would also be perceived as rejecting the person who asked the question.

If you prefer not to discuss your problem, an honest response on your part would be, "Thanks for your interest. I am facing some problems today. But I think things will work out." Such an answer would not involve you in a discussion of your personal problems.

Also, you would not be perceived as rejecting your co-worker. The same principle applies equally well to personal relationships.

Express an Interest in the Work of Others

Almost everyone is self-centred to some extent. Thus, topics of conversation that are favoured are ones closely related to people themselves, such as their children, friends, hobbies, work, or possessions. Sales representatives rely heavily on this fact in cultivating relationships with established customers. They routinely ask the customer about his or her hobbies, family members, and work activities. ("Say, how's your coin collection going?") You can capitalize on this simple strategy by asking co-workers and friends questions such as these:

- How is your work going? (*Highly recommended.*)
- How are things going for you?
- How did you gain the knowledge necessary for your job?
- How does the company use the output from your department?
- How does your present job fit in with your career plans?
- How did Leticia do in the county cat show?

A danger in asking questions about other people's work is that some questions may not be perceived as well-intentioned. There is a fine line between honest curiosity and snooping. You must stay alert to this subtle distinction.

Be a Good Listener

After you ask questions, you must be prepared to listen to the answers. The simplest technique for getting along with co-workers, friends, and acquaintances is to be a good listener. The topics you should be willing to listen to during working hours include job problems and miscellaneous complaints. Lunch breaks, coffee breaks, and after hours are better suited to listening to people talk about their personal lives, current events, sports, and the like.

Becoming an effective listener takes practice. As you practise your listening skills, try the suggestions offered in Chapter 7. The payoff is that listening builds constructive relationships both on and off the job. Too often, people take turns talking rather than listening to each other. The result is that neither party feels better as a result of the conversation.

Use Appropriate Compliments

An effective way of developing good relationships with co-workers and friends is to compliment something with which they closely identify, such as their children, spouse, hobbies, or pets. Paying a compliment is a form of **positive reinforcement**, rewarding somebody for doing something right. The right response is therefore strengthened, or reinforced. A compliment is a useful multipurpose reward.

Another way of complimenting people is through recognition. The suggestions made earlier about making people feel important are a way of recognizing people, and therefore compliments. Investing a small amount of time in recognizing a co-worker can pay large dividends in terms of cultivating an ally. Recognition and compliments are more likely to create a favourable relationship when they are appropriate. Appropriate in this context means that the compliment fits the accomplishment. Praise that is too lavish may be interpreted as belittling and patronizing.

Deal Effectively with Difficult People

A major challenge in getting along well with co-workers is to deal constructively with difficult people. These co-workers may be in your work group or team or elsewhere in your business or organization. A co-worker is classified as difficult if he or she is uncooperative, touchy, defensive, hostile, or even very unfriendly. Also, the various negative team roles that are discussed in a later section of this chapter describe behaviours of difficult co-workers. Here we present five widely applicable approaches to dealing with such individuals.

Take Problems Professionally, Not Personally A key principle in dealing with a variety of personalities is to take what they do professionally, not personally. Difficult people are not necessarily out to get you. You may just represent a stepping-stone for them to get what they want.[6] For example, if a co-worker insults you because you need his help Friday afternoon, he probably has nothing against you personally. He might just prefer to become mentally disengaged from work on Friday afternoons. Your request distracts him from mentally phasing out of work as early as he would like.

Give Ample Feedback The primary technique for dealing with counterproductive behaviour is to offer feedback to the difficult person regarding how his or her behaviour affects you. Focus on the person's behaviour rather than on characteristics or values. If a co-worker is annoying you by constantly pointing out potential disasters, say something to this effect: "I have difficulty maintaining my enthusiasm when you so often point out the possible negatives." Such a statement will engender less resentment than saying, "I find you to be a total pessimist, and it annoys me."

Use Tact and Diplomacy in Dealing with Annoying Behaviour Co-workers who irritate you rarely do annoying things on purpose. Tactful actions on your part can sometimes take care of these annoyances without your having to confront the problem. Close your door, for example, if noisy co-workers are gathered outside. Or, try one woman's method of getting rid of office pests: She keeps a file open on her computer screen and gestures to it apologetically when someone overstays a visit.

Sometimes subtlety doesn't work, and it may be necessary to diplomatically confront the co-worker who is annoying you. Jane Michaels suggests that you precede a criticism with a compliment. Here is an example of this approach: "You're one of the best people I've ever worked with, but one habit of yours drives me bananas. Do you think you could let me know when you're going to be late getting back to the office after lunch?"[7]

Use Humour Nonhostile humour can often be used to help a difficult person understand how his or her behaviour is blocking others.[8] Also, the humour will help defuse conflict between you and that person. The humour should point to the person's unacceptable behaviour yet not belittle him or her. Imagine that Kevin (who in your opinion is a difficult person) says that he will not sign off on your report because instead of using the metric system you used imperial measures. You need Kevin's approval because the boss wants a consensus report from the group. You ask Kevin again the next day, and he still refuses to sign.

To gain Kevin's cooperation, you say: "I'm sorry we upset your scientific mind. But I swear on a stack of Bibles, one metre high, all future reports will use the metric system. Will you please affix your signature one centimetre below mine? By the way, did you see that 45-metre field goal the Alouettes kicker made in yesterday's game?" With a grin on his face, Kevin replies, "OK, give me the report to sign." (The touch of humour here indicates that you respect Kevin's desire to use the metric system, but you also acknowledge that it can sometimes be impractical.)

Reinforce Civil Behaviour and Good Moods In the spirit of positive reinforcement, when a generally difficult person is behaving acceptably, recognize the behaviour in some way. Reinforcing statements would include "It's fun working with you today" and "I appreciate your professional attitude."

Listen and Respond As usual, active listening improves many problems in human relations. Give the difficult person ample opportunity to express his or her concerns, doubts, anger, or other feelings. Then acknowledge your awareness of the person's position.[9] An example: "OK, you tell me that management is really against us and, therefore, we shouldn't work so hard." After listening, present your perspective in a way such as this: "Your viewpoint may be valid based on your experiences. Yet so far, I've found management here to be on my side." This exchange of viewpoints is less likely to lead to failed communication than if you are judgmental with a statement such as, "You really shouldn't think that way."

The tactics for dealing with difficult people just described require practice to be effective. Also, you may have to use a combination of the six tactics described in this section to deal effectively with a difficult person. The point of these tactics is not to out-manipulate or subdue a difficult person, but to establish a cordial and productive working relationship.

TEAMS IN THE WORKPLACE

The strategies that we have just discussed will assist you in getting along more effectively with co-workers, whether they are members of your work group, work team, or other members of your organization. An essential strategy for developing good relationships with co-workers is to be a team player. A **team player** is one who emphasizes group accomplishment and cooperation rather than individual achievement and not helping others. Team play has surged in importance because of the emphasis on having teams of workers decide how to improve productivity and quality. You will also have to be a team player if you reach the pinnacle of power in your organization. Here we want to focus exclusively on teams. With continued emphasis on teams in the workplace, you will benefit from developing a better understanding of what teams are, the stages of team development, and strategies for you to become a more effective team player. See the Canada Today box for a sample of Canadian companies that rely heavily on teams to meet organizational goals.

Canada Today

Successful Companies That Rely on the "Team" Approach

Here is a small sampling of the companies in Canada that rely heavily on teams, particularly self-managed teams. Self-managed teams are specialized teams that assume all or most of the responsibility for their performance as well as doing their own performance reviews. Each team is responsible for all aspects of its performance. Leadership within the team may vary according to required tasks, or leadership may be done on a rotating basis. To be a truly self-managed team, the team must manage all tasks required for its performance. Many of these companies, such as Milltronics, gave their employees formal training to assist in the development of teams.

Investing in the team approach has paid off for many companies. The key is to train staff in the techniques of working effectively in groups. These skills are not hard to learn and usually involve basic communication skills, conflict resolution skills, skills in managing change, and decision-making and problem-solving skills. These companies are not presented in any type of order. The common thread is that teams are the core of how these companies "do business."

Company	Location	Product
Pratt and Whitney	Longueuil, Quebec	PW500 turbofan engine
Asea Brown Boveri Canada	Guelph, Ontario	power transformers
Siemens Milltronics	Peterborough, Ontario	measuring equipment
AMP of Canada	Markham, Ontario	electrical connectors and interconnection systems
Steelcase Canada Ltd.	Markham, Ontario	office furniture and equipment

Sources: Brian D. Harrison, Henry P. Conn, Barrie Whittaker, and James Mitchell, "Mobilizing Abilities Through Teamwork," *Canadian Business Review*, 21, 1994, pp. 20–24; and Steven L. Mcshane, *Canadian Organizational Behaviour* (Toronto: Richard D. Irwin Inc., 1995).

What Are Teams?

With such an emphasis in the workplace on working on teams, we need to be clear about what makes up a true workplace team.

A team starts out as a group of co-workers put together to achieve organizational goals but over time reaches a new level of quality. Special feelings are created among members, and a team creates its own processes and takes leadership for its own development and performance.[10] A work team has some special characteristics.[11]

- *A team is a diverse group of people*. In order to achieve its goal(s), a team is made up of people with specific abilities and resources. For instance, a marketing team may have members from finance, product development, as well as marketing specialists in advertising.
- *Members share leadership responsibility*. Because of the diversity of talents and abilities, each member must assume leadership as required for the task. For example, the individual from product development may assume a leadership role as he or she demonstrates and discusses the product for the rest of the team. At this point, this member gives direction to the other, less knowledgeable members.

- *A team creates an identity.* More than an ordinary group, teams develop specific self-images. This image creates cohesiveness and helps to motivate the team. Members begin to see themselves as the "Widget Creative Team."
- *Team efforts are interconnected.* A team continuously weaves and interconnects the efforts of individual team members to develop a tighter energy and higher focus than most groups have. Each team member's efforts become an integral part of the team effort.
- *Members work to achieve a mutually defined goal.* Team goals may involve intensive communication to develop a consensus as to what the goals are and how they should be achieved. A team's goal may be to get the product on the shelves before the Christmas season. As such, each member has his or her own goals to bring back to his or her own team and department.

When these factors are put together, a **team** can be defined as "*a diverse group of people who share leadership responsibility for creating a group identity and an interconnected effort to achieve a mutually defined goal within the context of other groups and systems.*"[12] In general then, teams are often tightly knit and cohesive, more focused on mutually defined goals, have more diverse members' backgrounds, and are usually formed for a specific purpose. There are many different types of teams in the workplace. Some teams, such as many task forces, have a formalized structure with a recognized leader (such as a chairperson or coordinator) and are temporary. Other teams are more informal, such as a teaching team at a college or a marketing team within an organization. Within any business or firm there may be many highly specialized teams, and employees may belong to more than one team. On the other hand, a small business may consist of one team. Successful small businesses often have a close group of people that work together to ensure continued company success.

How Teams Develop

Teams and groups do not "just happen." Teams, in particular, go through a series of developmental stages that can be identified. There are several theories of group development, including the four stages of group development by Tuckman[13] and the four phases of decision-making groups by Fisher.[14] We will examine the four stages of the Tuckman model, which includes the stages of forming, storming, norming, and performing. A fifth stage, adjourning, has been added to these four stages.[15]

The *forming stage* usually occurs when the group or team is new or there are a number of new members. Members are cautious and uncomfortable as they attempt to determine personal relationships and define their tasks. Little work is accomplished. Once the group or team has some idea about goals and responsibilities, the *storming stage* begins. During this stage, members may argue or become more emotional, and conflicts and differences of opinion emerge during team meetings. Important issues and ideas are tabled and emotions may run high. The *norming stage* can be identified as the period when conflicts are resolved and the group develops approaches for goal completion. The *performing stage* is entered when the group focuses its energy on tasks to attain goals. Decisions are reached, problems solved, and the group is now a fully functioning team.

A final stage can be added to this model: the *stage of adjourning*. Some teams, such as task forces and ad hoc committees, may be disbanded once the task has been completed or the goal has been reached. During adjournment, group members may experience several different emotions. They may be sad that the group is now about to be disbanded and may actually experience emotions similar to the grieving process. There may also be relief that the work is now completed and members can focus their energy elsewhere. Members may also feel proud of their accomplishments.[16]

It should be noted that team development does not always run a smooth course as these stages seem to suggest. In reality, the development may falter. For example, a team may quickly go through forming and storming and then get mired in the norming stage with conflicts. Some teams never get beyond storming and other teams perform well for a period of time until conflict erupts or the team encounters an internal or external change. What we have presented here is a framework to assist you in understanding some of the processes that occur as teams develop, mature, and hopefully make efficient progress toward organizational goals.

Barriers to Effective Team-Building

Why don't teams always reach the performing stage? In other words, what are the barriers that slow teams down and inhibit team development and performance? Some of these barriers may be imposed upon the group by outside forces that the group may not be able to control (such as downsizing). Other barriers are internal and result from group interaction and processes (such as new hires on the team and personal problems that interfere with working). Here we will review some of these barriers.

Time Constraints When a work group or team does not have sufficient time to make a decision, complete goals or tasks, or solve a problem, the members may not put forth their best efforts. This type of pressure can create stress and work overload. Conflicts may erupt. As a result, the group may perform poorly.

Conflicting Goals of Group Members When people join a team or group, they also bring different motives or goals with them. Some members may be there to sabotage any group efforts. Others may want to assume leadership or display power. Some people may want to put in as little effort as possible. Some team members may have **hidden agendas** that may ultimately interfere with team performance. Hidden agendas are personal goals that a member keeps to himself or herself and that may or may not be harmful to group efforts. The problem with personal agendas is that they work against open communication in the group and destroy trust within the group. Even members with positive goals and motives in mind may have differences over such issues as how the group should proceed, which goals should be given top priority, and how various tasks should be divided among members.

Roles That Interfere with Group Processes In an ideal workplace, all team members value each other and treat each other and the team experience as valued parts of the job. Unfortunately, the reality is that some people also assume roles and play games in groups or teams that negatively affect the group. There are many reasons why people behave in these negative ways, ranging from inexperience in a team environment to darker motives such as a desire to hurt the organization itself. These roles hurt group members and group performance. Some of these roles are summarized here.[17] Near the end of the chapter, there are suggestions to assist you with dealing with difficult co-workers, including these types of difficult team members.

- *Dominator.* This person demands attention, tries to control the discussion, interrupts, and tries to control others. He or she monopolizes the discussion and prevents the team from concentrating on its tasks.
- *Aggressor.* Similar to the dominator, this person wants control. However, he or she puts down other team members, using sarcasm, name-calling, and other negative means to get what he or she wants.
- *The Know-It-All.* This person thinks he or she knows everything (though often that's not the reality) and tries to impose the knowledge on the group. This person may use age, experience, education, or any other thing in his or her background to prove that he or she is correct and everyone else is wrong.
- *Distractor.* While distraction can be useful when members are stressed, overuse of this role results in poor team performance. This person may clown around by teasing and joking, change topics and get the group off-task, and generally "act up."
- *Nonparticipator.* This person can be a psychological deserter who may appear bored with or above the pettiness of group interaction. He or she may doodle, daydream, or in other ways nonverbally signal his or her lack of interest in the group work. These people can also be physical deserters by announcing they have to leave early, arriving late, not arriving at all, or arriving completely unprepared.
- *The Mean and Unethical Player.* This person can be unethical, dishonest, conniving, prejudicial, and nasty and behaves this way consistently. He or she may lie, cheat, take credit for others' efforts, belittle others, and engage in other unacceptable behaviours that harm team members, hurt team spirit, and discourage group efforts.
- *The "Yes, But" Player.* This person is basically irresponsible for his or her part on the team. The behaviours of this person—always accompanied by excuses—include not finishing a task, being late, missing meetings, obtaining the wrong data, and doing the wrong thing. At first, these excuses may sound legitimate, but as time wears on, it becomes obvious this person is an irresponsible team member who refuses to do his or her part. For example, "I would have been here on time, but the traffic was bad"; then at the next meeting, "I tried to get here but the phone kept ringing"; followed at the next meeting with "I was so busy with my other work, I lost track of time"; and so on.
- *The Whiner/Complainer.* This person undermines the entire spirit of the group with continual complaining and whining. Every idea from others is met with a list of reasons why the idea would never work. This person may complain about personal problems and other injustices that he or she is currently having to manage in his or her life.

Competition Instead of Cooperation In a society that values individualism, competitiveness, and "doing your own thing," cooperation may be difficult for some people. A barrier that hinders group and team work is a structure that fosters competition among group members instead of cooperation. Many well-meaning organizations have employee awards that go to a single individual rather than the entire team. People who want these awards may compete against their very own team members to achieve this recognition. Team awards foster cooperation among team members and are currently used in many organizations that foster the team approach.

Social Loafing Have you ever been in a group or on a team where one or two members did very little work? These members were content to ride along for free and did very little to help the group obtain its goals. Social loafing is the tendency for people to perform at a lower level when working in groups than when working alone.[18] Social loafers do not try as hard in a group as they do when they are alone. Social loafing occurs more often when individual contributions are not monitored or identified in some way and in larger teams where individual efforts are less noticeable.[19] Witnessing such loafing and lack of effort can demoralize other team members and reduce motivation.

How to Become a More Effective Team Member

Now that you have an idea about the importance of teams in the workplace, the characteristics of teams, how teams develop, and some of the barriers to effective development, let's turn our focus onto strategies for becoming an effective team player including positive team member roles.

Here we describe a representative group of behaviours that contribute to team play. In addition, engaging in such behaviour helps one be perceived as a team player.

1. *Share Credit with Co-Workers*. A direct method of promoting team play is to share credit for good deeds with other team members. Instead of focusing on yourself as the person responsible for a work achievement, point out that the achievement was the product of a team effort.
2. *Display a Helpful, Cooperative Attitude*. Working cooperatively with others is virtually synonymous with team play. Cooperation translates into such activities as helping another worker with a computer problem, covering for a teammate when he or she is absent, and making sure a co-worker has the input required from you on time. A helpful cooperative attitude is the main component of organizational citizenship behaviour.
3. *Share Information and Opinions with Co-Workers*. Teamwork is facilitated when group members share information and opinions. This is true because one of the benefits of group effort is that members can share ideas. The result is often a better solution to problems than would have been possible for people working alone. The group thus achieves synergy—a product of group effort whereby the output of the group exceeds the output possible if the members worked alone.
4. *Provide Emotional Support to Co-Workers*. Good team players offer each other emotional support. Such support can take the form of verbal encouragement for ideas expressed, listening to a group member's concerns, or complimenting achievements. An emotionally supportive comment to a co-worker who appears to be under stress might be "This doesn't look like one of your better days. What can I do to help?"
5. *Follow the Golden Rule*. The ancient adage "Treat others the way you would like them to treat you" provides a firm foundation for effective team and group work. Although some may dismiss the golden rule as a syrupy platitude, it still works. For example, you would probably want someone to help you with a perplexing problem, so you take the initiative to help others when they need your expertise to solve a problem.

6. *To Establish Trust, Keep Confidential Information to Yourself.* Confidential information shared with you by a teammate should not be shared with others. Trust is essential to effective teamwork and can be exceedingly difficult to regain after a person is betrayed. Other teammates may also lose faith and trust in you if you breach even one member's trust.
7. *Avoid Actions That Could Sabotage or Undermine the Group or Team in Any Way.* Frequently criticizing group members directly or complaining about them to outsiders works against the best interest of the group. Members within the group, as well as the team or group leader, will most likely hear that you criticized them to an outsider, thus doing severe damage to your ability to work cooperatively with them.
8. *Attend Company-Sponsored Social Events.* A worker's reputation as a team player is often judged both on the job and in company-sponsored social events, such as parties, picnics, and athletic events. If you attend these and participate fully, your reputation as a team player will be enhanced. Company-sponsored social events are also important because they provide an opportunity to build rapport with co-workers. Rapport, in turn, facilitates teamwork.
9. *Share the Glory.* You will make a poor team player if you try to grab all the glory for ideas that work and distance yourself from ideas that do not work. An effective team member wants all other members to succeed. You will stand out by praising the people you work with rather than hogging any praise for the team.[20]
10. *Avoid Backstabbing.* A special category of disliked behaviour is **backstabbing**, an attempt to discredit by underhanded means such as innuendo, accusation, or the like. A backstabber might drop hints to the boss, for example, that a co-worker performs poorly under pressure or is looking for a new job. Sometimes the backstabber assertively gathers information in order to backstab a co-worker. He or she might engage another worker in a derogatory discussion about the boss and then report the co-worker's negative comments back to the boss. A person who develops a reputation as a backstabber will receive poor cooperation from co-workers. The person might also be considered untrustworthy by management, thus stalling his or her own career.

Observing the ten points just made and using your increased understanding of teams and groups in the workplace will help you become an effective team member. Recognize also that all other actions directed toward good co-worker relationships will also enhance team and group performance.

Team Member Roles

A major challenge in learning to become an effective team member is to choose the right roles to occupy as opposed to the negative roles discussed earlier. It is helpful for the leader to understand these roles as he or she attempts to get the group working together smoothly. For example, the leader might want to make sure that all positive roles are filled. If you carry out positive roles, you will be perceived as a contributor to team effort. If you neglect carrying out these roles, you will be perceived as a poor contributor. Human Relations Self-Assessment Quiz 11-2 will help you evaluate your present inclinations toward occupying effective roles as a team member. In this section we describe a number of the most frequently observed positive roles played by team members.

Human Relations Self-Assessment

QUIZ 11-2 Team Player Roles

For each of the following statements about team activity, check Mostly Agree or Mostly Disagree. If you have not experienced such a situation, imagine how you would act or think if placed in that situation. In responding to the statements, assume that you are taking the questionnaire with the intent of learning something about yourself.

	Mostly Agree	***Mostly Disagree***
1. It is rare that I ever miss a team meeting.	_____	_____
2. I regularly compliment team members when they do something exceptional.	_____	_____
3. Whenever I can, I avoid being the note taker at a team meeting.	_____	_____
4. From time to time, other team members come to me for advice on technical matters.	_____	_____
5. I like to hide some information from other team members so I can be in control.	_____	_____
6. I welcome new team members coming to me for advice and learning the ropes.	_____	_____
7. My priorities come first, which leaves me with very little time to help other team members.	_____	_____
8. During a team meeting, it is not unusual for several other people at a time to look toward me for my opinion.	_____	_____
9. If I think the team is moving in an unethical direction, I will say so explicitly.	_____	_____
10. Rarely will I criticize the progress of the team even if I think such criticism is deserved.	_____	_____
11. It is not unusual for me to summarize the progress in a team meeting, even if not asked.	_____	_____
12. To conserve time, I attempt to minimize contact with my teammates outside of our meetings.	_____	_____
13. I intensely dislike going along with a consensus decision if the decision runs contrary to my thoughts on the issue.	_____	_____
14. I rarely remind teammates of our mission statement as we go about our work.	_____	_____
15. Once I have made up my mind on an issue facing the team, I am unlikely to be persuaded in another direction.	_____	_____
16. I am willing to accept negative feedback from team members.	_____	_____
17. Simply to get a new member of the team involved, I will ask his or her opinion.	_____	_____
18. Even if the team has decided on a course of action, I am not hesitant to bring in new information that supports another position.	_____	_____
19. Quite often I talk negatively about one team member to another.	_____	_____
20. My teammates are almost a family to me because I am truly concerned about their welfare.	_____	_____
21. When it seems appropriate, I joke and kid with teammates.	_____	_____
22. My contribution to team tasks is as important to me as my individual work.	_____	_____
23. From time to time I have pointed out to the team how we can all improve in reaching our goals.	_____	_____

(*continued*)

24. I will fight to the last when the team does not support my viewpoint and wants to move toward consensus. ______ ______

25. I will confront the team if I believe that the members are thinking too much alike. ______ ______

Total score ______

Scoring and Interpretation

Give yourself one point (+1) for each statement you gave in agreement with the keyed answer. The keyed answer indicates carrying out a positive, as opposed to a negative, role.

1. Mostly agree
2. Mostly agree
3. Mostly disagree
4. Mostly agree
5. Mostly disagree
6. Mostly agree
7. Mostly disagree
8. Mostly agree
9. Mostly agree
10. Mostly disagree
11. Mostly agree
12. Mostly disagree
13. Mostly disagree
14. Mostly disagree
15. Mostly disagree
16. Mostly agree
17. Mostly agree
18. Mostly agree
19. Mostly disagree
20. Mostly agree
21. Mostly agree
22. Mostly agree
23. Mostly agree
24. Mostly disagree
25. Mostly agree

20–25 You carry out a well above average number of positive team roles. Behaviour of this type contributes substantially to being an effective team player. Study the roles in this chapter to further build your effectiveness as a team member.

10–19 You carry out an average number of positive team roles. Study carefully the roles described in this chapter to search for ways to carry out a greater number of positive roles.

0–9 You carry out a substantially above average number of negative team roles. If becoming an effective team player is important to you, you will have to diligently search for ways to play positive team roles. Study the information about roles in this chapter carefully.

According to the role theory developed by Meredith Belbin and his group of researchers at Belbin Associates, there are nine frequent roles occupied by team members.[21] All of these roles are influenced to some extent by an individual's personality.

1. *Plant.* The plant is creative, imaginative, and unorthodox. Such a person solves difficult problems. A potential weakness of this role is that the person tends to ignore fine details and becomes too immersed in the problem to communicate effectively.
2. *Resource investigator.* The resource investigator is extroverted, enthusiastic, and communicates freely with other team members. He or she will explore opportunities and develop valuable contacts. A potential weakness of this role is that the person can be overly optimistic and may lose interest after the initial enthusiasm wanes.
3. *Coordinator.* The coordinator is mature, confident, and a natural team leader. He or she clarifies goals, promotes decision making and delegates effectively. A downside to occupying this role is that the person might be seen as manipulative and controlling.

Some coordinators delegate too much by asking others to do some of the work they (the coordinators) should be doing.

4. *Shaper*. The shaper is challenging, dynamic, and thrives under pressure. He or she will use determination and courage to overcome obstacles. A potential weakness of the shaper is that he or she can be easily provoked and may ignore the feelings of others.
5. *Monitor-evaluator*. The monitor-evaluator is even tempered, engages in strategic (big picture and long-term) thinking, and makes accurate judgments. He or she sees all the options and judges accurately. A potential weakness of this role occupant is that he or she might lack drive and the ability to inspire others.
6. *Team worker*. The team worker is cooperative, focuses on relationships, and is sensitive and diplomatic. He or she is a good listener who builds relationships, dislikes confrontation, and averts friction. A potential weakness is that the team worker can be indecisive in a crunch situation or crisis.
7. *Implementer*. The implementer is disciplined, reliable, conservative and efficient. He or she will act quickly on ideas, and convert them into practical actions. A potential weakness is that the implementer can be inflexible and slow to see new opportunities.
8. *Completer-finisher*. The completer-finisher is conscientious and anxious to get the job done. He or she has a good eye for detail and is effective at searching out errors. He or she can be counted on for finishing a project and delivering on time. A potential weakness is that he or she can be a worrier and reluctant to delegate.
9. *Specialist*. The specialist is a single-minded self-starter. He or she is dedicated and provides knowledge and skill in rare supply. A potential weakness of the specialist is that he or she can be stuck in a niche with little interest in other knowledge and may dwell on technicalities.

The weaknesses in the first nine roles point to problems the team leader or manager can expect to emerge, and, therefore, allowances should be made. Belbin refers to these potential problems as allowable weaknesses because allowances should be made for them. To illustrate, if a team worker has a tendency to be indecisive in a crisis, the team should not have high expectations of the team worker when faced with a crisis. Team workers will be the most satisfied if the crisis is predicted and decisions involving them are made before the pressure mounts.[22]

Another perspective on team roles is that team members will sometimes engage in self-oriented roles. Members will sometimes focus on their own needs rather than those of the group. The individual might be overly aggressive because of a personal need, such as wanting a bigger budget on his or her project. The individual might hunger for recognition or power. Similarly, the person might attempt to dominate the meeting, block others from contributing, or serve as a distraction. One of the ploys used by distracters recently is to engage in cell phone conversations during a meeting and blaming it on "those people who keep calling me."

The many roles just presented overlap somewhat. For example, the implementer might engage in specialist activities. Do not be concerned about the overlap. Instead, pick and choose from the many roles as the situation dictates—regardless of whether overlap exists.

The behaviour associated with the roles just described is more important than remembering the labels. For example, remembering to be creative and imaginative is more important than remembering the specific label name or title.

Face Maturely the Challenge of the Office Romance

Working closely with others, either as co-workers or on a team, may lead to romance for some individuals. Office romances can be disruptive to morale and productivity. Co-worker romances are a more widespread potential problem because more romances take place between co-workers on the same level than between superiors and subordinates. As more women have entered the workforce in professional positions and as professionals work longer hours, the office has become a frequent meeting place. People often work closely in teams and other joint projects, thus creating the conditions for romance to take place. Another basic reason why office romances are so frequent is that familiarity builds emotional and physical attraction. Based on research spanning 20 years, Cindy Hazan, an associate professor of human development, concludes that people need attachment. And proximity breeds attachment. "Proximity is really the core of attachment. Familiar people have a calming, soothing effect on us."[23]

Many companies have policies against managers dating people below them in the hierarchy, but few companies attempt to restrict same-level romantic relationships. About 72 percent of companies do not have written policies about dating, yet about 14 percent have an unwritten understanding.[24] Managers widely accept the idea of employees dating each other, with nearly 68 percent of managers of all ages saying it is acceptable, according to an American Management Survey.[25] Nevertheless, sensitivity is required to conduct an office romance that does not detract from your professionalism.

Many companies are concerned about information leakage within their organization. If you date a person who has access to confidential information (such as trade secrets), management might be concerned that you are a security risk. You, therefore, might miss out on some opportunities for better assignments. Companies also worry about negative consequences stemming from office romances, such as sexual harassment claims, low morale of co-workers, lowered productivity from the couple involved in the romance, and an unprofessional atmosphere. Yet an important positive consequence to employers from an office romance is that while the relationship is working well, the couple may have a heightened interest in coming to work. Also, romance can trigger energy that leads to enhanced productivity.

It is important not to abuse company tolerance of the co-worker romance. Do not invite the person you are dating to meals at company expense, take him or her on nonessential business trips, or create projects to work on jointly. Strive to keep the relationship confidential and restricted to after hours. Minimize talking to co-workers about the relationship. Such behaviour as holding hands or kissing in public view is regarded as poor office etiquette. Disappearing acts together during working hours are taboo.

Should your co-worker romance terminate, you face a special challenge. You must now work together cooperatively with a person toward whom you may have angry feelings. Few people have the emotional detachment necessary to work smoothly with a former romantic involvement. Extra effort, therefore, will be required on both your parts.

What should you do if you and your boss seem suited for a long-term commitment? Why walk away from Mr. or Ms. Right? My suggestion is that if you do become romantically involved, one person should request a transfer to another department. Many office romances do lead to happy marriages and other long-term relationships. At the start of the relationship, however, use considerable discretion. Engaging in personal conversations during work time or holding hands in the company cafeteria is unprofessional and taboo.

Human Relations in Practice

Human Resources Specialist Advises on Office Romance

Professionals who advise company owners and managers about office romances say the owner or manager, on learning of the relationship, needs to talk to the couple. "You should immediately meet with those people and set some guidelines for appropriate workplace behavior," says Arlene Vernon, a human resources consultant in Eden Prairie, Minnesota. "You need to tell them, 'This is not your place for any of the fooling around that might go on—sneaking, hand-holdings, hugging in the corner, passing little notes.'"

But you shouldn't try to forbid the couple from having the relationship. As the lawyer John Robinson puts it, "You can't stop biology." And Vernon said that trying to force an end to a relationship can create an unpleasant atmosphere for everyone, including other employees who wouldn't want similar interference in their personal lives. She suggests telling the couple, "I'm glad you met and that things are going well, but this is what I expect in the workplace."

Source: Excerpted from Joyce M. Rosenberg, "Office Romances Can Pose Problems," Associated Press, February 6, 2004.

To help deal with the complexity and the positive and negative aspects of office romance, some companies have established policies covering such relationships. To prevent charges of sexual harassment, a policy about office romance is likely to emphasize that both parties must mutually and voluntarily consent to the social relationship. Furthermore, the policy states that the social relationship must not affect job performance or negatively impact the company's business.[26] The accompanying Human Relations in Practice box offers some additional professional advice about the conduct of office romances.

BUILDING GOOD RELATIONSHIPS WITH CUSTOMERS

Success on the job also requires building good relationships with both external and internal customers. *External customers* fit the traditional definition of customer that includes clients and guests. External customers can be classified as either retail or industrial. The latter represents one company buying from another, such as purchasing steel from a manufacturer. *Internal customers* are the people you serve within the organization, or those who use the output from your job. For example, if you design computer graphics, the other people in the company who receive your graphics are your internal customers.

An overall approach to dealing effectively with customers is to be a good organizational citizen with respect to customer relationships. You gear a lot of your out-of-the-way effort into customer relationships. Specific behaviours of this type are presented in Figure 11-1. Time-tested suggestions for high-level customer service are presented next.[27] Taken together, these suggestions will help you bond with a customer, referring to a close and valued ongoing relationship. You will be able to implement principles of good service more readily if you are treated well by your employer. When workers feel valued, and are adequately compensated, they usually spread the sunshine to customers. Satisfied employees create satisfied customers.[28] One of the key reasons for the enviable success of Westjet Airlines is that all workers are treated well, and they, in turn, treat customers well.

1. *Establish customer satisfaction goals*. Decide jointly with your manager how much you intend to help customers. Find answers to questions such as the following: Is your

1. Tells outsiders this is a good place to work.
2. Says good things about the organization to others.
3. Generates favourable goodwill for the company.
4. Encourages friends and family to use the firm's products and services.
5. Actively promotes the firm's products and services.
6. Follows customer service guidelines with extreme care.
7. Conscientiously follows guidelines for customer promotions.
8. Follows up in a timely manner to customer requests and problems.
9. Performs duties with unusually few mistakes.
10. Always has a positive attitude at work.
11. Regardless of circumstances, exceptionally courteous and respectful to customers.
12. Encourages co-workers to contribute ideas and suggestions for service improvement.
13. Contributes many ideas for customer promotions and communications.
14. Makes constructive suggestions for service improvement.
15. Frequently presents to others creative solutions to customer problems.
16. Takes home brochures to read up on products and services.

Figure 11-1 Service-Oriented Organizational Citizenship Behaviours

Source: Portion of a table from Lance A. Bettencourt, Kevin P. Gwinner, and Matthew L. Meuter, "A Comparison of Attitude, Personality, and Knowledge Predictors of Service-Oriented Organizational Citizenship Behaviors," *Journal of Applied Psychology*, February 2001, p. 32.

company attempting to satisfy every customer within ten minutes of his or her request? Are you striving to provide the finest customer service in your field? Is your goal zero defections to competitors? Your goals will dictate how much and the type of effort you put into pleasing customers.

2. *Understand your customer's needs and place them first.* The most basic principle of selling is to identify and satisfy customer needs. Many customers may not be able to express their needs clearly. Also, they may not be certain of their needs. To help identify customer needs, you may have to probe for more information. For example, the associate in a consumer electronics store may have to ask, "What uses do you have in mind for your television receiver aside from watching regular programs? Will you be using it to display electronic photographs? Will you be using it to surf the internet?" Knowing such information will help the store associate identify which television set will satisfy the customer's needs.

   After you have identified customer needs, focus on satisfying them rather than doing what is convenient for you or your firm. Assume, for example, the customer says, "I would like to purchase nine reams of copier paper." The sales associate should not respond, "Sorry, the copying paper comes in boxes of ten, so it is not convenient to sell you nine reams." The associate might, however, offer a discount for the purchase of the full ten-ream box if such action fits company policy.

3. *Show care and concern.* During contacts with your customer, show concern for his or her welfare. Ask questions such as "How have you enjoyed the television set you bought here a while back?" or just "How are you feeling today?" After asking the

question, project a genuine interest in the answer. A strictly business approach to showing care and concern is to follow up on requests. A telephone call or email to the requester of your service is usually sufficient follow-up. A follow-up is effective because it completes the communication loop between two people.

4. *Communicate a positive attitude*. A positive attitude is conveyed by factors such as appearance, friendly gestures, a warm voice tone, and good telephone communication skills. If a customer seems apologetic about making a heavy demand, respond, "No need to apologize. My job is to please you. I'm here to serve."
5. *Make the buyer feel good*. A fundamental way of building a customer relationship is to make the buyer feel good about himself or herself. Also, make the buyer feel good because he or she has bought from you. Offer compliments about the customer's healthy glow, or a report that specified vendor requirements (for an industrial customer). An effective feel-good line is "I enjoy doing business with you."
6. *Display strong business ethics*. Ethical violations receive so much publicity that one can impress customers by being conspicuously ethical. Look for ways to show that you are so ethical that you would welcome making your sales tactics public knowledge. Also, treat the customer the same way you would treat a family member or a valued friend.
7. *Be helpful rather than defensive when a customer complains*. As described earlier, look at a complaint professionally rather than personally. Listen carefully and concentrate on being helpful. The upset customer cares primarily about having the problem resolved, not whether you are at fault. Use a statement such as this one: "I understand that this mistake is a major inconvenience. I'll do what I can right now to solve the problem." Remember also that complaints that are taken care of quickly and satisfactorily will often create a more positive impression than mistake-free service. If your company has a website where customers can email complaints, respond promptly and be helpful as if the person was there with you. Nygard, a Canadian company that sells clothing and other wares on the Web, responds quickly to customer complaints via email, often following up with a phone call.
8. *Invite the customer back*. The Southern expression "Y'all come back, now!" is well suited for good customer service. Specific invitations to return may help increase repeat business. The more focused and individualized the invitation, the more likely that it will have an impact on customer behaviour. ("Y'all come back, now!" is sometimes used too indiscriminately to be effective.) Pointing out why you enjoyed doing business with the customer and what future problems you could help with is an effective technique.
9. *Avoid rudeness*. Although rudeness to customers is obviously a poor business practice, the problem is widespread. Rudeness by customer-contact personnel is a major problem from the employer's standpoint. Be aware of subtle forms of rudeness such as complaining about your job or working hours in front of customers. To elevate your awareness level about rudeness among customer-contact personnel, do Human Relations Self-Assessment Quiz 11-3.

All of the 9 points just made emphasize the importance of practising good human relations with customers. Good customer service stems naturally from practising good human relations. Human Relations Skill-Building Exercise 11-1 gives you an opportunity to practise two techniques for building customer relationships.

Human Relations Self-Assessment

QUIZ 11-3 Am I Being Rude?

Directions: Following is a list of behaviours of customer-contact workers that would be interpreted as rude by many customers. Indicate whether you have engaged in such behaviour in your dealings with customers—or whether you would be likely to do so if your job involved customer contact.

	Yes	***No***
1. I talk to a co-worker while serving a customer.	______	______
2. I conduct a telephone conversation with someone else while serving a customer.	______	______
3. I address customers by their first names without having their permission.	______	______
4. I address customers as "you guys."	______	______
5. I chew gum or eat candy while dealing with a customer.	______	______
6. I laugh when customers describe an agonizing problem they are having with one of our company's products or services.	______	______
7. I minimize eye contact with customers.	______	______
8. I say the same thing to every customer, such as "Have a nice day," in a monotone.	______	______
9. I accuse customers of attempting to cheat the company before carefully investigating the situation.	______	______
10. I hurry customers when my break time approaches.	______	______
11. I comment on a customer's appearance in a flirtatious, sexually oriented way.	______	______
12. I sometimes complain about or make fun of other customers when I am serving a customer.	______	______

Interpretation: The more of these behaviours you have engaged in, the ruder you are and the more likely it is that you are losing potential business for your company. If you have not engaged in any of these behaviours, even when faced with a rude customer, you are an asset to your employer. You are also tolerant.

Human Relations Skill Building

Exercise 11-1 Giving Good Customer Service

Role players in this exercise will demonstrate two related techniques for giving good customer service.

Scenario 1: Show care and concern. A sales representative meets with two company representatives to talk about installing a new information system for employee benefits. One of the company representatives is from the human resources department and the other from the telecommunications department. The sales representative will attempt to show care and concern for both company representatives during the same meeting.

Scenario 2: Make the buyer feel good. A couple, played by two role players, enters a new-car showroom to examine a model they have seen advertised on television. Although they are not in urgent need of a new car, they are strongly interested. The sales representative is behind quota for the month and would like to close a sale today. The rep decides to use the tactic "Make the buyer feel good" to help form a bond.

SUMMARY

Getting along with co-workers is important for performing your job satisfactorily or better. Methods and tactics for building good co-worker relationships include the following:

1. Develop allies through being civil.
2. Make other people feel important.
3. Maintain honest and open relationships.
4. Express an interest in the work of others.
5. Be a good listener.
6. Use appropriate compliments.
7. Deal effectively with difficult people (including handling problems professionally, giving ample feedback, employing tact and diplomacy, using humour, reinforcing civil behaviour, and listening and responding).

An important part of getting along with co-workers is to understand the importance of teams and groups and to be able to effectively work as part of a team or group. Work teams are a special type of group that is brought together to perform specific tasks and goals. Groups and teams go through stages of development, which consist of forming, storming, norming, performing, and often, adjourning. Several barriers can inhibit team development, including time constraints, conflicting goals, roles that interfere with team progress, competing team members, and social loafing. Suggestions for being a good team player and working effectively on a team include these: share credit; display a helpful, cooperative attitude; share information; provide emotional support; follow the golden rule; keep confidential information to yourself; avoid actions that may sabotage the team; share the glory; and avoid backstabbing. Team members occupy various positive roles, including the following: resource investigator, coordinator, monitor-evaluator, completer-finisher and specialist. The challenge of office romances must also be handled maturely.

Success on the job also requires building good relationships with both internal and external customers. Representative techniques for building constructive customer relationships include (1) establish customer-satisfaction goals, (2) understand customer needs, (3) show care and concern, (4) communicate a positive attitude, (5) make the buyer feel good, (6) display strong business ethics, (7) be helpful rather than defensive in response to complaints, (8) invite the customer back, and (9) avoid being rude.

QUESTIONS AND ACTIVITIES

1. A critic of this chapter said, "A lot of ruthless people get ahead in business. So getting along with your co-workers may not really be that important." What do you think?
2. Why study about getting along with co-workers and customers? Isn't common sense good enough to develop smooth working relationships with people?
3. Make up an emotionally supportive statement to offer a co-worker whose wedding plans were cancelled one week before the marriage date.
4. Should companies have a policy about backstabbing? Explain.

5. What are the advantages of meeting a potential mate in the office rather than through friends or in public places such as bars or dances?
6. Many companies train employees in team skills. Why is such training essential for company success?
7. Many students dislike group assignments. What are some advantages and disadvantages of working in groups that you have experienced? Which strategies presented here would have helped you to overcome these disadvantages?
8. Have you ever been part of a team in the "performing" stage of development? If so, describe the experience to other classmates.
9. How might placing too much emphasis on being a good team player and fitting in with the group hurt a person's chances of becoming an executive?
10. If rudeness is so widespread today, why bother being polite and considerate on the job?

INTERNET SKILL BUILDER

Interpersonal Skills at Home Depot

Visit http://careers.homedepot.com, and proceed to "Living our values." Identify which skills mentioned relate to workplace relationships, including communication skills and self-understanding. Reflect back on any time you have visited a Home Depot or a competitor's store. How realistic is Home Depot about the interpersonal and personal skills required for a sales associate? If you happen to know a Home Depot employee, obtain his or her input in formulating your answer to the preceding question.

Log on to the **Companion Website** at **www.pearsoncanada.ca/dubrin** to access additional resources for this chapter.

CASE STUDY 11-1 HUMAN RELATIONS

The Unbalanced Team

Bluestone Security Systems is one of the largest security systems distributors in its city, with annual sales of $20 million. Two years ago, Bill Scovia, vice president of marketing and sales, reorganized the sales force. Previously, the sales force consisted of inside sales representatives (who took care of phone-in orders) and outside sales representatives (who called on accounts). The reorganization divided the outside sales force into two groups: direct sales and major accounts. The direct sales representatives were made responsible for small commercial customers and individual homeowners. As before, they would service existing customers and prospect for new accounts. Servicing existing customers usually involves adding fire protection to burglary protection and upgrading burglary systems.

In addition, Bluestone established a website to help sell its systems. A sales representative handling accounts generated by the website would receive one-half the ordinary commission. Although the representative would have to follow up on the web order or inquiry, top management felt that this would be an easy sale for a sales representative. The website was managed by a coordinator who would assign orders and inquiries to sales representatives in equal turns.

Three people who were direct sales representatives were promoted to major account executives. The account executives would service Bluestone's largest accounts, including prospecting for new business with these accounts. An example would be expanding the security system to a retailer's other stores. To promote teamwork and cooperation, Scovia assigned group sales quotas, including web sales, to account representatives. Collectively, their goal was to bring in 25 new large accounts per month, internet-generated sales included.

Given that the sales quota was a group quota, the account representatives were supposed to work together on strategy for acquiring new accounts. If a particular account executive did not have the expertise to handle his or her customer's problems, another account executive was supposed to offer help. Brian Marcus, for example, was the resident expert on the unique security problems of warehouses. If invited, Brian would join one of the two other account executives to call on a customer who owned a warehouse.

After the new sales organization had been in place 19 months, Elizabeth Kato, an account executive, was having lunch with Larry Starks, the manufacturing director at Bluestone. "I've about had it," said Elizabeth. "I'm tired of single-handedly carrying the team."

"What do you mean, you are single-handedly carrying the team?" asked Larry.

"You're a trusted friend, Larry. So let me lay out the facts. Each month the group is supposed to bring in 25 new sales. If we don't average those 25 sales per month, including web sales, we don't get our semi-annual bonus. That represents about 25 percent of my income. So a big chunk of my money comes from group effort.

"My average number of new accounts brought in for the last 12 months has been 14. And we are averaging about 21 sales per month. This translates into the other account execs averaging about seven sales among them. I'm carrying the group, but overall sales are still below quota. This means I didn't get my bonus last month.

"The other account execs are friendly and helpful in writing up proposals. But they just don't bring in their share of accounts."

Larry asked, "What does your boss say about this?"

"I've had several conversations with him about the problem. He tells me to be patient and to remember that the development of a fully balanced team requires time. He also tells me that I should develop a stronger team spirit. My problem is that I cannot pay my bills with team spirit."

Questions

1. What does this case illustrate about teamwork?
2. How effective is Elizabeth as a team player?
3. To what extent are Elizabeth's complaints justified?

CASE STUDY 11-2 HUMAN RELATIONS

Procter & Gamble Gives Time Off for Good Behaviour

On a Monday morning in late March a few years ago, A. G. Lafley, chair of Procter & Gamble (P&G), thrashed out a business decision with other key executives. By the first Wednesday in May, the plan had been orchestrated, and managers were directed to announce it at staff meetings at 11 a.m. Cincinnati time so that most of the company's 98,000 employees would find out at once.

The announcement wasn't a merger, a crucial new product rollout, or a reformulation of Tide. Instead, it was a sort of corporate parole: time off for good behaviour. In their meetings, P&G workers learned they had been granted a two-day vacation bonus, a reward for the company's sustained excellent performance over the previous four years, during which time P&G's stock nearly doubled in price. "We've never before offered a company performance award such as this, but you've earned it," Lafley wrote to employees in an e-mail.

Employees will have the option of taking two days pay instead of the time off, but that was hardly mentioned in newspaper headlines across the country that trumpeted the announcement.

Terry Loftus, a spokesperson for P&G says that the cost of the bonus "will be in the millions, though it isn't material from an accounting standpoint." The cash involved would be equivalent to less than 1 percent bonus, Loftus says. Nevertheless, P&G's gesture had people pondering the value of time off as a motivational tool.

Questions

1. How effective do you think the reward of two days off from work will be in motivating P&G employees to higher levels of performance?
2. How effective do you think the reward of two days pay will be in motivating P&G employees to higher levels of performance?
3. How will P&G know if time off from work (or two days pay) is actually an effective motivator?
4. What employee needs might be satisfied by having two days off from work?

Source: Joe Mullich, "Giving Employees Something They Can't Buy with a Bonus Check," Workforce Management, July 2004, p. 66.

Chapter 12

Developing Self-Confidence and Leadership Skills

Learning Outcomes

After studying the information and doing the exercises in this chapter, you should be able to

- develop a strategy for increasing your self-confidence if you think it is desirable to do so;
- understand the relationship of self-confidence to leadership;
- identify a number of personal traits and characteristics of effective leaders;
- identify a number of behaviours of effective leaders;
- map out a tentative program for developing your leadership potential and skills.

Katrina Makowski worked for several years as a member of the central support staff in a large law firm. One afternoon, office manager Georgette Dixon entered Katrina's work area. With a warm smile, she said, "Congratulations Katrina. On behalf of the rest of the managers in our firm, we are pleased to announce that you are the successful candidate for the team leader position of support services." Katrina said she was thrilled to accept the appointment, yet she asked, "Why me? I thought I was a real long-shot for this position. I'm not the most experienced support specialist in the group." Georgette replied, "Don't be so modest. You have managed many difficult situations very well. You're always on top of everything, take everything in stride, and maintain control. We want someone with your self-confidence in this team leader position."

The situation surrounding Katrina's promotion illustrates the importance of personal qualities to leadership—qualities such as a take-charge attitude, the ability to manage difficult situations, and self-confidence. While getting along with your manager, co-workers, and customers is essential for dealing effectively with people, if you wish to move up the "ladder" or work in supervisory positions, you will need to develop skills and abilities for assuming leadership roles.

Leadership occurs at all levels in an organization and can happen when people come to respect your opinion and personal characteristics and thus are influenced by you. Another way of becoming a leader is to be appointed to a formal position, such as supervisor or team leader, in which it is natural to exert leadership. Your greatest opportunity for exerting leadership, however, will come about from a combination of these methods of influence and learning the proper skills. You need to develop the "soft skills," as one author puts it. These skills include a blend of cognitive, emotional, and social skills as well as the managerial and technical skills required for a leadership position.[1] As a result, an individual with such appealing personal characteristics who is placed in a position of authority will find it relatively easy to exert leadership.

Our study of leadership will first focus on self-confidence because of its close relationship to, and requirement for, leadership. We then focus on the characteristics of leaders, their actions and attitudes, followed by an overview of how to develop your leadership potential, including some of those soft skills.

THE IMPORTANCE OF SELF-CONFIDENCE AND SELF-EFFICACY

Self-confidence is necessary for leadership because it helps assure group members that things are under control. Assume you are a manager in a company that is rumoured to be facing bankruptcy. At a meeting you attend, the president tearfully confesses, "I'm sorry, I'm just no good in a crisis. I don't know what's going to happen to the company. I don't think I can get us out of this mess. Maybe one of you would like to try your hand at turning around a troubled company."

In this situation, company employees would feel insecure. Many would be so preoccupied with finding new employment that they couldn't concentrate on their work. You would want the president to behave in a confident, assured manner. Yet, if the president were too arrogant about things, if he or she dismissed the problem too lightly, you might not feel secure then, either.

In other leadership situations as well, the leader who functions best is self-confident enough to reassure others and to appear in control. But if the leader is so self-confident that he or she will not admit errors, listen to criticism, or ask for advice, that too creates a problem.

An appropriate amount of self-confidence is also important because it contributes to **self-efficacy**, the belief in one's capability to perform a task. Various studies have shown that people with a high sense of self-efficacy tend to have good job performance. They also set relatively high goals for themselves.[2] Self-efficacy is thus related to self-confidence but is tied more directly to performing a task. A straightforward implication of self-efficacy is that people who think they can perform well on a task do better than those who think they will do poorly. Self-efficacy contributes to leadership effectiveness because a leader with high self-efficacy will usually believe that a task is doable. As a result, the leader can inspire others to carry out a difficult mission such as correcting a serious customer problem.

An encouraging note is that self-efficacy can be boosted through training. In an experiment, 66 unemployed people participated in a self-efficacy workshop. The group included bookkeepers, clerks, teachers, skilled mechanics, and technicians. The workshop featured watching video clips of people successfully performing job-search behaviours, followed by encouragement from the trainer and peers. In contrast to unemployed people who did not attend the workshop, the people who were trained in self-efficacy became more involved in job searches.[3] Being involved in job searches included telephoning about a job and obtaining an interview.

Research by college professors and psychological consultants George P. Hollenbeck and Douglas T. Hall suggests that our feelings of self-confidence stem from five sources of information.[4] The first source is the actual experience, or things we have done. Having done something before and succeeded is the most powerful way to build self-confidence. If you successfully inserted a replacement battery in your watch without destroying the watch, you will be confident in making another replacement.

The second source of self-confidence is the experiences of others, or modelling. You can gain some self-confidence if you have carefully observed others perform a task, such as resolving conflict with a customer. You might say to yourself, "I've seen Tracy calm down the customer by listening and showing sympathy, and I'm confident I can do the same thing." The third source of self-confidence is social comparison, or comparing yourself to others. If you see other people with capabilities similar to your own perform a task well, you will gain in confidence. A person might say to himself or herself, "If that person can learn how to work with enterprise software, I can do it also. I'm just as smart."

The fourth source of self-confidence is social persuasion, the process of convincing another person. If a credible person convinces you that you can accomplish a particular task, you will often receive a boost in self-confidence large enough to give the task a try. If the encouragement is coupled with guidance on how to perform the task, your self-confidence gain will be higher. So the boss or teacher who says, "I know you can do it, and I'm here to help you," knows how to build self-confidence.

The fifth source of information for making a self-confidence judgment is emotional arousal, or how you feel about events around you and manage your emotions. People rely somewhat on inner feelings to know if they are self-confident enough to perform the task. Imagine a person standing on top of a high mountain ready to ski down. However, he or she is trembling and nauseous with fear. Contrast this beginner to another person who simply feels mildly excited and challenged. Skier number one has a self-confidence problem, whereas skier number two has enough confidence to start the descent. (Have your emotional sensations ever influenced your self-confidence?)

The more of these five sources of self-confidence are positive for you, the more likely your self-confidence will be positive. Human Relations Self-Assessment Quiz12-1 provides some insight into your level of self-confidence.

DEVELOPING AND ENHANCING SELF-CONFIDENCE

Self-confidence is generally achieved by succeeding in a variety of situations. A confident sales representative may not be generally self-confident unless he or she also achieves success in activities such as taking exams, forming good personal relationships, navigating complex software, composing a letter, and displaying athletic skills.

Although this general approach to self-confidence building makes sense, it does not work for everyone. Some people who seem to succeed at everything still have lingering

Human Relations Self-Assessment

QUIZ 12-1 How Self-Confident Are You?

Indicate the extent to which you agree with each of the following statements: disagree strongly; disagree; neutral; agree; agree strongly.

	DS	*D*	*N*	*A*	*AS*
1. I frequently say to people, "I'm not sure."	5	4	3	2	1
2. I perform well in most situations in life.	1	2	3	4	5
3. I willingly offer advice to others.	1	2	3	4	5
4. Before making even a minor decision I usually consult with several people.	5	4	3	2	1
5. I am generally willing to attempt new activities for which I have very little related skill or experience.	1	2	3	4	5
6. Speaking in front of the class or other group is a frightening experience for me.	5	4	3	2	1
7. I sweat a lot when people challenge me or put me on the spot.	5	4	3	2	1
8. I feel comfortable attending a social event by myself.	1	2	3	4	5
9. I'm much more of a winner than a loser.	1	2	3	4	5
10. I am cautious about making any substantial change in my life.	5	4	3	2	1
Total score:					

Scoring and Interpretation: Calculate your total score by adding the numbers circled. A tentative interpretation of the scoring is as follows:

45–50: Very high self-confidence with perhaps a tendency toward arrogance
38–44: A high, desirable level of self-confidence
30–37: Moderate, or average, self-confidence
10–29: Self-confidence needs strengthening

self-doubt. Low self-confidence is so deeply ingrained in this type of personality that success in later life is not sufficient to change things. The following are some specific strategies and tactics for building and elevating self-confidence. They will generally work unless the person has deep-rooted feelings of inferiority. The tactics and strategies are arranged approximately in the order in which they should be tried to achieve best results.

Take an Inventory of Personal Assets and Accomplishments

Many people suffer from low self-confidence because they do not appreciate their own good points. Therefore, a starting point in increasing your self-confidence is to take an inventory of personal assets and accomplishments. This same activity was offered in Chapter 1 as a method of developing self-esteem. Personal assets should be related to characteristics and behaviours, rather than tangible assets such as an inheritance or an antique car. Accomplishments can be anything significant in which you played a key role in achieving the results. Try not to be modest in preparing your list of assets and accomplishments. You are looking for any confidence booster you can find.

Two lists prepared by different people will suffice to give you an idea of the kinds of assets and accomplishments that might be included:

Lillian

Good listener; most people like me; good handwriting; good posture; inquisitive mind; good at solving problems; good sense of humour; patient with people who make mistakes; better-than-average appearance. Organized successful fund drive that raised $30,000 for church; graduated tenth in high-school class of 500; achieved first place in industrial bowling league; daughter has an excellent career.

Angelo

Good mechanical skills; work well under pressure; good dancer; friendly with strangers; strong as an ox; good cook; can laugh at my own mistakes; great-looking guy; humble and modest. Made award-winning suggestion that saved company $25,000; scored winning goal in college basketball tournament; dragged child out of burning building.

The value of these asset lists is that they add to your self-appreciation. Most people who lay out their good points on paper come away from the activity with at least a temporary boost in self-confidence. The temporary boost, combined with a few success experiences, may lead to a long-term gain in self-confidence.

An important supplement to listing your own assets is hearing the opinion of others on your good points. This tactic has to be used sparingly, however, and mainly with people who are personal-growth-minded. A good icebreaker is to tell your source of feedback that you have to prepare a list of your assets for a human relations exercise (the one you are reading about right now!). Since that person knows of your work or your capabilities, you hope that he or she can spare a few minutes for this important exercise.

For many people, positive feedback from others does more for building self-confidence than does feedback from oneself. The reason is that self-esteem depends to a large extent on what we think others think about us. Consequently, if other people—whose judgment you trust—think highly of you, your self-image will be positive.

Develop a Solid Knowledge Base

A bedrock for projecting self-confidence is to develop a base of knowledge that enables you to provide sensible alternative solutions to problems. Intuition is very important, but working from a base of facts helps you project a confident image. Formal education is an obvious and important source of information for your knowledge base. Day-by-day absorption of information directly and indirectly related to your career is equally important. A major purpose of formal education is to get you in the right frame of mind to continue your quest for knowledge.

In your quest for developing a solid knowledge base to project self-confidence, be sensitive to the potential for abusing this technique. If you bombard people with quotes, facts, and figures, you are likely to be perceived as an annoying know-it-all.

Use Positive Self-Talk

A basic method of building self-confidence is to engage in **positive self-talk**, saying positive things about oneself to oneself. As explained by Jay T. Knippen and Thad B. Green, the first step in using positive self-talk is to objectively state the incident that is casting doubt about self-worth.[5] The key word here is *objectively*. Louis, who is fearful of poorly executing a report-writing assignment, might say, "I've been asked to write a report for the company, and I'm not a good writer."

The next step is to objectively interpret what the incident *does not* mean. Louis might say, "Not being a skilled writer doesn't mean that I can't figure out a way to write a good report, or that I'm an ineffective employee."

Next, the person should objectively state what the incident *does* mean. In doing this, the person should avoid put-down labels such as "incompetent," "stupid," "dumb," "jerk," or "airhead." All these terms are forms of negative self-talk. Louis should state what the incident does mean: "I have a problem with one small aspect of this job, preparing professional-level reports. This means I need to improve my report-writing skills."

The fourth step is to objectively account for the cause of the incident. Louis would say, "I'm really worried about writing a good report because I have very little experience in writing along these lines."

The fifth step is to identify some positive ways to prevent the incident from happening again. Louis might say, "I'll get out my textbook on business communications and review the chapter on report-writing," or "I'll enroll in a course or seminar on business report-writing."

The final step is to use positive self-talk. Louis imagines his boss saying, "This report is really good. I'm proud of my decision to select you to prepare this important report."

Positive self-talk builds self-confidence and self-esteem because it programs the mind with positive messages.[6] Making frequent positive messages or affirmations about the self creates a more confident person. An example would be, "I know I can learn this new equipment rapidly enough to increase my productivity within five days." If you do make a mistake, your positive self-talk might be, "It's taken me more time than usual to learn how to use this new equipment. I know I'll have the problem licked in a few days."

Business coach Gary Lockwood emphasizes that positive self-talk is also useful for getting people past difficult times. "It's all in your head," he said. "Remember you are in charge of your feelings. You are in control of your attitude." Instead of berating yourself after making a mistake, learn from the experience and move on. Say to yourself, "Everyone makes mistakes," "Tomorrow is another day," or "What can I learn from this?"[7]

Avoid Negative Self-Talk

As mentioned above, you should minimize negative statements about yourself in order to bolster self-confidence. A lack of self-confidence is reflected in statements such as, "I may be stupid but . . . ," "Nobody asked my opinion," "I know I'm usually wrong, but . . . ," and "I know I don't have as much education as some people, but . . . ." Self-effacing statements like these serve to reinforce low self-confidence.

It is also important not to attribute to yourself negative, irreversible traits such as "idiotic," "ugly," "dull," "loser," and "hopeless."[8] Instead, look upon your weak points as areas for possible self-improvement. Negative self-labelling can do long-term damage to your self-confidence. If a person stops that practice today, his or her self-confidence may begin to increase.

Use Positive Visual Imagery

Assume you have a situation in mind in which you would like to appear confident and in control. An example would be a meeting with a major customer who has told you over the telephone that he is considering switching suppliers. Your intuitive reaction is that if you cannot handle his objectives without fumbling or appearing desperate, you will lose the account. An important technique in this situation is **positive visual imagery**, or picturing a positive outcome in your mind. To apply this technique in this situation, imagine yourself engaging in a convincing argument about retaining your customer as the primary supplier. Imagine yourself talking in positive terms about the good service your company offers and how you can rectify any problems.

Visualize yourself listening patiently to your customer's concerns and then talking confidently about how your company can handle these concerns. As you rehearse this moment of truth, create a mental picture of you and the customer shaking hands over the fact that the account is still yours.

Positive visual imagery helps you appear self-confident because your mental rehearsal of the situation has helped you prepare for battle. If imagery works for you once, you will be even more effective in subsequent uses of the technique.

Set High Expectations for Yourself (The Galatea Effect)

If you set high expectations for yourself, and you succeed, you are likely to experience a temporary or permanent boost in self-confidence. The **Galatea effect** is a type of self-fulfilling prophecy in which high expectations lead to high performance. Similar to positive self-talk, if you believe in yourself, you are more likely to succeed. You expect to win, so you do. The Galatea effect does not work all the time, but it does work some of the time for many people.

Workplace behaviour researchers D. Brian McNatt and Timothy A. Judge studied the Galatea effect with 72 auditors within three offices of a major accounting firm for a three-month period. The auditors were given letters of encouragement to strengthen their feelings of self-efficacy. Information in the letters was based on facts about the auditors, such as information derived from their résumés and company records. The results of the experiment showed that creating a Galatea effect bolstered self-efficacy, motivation, and performance. However, the performance improvement was temporary suggesting that self-expectations need to be boosted regularly.[9]

Strive for Peak Performance

A key strategy for projecting self-confidence is to display **peak performance**. The term refers to much more than attempting to do your best. To achieve peak performance you must be totally focused on what you are doing. When you are in the state of peak performance you are mentally calm and physically at ease. Intense concentration is required to achieve this state. You are so focused on the task at hand that you are not distracted by extraneous events or thoughts.

The mental state achieved during peak performance is akin to a person's sense of deep concentration when immersed in a sport or hobby. On days when tennis players perform way above their usual game, they typically comment, "The ball looked so large today, I could read the label as I hit it." On the job, the focus and concentration allow you to sense and respond to relevant information coming from within the mind and from outside stimuli. While turning in peak performance, you are experiencing a mental state referred to as *flow*.

Although you are concentrating on an object or sometimes on another person during peak performance, you still have an awareness of the self. You develop a strong sense of the self, similar to self-confidence and self-efficacy, while you are concentrating on the task. Peak performance is related to self-confidence in another important way. Achieving peak performance in many situations helps you develop self-confidence. Here are two representative examples of peak performance:

- A real estate agent sells $17 million of homes in her region in one year, 40 percent higher than any other agent in her area.
- A manufacturing technician becomes certified as a Black Belt in the quality-improvement process called Six Sigma, and then leads a team that moves a call centre from a customer satisfaction rating of 75 to 98 percent.

Bounce Back from Setbacks and Embarrassments

An effective self-confidence builder is to convince yourself that you can conquer adversities such as setbacks and embarrassments, thus being resilient. The vast majority of

Human Relations in Practice

Eddie Lampert Uses Self-Confidence to Make Billions and Escape Kidnappers

By the time financier Eddie Lampert was 42 years old he had amassed a fortune estimated at nearly $2 billion. He is the owner of the private investment fund, ESL Investments. After his fund acquired the bankrupt discounter Kmart, Lampert then acquired Sears Roebuck & Co. to form Sears Holding Company—with Lampert as chair. In his dealings with business associates, Big Eddie brims with self-confidence in his decision making. During a meeting with Sears Executives, he asked again and again, "What's the benefit of that?" or "Why invest in that?" He shot down a modest $2 million proposal to improve lighting in the stores.

In 2003, he was kidnapped at gunpoint in a parking garage by four hoodlums who had been searching for wealthy people on the Internet. He was held bound in a bathtub at a motel. The men told Lampert they had been hired to kill him for $5 million but would let him go for $1 million. As the kidnappers became increasingly nervous, Lampert convinced them that if they would release him, he would pay them $40,000 a couple of days later. The hoodlums let him off on the side of a road in Greenwich, Connecticut. "It was very much like going to your own funeral," he says. Two days later Lampert was back in Kmart negotiations, with all the more confidence in his negotiating skills.

Source: Patricia Sellers, "Eddie Lampert: The Best Investor of His Generation," *Fortune*, Investor's Guide February 6, 2006; Robert Berner, "The Next Warren Buffet," *BusinessWeek*, November 22, 2004, pp. 144–154.

successful leaders have dealt successfully with at least one significant setback in their careers, such as being fired or demoted. In contrast, crumbling after a setback or series of setbacks will usually lower self-confidence. Two major suggestions for bouncing back from setbacks and embarrassments are presented next.

Get Past the Emotional Turmoil Adversity has enormous emotional consequences. The emotional impact of severe job adversity can rival the loss of a personal relationship. The stress from adversity leads to a cycle in which adversity is followed by stress, which is followed by more adversity. A starting point in dealing with the emotional aspects of adversity is to *accept the reality of your problem.* Admit that your problems are real and that you are hurting inside. A second step is *not to take the setback personally.* Remember that setbacks are inevitable so long as you are taking some risks in your career. Not personalizing setbacks helps reduce some of the emotional sting.

If possible, *do not panic.* Recognize that you are in difficult circumstances under which many others panic. Convince yourself to remain calm enough to deal with the severe problem or crisis. Also, *get help from your support network.* Getting emotional support from family members and friends helps overcome the emotional turmoil associated with adversity.

Find a Creative Solution to Your Problem An inescapable part of planning a comeback is to solve your problem. You often need to search for creative solutions, using the problem-solving and decision-making steps described in Chapter 3. Suppose a person faced the adversity of not having enough money for educational expenses. The person might search through standard alternatives such as applying for financial aid, looking for more lucrative part-time work, and borrowing from family members. Several students have solved this problem more creatively by asking strangers to lend them money as intermediate-term investments. An option the investors have is to receive a payback based on the future earnings of the students.

LEADERSHIP AND BEING A LEADER

So far we have emphasized the importance of developing self-confidence so that you are able to provide leadership to others. **Leadership** is the process of bringing about positive changes and influencing others to achieve organizational goals. Self-confidence makes a contribution to leadership because people tend to be influenced by a person of high—but not unreasonable—self-confidence.

The key words in understanding leadership are *change* and *influence.* A leader often challenges the status quo and brings about improvements. A leader also influences people to do things, such as achieve a higher performance level, that they would not do in his or her absence. If influence is not exerted, then strictly speaking, there is no leadership.

Effective leadership at the top of organizations is necessary for their prosperity and even survival.[10] Effective leadership is also important throughout the organization, particularly in working with entry-level workers. Good supervision is needed to help employees deal with customer problems, carry out their usual tasks, and maintain high quality.

Before studying the personal qualities and behaviours of effective leaders, take Human Relations Self-Assessment Quiz 12-2. The exercise will help you understand how ready you are to assume a leadership role. Taking the quiz will also give you insight into the type of thinking that is characteristic of leaders.

Human Relations Self-Assessment

QUIZ 12-2 Readiness for the Leadership Role

Indicate the extent to which you agree with each of the following statements. Use a one-to-five scale: (1) disagree strongly; (2) disagree; (3) neutral; (4) agree; (5) agree strongly. If you do not have leadership experience, imagine how you might react to the questions if you were a leader.

Statement					
1. It is enjoyable having people count on me for ideas and suggestions.	1	2	3	4	5
2. It would be accurate to say that I have inspired other people.	1	2	3	4	5
3. It's a good practice to ask people provocative questions about their work.	1	2	3	4	5
4. It's easy for me to compliment others.	1	2	3	4	5
5. I like to cheer people up even when my own spirits are down.	1	2	3	4	5
6. What my team accomplishes is more important than my personal glory.	1	2	3	4	5
7. Many people imitate my ideas.	1	2	3	4	5
8. Building team spirit is important to me.	1	2	3	4	5
9. I would enjoy coaching other members of the team.	1	2	3	4	5
10. It is important to me to recognize others for their accomplishments.	1	2	3	4	5
11. I would enjoy entertaining visitors to my firm even if it interfered with my completing a report.	1	2	3	4	5
12. It would be fun for me to represent my team at gatherings outside our department.	1	2	3	4	5
13. The problems of my teammates are my problems too.	1	2	3	4	5
14. Resolving conflict is an activity I enjoy.	1	2	3	4	5
15. I would cooperate with another unit in the organization even if I disagreed with the position taken by its members.	1	2	3	4	5
16. I am an idea generator on the job.	1	2	3	4	5
17. It's fun for me to bargain whenever I have the opportunity.	1	2	3	4	5
18. Team members listen to me when I speak.	1	2	3	4	5
19. People have asked me to assume the leadership of an activity several times in my life.	1	2	3	4	5
20. I've always been a convincing person.	1	2	3	4	5
Total score:					

Scoring and Interpretation: Calculate your total score by adding the numbers circled. A tentative interpretation of the scoring is as follows:

- 90–100 High readiness for the leadership role
- 60–89 Moderate readiness for the leadership role
- 40–59 Some uneasiness with the leadership role
- 39 or less Low readiness for carrying out the leadership role

If you are already a successful leader and you scored low on this questionnaire, ignore your score. If you scored surprisingly low and you are not yet a leader or are currently performing poorly as a leader, study the statements carefully. Consider changing your attitude or your behaviour so that you can legitimately answer more of the statements with a 4 or a 5. Studying the rest of this chapter will give you additional insights into the leader's role that may be helpful in your development as a leader.

TRAITS AND CHARACTERISTICS OF EFFECTIVE LEADERS

A major part of understanding leaders and leadership is to recognize that effective leaders have the "right stuff." In other words, certain inner qualities contribute to leadership effectiveness in a wide variety of situations. **Effectiveness** in this situation means that the leader helps the group or team accomplish its objectives without neglecting satisfaction and morale. The characteristics that contribute to effectiveness depend somewhat on the situation. A supervisor in a meat-packing plant may need some different characteristics from a supervisor in an information technology department. The situation includes such factors as how experienced the people being supervised are, the job or tasks being performed, the company, and the cultural background of the employees. In the next several pages, we describe some of the more important traits and characteristics of leaders. Many of these characteristics and traits are capable of development and refinement. Figure 12-1 outlines these key traits.

Self-Confidence and Courage

Self-confidence is necessary for leadership because it helps assure group members that activities are under control. Assume you are a manager in a company that is facing bankruptcy. At a meeting you attend, the chief executive officer sobs, "I'm sorry, I'm just no good in a crisis. I don't know what's going to happen to the company. I don't think I can get us out of this mess. Maybe one of you would like to try your hand at

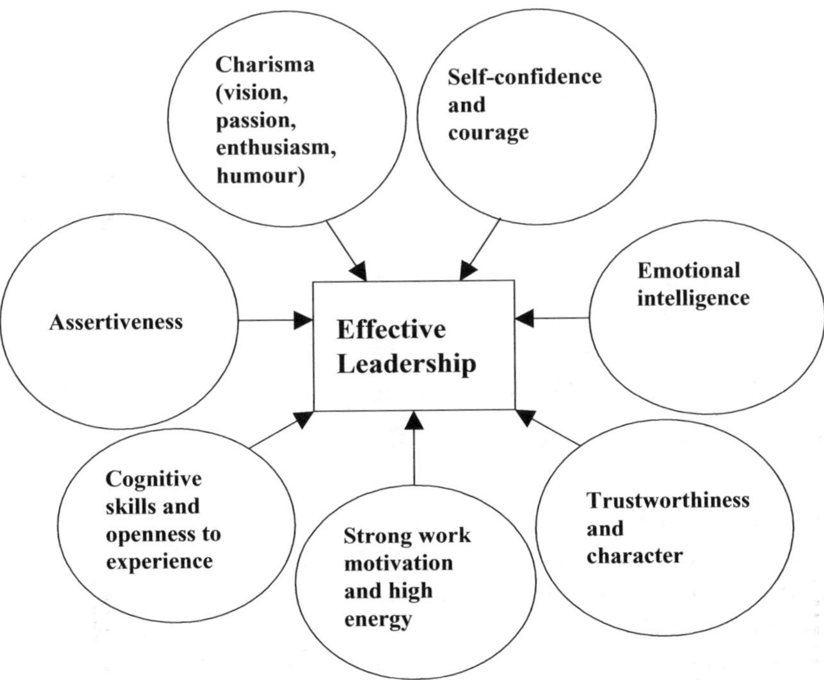

Figure 12-1 Seven Key Leadership Traits

turning around the company." You would probably prefer that the CEO behave in a confident, assured manner.

In other leadership situations as well, the leader who functions best is self-confident enough to reassure others and to appear in control. But if the leader is so self-confident that he so she will not admit errors, listen to criticism, or ask for advice, that too creates problems. Being too self-confident can lead to the person to ignore potential problems, thinking, "I can handle whatever comes my way."

Self-confidence often takes the form of the courage to face the challenges of taking prudent risks and taking initiative in general. Courage comes from the heart, as suggested by the French word for heart, le coeur. Leaders must be able to face up to responsibility and be willing to put reputations on the line, even if this means taking a course of action others would not advise.

Emotional Intelligence

Receiving more and more support is the idea that **emotional intelligence** is key to the development of a healthy personality, including one's ability to demonstrate effective leadership. Emotional intelligence is considered a major contributor to leadership effectiveness. In review (refer to Chapter 6), the concept refers to managing ourselves and our relationships effectively with an emphasis on dealing with emotion. The traits and behaviours of emotional intelligence directly related to leadership include self-confidence, empathy, and visionary leadership.[11] Also, effective leaders demonstrate emotional calm in crises and control their negative emotions. Recent Canadian political blunders—verbal attacks on the United States—demonstrate that the inability to control emotions and not say whatever "pops" into one's head can have very negative repercussions. One example of such a blunder was the remark by MP Carolyn Parrish, who blurted out, "Damn Americans. I hate those bastards," unaware that she was being taped. This remark jeopardized her re-election as a NATO association chair.[12]

Emotional intelligence can be developed through working on some of its components, such as finding work you are passionate about, developing self-confidence, and developing empathy. It is also important to develop the habit of trying to understand the feelings and emotions of people around you. Ask yourself such questions as, Why is the person feeling like this? What are the person's possible motives? Why is this person telling me what he or she is telling me? Effective leaders look beneath the surface to develop a deeper understanding of situations.

Trustworthiness and Character

Group members consistently believe that leaders must display honesty, integrity, and credibility. Leaders themselves believe that honesty and integrity make a difference in their effectiveness. Researchers and observers also share these views. Warren G. Bennis, a leadership authority, interviewed more than 100 corporate leaders and 50 private-sector leaders during a 13-year period. One of the common threads he found was the capacity of leaders to generate and sustain trust. He observed a consistency among what leaders think, feel, and do. Bennis said it drives people crazy when bosses don't walk their talk.[13] How would you feel if you worked for a boss you couldn't trust?

It takes a leader a long time to build trust, yet one brief incident of untrustworthy behaviour can destroy it. An example of untrustworthy behaviour would be using company money for private purposes or sexually harassing a team member. Leaders are usually allowed a fair share of honest mistakes. In contrast, dishonest mistakes quickly erode leadership effectiveness. Meg Whitman, the CEO of eBay, exemplifies a leader who many people—employees and members of the eBay community—trust. Part of the trust comes from her being self-effacing and low key, and the fact that she responds directly to email messages from buyers and sellers.[14] The small percentage of frauds who prey on eBay users have not diminished trust in Whitman because the criminals are not eBay employees.

Having certain character traits contributes to being trustworthy and being perceived as a trustworthy person. **Character** in this context refers to doing the right things despite outside pressures to do the opposite. Being of good character also includes leaving enduring marks that set one apart from another.[15] To be of good character is to be moral and to treat others respectfully and fairly.

Strong Work Motivation and High Energy

Leadership positions tend to be both physically and mentally demanding. A successful leader must be willing to work hard and long to achieve success. Many leaders appear to be driven by a need for self-fulfillment. Another fundamental reason strong work motivation is required for effectiveness is that a person has to be willing to accept the heavy responsibility that being a supervisor entails. As one department manager said, "Whoever thought being a manager would mean that I would have to fire a single parent who has three children to feed and clothe?"

Cognitive Skills and Openness to Experience

Mental ability and personality are important for leadership success. To inspire people, bring about constructive changes, and solve problems creatively, leaders need to be mentally sharp. Problem-solving and intellectual skills are referred to collectively as **cognitive factors**. The term *cognition* refers to the mental process or faculty by which knowledge is gathered.

A cognitive skill of major importance is *knowledge of the business*, or technical competence. An effective leader has to be technically or professionally competent in some discipline, particularly when leading a group of specialists. It is difficult for the leader to establish rapport with group members when he or she does not know what they are doing. A related damper on leadership effectiveness is when the group does not respect the leader's technical skill. Having good practical intelligence (*street smarts*) is also part of an effective leader's intellectual makeup. A leader with high practical intelligence could size up a good opportunity without spending an extensive amount of time analyzing what could possibly go wrong.

Closely related to cognitive skills is the personality characteristic of **openness to experience**, a positive orientation toward learning. People who have considerable openness to experience have well-developed intellects. Traits commonly associated with this dimension of the intellect include being imaginative, cultured, curious, original, broad-minded, intelligent, and artistically sensitive.

Assertiveness

Assertiveness is a widely recognized leadership trait. If you are self-confident, it is easier to be assertive with people. An assertive leader might say, "I know that the ice storm put us out of business for four days, but we can make up the time by working smart and pulling together. Within 30 days, we will have met or surpassed our goals for the quarter." This statement reflects self-confidence in leadership capabilities and assertiveness in expressing thoughts.

Assertiveness helps leaders perform many tasks and achieve goals. Among them are confronting group members about their mistakes, demanding higher performance, and setting high expectations. An assertive leader will also make demands on higher management, such as asking for equipment needed by the group.

Charisma

An important quality for a high-level leader is **charisma**, a type of charm and magnetism that inspires others. Not every leader has to be charismatic, yet to be an effective leader you need some degree of this intangible personal quality.[16] A leader's charisma is determined by the subjective perception of him or her by other people. It is therefore impossible for even the most effective leaders to inspire and motivate everyone. Even popular business leaders are disliked by some of their employees. Charisma encompasses many traits and characteristics. Here we focus on vision, enthusiasm and excitement, and humour.

Vision Top-level leaders need a visual image of where the organization is headed and how it can get there. The progress of the organization is dependent on the top executive having this vision. Effective leaders project ideas and images that excite people and therefore inspire employees to do their best. At a Conference Board of Canada conference in 2001, the new president of the board at that time stated that leaders need the capacity to see the "bigger picture."[17] Leadership positions of lesser responsibility also call for some vision or that ability to see the bigger picture. Each work group in a progressive company might be expected to form its own vision, as in this vision statement: "We will become the best accounts receivable group in the entire desk-manufacturing industry."

Passion, Enthusiasm, and Excitement Charismatic leaders are passionate about their work and their group members. Part of the reason charismatic leaders can readily be passionate, enthusiastic, and excited is that they tend to be extraverted. The extraversion is most strongly associated with the type of charismatic leader who brings about major changes in the organization or an organizational unit.[18] The charismatic business owner is likely to think about the company's product or service day and night. Because of their contagious excitement, charismatic leaders stimulate group members. Workers respond positively to enthusiasm, especially because enthusiasm may be perceived as a reward for good performance. Enthusiasm is also effective because it helps build good relationships with group members. Spoken expressions of enthusiasm include such statements as "great job" and "I love it." Andrea Jung, the stylish and inspirational chief executive officer of Avon Products, tells Avon representatives at company meetings that she loves them. The leader can express enthusiasm nonverbally through gestures, nonsexual touching, and so forth.

Sense of Humour Humour is a component of charisma and a contributor to leadership effectiveness. Humour helps leaders influence people by reducing tension, relieving boredom, and defusing anger.[19] The most effective form of humour by a leader is tied to the leadership situation. It is much less effective for the leader to tell rehearsed jokes. A key advantage of a witty, work-related comment is that it indicates mental alertness. A canned joke is much more likely to fall flat.

A sales manager was conducting a meeting about declining sales. He opened the meeting by saying, "Ladies and gentlemen, just yesterday I completed a spreadsheet analysis of our declining sales. According to my spreadsheet analysis, if we continue our current trend, by the year 2014 we will have sales of negative $2,750,000. No company can support those figures. We've got to reverse the trend." The manager's humour helped dramatize the importance of reversing the sales decline.

Although inherited characteristics such as energy contribute to charisma, most people can develop some charismatic qualities. Exhibit 12-1 presents suggestions for acquiring more charisma.

Exhibit 12-1
Suggestions for Becoming More Charismatic

The following are a number of suggestions for behaving charismatically, all based on characteristics and behaviours often found among charismatic people.

1. *Communicate a vision.* A charismatic leader offers an exciting image of where the organization is headed and how to get there. A vision is more than a forecast because it describes an ideal version of the future of an entire organization or an organizational unit such as a department. The supervisor of paralegal services might communicate a vision such as, "Our paralegal group will become known as the most professional and helpful paralegal group in Alberta."
2. *Make frequent use of metaphors and analogies.* To inspire people, the charismatic leader uses colourful language and exciting metaphors and analogies. Develop metaphors to inspire people around you. To pick up the spirits of her maintenance group, a maintenance supervisor told the group, "We're a lot like the heating and cooling system in a house. A lot of people don't give us much thought, but without us their lives would be very uncomfortable."
3. *Inspire trust and confidence.* Make your deeds consistent with your promises. As mentioned earlier in this chapter, being trustworthy is a key leadership trait. Get people to believe in your competence by making your accomplishments known in a polite, tactful way.
4. *Be highly energetic and goal-oriented.* Impress others with your energy and resourcefulness. To increase your energy supply, exercise frequently, eat well, and

(*continued*)

get ample rest. You can also add to an image of energy by raising and lowering your voice frequently and avoiding a slow pace.

5. *Be emotionally expressive and warm.* A key characteristic of charismatic leaders is the ability to express feelings openly. In dealing with team members, refer to your feelings at the time, such as "I'm excited because I know we are going to hit our year-end target by mid-October." Nonverbal emotional expressiveness, such as warm gestures and frequent touching (nonsexual) of group members also exhibits charisma.
6. *Make ample use of true stories.* An excellent way of building rapport is to tell stories that deliver a message.[20] Storytelling adds a touch of warmth to the teller and helps build connections among people who become familiar with the same story.
7. *Smile frequently, even if you are not in a happy mood.* A warm smile seems to indicate a confident, caring person, which contributes to a perception of charisma.[21]
8. *Be candid.* Practise saying directly what you want rather than being indirect and evasive. If you want someone to help you, don't ask, "Are you busy?" Instead ask, "Can you help me with a problem I'm having right now?"
9. *Make everybody you meet feel that he or she is quite important.* For example, at a company social gathering, shake the hand of every person you meet. Also, thank people frequently both orally and by written notes.
10. *Stand up straight and also use other nonverbal signals of self-confidence.* Practise good posture. Minimize fidgeting, scratching, foot tapping, and speaking in a monotone. Walk at a rapid pace without appearing to be panicked. Dress fashionably without going to the extreme that people notice your clothes more than they notice you.
11. *Be willing to take personal risks.* Charismatic leaders are typically risk takers, and risk taking adds to their charisma. Risks you might take would include suggesting a bright but costly idea and recommending that a former felon be given a chance in your firm.

BEHAVIOURS AND SKILLS OF EFFECTIVE LEADERS

The personal traits, skills, and characteristics just discussed help create the potential for effective leadership. A leader also has to do things that influence group members to achieve good performance. The behaviours or actions of leaders described next contribute to productivity and morale in most situations.

Practise Strong Ethics

Being trustworthy as a leader facilitates the practice of strong (or good) **ethics**. Ethics is the study of moral obligation, or separating right from wrong. Ethical leadership is about doing the right thing by employees, customers, the environment, and the law.[22] Practising good ethics contributes to effective leadership for several reasons. Workers are more likely to trust an ethical than an unethical leader, which helps the leader gain the support of the group. Good ethics serves as a positive model for group members, thus strengthening the organization. Also, ethical leaders help group members avoid common ethical pitfalls in the workplace. Many of these unethical practices, as listed next, can lead to lawsuits against the company:

- Lying or misrepresenting facts
- Blaming others for your mistakes
- Divulging personal or confidential information to others in the company to promote yourself
- Permitting or failing to report violations of legal requirements
- Protecting substandard performers from proper discipline
- Condoning or failing to report theft or misuse of company property
- Suppressing grievances and complaints
- Covering up accidents and failing to report health and safety hazards
- Ignoring or violating higher management's commitments to employees
- Taking credit for the ideas of others[23]

To simplify a complex issue, an effective leader practises the golden rule: *Do unto others as you would have others do unto you.* Similarly, Steven Covey encourages leaders to follow natural principles such as doing only good things.[24] He urges corporate executives, for example, to establish only those goals that will benefit people.

Direction Setting

Given that leaders are supposed to bring about change, they must point people in the right direction. Setting a direction includes the idea of establishing a vision for the organization or a smaller group. An example of direction setting by a top-level manager would be for the chief executive officer of a toy company to decide that the company should now diversify into the bicycle business. Direction setting by a team leader would include encouraging the group to strive toward error-free work from this point forward or to collaborate more with each other to form a true team.

Develop Partnerships with People

Leadership is now regarded as a long-term relationship, or partnership, between leaders and group members. According to Peter Block, in a **partnership** the leader and group members are connected in such a way that the power between them is approximately balanced. To form a partnership, the leader has to allow the group members to share in decision making. Four conditions are necessary to form a true partnership between the leader and group members:

1. *Exchange of purpose* The leader and team member should work together to build a vision.
2. *A right to say no* In a partnership each side has the right to say no without fear of being punished.
3. *Joint accountability* Each person takes responsibility for the success and failure of the group.

4. *Absolute honesty* In a partnership, not telling the truth to each other is an act of betrayal. When group members recognize that they have power, they are more likely to tell the truth because they feel less vulnerable to punishment.[25]

Help Group Members Reach Goals and Achieve Satisfaction

Effective leaders help subordinates in their efforts to achieve goals.[26] In a sense, they smooth out the path to reaching goals. One important way to do this is to provide the necessary resources to subordinates. An important aspect of a leader's job is to ensure that subordinates have the proper tools, equipment, and personnel to accomplish their objectives.

Another way of helping group members achieve goals is to reduce frustrating barriers to getting work accomplished. A leader who helps group members cut through minor rules and regulations would be engaging in such behaviour. In a factory, a supervisory leader has a responsibility to replace faulty equipment, make sure unsafe conditions are corrected, and see that troublesome employees are either rehabilitated or replaced.

Another important general set of actions characteristic of an effective leader is looking out for the satisfaction of the group. Small things sometimes mean a lot in terms of personal satisfaction. One office manager fought for better coffee facilities for her subordinates. Her thoughtfulness contributed immensely to their job satisfaction.

Giving group members emotional support is another effective way of improving worker satisfaction. An emotionally supportive leader would engage in activities such as listening to subordinates' problems and offering them encouragement and praise. Again, basic human relations skills contribute to leader effectiveness.

Set High Expectations

In addition to making expectations clear, it is important for leaders to set high expectations for group members. If you as a leader expect others to succeed, they are likely to live up to your expectations. This mysterious phenomenon has been labelled the **Pygmalion effect**. According to Greek mythology, Pygmalion was a sculptor and king of Cyprus who carved an ivory statue of a maiden and fell in love with it. The statue was soon brought to life in response to his prayers.

The point of the Pygmalion effect is that the leader can elevate performance by the simple method of expecting others to perform well. The manager's high expectations become a self-fulfilling prophecy. Why high expectations lead to high performance could be linked to self-confidence. As the leader expresses faith in the group members' ability to perform well, they become more confident of their skills.

Give Frequent Feedback on Performance

Effective leaders inform employees how they are progressing on the job. They know how to recognize progress and how to reward success. They give feedback on progress in such a manner as to encourage the employee to improve and use praise for things done right.[27] Less effective leaders, in contrast, often avoid confrontation and give limited positive feedback. An exception is that some ineffective leaders become involved in many confrontations—they are masters at reprimanding people!

Manage a Crisis Effectively

When a crisis strikes, that's the time to have an effective leader around. When things are running very smoothly, you may not always notice whether your leader is present. Effectively managing a crisis means giving reassurance to the group that things will soon be under control, specifying the alternative paths for getting out of the crisis, and choosing one of the paths.

Ask the Right Questions

As in the example just presented, leaders do not need to know all the answers. Instead, a major contribution can be to ask the right questions. Although being knowledgeable about the group task is important, there are many times when asking group members penetrating questions is more important. In today's complex and rapidly changing business environment, the collective intelligence of group members is needed to solve problems.[28] Asking questions, rather than giving answers, is the natural method of helping group members become better problem solvers. Here are sample questions a leader might ask group members to help them meet their challenges:

- What are you going to do differently to reduce by 50 percent the time it takes to fill a customer order?
- Top management is thinking of getting rid of our group and subcontracting the work we do to outside vendors. What do you propose we do to make us more valuable to the company?
- Can you figure out why the competition is outperforming us?

Be a Servant Leader

A humanitarian approach to leadership is to be a **servant leader**, one who serves group members by working on their behalf to help them achieve their goals, not the leader's goals. The idea behind servant leadership, as developed by Robert K. Greenleaf, is that leadership stems naturally from a commitment to service. Serving others, including employees, customers, and the community, is the primary motivation for the servant leader.[29] Servant leadership encompasses many different acts, all designed to make life easier or better for group members. Several acts of servant leadership are mentioned next.

A good starting point is for the leader to see himself or herself as a humble servant. ("I'm here to serve you.") Servant leaders also look for the opportunity to lend assistance directly to employees—for example, a supermarket manager bagging groceries during an unanticipated rush of business. On Lawrence Weinbach's first day as CEO of computer-maker Unisys Corp., he opened a door for an employee carrying a computer and picked up a piece of paper she dropped.[30] A servant leader would also provide the tools people need to accomplish their work, such as fighting for a budget big enough to cover expensive new equipment.

Although a servant leader is idealistic, he or she recognizes that one individual cannot accomplish everything. So the leader listens carefully to the array of problems facing group members and then concentrates on a few. As the head of a nurse's union told the group: "I know you are hurting in many ways. Yet I think that the work overload issue is the biggest one, so we will head into negotiations working on obtaining sensible workloads. After that we will work on job security."

Canada Today

Six New Carrots, or How to Keep Your Staff Around

A Canadian book, *Values Shift: The New Work Ethic and What It Means for Business,* tries to tackle the problem of motivating and inspiring employees in a time when traditional values and ideas may no longer be valued by employees. What can leaders or managers do to keep employees in an era when promotions and big pay raises may not be possible? The authors have some interesting ideas on how to maintain and even excite current workers!

1. **Be proactive in offering workers a better work/life balance.** In the last 20 years, time spent on the job in a given year has increased by 163 hours while leisure time has declined by one-third. Freedom to take extended leave or sabbaticals has been identified as a key workplace benefit. Managers who help employees achieve better balance so that personal time can also be enjoyed will be seen as better leaders.
2. **Promote the sense of deeper cause.** Helping employees achieve deeper levels of satisfaction than just company profitability leads to happier and more motivated employees. Many companies, such as Americredit (including its Canadian location), give employees paid time for volunteer work, something that many find personally fulfilling.
3. **Promote professional growth and development.** Employees want the opportunity to learn and grow. A 1999 Gallup poll found that lacking such opportunity was one of the top three reasons for employee dissatisfaction. Managers who provide such opportunities including such activities as mentoring programs will be more successful.
4. **Treat employees like partners.** Workers who feel that their opinions and ideas matter enjoy their work more and are more likely to contribute enthusiastically and be more dedicated. Only 27 percent of employees in a 1999 Watson Wyatt Canada survey reported that they felt they were treated as valued business partners by their bosses.
5. **Encourage community-building in the workplace.** With longer work hours, technology in the workplace, flexible work hours, telecommuting, and other advances that tend to isolate people, many employees feel disconnected (and thus discontent) from the workplace and from each other. Leaders and workplaces who create opportunities for interaction will have happier employees.
6. **Start rebuilding trust.** Only 37 percent of employees rated the level of honesty in their organizations as high or very high. And only 14 percent felt that they could trust each other! Leaders not only need to work harder to gain the trust of their subordinates but also to work in ways that help employees trust each other.

What does this mean for you? Developing leadership skills and behaviours is very important. However, leadership takes place within organizational cultures, and it is obvious that not all organizations warmly embrace organizational goals and the leadership to guide employees to achieve these goals. Leadership is much more than management, and a more holistic approach is required if you are going to be an effective leader in today's organizations.

Sources: Pam Withers, "Managing Discontent," *BC Business,* January 2001, vol. 29(1), pp. 26–32. Used with permission of the author. This article is adapted from John P. Izzo and Pam Withers, *Values Shift: The New Work Ethic and What It Means for Business* (Prentice Hall Canada, 2000).

Servant leadership has been put into practice by many managers as well as business corporations. Such companies as Southwest Airlines, The Toro Company, Men's Warehouse, and Starbucks have adapted the philosophy of servant-leadership into their cultures and mission statements (a statement of purpose). All of these firms emphasize treating employees humanely, and allowing for profit sharing.[31]

The Canada Today feature above lists six things that current leaders can do to keep their staff in the current climate of uncertainty. As a future (or perhaps current) leader, this may be of interest.

DEVELOPING YOUR LEADERSHIP POTENTIAL

How to improve your potential for becoming a leader is a topic without limits. Almost anything you do to improve your individual effectiveness will have some impact on your ability to lead others. If you strengthen your self-confidence, improve your memory for names, study this book carefully, read studies about leadership, or improve your physical fitness, you stand a good chance of improving your leadership potential. Seven general strategies might be kept in mind if you are seeking to improve your leadership potential:

1. *Having general education and specific training* Almost any program of career training or education can be considered a program of leadership development. Courses in human relations, management, or applied psychology have obvious relevance for someone currently occupying or aspiring toward a leadership position. Many of today's leaders in profit and nonprofit organizations hold formal degrees in business. Specific training programs will also help you improve your leadership potential. Among them might be skill development programs in interviewing, employee selection, listening, assertiveness training, budgeting, planning, improving work habits, resolving conflict, and communication skills. After acquiring knowledge through study, you then put the knowledge into practice as a leader.
2. *Attending leadership development programs* A focused way of improving your leadership potential is to attend development programs designed specifically to improve your ability to lead others and develop self-confidence. A popular type of leadership development program called *outdoor training* places people in a challenging outdoor environment for a weekend or up to ten days. Participants are required to accomplish physical feats such as climbing a mountain, whitewater canoeing, building a wall, or swinging between trees on a rope.[32] Participants in these outdoor programs learn such important leadership skills and attitudes as teamwork, trusting others, and confidence in their ability to accomplish the seemingly impossible.
3. *Gaining leadership experience* No program of leadership improvement can be a substitute for leadership experience. Because leadership effectiveness depends somewhat on the situation, a sound approach is to attempt to gain leadership experience in different settings. A person who wants to become an executive is well advised to gain supervisory experience in at least two different organizational functions (such as customer service and finance).

   First-level supervisory jobs are an invaluable starting point for developing your leadership potential. It takes considerable skill to manage a fast-food restaurant effectively or to direct a public playground during the summer. A first-line supervisor frequently faces a situation in which subordinates are poorly trained, poorly paid, and not well motivated to achieve company objectives.
4. *Modelling effective leaders* Are you committed to improving your leadership skill and potential? If so, carefully observe a capable leader in action and incorporate some of his or her approaches into your own behaviour. You may not be able to or want to become that person's clone, but you can model (imitate) what the person does. For instance, most inexperienced leaders have a difficult time confronting others with

bad news. Observe how a good confronter handles that situation and try that person's approach the next time you have some unfavourable news to deliver.

5. *Pursuing self-development of leadership characteristics and behaviour* Study the leadership characteristics and behaviours described in this chapter. As a starting point, identify several attributes you think you could strengthen within yourself given some self-determination. For example, you might decide that with effort you could improve your enthusiasm. You might also believe that you could be more emotionally supportive of others. It is also helpful to obtain feedback from reliable sources about which traits and behaviours you particularly need to develop.
6. *Practicing self-leadership* One of the most effective ways of becoming a leader is to begin by leading yourself, or practicing **self-leadership**. According to this concept, all organizational members are capable of leading themselves to some extent. You influence yourself without waiting for an external leader to lead you, much like taking the initiative to accomplish something worthwhile or being a good organizational citizen. According to Charles C. Manz, a professor of business leadership, self-leadership extends as far as setting your own standards and objectives. "It addresses what should be done, and why it should be done, in addition to how to do it." Recognize, however, you still have to accomplish what your leader wants you to accomplish, but you can go beyond the minimum required in your job.
7. *Becoming an integrated human being* A philosophical approach to leadership suggests that the model leader is first and foremost a fully functioning person. According to William D. Hitt, mastering the art of leadership comes with self-mastery. Leadership development is the process of self-development. As a result, the process of becoming a leader is similar to the process of becoming an integrated human being. For example, you need to develop values that guide your behaviour before you can adequately guide the behaviour of others.

The model (or ideal) leader, according to Hitt, must possess six character traits: identity ("know thyself"), independence, authenticity, responsibility, courage, and integrity.[33] All of these traits have everyday meanings, but they can also have personal meanings. Part of becoming an integrated person is to answer such questions as, "What do I mean when I say I have integrity?" As we stated in the beginning of the chapter, this softer side or set of soft skills is an essential component of effective leadership.

SUMMARY

Before most people can exert leadership, they need to develop an appropriate amount of self-confidence. Self-confidence is necessary for leadership because it helps assure group members that things are under control. A leader who is too self-confident, however, may not admit to errors, listen to criticism, or ask for advice. Also, you may appear insecure if you are too self-confident.

A general principle of boosting your self-confidence is to experience success (goal accomplishment) in a variety of situations. As you achieve one set of goals, you establish slightly more difficult goals, thus entering a success cycle. The specific strategies for building self-confidence described here are these:

1. Take an inventory of personal assets and accomplishments.
2. Develop a solid knowledge base.
3. Develop positive self-talk.
4. Avoid negative self-talk.
5. Use positive visual imagery.
6. Set high expectations for yourself (Galatea effect)
7. Strive for peak performance.
8. Bounce back from setbacks and embarrassments.

Leadership is the process of bringing about positive changes and influencing others to achieve organizational goals. Effective leadership is needed at the top of organizations, but supervisors and team leaders also need to provide effective leadership. Effective leaders have the "right stuff."

Certain traits and characteristics contribute to leadership effectiveness in many situations. Among them are self-confidence and courage; emotional intelligence; trustworthiness and character; strong work motivation and high energy; cognitive skills and openness to experience; assertiveness; and charisma (including vision, enthusiasm and excitement, and a sense of humour).

Behaviours and skills of an effective leader (one who maintains high productivity and morale) include the following:

1. Practise strong ethics.
2. Direction setting.
3. Develop partnerships with people (emphasizing power sharing).
4. Help group members reach goals and achieve satisfaction.
5. Set high expectations.
6. Give frequent feedback on performance.
7. Manage a crisis effectively.
8. Ask the right questions.
9. Be a servant leader.

Many activities in life can in some way contribute to the development of a person's leadership potential. Five recommended strategies for improving your leadership potential or leadership skills are (1) general education and specific training, (2) participation in leadership development programs, (3) acquisition of leadership experience, (4) modelling experienced leaders, (5) self-development of leadership characteristics and behaviour, and (6) practising self-leadership, and (7) becoming an integrated human being.

QUESTIONS AND ACTIVITIES

1. When you meet a person, how can you tell whether he or she is self-confident?
2. What is the difference between "trying your hardest" and "achieving peak performance"?

3. What positive self-talk can you use after you have failed on a major assignment?
4. How does the emphasis on developing strong ethics for leaders fit with the general stereotype of business executives?
5. Give an example of a specific action taken by a present or former boss that helped cultivate good relationships with subordinates. Also, identify an action that hurt relationships with subordinates.
6. Provide an example of something a leader motivated or inspired you to do that you would not have done without his or her presence.
7. Create a vision for your present or past employer (or any other company of your choosing).
8. Identify three areas in life in which being charismatic would help a person achieve his or her goals.
9. How might your current program of study contribute to your development as a leader?

INTERNET SKILL BUILDER

Becoming More Charismatic

You have already received in this chapter, suggestions for developing your charisma. Visit www.core-edge.com to search for additional ideas for charisma development. Go to the section on charismatology, and read a couple of the case histories to uncover ideas you might try to enhance your charisma. After digging through core-edge.com, list two concrete ideas you might implement to enhance your charisma.

Log on to the **Companion Website** at **www.pearsoncanada.ca/dubrin** to access additional resources for this chapter.

CASE STUDY 12-1 HUMAN RELATIONS

Charismatically Challenged Colleen

Twenty-seven-year-old Colleen McFerguson worked as a merchandising specialist for ValuMart, one of the largest international retail chains. Based in the United States, ValuMart also has a strong presence in Canada, Europe, Japan, and Hong Kong. Colleen began her employment with ValuMart as a cashier, and two years later she was invited into the training program for merchandising specialists.

Colleen performed well as a merchandising trainee in the soft-goods line. Her specialty areas included men's, women's, and children's clothing; linens and bedding; men's and women's jewellery; and home decorations. For several years in a row, Colleen received performance evaluation ratings of above average or outstanding. Among the write-in comments made by her supervisors were "diligent worker," "knows the tricks of merchandising," "good flair for buying the right products at the right price," and "fits right into the team."

Despite the positive performance appraisals supported with positive comments, Colleen had a gnawing discontent about her career at ValuMart. Despite five years of good performance, she was still not invited to become a member of the ValuTrackers, a group of merchandising and operations specialists who are regarded as being on the fast track to becoming future ValuMart leaders. The leaders hold high-level positions such as head merchandiser, regional vice-president, and store manager.

Several times when Colleen inquired about why she was not invited to join the ValuTrackers, she was told that she was not quite ready to be included in this elite group. She was also told not to be discouraged because the company still valued her contribution.

One day Colleen thought to herself, "I'm heading toward age 30, and I want a great future in the retail business now." So she convinced her boss, merchandising supervisor Evan Tyler, to set up a career conference with three people: Colleen, the boss, and her boss's boss, Heather Bridges, the area merchandising manager. She let Evan know in advance that she wanted to talk about her potential for promotion.

Evan started the meeting by saying, "Colleen, perhaps you can tell Heather and me again why you requested this meeting."

Colleen responded, "Thanks for asking, Evan. As I mentioned before, I'm wondering what you think is wrong with me. I receive a lot of positive feedback about my performance, but I'm not a ValuTracker. Also, you seem to change the subject when I talk about wanting to become a merchandising supervisor and eventually a merchandising executive. What am I doing wrong?"

Heather responded, "Evan and I frequently talk about the performance and potential of all our merchandising specialists. You're a good performer, Colleen, but you lack that little spark that makes a person a leader. You go about your job efficiently and quietly, but that's not enough. We want future leaders of ValuMart to make an impact."

Evan added, "I go along with Heather's comments. Another point, Colleen, is that you rarely take the initiative to suggest ideas. I was a little shocked by your request for a three-way career interview because it's one of the few initiatives you have taken. You're generally pretty laid-back."

"Then what do I have to do to convince you two that I should be a ValuTracker?" asked Colleen.

Heather replied, "Start acting more like a leader. Be more charismatic." Evan nodded in agreement.

Questions

1. What career advice can you offer Colleen McFerguson?
2. What might Colleen do to develop more charisma?
3. What is your opinion of the fairness of the ValuTracker program?

CASE STUDY 12-2 HUMAN RELATIONS

So Is This How You Learn Leadership?

Len Olsen, age 23, was proud to be selected as part of the leader's program at a national chain of family restaurants. Workers selected for the leadership program are considered to be in line for running individual restaurants and as potential candidates in the long run for leadership positions in corporate headquarters. Before entering the key phase of the leadership program, all candidates must first work a minimum of one year as a server or bartender at one of the company stores (restaurants).

Olsen worked one year as a server in a downtown Edmonton restaurant and then was assigned to another Edmonton restaurant to begin his formal leadership training as an assistant manager. Olsen's assignments as an assistant manager included scheduling the wait staff, conducting preliminary screening interviews of job applicants, and resolving problems with customers. After three months on the job, Olsen was asked by a member of the corporate human resources staff how his leadership training program was going. Olsen replied, "I'm a little bit skeptical. I don't think I'm learning much about leadership."

When asked why he didn't think he was learning much about leadership, Olsen listed what he considered three recent examples of the type of responsibilities he faced regularly:

- At 11 yesterday morning, I received a phone call from Annie, one of the servers. She told me she wouldn't be to work that afternoon because her Labrador retriever had become quite ill and she had to take the Lab to the vet. I told Annie that we desperately needed her that afternoon because of a large luncheon party. Annie told me her dog was more important to her than the job.
- Two weeks ago, Gus, one of our salad chefs showed up to work absolutely drunk. I told him that working while drunk was absolutely against company rules. He got a little belligerent, but I did get him to take a taxi home at company expense.
- Two days ago a customer in the restaurant spilled a cup of hot coffee on herself while answering a call on her cell phone. She told me that the coffee was too hot and that she was going to sue the restaurant. I explained to her tactfully that unless she was truly burned, she had no claim. I offered to have the restaurant pay for her dry cleaning, and then she calmed down.

Olsen then said to the human resources manager, "What has stuff like this got to do with leadership? I mean, I'm not creating great visions or inspiring hordes of people. In what way am I becoming a leader?"

Questions

1. What is your opinion of the contribution of Olsen's representative experiences to his development as a leader?
2. What else can the restaurant chain do to help Olsen, and others in the leadership program, develop as leaders?

Chapter 13

Choosing a Career and Developing a Portfolio Career

Learning Outcomes

After studying the information and doing the exercises in this chapter, you should be able to

- make a tentative career choice if you have not already done so;
- identify skills that could serve as the basis for your career;
- appreciate the complexity of choosing a career;
- search for useful information about occupations and careers;
- explain the basics of career switching and developing a portfolio career.

Vincent Langlois was recently promoted to a supervising teller position in a bank, putting him on track to becoming a bank manager. Vincent enjoys his work and is proud of his accomplishments. Asked how he chose to launch his career as a teller, Vincent explained: "Four years ago as graduation was fast approaching, I didn't have a clue as to what aspect of business I would enter. Like many others, I decided to use the Internet to start my job search. After surfing different directions, I hit Human Resources Development Canada's Job Bank. One of the jobs being advertised was a teller position. I had also heard that one way to get yourself known was to go into a nontraditional field. I thought being a male teller would be nontraditional, as most tellers are women.

"I figured that if I became a teller, maybe I would stand out because of being a man. Also, I always liked banks because the work they do is important. Next, I followed through by applying to the bank and I got it!"

Vincent's success in finding a career that is working for him illustrates a major theme of this chapter. For many people, finding the right career requires careful thinking and systematic effort. If you have not already chosen a career or are thinking of changing careers, this chapter is especially important. If you are content with your career, this chapter can be read with the intention of learning more about that vital part of your life. What a person does for a living is one of the key influences in his or her life. Your career is also a prime source of your self-concept and self-esteem.

The purpose of this chapter is to help you choose a career by describing systematic methods of career selection. For those who have already chosen a career field in general, this chapter may help you narrow down your career choice within your field. For example, a person entering the computer field might choose to emphasize those aspects of computers dealing heavily with people, such as computer sales or information systems.

SELF-KNOWLEDGE AND CHOOSING A CAREER

A **career** is a series of related job experiences that fit into a meaningful pattern. If you have a series of odd jobs all your working life, that is hardly a career. But if each job builds carefully on the previous one, we say you are "building a career." We assume that by making a sound initial choice of occupation, you will be on the first step toward building a real career. Chapters 14 through 16 provide information to help you advance in whatever career you have chosen.

A general strategy for making a sound career choice is to understand first the inner you, including what you have to offer. You then match that information with opportunities in the outside world. The Self-Knowledge Questionnaire presented in Chapter 1 asks many questions that are relevant to making a career choice. Almost any of the information provided by candid answers to those questions could help you make a sound career choice. Several specific illustrations are in order.

Question 1 asks, "How far have I gone in school?" If you answered, "Three years of high school," or "Four years of high school and two years of business school," you will need additional education to enter many fields. Among them are management, teaching, counselling, or social work.

Question 9 asks, "What aspect of these jobs did I enjoy?" Suppose you answered, "Anytime I was left alone to do some figuring or report writing I was happy. Thinking made me happy." Your answer could mean that you should search for a field in which working with ideas and data is more important than working with people or things. What about investigating laboratory work or financial analysis?

Question 31 asks, "What gives me satisfaction in life?" Suppose you answered, "Playing with my children, going fishing, and getting involved with my friends almost every day." However good for your mental health this answer might be, it certainly does limit the level of responsibility you can aspire to in most careers. A busy executive or professional person often comes out on the short end with respect to having ample time for family, fishing, and friends.

Some additional questions useful in clarifying the type of work you would prefer are presented in Human Relations Self-Assessment Quiz 13-1.

The Importance of Skills in Choosing a Career

In addition to other aspects of self-understanding, knowing which skills you possess—and enjoy performing—can be the basis for a successful career. A **skill** is a learned, specific

Human Relations Self-Assessment

QUIZ 13-1 The Career Development Inventory

Career development activities inevitably include answering some penetrating questions about yourself, such as the 12 questions that follow. You may need several hours to do a competent job answering these questions. After individuals have answered these questions by themselves, it may be profitable to hold a class discussion about the relevance of the specific questions. A strongly recommended procedure is for you to date your completed inventory and put it away for safekeeping. Examine your answers in several years to see (1) how well you are doing in advancing your career and (2) how much you have changed.

Keep the following information in mind in answering this inventory: People are generous in their self-evaluations when they answer career development inventories. So you might want to discuss some of your answers with somebody else who knows you well.

1. How would you describe yourself as a person?
2. What are you best at doing? Worst?
3. What are your two biggest strengths or assets?
4. What skills and knowledge will you need to acquire to reach your goals?
5. What are your two biggest accomplishments?
6. Write your obituary as you would like it to appear.
7. What would be the ideal job for you?
8. What career advice can you give yourself?
9. Describe the two peak work-related experiences in your life.
10. What are your five most important values (the things in life most important to you)?
11. What goals in life are you trying to achieve?
12. What do you see as your niche (spot where you best fit) in the modern world?

ability to do something such as write a report, prepare a website, or troubleshoot software problems. A vast number of skills could be exercised in a career, including such skills as selling, calculating currency exchanges, and coaching workers. Identifying your skills is important both in choosing a career and in finding a job. Employers want to know what a job prospect can actually *do*, or what skills he or she possesses.

An enlightening perspective is that your best skill represents your **core competency**, or whatever you do best. But there is more to core competency than what is suggested in your job title.[1] Your core competency is the aspect of your job that you perform particularly well. As a collection agent, your core competency might be obtaining partial payments with accounts so long overdue that others consider them almost uncollectible. If you have developed a core competency early in your schooling or temporary work experience, making a sound career choice is easier. An adolescent with superior skill in explaining to others how to use electronic devices might have the necessary core competency for a career in technical writing. (A big part of a technical writer's job is preparing operating manuals for equipment.)

Human Relations Self-Assessment

QUIZ 13-2 Skills Profile

Review the following skill areas and specific skills. In the space provided, write down each one you believe is a strong skill for you. You can also add a specific skill that was not included in the skill area listed at the left.

A Strong Skill	***Skill Area***	***A Specific Skill for Me***
Communication	writing, speaking, knowledge of foreign language, telephone skills, persuasiveness, listening	______
Creative	originating ideas, thinking up novel solutions	______
Interpersonal relations	ability to get along well with others, being a team player, diplomacy, conflict resolution, understanding others	______
Management	ability to lead, organize, plan, motivate others, make decisions, manage time	______
Manual and mechanical	mechanically inclined, build, operate, repair, assemble, install, drive vehicles	______
Mathematics	math skills, computers, analyzing data, budgeting, using statistical techniques	______
Office	keyboarding, filing, business math, bookkeeping, using spreadsheets, word processing, database management, record keeping	______
Sales	persuading others, negotiating, promoting, dressing fashionably	______
Scientific	investigating, researching, compiling, systematizing, diagnosing, evaluating	______
Service of customers	serving customers, handling complaints, dealing with difficult people	______
Service of patients	nurturing, diagnosing, treating, guiding, counselling, consoling, dealing with emergencies	______
Other skill area	______________________________	______

Source: Abridged and adapted from Julie Griffin Levitt, *Your Career: How to Make It Happen*, 2nd ed. (Cincinnati, Ohio: South-Western Publishing Co., 1990), pp. 19–21.

Julie Griffin Levitt has developed a useful way of identifying skills,[2] as outlined in Human Relations Self-Assessment Quiz 13-2. As you develop several of these skills to an above-average degree, they may become your core competency.

Getting Help from a Career Counsellor

In choosing a career or switching careers, an excellent method of learning more about yourself in relation to the world of work is to obtain help from a professional **career counsellor**. A counsellor usually relies on a wide variety of tests plus an interview to assist you in making a sound career choice. It is untrue that any single test will tell you what occupation you should enter. Tests are designed to provide useful clues, not to give you definite answers. Nor it is true that a career counsellor will tell you what occupation you should enter. Using tests and human judgment, the counsellor helps you become more aware of yourself and the alternatives that might suit your circumstances. This chapter emphasizes choosing a career by yourself. It is recommended, however, that you seek the help of a guidance counsellor, career counsellor, or counselling psychologist.

Interest Testing to Identify Careers of Interest

Career counselling emphasizes finding a career that suits a person's interests. The most widely used instrument for matching a person's interests with careers is the **Strong Interest Inventory (SII)**. The output of the SII is a computer-generated report that provides potentially useful information about making career choices.[3]

The SII asks 325 questions about your preferences (likes, dislikes, or indifferences) concerning occupations, school subjects, activities, amusements, and types of people. Exhibit 13-1 presents a sampling of such questions. A person's answers to these questions are used to compute three sets of scores: (1) general occupational themes, (2) basic interest scales, and (3) occupational scales. The Inventory is available online on a variety of career sites, but it is not free.

Scores on the Strong Interest Inventory

Each of the six occupational themes is associated with one or more basic interest scales as follows:

R Theme (Realistic) High scorers on this theme tend to be rugged, robust, practical individuals who are physically strong and frequently aggressive in outlook. The basic interest scales carrying the realistic theme are Agriculture, Nature, Adventure, Military Activities, and Mechanical Activities.

Exhibit 13-1
Type of Test Items Found on the Strong Interest Inventory

1. Actor	L	I	D
2. Aviator	L	I	D
3. Architect	L	I	D
4. Astronomer	L	I	D
5. Athletic director	L	I	D
6. Auctioneer	L	I	D
7. Author of novel	L	I	D
8. Author of scientific book	L	I	D
9. Auto sales representative	L	I	D
10. Auto mechanic	L	I	D

Note: In this section of the test, the subject indicates whether he or she would like (L), dislike (D), or be indifferent to (I) working in each occupation.

I Theme (Investigative) High scorers on this theme enjoy science and scientific activities, and are not particularly interested in working with others. They also enjoy solving abstract problems. The basic interest scales carrying the investigative theme are Science, Mathematics, Medical Science, and Medical Service.

A Theme (Artistic) High scorers on these themes are artistically oriented and like to work in settings where self-expression is welcome. The associated interest scales are Music/Dramatics, Art, and Writing.

S Theme (Social) High scorers on this theme are sociable, responsible, humanistic, and concerned with the welfare of others. The associated interest scales are Teaching, Social Service, Athletics, Domestic Arts, and Religious Activities.

E Theme (Enterprising) High scorers on this theme are skillful with words and use this capability to sell, dominate, and lead. The associated interest scales are Public Speaking, Law/Politics, Merchandising, Sales, and Business Management.

C Theme (Conventional) High scorers on this theme prefer the ordered activities, both verbal and numerical, that characterize office work. They are comfortable following the rules and regulations of a large firm. The associated interest scale is Office Practices.

The Strong Interest Inventory has 211 occupational scales, divided among the six general occupational themes and basic interest scales. For example, the following occupations are among those associated with the conventional theme and the office practices scales: accountant, banker, credit manager, business education teacher, food service manager, nursing home administrator, and secretary.

Interpreting the SII Profile With the assistance of a counsellor, a person looks for patterns of high and low scores. High scores indicate interests similar to people in occupational areas and occupations, whereas low scores suggest the opposite. Assume that a person scores very high on the Office Practices Scale and high on the occupations of banker and credit manager. The same person also scores very low on the Investigative theme, the Medical Service Interest Scale, and the medical, technical, and respiratory therapist Occupational Scales. We conclude that this person would be happier as an office manager than as an ambulance medic!

Note that *interest* is not the same as *ability*. Some people may not have the mental aptitude and skills to do well in the occupations they would enjoy. Interest is but one important factor contributing to successful performance. Being interested in your field makes the biggest contribution to keeping you motivated.

MATCHING YOUR CAREER TO YOUR LIFESTYLE

Another consideration in using self-knowledge to assist in choosing a career is to take into account your lifestyle preferences. Ideally, you should pursue a career that provides you with the right balance among work, leisure, and interaction with people. Some degree of compromise is usually necessary. If your preferred lifestyle is to take two-hour lunch breaks each workday, it would be difficult to attain a high level of responsibility. Executives, public relations specialists, and sales representatives who seem to spend considerable time at lunch are usually conducting business over their meal. They are not taking time out during the workday. If a cornerstone of your lifestyle is to remain in top physical and mental shape, you should probably avoid some of the high-pressure careers, such as ambulance paramedic or securities sales representative. On the other hand, you would want to avoid a career that provided too little challenge.

As just hinted, the term **lifestyle** can refer to many different key aspects of your life. In terms of making a career choice, it is helpful to regard lifestyle as the pattern by which a person invests energy into work and nonwork. Being the proverbial beach bum or ski bum is one lifestyle. So is being the 90-hour-a-week financial executive.

Today, an increasing number of people at different stages in their careers are making career choices that improve their chances of leading their preferred lifestyle. The general manager of a plant in a small town makes a revealing comment about modern lifestyles: "A number of years ago we couldn't get nearly the number of skilled people we needed to work here. The people who had a choice wanted to live in an area near a big city. Now we get loads of unsolicited résumés. It seems that a lot of people want access to camping and fishing. I think they're also worried about crime and pollution in the cities."

The move toward a healthy balance between work and nonwork might also be considered part of the movement toward a higher quality of life. For some people, living in a $1,800-a-month studio apartment in Vancouver or Montreal represents a high quality of life. Such city dwellers would, of course, have to aspire to a very high-paying occupation to support their preference. How will your preferred lifestyle influence your career decision-making?

Another key aspect of matching your career to your lifestyle is to choose a career that enables you to achieve the right balance between work and personal life. People vary widely in what they consider the right balance. Individuals who want to be home at regular hours and on weekends, with very little travel, will usually have to avoid industrial sales or managerial work. On the other hand, individuals who prefer the excitement of breakfast meetings, weekend meetings, and travel might choose the two occupations just mentioned.

Flexible work schedules are a major mechanism for matching preferred lifestyle to career choice. Many people whose preferred lifestyle does not permit full-time work seek opportunities to work part-time. Others, whose preferred lifestyle is to minimize commuting and working outside the home, seek careers that allow them to work from home via the internet.

Lastly, your career and job choices need to match your **values** and the things that are important to you in your life. While this may sound rather ideal, it is not unrealistic. If you value honesty and integrity, would you want to work for a company that has unethical business practices? The Web can be a valuable source here. Many companies post mission statements that incorporate the values the company wishes to embrace as its best practice. Below is the credo of Johnson & Johnson, a large company with many international locations including Canada. What values do you see in this credo? Does this company share some of your values?

However, you also need to be realistic. In an economy experiencing economic decline or recession, you may need to choose a job that enables you to pay your bills and eat. At times, being choosy is an erroneous career choice that may lead to long periods of unemployment, and for many older workers, despair and frustration. Many older workers, who have been laid off from long-time jobs, will be direct competition for younger workers with less experience. It is unwise, at times, to refuse employment, just because it does not match your values or career aspirations.

FINDING OUT ABOUT OCCUPATIONS

Whether or not you have already made a career choice, you should follow a fundamental rule of plotting your career—get the facts. Few people have valid information about careers they wish to pursue. A glaring example of occupational misinformation relates to the legal field. Many young people say, "I would like to be a lawyer. I'm good at convincing people. And I know I could sway a jury." Similarly, "I want to be a paralegal. I have the mind of a detective. I know I could break most of the tough cases I'd be given to research."

In reality, the work of a lawyer or paralegal includes the processing of much nonglamorous information. One example is figuring out how much money a bankrupt bakery owes to 27 different suppliers. Four general sources of occupational information are printed material and electronic information, computer systems, spoken information, and first-hand experience. Without this information, it is difficult to find a good fit between yourself and existing opportunities.

Printed and Web Information

Most libraries, bookstores, websites, and Human Resources Development Canada centres are well supplied with information about career opportunities. One of the most comprehensive source documents of occupational information is the National Occupational Classification (NOC). It contains the classification structure and descriptions of 522 occupational groups that constitute the Canadian labour market and is available online. The index contains over 25,000 occupational titles divided into ten major classifications.

Human Relations in Practice

Johnson & Johnson: "Our Credo"

We believe our first responsibility is to the doctors, nurses and patients, to mothers and fathers and all others who use our products and services.

In meeting their needs everything we do must be of high quality.

We must constantly strive to reduce our costs in order to maintain reasonable prices.

Customers' orders must be serviced promptly and accurately.

Our suppliers and distributors must have an opportunity to make a fair profit.

We are responsible to our employees, the men and women who work with us throughout the world.

Everyone must be considered as an individual.

We must respect their dignity and recognize their merit.

They must have a sense of security in their jobs.

Compensation must be fair and adequate, and working conditions clean, orderly and safe.

We must be mindful of ways to help our employees fulfill their family responsibilities.

Employees must feel free to make suggestions and complaints.

There must be equal opportunity for employment, development and advancement for those qualified.

We must provide competent management, and their actions must be just and ethical.

We are responsible to the communities in which we live and work and to the world community as well.

We must be good citizens—support good works and charities and bear our fair share of taxes.

We must encourage civic improvements and better health and education.

We must maintain in good order the property we are privileged to use, protecting the environment and natural resources.

Our final responsibility is to our stockholders.

Business must make a sound profit.

We must experiment with new ideas.

Research must be carried on, innovative programs developed and mistakes paid for.

New equipment must be purchased, new facilities provided and new products launched.

Reserves must be created to provide for adverse times.

When we operate according to these principles, the stockholders should realize a fair return.

Source: Permission to use credo, courtesy of Johnson & Johnson.

For the various occupations it lists, there is information on employment requirements, type of work performed, education required to perform the job, and so on. The most recent update, NOC 2006, has added many new occupations, particularly in the areas experiencing high technological changes. If you do not have computer access, these resources are available in Print.

Use of the internet's resources has been steadily growing in the past few years and will continue to do so in coming years. See the In Canada Box for a listing and description of specific Canadian information sites. Both the National Occupational Classification (NOC) and JobFutures, which uses the NOC, are excellent sources for detailed information on jobs. JobFutures also includes a searchable site for jobs and job shortages in your area. While not complete, it is a great starting point for examining careers and their availability in your area.

HRDC has an extensive site with several useful links, including an up to date Job Bank with literally thousands of postings. A career seeker can simply type in the job title sought, click onto geographical areas of interest, and read the list of available openings, many of which include contact names and salary schedules. HRDC also has extensive information on job skills, such as developing a résumé and preparing for a job interview. It

Canada Today

Job Information Sites

National Occupational Classification (NOC)

http://www5.hrsdc.gc.ca/noc/english/noc/2006/welcome.aspx

The NOC is the authoritative resource on occupational information in Canada. It is used daily by thousands of people to understand the jobs found throughout Canada's labour market. It is free of charge and easily searchable.

Job Futures

http://www.jobfutures.ca/

National Job Futures is currently being updated and has a new tool, **"The Working in Canada Tool" Explore Canada's Labour Market** and search for employment facts by occupation and location with the Working in Canada Tool. The Working in Canada Tool can tell you about job opportunities, wages, occupational demand, employment requirements, and much more.

Human Resources Development Canada

http://www.hrsdc.gc.ca

Although this site does have job ads, it is also a rich source for job information and job-helping ideas and strategies.

Information on Apprenticeships

http://www.edu.gov.on.ca/eng/training/apprenticeship/appren.html; (Ontario) http://www.itabc.ca/site3.aspx (British Columbia)

Apprenticeships are another pathway to a career (often not accessed). The Ministry of Training, Colleges, and Universities Ontario has site dedicates web page with links about apprenticeship. British Columbia has a similar site as do other provinces. Use your search engine and type in the province and "apprenticeships."

Workopolis

http://www.workopolis.com

Although a job search site, it is also a great site for job resources.

Workinfonet

http://onwin.ca/english/index.cfm?fuseaction=view_subcategories&CategoryID=1

Each province/territory has a workinfonet. This is the address for the resources on the Ontario Site. Another great source on jobs, job search, and job seeking preparation. Use your search browser, to access WorkInfoNet for the one in your province/territory.

is strongly recommended that you take a tour of this site and use it for job and career seeking. Two other sites of interest are WorkInfoNet and Campus WorkLink. Both sites offer job postings as well as information on acquiring job skills. WorkInfoNet has links to a vast array of career-related websites. Within this link are separate areas to explore, including jobs and recruiting, career planning, training, professional and community associations, and general information about the labour market. Campus WorkLink is also for job seekers as well as for employers wishing to hire new recruits. At this site, job seekers can post a résumé. Membership is free. A complete list of the site addresses mentioned here is provided at the end of this chapter. Another Canadian site, Career Discovery, is also very interesting and you can sign up for free (**www.careerdiscovery.ca**). There are many more sites that you can find on your own by typing in key words in your browser.

A new way to look at jobs or get jobs is through the use of Twitter and Facebook. There are many groups that you can join on Facebook for career assistance and leads and many people are reporting that they found their last job by using Twitter. Several sites such as Mashable.com give you techniques and tips to use Twitter to find a job. Some suggestions include using your job pitch in your Twitter bio, tweet that you are looking, and have a professional looking avatar.[4]

Speaking to People

An invaluable supplement to reading about occupations is speaking to people engaged in them. No matter what occupation interests you, search out a person actually employed in that kind of work. Most people welcome the opportunity to talk about themselves and the type of work they do. If you do not know anyone engaged in the career field that interests you, do some digging. A few inquiries will usually lead to a person you can contact. It is best to interview that person in his or her actual work setting to obtain a sense of the working conditions people face in that field.

Remember, however, that many people will probably say that although they are very happy in their work, there are better ways to make a living. Ask your dentist, doctor, lawyer, or plumber about his or her field, and you might be told, "Don't believe all those stories about people in this field being wealthy. We work long and hard for our money. And there's always the problem of people not paying their bills. I don't recommend that you enter this field."

Suppose you want to learn about the field of Total Quality Management, yet you do not know anyone who knows any person doing this kind of work. Try the cold-canvas method. Call one or two large companies and ask to speak to someone working in Total Quality. When you reach that department, indicate that you are trying to make a sound career choice and then proceed with your inquiry. The success ratio of this approach is remarkably high.

First-hand Experience

If you want to explore an occupation in depth, it is important to obtain some first-hand experience in that occupation. Part-time and temporary employment is particularly useful. One man who is a self-employed landscape consultant first tried out the field by working two summers for an established business. Some schools offer cooperative, or work-study, programs. However modest your cooperative employment, it can provide you with much valuable information. For instance, it is surprisingly helpful to observe whether or not people engaged in that type of work ever smile or laugh. If not, the work might be intense and dreary.

Temporary work in a field you might wish to enter could lead to a job offer. It is standard practice for employers to use part-time and temporary jobs as a way of screening prospective employees. A woman who is now a sales representative for a well-known business corporation presents this anecdote: "I took the most menial clerical position in the marketing department. My supervisor told her boss that I was a good worker—somebody who would give a fair shake to the company. Now I'm making more money and having more fun than I thought possible at my age."

A promising approach to gaining first-hand knowledge about a potential career is by directly observing a sampling of the career. **Job shadowing** is a way of gaining information about an occupation by spending a few hours with a professional in the workplace, observing first-hand what the job entails. Closely observing a professional in action will often lead to an enhanced understanding of what the work really entails. As practised at several schools, students get a four-hour shadowing opportunity at local business firms. Even when a student has chosen a career, the direct observation can help confirm that the choice was sound.[5]

CHOOSING A GROWTH OCCUPATION

Another important type of occupational information for career selection relates to growth opportunities within the field. An advantageous way of choosing a career is to pursue an occupation that appears to have growth potential, *provided work in that field matches your interests*. Entering a rapidly growing field will not do a person much good if he or she does not like the work, because it will be difficult to perform well in the long run.

Using the growth-occupation strategy, the career seeker searches for a match between his or her capabilities and a growth occupation in a growth field. For example, a person who likes to provide support to others and to work extensively with computers might choose systems analyst (a growth occupation).

How do you identify growth occupations? One way is to use the sources described in the section about finding career information. For instance, visit the Human Resources Development Canada site and find out what jobs have the most listings. Also, check out current magazines that discuss hiring and job hunting on a fairly regular basis, such as *Computing Canada*, and *Canadian Business*. They often have helpful articles to guide you in some career choices and ideas. Statistics Canada also gathers data on job growth areas. In the Spring of 2010, April's increases were widespread among services industries, with the largest gains in retail and wholesale trade; amusement, gambling and recreation; professional, scientific and technical services; and administrative and support services. There were also gains in the goods sector in April, as the number of jobs continued to grow in construction and in mining, quarrying and oil and gas extraction.[6]

DATA, PEOPLE, OR THINGS

A helpful way of looking at career choices is to characterize jobs according to the amount of time devoted to data (or ideas), people, or things. The National Occupational Classification (NOC) and Job Futures Canada, published by Human Resources Development Canada, use these categories of how time is spent on the job in describing all the occupational titles:

1. *Data/Information* Refers to working with facts, information, and ideas made from observations and interpretations. The activities involved in working with data are synthesizing, coordinating, analyzing, compiling, computing, copying, and comparing. Analyzing information generated by computers, for example, gives a person ample opportunity to work with data. This is now called Information Junkie.
2. *People* Refers to working with human beings, and also to working with animals as if they were human. The activities involved in working with people are mentoring, negotiating, instructing, supervising, diverting, persuading, speaking/signalling, serving, and taking instructions/helping. A customer service representative would have ample opportunity to work with people, as the representative regularly handles customer complaints.
3. *Things* Refers to work with inanimate objects such as tools, equipment, and products. The activities involved in working with things are setting up, precision working, operating/controlling, driving/operating, manipulating, tending, feeding/offbearing, and handling. An office equipment repair technician would have ample opportunity to work with things while making service calls.

Most jobs involve a combination of dealing with data, people, and things. It is usually a question of the relative proportion of each dimension. Managers, for example, have high involvement with data and people and a low involvement with things. Registered nurses have an average involvement with all three.

Understanding one's preferences for working with data, people, and things sharpens a career choice. Job satisfaction is likely to increase when the individual engages in work that fits his or her relative interest in data, people, and things. A person with a balanced preference for all three would probably enjoy a position selling business equipment that also required substantial preparation of sales reports.

DEVELOPING A PORTFOLIO CAREER AND CAREER SWITCHING

It is becoming increasingly common for people to either switch the emphasis of activities in their work or switch careers entirely. Particularly in a volatile career market, job and career switching is common and learning and emphasizing your skills is important. An example of switching the emphasis of activities would be a salesperson who is working with computers to shift to a new field in which he or she worked primarily with computers and did no selling. People modify their careers for a variety of reasons including job loss and wanting a new challenge. Here we look at two closely related approaches to changing direction in a career: developing a portfolio career and career switching.

Developing a Portfolio Career

Many people would like to change careers yet not be confined to focusing on one major type of job activity. To accomplish this, a growing number of people are developing a **portfolio career**, in which they use a variety of skills and earn money in several different ways. In addition to fulfilling a desire to diversify, a portfolio career helps many people when employment opportunities decrease and there are fewer full-time positions. In May 2010, the unemployment rate was at 8.1 percent.[7] In a challenging economy, many people will switch to part-time employment. To earn the equivalent of a full-time salary, many people are piecing together more than one part-time position. As more part-time positions pay benefits, working for more than one employer becomes more feasible.

According to career adviser Susan Larson, having a portfolio (or collection) of income-generating possibilities makes you more resistant to the effects of losing one job. You spread your risk by earning money in several ways. The career portfolio minimizes risks by accumulating groups of skills that can provide income. If one skill is not in demand, another might be.[8] A common example of a skill portfolio is that of a person with a full-time position who has a part-time position requiring different skills. A department manager within a retail store might install satellite dishes as a part-time activity.

An important part of developing a portfolio career is keeping your occupational skills current. Suppose a person is able to translate documents from Japanese to English and English to Japanese, but is currently not working as a translator. Translation skills fade rapidly, so the bilingual person should continue to practise this skill at home.

Increasing in popularity, are the use of actual portfolios to track skills and jobs. These can be done online and printed as needed. Many college programs include portfolio development as part of the program requirements for graduation. Keep these portfolios handy and keep adding to them as you advance in your career. Job employment centres offer portfolio development for displaced workers. If the trend continues, many interviewers may be asking to see your portfolio or components of it as part of the job interview.

Career Switching

From the perspective of career specialist Douglas T. Hall, the career of the twenty-first century will be driven more by the person than the organization. The ultimate career goal is psychological success that comes from attaining important goals such as achievement and family happiness. This stands in contrast to the older goal of climbing the corporate pyramid and making lots of money.[9] (Of course, this is still the major career goal for many people.) The new type of career emphasizes doing work that fits your major values in life. Whether in pursuit of psychological well-being or old-fashioned success, many people find it necessary to switch careers.

A major principle of career switching is to *be thorough*. Go through the same kind of thinking and planning that is recommended for finding a first career. Everything said in this chapter about choosing a first career is also relevant for choosing a later career. The advantage for the career switcher, however, is that the experienced person often has a better understanding of the type of work he or she does not want to do.

One of the first steps in making a career change is to assess your likes and dislikes. Career coach Randall S. Hansen advises that many people change careers because they dislike their job, their boss, and their company. Yet you also need to examine your likes. What work-related activities excite and energize you?[10] Many people learn more about their career preferences by taking a career assessment instrument combined with the guidance of a career counsellor. Three of the most scientifically developed career inventories are as follows:

- Campbell Interest and Skill Survey (www.pearsonassessments.com/tests/ciss.htm)
- Myers-Briggs Type® Indicator Career Report (www.cpp.com)
- 16PF Personal Career Development Profile Plus (www.Careers-By-Design.com)

A new career should be *built gradually*. Few people are able to leave one career abruptly and step into another. For most people who switch careers successfully, the switch is more of a transition than an abrupt change. A constructive approach would be to take on a few minor assignments in the proposed new field and then search for full-time work in that field after building skill. An electronics technician, for example, might request to visit customers with sales representatives to facilitate a switch to industrial selling.

Sometimes an interim assignment can offer a person useful ideas for a complete career change or at least a different emphasis. One such possibility is to fill in for a person who is on a company-paid leave of absence, referred to as a *sabbatical*. Another possibility for an interim assignment is filling in for someone who is on family leave because of the birth or adoption of a child. Filling in for the boss, for example, can give a person a first-hand feel for managerial work.[11]

A major reason why many employees consider a new career is that they crave more independence. As a consequence, an increasingly popular path for the career switcher is to *move from salaried employment to self-employment*. In 2000, nearly one worker out of six

Exhibit 13-2
A Sampling of Opportunities for Self-Employment, as Suggested by Entrepreneur Business Start-Up Guides

Computer-Based Businesses
Computer Consulting
Computer Repair Service
Web Page Design
Laser Printing Recharging & Repair

Financial Services
Cheque Cashing Service
Financial Aid Services
Financial Broker
Real Estate Investment

Cleaning/Maintenance Businesses
Apartment Preparation Service
Damage Restoration
Garage Detailing Service
Parking Lot Striping & Maintenance

Services to Business
Collection Agency
Language Translation Service
Medical Billing
Mobile Bookkeeping

Personal Services
Private Investigator
Event Planning Service
Home Staging
Operating a 900 Number

Service Businesses
Coffeehouse
Spa
Mobile Frozen Yogurt
Mobile Restaurant/Sandwich Truck

Wholesale Businesses
Import/Export Business
Web Site wholesaler
Wholesale Distribution Business
Marketing a Family Recipe

Retail Businesses
Antique Sales & Restoration
E-tailer (i.e., eBay)
Pet Hotel & Grooming Service
Self-Storage Centre

was self-employed according to the Statistics Canada Survey of Self-employment, indicating a strong growth in this career choice in Canada.[12] The prospective self-employed person needs to decide on which particular business to enter. For many people, self-employment means continuing to perform similar work, such as the company cafeteria manager entering the food catering business. Other formerly employed workers go into competition with their former employers, such as a print shop manager opening a print shop of her own. For those who lack specific plans of their own, prepackaged plans can be purchased. A sampling of these is listed in Exhibit 13-2.

Another self-employment possibility is to purchase a franchise, thus lowering the risk of a start-up business. Currently, franchises account for about one-third of retail sales in the United States and Canada. Yet franchises require a substantial financial investment, ranging from about $6,000 to $700,000. Another caution is that some franchise operators may work around 70 hours per week to earn about $18,000 per year.

EIGHT SUGGESTIONS FOR CAREER PREPARATION

Preparing for a career is closely related to choosing a career. To prepare is to make oneself ready to meet the challenges that lie ahead in whatever career you choose. Several of the points below[13] reinforce what you have already studied in this text or will study in Chapter 15.

1. *Be flexible*. You may have one career field in mind, such as business. Do not overlook the possibilities of applying your education and skills to a rapidly expanding field such as software development. Also, be flexible about the size of firm you hope to work for. Most of the job growth continues to take place in small and medium-sized firms.
2. *Develop interpersonal skills*. Good interpersonal skills, especially communication skills, are a foundation for many careers. Employers seek employees who speak and write well. Most jobs require contact with co-workers and customers, or working as part of a team—meaning that people skills are essential.
3. *Think globally*. Many jobs are becoming international jobs even if they do not involve travel. An increasing amount of business is being conducted with customers and suppliers from other countries. To capitalize on the globalization of business, polish your skills in your second language. (Some people may have to learn a second language for the first time.) It is also important to study the culture associated with your second language.
4. *Develop your technology skills*. This is more than your ability to surf the net or manage your Facebook. Computers have become an integral part of most jobs, including people-oriented jobs such as sales. Be able to use presentation software, spreadsheets, and wordprocessing. If you can also gain skills in leading Webinars or Web-based workshop software, you will have an additional skill that is gaining in popularity. Lack of computer skills, including recent technology tools, can be a career hindrance.
5. *Get an edge*. Although we may be on the verge of boom economic times, employers can still afford to be choosy. Any extra skill or knowledge can help distinguish you from other job applicants. Computer skills, foreign-language skills, and another degree are assets for most fields.
6. *Keep learning after you have chosen a field*. With technologies changing so rapidly, training has become a way of life in business and industry. Be prepared to take the initiative to acquire valuable new skills before the company offers you a training program.
7. *Be less concerned about promotions; it is what you know and how you apply it that really counts*. The corporate world today places much less emphasis on promotions than on acquiring skills and applying them well. *Promotion* in the new sense of the word often means getting to work on the most exciting projects and taking turns at being a team leader. Both of these activities can lead to higher compensation even if they do not lead to a change in job title.
8. *Strive for high-quality work*. Most employers assume that workers at all levels will strive to make high-quality goods and provide high-quality service. Many companies expect employees to apply quality principles to their work, so it is important to study books and articles about quality. Apply quality principles such as "Do it right the first time." Also, think of quality as simply being conscientious and terrific at what you do.

SUMMARY

For many people, finding the right career requires careful thinking and systematic effort. What a person does for a living is one of the key influences in his or her life. Your career is also a prime source of your self-concept and self-esteem. A general strategy for making a sound career choice is first to understand the inner you, including what you have to offer.

Knowing which skills and abilities you possess and enjoy using can be the basis for a successful career. Your best skill is your core competency. Skill areas can be divided into the following areas: communication, creativity, interpersonal relations, management, manual and mechanical skills, mathematics, office skills, sales, scientific skills, service of customers, and service of patients.

Career counselling, including interest testing, can be helpful in making a good career choice. Ideally, a person should choose a career that meshes with his or her preferred lifestyle.

A recommended strategy for making a sound career choice is to gather valid occupational facts. The three sources to be consulted are printed and Web information, knowledgeable people, and first-hand experience. The last category covers information gained from visiting places of work or from part-time or temporary employment. An advantageous way of choosing a career is to pursue an occupation that appears to have growth potential. Search for a match between your capabilities and interests and a growth occupation.

A helpful way of looking at occupations is to characterize every job by the proportion of time you devote to working with data, people, or things. It is best to choose an occupation or field that fits your preferences in these three work dimensions.

It is becoming increasingly common for people to either switch the emphasis of activities in their work or switch careers entirely. A portfolio career is one in which a person has a variety of skills that can be used to earn money in different ways. The skill portfolio is particularly useful when a person holds two or more part-time positions.

Career switching is necessary for many reasons including the pursuit of happiness. Switching careers follows many of the same principles as choosing a first career. A new career should be built gradually, often by phasing into the new career part-time. To satisfy a desire for independence, many people switch careers from being an employee to being self-employed.

At the same time you might be choosing a career, think of preparing for a career. Suggestions along these lines include these: be flexible; develop interpersonal skills; think globally; develop technology skills; get an edge; keep learning; focus more on skills and knowledge than promotions; and strive for high-quality work.

QUESTIONS AND ACTIVITIES

1. Why is choosing a career so difficult?
2. Now that you have read this chapter, what do you think you would do differently when choosing a career or career switching?
3. Which of the skills listed in Self-Assessment Quiz 13-2 do you think will take the longest time to develop? Why?
4. Why are technological skills important for career people who are not entering a technological field?

5. A friend of yours majoring in business administration will graduate in three months but still has no idea which career he (or she) would like to pursue. If you think this situation warrants concern, offer your friend some advice.
6. How might attempting to match your career to your lifestyle block your career progress?
7. What flaw do you detect in the strategy of choosing a career based on whether the field you select is a growth field?
8. In your own words, explain what is meant by a "portfolio career."
9. Which skills do you think would be the most important to develop before entering self-employment?
10. Speak to someone you think has a successful career to find out how that person made his or her career choice. Be ready to discuss your findings in class.

INTERNET SKILL BUILDER

Finding a Career That Matches Your Interests

The chapter provided some information about vocational interests and careers. Search for additional information about identifying your vocational interests and matching them to a career. As a start, try such search phrases as "vocational interests," "occupational interests," and "matching career with interests." After your research is complete, speculate about how well any of your occupational interests match your field or contemplated field.

Log on to the **Companion Website** at **www.pearsoncanada.ca/dubrin** to access additional resources for this chapter.

CASE STUDY HUMAN RELATIONS

Self-Esteem Building at Pyramid Remanufacturing

After reading the case and answering the questions that follow, try Human Relations Skill-Building Exercise 13-1.

Allison's Dilemma

One year before entering college, Allison engaged her family, friends, and high-school guidance counsellor in helping her make a good career decision. Allison was asked by her guidance counsellor what activities in life she enjoyed the most. Allison's answer to this question provided her with a strong clue to a possible career path.

Allison responded thoughtfully, "I've really enjoyed my vacations with my parents. I've always been impressed with the way hotels and cruise ships operate. The people in charge are so polite, well dressed, and well spoken. I would enjoy working with people in the hotel and travel field. I also like the atmosphere of hotels. It's kind of in my blood."

With this initial hunch about a career prospect, Allison next conducted serious research. She investigated programs of study in hospitality and tourism. She also telephoned anybody she thought might know of someone working at a professional level this field.

Allison arranged interviews with two hotel managers and one assistant hotel manager. She also spoke to a friend's brother who had worked as a photographer on a few cruises. Based on these interviews and her own observations, Allison decided to major in hospitality and tourism upon entering college.

Three weeks before the first fall semester at college, Allison asked her parents to reserve dinnertime one Friday night for serious conversation. "What's on your mind, Allison?" asked her dad.

Allison replied, "Mom and Dad, I'm not so sure I want to go into the hospitality and tourism field. I think the work is great, but the sacrifice might be too big."

"What sacrifice?" asked her mother.

"The sacrifice," said Allison, "is that I couldn't lead a normal life. When my friends were off from work, I'd be working. When other people would be on vacation, I would be busier than ever. Another problem is that if you do a good job as a hotel manager, you're moved around from hotel to hotel.

"How could I ever lead a normal social life? How could I ever get married and raise children?"

Allison's dad asked, "Are you telling me that nobody in the hotel field has friends or family?"

"Maybe they have friends," said Allison, "but they must all be working at hotels or restaurants. These people are probably a culture of their own."

Allison's mom replied, "If you feel that strongly, pick another major. Just drop the whole idea. Find a field like office management where you could lead a normal life."

"It's not that simple," responded Allison. "I still want to enter the hospitality and tourism field. I know I would love the work. It's just the work schedule that might ruin it.

"I'm going to have to give my career choice a lot more thought."

Questions

1. How serious is the career choice problem facing Allison?
2. In what way is Allison facing a conflict?
3. What advice can you give Allison for deciding whether to pursue a career in hospitality and tourism?

Human Relations Skill Building

Exercise 13-1 Role Play: The Uncertain Career Seeker

The above case serves as background information for this role play. One person plays the role of Allison, who visits her guidance counsellor to mull over her career choice dilemma. Allison has considerable emotion about making a career choice. Another student plays the role of the guidance counsellor, who wants to both ask Allison the right questions and give her concrete advice. Run the role play for 10 to 15 minutes.

Chapter 14
Conducting a Job Search

Learning Outcomes

After studying the information and doing the exercises in this chapter, you should be able to

- improve your chances of finding a suitable job;
- target your job search and recognize what qualifications employers are seeking;
- identify job-finding methods;
- prepare an effective cover letter, résumé, and follow-up letter;
- identify the types of tests and examinations an applicant is likely to take.

Shefika Ahman is a marketing consultant with a large firm in Vancouver. She would like to move to Ontario where her aging parents live, so she is looking for a new job there that will allow her to spend more time with them and with her children. While she enjoys her present position, the travelling and long hours have taken their toll. With young children and being a new single parent, Shefika wants a company that promotes home–work balance through programs such as flextime and wellness programs.

First Shefika heads to the internet to several job bank sites. When she finds a job that sounds promising, she stays on the internet and searches for information on the company at its own website (if it has one) as well as various newsgroups. If she is still intrigued, she then phones or emails career groups for women to find out how the company manages work–life balance and how flexible it is with working families. As she has found, some companies' promises of flexibility are only words and do not carry over into business practice. After three months of searching, she is flying to Ottawa for her first interview at a smaller company.

The job-search tactics of this professional illustrate an important point about finding a position: a systematic approach is advised. With careful planning and preparation (such as preparing answers to typical interview questions in advance), a job search is more likely to be successful. Job searches are important for several reasons. You may be starting your career; you may be tired of your present job; you may want to boost your career; or you might be downsized or fired. Another reason for conducting a job search is to find a new position within a large company. The purpose of this chapter is to provide the basic information you need to conduct a successful job search, including sources of job leads, preparation of a cover letter and résumé, and how to perform well in an interview. This chapter also presents a few fine points to help give you an edge over those who do the minimum necessary to find a suitable position. Although you probably already have some job-search knowledge, this chapter can be used as a refresher and a reminder to be systematic in searching for a new position.

TARGETING YOUR JOB SEARCH

A job search begins with a reasonably flexible description of the type of job or jobs you are looking for. Flexibility is called for because with so many different jobs available, it is counterproductive to exclude possibilities by being too specific. A reasonable objective might be something of this nature: "I am searching for a job in the numerical field, with a large employer, located within 50 kilometres of here. I prefer accounting work. My minimum salary would be $675 per week."

Your chances of finding suitable employment are directly proportional to the number of positions that will satisfy your job objectives. One person with an interest in the literary field might only be willing to accept a job as a newspaper reporter—always a difficult position to find. Another person with the same background is seeking a job as (1) a newspaper reporter, (2) a magazine staff writer, (3) a copywriter in an advertising agency, (4) a communications specialist in a firm, or (5) a copywriter in a public relations firm. The second person has a better chance than the first of finding a job.

Closely tied in with the type of work you are seeking is the type of organization in which you would prefer to work. Unless you have had exposure to different types of organizations, you may have only tentative answers to this question. Questioning people who work for different types of organizations can provide you with some useful clues. A vital source of input about a prospective employer is present and past employees. Further, public tours can provide valuable tips about what it is like to work in a particular firm.

Visits to stores, restaurants, and government agencies will provide informal information about the general nature of working conditions in these places. Using the internet to find facts about a company has become standard practice. The internet search includes the firm's website as well as news stories about the company. Run your prospective company through your favourite search engines and see what you come up with.[1] As you begin your job search, ask yourself these questions to help you identify the type of organization that *might* be right for you:

- Would I feel more comfortable working in an office with hundreds of other people? Or, would I prefer just a handful of co-workers?
- Would I prefer to work in a small town or in a busy metropolitan area?
- How important is access to stores and restaurants?
- Would it be best for me to work where I could rely on public transportation?
- Would I prefer an easygoing atmosphere or a highly competitive, "rat race" environment?
- How important are the social aspects of work to me? Would I be happy only in a place where I could meet prospective dates and make new friends?

Not every job candidate can afford to be so selective about a prospective employer. The more your skills are in demand, and the more prosperous the times, the more selective a person can be in choosing an employer.

QUALIFICATIONS SOUGHT BY EMPLOYERS

What you are looking for in an employer must be matched against what an employer is looking for in an employee. Job interviewers and employers do not all agree on the qualifications they seek in employees. Nevertheless, a number of traits, characteristics, skills, and accomplishments are important to many employers.[2]

The Conference Board of Canada's Corporate Council on Education has researched and identified an employability skills profile. which is widely used to identify skills and abilities sought after by employers.[3] Representatives from numerous Canadian companies have had input into developing this profile of skills, including Air Canada, Bell Canada, General Motors of Canada, IBM Canada, Shell Canada, and Xerox Limited, to name just a few. The profile of skills, Employability Skills 2000+, is presented in the Canada Today below.

Canada Today

Employability Skills 2000+

The skills you need to enter, stay in, and progress in the world of work—whether you work on your own or as a part of a team.

These skills can also be applied and used beyond the workplace in a range of daily activities.

Fundamental Skills

The skills needed as a base for further development

You will be better prepared to progress in the world of work when you can:

Communicate

- read and understand information presented in a variety of forms (e.g., words, graphs, charts, diagrams)
- write and speak so others pay attention and understand
- listen and ask questions to understand and appreciate the points of view of others
- share information using a range of information and communications technologies (e.g., voice, email, computers)

Personal Management Skills

The personal skills, attitudes, and behaviours that drive one's potential for growth

You will be able to offer yourself greater possibilities for achievement when you can:

Demonstrate Positive Attitudes & Behaviours

- feel good about yourself and be confident
- deal with people, problems, and situations with honesty, integrity, and personal ethics
- recognize your own and other people's good efforts
- take care of your personal health
- show interest, initiative, and effort

Teamwork Skills

The skills and attributes needed to contribute productively

You will be better prepared to add value to the outcomes of a task, project, or team when you can:

Work with Others

- understand and work within the dynamics of a group
- ensure that a team's purpose and objectives are clear
- be flexible: respect, be open to, and supportive of the thoughts, opinions, and contributions of others in a group
- recognize and respect people's diversity, individual differences, and perspectives

- use relevant scientific, technological, and mathematical knowledge and skills to explain or clarify ideas

Manage Information

- locate, gather, and organize information using appropriate technology and information systems
- access, analyze, and apply knowledge and skills from various disciplines (e.g., the arts, languages, science, technology, mathematics, social sciences, and the humanities)

Use Numbers

- decide what needs to be measured or calculated
- observe and record data using appropriate methods, tools, and technology
- make estimates and verify calculations

Think & Solve Problems

- assess situations and identify problems
- seek different points of view and evaluate them based on facts
- recognize the human, interpersonal, technical, scientific, and mathematical dimensions of a problem
- identify the root cause of a problem
- be creative and innovative in exploring possible solutions
- readily use science, technology, and mathematics as ways to think, gain and share knowledge, solve problems, and make decisions
- evaluate solutions to make recommendations or decisions
- implement solutions
- check to see if a solution works, and act on opportunities for improvement

Be Responsible

- set goals and priorities balancing work and personal life
- plan and manage time, money, and other resources to achieve goals
- assess, weigh, and manage risk
- be accountable for your actions and the actions of your group
- be socially responsible and contribute to your community

Be Adaptable

- work independently or as a part of a team
- carry out multiple tasks or projects
- be innovative and resourceful: identify and suggest alternative ways to achieve goals and get the job done
- be open and respond constructively to change
- learn from your mistakes and accept feedback
- cope with uncertainty

Learn Continuously

- be willing to continuously learn and grow
- assess personal strengths and areas for development
- set your own learning goals
- identify and access learning sources and opportunities
- plan for and achieve your learning goals

Work Safely

- be aware of personal and group health and safety practices and procedures, and act in accordance with these

- accept and provide feedback in a constructive and considerate manner
- contribute to a team by sharing information and expertise
- lead or support when appropriate, motivating a group for high performance
- understand the role of conflict in a group to reach solutions
- manage and resolve conflict when appropriate

Participate in Projects & Tasks

- plan, design, or carry out a project or task from start to finish with well-defined objectives and outcomes
- develop a plan, seek feedback, test, revise, and implement
- work to agreed quality standards and specifications
- select and use appropriate tools and technology for a task or project
- adapt to changing requirements and information
- continuously monitor the success of a project or task and identify ways to improve

Source: Employability Skills 2000+ Brochure 2000 E/F (Ottawa: The Conference Board of Canada, 2000) www.conferenceboard.ca

Human Relations Self-Assessment

QUIZ 14-1 Qualifications Sought by Employers

The following is a list of qualifications widely sought by prospective employers. After reading each qualification, rate yourself on a 1-to-5 scale on the particular dimension.

1 = very low; 2 = low; 3 = average; 4 = high; 5 = very high.

1.	Appropriate education for the position under consideration, and satisfactory grades	1	2	3	4	5
2.	Relevant work experience	1	2	3	4	5
3.	Communication and other interpersonal skills	1	2	3	4	5
4.	Motivation and energy	1	2	3	4	5
5.	Problem-solving ability (intelligence) and creativity	1	2	3	4	5
6.	Judgment and common sense	1	2	3	4	5
7.	Adaptability to change	1	2	3	4	5
8.	Emotional maturity (acting professionally and responsibly)	1	2	3	4	5
9.	Teamwork (ability and interest in working in a team effort)	1	2	3	4	5
10.	Positive attitude (enthusiasm about work and initiative)	1	2	3	4	5
11.	Customer service orientation	1	2	3	4	5
12.	Information technology skills	1	2	3	4	5
13.	Internet research skills	1	2	3	4	5
14.	Willingness to continue to study and learn about job, company, and industry	1	2	3	4	5
15.	Likeability and sense of humour	1	2	3	4	5
16.	Dependability, responsibility, and conscientiousness (including good work habits and time management)	1	2	3	4	5

Interpretation: Consider engaging in some serious self-development, training, and education for items that you rated low or very low. If you accurately rated yourself as 4 or 5 on all the dimensions, you are an exceptional job candidate.

These skills are divided into three areas: fundamental skills, teamwork skills, and personal management skills. According to the Council, these skills form the foundation of a high-quality Canadian workforce leading into the future. Human Relations Self-Assessment Quiz 14-1 lets you assess yourself in relation to some of the skills and qualifications sought by employers.

JOB-FINDING METHODS

Two cornerstone principles of conducting a job campaign are (1) use several different methods and (2) keep trying. These two principles should be applied because most approaches to job finding are inefficient yet effective. *Inefficient* refers to the fact that a person might have to make many contacts to find just one job. Yet, the system is *effective* because it does lead to a desired outcome—finding a suitable position.

Job-finding techniques are divided here into six types: (1) networking; (2) internet search; (3) unsolicited letter campaigns; (4) telesearches; (5) placement offices, employment agencies, and career fairs; (5) help-wanted ads; and (6) online social networking.

Exhibit 14-1 presents the results of a survey of 344 corporate executives about where they found current employees. Although classified ads are the major source of employees,

Exhibit 14-1
Sources of Employees According to Employers

Source	Percentage
Help-Wanted Ads	43%
Other	17%
Employee Referrals	13%
Employment Firms	12%
Temporary Firms	10%
Internet	5%

Note: Other studies typically find employee referrals to be a bigger source of candidates than help-wanted ads.

Sources: Information from Olsten Corporation survey reported in Mildred L. Culp, "Classifieds Still Important for Job Seekers," *WorkWise®*, syndicated column, August 29, 1999; and "Job Recruiters May Want to Go Online or Offline," Associated Press story, August 14, 2000.

it is possible that a larger proportion of more recent hires were found through the internet. Human Relations Skill-Building Exercise 14-1 will help sensitize you to the many ways of finding a suitable position.

Networking (Contacts and Referrals)

Developing a network of contacts is important for finding a job, obtaining promotions, or career switching (refer to Chapter 16 for more career advancement strategies). As a career advancement tactic, networking has several purposes. The contacts you establish can help you find a better position, offer you a new position, become a customer, become a valuable supplier, help you solve difficult problems, or find a mentor. People in your network can also offer you emotional support during periods of adversity.

A recommended approach to networking is to keep a list of at least 25 people whom you contact at least once a month. The contact can be as extensive as a luncheon meeting or as brief as an email message. The starting point in networking is to obtain an ample supply of

Human Relations Skill Building
Exercise 14-1 Creative Job-Finding Techniques

Job seekers often make the mistake of not exploring enough different methods for finding a job. After exploring a few conventional techniques, such as making a trip to the placement office, they sit back and wait for job offers to pour in. A better approach is to search for creative alternatives to finding a job. Think of every possibility, then sort out the workable from the unworkable later on. To accomplish this task, the class will be organized into brainstorming groups. The goal is to specify as large a number of job-finding techniques as possible. Follow the guidelines for brainstorming presented in Chapter 3.

After each group has assembled and edited its job-finding techniques, group leaders will present their findings to the rest of the class. Groups can then compare their job-finding suggestions.

business cards. You then give a card to any person you meet who might be able to help you now or in the future. While first developing your network, be inclusive. Later, as your network develops, you can strive to include a greater number of influential and successful people. People in your network can include relatives; people you meet while traveling, vacationing, or attending trade shows; online friends and acquaintances; and classmates.

Community activities and religious organizations can also be a source of contacts. Golf is still considered the number one sport for networking because of the high-level contacts the sport generates. A substantial amount of social networking also takes place on the internet. The range of potential people in your network is much greater over the internet than if networking is done locally and in person. The people in these groups can become valuable business contacts. Online networking includes newsgroups, mailing lists, chat rooms, and email. Corporate websites usually have a listing of contact people for a company, and it is possible that some of these people will become part of your network. Figure 14-1 offers some additional networking suggestions, and Human Relations Skill-Building Exercise 14-2 provides a worksheet for networking.

The following networking suggestions are gathered from a number of career counsellors and business writers. Select and choose from among the list those ideas that appear to fit your personality and circumstances.

- Expand and diversify your network. Everyone you come in contact with is a potential resource to help you in your career. Even someone whose sole purpose is to cheer you on during downturns can be a valuable ally. Keep filling your network with new contacts because older contacts may fade away. Retired people who have had successful careers can be a valuable source of contacts. Also, retired people typically enjoy assisting people at earlier stages in their careers.
- Add value as well as asking for assistance. Consider how you can help the other person and listen as much as you talk.
- When networking by email, include your telephone number and address. The other person may want to contact you by means other than an email. Also, be persistent because email messages may get deleted by accident or simply disappear because of technical problems.
- When approaching someone to be part of your network, explain how you received his or her name or refresh the person's mind as to how you met previously.
- If you attend a formal networking event (such as a professional meeting), "work the room." Engage in professional conversations with as many people as feasible.
- Create good relationships with your peers and fellow students. Some of them will occupy influential positions in the future. Stay in touch with your more promising classmates. In other words, "Look at the paws on those pups."
- Strive to develop a personal relationship with at least two people at higher levels in your place of work. Keep these people informed of what you are doing and ask for their advice.
- Be memorable for positive reasons. Making a lasting positive impression is a promising way of keeping a network alive.
- When you have a change of status, such as accepting a new position, let this be an opportunity to notify network members. Let everyone know should you change your email address or telephone number.

Source: Anita Bruzzese, "Restrain Yourself and Think When Networking by E-Mail," *Gannett News Service*, June 30, 2003; "Networking Isn't for Spectators: Meeting People, Discovering Trends, and Arriving Early Can Pay Dividends," Knight Ridder, February 24, 2003; Deb Koehn, "Networking Vital in Ever-Evolving Workplaces," *Rochester (NY) Democrat and Chronicle*, July 14, 2002, p. 4E; Deb Koehn, "Know Etiquette of Networking," *Rochester (NY) Democrat and Chronicle*, October 27, 2002, p. 4E; "'85 Broads' Shares Networking Tips," *Executive Leadership*, February 2002, p. 3; Anne Fisher, "How Do I Network When I Don't Even Know Anyone?" *Fortune*, July 22, 2002, p. 226.

Figure 14-1 Networking Suggestions

Human Relations Skill Building

Exercise 14-2 Building Your Network

Networking can be regarded as the process of building a team that works with you to achieve success. You can start the following exercise now, but it will probably take your entire career to implement completely. To start networking or make your present networking more systematic, take the following steps:

Step 1. Jot down your top three goals or objectives for the following three months, such as obtaining a new job or promotion, starting a small business, or doing a field research study.

1. ______________________________
____
2. ______________________________
____
3. ______________________________
____

Step 2. List family members, friends, or acquaintances who could assist you in meeting your goals or objectives. Prepare a contact card or database entry for each person on your list, including as many details as you can about the person and the person's family, friends, employers, and contacts.

Step 3. Identify what assistance you will request of your contact or contacts. Be realistic in light of your prior investment in the relationship. Remember, you have to be a friend to have a friend.

Step 4. Identify how you will meet your contact or contacts during the next month. Could it be for lunch or at an athletic field, nightclub, sports club, recreational facility on campus, cafeteria, and so forth? Learn more about your contacts during your face-to-face meetings. In some cases you may have to use the telephone or email to substitute for an in-person meeting. Look for ways to mutually benefit from the relationship. At the beginning of each week, verify that you have made a small investment in building these relationships.

Step 5. Ask for the help you need. A network must benefit you. Thank the contact for any help given. Jot down on your planner a reminder to make a follow-up call, letter, or email message to your contacts. In this way, you will have less work to do before you make another request for help.

Step 6. For each person in your network, think of a favor, however small, that you can return to him or her. Without reciprocity, a network fades rapidly.

Source: Adapted and expanded from Cheryl Kitter, "Taking the Work Out of Networking," Success Workshop, supplement to The Pryor Report, March 1998, pp. 1–2.

Networking is obviously beneficial in a field such as direct selling whereby you contact people you know to purchase your goods or services. For example, if you sell products such as financial services, Avon, or Tupperware, you are expected to capitalize on personal contacts. Almost any successful businessperson you meet uses networking, at least to some extent.

We caution again to be selective about your networking. Overreliance on networking, such as contacting people who probably have no interest in hearing from you, can be annoying to the recipient. Kenneth Norton, the director of product management at Yahoo! has coined the term snam (a mutant of spam) in reference to unwanted email generated by such social networking sites as Friendster, LinkedIn, and Tribe.[4]

The Internet

The internet is a standard part of job hunting. For little or no cost, the job seeker can post a résumé or scroll through thousands of job opportunities. There are many sites such as

Workopolis and Headhunters.com. For example, Headhunters.com and other sites mentioned in the previous chapter allow you to post an electronic résumé for no cost, or you can invest a few dollars and "locate" your résumé in a "better" area. If you are willing to move to another country, you can also visit many U.S. or international sites such as Careerbuilder.com. Careerbuilder.com (for United States postings) has many large employers' jobs such as General Electric and Bell. Résumé database sites allow employers to view résumés for potential employees. Employers usually pay some sort of fee to view these résumés and thus use these sites for serious employee searches.

Job hunting on the internet can lead to a false sense of security. Using the internet, a job search can cast a wide net, and hundreds of job postings can be explored. As a consequence, the job seeker may think that he or she can sit back and wait for a job offer to come through by email. In reality, the internet is just one source of leads that should be used in conjunction with other job-finding methods. Thousands of other job seekers can access the same job openings, and many of the positions listed have already been filled. Many employers hire résumé screening services (much like an employment agency) to sort through the thousands of posted résumés to find qualified applicants.

Unsolicited Letter Campaign

A standard and still current method of job finding is the **unsolicited letter campaign** or writing directly to a company you would like to work for. The plan is to come up with a master list of firms for whom you would like to work. You make up the list according to the categories most relevant to your situation, such as by industry or geographic location. Your list can be developed through the internet by using search engines to access such categories as "furniture makers, Quebec." Business directories in libraries, such as those published by Dun and Bradstreet and Standard and Poor, provide full addresses and names of key people in the firms listed.

When writing to a prospective employer, send the letter to a specific individual rather than Dear Sir, Madam, or Ms. The mailing should consist of a cover letter and résumé. A sensible approach is to scroll through company websites for employment information, as posted by most large employers. This approach automatically creates a contact person for you. Should somebody be interested in your letter, it could get you into the insider system. The person will either contact you directly or refer your letter and résumé to a hiring manager.

Telesearch

A related approach to the mail campaign is the **telesearch**, in which job leads are obtained by making unsolicited phone calls to prospective employers. Although not as popular as using the internet, this is still worth a try as one more job-seeking method. One of the author's daughters called a company recently and had a phone interview "on the spot" and received immediate employment, although there were no positions posted! The list of prospects can be assembled in the same manner as the mail campaign. Begin your inquiry into an organization by contacting the person who would be your boss if you landed the job you really want. A major goal of the telesearch is to establish direct contact with as many of these decision makers as you can.

If the person contacted has an opening or is interested in learning more about you, you will probably get an interview or be asked to send a résumé. Even if you fail to get an interview, you might be able to obtain a job lead from your contact. Inquire about other people who might be interested in hiring someone with your experience.

Placement Offices, Employment Agencies, and Career Fairs

Your placement office is a primary avenue to finding a job. Even if you do not find a job through the placement office, you will still gain insight into the job-finding process. If recruiters visit your campus, you can gain valuable experience in being interviewed. Placement offices also offer helpful suggestions for preparing résumés and cover letters.

Employment agencies can also lead you to the right position. Employers use employment agencies to advertise jobs and screen applicants, particularly in large cities. Agencies tend to be more valuable for people with about five to ten years of work experience than for newcomers. Not to be overlooked, however, is that many employment agencies specialize in temporary help. After about nine months, a temporary job might become permanent. A concern expressed about employment agencies is that they sometimes encourage applicants to accept less-than-ideal positions just so the agency can earn a placement fee.

Career (or job) fairs function somewhat like a temporary placement office. A large number of employers may visit the fair to recruit employees. At the same time, a large number of applicants register at the fair and present their résumés. In addition to their direct value as a means of finding jobs, career fairs are also useful for learning about employment trends and the skills required for certain positions and for developing your network of career contacts.

Help-Wanted Ads in Newspapers, Magazines, and Trade Journals

A thorough job search includes a careful scanning of the help-wanted section of classified ads. Many people find good jobs through this method. Help-wanted ads are found in local and national newspapers, such as *The Globe and Mail*, the *Toronto Star*, and *The Edmonton Sun*. Professional and trade magazines such as *Personnel Journal* often contain ads searching for workers in the field of interest covered by the publication.

Online Social Networking

While the internet has job sites and job sources, social media allows for more personalized networking and a way to reach more people quickly. Since you already belong to some social media networks such as Facebook and Twitter, these can become rich sources for job leads. Even YouTube has been used for finding jobs or at least becoming known in various fields such as music. In other words, put your computer and PDA to work. This means getting word out that your are job hunting on social sites like Facebook and MySpace, sending instant job-search updates via messaging feeds like Twitter, and meeting new people who might be able to lend a hand through Web-networking sites such as LinkedIn and Ryze.[5] Several sites will give you helpful hints as how to use Twitter successfully to find a job (see

Weblinks at the end of the chapter). Some suggestions for using Twitter include browsing Twitter directories to find professionals to follow and make yourself worth following.[6]

Blogging is also an excellent strategy. By using your blog as a résumé, you are putting yourself out to the widest group of potential employers. Your résumé blog could be more in-depth than your normal traditional résumé. You can also post stories about your major accomplishments, your education, the projects you are working on and any other topics that you are personally passionate about. Always communicate on your blog in both directions by encouraging and enabling comments on your résumé blog.[7]

Some job seekers have also had success with YouTube. You can post a video résumé on YouTube to get noticed quickly. With a YouTube video résumé you may stand out from the crowd and your competitors. Using keywords and keyword phrases that express your capabilities in the title of the video and the description will enable your résumé to be found on search engines. One suggestion is that once you have created and uploaded your résumé on YouTube, add the video to your blog as well.[8]

In addition to being aware of the various job-finding methods, it is also important to consider *when* to begin a job search. In general, the bigger the job, the longer the job campaign. Finding a position within 30 days is exceptional, whereas a total search time of about six months is typical. You will usually need several months to prepare your résumé and cover letter, pursue all the methods described in this section, and wait to hear from employers. When people are in a particularly in-demand field, a position can sometimes be found in several days just by posting a résumé online. Even more quickly, some in-demand people are recruited away from their present employers without making any effort to conduct a job search.

COVER LETTERS

While social media is becoming more popular for job hunting, most companies still require the traditional cover letter and résumé. Therefore, it is worthwhile to become proficient in writing good cover letters and résumés. A résumé or job application form is necessary but not sufficient for conducting an intelligent job campaign. You also need a cover letter to accompany such documents. The cover letter multiplies the effectiveness of the résumé because it enables you to prepare a tailor-made, individual approach to each position you pursue. The most important purpose of the cover letter is to explain why you are applying for the position in question. Simultaneously, you try to convince the prospective employer why you should be considered. Here we look at two effective types of cover letters.

Attention-Getting Cover Letters

Most job seekers use the conventional approach for writing a letter, attempting to impress the prospective employer with their backgrounds. A more effective approach is to capture the reader's attention with a direct statement of what you might be able to do for the company. Keep this "what I can do for you" strategy paramount in mind at every stage of finding a job. It works wonders in the job interview, as it will in the rest of your career.

After you have stated how you can help the employer, present a one-page summary of your education and the highlights of your work experience. A sample cover letter is presented in Exhibit 14-2.

Exhibit 14-2
Sample Cover Letter

Date of letter
27 Buttercup Lane
Toronto Ontario M6P 2N5

Mr. Bart Bertrand
Phone/Fax (416) 658-1000
President jj@igs.net
South View Dodge
258 Princess Blvd.
Toronto Ontario M1V 2P1

Dear Mr. Bertrand:

Without a good service department, a new-car dealership is in big trouble. An efficiency-minded person like myself who loves autos, and likes to help customers, can do wonders for your service department. Give me a chance, and I will help you maintain the high quality of after-sales service demanded by your customers.

The position you advertised in the *Sun* is an ideal fit for my background. Shortly, I will be graduating from Centennial College with an associate's degree in automotive technology. In addition, I was an automotive mechanics major at Harrison Vocational High.

My job experience includes three years of part-time general work at Manny's Petro Canada Service, and two years of clerical work at Brandon's Chrysler-Plymouth. Besides this relevant experience, I'm the proud owner of a mint condition 1980 sports coupe I maintain myself.

My enclosed résumé contains additional information about me. When might I have the opportunity to be interviewed?

Sincerely yours,

Jane Jenkins

Notice that the opening line is an attention-getter: "Without a good service department, a car dealership is in big trouble." You may not want to write an outrageous or flip cover letter, but it should have enough flair to attract the reader's attention.

Employment specialist Richard H. Beatty recommends a slightly different version of the attention-getting cover letter. He explains that an effective cover letter has five parts: an attention-grabbing introduction, a paragraph selling your value to the employer, a background summary paragraph, a compelling follow-up action statement, and an appreciative close. Beatty recommends mentioning a personal contact as part of the attention-grabber,[9] for example: "Meg Atwood, your computer operations manager, mentioned that you are looking for a talented person to manage your website. I would very much like to talk to you about this position."

The T-Form Cover Letter

A novel format for a cover letter is one that systematically outlines how the applicant's qualifications match up against the job requirements posted in the position announcement.[10] The T-form (or column) approach gives the reader a tabular outline of how the applicant's background fits the position description. The T-form cover letter, presented in Exhibit 14-3, is also recommended because it has an attention-getting format.

Exhibit 14-3
The T-Form Cover Letter

Nadir Simms
2127 Marketview Avenue
Downsview ON M1A W2C
Phone/Fax (416) 441-0761
gnc26@home.com

Sales Manager
Southeast Supply Corporation
200 Ashford Centre North, Suite 650
Toronto, ON M1V 2G6

Dear Sales Manager:

In response to your recent advertisement in the *Toronto Star* and on the EmployCanada website for telemarketing sales professionals, please consider the following:

Requirements	***My Qualifications***
Prior sales experience a must	Two years of full-time and part-time selling, including retail and magazine subscription renewals
Great communicator	Two different managers praised my communication skills; received an A in two communication skills courses
Self-motivated	Worked well without supervision; considered to be a self-starter
Reliable	Not one sick day in two years; never late with a class assignment

Your opportunity excites me, and I would be proud to represent your company. My résumé is enclosed for your consideration.

Sincerely,

Nadir Simms
enclosure

PREPARING AN EFFECTIVE JOB RÉSUMÉ

The major purpose of a résumé is to help you obtain a job interview, not a job. A résumé is needed when you are applying as an outside candidate and often when seeking a transfer within a firm. Effective résumés are straightforward, factual presentations of a person's experiences, education, skills, and accomplishments. Yet a résumé is much like art. People have different ideas about what constitutes an effective résumé. To add to the confusion, some people spell "résumé" with the acute accents (résumé is a French word), and some without. A challenge in preparing an effective résumé is to suit many different preferences.

The issue of résumé length illustrates how employers hold different opinions about the best résumé format. A national survey of employers indicated that 24 percent said the résumé should be "no longer than one page"; 42 percent said "no longer than two pages," and 34 percent, "determined by information."[11]

Regardless of length, a poorly written résumé will not get you an interview. A few general guidelines will be offered here to help you avoid serious mistakes. An overall perspective to keep in mind is, "If your résumé is not a winner, it's a killer."[12] Done properly, a résumé can lead to an interview with a prospective employer. Done poorly, it will block you from further consideration.

Three Types of Résumés

The three most commonly used résumé formats are the chronological, functional, and targeted. You might consider using one of these types, or a blend of them (the combination résumé), based on the information about yourself you are trying to highlight. Whichever format you choose, you must include essential information.

The **chronological résumé** presents your work experience, education, and interests, along with your accomplishments, in reverse chronological order. A chronological résumé is basically the traditional résumé with the addition of accomplishments and achievements. Some people say the chronological résumé is too bland. However, it contains precisely the information that most employers demand, and it is easy to prepare.

The **functional résumé** organizes your skills and accomplishments into the functions or tasks that support the job you are seeking. A section of a functional résumé might read:

> **SUPERVISION:** Organized the activities of five park employees to create a smooth-running recreation program. Trained and supervised four roofing specialists to help produce a successful roofing business.

The functional résumé is useful because it highlights the things you have accomplished and the skills you have developed. In this way, an ordinary work experience might seem more impressive. For instance, the tasks listed above under "supervision" may appear more impressive than listing the jobs "Playground supervisor" and "Roofing crew chief." One problem with the functional résumé is that it omits the factual information many employers demand. You might therefore appear to be hiding something about your background.

The **targeted résumé** focuses on a specific job target or position and presents only information about you that supports that target. Using a target format, an applicant for a sales position would list only sales jobs. Under education, the applicant would focus on sales-related courses such as communication skills and marketing. A targeted résumé is helpful in dramatizing your suitability for the position you are seeking. However, this résumé format omits other relevant information about you, and a new résumé must be prepared for each target position. The *combination résumé* combines a listing of your skills such as functional résumé and then describes your experience and education in reverse chronological order.

Whichever résumé format you choose, it is best to place your most saleable asset first.[13] If your work experience is limited, place education before work experience. If your skills are more impressive than your education or work experience, list them first.

A general-purpose résumé, following a chronological format, is presented in Exhibit 14-4. This person chose to place work experience before education. Although her résumé is chronological, it also allows room for accomplishments and skills. Many people have achieved good results with this format. However, do not restrict yourself.

The references section of the résumé is another area where opinion varies. One approach is to list several references on the résumé, giving complete identifying information so that the prospective employer can readily contact the references. A concern is that these references are often perceived as meaningless because you have identified friends. If you are a recent graduate, a slightly more objective approach is to indicate that references are on file in a placement office. References can also be provided with a cover letter or a follow-up letter. A sophisticated approach is to ask the prospective employer what types of references are preferred and then supply them promptly by email. Types of references include superiors, co-workers, and those outside work, such as athletic coaches and community leaders.

In preparing either a print or an electronic résumé, keep in mind that certain key words or references attract the attention of managers and specialists who scan résumés. The scanning may be done visually, electronically, or both. In today's market, key words and phrases include the following: *languages*, *computer, information technology, internet, ecommerce*, *etailing, experience*, *hard-working, overseas experience*, *flexible, task-oriented, team player,* and *customer-oriented*. A sensible tactic would be to mention those words that apply to you. Many of these words, such as *computer* and *team player,* are widely applicable.

The Electronic Résumé

A current development in résumé construction is to prepare one primarily for electronic databases. Many companies store résumés electronically, making it important to prepare one that is suitable for an electronic database. If a job-search website calls for an electronic résumé, it can be entered into the right place on the webpage. At other times an electronic résumé is printed and mailed to the employer, who in turn uses an optical scanner to enter the résumé in the company database. Note that attaching a word-processed résumé to an email is not the same as preparing an electronic résumé.

A distinguishing feature of an electronic résumé is that it contains keywords that fit the requirements of a keyword search. The job seeker should isolate keywords (nouns and adjectives) by placing them right under his or her name, address, and telephone

Exhibit 14-4
A General-Purpose Résumé

Jane Jenkins
27 Buttercup Lane
Toronto Ontario M6P 2N5
Phone/Fax (416) 658-1000
jj@igs.net

Qualification Summary	Experience in administrative support activities for automobile dealership. Education in office management and automotive repairs.
Job Objective	Management position in service department of new-car dealership.
Job Experience	
2001–present	Senior support specialist, Brandon-Chrysler Plymouth, Toronto. Responsible for receiving customer payments for service performed; preparing invoices; miscellaneous tasks as requested by service manager. • Set up database that saved space and reduced file-searching time.
1998–2001	Service station attendant, Manny's Petro Canada Service. Performed variety of light mechanical tasks such as assisting in brake relinings, installing mufflers and tailpipes, tune-ups, independent responsibility for lubrication and oil changes. • Increased sales of tires, batteries, and accessories by 18 percent during time periods on duty.
Formal Education	
1999–2001	Centennial College, Associate Degree, automotive technology, May 1998. Studied all phases of auto repair including computerized diagnostics, service department management. Attended school while working about 30 hours per week. Average grade, 92%.
1995–1999	Harrison Vocational Technical High School, Toronto. Graduated 10th in class of 137. Majored in automotive repair and maintenance. Also studied business education topics such as bookkeeping, business machines, and office systems and procedures.
Job-Related Skills	Word processing, spreadsheet analysis, development of databases. Can perform bookkeeping. Able to handle customer concerns and complaints in person or by phone. Know how to diagnose and repair wide range of automotive problems for domestic and imported vehicles.
Personal Interests and Hobbies	Enjoy automobile restoration and maintenance. Physical fitness enthusiast. Walt Disney movie buff. Read self-improvement books and current fiction; daily newspaper. Watch CNN and pro football on television.
References	On file with placement office at Centennial College. Permissible to contact present or former employer.

numbers. Zane K. Quible recommends that keywords be selected from among the following information:[14]

- Title of jobs held by applicant
- Names of job-related tasks performed by the applicant
- Industry jargon such as "zero defects," "customer delight," or "just-in-time inventory management" (also acronyms such as JIT for "just in time")
- Special skills or knowledge possessed by the applicant
- Degrees earned
- High school program or college major (for college graduates, delete information about the high school program)
- High schools or colleges attended
- Special awards or honours received
- Nature of interpersonal skills the applicant possesses

Most of this information, of course, should also be included in a conventional printed résumé. Many job sites may have online templates to build your résumé or you may need to file-attach your résumé with the online application. Despite the increasing popularity of electronic résumés, the serious job hunter also needs a conventional (paper) one. Exhibit 14-5 (on page 353) illustrates an electronic résumé.

How to Handle the Job Objective Section

On the résumé, a **job objective** is the position you are applying for now or intend to hold in the future. A job objective is also referred to as a *job target* or a *position objective*. Although stating a job objective seems easy, it is a trouble spot for many résumé writers. Early in their careers, many people feel compelled to state their long-range career objectives in the job objective section. A 21-year-old might state, "To become president of an international corporation." Certainly this is a worthy objective, but it is better to be more modest at the outset.

Employers will tend to interpret the job objective as a statement of your short-term plans. If you think your long-term objective should be stated, you might divide the section into "immediate objective" and "long-term objective." Current practice is to use the position under consideration as a job objective. Longer-term objectives can then be discussed during the job interview.

Another challenge with the job objective section is that your objective will often have to be tailored to the specific job under consideration. The job objective you have printed on your résumé may not fit exactly the job you are applying for. You might be considering a sales career. You find two good leads, one for selling an industrial product, and one for a consumer product. You would want your objective on one résumé to mention industrial sales, and on the other consumer sales.

By keeping your résumé on your computer, you can modify the objective section (and other sections as required) for a given job lead. Another approach is to omit the job objective section. Your cover letter can describe the link between you and the job under consideration. Notice how the cover letter in Exhibit 14-2 makes this link. (The same person, however, does include a job objective on her résumé.)

Exhibit 14-5
Electronic Résumé

Sara L. Adams
123 Elmwood Terrace
Vancouver BC V1G 2S2
(604) 332-1485 Fax (604) 372-4587
SLAdams@hmp.col

Keywords:	Accountant. Bookkeeper. Accounts receivable ledger. Accounts payable ledger. Financial reports. Business Administration. Lotus 1-2-3. Excel. Windows 2000. Word 2000. Team player. French. Supervision. President's Honour Roll. Superior oral communication skills. Superior written communication skills. Self-starter. Quick learner. Conscientious. Detail oriented. Reliable. Top 5 percent of class. IBM-compatible computers. Lakeville College, Winnipeg, MB.
Job objective:	To work as accountant or bookkeeper for private or public business, with the eventual goal of becoming supervisor of bookkeeping or accounting, or office manager.
Education:	Lakeville College, Winnipeg, MB, 1996–1998 Accounting major. Associate's degree in Business Administration with High Honours. East Winnipeg High School, National Honour Society, 1992.
Experience:	London's Department Store, Vancouver, BC, 1992–present. Full-time for four years, then part-time while attending college. Performed bookkeeping and cashier activities. Maintained accounts receivable and accounts payable ledgers. Prepared a variety of financial reports.
Key Accomplishment:	Developed a system of prompt payments which saved employer approximately $55,000 per year.
College Activities and Honours:	President of Accounting Club for two years. Team Leader of Student Misconduct Committee, President's Honour Roll, each semester, 1996–1998. Delta Phi Kappa Honorary, 1996–1998.

How Do You Write a Résumé When Your Background Does Not Fit the Position?

Job seekers sometimes lack the type of experience expected to qualify them for a position they seek. This lack of direct fit may occur when the applicant is switching fields or is entering the workforce after a long absence. In both instances, it is helpful to emphasize skills and experience that would contribute to success in the job under consideration.

Assume a person with five years of experience as a bookkeeper applies for a sales representative position at an office equipment company. The bookkeeper is advised to make these types of entries on his or her résumé: "Five years of experience in working directly with office equipment including computers, fax machines, and high-speed copiers"; "Able to size up equipment needs of accountants and bookkeepers"; "Accustomed to negotiating budgets with managers."

Assume a person has 20 years of experience managing a household but has not worked outside the home. The candidate applies for an assistant manager position in a restaurant. The person should list relevant skills such as "Able to plan and prepare holiday meals and parties for large groups of people." The candidate is also advised to describe his or her volunteer work because such experience may be job related. For example, "Coordinated church picnic for 250 people, including recruiting and supervising ten workers and raising the necessary funds."

What about the Creative-Style Résumé?

Since employers receive so many résumés, it is difficult to attract an employer's attention. The solution offered to this problem is a creatively prepared résumé. A **creative-style résumé** is one with a novel format and design.

If done in a way to attract positive attention to oneself, creative-style résumés have merit. The generally accepted approach, however, is for résumés to be conservative. In one study, 93 percent of college recruiters surveyed preferred white or ivory colour for the résumé paper. For the entry-level job applicant, the conservative approach is the safest bet.[15] If you are applying for a position in which creative talent is a primary factor, the creative-style résumé is helpful. Creative-style résumés work well for a variety of jobs in a hip industry such as fashion or dot-com companies. A more conventional job requires a more conventional résumé. Human resource specialists often object to oversized résumés because they are difficult to fit into standard files.

Avoid making your résumé visually distracting in an attempt to be different, for instance by using more than three fonts. A useful suggestion is to print your résumé on grey paper with a half-inch white border. (Grey will probably not be disliked by people who prefer ivory.) In this way, your résumé will communicate a classy, distinctive quality while remaining easy to read.[16]

Do not confuse the *creative* résumé with the *created* résumé, in which you "create" facts to make a favourable impression. Many employers check facts presented on a résumé. Evidence of distortion of the truth or outright lying usually leads to immediate disqualification of the applicant. If you made the sandwiches at a sub shop, do not list your job title as "master chef" or "vice-president of operations." And résumé misinformation uncovered after the applicant is hired can lead to immediate dismissal.

HAVING A SUCCESSFUL JOB INTERVIEW

A successful job campaign results in one or more employment interviews. Screening interviews are often conducted by telephone, particularly for customer-service positions requiring telephone skills. More extensive interviews are usually conducted in person. Many firms, however, also conduct group interviews in which the job candidates speak to several prospective work associates at the same time. Often the group interview is conducted in a casual environment, such as a restaurant or company cafeteria. The candidate may not be aware that meeting with the group is actually an interview and that he or she is being judged.

Exhibit 14-6
Questions Frequently Asked of Job Candidates

The following questions are of the same basic type and content encountered in most employment interviews. Practise answering them in front of a friend, video camera, or mirror.

1. Why did you apply for this job?
2. What are your short-term and long-term goals?
3. What do you expect to be doing five years from now?
4. What are your strengths? Areas for improvement?
5. Tell me about yourself.
6. How would other people describe you?
7. Why did you prepare for the career you did?
8. What makes you think you will be successful in business?
9. Why should we hire you?
10. Describe how well you work under pressure.
11. What has been your biggest accomplishment on the job?
12. What do you know about our firm?
13. Here's a sample problem. How would you handle it?

Another important development in employee interviewing is the **behavioural interview,** in which a candidate is asked how he or she handled a particular problem in the past. Examples of behavioural interview questions: "Describe a time when you didn't meet a deadline." "Tell me how you dealt with an angry customer. What was the problem and what was the outcome?"[17]

Becoming a skillful interviewee requires practice. You can acquire this practice as you go through the job-finding process. In addition, you can rehearse simulated job interviews with friends and other students. Practise answering the questions posed in Exhibit 14-6. You might also think of several questions you would not like to be asked and develop answers for them.

Videotaping the practice interviews is especially helpful because it provides feedback on how you handled yourself. In watching the replay, pay particular attention to your spoken and nonverbal communication skills. Then make adjustments as needed.

Suggestions for Performing Well in the Interview

A general guide for performing well in the job interview is to present a positive but accurate picture of yourself. Your chances of performing well in a job increase if you are suited for the job. Tricking a prospective employer into hiring you when you are not qualified is therefore self-defeating in terms of your career. The suggestions presented next will help you create a professional impact.

1. *Prepare in advance*. Be familiar with pertinent details about your background, including your employment history. Bring to the interview your social insurance number, driver's licence, résumé, and the names of references.[18] Prepare a statement in your mind of your uniqueness—what differentiates you from other job candidates. Sometimes the uniqueness is not strictly job related, such as being a champion figure skater. Being prepared in advance also means finding as much information about the company as you can. Many interviewers are impressed when candidates have thoroughly researched the company and can readily answer questions about the company such as products, locations, mission statement, and history of growth. Check if the company has a website and learn as much as you can about the company prior to the interview.
2. *Dress appropriately*. So much emphasis is placed on dressing well for job interviews that some people overdress. Instead of looking businesslike, they appear to be dressed for a wedding or a funeral. The safest tactic is to wear moderately conservative business attire when applying for most positions. Another important principle is to gear your dress somewhat to the type of prospective employer. If you have a job interview with an employer where sports attire is worn to the office regularly, dress more casually. Recognize also that dress standards have more latitude than in the past. If you are asked to wear business casual clothing to the interview, accept the suggestion.
3. *Focus on important job factors*. Inexperienced job candidates often ask questions about noncontroversial topics such as paid holidays, benefits, and company-sponsored social activities. All these topics may be important to you, but explore them after the basic issue—the nature of the job—has been discussed. In this way, you will project a more professional image.
4. *Be ready for a frank discussion of your strengths and areas for improvement*. Almost every personnel interviewer and many hiring supervisors will ask you to discuss your strengths and areas for improvement (weaknesses). Everyone has weaknesses, or at least needs to improve in certain areas. To deny them is to appear uninsightful or defensive. However, you may not want to reveal weaknesses that are unrelated to the job (such as recurring nightmares or fear of swimming). A mildly evasive approach is to emphasize weaknesses that could be interpreted as strengths. A case in point: "Sometimes I'm too impatient when I see others do sloppy work."
5. *Do not knock former employers*. To justify looking for a new position, or having left a position in the past, job candidates often make negative statements about former employers. Employer-bashing makes one appear unprofessional. Take a positive approach by explaining what went wrong, such as a change in your job that left you without the opportunity to use the skills you were hired for.
6. *Ask a few good questions*. An intelligent interviewee asks a few good questions. An employment specialist for managers said, "The best way to impress somebody on

an interview is to ask intelligent questions."[19] Here are a few questions worth considering:

a. If hired, what kind of work would I actually be doing?
b. What would I have to accomplish in this job to be considered an outstanding performer?

7. *Let the interviewer introduce the topic of compensation.* Often the interviewer will specify the starting salary and benefits to the interviewee, allowing little room for questioning. If asked what starting salary you are looking for, mention a realistic salary range—one that makes you appear neither desperate nor greedy. If the interviewer does not mention salary, toward the end of the interview ask a question such as, "By the way, what is the starting salary for this position?"
8. *Smile and exhibit a positive attitude.* People who smile during job interviews are more likely to receive a job offer.[20] It is also important to express a positive attitude in other ways, such as agreeing with the interviewer and being impressed with facts about the company. If you want the job, toward the conclusion of the interview explain why you see a good fit between your qualifications and those demanded by the job. For example, "The way I see it, this job calls for somebody who is really devoted to improving customer service. That's me. I love to take good care of customers." Smiling also helps you appear relaxed.
9. *Emphasize how your skills can benefit the employer.* To repeat, an effective job-getting tactic is to explain to a prospective employer what you think you can do to help the company. Look for opportunities to make **skill-benefit statements**, brief explanations of how your skills can benefit the company.[21] Preparing these skill-benefit statements requires considerable self-examination. Practice is required to make the statements smoothly and confidently without appearing pompous or arrogant.
10. *Ask for the job and follow through.* If you want the job in question, be assertive. Make a statement such as, "I'm really interested. What is the next step in the process? Is there any other information I could submit that would help you complete your evaluation of me?" Part of asking for the job is to follow through. Mail a follow-up letter or send an email message within three working days after the interview. Even if you decide not to take the job, a brief thank-you letter is advisable. You may conceivably have contact with that firm in the future. A sample follow-up letter is shown in Exhibit 14-7 on page 358.

A final note here about job finding is to avoid widely practised tactics that disqualify candidates. Executive coach and corporate trainer Jim Pawiak spoke to a panel of HR specialists and hiring managers on how not to get a job. His findings encompass much wisdom.

> Being rude to the receptionist or administrative assistant, "cute" email account names (e.g., babygirl44@, and bookworm@); busy signals (use voice mail rather than an answering machine); taking a call waiting interruption while talking with an employer; smelling like tobacco smoke, wearing perfume or aftershave lotion when interviewing; the dead-fish handshake; not making eye contact; not asking questions; not knowing anything—asking anything about the company; not saying "Thank you" at the end of the interview.[22] (Also, complaints are surfacing of job candidates who receive cell-phone calls while being interviewed.)

Exhibit 14-7
Sample Follow-up Letter

Date of Writing Letter
27 Buttercup Lane
Toronto Ontario M6P 2N5
Mr. Bart Bertrand
Phone/Fax (416) 658-1000
President jj@igs.net
South View Dodge
258 Princess Blvd.
Toronto Ontario M1V 2P1

Dear Mr. Bertrand:

Thank you for my recent chance to discuss the assistant service manager position with you and Mr. Ralph Alexander. It was illuminating to see what a busy, successful operation you have.

I was impressed with the amount of responsibility the assistant service manager would have at your dealership. The job sounds exciting and I would like to be part of the growth of the dealership. I realize the work would be hard and the hours would be long, but that's the kind of challenge I want and can handle.

My understanding is that my background is generally favourable for the position, but that you would prefer more direct experience in managing a service operation. Since the car repair and service business is in my blood, I know I will be a fast learner. You said that about two weeks would be needed to interview additional candidates. Count on me to start work on July 1, should you extend me a job offer.

Sincerely,

Jane Jenkins

PSYCHOLOGICAL TESTING AND THE PHYSICAL EXAMINATION

Psychological testing and the physical examination are two further challenges facing many job candidates who have made it through the interview. Psychological tests (sometimes called personnel or employment testing) can help both the employer and job candidate find a mutually satisfactory fit. The good fit is most likely to be found when the tests are accurate and fair and the candidate answers them accurately. It is best to take these tests with a positive, relaxed attitude. Being physically and mentally well rested is the best preparation. Specialists who develop the test profiles of successful candidates are not expecting an incredible display of human attributes. Also, psychological tests and the physical exam are but two factors in making hiring decisions.

Psychological Testing

Five types of personnel and psychological tests are widely used: achievement, aptitude, personality, interest, and integrity (honesty) tests. The fifth category is used particularly in the retail and financial services industry. A recent trend in psychological testing is for the tests and application forms to be done by computer. The computer screening is popular with candidates and with employers because of its efficiency and apparent fairness. Test results, along with recommendations for hiring or not hiring, can be sent back to a client within ten minutes. Information about good applicants is readily transferred from one company location to another, such as between Blockbuster Video branches.[23]

1. *Achievement tests* sample and measure the applicant's knowledge and skills. They require applicants to demonstrate their competency on job tasks or related subjects. A person applying for a position as a paralegal might be given a test about real-estate and matrimonial law. Giving an applicant a sample of work to perform, such as making a sales pitch, is based on the same idea as a paper-and-pencil or computerized achievement test.
2. *Aptitude tests* measure an applicant's capacity or potential for performing satisfactorily on the job, given sufficient training. Mental-ability tests are the best-known variety of aptitude test. They measure ability to solve problems and learn new material. Mental-ability tests measure such specific aptitudes as verbal reasoning, numerical reasoning, and spatial relations (visualizing three dimensions). Scores on mental-ability tests are related to success in most jobs in which problem-solving ability is important.
3. *Personality tests* measure personal traits and characteristics that could be related to job performance. Among the many personal characteristics measured by these tests are conscientiousness, self-confidence, and emotional maturity. A more recent development is to measure emotional intelligence, including such factors as impulse control and optimism. Critics of personality tests are concerned that these tests invade privacy and are too imprecise to be useful.
4. *Interest tests* measure preferences for engaging in certain activities such as mechanical, numerical, literary, or managerial work. They also measure a person's interest in specific occupations such as accountant, social worker, or sales representative. Interest tests are designed to indicate whether a person would enjoy a particular activity or occupation. They do not attempt, however, to measure a person's aptitude for that activity or occupation. The Strong Interest Inventory described in Chapter 13 is an interest test.
5. *Integrity (honesty) tests* are of two types: paper-and-pencil and polygraph tests (often referred to as lie-detector tests). Paper-and-pencil honesty tests ask people questions that directly or indirectly measure their tendency not to tell the truth. A direct question would be, "Should an employee be disciplined for stealing ten dollars' worth of supplies from the company?" (A dishonest person would answer no.) An indirect question would be, "Do you read the editorial page of the local newspaper every day?" (Only a dishonest person would answer yes. Almost nobody can claim a perfect record in this regard.)[24]

   Polygraphs record a person's internal physiological responses, such as heart rate and breathing rate, in response to questions. The level of emotional response to neutral questions is compared with responses to key questions. In Canada, polygraph tests might be used as a screening device by law enforcement agencies and some other employers when selecting candidates for particularly sensitive jobs.

However, their use has been challenged on ethical grounds, and it should be noted that they are illegal in certain provinces, including Ontario.

The Physical Examination and Drug Testing

Employment-related medical examinations and drug testing are areas of controversy in many provinces. The Canadian Human Rights Commission and some provincial commissions have issued policies on medical examinations and drug and alcohol testing. Medical examinations should only be administered after a conditional offer of employment has been made, preferably in writing. Employment-related medical examinations are to be limited to determining the individual's ability to perform the essential duties of the job. The employer must disclose to the potential employee the use of medical examinations and drug testing prior to hiring.

MANAGING THE DOWNSIDE OF CONDUCTING A JOB SEARCH

For some people, finding a job is an easy task, particularly if they happen to be in a field in which the number of positions available is far greater than the number of job applicants. For many other people, the job search can be a mixed experience: some joy and some frustration. This is especially frustrating for workers who have been laid off after working in a job for many years. Much rejection can be expected. Few people are wanted by every employer. You have to learn to take rejection in stride, remembering that a good deal of personal chemistry is involved in being hired. Suppose the person doing the hiring likes you personally. You then have a much greater chance of being hired for the position than does another individual of comparable merit. If the interviewer dislikes you, the reverse is true.

Rejection and rudeness are frequently encountered in job hunting, which can easily create discouragement. Keep pressure on yourself to avoid slowing down because you are discouraged. Research documents the fact that assertive behaviours are associated with success in finding a job, even when the job hunter has average qualifications.[25] One study showed that unemployed people who maintain good control of their motivation through such means as goal setting are more likely to keep up the intensity of their job search. Also, job seekers who maintain control over anxiety and worry are more likely to keep trying.[26] Each lead processed takes you one step closer to finding work. And all you are looking for is one job.

SUMMARY

Job-search skills may be used at different stages in your career. The job search begins with a reasonably flexible statement of the type of job you are seeking (your job objective). Knowing what type of organization you would prefer to work for will help focus your job search. The qualifications listed in Self-Assessment Quiz 14-1 are frequently sought by employers; they should be kept in mind during the job search.

A systematic job search uses many job-finding methods, including networking (contacts and referrals); the internet; an unsolicited letter campaign; a telesearch; placement offices, employment agencies, and career fairs; help-wanted ads, and online social networking. The number of job offerings on the internet continues to increase.

A cover letter should accompany a résumé and application form. An attention-getting cover letter should explain why you are applying for a particular position and identify your potential contribution to the employer. A T-form cover letter systematically outlines how the applicant's qualifications match up against the job requirements posted in the position announcement. The T-form approach gives the reader a tabular outline of how the applicant's background fits the position description.

The major purpose of a résumé is to help you obtain a job interview. There is no one best way to prepare a résumé. Effective résumés are straightforward, factual presentations of a person's experiences, skills, and accomplishments.

The chronological résumé presents your work experience, education, and interests, along with your accomplishments, in reverse chronological order. The functional résumé organizes your skills and accomplishments into the functions or tasks that support the job you are seeking. The targeted résumé focuses on a specific job or position, and presents only information that supports the target. A distinguishing feature of an electronic résumé is that it contains keywords that fit the requirements of a keyword search. Keywords should be placed right under the information identifying the individual.

The job objective on your résumé should describe the position you are seeking now or in the short-term future. When your credentials do not closely fit the position description, emphasize on your résumé those skills from other experiences that would help you succeed in the position. Creative-style résumés bring favourable attention to your credentials but should be used with discretion.

Rehearse being interviewed and then present yourself favourably but accurately in the interview. Specific interview suggestions include these: (1) prepare in advance; (2) dress appropriately; (3) focus on important job factors; (4) be prepared to discuss your strengths and areas for improvement; (5) do not knock former employers; (6) ask good questions; (7) let the interviewer introduce the topic of compensation; (8) smile and exhibit a positive attitude; (9) emphasize how your skills can benefit the employer; and (10) ask for the job and follow through.

Psychological testing may be part of the employment process, with five types of tests being widely used: achievement, aptitude, personality, interest, and integrity (or honesty) tests. The physical exam, including possible drug testing (a very controversial area), is another key step on the way to being hired.

Conducting a job campaign is typically inefficient but ultimately effective. Follow up every lead, and try not to take rejection and rudeness personally.

QUESTIONS AND ACTIVITIES

1. During times when there is a shortage of skilled workers, why is it still important to study how to conduct a job campaign?
2. Does it seem that most employers have unrealistic expectations of job candidates?
3. Which job-hunting technique is used most frequently by people you know? What accounts for its popularity?

4. How has the internet changed job finding?
5. What are some drawbacks of using the internet for employment opportunities?
6. Some job seekers send email messages instead of postal mail when conducting an unsolicited letter campaign. Identify an advantage and disadvantage of using email messages for this purpose.
7. What special challenges do voice-mail systems present for job seekers?
8. Given that people have so many different opinions about what makes an effective résumé, what kind of résumé should a job seeker prepare?
9. Many employers use telephone screening interviews before inviting a candidate for an in-person interview. What special communication challenges does this present for the job seeker?
10. Assume you are being interviewed for a position you really want, and the interviewer asks you several questions that could be considered in violation of employment law. How would you respond to his or her questions?

INTERNET SKILL BUILDER

How Much Am I in Demand?

So many job boards exist on the internet that conducting a Web-based job search can be baffling. A direct approach is to visit a site and investigate it. Go to *Workopolis* (Workopolis.com) and enter three specific job titles of interest to you. You will be directed to loads of job opportunities closely matching the job titles you entered. It may be helpful to enter variations of the same job title, such as both "office manager" and "administrative assistant." Your assignment is to identify five jobs for which you appear to be qualified. Even if you have no interest in conducting a job search, it is informative to be aware of job opportunities in your field.

Seek answers to the following questions:

1. Do I appear to have the qualifications for the type of job I am seeking?
2. Is there a particular geographic area where the job or jobs I want are available?
3. How good are opportunities in my chosen field?

Log on to the **Companion Website** at **www.pearsoncanada.ca/dubrin** to access additional resources for this chapter.

CASE STUDY 14-1 HUMAN RELATIONS

Why Isn't My Résumé Getting Results?

Kaled Naqui was working in the family business as a manufacturing technician while he attended career school. Although he got along well with his family members, Kaled wanted to find employment elsewhere so he could build a career on his own. Kaled's job objective was a position in industrial sales. He compiled a long list of prospective employers. He developed the list from personal contacts, classified ads in newspapers, and job openings on the internet. Kaled clipped a business card with a brief handwritten note to each résumé. The note usually said something to the effect, "Job sounds great. Let's schedule an interview at your convenience." The résumé is shown in Exhibit 14-8.

After mailing out 100 résumés and emailing an additional 100 copies, Kaled still did not have an interview. He asked his uncle and mentor, the owner of the family business, "Why isn't my résumé getting results?"

Questions

1. What suggestions can you make to Kaled for improving his résumé? Or, does it require improvement?
2. What is your evaluation of Kaled's approach to creating a cover letter?

Exhibit 14-8
Résumé of Kaled Naqui

Kaled Naqui
275 Birdwhistle Lane
Toronto Ontario M2M 2M2
(416) 614-7512 (Please call after 7 p.m. weekday nights)
Kaled@naqui.com

Objective

Long-range goal is Vice President of sales of major corporation. For now, industrial sales representative paid by salary and commission.

Job Experience

Five years experience in Naqui Industries as manufacturing technician, tool crib attendant, shipper, and floor sweeper. Voted as "employee of the month" twice.

Two years of experience in newspaper delivery business. Distributed newspapers door to door, responsible for accounts receivable and development of new business in my territory.

Education

George Brown College of Applied Arts and Technology, business administration major with manufacturing technology minor. Expect degree in June 2001. 68% average. Took courses in sales management and selling. Received a B+ in professional selling course.

Birdwhistle Lane High School, business and technology major, 1994–1998. Graduated 45th in class of 125. 82% average.

Skills and Talents

Good knowledge of manufacturing equipment; friends say I'm a born leader; have been offered supervisory position in Naqui Industries; real go getter.

References

OK to contact present employer except for my immediate supervisor, Jill Baxter, with whom I have a personality clash.

CASE STUDY 14-2 HUMAN RELATIONS

Stacy Sings the Blues

Stacy, age 27, was proud to be an architectural technician student. She liked the idea of combining her interest in art with being part of something important. As she reasoned, "I will be helping architects erect skyscrapers, small office buildings, and houses that will last for a century. I will help provide beautiful environments in which fellow human beings will work and live."

To help fund her schooling and pay her living expenses while at career school, Stacy tended bar at the Big Boar Inn, a trendy bar frequented mostly by young people. Stacy had worked on and off as a bartender before attending career school. For several years after high school, she travelled around the world finding work at bars and resorts wherever she could. During her travels, Stacy made notes of the designs of buildings and prepared many sketches of her own ideas about building designs. She knew that she wanted someday to work in the field of architecture.

Several months before graduation, Stacy's father and several friends asked her when she would be starting her job hunt. Stacy explained that she was too busy finishing her studies at school and working at the Big Boar to get seriously involved in a job hunt. "After graduation in May, I'll take a couple of months to unwind and then begin searching for a job. Besides, most architectural firms don't get serious about hiring recent graduates until after Labor Day." Stacy's dad thought she was being a little laid back in her job-hunting approach but did not think he was in a position to tell her what to do.

After graduation, Stacy continued to work at the Big Boar about 25 hours per week. She spent a lot of time at the beach and developed a deep skin tan. One day she ran into her mentor, Professor Bill Byron, at the supermarket. Byron asked Stacy how her job search was going.

Stacy replied, "I will be getting to working on my résumé soon. With the job market for architectural technicians being soft right now, I didn't see any need to rush. Would it be OK to drop by your office to get some advice on my résumé?"

Stacy met with Mr. Byron a week later. He gave Stacy a few suggestions about résumé construction and also noted that her portfolio of architectural renderings needed more work before she could present the portfolio to prospective employers. Stacy then decided to sharpen her portfolio before beginning her job search.

At the urging of a friend, Stacy bought a few out-of-town newspapers to search the classified sections. She chose just Vancouver as she thought she might like the more temperate climate. Stacy spotted a total of three openings for architectural technicians and sent a résumé and cover letter to the addresses indicated in the ads.

Two months passed, and Stacy had not heard back from any of the firms to which she sent letters. Stacy's next approach was to give a copy of her résumé to a friend who sold furniture to an architectural firm in Halifax. The friend said he would give the résumé to a personal contact he had at the firm.

During a work break at the Big Boar, a server asked Stacy how her job hunt was proceeding. Stacy replied, "Right now, I'm just sitting back and waiting to hear. There's not much else I can do."

Questions

1. What is your evaluation of the effectiveness of Stacy's job campaign?
2. What recommendations can you make to Stacy to help her find a position as an architectural technician?
3. You be the career counsellor. Does Stacy really want to leave her job as a bartender at the Big Boar Inn and become an architectural technician?

Chapter 15
Developing Good Work Habits

Learning Outcomes

After studying the information and doing the exercises in this chapter, you should be able to

- appreciate the importance of good work habits and time management;
- decrease any tendencies you might have toward procrastination;
- develop attitudes and values that will help you become more productive;
- develop skills and techniques that will help you become more productive;
- overcome time-wasting practices.

Annick Baudot-Mohageg says she often had trouble saying no to her bosses and colleagues at Adobe Systems, which is probably why her workweek typically averaged 45 to 50 hours. Then her company cut its workforce, and Baudot-Mohageg, a senior marketing manager, found herself feeling even more overworked, with little energy left for her husband, Michael, and son, Lucas.

That was more than one year ago. She says she is feeling much less frazzled these days, having participated during the past year in a mentoring program sponsored by Adobe, which is based in San Jose, California. The program—intended, among other things, to help budget time—included monthly workshops with other women executives and one-to-one meetings with her own mentor from outside Adobe.

Baudot-Mohageg, 40, says she has learned to focus on details of projects that are relevant only to her, rather than trying to do other people's work for them, and to conduct staff meetings more efficiently. As a result, she estimates, her productivity has increased 50 percent. She says she also has more time to spend with her family. "Mentoring helped me set objectives in life," she said.[1]

As the story presented illustrates, learning to be productive, including more effective budgeting of time, is an important part of holding down an executive position as well as having time left over for personal life. Because good work habits and time management (including concentrating carefully on the task at hand) improve productivity, they contribute to success in business. **Work habits** refer to a person's characteristic approach to work, including such things as organization, priority setting, and handling of paperwork and email. Poor work habits also interfere with social life because of such problems as cancelled social engagements or missed time with family.

People with good work habits tend to achieve greater career success and have more time to invest in their personal lives. They also enjoy their personal lives more because they are not preoccupied with unfinished tasks. Effective work habits are also beneficial because they eliminate a major stressor—the feeling of having very little or no control over your life. Being in control also leads to a relaxed and confident approach to work.

Good work habits and time management are more important than ever because of today's emphasis on **productivity**, the amount of quality work accomplished in relation to the resources consumed. Good work habits and time management lead to high personal productivity.

The goal of this chapter is to help you become a more productive person who is still flexible. Someone who develops good work habits is not someone who becomes so obsessed with time and so rigid that he or she makes other people feel uncomfortable. Ideally, a person should be well organized yet still flexible.

Information about becoming more productive is organized here into four related categories. One is overcoming procrastination, a problem that plagues almost everybody to some extent. The second is developing attitudes and values that foster productivity. The third category is the lengthiest: developing skills and techniques that lead to personal productivity. The fourth category deals with overcoming time wasters.

DEALING WITH PROCRASTINATION

The leading cause of poor productivity and career self-sabotage is **procrastination**, delaying a task for an invalid or weak reason. Procrastination is the major work-habit problem for most workers and students. The presence of computers at work increases the risk of procrastination, which is why so many companies restrict access to such sites as Facebook and instant messaging. Unproductive people are the biggest procrastinators, but even productive people have problems with procrastination. Think of all the people who fail to file their income tax returns on time even when the government owes them money.

Why People Procrastinate

People procrastinate for many different reasons. One is that we perceive the task to be done (such as quitting a job) as unpleasant. Another reason we procrastinate is that we find the job facing us to be overwhelming, such as starting a major essay. To avoid an overwhelming or taxing task, some people flood their workday with small, easy-to-do tasks. As a result, these people do not appear to be procrastinators on the surface.[2] Another major cause of procrastination is a fear of the consequences of our actions.

One possible consequence is a negative evaluation of your work. For example, if you delay preparing a report for your boss or instructor, that person cannot criticize its quality. Bad news is another negative consequence that procrastination can sometimes delay. If you think your personal computer needs a new disk drive, delaying a trip to the computer store means you will not have to hear the diagnosis: "Your disk drive needs replacement. We can do the job for about $300."

Another reason some people procrastinate is that they **fear success**. People sometimes believe that if they succeed at an important task, they will be asked to take on more responsibility in the future. They dread this possibility. Some students have been known to put off completing their degree requirements to avoid taking on the responsibility of a full-time position.

People frequently put off tasks that do not appear to offer a meaningful reward. Suppose you decide that your hard drive needs a thorough updating, including deleting inactive files. Even if you know this task should be done, the accomplishment of updated files might not be a particularly meaningful reward.

Many people often procrastinate as a way of rebelling against being controlled. Procrastination, used in this way, is a means of defying unwarranted authority.[3] Rather than submit to authority, a person might tell himself, "Nobody is going to tell me when I should get a report done. I'll do it when I'm good and ready."

A curious reason for procrastination is to achieve the stimulation and excitement that stems from rushing to meet a deadline.[4] Some people, for example, enjoy fighting their way through traffic or running through an airline terminal so they can make an appointment or airplane flight barely on time. They appear to enjoy the rush of adrenaline, endorphins, and other hormones associated with hurrying.

Finally, some people procrastinate because they are perfectionists. They attempt to perfect a project before submitting it. As a result, the person procrastinates, not in beginning a project, but in letting go of it. When asked, "Have you finished that project?" the perfectionist replies, "No, there are a few small details that still need to be worked out." Being a perfectionist can also block starting new projects because the perfectionist will often want to keep working on the present project. Perfectionism comes in degrees: slight perfectionists may simply be extremely conscientious; heavy-duty perfectionists may be almost stalled in their actions. Human Relations Self-Assessment Quiz 15-1 gives you an opportunity to measure your degree of perfectionism.

Techniques for Reducing Procrastination

To overcome, or at least minimize, procrastination we recommend a number of specific tactics. A general approach, however, is simply to be aware that procrastination is a major drain on productivity. Being aware of the problem will remind you to take corrective action in many situations. When your accomplishment level is low, you might ask yourself, "Am I procrastinating on anything of significance?" The Canada Today feature that appears later in this chapter also offers some valuable tips on reducing your tendencies toward procrastination.

Calculate the Cost of Procrastination You can reduce procrastination by calculating its cost.[5] One example is that you might lose out on obtaining a high-paying job

Human Relations Self-Assessment

QUIZ 15-1 Tendency toward Perfectionism?

Many perfectionists hold some of the following behaviours and attitudes. To help understand your tendencies toward perfectionism, rate how strongly you agree with each of the statements below on a scale of 0 to 4: 0=disagree strongly; 1=disagree; 2=neutral; 3=agree; 4=strongly agree.

1. Many people have told me that I am a perfectionist.	0	1	2	3	4
2. I often correct the speech of others.	0	1	2	3	4
3. It takes me a long time to write an email because I keep checking and rechecking my writing.	0	1	2	3	4
4. I often criticize the colour combinations my friends are wearing.	0	1	2	3	4
5. When I purchase food at a supermarket, I usually look at the expiration date so I can purchase the freshest.	0	1	2	3	4
6. I can't stand when people use the term "remote" instead of "remote control."	0	1	2	3	4
7. If a company representative asked me "What is your *social?* " I would reply something like, "Do you mean my *Social Insurance?*"	0	1	2	3	4
8. I hate to see dust on furniture.	0	1	2	3	4
9. I like the Martha Stewart idea of having every decoration in the home just right.	0	1	2	3	4
10. I never put a map back in the glove compartment until it is folder just right.	0	1	2	3	4
11. Once an eraser on a pencil of mine becomes hard and useless, I throw the pencil away.	0	1	2	3	4
12. I adjust all my watches and clocks so they show exactly the same time.	0	1	2	3	4
13. It bothers me that clocks on personal computers are often wrong by a few minutes.	0	1	2	3	4
14. I clean the keyboard on my computer at least once a week.	0	1	2	3	4
15. I organize my email messages and computer documents into many different, clearly labelled files.	0	1	2	3	4
16. You won't find old coffee cups or soft-drink containers on my desk.	0	1	2	3	4
17. I rarely start a new project or assignment until I have completed my present project or assignment.	0	1	2	3	4
18. It is very difficult for me to concentrate when my work area is disorganized.	0	1	2	3	4
19. Cobwebs in chandeliers and other lighting fixtures bug me.	0	1	2	3	4
20. It takes me a long time to make a purchase such as a digital camera because I keep studying the features on various models.	0	1	2	3	4
21. When I balance my checkbook, it usually comes out right within a few dollars.	0	1	2	3	4
22. I carry enough small coins and dollar bills with me so when I shop I can pay the exact amount without requiring change.	0	1	2	3	4

(*continued*)

23. I throw out any underwear or T-shirts that have even the smallest holes or tears.	0	1	2	3	4
24. I become upset with myself if I make a mistake.	0	1	2	3	4
25. When a fingernail of mine is broken or chipped, I fix it as soon as possible.	0	1	2	3	4
26. I am carefully groomed whenever I leave my home.	0	1	2	3	4
27. When I notice packaged goods or cans on the floor in a supermarket, I will often place them back on the shelf.	0	1	2	3	4
28. I think that carrying around antibacterial cleaner for the hands is an excellent idea.	0	1	2	3	4
29. If I am with a friend, and he or she has a loose hair on the shoulder, I will remove it without asking.	0	1	2	3	4
30. I know that I am a perfectionist.	0	1	2	3	4

Scoring and Interpretation

91 or over You have strong perfectionist tendencies to the point that it could interfere with your taking quick action when necessary. Also, you may annoy many people with your perfectionism.

61–90 Moderate degree of perfectionism that could lead you to produce high-quality work and be a dependable person.

31–60 Mild degree of perfectionism. You might be a perfectionist in some situations quite important to you but not in others.

0–30 Not a perfectionist. You might be too casual about getting things done right, meeting deadlines, and being aware of details.

you really want by not having your résumé and cover letter ready on time. Your cost of procrastination would include the difference in salary between the job you do find and the one you really wanted. Another cost would be the loss of potential job satisfaction.

Counterattack Forcing yourself to do something overwhelming, frightening, or uncomfortable helps to prove that the task was not as bad as initially perceived.[6] Let's say you've accepted a new position but have not yet resigned from your present one because resigning seems so uncomfortable. Set up a specific time to call your manager, or his or her assistant, to schedule an appointment. Force yourself further to show up for the resignation appointment. After you break the ice with the statement, "I have something important to tell you," the task will be much easier.

Jump-Start Yourself You can often get momentum going on a project by giving yourself a tiny assignment to get started. One way to get momentum going on an unpleasant or overwhelming task is to set aside a specific time to work on it. If you have to write a report on a subject you dislike, you might set aside Saturday from 3 p.m. to 5 p.m. as your time to first attack the project. If your procrastination problem is particularly intense, giving yourself even a five-minute task, such as starting a new file, might help you gain momentum. After five minutes, decide whether to continue for another five minutes. The five-minute chunks will help you focus your energy.

Peck Away at an Overwhelming Task. Assume that you have a major project that does not have to be accomplished in a hurry. A good way of minimizing procrastination is to peck away at the project in 15- to 30-minute bits of time. Bit by bit the project will get down to manageable size and therefore not seem so overwhelming.

A related way of pecking away at an overwhelming task is to subdivide it into smaller units. For instance, you might break down moving into a series of tasks such as filing change-of-address notices, locating a mover, and packing books. Pecking away can sometimes be achieved by setting aside as little as five minutes to work on a seemingly overwhelming task. When the five minutes are up, either work five more minutes on the task or reschedule the activity for sometime soon.

Motivate Yourself with Rewards and Punishments. Give yourself a pleasant reward soon after you accomplish a task you would ordinarily procrastinate about. You might, for example, jog through the woods after having completed a tough take-home exam. The second part of this tactic is to punish yourself if you have engaged in serious procrastination. How about eating only oatmeal for five days?

Follow the WIFO Principle. Personal-effectiveness coach Shale Paul recommends that you use the technique of *worst in, first out* for dealing with unpleasant tasks you would prefer to avoid. After you finally get the task done, Paul says, "Chances are, you'll find that you spent nearly as much time worrying and rescheduling it as you did actually doing it." If the task sits high enough on your list of priorities, simply get it done and out of the way.[7] A related motivational principle is that, after completing the unpleasant task, moving on to a more pleasant (or less unpleasant) task functions as a reward.

Make a Commitment to Other People. Put pressure on yourself to get something done on time by making it a commitment to one or more other people. You might announce to co-workers that you are going to get a project of mutual concern completed by a certain date. If you fail to meet this date, you may feel embarrassed.

Express a More Positive Attitude about Your Intentions. Expressing a more positive attitude can often lead to change in behaviour. If you choose words that express a serious intention to complete an activity, you are more likely to follow through than if you choose more uncertain words. If a co-worker says, "I *might* get you the information you need by next Friday," you probably won't be surprised if you don't receive the information by then. In contrast, if your co-worker says, "I *will*. . . Friday," there is less likelihood the person will procrastinate. Psychologist Linda Sapadin believes that you are less likely to procrastinate if you change your "wish" to "will," your "like to" to "try to," and your "have to" to "want to."[8]

DEVELOPING THE PROPER ATTITUDES AND VALUES

Developing good work habits and time-management practices is often a matter of developing proper attitudes toward work and time. For instance, if you think that your job is important and that time is valuable, you will be on your way toward developing good work habits. In this section, we describe a group of attitudes and values that can help improve your productivity through better use of time and improved work habits.

X Jan 17

Develop a Mission, Goals, and a Strong Work Ethic

A mission, or general purpose in life, propels you toward being productive. Assume that a person says, "My mission is to become an outstanding professional in my career and to be a loving, constructive parent." The mission serves as a compass to direct your activities, such as being well-organized in order to attain a favourable performance appraisal.

Goals are more specific than mission statements. The goals support the mission statement, but the effect is the same. Stephen Covey, a popularizer of time management techniques, expresses the importance of both a mission and goals in his phrase "Begin with the end in mind." He recommends you develop your mission statement by first thinking about what people who know you well would say at your funeral if you died three years from now. Also, list your various roles in life such as spouse, child, family member, professional, and soccer player. For each role, think of one or two major lifetime goals you have in that area. Then develop a brief mission statement describing your life's purpose that incorporates these goals.[9]

Say that your mission is to become an outstanding professional person. Your goals to support that mission might include achieving advanced certification in your field, becoming an officer in a professional organization, and making large donations to charity. When you're deciding how to spend your time each day, give top priority to goals related to your mission.

Closely related to establishing a mission and goals is developing a strong work ethic, as described in Chapter 12. Developing a strong work ethic may lead to even higher productivity than goal setting alone. For example, a goal of earning a high income might lead to some good work habits but not necessarily a high commitment to quality.

Value Good Attendance and Punctuality

On the job, in school, or in personal life, good attendance and punctuality are essential for developing a good reputation. Also, you cannot accomplish much if you are not present. Poor attendance and consistent lateness are the most frequent reasons for employee discipline. Furthermore, many managers interpret high absenteeism and lateness as signs of emotional immaturity.

An important myth about attendance and punctuality should be challenged early in your career. One is that a certain number of sick days are owed an employee. Some employees who have not used up their sick days will find reasons to be sick at the end of the year.

The causes of chronic lateness follow those of the causes of procrastination. Time-management specialist Diane DeLonzor says that the motivations are often subconscious, related to personality characteristics such as lack of self-control and a desire for thrill seeking. Some people are drawn to the adrenaline rush of that last minute sprint to the meeting (or class), while others receive an ego boost from over-scheduling and filling each moment with activity. Trying to get one more thing done before leaving for an appointment will often lead to being late. Keeping a time log (as described later in the chapter) can help control lateness because the result can be a more accurate estimation of the amount of time necessary to complete various activities. For example, if it takes a person 45 minutes to commute to work, he or she must leave the residence about 55 minutes before an important meeting.[10]

Value Your Time

People who place a high value on their time are propelled into making good use of time. If a person believes that his or her time is valuable, it will be difficult to engage that person in idle conversation during working hours. Valuing your time can also apply to personal life. The yield from clipping or gathering grocery coupons is an average of $9 per hour—assuming that purchasing national brands is important to you. Would a busy professional person, therefore, be better off clipping and gathering coupons or engaging in self-development for the same amount of time? Being committed to a mission and goals is an automatic way of making good use of time.

Value Neatness, Orderliness, and Speed

Neatness, orderliness, and speed are important contributors to workplace productivity and therefore should be highly valued. An orderly desk, file cabinet, or work area does not inevitably signify an orderly mind. Yet orderliness does help most people become more productive. Less time is wasted and less energy is expended if you do not have to hunt for missing information. Knowing where information is and what information you have available is a way of being in control of your job. When your job gets out of control, you are probably working at less than peak efficiency.

Being neat and orderly helps you achieve good performance. Frequently breaking your concentration for such matters as finding a memo or a computer manual inhibits high performance.

Neatness is linked to working rapidly because clutter and searching for misplaced items consumes time. Employers emphasize speed today to remain competitive in such matters as serving customers promptly and bringing new products and services to the market. Speed is widely considered to be a competitive advantage. In the words of organizational consultant Price Pritchett:

> So you need to operate with a strong sense of urgency. Accelerate in all aspects of your work, even if it means living with a few more ragged edges. Emphasize *action*. Don't bog down in endless preparation trying to get things perfect before you make a move. Sure, high quality is crucial, but it must come quickly. You can't sacrifice speed. Learn to fail fast, fix it, and race on.[11]

The best approach to maintaining a neat work area and enhancing speed is to convince yourself that neatness and speed are valuable. You will then search for ways to be neat and fast, such as putting back a computer manual immediately after use or making phone conversations brief. The underlying principle is that an attitude leads to a change in behaviour.

Work Smarter, Not Harder

People caught up in trying to accomplish a job often wind up working hard, but not in an imaginative way that leads to good results. Much time and energy are thus wasted. A working-smart approach also requires that you spend a few minutes carefully planning how to implement your task. An example of working smarter, not harder, is to invest a few minutes of critical thinking before launching an internet search. Think through carefully what might be the key words that will lead you to the information you need. In this way, you will minimize conducting your search with words and phrases that will lead to irrelevant information. For example, suppose you want to conduct research on back-stabbing as negative office politics. If you simply use the term back-stabbing, the search engine will direct you to such topics as street crime and medical treatment for wounds. Working smarter is to try "back-stabbing in the office."

A modern approach to working smarter is to avoid doing work that is already being accomplished in another part of the organization by using information technology designed to foster collaboration. Some programs make it easier to find out what co-workers in other parts of a far-flung company are working on, thus avoiding duplication. Company blogs can also be helpful in identifying other workers who are engaged in a similar project. For example, you might be mining data attempting to discover which customers are likely to buy a variety of products from your employer.[12] A blog might tell you that Sally in Montreal, is working on the same project. If you then collaborate, you will save lots of time—and work smarter.

Become Self-Employed Psychologically

A distinguishing characteristic of many self-employed people is that they care deeply about what they accomplish each day.[13] Most of their job activities directly or indirectly affect their financial health. Additionally, many self-employed people enjoy high job satisfaction because they have chosen work that fits their interests. Because of the factors just mentioned, the self-employed person is compelled to make good use of time. Also, the high level of job satisfaction typical of many self-employed people leads them to enjoy being productive.

If a person working for an employer regards his or her area of responsibility as self-employment, productivity may increase. To help regard employment by others as self-employment, keep this thought in mind: every employee is given some assets to manage to achieve a good return on investment. If you managed the printing and copying centre for your company, you would be expected to manage that asset profitably.

Appreciate the Importance of Rest and Relaxation

A productive attitude to maintain is that overwork can be counterproductive and lead to negative stress and burnout. Proper physical rest contributes to mental alertness and improved ability to cope with frustration. Constant attention to work or study is often inefficient. It is a normal human requirement to take enough rest breaks to allow oneself to approach work or study with a fresh perspective. Each person has to establish the right balance between work and leisure within the bounds of freedom granted by the situation. Neglecting the normal need for rest and relaxation can lead to **workaholism**, an addiction to work in which not working is an uncomfortable experience. Some types of workaholics are perfectionists who are never satisfied with their work and therefore find it difficult to leave work behind. One career counsellor notes, "Workaholics put the job before family, friends, and their own health. And even if they're spending time with their families, their mind is on work."[14] Not only is the negative type of workaholic preoccupied with work but also he or she derives relatively little satisfaction from passing time with family, friends, health, and hobbies.[15] In addition, the workaholic who is a perfectionist may become heavily focused on control, leading to rigid behaviour.

However, some people who work long and hard are classified as achievement-oriented workaholics who thrive on hard work and are usually highly productive.[16] Furthermore many people who work long and hard to be successful in their careers also intensely enjoy other activities. Warren Buffett, the legendary investor who is one of the world's richest people, carries an enormous workload. However, he is also a fanatic about bridge and regularly interrupts his workday to play bridge on the computer.

TIME-MANAGEMENT TECHNIQUES

So far we have discussed improving productivity from standpoints of dealing with procrastination and developing the right attitudes and values. Skills and techniques are also important for becoming more productive. Here we describe some well-established methods of work-habit improvement, along with several new ones. For these techniques to enhance productivity, most of them need to be incorporated in our daily lives and practised regularly. This is particularly true because many of these techniques are habits, and habits have to be programmed into the brain through repetition. The Canada Today feature (on page 377) offers some valuable tips on time management, organization, and procrastination from a well-known productivity consultant.

Clean Up and Get Organized

An excellent starting point for improving work habits and time management is to clean up your work area and arrange things neatly. Eliminate clutter by throwing out unnecessary paper and deleting computer files that will probably never be used again. The idea is to learn to simplify the work area so that there are fewer distractions and the brain can be more focused. In addition, finding important files becomes easier. According to the Delphi Group, a consultancy firm, about 15 percent of all paper handled in business becomes lost, and 30 percent of all employee's time is spent trying to find lost documents.[17] (We assume that the lost documents are both paper and electronic.)

Desktop search software such as Google's Desktop Search or Apple's Spotlight can help you find many missing documents. However, there is still a productivity advantage to having fewer obsolete documents and files in your computer including a front page with dozens of icons with similar-sounding names. Conducting an electronic search to find your expense report is one more task on your to-do list.

Getting organized includes sorting out which tasks need doing, including assignments and projects not yet completed. Getting organized can also mean sorting through the many small paper notes attached to the computer and on the wall. A major cleanup principle is, therefore, to discard anything that is no longer valuable. A suggestion worth considering is to throw out at least one item every day from the office and home—even if the item thrown out is as humble as an empty ball pen. Because new items come into the office and home almost daily, you will always have possessions left.

Plan Your Activities

The primary principle of effective time management is **planning**: deciding what you want to accomplish and what you will do to make it happen. The most elementary—and most important—planning tool is a list of tasks that need doing. Almost every successful person works from a to-do list. These lists are similar to the daily goals described in Chapter 2. Before you can compose a useful list, you need to set aside a few moments each day to sort out the tasks at hand.

Where Do You Put Your Lists? Some people dislike having small to-do lists stuck in different places. One reason is that these lists are readily lost among other papers. Many people therefore put lists on desk calendars or printed forms called *daily planners*. Software is also available to help you keep track of your activities.

How Do You Set Priorities? Faced with multiple tasks to do at the same time, it is possible to feel overwhelmed and freeze as a result. A time-tested prioritizing system is to use *A* to signify critical or essential items, *B* to signify important items, and C for the least important ones. Although an item might be regarded as a C (for example, refilling your stapler), it still has a contribution to make to your productivity and sense of well-being. Many people report that they obtain a sense of satisfaction from crossing an item, however trivial, off their list. Second, if you are at all conscientious, small undone items will come back to interfere with concentration. The key is to set priorities and follow some sort of system to assist you in accomplishing your tasks.

How Do You Schedule and Follow Through? To be effective, a to-do list must be an action tool. To convert your list into action, prepare a schedule of when you are going to do each of the things on the list. Follow through by doing things according to your schedule, checking them off as you go along.

Get Off to a Good Start

Get off to a good beginning, and you are more likely to have a successful, productive day. Start poorly, and you will be behind most of the day. According to Merrill Douglass, people who get going early tend to be in the right place at the right time more often, thus seeming to be lucky. "When you start early, you are lucky enough to get a good parking spot. You are lucky enough to avoid traffic jams. You are lucky enough to finish your job by the end of the day."[18] To get off to a good start regularly, it is important to start the day with the conscious intention of starting strong.

An effective way of getting off to a good start is to tackle the toughest task first because most people have their peak energy in the morning. (You will recall that a variation of this technique is useful in combating procrastination.) With a major task already completed, you are off to a running start on a busy workday.

Make Good Use of Office Technology

The productivity of workers has increased because of effective use of information and office technology. Used properly, most high-tech devices in the office can improve

Canada Today

Tips for Increasing Productivity with Effective Time Management

Mark Ellwood, president of Pace Productivity, Toronto, is no stranger to the problems people have in maintaining a high level of productivity through time management. In 1989, Mr. Ellwood established Pace Productivity and designed his unique TimeCorder, a time-tracking system to assist in the development of sound time-management practices. His basic idea is that productive people are organized, manage procrastination, know how to use time effectively, manage paperwork and email, and are prepared to handle workplace challenges. As a consultant, he has helped many companies increase productivity by assisting employees in these areas. Companies that have benefited from his training include Metropolitan Life, the Royal Bank of Canada, Starbucks and Nortel, to name a few. Below is a list of some of the tips that he offers on his website. A visit to this site, found at **www.GetMoreDone.com,** will be well worth your time.

Some strategies for time management:

- Stop spending time on trivia such as recording a new voice-mail message daily.
- Block off time for important activities by making an appointment with yourself and keep it.
- Don't be a slave to technology. Leave your cell phone at home. People do not have to be able to reach you all of the time!
- Have the courage to say no.

Some strategies to manage paperwork:

- Create a block of time during non-prime time to handle paperwork. Schedule it and stick to it.
- Throw away previous drafts. They serve no purpose.
- Cut back on sending memos or emails. Use a phone call instead.
- Throw out last month's magazines when the new ones arrive.

Some strategies for handling email:

- Block off times to process your email. Twice per day should be enough.
- Check your spelling and grammar before sending email.
- Don't waste time reading unsolicited email, and if you are on a mailing list that you have no interest in, reply by writing "unsubscribe" or "remove" in the comment box.
- Don't attach large files without getting permission from the recipient of the email.

Some strategies to manage procrastination (not covered above):

- Make a deadline if you are procrastinating about making a decision and share the deadline with someone else. Stick to it.
- Make a game out of unpleasant tasks. Give yourself points as you complete it.
- Reward yourself for accomplishments. But if you do not finish by your deadline, do not take the reward anyway.
- Tailor your environment for work. Close your door and tidy your desk.

Source: This information is presented with the permission of Mark Ellwood, President, Pace Productivity Inc.

productivity. Among the most productivity-enhancing devices are word processors, spreadsheets, voice mail, and personal digital assistants. How you use these devices is the key to increased productivity. A major consideration is that the time saved using office technology must be invested in productive activity to attain a true productivity advantage. Assume that you save two hours by ordering office equipment over the internet. If you invest those two hours in activity such as finding ways to save the company money, you are more productive.

Concentrate on One Key Task at a Time

Effective people have a well-developed capacity to concentrate on the problem or person facing them, however surrounded they are with potential distractions. The best results from concentration are achieved when you are so absorbed in your work that you are aware of virtually nothing else at the moment. As described in Chapter 3, this is the flow experience. Another useful by-product of concentration is that it helps reduce absent-mindedness. If you really concentrate on what you are doing, the chances that you will forget what you intended to do diminish.

Note that the suggestion here is to concentrate on one *key* task at a time. As described later in this chapter, sometimes doing two or three minor tasks at the same time can help save time. In general younger people are more effective at multitasking than much older people, yet being distracted can lower performance for both groups. The experimental psychologists Moshe Naveh-Benjamin of the University of Missouri at Columbia, and Fergus Craik of the Rotman Research Institute in Toronto tested a group of undergraduates and a group of people averaging 70 years old on a word recall task. (For example, the participants were asked to remember "waiter–kitchen" and "paper–apple.") Half of the groups were asked to follow a green asterisk moving across a computer screen while memorizing the word pairs. The students did better than the seniors, yet both groups who learned word pairs while their attention was divided performed more poorly when recalling the words.[19]

Time management consultant Stephanie Winston also points to the problems of multitasking while performing important work. She notes that the biggest work habit problem for most people is multitasking. "Successful CEOs do not multitask. They concentrate intensely on one thing at a time," she says.[20]

The accompanying Human Relations in Practice illustrates how workers might make good use of office technology and prevent multitasking from lowering productivity.

Streamline Your Work and Emphasize Important Tasks

As companies continue to operate with fewer workers than in the past, more nonproductive work must be eliminated. Remember the story about Kodak's Work-Out program? Every employee is expected to get rid of work that does not contribute to productivity or help customers. If you get rid of work that is of little consequence, you will have more time to concentrate on value-contributing tasks. Getting rid of such unproductive work is part of *re-engineering*, in which work processes are radically redesigned and simplified. Here are typical examples of work that does not add value:

- Email or paper messages that almost nobody reads
- Sending receipts and acknowledgments to people who do not need them
- Writing and mailing reports that nobody reads or needs
- Meetings that do not accomplish work, exchange important information, or improve team spirit
- Checking up frequently on the work of competent people

Human Relations in Practice

COO John Seiple Stays Focused and Emphasizes Productive Use of Office Technology

John Seiple, president and chief operating officer of North American operations at ProLogis, a Denver-based distribution-facilities company, tries to stay focused on work that helps boost the bottom line. That means keeping paperwork to a minimum to free up time with customers. To help managers do more work with less staff, Seiple's staff streamlined work processes such as the company's accounts payable system. He discourages multitasking as unproductive. He insists that cell phones and Blackberry's are turned off during meetings. "It's so we can all focus and get through our agenda in 15 or 30 minutes instead of an hour," he says.

He checks his own emails early in the morning and late at night after his children go to sleep so he doesn't spend his workday in front of a computer screen. "I want to make sure we're using technology rather than have technology use us," he says. He asks managers to spend at least half their time conferring with customers. Seiple believes it's important for executives to master how to compartmentalize tasks. "When a customer presents you with a new opportunity, you give that your total focus and stop thinking about the problem you were tackling 10 minutes before," he says. Staying focused in the moment requires discipline and some tricks. Whenever someone comes into his office to chat, Seiple moves to another chair. "That's my way of reminding myself that I'm starting a new conversation," he says.

Source: Carol Hymowitz, "Doing More with Less, Avoiding Shoddy Work and Burned-Out Staff," *The Wall Street Journal*, February 20, 2003, p. B1.

In general, to streamline or re-engineer your work, look for duplication of effort and waste for both you and your clients. An example of duplication of effort would be to routinely send people both emails and faxes covering the same topic. An example of waste would be to call a meeting for disseminating information that could easily be communicated by email.

Important (value-contributing) tasks are those in which superior performance could have a large payoff. No matter how quickly you take care of making sure that your store pays its bills on time, for example, this effort will not make your store an outstanding success. If, however, you concentrate your efforts on bringing unique and desirable merchandise into the store, this action could greatly affect your business success.

In following the *A-B-C* system, you should devote ample time to the essential tasks. You should not pay more attention than absolutely necessary to the C (trivial) items. Many people respond to this suggestion by saying, "I don't think concentrating on important tasks applies to me. My job is so filled with routine that I have no chance to work on the big breakthrough ideas." True, most jobs are filled with routine requirements. What a person can do is spend some time, perhaps even one hour a week, concentrating on tasks of potentially major significance.

Work at a Steady Pace

In most jobs, working at a steady clip pays dividends in efficiency. The spurt worker creates many problems for management. Some employees take pride in working rapidly, even when the result is a high error rate. At home, too, a steady pace is better than spurting. A spurt houseworker is one who goes into a flurry of activity every so often. An easier person to live with is someone who does his or her share of housework at an even pace throughout the year.

Another advantage of the steady-pace approach is that it accomplishes much more than putting out extra effort just once in a while. The completely steady worker would accomplish just as much the day before a holiday as on any Monday. That extra hour or so of productivity adds up substantially by the end of the year. Despite the advantages of maintaining a steady pace, some peaks and valleys in your work may be inevitable. Tax accounting firms, for example, have busy seasons.

Create Some Quiet, Uninterrupted Time

Many office workers find their days hectic, fragmented, and frustrating. Incessant interruptions make it difficult to get things done. The constant start-stop-restart pattern lengthens the time needed to get jobs done. Quiet time can reduce the type of productivity drain just described. To achieve quiet time, create an uninterrupted block of time enabling you to concentrate on your work. This could mean turning off the telephone, not accessing your email, and blocking drop-in visitors during certain times of the workday.

Quiet time is used for such essential activities as thinking, planning, getting organized, doing analytical work, writing reports, and doing creative tasks. One hour of quiet time might yield as much productive work as four hours of interrupted time.[21]

Quiet time is difficult to find in some jobs, such as those involving customer contact. An agreement has to be worked out with the manager about when and where quiet time can be taken.

Make Use of Bits of Time and Use Multitasking for Routine Work

A truly productive person makes good use of miscellaneous bits of time, both on and off the job. While waiting in line at a post office, you might update your to-do list; while waiting for an elevator, you might be able to read a brief report; and if you have finished your day's work ten minutes before quitting time, you can use that time to clean out a file. When travelling for business, bring as much work as you can comfortably carry. Spare time at airports because you arrive early or because of flight delays provides a good opportunity to perform routine work. Many airports offer free wireless to check and reply to emails. By the end of the year your productivity will have increased much more than if you had squandered these bits of time.

Some forms of making use of bits of time, such as reviewing your to-do list as you ride the elevator, are a form of multitasking. Doing two or more routine chores simultaneously can sometimes enhance personal productivity. While exercising on a stationary bike, you might read work-related information; while commuting, listen to the radio for information of potential relevance for your job. Also, while reading email, you might clean the outside of your computer; while waiting for a file to download, you might arrange your work area or read a brief report.

Despite searching for productivity gains through multitasking, it is important to avoid rude or dangerous acts or a combination of the two. A rude practice is doing paperwork while on the telephone or sitting in class. A dangerous practice is engaging in an intense conversation over the cell phone while driving (which is illegal in many provinces, including Ontario, unless it is hands-free). Checking out email on a laptop or onboard computer is more dangerous because you are forced to lose full eye contact with the road.

Stay in Control of Paperwork, the In-Basket and Email

Despite the major shift to the use of electronic messages, the workplace is still overflowing with printed messages, including computer printouts. Paperwork essentially involves taking care of administrative details such as correspondence, expense account forms, and surveys. Responding to email messages creates additional administrative details that require handling, even though it's *electronic work* rather than paperwork.

Unless you handle paperwork and email efficiently, you may lose control of your job or home life, which could lead to heavy stress. Ideally, a small amount of time should be invested in paperwork every day. Non-prime time (when you are at less than peak efficiency, but not overly fatigued) is the best time to take care of administrative routine work.

OVERCOMING TIME WASTERS

Another basic thrust to improved personal productivity is to minimize wasting time. Many of the techniques already described in this chapter help save time. The tactics and strategies described next, however, are directly aimed at overcoming the problem of wasted time.

Minimize Daydreaming

"Taking a field trip" while on the job is a major productivity drain. Daydreaming is triggered when the individual perceives the task to be boring—such as reviewing another person's work for errors. Unresolved personal problems are an important source of daydreaming, thus blocking your productivity. This is especially true because effective time utilization requires good concentration. When you are preoccupied with a personal or business problem, it is difficult to give your full efforts to a task at hand.

The solution is to do something constructive about whatever problem is sapping your ability to concentrate. Sometimes a relatively minor problem, such as driving with an expired operator's licence, can impair your work concentration. At other times, a major problem, such as how best to take care of a parent who has suffered a stroke, interferes with work. In either situation, your concentration will suffer until you take appropriate action.

Avoid Unproductive Use of Computers

An unproductive use of computers is to tinker with them to the exclusion of useful work. Many people have become intrigued with computers to the point of diversion. They become habituated to creating new reports or exquisite graphics and making endless changes. It is easy to become diverted by the thousands of commands in a program such as

Microsoft Word or PowerPoint. Some managers spend so much time with computers that they neglect leadership responsibilities, thus lowering their productivity.

In addition to these problems, internet surfing for purposes not strictly related to the job has become a major productivity drain. According to the Accountemps survey of senior executives mentioned previously, workers spend an average of 56 minutes per day with non work-related internet use.[22] Figure 15-1 based on a survey of 2,400 workers by *Cerbian.com* digs further into the specific categories of **computer surfing** unrelated to work. (Surfing in the context of the internet refers to browsing through websites with no specific work goal in mind.) In defence of some of these surfers, some of the activity could enhance job performance, such as being informed of business trends.

The general message is straightforward: to plug one more potential productivity drain, avoid being a computer goof-off.

Keep Track of Important Names, Places, and Things

How much time have you wasted lately searching for such items as a telephone number you jotted down somewhere, your keys, or an appointment book? A supervisor suddenly realized he had forgotten to show up for a luncheon appointment. He wanted to call and apologize but was unable to locate the person's name and phone number. Standard solutions to overcoming these problems are to keep a wheel file (such as the type made by Rolodex) of people's names and companies. It is difficult to misplace such a file. Many managers and professionals store such information in a database or even in a word processing file. Such files are more difficult to misplace than a pocket directory.

Two steps are recommended for remembering where you put things. First, have a parking place for everything. This would include putting your keys and appointment book back in the same place after each use. Second, make visual associations. To have something register in your mind at the moment you are doing it, make up a visual association with that act. Thus, you might say, "Here I am putting my résumé in the back section of my canvas bag."

Set a Time Limit for Certain Tasks and Projects

Spending too much time on a task or project wastes time. As a person becomes experienced with certain projects, he or she is able to make accurate estimates of how long a project will take to complete. A paralegal might say, "Getting this will drawn up for the lawyer's approval should take two hours." A good work habit to develop is to estimate how long a job should take and then proceed with strong determination to get that job completed within the estimated time period.

A productive version of this technique is to decide that some low- and medium-priority items are worth only so much of your time. Invest that much time in the project, but no more. Preparing a file on advertisements that come across your desk is one example.

Schedule Similar Tasks Together: Clustering

An efficient method of accomplishing small tasks is to group them together and perform them in one block of time. Clustering of this type has several applications. If you are

For nonjob-related surfing, where do you spend most of your time (please rank in order your top five categories)?

	Response Percentage	Response Total
News	56	1,342
Research	44	1,052
Web email (e.g., Hotmail)	40	969
Online banking	33	792
Business and economy	29	704
Retail shopping	27	655
Auction (e.g., eBay)	25	595
Arts/entertainment	25	591
Sports	22	527
Travel	20	486
Education/culture	17	416
Chat/instant messaging	16	393
Brokerage/trading	13	313
Health/medical	11	276
Gaming	6	155
Pornography	3	74
Other	3	63
I'm not allowed to surf for personal reasons	2	59
Gambling	1	21

Figure 15-1 Categories of Nonjob-Related Computer Surfing

Source: "Personal Surfing and Porn Plague the Office," available at www.computertimes.com/webusageporn.htm, retrieved May 1, 2006. June 2004.

visiting an office supply store, think of what else you need there to avoid an unnecessary repeat visit. A basic way of scheduling similar tasks together is to make most of your telephone calls in relation to your job from 11:00 to 11:30 each morning. Or, you might reserve the last hour of every workday for routine tasks such as responding to email and other correspondence.

Bounce Quickly From Task to Task

Much time is lost when a person takes a break between tasks. After one task is completed, you might pause for ten minutes to clear your work area and adjust your to-do list. After the brief pause, dive into your next important task. A compliance officer at a mutual fund says that he turns over an hourglass when he needs to decompress after handling an urgent situation. When the sand runs out, he moves to the next priority.[23]

Now that you have studied various ways to improve your personal productivity, do Human Relations Skill-Building Exercise 15-1. Incorporating many of these ideas in this chapter will help you achieve peak performance or exceptional accomplishment.

Human Relations Skill Building

Exercise 15-1 The Personal Productivity Checklist

Each class member will use the four headings below (in italics) to identify two areas where he or she is experiencing problems in developing productivity in the areas of work habits and time management. The problems could apply to work, school, or personal life.

In addition to identifying the problem area, each student will check off at least two solutions and then develop a brief action plan about how to overcome the problem by using these solutions. For instance, "One of my biggest problems is that I tend to start a lot of projects but finish very few of them. Procrastination is obviously a big problem area for me. Now that I am more aware of it, I am going to give myself a strict deadline for completing college papers. If I complete the paper before a deadline, I am going to reward myself with a new DVD."

Students then present their problems and action plans to the class. After each student has made his or her presentation, hold a class discussion to reach conclusions and interpretations about the problems revealed. For instance, it might be that one or two time-management problems are quite frequent.

Overcoming Procrastination	***Especially Applicable to Me***
1. Increase awareness of the problem.	________
2. Calculate cost of procrastination.	________
3. Jump-start yourself.	________
4. Peck away at an overwhelming task.	________
5. Motivate yourself with rewards and punishment.	________
6. Make a commitment to other people.	________
7. Express a more positive attitude about your intentions.	________
8. Use subliminal messages about overcoming procrastination.	________

Developing Proper Attitudes and Values

1. Become a goal-oriented person and value your time. ____________
2. Value good attendance and punctuality. ____________
3. Value neatness, orderliness, and speed. ____________
4. Develop an ethic of effectiveness and quality. ____________
5. Work smarter, not harder. ____________
6. Become self-employed psychologically. ____________
7. Appreciate the importance of rest and relaxation. ____________

Developing the Proper Skills and Techniques

1. Clean up and get organized. ____________
2. Plan your activities (including a to-do list with priority setting). ____________
3. Get off to a good start. ____________
4. Make good use of office technology. ____________
5. Concentrate on one task at a time. ____________
6. Streamline your work and emphasize important tasks. ____________
7. Tackle distasteful tasks first. ____________
8. Work at a steady pace. ____________
9. Create some quiet, uninterrupted time. ____________
10. Make use of bits of time. ____________
11. Stay in control of paperwork and email. ____________

Overcoming Time Wasters

1. Minimize daydreaming. ____________
2. Prepare a time log to evaluate your use of time. ____________
3. Avoid being a computer goof-off. ____________
4. Keep track of important names, places, and things. ____________
5. Set a time limit for certain tasks and projects. ____________
6. Be decisive and finish things. ____________

SUMMARY

People with good work habits tend to be more successful in their careers than poorly organized individuals, and they tend to have more time to spend on personal life. Good work habits are more important than ever because of today's emphasis on productivity and quality.

Procrastination is the major work habit problem for most employees and students. People procrastinate for many reasons, including their perception that a task is unpleasant, overwhelming, or may lead to negative consequences. Fear of success can also lead to procrastination. Awareness of procrastination may lead to its control. Eight other techniques for reducing procrastination are (1) calculate the cost of procrastination; (2) counterattack the burdensome task; (3) jump-start yourself; (4) peck away at an overwhelming task; (5) motivate yourself with rewards and punishments; (6) follow the WIFO principle; (7) make a commitment to other people; and (8) express a more positive attitude about your intentions.

Developing good work habits and time-management practices is often a matter of developing proper attitudes toward work and time. Seven such methods are (1) develop a mission, goals, and a strong work ethic; (3) value good attendance and punctuality; (4) value neatness, orderliness, and speed; (5) work smarter, not harder; (6) become self-employed psychologically; and (7) appreciate the importance of rest and relaxation.

Nine skills and techniques to help you become more productive are (1) plan your activities; (2) get off to a good start; (3) make good use of office technology; (4) concentrate on one key task at a time; (5) streamline your work and emphasize important tasks; (6) work at a steady pace; (7) create some quiet, uninterrupted time; (8) make use of bits of time and use multitasking for routine work; and (9) stay in control of paperwork and email.

Six suggestions for overcoming time wasting are (1) minimize daydreaming; (2) avoid unproductive use of computers; (3) keep track of important names, places, and things; (4) set time limits for certain tasks and projects; (5) schedule similar tasks together; and (6) bounce quickly from task to task.

QUESTIONS AND ACTIVITIES

1. In recent years, companies that sell desk planners and other time-management devices have experienced all-time peak demands for their products. What factors do you think created this boom?
2. What factors about a person's appearance might be accurate indicators of his or her work habits and time-management skills?
3. Many tidy, well-organized workers never attain much in the way of career success. Which principle of work habits and time management described in this chapter might they be neglecting?
4. Some students contend that because they work best when they put things off until the last moment, procrastination probably will not hurt them in their career. What is wrong with their reasoning?
5. What type of bad work habits might result from having very low tendencies toward perfectionism?
6. Give an example of any work you have ever performed, or heard of someone else performing, that could be eliminated because it is unproductive.
7. What is your opinion of the honesty of the responses to the survey about non job-related computer surfing? For example, do more people spend time visiting sports websites and gambling websites than they admit?
8. Identify five bits of time you could put to better use.
9. Complaints are mounting that the frequent use of email and the internet is lowering productivity for many workers. What might be the problem?
10. Ask an experienced business person how he or she uses the computer to improve his or her work habits and time management. Be prepared to discuss your findings in class.

INTERNET SKILL BUILDER

What Are You Doing With Your Time?

Go to www.getmoredone.com/tabulator.html to find the Pace Productivity Tabulator. This interactive module enables you to enter the time you spend on 11 major activities (such as employment, eating, sleeping, and television watching) and compare your profile to others. You are also able to enter your ideal profile to see where you would like to be. Simply follow the straightforward instructions. After arriving at your personal pie chart, ask yourself, "What have I learned that will enhance my personal productivity?"

Log on to the **Companion Website** at **www.pearsoncanada.ca/dubrin** to access additional resources for this chapter.

CASE STUDY 15-1 HUMAN RELATIONS

A Case of Not Getting It Done

Carol Winchester sat nervously outside the office of Daniel Delvin, a time-management consultant and personal coach. She kept thinking about how self-conscious she felt seeking professional help just because she was having a little trouble getting started on projects and finishing projects she had started. Carol said to herself, "This counsellor is going to think there's something really wrong with me just because I have a small procrastination problem."

Winchester's thought pattern was interrupted by a warm welcome from Daniel Delvin, a neatly dressed, middle-aged counsellor. With a smile and an extended hand, Delvin said, "Hi. You must be Carol Winchester. I'm Dan Delvin. Come in and have a seat near the coffee table. That's where we'll be talking." Delvin sat in a chair a few feet away from Winchester.

"What kind of help do you want from me?" asked Delvin.

"The reason I'm here," answered Winchester, "is that both my boss and my boyfriend think I'm a procrastinator—big time. I don't disagree entirely, but I don't think I'm quite the basket case they think I am."

Delvin replied, "I doubt you're a basket case, but I don't think you would be here if you weren't experiencing a little pain. Hurting a little bit and admitting that you have a problem are the beginning points for overcoming your problem. Let's get started, Carol, by you telling me about some of the ways in which you procrastinate."

"I've got a few horror stories to tell you," said Winchester with a nervous laugh. "A recent example is that it took me four months to make this appointment with you. [They both laugh.] I kept looking at my calendar and saying to myself that I was too busy to get help. I would pick up the phone to make an appointment. Then I would think of all the other things I needed to do. I finally set April 15 as an absolute firm date to call you. Then I realized I only had two more weeks to prepare my income tax forms for last year. I guess you could say that I even procrastinated on my income tax. But I finally did get it in on May 15, and the penalty amounted to only about $65. Those are two examples for you."

"Yes, they are two good examples. But I need more examples of your procrastination so I can better understand your problem."

"Okay, you asked for it," responded Winchester. "Lance, my boyfriend, whom I love very much, proposed to me one year ago. We were in a beautiful Greek restaurant called Acropolis. He pulled a ring out of the box. The group at the table across from us were watching intently. They were ready to clap when I said yes. Lance just assumed I would say yes. I didn't say yes, but I didn't say no. I just said I wasn't ready to make a decision that night.

"Two months later, when the engagement came up for about the tenth time in conversation, I did say yes. I know that by delaying my decision I took some of the romance out of Lance's proposal. His feelings are still a little hurt, but it didn't change his mind about wanting to marry me."

"Hold on a second," said Delvin. "Have you two agreed on a wedding date yet?"

"Lance has been pressing me a little, but I'm just not ready to be that specific about getting married."

"Let's switch channels now," said Delvin. "What about on the job? What has prompted your boss to think you have a major procrastination problem?"

"It would be fair to say that I need more time than most people to get my projects done. I'm the assistant sales promotion manager. I have to do things like make some of the arrangements for trade shows and work with printers to have brochures ready. My boss says that I wait so long to make arrangements for booking hotels that we often have to pay premium rates. I think he exaggerates that problem. I'm very thorough and that can be a big asset.

"A few times I've been late in getting computer disks ready for the printer so they can do their job on time. Yet, since we're supposed to be the customer, I think they should be adapting to our schedule. I can think of another recent example. We were going to hire a new assistant for the office. We all agreed she was the right person to do the job. My boss had to go out of town for an important sales meeting, so he told me to contact this woman and tell her about the job offer.

"I got so busy with other stuff that I didn't call her for a week. By that time she had accepted another job. My boss was upset and blamed losing her on my procrastination. My take on it is a little different. If that woman really wanted to work for us, she could have waited for the job offer instead of taking another position."

Delvin asked, "Carol, why do you think you procrastinate so much?"

Carol replied, "You're a little bit like my boss and my boyfriend. You assume that every time I delay doing something, it's procrastination. Sometimes something else very important comes up that prevents me from going down a particular path. At other times I might be just a little forgetful, like filing the taxes on time."

Questions

1. What do you see as some of the reasons behind Carol Winchester's procrastination?
2. What evidence do you find that Winchester might be defensive about her problem or denying its reality?
3. What advice can you offer Winchester for overcoming her procrastination problem?

CASE STUDY 15-2 HUMAN RELATIONS

The Cubicle Blues

Paul Chen works as a design technician for DesignTrend, a furniture manufacturer in Vancouver. His major responsibility is to design support devices for home and office furniture, such as the arms, legs, and frames. His employer has configured the office into cubicles, with even the company executives being assigned to cubicles. When the creative staff needs more space, such as when laying out blueprints for an office, a common area with large drawing tables is available. Because most design work is computer aided, the creative staff does most of their work in the assigned cubicles.

Previous to the reconfiguration of the office, design engineers and technicians were assigned to small private offices with doors. In this way, the engineers and technicians could work relatively uninterrupted without colleagues frequently conversing with them. The offices also closed off most sounds so a creative worker could avoid hearing office chatter, including telephone conversations.

CEO Kenneth Yang decided to change from closed offices to cubicles to enhance communication and idea sharing among all staff members. Yang opined, "Unstructured communication leads to an exchange of ideas that is vital for creativity. I don't want the staff holed up in offices and minimizing communication with each other."

Chen became increasingly troubled by life in his cubicle. He grumbled to co-workers, friends, and family members about working in a cubicle farm. He disliked the distractions, and he was having difficulty concentrating on creative tasks. One day when his supervisor dropped by his cubicle, Chen explained his problem:

"How can Yang expect the creative staff to be creative when assigned to these cubicles? I hear every conversation that's going on up to two cubicles down. When I am working on a design I need to concentrate. I need to reflect. I don't want to be interrupted by a neighbor telling her husband over the phone to pick up a pizza on the way home. I enjoy working for DesignTrend, but the cubicles have made my days insufferable."

The supervisor replied, "I'm in no position to assign you a private office. Even Ken Yang works out of a cubicle. Yet, I will give some thought to your problem."

Questions

1. Is Paul Chen offering a valid complaint that creative thought is difficult without privacy?
2. What advice can you offer Chen to help him manage interruptions better?
3. What should Chen's supervisor advise him to do?

Source: A few of the facts in this case are from Linda Tischler, "Death to the Cubicle," Fast Company, June 2005, pp. 29–32.

Chapter 16
Getting Ahead in Your Career

Learning Outcomes

After studying the information and doing the exercises in this chapter, you should be able to

- explain the new model of career advancement in organizations;
- select several strategies and tactics for getting ahead in your career by taking control of your own behaviour;
- select several strategies and tactics for advancing your career by exerting control over your environment.

Mindy Gikas was interviewing a senior-level manager on the phone when suddenly the job candidate paused. He said he was reading an email, recalls Ms. Gikas, a managing director for Ogilvy Public Relations Worldwide, a unit of WPP Group of London. "It showed me that his conversation with me wasn't very important," she explains. He wasn't invited to interview in person.[1]

You might be saying to yourself, "How could any senior-level manager be so stupid when conducting a job search? Doesn't he have any common sense? Doesn't he know any telephone etiquette?" In reality, when it comes to job finding and career management many people can use a refresher about the basics.

In this chapter we focus on strategies, tactics, and attitudes that will help you achieve promotion or hold on to a position you enjoy including those important career change and career advancement strategies. The same approaches will enable you to achieve **career portability**, the ability to move from one employer to another when necessary.

We have divided the vast information about career advancement divided into three sections. The first section describes the new model, or concept, of career advancement or **career pathing**.

The second section deals with approaches to managing or taking control of your own behaviour to advance or to retain a good position. The third section deals with approaches to exerting control over your environment to improve your chances for success.

THE NEW MODEL OF CAREER ADVANCEMENT

Career advancement has acquired a shift in emphasis in recent years to accommodate new organizational structures. The major shift has been away from vertical mobility, or moving up the ladder, toward lateral growth, or advancing by learning more. Here, we look briefly at the key components of the new model of career advancement.

1. *More emphasis on horizontal growth.* As just mentioned, the major shift in career advancement has been toward more emphasis on learning new skills and acquiring new knowledge in a position at the same organizational level. Many companies even give pay raises to employees who learn new job-related skills. Despite the emphasis on horizontal growth, many workers still aspire to climb the organizational ladder. Also, many companies offer promotion to a higher-level position as a reward for good performance.
2. *More emphasis on temporary leadership assignments.* In the traditional model of career advancement, an individual would strive to be promoted to a management or leadership position. The person would then hold on to that position unless demoted or fired. Today, many leadership positions are temporary, such as working as the head of a project to launch a new product. After the product is launched, the person might return to his or her position as a group member (individual contributor). Or, a person might be assigned as a committee head because of his or her expertise. After the committee has completed its work, the person returns to a non-leadership position.
3. *Climbing the ladder of self-fulfillment.* For an increasing number of people, doing work that contributes to self-fulfillment is more important than a focus on promotion or earnings growth. To advance in your career would be to find work that provides more self-fulfillment. Individual preferences determine what type of work is self-fulfilling.
4. *Continuous learning.* According to the career expert Douglas T. Hall, careers for the twenty-first century will consist of a series of short learning stages. *Career age*, or how long a person has been engaged in a type of work, will become more important than chronological age.[2] At one point in your career you might need to rapidly learn how to conduct research on the internet; at another stage, you might need to learn how to organize a trade show.
5. *Being promoted as much for learn-how as know-how.* Hall also predicts that in the twenty-first century, demand in the labour market will shift from those with know-how (present skills) to those with learn-how (learning capability).[3] A track record of being able to learn will give people the portability mentioned at the start of this chapter. Being able to learn rapidly makes continuous learning possible. The reason that learn-how is so important is that organizations face such rapid technological change.

The new model of career advancement is compatible with a modern definition of success. **Career success** as used here means attaining the twin goals of organizational rewards

Human Relations Self-Assessment

QUIZ 16-1 The Career-Development Inventory

Career-development activities inevitably include answering some penetrating questions about yourself. The following are 12 representative questions to be found on career-development inventories. You may need several hours to do a competent job of answering these questions. After individuals have answered these questions by themselves, it may be profitable to hold a class discussion about the relevance of the specific questions. A strongly recommended procedure is for you to date your completed inventory and put it away for safekeeping. Examine your answers in several years to see (1) how well you are doing in advancing your career and (2) how much you have changed.

Keep the following information in mind in answering this inventory: People are generous in their self-evaluations when they answer career-development inventories, so you might want to discuss some of your answers with somebody who knows you well.

1. How would you describe yourself as a person?
2. What are you best at doing? worst?
3. What are your two biggest strengths or assets?
4. What are the two traits, characteristics, or behaviours of yours that need the most improvement?
5. What are your two biggest accomplishments?
6. Write your obituary as you would like it to appear.
7. What would be the ideal job for you?
8. What career advice can you give yourself?
9. Describe the two peak work-related experiences in your life.
10. What are your five most important values (the things in life most important to you)?
11. What goals in life are you trying to achieve?
12. What do you see as your niche (spot where you best fit) in the modern world?

and personal satisfaction. Organizational rewards include such things as higher-ranking positions, more money, and challenging assignments. Personal satisfaction refers to enjoying, or liking, what you are doing. If your employer highly values your contribution and your job satisfaction is high, you are experiencing career success. However, success in general also includes accomplishments and satisfaction in personal life.

To begin relating career development to yourself, do Human Relations Self-Assessment Quiz 16-1.

TAKING CONTROL OF YOURSELF

The unifying theme to the strategies, tactics, and attitudes described in this section is that you must attempt to control your own behaviour. You can advance your career by harnessing the forces under your control. Such a perspective is helpful because individuals have the primary responsibility for managing their own careers. The organization may help, but managing your career is your responsibility.

The following section concentrates on getting ahead by trying to control your external environment in some small way. Do not be concerned about overlap between the general categories of controlling yourself versus controlling the environment. Instead, focus on the meaning and application of the strategies and tactics. Recognize also that the information presented throughout this chapter will help you take responsibility for managing your career.

Develop Outstanding Interpersonal Skills

Getting ahead in business-related fields is exceedingly difficult unless you can relate effectively to other people. Workers are bypassed for promotion generally because someone thinks they cannot effectively be responsible for the work of others. Workers are more likely to be terminated for poor interpersonal skills than for poor technical skills.

Effective interpersonal or human relations skills refer to many specific practices. At a meeting, if you crack a joke that relieves tension and serves as an icebreaker, you are showing good interpersonal skills. If, as the team leader, you convince other team members to strive harder for quality, you are showing good interpersonal (and leadership) skills.

Chapters 7 through 12 of this book focused on important interpersonal skills such as communication, resolving conflict, being assertive, exerting leadership, behaving with self-confidence, and listening to customers.

Develop Expertise, Passion, and Pride

A starting point in getting ahead is to develop a useful job skill. This tactic is obvious if one is working as a specialist, such as an insurance underwriter. Being skilled at the task performed by the group is also a requirement for being promoted to a supervisory position. After one is promoted to supervisor or another managerial job, expertise is still important for further advancement. It helps a manager's reputation to be skilled in such things as memo writing, computer applications, preparing a budget, and interviewing job candidates.

Although expertise in one's field is highly recommended, the workplace also demands that a person perform a variety of tasks outside that field. A recommended approach is to have depth in your primary field, but also to have breadth by having several lesser areas of expertise. A widespread example is that no matter what your specialty field, you are also expected to have information-technology skills.

Passion goes hand in hand with expertise; it contributes to problem solving and is a major requirement for being an effective leader. It is difficult to sustain expertise if you are not passionate about your specialty field. A work-passionate person, for example, would regularly read printed and electronic information about his or her specialty. In support of job passion, career coach and author Cynthia Shapiro advises that "Companies are running scared. They're looking for the kind of passion that creates a competitive edge. Employers rarely get rid of cheerleaders. Even in a drastic layoff, their jobs are safe." [4]

Developing expertise and being passionate about your work leads naturally to being proud of what you produce. People who take pride in their work are likely to achieve higher quality and a good reputation. From the standpoint of management, proud workers are major contributors because their pride motivates them to excel.

Develop a Code of Professional Ethics

Another solid foundation for developing a career is to establish a personal ethical code. An ethical code determines what behaviour is right or wrong, good or bad, based on values. The values stem from cultural upbringing, religious teachings, peer influences, and professional or industry standards. A code of professional ethics helps a worker deal with such issues as accepting bribes, back-stabbing co-workers, and sexually harassing a work associate.

Perform Well Including Going beyond Your Job Description

Good job performance is the bedrock of a person's career. In rare instances, a person is promoted on the basis of favouritism alone. In all other situations an employee must have received a favourable performance appraisal to be promoted. Before an employee is promoted, the prospective new boss asks, "How well did this person perform for you?" To be an outstanding performer, it is also necessary to go outside your job description by occasionally taking on tasks not expected of you. Going beyond your job description is part of being a good organizational citizen. Another way of looking at the same issue is that people tend to get promoted not because they perform their jobs well but because they take the initiative to do more than expected.

Performing well on all your assignments is also important because it contributes to the **success syndrome**, a pattern in which the worker performs one assignment well and then has the confidence to take on an even more difficult assignment. Each new assignment contributes to more self-confidence and more success. As you succeed in new and more challenging assignments, your reputation grows within the firm.

Develop a Proactive Personality

If you are an active agent in taking control of the forces around you, you stand a better chance of capitalizing on opportunities. Also, you will seek out opportunities such as seeing problems that need fixing. A proactive personality is a person relatively unconstrained by forces in the situation and who brings about environmental change. People who are highly proactive identify opportunities and act on them, showing initiative, and keep trying until they bring about meaningful change. One reason proactive personalities perform better is that they develop the social networks they need to help them achieve their goals. For example, the person with a proactive personality would know whom to contact for help with a specific business or technical problem.[5]

A health and safety specialist with a proactive personality might identify a health hazard others had missed. She would identify the nature of the problem and urge management for funding to control the problem, making use of her network. Ultimately, her efforts in preventing major health problems would be recognized. Having a proactive personality makes it easier for a person to be a good corporate citizen because such behaviour is "built into your DNA."

Managers prefer workers with a proactive personality because these workers become proactive employees, or those who take the initiative to take care of problems. Today's employee is supposed to be enterprising. Instead of relying solely on the manager to figure out what work needs to be accomplished, he or she looks for projects to undertake. The proactive employee, however, may clash with an old-fashioned manager who believes that an employee's job is strictly to follow orders. A study conducted with close to 500 men and women workers in diverse occupations examined the relationship between career success and a proactive personality. Proactive personality, as measured by a test, was related to salary, promotions, and career satisfaction.[6] It may not be easy to develop a proactive personality, but a person can get started by taking more initiative to fix problems and attempt to be more self-starting.

Create Good First Impressions and a Favourable Appearance

Every time you interact with a new person inside or outside your company, you create a first impression. Fair or not, these first impressions have a big impact on your career. If your first impression is favourable, you will often be invited back by an internal or external customer. Your first impression also creates a "halo" that may influence perceptions about the quality of your work in the future. If your first impression is negative, you will have to work extra hard to be perceived as competent later on.

Looking successful contributes to a positive first impression. Your clothing, your desk and office, and your speech should project the image of a successful, but not necessarily flamboyant, person. Your standard of dress should be appropriate to your particular career stage and work environment. At the extreme, highly placed business executives often dress as if they were walking advertisements for the beauty and fashion industry.

Appropriate dress for an inventory specialist is not the same as for an outside salesperson dealing with industrial customers. Yet, in the past few years, more formal business attire, such as suits for men and women, is making a comeback. Many salespeople and managers today maintain a flexible clothing style by such means as keeping a jacket and extra jewellery in the car or office. When an unanticipated meeting with a customer or some other special occasion arises, a quick modification of clothing style is possible.[7] Appearing physically fit is also part of the success image.

Projecting a sense of control is another key factor contributing to a positive first impression. Show that you are in control of yourself and the environment. Avoid letting your body language betray you—nonverbal messages are sent by fidgeting or rubbing your face. Make your gestures project self-assurance and purpose.[8] A verbal method of appearing in control is to make a positive assertion such as, "This is a demanding assignment and I welcome the challenge."

The factors mentioned so far contribute to a favourable appearance, which can be an asset in a career. Physical attractiveness continues to play a major role in many employment decisions—especially for workers who are in contact with customers and clients.

Patrick Hicks, an attorney in a Las Vegas employment law firm, notes, "Everything else being equal, certain businesses—retail is the best example—would prefer people who are physically attractive."[9]

Body art in the form of tattoos and piercing often figures into physical appearance. More companies today accept such decorations as a fact of modern culture. Tatooing is one of the faster-growing retail businesses in North America. Ford Motor Co. permits employees from the most senior executives on down to have tattoos and piercings—except those that could endanger factory workers. Despite this general acceptance of body art, excessive decoration in visible places could be a career deterrent.[10] Visualize a man with a pierced tongue and snake tattooed on his neck applying for a sales representative position at Hewlett Packard!

Document Your Accomplishments

Keeping an accurate record of what you have accomplished on the job can be valuable when you are being considered for promotion, transfer, or assignment to a team or project. Documenting your accomplishments can also be used to verify new learning. In addition, a record of this type is also useful when your performance is being evaluated. You can show your manager what you have done for the organization lately. Many professional-level workers maintain a portfolio of their accomplishments, such as samples of successful work. The portfolio is much like that used by photographers, artists, and models when applying for a job and is gaining in popularity. Many colleges and universities have students design their portfolios in various courses. These portfolios can then be added to over time. Accomplishments do not have to be "on the job," as many skills are learned outside the office and should be included. Here are three examples of documented accomplishments from different types of jobs and a volunteer assignment:

1. A bank teller suggested that at least one person in the bank should be fluent in American Sign Language to facilitate serving hearing impaired customers. After implementing the idea, the bank attracted many more deaf customers.
2. A maintenance supervisor decreased fuel costs in her office by 27 percent in one year by installing ceiling fans.

After documenting your accomplishments, it pays to advertise. Let key people know in a tasteful way of your tangible accomplishments. You might request an opportunity to make a presentation to your boss to review the status of one of your successful projects, or if it would be presumptuous for you to request a special meeting to discuss your accomplishments, use email for the same purpose.

Keep Growing through Continuous Learning and Self-Development

Given that continuous learning is part of the new model of career advancement, engaging in regular learning will help a person advance. Continuous learning can take many forms, including formal schooling, attending training programs and seminars, and self-study. It is particularly important to engage in new learning in areas of interest to the company, such as developing proficiency in a second language if the company has customers or employees in areas where that language is spoken. Many companies support continuous learning, making it easier for you to implement the tactic of growth through continuous learning. Today it is even easier to engage in continuous learning in a wide variety of fields. Many courses are offered online for little cost and many are free of charge. For example, Brandon Hall Research offers a variety of free webinars (small training sessions online) as well as ones that are fee-based on a variety of topics including training. Your employer may be much more amenable to pay for an online course or webinar than pay for you to travel to training in another location.

Self-development can include any type of learning but often emphasizes personal improvement and skill development. Improving your work habits or team leadership skills would be job-relevant examples of self-development.

Observe Proper Etiquette

Proper etiquette is important for career advancement because such behaviour is considered part of acting professionally. **Business etiquette** is a special code of behaviour required in work situations. The term *manners* has an equivalent meaning. Both etiquette and manners refer to behaving in an acceptable and refined way. In the digital era, etiquette is just as important as ever because of the new challenges that high-tech devices bring. For example, is it good etiquette to read the information on a co-worker's computer screen when visiting his or her cubicle? The globalization of business also creates challenges—for example, knowing whether handshakes are acceptable when visiting another country.

Figuring out what constitutes proper etiquette and business manners requires investigation. One approach is to use successful people as models of behaviour or sources of information. Another approach is to consult a current book about business etiquette. Many of the suggestions offered in these books follow common sense, but many others would not be obvious to an inexperienced career person.

The basic rules of etiquette are to make the other person feel comfortable in your presence, to be considerate, and to strive not to embarrass anyone. Also, be cordial to all, remembering that everyone deserves our respect.[11] Specific guidelines stem from these basic rules. Exhibit 16-1 presents examples of good business etiquette and manners.

Take Sensible Risks

An element of risk taking is necessary to advance very far in a career. Almost all successful people have taken at least one moderate risk in their careers. These risks include starting a new business with mostly borrowed money, joining a fledgling firm, or submitting a groundbreaking idea to management. Terrie M. Williams, founder of a public relations firm, believes that risk taking is the most essential ingredient in advancing a career. Not risking anything can mean risking even more, including inhibiting your career. Williams offers this explanation:

> When I'm approaching an important meeting, I sometimes find myself thinking, "I'm scared. I don't know if I can carry this off." Whenever I feel that way, I make a conscious effort to remind myself that being scared is good. It means I'm embarking on something new and different, and I can only go to the next level.[12]

Exhibit 16-1
Business Etiquette and Manners

Below are 13 specific suggestions about office etiquette and business manners that should be considered in the context of a specific job situation. For example, the rule "Shouting is out" would not apply to traders on the floor of a stock exchange, where shouting is routine.

1. *Be polite to people in person.* Say "good morning" and "good night" to work associates at all job levels. Smile frequently. Offer to bring coffee or another beverage for a co-worker if you are going outside to get some for yourself.
2. *Write polite letters and email messages.* An important occasion for practising good etiquette is the writing of business and personal letters. Include the person's job title in the inside address; spell the person's name correctly. Use supportive rather than harsh statements. (For example, say "It would be helpful if you could" rather than "You must.") Avoid right-margin justification because it is much more severe looking than ragged right (uneven) text. Thank you notes for gifts should be handwritten rather than sent by email, but at least an email is better than not offering thanks.
3. *Practise good table manners.* Avoid smacking your lips or sucking your fingers. If someone else is paying the bill, do not order the most expensive item on the menu (such as a $150 bottle of Dom Pérignon champagne!). Offer to cut bread for the other person, and do not look at the bill if another person is paying.
4. *Remember names.* It is both good manners and good human relations to remember the names of work associates, even if you see them only occasionally.
5. *Treat males and females equally.* Amenities extended to females by males in a social setting are minimized in business settings today. During a meeting, a male is not expected to hold a chair or a door for a woman, nor does he jump to walk on the outside when the two of them are walking down the street. Many women resent being treated differently from males with respect to minor social customs. In general, common courtesies should be extended by both sexes to one another.
6. *Shouting is out.* Emotional control is an important way of impressing superiors. Following the same principle, shouting in most work situations detracts from your image.
7. *The host or hostess pays the bill.* An area of considerable confusion about etiquette surrounds business lunches and who should pay the cheque. The rule of etiquette is that the person who extends the invitation pays the bill.
8. *Introduce the lower-ranking person to the higher-ranking person.* In other words, the higher-ranking person is the centre of attention, and others are introduced *to* him or her. For instance, you introduce the younger person *to* the older person: "[Older person's name], I'd like you to meet [younger person's name]." Similarly, co-workers are introduced *to* a client. Also, when introducing more than one person at a time, introduce higher-ranking people first; your boss's name should be mentioned before a co-worker's.
9. *Address superiors and visitors in their preferred way.* As the modern business world has become more informal, a natural tendency has developed to address people at all levels by their first names. It is safer to first address people by a title and their last name and then wait for them to correct you if they desire.
10. *Make appointments with high-ranking people rather than dropping in.* It is taboo in most firms for lower-ranking employees to casually drop in on an executive.
11. *When another person is opening a door to exit a room or building, do not jump in ahead of him or her.* In recent years, many people have developed the curious habit of quickly jumping in past another person (moving in the opposite direction) who is exiting. Not only is this practice rude, it can lead to an uncomfortable collision.

12. *Be sensitive to cross-cultural differences in etiquette.* When dealing with people from different cultures, regularly investigate possible major differences in etiquette. For example, using the index finger to point is considered rude in most Asian countries. The American sign for OK (thumb and index finger forming a circle) is considered a vulgarity in most other countries. Another example is that Finns are very private people, so don't ask questions about their private lives unless they bring up the topic first. Instead, talk about the safe topic of sports. Don't blow your nose in public in Belgium, where it is considered an offensive gesture. (It's not too cool elsewhere, either.)
13. *Minimize social kissing in an American or Canadian workplace, but welcome it in Europe.* Kissing in business is generally regarded as rude except among close acquaintances, yet is more frequent in Europe. However, European kissing amounts to pecks on both cheeks, or tom of the head, and never on the lips.

Caution: Although all these points could have some bearing on the image you project, violation of any one of them would not necessarily have a negative impact on your career. It is the overall image you project that counts the most. Therefore, the general principle of being considerate of work associates is much more important than any one act of etiquette or manners.

Sources: Jim Rucker and Jean Anna Sellers, "Changes in Business Etiquette," *Business Education Forum,* February 1998, p. 45; "Business Etiquette: Teaching Students the Unwritten Rules," *Keying In,* January 1996, pp. 1–2; "Meeting and Greeting," *Keying In,* January 1996, p. 3; Lisa Lee Freeman, "Re-Finishing School," *Working Woman,* February 1999, pp. 84–85; compilation from other sources in Andrea Sachs, "Corporate Ps and Qs," *Time,* November 1, 1999, Special Business Section, p. 23.

Learn to Manage Adversity

Some adversity is almost inevitable in an ambitious person's career. It is difficult to get through a career without at least once being laid off, fired, demoted, transferred to an undesirable assignment, or making a bad investment. Company mergers and takeovers also contribute to adversity because so many people are laid off in the process or assigned to lesser jobs.

Personal resilience—the capacity to bounce back from setback—is necessary to overcome adversity. A general-purpose way of handling adversity is to first get emotional support from a friend or family member, and then solve the problem systematically. You can follow the decision-making steps described in Chapter 3.

Two other points about managing adversity are particularly relevant here. First, attempt not to be bitter and cynical about your problem. Bitterness and cynicism can freeze a person into inaction. Second, look to minimize the self-doubt that grows from a mental script called the *fear narrative*. According to Kenneth Ruge, this is a narrative in which you tell yourself that if you try again, something terrible will happen. "The word *can't* becomes the operative word and you become its prisoner." The best antidote is to create an opposite narrative whereby you think, "How can I use my imagination and creativity to move beyond this *can't* to achieve my goals?"[13]

Develop the Brand Called "You"

Well-known consultant Tom Peters urges all career-minded people to develop their credentials and their reputation to the extent that they stand out like a brand name. Although the analogy of each person becoming a recognizable brand name like Nike is far-fetched, the idea of becoming a trusted person with value is sound. As Peters sees it,

Canada Today

Canadian Websites for Some Sound Career Advice

The internet is an excellent source for valuable ideas and strategies to help you develop and get ahead in your career. Below are a few Canadian sites and some advice and ideas.

Barbara Moses is a Canadian career-management consultant and author of four books on life career success. One of her interesting rules out of her 12 rules for success is that you need to become a career activist. A career activist is just that; someone who is vigilant and active in developing a career path. Identify and prepare for opportunities. Stay informed and alert. In other words, create your own opportunities rather than waiting for them to come to you. You can access many of her ideas at her website at **www.bbmcareerdev.com.**

From Queen's University, you can access a site with everything from ways to find a job to how to dress for that important interview. While it is for Queen's students, there are many helpful tips and ideas that make this site well worth the trip. Find it at http://careers.queensu.ca/

Chatelaine, a Canadian women's magazine available online, has a section on work, including archives of work-related articles. Many of the articles are written by women who have managed career problems such as balancing career and home life or changing careers. Although, targeted for women, many of the job articles are suitable for anyone pursuing a career, switching careers, or trying to advance in your current company.

A site from Quebec that is excellent is **www.jobboom.com.** This site includes a Career and Orientation Profile, the Campbell Interest and Skills Survey, and other self-tests to help you in understanding yourself. Other sections include many career management sections including finding the right job for you, hot careers, and working for yourself. This site contains many valuable career development ideas and is also available in French.

These are just a few good Canadian sources to help you with your career aspirations!

you don't belong to any company for life, and your chief affiliation isn't any particular function or department (such as accounting). You are not defined by your job title or your job description. "Starting today, you are a brand."[14]

You begin developing brand You by identifying the qualities or characteristics that distinguish you from co-workers. What have you done recently to make You stand out? What benefit do you offer? Do you deliver high-quality work on time? Are you a creative problem solver? Next, you make yourself visible so you can cash in on your uniqueness (your brand). Almost all the ideas in this chapter will help you develop brand You!

The Canada Today feature above offers some other tips and ideas about developing your career and the brand "You."

EXERTING CONTROL OVER THE OUTSIDE WORLD

Here we emphasize strategies and tactics requiring you to exert some control over the outside environment. If you do not fully control it, at least you can try to juggle it to your advantage. For instance, "Find a Mentor" suggests that you search out a friendly and supportive person in your field who can help you advance in your career.

Develop a Flexible Career Path

Planning your career inevitably involves some form of goal setting. If your goals are laid out systematically to lead you to your ultimate career goal, you have established a career path. A **career path** is thus a sequence of positions necessary to achieve a goal.[15]

Here we describe two types of career paths. One type emphasizes climbing up the ladder in a traditional organization. The other emphasizes the horizontal movements that characterize the new model of career advancement.

The Traditional Career Path A traditional (or vertical) career path is based on the assumption that a person will occupy a series of positions, each at a higher level of responsibility than the previous one. A person thus climbs the organizational ladder or hierarchy. If a career path is laid out in one firm, it must be related to the present and future demands of that firm. If you aspire toward a high-level manufacturing position, you would need to know the future of manufacturing in that company. Many U.S. and Canadian firms, for example, plan to conduct more of their manufacturing in the Pacific Rim or Mexico. If you were really determined, you might study the appropriate language and ready yourself for a global position.

Before establishing the goals on the career path, it is helpful to clarify your values. These are probably the same values that enabled you to choose a career in the first place. Questions to think about include these: "Can you name the three things most important to your job satisfaction? What do you really look for in a job? Do you want to be part of a team? To think creatively? Are you passionate about helping people and improving the world? Do you want to carefully follow directions, or do you prefer to decide which tasks are important?"[16]

While sketching out a career path you should list your personal goals. They should mesh with your work plans to help avoid major conflicts in your life. Some lifestyles, for example, are incompatible with some career paths. You might find it difficult to develop a stable home life (spouse, children, friends, community activities, garden) if you aspire to holding a sales position in the Far East.

Your career path is a living document and may need to be modified as your circumstances change. Keep in mind changes in your company and industry. If becoming a branch manager is an important step in your career path, check to see if your company or industry still has branch managers. The changing preferences of your family can also influence your career path. A family that once wanted to stay put may now be willing to relocate, which could open up new possibilities on your career path.

Contingency ("what if?") plans should also be incorporated into a well-designed career path. For instance, "If I don't become an agency supervisor by age 35, I will seek employment in the private sector." Or, "If I am not promoted within two years, I will enroll in a business school program."

Career paths can also be laid out graphically, as shown in Figure 16-1. One benefit of a career path laid out in chart form is that it gives a clear perception of climbing steps toward your target position. As each position is attained, the corresponding step can be shaded in colour or cross-hatched.

Most of the goals just mentioned include a time element, which is crucial to sound career management. Your long-range goal might be clearly established in your mind (such as owner and operator of a health spa). At the same time you must establish short-range goals (get any kind of job in health spa) and intermediate-range goals (manager of a health spa by age 30). Goals set far in the future that are not supported with more immediate goals may lose their motivational value.

The career path shown in Figure 16-1 features a steady progression of promotions, yet a reasonable number of years in each position. Such planning is realistic because promotions often take a long time to achieve.

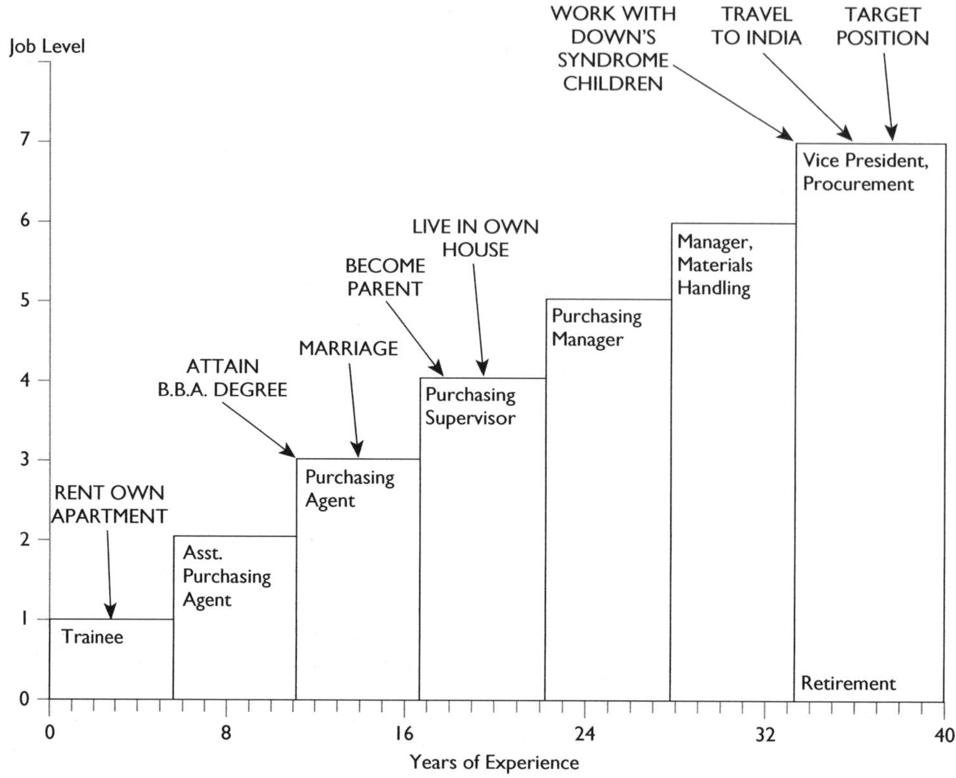

Figure 16-1 A Traditional Career Path

The Horizontal Career Path Many organizations today have structures that don't lend themselves to fixed career paths. Instead of plotting a series of moves over a long time period, many individuals can only make predictions about one or two years into the future. A significant feature of the horizontal career path is that people are more likely to advance by moving sideways than moving up. Or, at least, people who get ahead will spend a considerable part of their career working in different positions at or near the same level. In addition, they may occasionally move to a lower-level position to gain valuable experience. With a horizontal career path, the major reward is no longer promotion but the opportunity to gain more experience and increase job skills.

As with a traditional (or vertical) career path, a horizontal career path does not necessarily mean the person stays with the same firm. For example, a worker might spend three years in one company as an electronics technician, three years in another as an ecommerce coordinator, and then three years as a customer service specialist in a third company. All three positions would be approximately at the same level. The third company then promotes the individual to a much-deserved position as the marketing team leader. Figure 16-2 presents a horizontal career path. After you've studied the two types of career paths, do Human Relations Skill-Building Exercise 16-1.

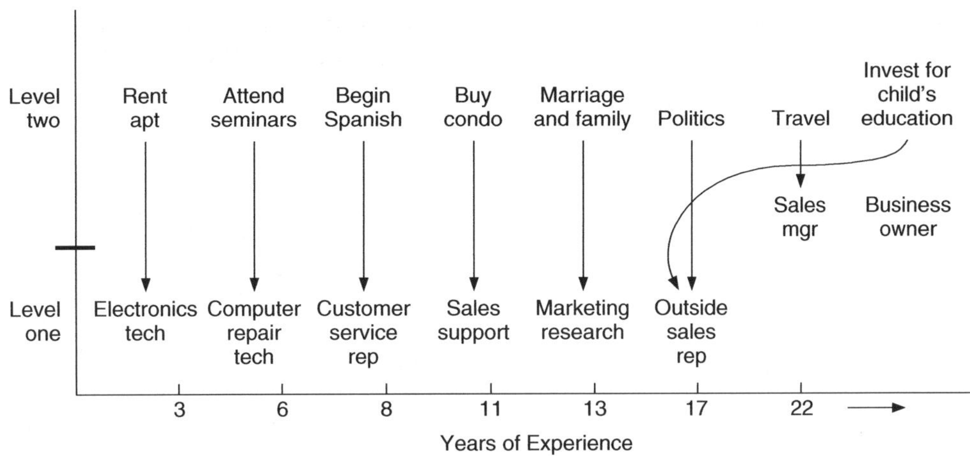

Figure 16-2 A Horizontal Career Path

Achieve Broad Experience

Most people who land high-ranking positions usually have broad experience. Therefore, a widely accepted strategy for advancing in responsibility is to strengthen your credentials by broadening your experience. Workers who follow the alternative model of career advancement, as illustrated by the horizontal career path, are automatically achieving broad experience. It is best to achieve breadth early in your career because it is easier to transfer when an individual's compensation is not too high. Broadening can come about by performing a variety of jobs or sometimes by performing essentially the same job in different organizations. You can also achieve breadth by working on committees and special assignments.

Breadth can also be attained through self-nomination. Have the courage and assertiveness to ask for a promotion or a transfer. Your manager or team leader may not

Human Relations Skill Building

Exercise 16-1 Career Pathing

1. Each class member will develop a tentative career path, perhaps as an outside assignment. About six volunteers will then share their paths with the rest of the class. Feedback of any type will be welcomed. Class members studying the career paths of others should keep in mind such issues as:
   - How logical does the plan appear?
   - Is this something the person really wants or is it simply an exercise in putting down on paper what the ambitious person is supposed to want?
   - How well do the individual's work plans mesh with personal plans?
2. Each class member will interview an experienced working person outside class about his or her career path. Most of the people interviewed will have already completed a portion of their path. They will therefore have less flexibility (and perhaps less idealism) than people just getting started in their careers. The conclusions reached about these interviews will make a fruitful class discussion. Among the issues raised might be these:
   - How familiar were these people with the idea of a career path?
   - How willing were they to talk about themselves?
   - Were many actual "paths" discovered, or did a series of jobs simply come about by luck or "fate"?

know that you are actually seeking more responsibility. An effective method of convincing him or her is to volunteer for specific job openings or for challenging assignments. A boss may need convincing because many more people will be seeking advancement than are actually willing to handle more responsibility.

A major benefit of broad experience is that you achieve more career portability, allowing you to move to another employer should the need exist. The employability derives from being a more flexible person with a broader perspective. A person, for example, who has worked in both the underwriting (setting rates for risks) and the claims aspects of insurance would be well regarded by insurance companies.

Have an Action Plan to Reach Your Goals

As described in Chapter 2, a useful goal is backed up by a logical plan for its attainment. A recommended practice is to supplement your career path with a description of your action plans.

Action plans can be drawn up in minute detail. As with any other aspect of career planning, however, avoid becoming too rigid in your thinking. Career paths and career plans are only tentative. A different path to your goal might fall right in your lap. Ten years from now, for instance, Lisa might receive a telephone call from an executive employment agency. The caller might say: "My client has engaged me to find a materials manager who is competent. Your name was given to us. Could you possibly meet me for lunch to discuss this exciting career opportunity?"

Practise Networking

Developing a network of contacts was recommended in Chapter 14 as a method of finding a job. Currently the most popular career-advancement tactic, networking has several purposes. The contacts you establish can help you find a better position, offer you a new position, become a customer, become a valuable supplier, or help you solve difficult problems. People in your network can also offer you emotional support during periods of adversity.

A recommended approach to networking is to keep a list of at least 25 people whom you contact at least once a month in person or via the intenet. The contact can be as extensive as a luncheon meeting or as brief as an email message. The starting point in networking is to obtain an ample supply of business cards. You then give a card to any person you meet who might be able to help you now or in the future. While first developing your network, be inclusive. Sandy Vilas says, "Remember the 3-foot rule—anyone within three feet of you is someone you can network with."[17] We can also now add "anyone who is a click away" on the internet such as Twitter and other social networking sites. Later, as your network develops, you can strive to include a greater number of influential and successful people.

Human Relations Skill-Building Exercise 16-2 (also offered in Chapter 14) recommends a systematic approach to networking to help you capitalize on its potential advantages.

Find a Mentor

Most successful career people have had one or more mentors during their careers. A **mentor** is a more experienced person who guides, teaches, and coaches another individual. In years past, mentors were almost always higher-ranking people. Today mentors can be peers and even lower-ranking individuals. A lower-ranking individual, for example, can

Human Relations Skill Building

Exercise 16-2 Building Your Network

Networking can be regarded as the process of building a team that works with you to achieve success. You can start the following exercise now, but it will probably take your entire career to implement completely. To start networking, or to make your present networking more systematic, take the following steps:

Step 1. Jot down your top three goals or objectives for the coming three months, such as obtaining a new job or promotion, starting a small business, or doing a field research study.

1. ____

____

2. ____

____

3. ____

____

Step 2. List family members, friends, or acquaintances who could assist you in meeting your goals or objectives. Prepare a contact card or database entry for each person on your list, including as many details as you can about the person, the person's family, friends, employers, and contacts. Do not forget to include your contacts and people you know through the internet.

Step 3. Identify what assistance you will request of your contact or contacts. Be realistic in light of your prior investment in the relationship. Remember, you have to be a friend to have a friend.

Step 4. Identify how you will meet your contact or contacts during the next month. Could it be for lunch, or at an athletic field, nightclub, sports club, recreational facility on campus, or cafeteria? Learn more about your contacts during your face-to-face meetings. In some cases you may have to use the telephone or email instead of an in-person meeting. Look for ways to mutually benefit from the relationship. At the beginning of each week, verify that you have made a small investment in building these relationships.

Step 5. Ask for the help you need. A network must benefit you. Thank the contact for any help given. Jot down in your planner a reminder to follow up with a call, letter, or email message to your contacts. In this way you will have less work to do before you make another request for help.

Step 6. For each person in your network, think of a favour, however small, you can return to him or her. Without reciprocity, a network fades rapidly.

Source: Adapted and expanded from Cheryl Kitter, "Taking the Work out of Networking," Success Workshop, supplement to *The Pryor Report,* March 1998, pp. 1–2.

educate you on how other parts of the organization work—something you may need to know to advance. Sometimes you are able to develop a mentor from the contacts you make on the internet. After the person becomes your mentor, much of the mentoring can take place through email and messaging. (Busier mentors may prefer email because they can respond at their leisure.) E-mentoring will sometimes increase the pool of potential mentors and allow relationships to develop without social bias, such as people being suspicious of the nature of a mentoring relationship between a middle-age man and a young woman.[18]

Mentorship is an important development process in many occupations: master–apprentice, physician–intern, teacher–student, and executive–junior executive. An emotional tie exists between the less experienced person (the protégé) and the mentor. The mentor serves as a positive model and a trusted friend. In return, the person being mentored expresses appreciation, gives positive feedback to the mentor, and shares victories. It is also important to offer a concrete service in return for the mentor's advice. Possibilities include offering to collect information, prepare computer graphics, or run a few errands.

Finding a mentor involves the same process as networking (described later in this chapter). One possibility to mention for now is that you can ask people you already know if they could think of a possible mentor for you. With e-mentoring, geographic distance does not create a substantial barrier. With any prospective mentor, it is best to begin gradually by asking for some advice and then see how the relationship develops. The accompanying Human Relations in Practice box insert provides an example of e-mentoring.

The advantages of being mentored are widely accepted by managers and human relations specialists, so it is encouraging to know that data-based research supports the contention that mentoring can benefit a protégé's career. A team of five researchers synthesized a group of studies covering more than 10,000 individuals. It was found that compensation and promotions were slightly higher for mentored than nonmentored individuals. Also, the mentored individuals were more satisfied with their career, felt more optimistic about promotions, and were more committed to their careers. Two key reasons that mentoring helps protégés is that they receive good suggestions from mentors about career advancement and they use the mentors as positive models.[19]

Balance Your Life

Balancing your life among the competing demands of work, social life, and personal interests can help you advance your career. As mentioned in several places in this book, having balance gives you additional energy and vitality, which will help you in your career. Without balance, a career person runs the risk of burnout and feeling that work is not worthwhile. Stephen Covey, the popular leadership and family-living guru, offers this perspective:

> Always being the last to leave the office does not make you an indispensable employee. In fact, those who work long hours for extended periods are prone to burnout. The trick is to have your priorities clear, honour your commitments and keep a balance in life.[20]

Human Relations in Practice

KPMG Offers Employees Online Mentoring

KPMG LLP, a New York-based tax and audit firm with about 18,200 employees in the United States, has attained success using an on-line mentoring database. Although informal mentoring was taking place (partners mentored junior staff to help them move through the ranks), the company enacted a more formal voluntary nationwide mentoring program in 2004. "For a variety of reasons, wanted to expand on informal mentoring," says Barbara Wankoff, KPMG's director of workplace solutions, which is part of HR. "We set out to encourage people and establish mentoring relationships."

The KPMG program is on the company's HR Web site and is "customized to match our competencies," says Wankoff. The system uses key words such as "boardroom skills" or "negotiation" to help find suitable mentors for employees who seek mentoring. And before accepting an assignment, a mentor agrees to terms that include confidentiality.

KPMG officials describe the on-line program as "user friendly" and easy to navigate, with information that is prominently displayed and readily accessible. "We feel the message is being put out there," says Wankoff. Employees know we support this and it's available to them if they want it. We also recognize not everyone is ready and willing to commit to mentoring, but we hope to see it grow and increase greatly." So far, there's been a positive response—about 6,000 mentoring relationships have been formed.

Source: Donna M. Owens, "Virtual Mentoring," *HR Magazine*, March 2006, p. 106.

SUMMARY

Career advancement has witnessed a major shift in emphasis in recent years to accommodate the new organizational structures. This shift has involved less emphasis on vertical mobility and focuses more on lateral growth, or advancing by learning more. The new model also shows more emphasis on temporary leadership assignments, more self-fulfillment, continuous learning, and ability and willingness to learn.

One set of strategies and tactics for getting ahead can be classified as taking control of your own behaviour. Included are the following points:

1. Develop outstanding interpersonal skills.
2. Develop expertise, passion, and pride.
3. Perform well including going beyond your job description.
4. Develop a proactive personality.
5. Create good first impressions and a favourable appearance.
6. Document your accomplishments.
7. Keep growing through continuous learning and self-development.
8. Observe proper etiquette.
9. Take sensible risks.
10. Learn to manage adversity.
11. Develop the brand called *You*.

Another set of strategies and tactics for getting ahead centre on taking control of your environment, or at least adapting it to your advantage. The strategies include the following:

1. Develop a flexible career path.
2. Have an action plan to reach your goals.
3. Practise networking.
4. Achieve broad experience.
5. Find a mentor.
6. Balance your life.

QUESTIONS AND ACTIVITIES

1. Explain in your own words the new model of career advancement in organizations.
2. What are some of the organizational rewards that a successful person can hope to attain?
3. Why not simply do a good job and forget about all the other strategies and tactics described in this chapter?
4. Some students in computer-related fields are now being recruited out of career schools and colleges to accept full-time employment. Some of the more talented students are even being recruited while in high school for full-time positions after they graduate. What career mistake could most of these students be making by failing to finish school?
5. In the beginning of their careers job seekers often comment that employers are looking for specialists, not generalists. Which career-advancement tactic does this comment support?

6. Describe an incident in which you or somebody you know displayed a proactive personality or was a proactive employee.
7. Identify several jobs for which observing good business etiquette would be particularly important.
8. Use the internet to search for a good career-advancement suggestion. Be prepared to share your findings with the class.
9. Identify several tactics you would be willing to use to become more visible in a large company.
10. How might a person go about networking for career advancement in an airport or on an airplane?

INTERNET SKILL BUILDER

Training through Webinars

Use the internet to search sites that offer webinars in various job skills. For example, some skills may be to develop training skills or to learn basic marketing principles. Are they free or are there costs? What are the positive aspects of webinars? What do you see as some potential problems with using webinars to learn new skills?

Log on to the **Companion Website** at **www.pearsoncanada.ca/dubrin** to access additional resources for this chapter.

CASE STUDY 16-1 HUMAN RELATIONS

I'll Take That Old-Time Economy

Jeff Pequin, a 37-year-old accountant, worked for a paper company in Vancouver, British Columbia. The father of three, he was barely making enough money to get by, and he drove around in an old family car. He liked many aspects of his job, including a management team that treated its employees fairly. His work was not filled with excitement in the stable environment of the paper industry, but he had enough professional challenges to make the work interesting.

Pequin appreciated the fact that his job gave him enough time to spend with his family. Except when it was time to help prepare quarterly reports, Pequin was able to accomplish his work in about 45 hours per week. He also had enough free time to serve as an officer in the local chapter of the Institute of Management Accountants.

Despite his reasonable overall job satisfaction, a mild feeling of discontent kept running through Pequin's mind. People he read about, and many people he knew personally, were making it big in the New Economy. And he was stuck in the Old Economy.

As he explained to his wife over dinner at a Chinese restaurant one night: "Susie, I think that you, I, and the kids deserve better. Look at some of the Gen-X types who are making six- and seven-figure incomes in those dot-com companies. Look at the cars they drive: $60,000 SUVs, $150,000 sports cars, and exotic European convertibles. I love our old car, but it's approaching 150,000 kilometres."

Susie replied, "So what else about these dot-com types is bugging you?"

As he slowly exhaled, Jeff responded, "Those stock options are out of sight. I heard about a 26-year-old who sold some of the stock she accumulated through options and bought a $600,000 house for *cash*. I'm an accountant, so I should be a good money manager. Instead, we still have 22 years of payments left on our mortgage."

"So, what's really on your mind Jeff?" asked Sue.

"With your blessing, I'm starting a job search tomorrow," answered Jeff.

Starting that night, Jeff began exploring internet job sites and the classified advertisements in the Seattle newspapers. Over the next few days, Jeff also developed a list of employment agencies and executive placement services that specialize in finding talent for information technology-based companies.

Within three weeks, Jeff had four job offers. One position appeared to offer the greatest promise of excitement and wealth. He accepted a position as a controller at Homelectronics.com (a fictional, non-existent company), an e-tailer specializing in consumer electronics. He was offered a 12 percent pay hike over his salary at the paper company, plus stock options. At the time, dot-com companies were in big favour with many investors, and the future held great promise. Jeff had dreams of paying off his mortgage debt, buying a BMW, starting an investment program for the children's college expenses, and taking fabulous family vacations.

The first day on the new job at Homelectronics.com, Jeff was greeted hurriedly by the management team. He was assigned to a cubicle in a large, overcrowded room. As the controller, Jeff had a staff that consisted of one accountant, one bookkeeper, and an assistant shared with 10 other workers. Jeff shrugged off the uncomfortable surroundings as a natural part of being a new e-tailer.

Soon Jeff noticed that most of the company's financial information was in a state of chaos. When he asked the CEO about the problem, the CEO said, "We wouldn't have hired you if we didn't need somebody to clean up the mess. Besides, that's just paperwork. What's really important here is to grow our brand and our business."

As the days and weeks passed, Jeff became increasingly uncomfortable with what he saw at Homelectronics.com. He discovered that the company executives had been altering the financial statements for the bank and fabricating reasons for late payments to vendors. The company was also way behind on payments to advertisers, including other websites that served as links to Homelectronics.com. (The other websites were due commissions for referrals.)

Jeff was also perturbed about the standard operating procedure of charging customers' credit cards before the goods were even in stock—instead of when they were shipped. Several customers complained that they were paying interest on credit cards for home-entertainment centres they had not yet received.

Equally disturbing to Jeff was the fact that Homelectronics.com spent $3 in marketing and administrative costs for every $1 in sales. "They were doing virtual business with virtual money," he said.

Three months into his new job, Jeff realized he had made a mistake. In the pursuit of New Economy riches, he had jumped into a position that was giving him sleepless nights. As he explained to Sue, "The management team at Homelectronics.com is ethically challenged. If I jump ship right now, it might hurt my career. I wish I had never left that good old-time economy. I'm wondering whether to stick around for a while to see what happens, or should I start another job hunt right now?"

Questions

1. What career advice can you offer Jeff Pequin?
2. What should Jeff do about conducting a job search?
3. What career advice can you offer the top-management team at Homelectronics.com?

Source: Some of the facts in this case are derived from Michelle Conlin, "Give Me that Old-Time Economy: Boomerang: Disenchanted dot-com Workers Return to Corporate America," *Business Week*, April 24, 2000, p. 99.

CASE STUDY 16-2 HUMAN RELATIONS

San Deep Wants the Fast Track

At age 25, San Deep already had impressive leadership experience. She was the head of her Girl Scout troop at age 11, the president of the Asian Student Association in high school, and the captain of her soccer team in both high school and college. She also organized a food drive for homeless people in her hometown for three consecutive summers. Deep believed that these experiences, in addition to her formal education, were preparing her to be a corporate leader. At college, Deep majored in information systems and business administration.

Deep's first position in industry was a business analyst at a medium-size consulting firm that helped clients implement large-scale systems, such as enterprise software. She explained to her team leader at the outset that she wanted to be placed on a management track rather than a technical track because she aspired to becoming a corporate executive. Deep's team leader explained, "San, I know you are in a hurry to get ahead. Lots of capable people are looking to climb the ladder. But you first have to build your career by proving that you are an outstanding analyst."

Deep thought, "It looks like the company may need a little convincing that I'm leadership material, so I'm going to dig in and perform like a star." And Deep did dig in, much to the pleasure of her clients, her team leader, and her co-workers. Her first few performance evaluations were outstanding, yet the company was still not ready to promote San to a team leader position. Deep's team leader explained, "Bob [the team leader's manager] and I both agree that you are doing an outstanding job, but promotions are hard to come by in our company these days. The company is shrinking more than expanding, so talks about promotion are a little futile right now."

Deep decided that it would take a long time to be promoted to team leader or manager in her present company, so she began to quietly look for a new position in her field. Her job hunt proceeded more swiftly than she anticipated. Through a sports club contact, Deep was granted a job interview with a partner in a larger consulting firm offering similar services. After a series of four interviews, Deep was hired as a senior business analyst performing work on a system similar to the one she had been working with for two years. During her interviews, Deep emphasized her goals of occupying a leadership position as soon as the company believed that she was ready for such a role. Her first client assignment would be helping a team of consultants install a state income tax call centre.

After a one-month-long orientation and training program, Deep was performing billable work at her new employer. At the outset, she reminded her new manager and team leader again that she preferred the managerial route to remaining in a technical position. After six months of hard work, Deep looked forward to her first formal performance evaluation. Deep's team leader informed her that her performance was better than average but short of outstanding. Deep asked for an explanation of why her performance was not considered outstanding. She informed her team leader and manager, "I need an outstanding rating to help me achieve my goals of becoming a leader in our company."

The manager replied, "Our performance evaluations are based on your contribution to the company. We care much less about writing performance evaluations to help a senior business analyst reach her career goals. Besides, San, you've made your point enough about wanting to be a leader in our firm. Let your performance speak for itself."

That evening, Deep met with her fiancé, Ryan, to discuss her dilemma. "The problem, Ryan, is that they don't get it. I'm leadership material, and they don't see it yet. I'm performing well and letting my intentions be known, but my strategy isn't working. The company is missing out on a golden opportunity by not putting me on a fast leadership track. I have to convince them of their error in judgment."

Ryan, a human resources specialist, replied, "I'm listening to you, and I want to give you good advice. Let me be objective here despite the fact that I love you. What have you done lately to prove to the company that you are leadership material?"

Questions

1. Who has the problem here, San or the consulting firm in question?
2. What advice can you offer San to help her increase her chances of being promoted to a formal leadership position in the company?
3. What is your evaluation of the validity of the advice Ryan offered San?

Glossary

Acculturation The process whereby one culture is modified by contact with another culture.

Achievement need The need to accomplish something difficult, to win over others.

Action plan A description of how a person is going to reach a goal.

Active listener A person who listens intensely, with the goal of empathizing with the speaker.

Adolescence The period in life from approximately age 13 to 20; from a biological standpoint, adolescence begins with puberty.

Affective component (of attitude) The emotion connected with an object or a task.

Aggressive Acting in an overbearing, pushy, obnoxious, and sometimes hostile manner.

Aggressive personalities People who verbally and sometimes physically attack others frequently.

Alternate dispute resolution A formalized type of mediation, usually involving a hired professional who mediates in a conflict.

Anger A feeling of extreme hostility, indignation, or exasperation.

Artifacts Personal objects that we select to personalize our environments.

Assertive Stating clearly what one wants or how one feels in a given situation without being abusive, abrasive, or obnoxious.

Attitude A predisposition to respond that exerts an influence on a person's response to a person, a thing, an idea, or a situation.

Backstabbing An attempt to discredit by underhanded means such as innuendo, accusation, or the like.

Balance theory An explanation of attraction, stating that people prefer relationships that are consistent or balanced.

Behaviour The tangible acts or decisions of people, including both their actions and words.

Behavioural component (of attitude) How a person acts.

Behavioural interview A job interview in which the candidate is asked how he or she handled a particular problem in the past.

Behaviour modification (mod) A system of motivating people that emphasizes rewarding them for doing the right things and punishing them for doing the wrong things.

Beliefs The things that a person holds as true or false.

Bias A prejudgment toward another person or group based on something other than fact.

Blended family A family composed of adult partners and children from current and/or previous marriages.

Body image One's perception of one's body.

Body language Movements and gestures that reflect an individual's mood and feelings at any given moment.

Brainstorming A technique by which group members think of multiple solutions to a problem.

Brainwriting (or solo brainstorming) Arriving at creative ideas by jotting them down oneself.

Broken-record technique An assertive skill of calmly repeating one's position over and over again without showing signs of anger or irritation.

Burnout A condition of emotional, mental, and physical exhaustion, along with cynicism, in response to long-term job stressors.

Business etiquette A special code of behaviour required in work settings.

Cannabis A class of drugs, derived from the hemp plant, that generally produce a state of mild euphoria.

Career A series of related job experiences that fit into a meaningful pattern.

Career counsellor A specialist whose professional role is to provide counselling and guidance to individuals about their careers.

Career path A sequence of positions necessary to achieve a goal.

Career portability The ability to move from one employer to another when necessary.

Career success Attaining the twin goals of organizational rewards and personal satisfaction.

Carpal tunnel syndrome A condition that occurs when repetitive flexing and extension of the wrist causes the tendons to swell, thus trapping and pinching the median nerve.

Character Doing the right things despite outside pressures to do the opposite; includes leaving enduring marks that set one apart from another; being moral.

Charisma A type of charm and magnetism that inspires others.

Chronemics How people perceive and use time.

Chronological résumé A job résumé that presents work experience, education, and interests, along with accomplishments, in reverse chronological order.

Co-culture A culture that exists within a larger culture.

Cognitive factors A set of skills, including problem-solving and intellectual skills.

Cognitive Component The component of an attitude that is the knowledge or intellectual beliefs an individual might have about an object (an idea, a person, a thing, or a situation).

Cognitive dissonance A situation in which the pieces of knowledge, information, attitudes, or beliefs held by an individual are contradictory.

Cognitive restructuring A way of dealing with conflict in which a person mentally converts negative aspects into positive ones by looking for the positive elements in a situation.

Collectivistic cultures Cultures that emphasize the importance of the group rather than individuals. People see themselves as members of a group rather than as separate individuals.

Communication The sending and receiving of messages.

Communication (information) overload A condition in which the individual is confronted with so much information to process that he or she becomes overwhelmed and therefore does a poor job of processing information.

Competence As part of wellness, the presence of both job skills and social skills, including the ability to solve problems and control anger.

Compulsiveness A tendency to pay careful attention to detail and to be neat.

Computer surfing In the context of the Internet, browsing through Web sites with no specific work goal in mind; unrelated to work.

Computer-mediated communication (CMC) Communication between people using the medium of computers.

Conflict A condition that exists when two sets of demands, goals, or motives are incompatible.

Confrontation and problem solving A method of identifying the true source of conflict and resolving it systematically.

Core competency With respect to a person, whatever he or she does best.

Creative-style résumé A job résumé with a novel format and design.

Creativity The ability to develop good ideas that can be put into practice.

Cultural intelligence (CQ) An outsider's ability to interpret someone's unfamiliar and ambiguous behaviour the same way that person's compatriots would.

Cultural mosaic An individual's unique mixture of multiple cultural identities that yields a complex picture of the cultural influences on that person.

Cultural sensitivity An awareness of and a willingness to investigate the reasons people of another culture act as they do.

Cultural training A set of learning experiences designed to help employees understand the customs, traditions, and beliefs of another culture.

Cultural values A set of central and enduring goals in life and ways of life that are important to a specific culture.

Culture A learned and shared system of knowledge, beliefs, values, attitudes, and norms.

Database A systematic way of storing files for future retrieval.

Decision making Selecting one alternative from the various solutions or courses of action that can be pursued.

Decision-making software Any computer program that helps the decision maker work through the problem-solving and decision-making steps.

Decoding The process whereby the receiver interprets the message and translates it into meaningful information.

Defensive communication The tendency to receive messages in such a way that our self-esteem is protected.

Denial The suppression of information that a person finds uncomfortable.

Depressant A drug that slows down vital body processes.

Depression A widespread emotional disorder in which the person has such difficulties as sadness, changes in appetite, sleeping difficulties, and a decrease in activities, interests, and energy.

Developmental opportunity A positive way of identifying a person's area of weakness (or need for improvement).

Differentiation of self Emotional security in which one is not desperate for signals of approval and affection from others.

Disarm the opposition A method of conflict resolution in which a person disarms the criticizer by agreeing with valid criticism directed at himself or herself.

Discrimination Unjustifiable negative behaviour directed towards members of a group.

Diversity awareness training A program that provides an opportunity for employees to develop the skills necessary to deal effectively with each other and with customers in a diverse environment.

Dopamine A neurotransmitter that is associated with pleasure and elation. (A *neurotransmitter* is a molecule that transports messages from one neuron in the brain to another across a synapse.)

Downshifter A worker who chooses shorter hours and less-demanding work to allow more time for other activities.

Downsizing (or rightsizing) A method of reducing the number of employees to save money and improve efficiency.

Effectiveness In relation to leadership, a situation in which the leader helps the group accomplish its objectives without neglecting satisfaction and morale.

Effectiveness ethic A focus on the need for excellent work and doing work the best way.

Emotional intelligence A cluster of traits related to the emotional side of life, including regulating emotions, controlling impulses, recognizing how others feel, and interpersonal communication skill.

Emotional labour The process of regulating both feelings and expressions to meet organizational goals.

Empathy Understanding another person's point of view, or placing oneself in another's shoes.

Encoding The process of organizing ideas into a series of symbols, such as words and gestures, designed to communicate with the receiver.

Enculturation The process whereby culture is transmitted from one generation to another.

Ethics A code of conduct that separates morally right actions from those that are wrong; also a study of moral obligation.

Ethnocentrism A belief or conviction that the way that one's own culture does things is superior to another culture's ways.

Exit Strategy Determining a method of getting out of a bad decision.

Expectancy theory of motivation An explanation of motivation stating that people will be motivated if they believe that their effort will lead to desired outcomes.

External locus of control A belief that external forces control one's fate.

Fear of success The belief that if one succeeds at an important task, one will be asked to take on more responsibility in the future.

Feedback Information that tells one how well one has performed and helps one make corrections where indicated.

Feeling-type individuals People who have a need to conform and who attempt to adapt to the wishes of others.

Fight-or-flight response The body's battle against a stressor that helps one deal with emergencies.

Flatlining Reducing middle management.

Flow experience Total absorption in one's work.

Forced-association technique The process of individuals or groups solving a problem by making associations between the properties of two objects.

Frame of reference A model, framework, viewpoint, or perspective.

Frustration A blocking of need or motive satisfaction, or a blocking of a need, wish, or desire.

Functional résumé A job résumé that organizes one's skills and accomplishments into the functions or tasks that support the job one is seeking.

Galatea effect Improving one's performance through raising one's own expectations.

Glass ceiling An invisible but difficult-to-penetrate barrier to promotion based on subtle attitudes and prejudices.

Goal An event, circumstance, object, condition, or purpose for which a person strives. Also, a conscious intention to do something.

Group Two or more people who are aware of each other, influence each other, have a relationship, share common goals, and who view themselves as belonging to the group.

Group norms The unwritten set of expectations for group members—what people ought to do.

Groupthink The situation that occurs when group members strive so hard to get along that they fail to critically evaluate each other's ideas.

Grudge Unresolved or unrepressed anger felt toward someone who we believe has wronged us.

Hallucinogens A class of drugs that in small doses produce visual effects similar to hallucinations.

Hidden agenda Personal goals that are not shared with the group, which may interfere with team performance.

Human relations The art of using systematic knowledge about human behaviour to improve personal, job, and career effectiveness.

Identity crisis Adolescent struggle to establish a reliable self-concept, or personal identity, including concerns over ethnic identity, the need to keep close ties with the family or develop peer relations, sexuality, and body image.

Information (or communication) overload A condition in which the individual is confronted with so much information to process that he or she becomes overwhelmed and therefore processes it poorly.

Insight A depth of understanding that requires considerable intuition and common sense.

Interference Noise in the communication process that distorts or blocks a message and leads to misinterpretation by the receiver.

Internal locus of control A belief that one is the primary cause of events happening to oneself.

Internet addiction (dependence) A condition whereby a person spends so much time on the internet that work and personal life often suffer, usually through neglect.

Interpersonal Anything relating to the interactions between and among people.

Intrinsic motivation The natural tendency to seek out novelty and challenges, to extend one's capacities, to explore, and to learn.

Intuition A method of arriving at a conclusion by a quick judgment or "gut feel."

Intuitive-type individuals People who prefer an overall perspective, or the big picture.

Job objective The position one is applying for now or a job one intends to hold in the future.

Job shadowing A way of gaining information about an occupation by spending a few hours with a professional in the workplace and observing first-hand what the job entails.

Lateral move Transferring to a job at the same level and approximate salary as the present one.

Lateral thinking Thought process whereby an individual seeks out many alternative solutions to a problem. Lateral thinking is creative and broad-based, as opposed to *vertical thinking*, which zeroes in on a single best solution.

Leadership The process of influencing others to achieve certain goals.

Leading task An easy warm-up activity that helps one get started on a project that one might otherwise procrastinate in doing.

Life-change units A scale of values assigned to the impact caused by certain life events, representing the average amount of social readjustment considered necessary to cope with a given change, such as the death of a spouse. The higher the number of life-change units, the greater the stress.

Lifestyle A person's typical approach to living, including moral attitudes, clothing preferences, and ways of spending money.

Maslow's need hierarchy A widely accepted theory of motivation emphasizing that people strive to fulfill needs. These needs are arranged in a hierarchy of importance: physiological, safety, belongingness, esteem, and self-actualization. People tend to strive for need satisfaction at one level only after satisfaction has been achieved at the previous one.

Mediation A type of conflict resolution whereby the two parties appeal to a third party to assist in arriving at a solution to the conflict.

Mediator A person who has received special training in order to assist two conflicting parties to arrive at a resolution that satisfies the needs of each party.

Mentors Bosses who take subordinates under their wings and guide, teach, and coach them.

Metacommunicate To communicate about the actual style of communicating or about how one is communicating. Often metacommunication involves clarifying the nonverbal elements of a message.

Microinequity Small, semiconscious message sent with a powerful impact on the receiver.

Micromanagement The close monitoring of most aspects of group members' activities by the manager.

Midlife crisis Time adults in their forties face when they feel unfulfilled and search for a major shift in career or lifestyle.

Midlife transition Adults taking stock of their lives and formulating new goals; among dozens of other personality and social challenges facing adults are the loss of a youthful appearance and a decreased reproductive or sexual capacity.

Mirroring A form of nonverbal communication in which one person subtly imitates another, such as following the other person's breathing pattern.

Mixed signals Different messages to different audiences about the same topic.

Motive An inner drive that moves a person to do something.

Multitasking Doing two or more routine chores simultaneously that can sometimes enhance personal productivity.

Multicultural identities Individuals who incorporate the values of two or more cultures because they identify with both their primary culture and another culture or cultures.

Multicultural worker One who can work effectively with people of different cultures.

Narcotic A drug that dulls the senses, facilitates sleep, and becomes addictive with long-term use.

Need An internal striving or urge to do something. (Or a deficit within an individual that creates a craving for its satisfaction.)

Need for intimacy An explanation of love centring on the idea that people crave intimacy.

Negative affectivity A tendency to experience aversive (intensely disliked) emotional states.

Negative inquiry The active encouragement of criticism in order to use helpful information or exhaust manipulative criticism.

Negotiation and bargaining Conferring with another person to resolve a problem.

Networking The process of establishing a group of contacts who can help a person in his or her career.

Neurobiological disorders A quirk in the chemistry or anatomy of the brain that creates a disability.

Noise An unwanted interference that can distort or block a message.

Nonassertive Exhibiting a passive type of behaviour in which people let things happen to them without letting their feelings be known.

Nonpossessive relationship A relationship in which both people maintain separate identities and strive for personal fulfillment.

Nonverbal communication Sending messages other than by direct use of words, such as in writing and speaking with gestures.

Nonverbal feedback The signs other than words that indicate whether or not the sender's message has been delivered.

Norms A set of rules (usually unwritten) that set out guidelines for behaviour in a group setting.

Openness to experience A positive orientation toward learning.

Opiate A drug that dulls the senses, facilitates sleep, and is addictive with long-term use.

Organizational citizenship behaviour The willingness to work for the good of the organization, even without the promise of a specific reward.

Organizational culture The values and beliefs held by members of an organization.

Organizational effectiveness The extent to which an organization is productive and satisfies the demands of interested parties, such as employees, customers, and investors.

Paralanguage Vocal cues beyond the meaning of spoken words, including voice volume, tone, pitch, and intensity.

Paraphrase In listening, to repeat in one's own words what the sender says, feels, and means.

Participative leader A person in charge who shares power and decision making with the group.

Partnership In leadership, when the leader and group members are connected in such a way that the power between them is approximately balanced.

Peak performance The mental state necessary for achieving maximum results from minimum effort.

Peer evaluations A system in which co-workers contribute to an evaluation of a person's job performance.

Perfectionism A pattern of behaviour in which the individual strives to accomplish almost unattainable standards of flawless work.

Performance standard A statement of what constitutes acceptable performance.

Personal board of directors A group of people who meet with a person to discuss his or her career progress and problems faced.

Personality clash An antagonistic relationship between two people based on differences in personal attributes, preferences, interests, values, or styles.

Planning Deciding what needs to be accomplished and the actions needed to make it happen.

Political skills An interpersonal style that combines awareness of others with the ability to communicate well.

Portfolio career A career in which people use a variety of skills to earn money in several different ways.

Positive mental attitude A strong belief that things will work in one's favour.

Positive reinforcement Rewarding somebody for doing something right.

Positive self-talk Saying positive things about oneself to oneself to build self-confidence.

Positive visual imagery Picturing a positive outcome in one's mind.

Prejudice An unjustifiable negative attitude toward a group and its members.

Private self The actual person that one is.

Proactive personality A trait that leaves a person less constrained than others by forces in the situation, and that motivates him or her to bring about environmental change; highly proactive people identify opportunities and act on them, showing initiative, and keep trying until they bring about meaningful change.

Problem A gap between what exists and what one wants to exist.

Procrastination Putting off a task for no valid reason.

Productivity The amount of quality work accomplished in relation to the resources consumed.

Proxemics The study of personal space.

Psychological hardiness Describes an individual who tends to profit from stressful situations instead of developing negative symptoms.

Psychotherapy A method of overcoming emotional problems through discussion with a mental health professional.

Public self What the person is communicating about himself or herself, and what others actually perceive about the person.

Pygmalion effect The mysterious phenomenon that occurs when group members succeed because their leader expects them to (i.e., a group tends to live up to the leader's expectations).

Quest fatigue The demoralization and disappointment that takes place when all one's efforts at finding a date or a mate fail.

Realistic goal One that represents the right amount of challenge for the person pursuing the goal.

Reflected appraisal Your view of yourself, based on the assessment of others.

Relationship management The interpersonal skills of being able to communicate clearly and convincingly, disarm conflicts, and build strong personal bonds.

Relaxation response A bodily reaction in which the person experiences a slower respiration and heart rate, lowered blood pressure, and lowered metabolism.

Resilience The ability to withstand pressure and emerge stronger for it.

Role ambiguity A condition in which a job holder receives confusing or poorly defined expectations.

Role conflict The state that occurs when a person has to choose between two competing demands or expectations.

Role confusion Uncertainty about the role one is carrying out. For example, socializing with one's boss may create fuzzy demarcation lines at work.

Role overload A burdensome work load that can lead to stress.

Role underload Having too little to do. Can sometimes create stress similar to that of role overload.

Seasonal affective disorder (SAD) A form of depression that develops during the fall and winter months and disappears as the days lengthen in the spring.

Self A person's total being or individuality.

Self-awareness The ability to understand moods, emotions, and needs as well as their impact on others; self-awareness also includes using intuition to make decisions you can live with happily.

Self-concept What one thinks of oneself; the person that one thinks one is.

Self-defeating behaviour A behaviour pattern in which the person intentionally or unintentionally engages in activities or harbours attitudes that work against his or her best interests.

Self-determining work Work that allows the person performing the task some choice in initiating and regulating his or her own actions.

Self-discipline The ability to work systematically and progressively toward a goal until it is achieved.

Self-disclosure The process of revealing one's inner self to others.

Self-leadership Leading oneself; influencing oneself without waiting for an external leader to lead one; all organizational members are capable of leading themselves to some extent.

Self-management The ability to control one's emotions and act with honesty and integrity in a consistent and acceptable manner.

Self-efficacy The belief in one's capability to perform a task.
Self-esteem The sense of feeling worthwhile and the pride that comes from a sense of self-worth.
Self-respect How one thinks and feels about oneself.
Self-understanding Knowledge about oneself, particularly with respect to mental and emotional aspects.
Sensation-type individuals People who prefer routine and order.
Sensitivity Taking people's needs and feelings into account when dealing with them.
Servant leader A type of leader who serves group members by working on their behalf to help them achieve their goals, not the leader's goals.
Sexual harassment Behaviour of a sexual nature in the workplace that is offensive to an individual and that interferes with that person's ability to perform the job.
Shyness A feeling of discomfort, anxiety, or inhibition in social settings that ranges from mild to extreme.
Skill A learned, specific ability to perform a task competently (for example, writing a report, conducting a statistical analysis, or troubleshooting software problems).
Skill-benefit statement A brief explanation of how an individual's skills can benefit the company.
Social awareness Having empathy for others and having intuition about work problems.
Social comparison Comparing ourselves to others around us, and obtaining information as to how similar or dissimilar we are to them.
Social exchange theory The idea that human relationships are based mainly on self- interest; therefore, people measure their social, physical, and other assets against a potential partner's.
Social loafing Individual efforts that are reduced by membership in a group or team.
Social phobia An extreme type of shyness that interferes with social relations.
Sponsor A higher-ranking individual who is favourably impressed with a person and therefore recommends him or her for promotion and choice assignments.
Stereotypes Separate and distinct categories for people based on broad generalizations and assumptions.
Stimulants A class of drugs that produce feelings of optimism and high energy.
Stress An internal reaction to any force that threatens to disturb a person's equilibrium.
Stress interview A deliberate method of placing a job applicant under considerable pressure and then observing his or her reactions.
Stressor The external or internal force that brings about the stress.
Strong Interest Inventory (SII) The most widely used instrument for matching a person's interests with careers.
Style A person's characteristic way of doing things.
Substance abuse The overuse of any substance that enters the bloodstream.
Substance dependence A compulsion to use substances or engage in activities that lead to psychological dependence, and to withdrawal symptoms when use is discontinued.
Success Used in this book to mean attaining the twin goals of organizational rewards and personal satisfaction.
Success syndrome A pattern in which the worker performs one assignment well and then has the confidence to take on even more difficult assignments.
Summarization The process of clarifying and condensing what a speaker has said in order to demonstrate understanding of the speaker's message.
Support system A group of people a person can rely on for encouragement and comfort.
Swim against the tide To advance one's career by taking an unconventional path to career success.
Synergy Energy that results from the combined efforts and contributions of individual team members.

Targeted résumé A job résumé that focuses on a specific job target or position and presents only information that supports the target.
Team A diverse group of people who share leadership responsibility for creating a group identity and an interconnected effort to achieve goals.
Team leader A person who facilitates and guides the efforts of a small group that is given some authority to govern itself.
Team player A person who emphasizes group accomplishment and cooperation rather than individual achievement and self-interest.
Technical competence In leadership, being skilled in the actual work of the group.
Technostress A stress reaction caused by an inability to cope with computer technologies in a constructive manner.
Telesearch A job search in which job leads are obtained through unsolicited phone calls to prospective employers.
Teleworking (telecommuting) A work arrangement in which employees work at a location outside the workplace, usually at home, full time or part time, and send output electronically to a central office.
Theory of reasoned action One theory that discusses the link between attitudes and behaviour.
Thinking-type individuals People who rely on reason and intellect to deal with problems.
Tolerance Awareness that cultural differences do exist, and the ability to cope with them through understanding and empathy.
Total Quality Management (TQM) A system of management in which all activities are directed toward satisfying external and internal customers.
Traditional mental set A fixed way of thinking about objects and activities.

Type A behaviour A pattern of being aggressively involved in a chronic, incessant struggle to achieve more in less time.

Unsolicited-letter campaign A job search method in which the job seeker sends letters to prospective employers without knowing if a job opening exists.

Value(s) A set of central and enduring goals in life and ways of living that a person feels are important, right, and true.

VDT stress An adverse physical and psychological reaction to prolonged work at a video display terminal.

Vertical thinking An analytical, logical thought process whereby an individual is seeking a single best solution to a problem. Narrower than *lateral thinking* because it results in fewer solutions.

Visualization As a stress-management technique, picturing oneself doing something one would like to do. In general, a method of imagining oneself behaving in a particular way in order to achieve that behaviour.

Wellness A formalized approach to preventive health care.

Win–win The belief that, after conflict has been resolved, both sides should gain something of value.

Workaholism An addiction to work in which not working is an uncomfortable experience.

Work ethic A firm belief in the dignity and value of work.

Work–family conflict A situation that occurs when the individual has to perform multiple roles: worker, spouse or partner, and often parent.

Work habits A person's characteristic approach to work, including such things as organization, handling of paperwork, and the setting of priorities.

Worst-case scenario The most dreadful result possible in a decision-making situation.

References

Chapter One

1. David Neeleman, "My Golden Rule: Never, Ever Forget That You Are a Servant," *Business 2.0*, December 2005, p. 122.
2. Steven Kent, "Happy Workers Are the Best Workers," The *Wall Street Journal*, September 6, 2005, p. A20.
3. Jeffery Pfeffer, The Human Equation (Boston: Harvard Business School Press, 1998), p. 59; Pfeffer, "Producing Sustainable Competitive Advantage through the Effective Management of People," *Academy of Management Executive*, November 2005, pp. 95–108.
4. Timothy A. Judge and Remus Ilies, "Affect and Job Satisfaction: A Study of Their Relationship at Work and Home," *Journal of Applied Psychology*, August 2004, pp. 661–673.
5. Timothy A. Judge and Shinichiro Watanabe, "Another Look at the Job Satisfaction–Life Satisfaction Relationship," *Journal of Applied Psychology*, December 1993, pp. 939–48.

6, 7. C.R. Snyder, "So Many Selves," *Contemporary Psychology*, January 1988, p. 77.

8. John Hattie, *Self-Concept* (Hillsdale, NJ: Erlbaum, 1992).
9. Marilyn E. Gist, "Self-Efficacy: Implications for Organizational Behaviour and Human Resource Management," *Academy of Management Review*, July 1987, pp. 472–85.
10. Cited in Scott Sleek, "People Craft Their Self Image from Groups," *The APA Monitor*, November 1993, p. 22.
11. Nathaniel Branden, *Self-Esteem at Work: How Confident People Make Powerful Companies* (San Francisco: Jossey-Bass, 1998).
12. Cited in Wayne Weiten and Margaret Lloyd, *Psychology Applied to Modern Life* (Pacific Grove, CA: Brooks/Cole Publishing, 1994), p. 51.
13. Janis Miller, "The Value of Self-Respect," available at www.foryoumagazine.com/summer02/selfrespect.html. February 5, 2006.
14. "Better Self-Esteem," available at www.utexas.edu/student/cmhc/booklets/selfesteem/selfest.html. February 1, 2006.
15. Randall Edwards, "Is Self-Esteem Really All That Important?," *The APA Monitor*, May 1995, p. 43.
16. David De Cremer et al., "Rewarding Leadership and Fair Procedures as Determinants of Self-Esteem," *Journal of Applied Psychology*, January 2005, pp. 3–12.
17. Eugene Raudsepp, "Strong Self-Esteem Can Help You Advance," CareerJournal.com (*The Wall Street Journal*), August 10, 2004.
18. Larry Werner, "Coffee with Retired Toro CEO Kendrick Melrose," Minneapolis, *Minnesota Star Tribune*, May 23, 2005, as reprinted by Center for Ethical Business Culture, available at www.cebeglobal.org. February 7, 2006.
19. Jon L. Pierce, Donald G. Gardner, Larry L. Cummings, and Randall B. Dunham, "Organization-Based Self-Esteem: Construct Definition, Measurement, and Validation," *Academy of Management Journal*, September 1989, p. 623.
20. Branden, Self-Esteem at Work; Timothy A. Judge and Joyce E. Bono, "Relationship of Core Self-Evaluations Traits—Self-Esteem, Generalized Self-Efficacy, Locus of Control, and Emotional Stability—With Job Satisfaction and Job Performance: A Meta-Analysis," *Journal of Applied Psychology*, February 2001, pp. 80–92.
21. Cited in Julia M. Klein, "The Illusion of Rejection," *Psychology Today*, January/February 2005, p. 30.
22. Research reported in Melissa Dittmann, "Self-Esteem That's Based on External Sources Has Mental Health Consequences, Study Says," *Monitor on Psychology*, December 2002, p. 16.
23. Research mentioned in book review by E.R. Snyder in *Contemporary Psychology*, July 1998, p. 482.
24. Daniel L. Araoz, "The Manager's Self-Concept," *Human Resources Forum*, July 1989, p. 4.
25. "Self-Esteem: You'll Need It to Succeed," *Executive Strategies*, September 1993, p. 12.

26, 27. Douglas McGregor, *The Human Side of Enterprise* (New York: McGraw-Hill, 1960), pp. 33–48.

Chapter Two

1. Phil Ebersole, "Our Work Ethic: Many Companies Thrive Despite What Polls Say," *Rochester Democrat and Chronicle*, March 10, 1997, p. 6 of *Monday Business*. Updated with telephone interview August 15, 2000.
2. Robert A. Baron, Bruce Earhard, and Marcia Ozier, *Psychology: Canadian Edition* (Scarborough, ON: Allyn and Bacon Canada, 1995).
3. For a theoretical explanation of the principle of self-interest, see Dale T. Miller, "The Norm of Self-Interest," *American Psychologist*, December 1999, pp. 1053–1060.
4. David C. McClelland and Richard Boyatzis, "Leadership Motive Pattern and Long-Term Success in Management," *Journal of Applied Psychology*, December 1982, p. 737.
5. Some of the research on risk taking and thrill seeking is reviewed in Karl Taro Greenfield, "Life on the Edge," *Time*, September 6, 1999, pp. 28–36.
6. Scott Hays, "Generation X and the Art of Reward," *Workforce*, November 1999, pp. 44–48.

7. The original statement of this famous explanation of human motivation is from Abraham H. Maslow, "A Theory of Human Motivation," *Psychological Review*, July 1943, pp. 370–96. See also Maslow, *Motivation and Personality* (New York: Harper & Row, 1954).
8. "Getting There: 1983 Success Magazine Goal-Setting Guide," *Success!*, January 1983, p. A10.
9. Patrick M. Wright, "Operationalization of Goal Difficulty as a Moderator of the Goal Difficulty–Performance Relationship," *Journal of Applied Psychology*, June 1990, p. 227.
10. Don VandeWalle and Larry L. Cummings, "A Test of the Influence of Goal Orientation on the Feedback-Seeking Process," *Journal of Applied Psychology*, June 1997, pp. 390–400.
11. Don VandeWalle, Steven P. Brown, William L. Cron, and John W. Slocum Jr., "The Influence of Goal Orientation and Self-Regulation Tactics on Sales Performance: A Longitudinal Field Test," *Journal of Applied Psychology*, April 1999, pp. 249–59.
12. Onne Janssen and Nico W. Van Yperen, "Employee Goal Orientations, The Quality of Leader–Member Exchange, and the Outcomes of Job Performance and Job Satisfaction," *Academy of Management Journal*, June 2004, pp. 368–384.
13. Gerard H. Seijts and Gary P. Latham, "Learning versus Performance Goals: When Should Each Be Used?" *Academy of Management Executive*, February 2005, p. 130.
14. William B. Werther Jr., "Workshops Aid in Goal Setting," *Personnel Journal*, November 1989, p. 34.
15. Stephen Sprinkel, "Not Having Fantasies Can Be Hazardous to Your Health, Counselor Says," *Gannett News Service*, April 10, 1982.
16. VandeWalle and Cummings, "A Test of the Influence of Goal Orientation," p. 392.
17. Edward L. Deci, James P. Connell, and Richard M. Ryan, "Self-Determination in a Work Organization," *Journal of Applied Psychology*, August 1989, p. 580.
18. Earley and Lituchy, "Delineating Goals and Efficacy Effects," p. 96.
19. Dov Eden and Joseph Kinnar, "Modeling Galatea: Boosting Self-Efficacy to Increase Volunteering," *Journal of Applied Psychology*, December 1991, pp. 770–80.
20. Michael S. Cole, Hubert S. Field, and Stanley G. Harris, "Student Learning Motivation and Psychological Hardiness: Interactive Effects on Students' Reactions to a Management Class," *Academy of Management Learning and Education*, March 2004, pp. 64–85. The definition of psychological hardiness is from citations on page 66 of the same source.
21. Bill Palmroth, "Aspire to Self-Organization," *The American Salesman*, 44(8), August 1999, pp. 26–30; Sherill Tapsell, "How Do I Know They're Working?," *Management*, 46(8), July 1999.
22. Tapsell, "How Do I Know They're Working?"
23. Andrew J. DuBrin, "Career-Related Correlates of Self-Discipline," *Psychological Reports*, 2001, Vol. 89, pp. 107–110.

Chapter Three

1. Ben Rand, "Kodak Seeks Digital's Future via Past: V570's Dual Lenses Harken to 'Turret' Cameras," Rochester, New York, *Democrat and Chronicle*, March 12, 2006, pp. 1E, 4E.
2. *Employability Skills 2000+*, brochure (Ottawa: The Conference Board of Canada, 2000).
3. Daniel Goleman, *Working with Emotional Intelligence* (New York: Bantam, 1998).
4. Eugene Sadler-Smith and Erella Shefy, "The Intuitive Executive: Understanding and Applying 'Gut Feel' in Decision-Making," *Academy of Management Executive*, November 2004, p. 76
5. Quoted in Bill Breen, "What's Your Intuition?," *Fast Company*, September 2000, p. 300.
6. Quoted in Bill Breen, "What's Your Intuition?" *Fast Company*, September 2000, p. 300.
7. Malcolm Gladwell, Blink: The Power of Thinking without Thinking (New York: Little, Brown, 2005).
8. Lea Winerman, "What We Know without Knowing," *Monitor on Psychology*, March 2005, p. 52.
9. John S. Hammond, Ralph L. Keeney, and Howard Rafia, "The Hidden Traps in Decision Making," *Harvard Business Review*, September–October 1998, p. 50.
10. The Myers-Briggs Type Indicator (MBTI) is published by Consulting Psychological Press, Inc., Palo Alto, CA 94306; David A. Whetton and Kim S. Cameron, *Developing Management Skills*, 2nd ed. (New York: HarperCollins, 1991), p. 66.
11. Paul C. Nutt, "Surprising but True: Half the Decisions in Organizations Fail," *Academy of Management Executive*, November 1999, pp. 75–90.
12. Mark A. Runco and Steven R. Pritzker, eds., Encyclopedia of Creativity, vol. 1 (San Diego: Academic Press, 1999), p. xv.
13. Richard W. Woodman, John E. Sawyer, and Ricky W. Griffin, "Toward a Theory of Organizational Creativity," *The Academy of Management Review*, April 1993, pp. 293–321; Robert R. Godfrey, "Tapping Employee's Creativity," *Supervisory Management*, February 1986, pp. 17–18; Greg R. Oldham and Anne Cummings, "Employee Creativity: Personal and Contextual Factors at Work," *Academy of Management Journal*, June 1996, pp. 607–34; Mihaly Csikzentmihalyi, "If We Are So Rich, Why Aren't We Happy?," *American Psychologist*, October 1999, p. 824.
14. Reprinted and updated with permission from Eugene Raudsepp with George P. Hough, Jr., *Creative Growth Games* (New York: Harcourt Brace Jovanovich, 1977).

15. Robert J. Sternberg, ed., Handbook of Creativity (New York: Cambridge University Press, 1999).
16. "Why Kids Beat Adults at Video Games: Two Types of Intelligence," *USA Weekend,* January 1–3, 1999, p. 5.
17. Teresa M. Amabile, "How to Kill Creativity," *Harvard Business Review,* September–October 1998, pp. 78–79.
18. Research cited in "What Happens in the Brain of an Einstein in the Throes of Creation?," *USA Weekend,* January 1–3, 1999, p. 11.
19. "Cows Now Count Sheep on Comfy Mattresses," Knight-Ridder, May 11, 1997.
20. Robert I . Sutton, "The Weird Rules of Creativity," *Harvard Business Review,* September 2001, p. 101.
21. Linda Tischler, "Join the Circus," *Fast Company,* July 2005, p. 56.
22. Cited in Robert McGarvey, "Turn It On," *Entrepreneur,* November 1996, pp. 156–57.
23. Research cited in Bridget Murray, "A Ticking Clock Means a Creativity Drop," *Monitor on Psychology,* November 2002, p. 24; Interview with Teresa M. Amabile in Bill Breen, "The 6 Myths of Creativity," *Fast Company,* December 2004, pp. 77–78.
24. Marissa Ann Mayer, "Creativity Loves Constraints," *Business Week,* February 13, 2006, p. 102.
25. Frederick D. Buggie, "Overcoming Barriers to Creativity," *Innovative Leader,* May 1997, p. 5.
26. Quoted in Mark Hendricks, "Good Thinking: Knock Down the Barriers to Creativity—and Discover a Whole World of New Ideas," *Entrepreneur,* May 1996, p. 158.
27. "Be a Creative Problem Solver," *Executive Strategies,* June 6, 1989, pp. 1–2.

Chapter Four

1. Roger M. Mason, "Taking Health Care to Factory Floor Proves Smart Move for Growing Ontario Company," *Canadian Medical Association Journal,* 157(10), November 1997, pp. 1423–25.
2. Terry O'Neill, "Crunch Time for Families," *Citizen Centre Report,* 30(4), February 17, 2003, pp. 36–41.
3. Steve M. Jex, Terry A. Beehr, and Cathlyn K. Roberts, "The Meaning of Occupational Stress Items to Survey Respondents," *Journal of Applied Psychology,* October 1992, p. 623.
4. Dot Yandle, "Staying Well May Be up to You," *Success Workshop Folio* (a supplement to The Pryor Report Management Newsletter), February 1994, pp. 2–3.
5. Cary L. Cooper and Roy Pane (eds.), *Personality and Stress: Individual Differences in the Stress Process* (New York: John Wiley & Sons, 1991).
6. Statistics Canada, *Exercise Frequency, 1996–1997,* Catalogue No. 82F007XCB.
7. Statistics Canada, "How Healthy Are Canadians? 2001 Annual Report," *Health Reports,* Vol. 12(3), Catalogue No. 82-003-XIE.
8. Philip L. Rice, *Stress and Health: Principles and Practice for Coping and Wellness* (Monterey, CA: Brooks/Cole Publishing Company, 1987), pp. 353–54.
9. Jay Kimiecik, "Learn to Love Exercise," *Psychology Today,* January/February 2000, p. 20.
10. Research cited in Stephenie Overman, "Rise and Sigh," *HR Magazine,* May 1999, p. 68.
11. Canada's Food Guide to Healthy Eating, *Agriculture and Agri-Food Canada,* 1994.
12. W. Gifford Jones, MD, "The Doctor Game," *Peterborough Examiner,* January 9, 1997.
13. Margot Shields, et. al., "Fitness of Canadian Adults: Results from the 2007-2009 Canadian Health Measures Survey," *Statistics Canada Health Reports,* 21(1), March 2010 accessed April 24 at http://www.statcan.gc.ca/pub/82-003-x/2010001/article/11064-eng.pdf
14, 15. Emory L. Cowen, "In Pursuit of Wellness," *American Psychologist,* April 1991, p. 406.
16. Daniel Goleman, "Leadership That Gets Results," *Harvard Business Review,* March–April 2000, p. 80.
17. Research summarized in "Study: Sexes React Differently to Stress," *The Washington Post,* May 19, 2000. (Study published by Shelley Taylor, *Psychological Review,* 2000.)
18. Jeffrey R. Edwards, "A Cybernetic Theory of Stress, Coping, and Well-Being in Organizations," *Academy of Management Review,* April 1992, p. 248.
19. Research cited in "Mental Stress Is Linked to Blocked Blood Vessels," *APA Monitor,* February 1998, p. 7.
20. Jeffrey A. LePine, Marcie A. LePine, and Christine L. Jackson, "Challenge and Hindrance Stress: Relationships with Exhaustion, Motivation to Learn, and Learning Performance," *Journal of Applied Psychology,* October 2004, pp. 883–891.
21. R. Douglas Allen, Michael A. Hitt, and Charles R. Greer, "Occupational Stress and Perceived Organizational Effectiveness: An Examination of Stress Level and Stress Type," *Personnel Psychology,* Summer 1982, pp. 359–70.
22. Unpublished research reported in Claudia Wallis and Sonja Steptoe, "Help! I've Lost My Focus," *Time,* January 16, 2006, p. 75.
23. Palmer, Stephen, Cary Cooper and Kate Thomas, "A Model of Work Stress," *Counselling at Work.* Winter 2004, p. 5.
24. Raymond T. Lee and Blake E. Ashforth, "A Meta-Analytic Examination of the Correlates of Three Dimensions of Job Burnout," *Journal of Applied Psychology,* April 1996, p. 123.
25. Lee and Ashforth, "A Meta-Analytic Examination"; Joanne Cole, "An Ounce of Prevention Beats Burnout," *HRfocus,* June 1999, pp. 1, 14–15.

26. Rabi S. Bhagat, "Effects of Stressful Life Events on Individual Performance and Work Adjustment Processes within Organizational Settings: A Research Model," *Academy of Management Review*, October 1983, pp. 660–71.

27. "Building Self-Esteem," www.ashland.com/education/self-esteem/best_shot.html.

28. Michael E. Cavanagh, "What You Don't Know about Stress," *Personnel Journal*, July 1988, p. 55.

29. Robert Oswalt and Kelly Silberg, "Self-Perceived Stress in College: A Survey," *Psychological Reports*, December 1995, p. 985.

30. T.M. Dembrowski and P.T. Costa, Jr., "Coronary-Prone Behavior: Components of the Type A Pattern and Hostility," *Journal of Personality*, 55, 1987, pp. 211–35; Ray H. Rosenman, *Type A Behavior and Your Heart* (New York: Fawcett, 1975).

31. Peter Y. Chen and Paul E. Spector, "Negative Affectivity as the Underlying Cause of Correlations between Stressors and Strains," *Journal of Applied Psychology*, June 1991, p. 398.

32. Paul E. Spector, Peter Y. Chen, and Brian J. O'Connell, "A Longitudinal Study of Relations between Job Stressors and Job Strains While Controlling for Prior Negative Affectivity and Strains," *Journal of Applied Psychology*, April 2000, p. 216.

33, 34. Marilyn L. Fox, Deborah J. Dwyer, and Daniel C. Ganster, "Effects of Stressful Job Demands and Control on Physiological and Attitudinal Outcomes in a Hospital Setting," *Academy of Management Journal*, April 1993, pp. 290–91.

35. John Schaubroeck and Deryl E. Merritt, "Divergent Effects of Job Control on Coping with Work Stressors: The Key Role of Self-Efficacy," *Academy of Management Journal*, June 1997, pp. 738–54.

36. Terry O'Neill, "Crunch Time for Families," *Citizen Centre Report*, 30(4) February 17, 2003.

37. Craig Bond, *Technostress: The Human Cost of the Computer Revolution* (Reading, MA: Addison Wesley, 1984), p. 16.

38. James D. Brodzinski, Robert P. Scherer, and Karen A. Goyer, "Workplace Stress: A Study of the Internal and External Pressures Placed on Employees," *Personnel Administrator*, July 1989, pp. 77–78.

39. Alicia A. Grandey, "Emotion Regulation in the Workplace: A New Way to Conceptualize Emotional Labor," *Journal of Occupational Health Psychology*, Vol. 5, No. 1, 2000, pp. 95–110.

40. "Making Stress Work for You," *Executive Strategies*, October 3, 1989, p. 5.

41. Philip Morgan and H. Kent Baker, "Building a Professional Image: Dealing with Job Stress," *Supervisory Management*, September 1985, p. 38.

42. Andrew Weil, "Beating Stress," *USA Weekend*, December 26–28, 1997, p. 4.

43. "Canadian Workers among Most Stressed," *Worklife* (14)2, 2002.

44. Herbert Benson (with William Proctor), *Beyond the Relaxation Response* (New York: Berkley Books, 1995), pp. 96–97.

45. Sue McDonald, "Take a Deep Breath," *The Cincinnati Enquirer*, October 24, 1995, p. D3.

46. Quoted in "Forget about Eliminating Stress; Learn to Live with It Instead," *Knight-Ridder story*, October 5, 1999.

Chapter Five

1. Erick H. Erikson, *Childhood and Society* (New York: Norton, 1963); *Child Development Institute*, "Stages of Social-Emotional Development In Children and Teenagers," available at www.childdevelpmentinfo.com, retrieved May 6, 2006.

2. Our discussion of the challenges of adolescence and adulthood follows closely Saul Kassin, Psychology, 3rd ed. (Upper Saddle River, NJ: Prentice Hall, 2001), pp. 406–440; and Charles G. Morris and Albert A. Maisto, Psychology: An Introduction, 11th ed. (Upper Saddle River, NJ: Prentice Hall, 2002), pp. 418–441.

3. Lawrence Kohlberg, Essays on Moral Development: Vol. 2. *The Psychology of Moral Development* (New York: Harper & Row, 1984).

4. Research from *The New England Journal of Medicine* summarized in Sharon Begley, "Oops! Mental Training, Crosswords Fail to Slow Decline of Aging Brain," *The Wall Street Brain*, April 21, 2006, p. B1; Begley, "Studies on Dementia Often Confuse Causes with Consequences," *The Wall Street Journal*, April 28, 2006, p. B1.

5. Research reported in Joseph Pereira, "A Daily Drink May Help Prevent Cognitive Decline as Women Age," *The Wall Street Journal*, January 20, 2005, p. D5.

6. Research summarized in Karen Kersting, "Happiness in Men Usually Drops after Age 65, Study Finds," *Monitor on Psychology*, March 2005, p. 10.

7. Brian Scott Ehrlich and Derek Isaacowitz, "Does Subjective Well-Being Increase with Age?" *Perspectives in Psychology*, Spring 2002, pp. 20–26.

8. Kassin, Psychology, p. 435.

9. "U.S. Job Satisfaction Keeps Falling, The Conference Board Reports Today," available at www.conference-board.org, retrieved February 8, 2005.

10. Michael Drafke, The Human Side of Organizations, 9th ed. (Upper Saddle River, NJ: Pearson Prentice Hall, 2006), p. 335.

11. The first two items noted are from Fred Pryor, "What Have You Learned from Change?" Managers Edge, September 1998, p. 2.

12. Al Siebert, The Resiliency Advantage (San Francisco, CA: Berrett-Koehler, 2005).
13. Thomas L. Friedman, The World Is Flat: A Brief History of the Twenty-First Century (New York: FSG, 2005).
14. Peter Svensson, "Hands-On Jobs May Be the Safest," *Associated Press*, July 4, 2004.
15. John Wareham, *Wareham's Way: Escaping the Judas Trap* (New York: Atheneum, 1983), p. 107.
16. Thomas A. Widiger and Allen J. Frances, "Controversies Concerning the Self-Defeating Personality Disorder," in Rebecca C. Curtis, ed., *Self-Defeating Behaviors* (New York: Plenum Press, 1989), p. 304.
17. Seth Allcorn, "The Self-Protective Actions of Managers," *Supervisory Management*, January 1989, pp. 3–7.
18. Connirae Andreas and Steve Andreas, *Heart of the Mind* (Moab, UT: Real People Press, 1991).
19. Andrew J. DuBrin, *Bouncing Back: How to Handle Setbacks in Your Work & Personal Life* (Englewood Cliffs, NJ: Prentice Hall, 1982), pp. 85–102; Melba Colgrove, Harold H. Bloomfeld, and Peter McWilliams, *How to Survive the Loss of a Love* (New York: Bantam Books, 1976).
20. Publice Health *Agency of Canada, Report on Mental Illnesses in Canada*, 2002 http://www.phac-aspc.gc.ca/publicat/miic-mmac/index-eng.php
21. Statistics Canada, *Health Reports*, Vol. 12, No. 3, April 2001, Ottawa: Ministry of Industry, Catalogue No. 82-003.
22. Anthony J. Levitt, Michael H. Boyle, Russell T. Joffe, and Zillah Baumal, "Estimated Prevalence of the Seasonal Subtype of Major Depression in a Canadian Community Sample," *Canadian Journal of Psychiatry, (45)*7, September 2000, pp. 650–54.
23. John Lawrie, "Coping with Depression on the Job," *Supervisory Management*, June 1992, pp. 6–7.
24. Peggy Stuart, "Tracing Workplace Problems to Hidden Disorders," *Personnel Journal*, June 1992, p. 84. Our discussion of neurobiological disorders is based on the Stuart article.
25. Daniel Goleman, *Emotional Intelligence: Why It Can Matter More Than IQ* (New York: Bantam Books, 1995).
26. Fred Pryor, "Is Anger Really Healthy?," *The Pryor Report Management Newsletter*, February 1996, p. 3.
27. John Cloud, "Classroom for Hotheads," *Time*, April 10, 2000, p. 53.

Chapter Six

1. "Leading by Feel: Seek Frank Feedback," Harvard Business Review, January 2004, p. 31
2. Quoted in "Leading by Feel: Be Realistic," *Harvard Business Review*, January 2004, p. 28.
3. Daniel Goleman, Richard Boyatzis, and Annie McKee, "Primal Leadership: The Hidden Driver of Great Performance," *Harvard Business Review*, December 2001, pp. 42–51.
4. David A. Morand, "The Emotional Intelligence of Managers: Assessing the Construct Validity of a Nonverbal Measure of, 'People Skills,'" *Journal of Business and Psychology*, Fall 2001, pp. 21–23.
5. Peter J. Jordan, Neal M. Ashkanasy, and Charmine E. J. Hartel, "Emotional Intelligence as a Moderator of Emotional and Behavioral Reactions to Job Insecurity," *Academy of Management Review*, July 2002, pp. 361–372.
6. "Leading by Feel: Train the Gifted," *Harvard Business Review*, January 2004, p. 31.
7. Based to some extent on information synthesized in Dodge Fernald, *Psychology* (Upper Saddle River, NJ: Prentice Hall, 1997), pp. 562–563.
8. L. A. Burke and L. A. Witt, "Personality and High-Maintenance Employee Behavior," *Journal of Business and Psychology*, Spring 2004, pp. 349–363.
9. Timothy A. Judge and Remus Ilies, "Is Positiveness in Organizations Always Desirable?" *Academy of Management Executive*, p. 152.
10. Ibid., pp. 153–155.
11. Profit Staff, "The 50 Best Small and Medium Employers in Canada," *Profit Magazine* April 2010 http://www.canadianbusiness.com/entrepreneur/human_resources/article.jsp?content=20100412_132458_5676
12. Mark C. Ehrant and Stefanie E. Nauman, "Organizational Citizenship Behavior in Work Groups: A Group Norms Approach," *Journal of Applied Psychology*, December 2004, pp. 960–974.
13. Philip M. Podsakoff, Michael Ahearne, and Scott B. MacKenzie, "Organizational Citizenship Behavior and the Quantity and Quality of Work Group Performance," *Journal of Applied Psychology*, April 1997, pp. 262–270.
14. Diane Swanbrow, "The Paradox of Happiness," *Psychology Today*, July/August 1989, p. 38.
15. The major sources of information for this list are Mihaly Csikzentmihalyi, "Finding Flow," *Psychology Today*, July/August 1997, pp. 46–48, 70–71; Swanbrow, "The Paradox of Happiness"; Martin Seligman, *What You Can Change and What You Can't* (New York: Knopf, 1994); Maury M. Breecher, "C'mon Smile!" *Los Angeles Times*, October 3, 1982.
16. David Meyers, *The Pursuit of Happiness* (New York: Morrow, 1997); Black and McCafferty, "The Age of Contentment," p. 6.
17. Based on research conducted by Tim Kasser, department of psychology, the University of Rochester, 1994.
18. Martin Seligman, "Don't Diet, Be Happy," *USA Weekend*, February 4–6, 1994, p. 12.
19. Steven Reiss, "Secrets of Happiness," *Psychology Today*, January/February 2001, pp. 50–52, 55–56.

20. Richard Carlson, *You Can Be Happy No Matter What: Five Principles Your Therapist Never Told You*, revised edition (Novato, CA: New World Library, 1997).

21. Ibid., p. 71.

22. Howard Halpern, "Single or Married People Share Same Joys and Problems," *syndicated column*, November 12, 1988.

23. Quoted in Gary Soulsman, "Looking for Love in All the Right Places," *The Wilmington News Journal, syndicated story*, May 4, 1991.

24. John M. Darley, Sam Glucksberg, and Ronald A. Kinchla, *Psychology*, 4th ed. (Englewood Cliffs, NJ: Prentice Hall, 1988), p. 681.

25, 26. Daniel Goleman, "Making a Science of Why We Love Isn't Easy," *The New York Times*, syndicated story, July 23, 1986.

27. Pam Janis, "The Science of Sex," *USA Weekend*, March 29–31, 1996, pp. 16–17; Theresa Crenshaw, *Guide to the Ingredients in Our Sex Soup* (New York: Putnam, 1996).

28. Jeannette Lauer and Robert Lauer, "Marriages Made to Last," *Psychology Today*, June 1985, p. 24.

29. Robert J. Sternberg, *Love Is a Story* (New York: Oxford University Press, 1998); Sternberg, "What's Your Love Story?," *Psychology Today*, July/August 2000, pp. 52–59.

30. John Gottman and Sybil Carrere, "Welcome to the Love Lab," *Psychology Today*, September/October 2000, pp. 42–43.

31. Janet E. East and Judith A. Frederick, "Working Arrangements and Time-Stress," *Canadian Social Trends*, Winter 1996, pp. 14–19.

32. Terry O'Neill, "Crunch Time for Families," *Citizen Centre Report* 30(4), February 17, 2003, pp. 36–41.

33. "What Makes Women Healthy or Unhealthy?," Final Report, Vol. 2, *Canada Health Action: Building on the Legacy: An Overview of Women's Health.*

34. Steven R. Covey, "Decide Your Priorities," *USA Weekend*, December 31, 1993–January 2, 1994, p. 9.

35. Harville Hendrix, "Love and Marriage," *Family Circle* syndicated story, March 17, 1990.

36. Cited in Murray Dubin, "The Knack of Marriage: You Can Learn the Skills, Say Those Rooting for Coupledom," *Philadelphia Inquirer* syndicated story, August 22, 2000.

37. Diane Vaughan, "The Long Goodbye," *Psychology Today*, July 1987, p. 39.

38. Francesca M. Cancian, *Love in America: Gender and Self-Development* (Cambridge, England: Cambridge University Press, 1987).

39. Peter D. Kramer, *Should You Leave?* (New York: Morrow, 1997).

Chapter Seven

1. Our communication model is a condensation of a widely used model. An example of such a model is Robert E. Coffee, Curtis W. Cook, and Phillip L. Hunsaker, *Management and Organizational Behaviour* (Burr Ridge, IL: Irwin, 1994), pp. 197–200.

2. Joseph A. DeVito, *Messages: Building Interpersonal Communication Skills*, 3rd ed. (New York: HarperCollins, 1996).

3. Rich Sorenson, Grace De Bord, and Ida Ramirez, Business and Management Communication: A Guide Book, 4th ed. (Upper Saddle River, NJ: Prentice Hall, 2001), pp. 6–10.

4, 5. Albert Mehrabian, *Silent Messages: Implicit Communication of Emotions and Attitudes*, 2nd ed. (Belmont, CA: Wadsworth, 1981).

6. Irene Hanson Frieze, Jospehine E. Olson, and June Russell, "Attractiveness and Business Success: Is It More Important for Women or Men?," paper presented at the *Academy of Management*, Washington DC, August 1989.

7. N.M. Henley, *Body Politics: Power, Sex and Nonverbal Communication* (Englewood Cliffs, NJ: Prentice-Hall, 1977).

8. Edward T. Hall, "Proxemics—A Study of Man's Spatial Relationships," in *Man's Image in Medicine and Anthropology* (New York: International Universities Press, 1963); Pauline E. Henderson, "Communication without Words," *Personnel Journal*, January 1989, pp. 28–29.

9. Joann Ellison Rodgers, "Flirting Fascination," *Psychology Today*, January–February, 1999.

10. Merrill E. Douglass, "Standing Saves Time," *Executive Forum*, July 1989, p. 4.

11. Roger E. Axtell, *Do's and Taboos of Hosting International Visitors* (New York: John Wiley and Sons, 1989).

12. Jeffrey Jacobi, *The Vocal Advantage* (Upper Saddle River, NJ: Prentice-Hall, 1996).

13. Daniel Araoz, "The Effective Boss," *Human Resources Forum*, November 1989, p. 4.

14. Rodger W. Griffeth, "Information Overload: A Test of the Inverted U Hypothesis with Hourly and Salaried Employees," *Academy of Management Best Papers Proceedings*, p. 234.

15. "Weed Out Wimpy Words," WorkingSMART, March 2000, p. 2; George Walther cited in "Power Up Your Persuasiveness," Executive Leadership, July 2003, p. 1.

16. Joe Neumaier, "Sweet Sounds of Success: Dialect Coach Sam Chwat Accents Hollywood's Best," USA Weekend, July 12–14, 2002, p. 12.

17. Sharon Lund O'Neill, "An Empowered Attitude Can Enhance Communication Skills," *Business Education Forum*, April 1998, pp. 28–30.

18. For more details about point 9 see Brian Fugere, Chelsea Hardaway, and Jon Warshawsky, Why Business People Speak Like Idiots (New York: Free Press, 2005).
19. Suzette Haden Elgin, *Genderspeak* (New York: Wiley, 1993).
20. Suzette Haden Elgin, Genderspeak (New York: Wiley, 1993).
21. Quoted in Jacquelyn Lynn, "Small Talk, Big Results," *Entrepreneur,* August 1999, p. 30.
22. Nancy B. Kurland and Lisa Hope Pelled, "Passing the Word: Toward a Model of Gossip and Power in the Workplace," *Academy of Management Review,* April 2000, pp. 428–438; Samuel Greengard, "Gossip Poisons Business: HR Can Stop It," *Workforce,* July 2001, pp. 24–28.
23. Daniel Araoz, "Right-Brain Management (RBM): Part 2," *Human Resources Forum,* September 1989, p. 4.
24. "Train Yourself in the Art of Listening," *Positive Leadership,* sample issue, Summer 2000, p. 10.
25. Erik Rautalinko and Hans-Olof Lisper, "Effects of Training Reflective Listening in a Corporate Setting," *Journal of Business and Psychology,* Spring 2004, pp. 281–299.

Chapter Eight

1. Joseph A. Devito, *Messages,* 3rd ed. (New York: HarperCollins College Publishers, 1996).
2. Geert Hofstede, *Culture's Consequences: International Differences in Work-Related Values* (Beverly Hills, CA: Sage, 1980; updated and expanded in "A Conversation with Geert Hofstede," *Organizational Dynamics,* Spring 1993, pp. 53–61; Jim Kennedy and Anna Everest, "Put Diversity in Context," *Personnel Journal,* September 1991, pp. 50–54.
3. Geert Hofstede, *Culture's Consequences: International Differences in Work-Related Values* (Beverly Hills, CA: Sage, 1980).
4, 5. Hofstede, *Culture's Consequences.*
6. S. Gaines, Jr., "Relationships among Members of Cultural Minorities," in J.T. Wood and S.W. Duck, eds., *Understanding Relationship Processes, 6: Off the Beaten Track: Understudied Relationships* (Thousand Oaks, CA: Sage, 1995) pp. 51–88.
7. Jeffrey Jensen Arnett, "The Psychology of Globalization," American Psychologist, October 2002, pp. 777–778.
8. Georgia T. Chao and Henry Moon, "The Cultural Mosaic: A Methodology for Understanding the Complexity of Culture," *Journal of Applied Psychology,* November 2005, pp. 1128–1140.
9. Quoted in "Discrimination Is Brain's Way," *Los Angeles Times* story, May 7, 1995.
10. Ronald P. Philipchalk, *Invitation to Social Psychology* (Orlando, FL: Harcourt Brace and Company, 1995).
11. Gary M. Stern, "Small Slights Bring Big Problems," Workforce, August 2002, p. 17.
12. John Gray, *Men Are from Mars, Women Are from Venus* (New York: HarperCollins, 1992).
13. Mary Crawford, *Talking Difference: On Gender and Language* (Newbury Park, CA: Sage Publications, 1995).
14. Deborah Tannen, *Talking from 9 to 5* (New York: William Morrow, 1994); Tannen, *You Just Don't Understand* (New York: Ballentine, 1990); Gray, *Men Are from Mars;* Tannen, "The Power of Talk: Who Gets Heard and Why," *Harvard Business Review,* September–October 1995, pp. 138–48.
15. Earley and Mosakowski, "Toward Cultural Intelligence: Turning Cultural Differences into Workplace Advantage," *Academy of Management Executive,* August 2004, pp. 154–155.
16. Todd Raphael, "Savvy Companies Build Bonds with Hispanic Employees," *Workforce,* September 2001, p. 19.
17. Samuel B. Bacharach, Peter A. Bamberger, and Dana Vashdi, "Diversity and Homophilly at Work: Supportive Relations among White and African-American Peers," *Academy of Management Journal,* August 2005, pp. 619–644.
18. Steven Greenhouse, "Abercrombie & Fitch Bias Case Is Settled," *The New York Times,* available at nytimes.com, retrieved November 17, 2004.
19. Gunnar Beeth, "Multicultural Managers Wanted," Management Review, May 1997, p. 17.
20. A few of these tasty morsels are from Lillian H. Chaney and Jeannette S. Martin, *Interpersonal Business Communication,* 3rd ed. (Upper Saddle River, NJ: Pearson Prentice Hall, 2004), p. 190.
21. Todd Henneman, "Acceptance of Gays, Lesbians, Is a Big Part of Kodak's Diversity Picture," *Workforce Management,* December 2004, p. 68.
22. Rick Borelli, "A Worldwide Language Trap," *Management Review,* October 1997, pp. 52–54.
23. David P. Tulin, "Enhance Your Multi-Cultural Communication Skills," *Managing Diversity,* 1, 1992, p. 5.
24. "Use Team's Diversity to Best Advantage, ExecutiveSTRATEGIES, April 2000, p. 2.
25. Siri Carpenter, "Why Do 'They All Look Alike'?" *Monitor on Psychology,* December 2000, p. 44.

Chapter Nine

1. Dominic A. Infante, Arguing Constructively (Prospects Heights, IL: Waveland Press, 1992); Siobhan Leftwich, "Hey, You Can't Say That! How to Cope with Verbally Abusive People," *Black Enterprise,* January 2006, p. 95.
2. Julie Ellis, "Knock Down Workplace Bullying; Improve Office Morale," *Managing Workplace Conflict* (The Dartnell Corporation sample issue, 2002), p. 6.

3. Statistics Canada, Crime and Justice: Violence in the Workplace, 2004, http://www.statcan.gc.ca/pub/11-402-x/2008000/pdf/crime-eng.pdf accessed June 6, 2010.

4. Angela Pirisi, "Teamwork: The Downside of Diversity," *Psychology Today*, November/December 1999, p. 18.

5. Jiatao Li and Donald C. Hambrick, "Factional Groups: A New Vantage on Demographic Faultlines, Conflict, and Disintegration in Work Teams," *Academy of Management Journal*, October 2005, pp. 794–813.

6. The examples, but not the interpretations, are from Julie Fawe, "Why Your Boss May Start Sweating the Small Stuff," *Time*, March 20, 2006, p. 80. See also, Joann S. Lublin, "How to Stop the Snubs that Demoralize You and Your Colleagues," *The Wall Street Journal*, December 7, 2004, p. B1.

7. Human Resources Development Canada, Information on Labour Standards, Pamphlet 12—Sexual Harassment [online], available at http://info.load-otea.hrdc-drhc.ca/~lsweb/harassmen.htm.

8. H.F. Schwind, H. Das, W. Werther, and K. Davis, *Canadian Human Resource Management*, 4th ed. (McGraw-Hill Ryerson Canada, 1995).

9. "Human Rights in Employment," pamphlet prepared by the *Canadian Human Rights Commission*, 1992.

10. Statistics Canada, Study: Hours and Earnings of Dual-earner Couples, *The Daily*, Friday April 24, 2009. http://www.statcan.gc.ca/daily-quotidien/090424/dq090424b-eng.htm

11. "Women's Stress Eased by Flextime," *The Globe and Mail*, January 8, 1997.

12. "Flexible Work Lessons 'Struggle to Juggle,'" *Worklife Report*, 11(2), pp. 8–9, 1998.

13. Stewart D. Friedman, Perry Christensen, and Jessica DeGroot, "Work and Life: The End of the Zero-Sum Game," *Harvard Business Review*, November–December 1998, pp. 119–29.

14. John D. Arnold, *When Sparks Fly: Resolving Conflicts in Your Organization* (New York: McGraw-Hill, 1993).

15. Shari Caudron, "Workplace Violence," *Workforce*, August 1998, pp. 44–52.

16. International Labour Organization, "Violence on the Job—A Global Problem," press release, Monday, July 20, 1998, at www.us.ilo.org/news/prsrls/violence.html.

17. Joseph D. O'Brian, "Negotiating with Peers: Consensus, Not Power," *Supervisory Management*, January 1992, p. 4.

18. Joseph P. Folger, Marshall Scott Poole, and Randall K. Stutman, *Working Through Conflict: Strategies for Relationships, Groups, and Organizations*, 4th ed., (Reading, MA: Addison Wesley Longman Inc., 2001).

19, 20, 21. Lynne Henderson and Philip Zimbardo, "Shyness," *Encyclopedia of Mental Health* (San Diego, CA: Academic Press, 1998).

22. Philip Zimbardo, *Shyness: What It Is, What to Do about It* (Reading, MA: Addison-Wesley, 1977), pp. 220–26; Kevin Shyne, "Shyness: Breaking through the Invisible Barrier to Achievement," *Success*, July 1982, pp. 14–16, 36–37, 51.

Chapter Ten

1. Gerald R. Ferris, Pamela L. Perrewé, William P. Anthony, and David C. Gilmore, "Political Skill at Work." *Organizational Dynamics*, Spring 2000, p. 25.

2. Robert Epstein, "The Key to Our Emotions," *Psychology Today*, July/August 1999, p. 20.

3. William A. Cohen and Nuritt Cohen, "Get Promoted Fast," *Success*, July/August 1985, p. 6.

4. George A. Neuman and Jill R. Kickul, "Organizational Citizenship Behaviors: Achievement Orientation and Personality," *Journal of Business and Psychology*, Winter 1998, pp. 263–64.

5. Anita Bruzzese, "Get the Boss to Take Notice of You," *Gannett News Service*, April 21, 1997.

6. Walter D. St. John, "Successful Communications between Supervisors and Employees," *Personnel Journal*, January 1983, p. 76.

7. John J. Gabarro and John P. Kotter, "Managing Your Boss," *Harvard Business Review*, May–June 1993, p. 152. (HBR Classic reprint of article originally published in January–February 1980.)

8. "Using Evaluation Time to Improve Your Own Job," *Success Workshop* (Supplement to Pryor Report), May 1996, p. 2.

9. Jay T. Knippen, Thad B. Green, and Kurt M. Sutton, "How to Handle Problems with Two Bosses," *Supervisory Management*, August 1991, p. 7.

10. Sandy J. Wayne and Gerald R. Ferris, "Influence Tactics, Affect, and Exchange Quality in Supervisor-Subordinate Interactions: A Laboratory Experiment and Field Study," *Journal of Applied Psychology*, October 1990, pp. 487–99.

11. J. Kenneth Matejka and Richard Dunsing, "Managing the Baffling Boss," *Personnel*, February 1989, p. 50.

12. "So You're Smarter Than the Boss? Yeah, Right," *Executive Leadership*, June 2000, p. 5.

13. Quoted in Kathleen Driscoll, "Is a Tyrannical Boss Getting You Down? Don't Be Afraid to Confront Her," Rochester, NY, *Democrat and Chronicle*, June 14, 1995, p. 10B.

14. "How's the View Back There?," *Working Smart*, December 1996, p. 1.

15. Matejka and Dunsing, "Managing the Baffling Boss."

16. *How to Win at Organizational Politics—Without Being Unethical or Sacrificing Your Self-Respect* (New York: The Research Institute of America, January 1985), pp. 7–8.

17. "How to Work with a Disorganized Boss," *The Office Professional*, January 1994, pp. 1, 3–4.

18. Adapted from George Milite, "Office Politics: It's Still out There," *Supervisory Management*, July 1992, pp. 6–7.

Chapter Eleven

1. Anne Fisher, "For Happier Customers, Call HR," *Fortune*, November 28, 2005, p. 272
2. Gerald R. Ferris, Pamela L. Perrewé, William P. Anthony, and David C. Gilmore, "Political Skill at Work." *Organizational Dynamics*, Spring 2000, p. 25.
3. Chris Lee, "The Death of Civility," *Training*, July 1999, p. 26.
4. Jared Sandberg, "Office Minstrels Drive the Rest of Us Nuts but Are Hard to Silence," *The Wall Street Journal*, February 14, 2006, p. B1+.
5. Sheila Murray Bethela, *Making a Difference* (New York: G. P. Putnam's Sons, 1989).
6. Dru Scott, *Customer Satisfaction: The Other Half of Your Job* (Los Altos, CA: Crisp Publications, 1991), p. 16.
7. Jane Michaels, "You Gotta Get Along to Get Ahead," *Woman's Day*, April 3, 1984, p. 60.
8. Kaye Loraine, "Dealing with the Difficult Personality," *Supervision*, April 1989, pp. 6–8.
9. Sam Deep and Lyle Sussman, *What to Say to Get What You Want* (Reading, MA: Addison Wesley, 1995).
10. D. C. Kinlaw, *Developing Superior Work Teams: Building Quality and the Competitive Edge* (Lexington, MA: Lexington Books, 1991).
11. Gay Lumsden and Donald Lumsden, *Communicating in Groups and Teams: Sharing Leadership*, 2nd ed. (Belmont, CA: Wadsworth Publishing Company, 1997).
12. Ibid., p. 15.
13. B. Tuckman and M. Jensen, "Stages of Small-Group Development," *Group and Organizational Studies*, 2, 1977, pp. 419–27.
14. B. A. Fisher, "Decision Emergence: Phases in Group Decision Making," *Speech Monographs*, 37, 1977, pp. 53–66.

15, 16. Marilyn E. Laiken, *The Anatomy of High Performing Teams: A Leader's Handbook* (Toronto: OISE Press, 1994).

17. Engleberg and Wynn, *Working in Groups;* Lumsden and Lumsden, *Communicating in Groups and Teams*.
18. R. Albanese and D.D. Van Fleet, "Rational Behaviour in Groups: The Free-Riding Tendency," *Academy of Management Review*, 10, 1985, pp. 565–81; Jennifer George, "Extrinsic and Intrinsic Origins of Perceived Social Loafing in Organizations," *Academy of Management Journal*, 35, 1992, pp. 191–202.
19. Steven L. McShane, *Canadian Organizational Behaviour* (Toronto: Richard D. Irwin Inc., 1995).
20. E.G. Bauer, "Are You a Good Team Player?," *Working Together*, sample issue, Dartnell Corporation, undated.
21. "R. Meredith Belbin," in *Business: The Ultimate Resource* (Cambridge, MA: Perseus, 2002), pp. 966–967; Belbin® Team-Roles, available at http://www.belbin.com/belbin-teamroles.htm. Retrieved March 12, 2005.
22. From a review of Meredith Belbin, Management Teams, by Colin Thomson appearing in http://www.accountingweb.co.uk. Retrieved March 13, 2005.
23. Carlin Flora, "Close Quarters: Why We Fall in Love with the One Nearby," *Psychology Today*, January/February 2004, p. 15.
24. Charlene Marmer Solomon, "The Secret's Out: How to Handle the Truth of Workplace Romance," *Workforce*, July 1998, p. 45.
25. Survey cited in Stephanie Armour, "Cupid Finds Work as Office Romance No Longer Taboo," *USA Today*, February 11, 2003.
26. Policy developed by law firm of Gutierrez, Preciado & House, LLP, available at www.gutierrez-preciado.com/Memos/romance.htm, retrieved April 15, 2003.
27. Linda Thornburg, "Companies Benefit from Emphasis on Superior Customer Service," *HR Magazine*, October 1993, pp. 46–49; Theodore Garrison, III, "The Value of Customer Service," in Rick Crandall, ed., *Celebrate Customer Service* (Corte Madera, CA: Select Press, 1999), pp. 3–22; Hal Hardy, "Five Steps to Pleasing Difficult, Demanding Customers," *First Rate Customer Service* (sample issue distributed by Briefings Publishing Group, 2002).
28. Anne Fisher, "A Happy Staff Equals Happy Customers," *Fortune*, July 12, 2004, p. 52.

Chapter Twelve

1. Felicity Somerset, "The Softer Side of Leadership," *CMA Management*, October 2001, Vol. 75(7), pp. 12–14.
2. Marilyn E. Gist and Terence R. Mitchell, "Self-Efficacy: A Theoretical Analysis of Its Determinants and Malleability," *Academy of Management Review*, April 1992, pp. 183–211.
3. Dov Eden and Arie Aviram, "Self-Efficacy Training to Speed Reemployment: Helping People to Help Themselves," *Journal of Applied Psychology*, June 1993, pp. 352–60.
4. George P. Hollenbeck and Douglas T. Hall, "Self-Confidence and Leader Performance," *Organizational Dynamics*, Issue 3, 2004, pp. 261–264.
5. Jay T. Knippen and Thad B. Green, "Building Self-Confidence," *Supervisory Management*, August 1989, pp. 22–27.
6. Wolf J. Rinke, "Maximizing Management Potential by Building Self-Esteem," *Management Solutions*, March 1988, p. 6.

7. "Entrepreneurs Need Attitude: Power of Being Positive Can Help You to Succeed in Spite of Setbacks," *Knight Ridder*, September 16, 2002.
8. Philip G. Zimbardo, *Shyness: What It Is, What to Do about It* (New York: Jove/HBJ, 1977), p. 209.
9. D. Brian McNatt and Timothy A. Judge, "Boundary Conditions of the Galeta Effect: A Field Experiment and Constructive Replication," *Academy of Management Journal*, August 2004, pp. 550–565.
10. Genevieve Capowski, "Anatomy of a Leader: Where Are the Leaders of Tomorrow?," *Management Review*, March 1994, pp. 10–17.
11. Daniel Goleman, "Leadership That Gets Results," *Harvard Business Review*, March–April 2000, p. 80.
12. Daniel LeBlanc, "NATO Job Could Be Yanked from MP Parrish, *The Globe and Mail*, March 6, 2003, p. A6.
13. Cited in Julie Cohen Mason, "Leading the Way into the 21st Century," *Management Review*, October 1992, p. 19.
14. Chris Taylor, "Builders & Titans," *Time*, April 26, 2004, pp. 74–75.
15. Cassie R. Barlow, Mark Jordan, and William H. Hendrix, "Character Assessment: An Examination of Leadership Levels," *Journal of Business and Psychology*, Summer 2003, p. 563.
16. Edwin A. Locke and Associates, *The Essence of Leadership: The Four Keys to Leading Successfully* (New York: Lexington/Macmillan, 1991), pp. 32–34.
17. Felicity Somerset, "The Softer Side of Leadership."
18. Joyce E. Bono and Timothy A. Judge, "Personality and Transformational and Transactional Leadership: A Meta-Analysis," *Journal of Applied Psychology*, October 2004, pp. 901–910.
19. Shari Caudron, "Humour Is Healthy in the Workplace," *Personnel Journal*, June 1992, p. 63.
20. Elizabeth Weil, "Every Leader Tells a Story," www. fast-company.com/online/15/rftf.html (accessed May 6, 1999).
21. Suggestions 7, 9, and 10 are from Roger Dawson, *Sources of Power Persuasion* (Upper Saddle River, NJ: Prentice Hall, 1992), pp. 181–83.
22. "Ethics—Business Educators Teach Students to. . . Do the Right Thing!", *Keying In*, January 1997, p. 1.
23. Robert B. Maddux and Dorothy Maddux, *Ethics in Business: A Guide for Managers* (Los Altos, CA: Crisp Publications, 1994).
24. George W. Fotis, "Interactive Personal Ethics," *Management Review*, December 1996, p. 46; "Covey Proposes Principle-Based Leadership," *Management Review*, September 1995, pp. 20–21.
25. Peter Block, *Stewardship: Choosing Service over Self-Interest* (San Francisco: Berrett-Koehler Publishers, 1993), pp. 27–32.
26. Robert T. Keller, "A Test of the Path-Goal Theory of Leadership with Need for Clarity as a Moderator in Research and Development Organizations," *Journal of Applied Psychology*, April 1989, pp. 208–12.
27. "Motivating Personnel: A Condition Essential to Business Growth." Federal Office of Regional Development (Quebec), Dec. 1995.
28. Ronald A. Heifetz and Donald L. Laurie, "The Work of Leadership," *Harvard Business Review*, January–February 1997, p. 124.
29. Robert K. Greenleaf, *The Power of Servant Leadership: A Journey into the Nature of Legitimate Power and Greatness* (San Francisco: Berrett-Koehler Publishers, Inc., 1998).
30. "Blueprint for a Servant Leader," *Executive Strategies*, March 2000, p. 7.
31. Book review of Larry Spears and Michelle Lawrence (eds.), Practicing Servant-Leadership: Succeeding through Trust, Bravery, and Forgiveness (San Francisco: Jossey-Bass, 2004). The review by Frank Hamilton, appears in *Academy of Management Review*, October 2005, pp. 875–877.
32. Jennifer J. Laabs, "Team Training Goes Outdoors," *Personnel Journal*, June 1991, p. 59.
33. William D. Hitt, *The Model Leader: A Fully Functioning Person* (Columbus, OH: Battelle Press, 1993).

Chapter Thirteen

1. "Your Personal Core Competency," *Executive Strategies*, February 1996, p. 11.
2. Updated from Julie Griffin Levitt, *Your Career: How to Make It Happen*, 2nd ed. (Cincinnati, OH: South-Western College Publishing, 1990), pp. 11–21.
3. The description of the Strong Interest Inventory is based on James G. Clawson, John P. Kotter, Victor A. Faux, and Charles C. McArthur, *Self-Assessment and Career Development*, 3rd ed. (Englewood Cliffs, NJ: Prentice Hall, 1992), pp. 125–35.
4. One such site is Sarah Evans, "How to Find a Job on Twitter," Mashable/ Business http://mashable.com/2009/03/13/twitter-jobs/ accessed July 1, 2010.
5. Carol Klieman, " 'Shadowing' Offers a Few Hours of On-the-Job Learning," *Chicago Tribune* (Jobs Section), September 28, 1997, p. 1.
6. Statistics Canada, "Labour Force Survey," *The Daily*,Friday June 25, 2010. http://www.statcan.gc.ca/daily-quotidien/100625/dq100625a-eng.htm
7. Statistics Canada, "Labour Force Survey," *The Daily*,June 4, 2010. http://www.statcan.gc.ca/bsolc/olc-cel/olc-cel?catno=71-001-XWE&lang=eng
8. Quoted in Kathleen Driscoll, "Portfolio Career May Be the Way to Reinvent Your Future," Rochester, NY, *Democrat and Chronicle*, February 17, 1997, p. 5.

9. Douglas T. Hall, "Protean Careers of the 21st Century," *Academy of Management Executive*, November 1996, p. 8.
10. Randall S. Hansen, "Quintessential Careers: The 10-Step Plan to Career Change," www.quintcareers.com, retrieved April 13, 2006.
11. Mildred Culp, "Filling In Can Boost Career, but Be Wary of Guarantees," syndicated column, February 20, 2000.
12. Statistics Canada, The Survey of Self-Employment, abstract, January 29, 2002, Catalogue No. 71M0017XCB.
13. "Seven Tips for Career Preparation," *NBEA Keying In*, November 1993, p. 8; Anne Fisher, "Six Ways to Supercharge Your Career," *Fortune*, January 13, 1997, pp. 46–47.

Chapter Fourteen

1. "Reference Check Mates," *Working Woman*, August 2000, p. 84.
2. Based in part on Bob Weinstein, "What Employers Look For," in *The Honda How to Get a Job Guide* (*Business Week's Guide to Careers*, 1985), p. 24; Julie Griffin Levitt, *Your Career: How to Make It Happen* (Cincinnati, OH: South-Western, 1990), pp. 129–31.
3. *Employability Skills Profile 2000+*, The Conference Board of Canada, May 2000, www.conferenceboard.ca.
4. Scott Kirsner, "Networking Overload," *Fast Company*, April 2004, p. 38.
5. Barbara Kmat, "Using Twitter and Facebook to Find a Job," *Time*, Monday June 8, 2009 http://www.time.com/time/business/article/0,8599,1903083,00.html
6. Jacob Share, "The Beginner's Guide to Finding a Job Using Twitter," http://jobmob.co.il/blog/beginners-guide-find-a-job-with-twitter/ accessed July 8, 2010.
7. Anton Koekemoer, "Use Social Media Tools and Channels to Find the Perfect Job," Posted May 25, 2010, http://blog.wsioms.co.za/index.php/social-media-marketing/use-social-media-tools-and-channels-to-find-the-perfect-job/
8. Anton Koekemoer, ibid.
9. Richard H. Beatty, *The Perfect Cover Letter* (New York: John Wiley and Sons, 1997).
10. Based on form used by Garett Associates, Alexandra, Virginia.
11. Mary Alice Griffin and Patricia Lynn Anderson, "Résumé Content," *Business Education Forum*, February 1994, p. 11.
12. Peggy Schmidt, "When to Start Looking for a Job," *Business Week's Guide to Careers*, February 1986, p. 71.
13. R. Neil Dortch, "Résumé Preparation," *Business Education Forum*, April 1994, pp. 47–48.
14. Zane K. Quible, "Job Seeking Process," in *The Changing Dimensions of Business Education* (Reston, VA: National Business Education Association, 1997), p. 176.
15. Dortch, p. 47.
16. "Quick Career Booster," *WorkingSmart*, January 1998, p. 3.
17. "Helping Students Prepare for New Interviewing Tactics," *Keying In*, January 2000, pp. 1, 5.
18. Seth Godin, ed., *The 1994 Information Please Business Almanac & Desk Reference* (Boston: Houghton Mifflin, 1994), p. 354.
19. "Talking with Lynn Bignell about Job Hunting," *Working Smart*, November 1991, p. 7.
20. Susan Kleinman, "Is Your Attitude Killing Your Career?" *Cosmopolitan*, May 1994, p. 225.
21. Ellen Forman, "Surviving under the Microscope," *Sun-Sentinel* syndicated story, April 21, 1997; Nancy K. Austin, "The New Job Interview: Beyond the Trick Question," *Working Woman*, March 1996, pp. 23–24.
22. Jim Pawlak, "Interviewing 101: How Not to Get a New Job," *The Detroit News*, available at detnews.com, retrieved September 30, 2005.
23. "Screening by Computer Speeds Hiring Process," Knight-Ridder, August 6, 2000.
24. Larry Reynolds, "Truth or Consequences," *Personnel*, January 1991, p. 5; Paul R. Sackett, Laura R. Burris, and Christine Callahan, "Integrity Testing for Personnel Selection: An Update," *Personnel Psychology*, Autumn 1989, p. 493.
25. Mark J. Schmitt, Elise L. Amel, and Ann Marie Ryan, "Self-Reported Assertive Job-Seeking Behaviors of Minimally Educated Job-Hunters," *Personnel Psychology*, Spring 1993, p. 119.
26. Connie R. Wanberg, Ruth Kanfer, and Maria Rotundo, "Unemployed Individuals: Motives, Job-Search Competencies, and Job-Search Constraints as Predictors of Job Seeking and Reemployment," *Journal of Applied Psychology*, December 1999, pp. 897–910.

Chapter Fifteen

1. Laura Koss-Feder, "Slowing Down the Treadmill, with Help," available at *NYTimes.com*, retrieved June 29, 2003.
2. Research of Timothy A. Psychl, reported in Danielle Kost, "Professor Says Putting Off Chores Is a Breakable Habit," Rochester (NY), *Democrat and Chronicle*, September 22, 2002, p. D3.
3. Theodore Kurtz, "10 Reasons Why People Procrastinate," *Supervisory Management*, April 1990, pp. 1–2.
4. "When to Procrastinate and When to Get Going?" *Working Smart*, March 1992, pp. 1–2.
5. Alan Lakein, *How to Gain Control of Your Time and Your Life* (New York: Wyden Books, 1973), pp. 141–51.
6. "Don't Procrastinate," *Practical Supervision*, January 1989, p. 3.

7. Cited and quoted in "Get with It: Nip Your Procrastination Right in the Bud," *Entrepreneur*, September 1998, p. 94.
8. Linda Sapadin, *It's about Time! The Six Styles of Procrastination and How to Overcome Them* (New York: Viking, 1996).
9. Stephen R. Covey with Elaine Pofeldt, "Why Is This Man Smiling?" *Success*, January 2000, pp. 38–40.
10. Cited in Alfred A. Edmond, Jr., "Alone in Your Time Zone," *Black Enterprise*, December 2004, pp. 154–155.
11. Price Pritchett, *The Employee Handbook of New Work Habits for a Radically Changing World* (Dallas, TX: Pritchett and Associates, Inc., 1997), p. 11.
12. Michael Mandel, "The Real Reasons You're Working So Hard . . . and What You Can Do about It," *Business Week*, October 3, 2005, p. 62.
13. Raymond P. Rood and Brenda L. Meneley, "Serious Play at Work," *Personnel Journal*, January 1991, p. 90.
14. Quoted in Carrie Ferguson, "The Wages of a Workaholic," *Gannett News Service*, May 23, 2000.
15. Brenda Goodman, "A Field Guide to the Workaholic," *Psychology Today*, May/June 2006, p. 40.
16. Mildred L. Culp, "Working Productively with Workaholics While Minimizing Legal Risks," syndicated column, Passage Media, 1997.
17. Survey reported in Jane M. Von Bergen, "Getting Organized at the Office," available at www.philly.com, retrieved February 26, 2006.
18. Merrill Douglass, "Timely Time Tips: Ideas to Help You Manage Your Time," *Executive Management Forum*, September 1989, p. 4.
19. Research reported in Mark Greer, "Older Adults Need Full Attention to Juggle Multiple Tasks," *Monitor on Psychology*, June 2005, p. 19.
20. Quoted in Anne Fisher "Get Organized at Work—Painlessly," *Fortune*, January 10, 2005, p. 30.
21. Douglass, "Timely Time Tips," p. 4.
22. Survey cited in "Workers Dawdle on Net an Hour a Day, Firm Says," Rochester (NY), *Democrat and Chronicle*, August 22, 2005, p. 10D.
23. "Beating the Clock: Time Management When You Are under the Gun," *Working Smart*, March 1999, p. 1.

Chapter Sixteen

1. Sarah E. Needleman, "Be Prepared When Opportunity Calls," *The Wall Street Journal*, February 7, 2006, p. B4.
2. Douglas T. Hall, "Protean Careers of the 21st Century," *Academy of Management Executive*, November 1996, p. 9.
3. Ibid., p. 10.
4. Quoted in Anne Fisher, "Disaster-Proofing Your Career," *Fortune*, October 3, 2005, p. 174.
5. Jeffery A. Thompson, "Proactive Personality and Job Performance: A Social Capital Perspective," *Journal of Applied Psychology*, September 2005, pp. 1011–1017.
6. Scott E. Seibert, J. Michael Crant, and Maria L. Kraimer, "Proactive Personality and Career Success," *Journal of Applied Psychology*, June 1999, pp. 416–427.
7. Jacquelyn Lynn, "Apparel Perils: 'Dress for Success' Isn't So Cut and Dried Anymore," *Entrepreneur*, June 1999, p. 36.
8. "First Impressions: You Have to Make Them Count," *Executive Strategies*, December 1992, p. 10.
9. Quoted in Michael Barrier, "Should Looks Count: Are You Discriminating against Employees Because of Their Appearance?" *HR Magazine*, September 2004, p. 66.
10. Mielikki Org, "The Tatooed Executive: Body Art Gains Acceptance in Once-Staid Office Settings; Corporate Counsel's Yin-Yang" *The Wall Street Journal*, August 28, 2003, pp. D1, D 15; Karen Dybis, "While No Longer Taboo, Body Art Still Can Be a Sticky Issue at Work," *Detroit News*, available at detnews.com, June 21, 2005;
11. "Business Etiquette: Teaching Students the Unwritten Rules," *Keying In*, January 1996, p. 2.
12. "When the Knot in Your Stomach Is a *Good* Thing," *Executive Strategies*, July 1996, p. 5.
13. "The Bounce-Back Factor: Regain Lost Confidence and Charge Ahead," *Executive Strategies*, June 1997, p. 6.
14. Tom Peters, "The Brand Called You: You Can't Move Up If You Don't Stand Out," *Fast Company*, August/September 1997, pp. 83–94. The quotation is from p. 86.
15. Ray J. Friant, Jr., "Leadership Training for Long-Term Results," *Management Review*, July 1991, pp. 52–53.
16. Deb Koen, "Identifying Values Clarifies Career Goals," Rochester, NY, *Democrat and Chronicle*, June 4, 2000.
17. Quoted in "Network Your Way Up," *Working Smart*, February 1997, p. 4.
18. Betti A. Hamilton and Terri A. Scandura, "E-Mentoring: Implications for Organizational Learning and Development in a Wired World," Organizational Dynamics, 32, no. 4, 2003, p. 388; Donna M. Owens, "Virtual Mentoring," *HR Magazine*, March 2006, pp. 105–107.
19. Tammy D. Allen et al., "Career Benefits Associated with Mentoring for Protégés: A Meta-Analysis," *Journal of Applied Psychology*, February 2004, pp. 127–136.
20. Stephen Covey, "How to Succeed in Today's Workplace," *USA Weekend*, August 29–31, 1997, pp. 4–5.

Index

D

E

F

I

J

K

L

M

N

Q

R

T

U

V

W

Y

Z